UK COMPANY LAW

UK COMPANY LAW

Nicholas Grier MA, LLB, Solicitor, Writer to HM Signet
Department of Law, Napier University, Edinburgh

Consultant Editors:
Stephen Griffin, University of Wales, Aberystwyth
David Capper, Queen's University, Belfast

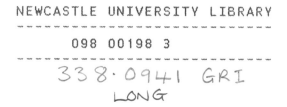
JOHN WILEY & SONS

Chichester • New York • Weinheim • Brisbane • Singapore • Toronto

Other Wiley Editorial Offices

John Wiley & Sons, Inc., 605 Third Avenue
New York, NY 10158-0012, USA

WILEY-VCH Verlag GmbH, Pappelallee 3,
D-69469 Weinheim, Germany

Jacaranda Wiley Ltd, 33 Park Road, Milton,
Queensland 4064, Australia

John Wiley & Sons (Asia) Pte Ltd, 2 Clementi Loop #02-01,
Jin Xing Distripark, Singapore 129809

John Wiley & Sons (Canada) Ltd, 22 Worcester Road,
Rexdale, Ontario M9W 1L1, Canada

British Library Cataloguing in Publication Data

A catalogue record for this book is available from the British Library

ISBN 0-471-95836-0

Typeset in 11/13pt Times by Poole Typesetting (Wessex) Ltd, Bournemouth, Dorset
Printed and bound in Great Britain by Biddles Ltd, Guildford and King's Lynn
This book is printed on acid-free paper responsibly manufactured from sustainable forestry, in which at least
two trees are planted for each one used for paper production.

CONTENTS

PREFACE

This book is written primarily as a textbook for students studying company law as part of professional examinations or as part of a university degree. Throughout this book, the emphasis will be on the practical effect of the law as drafted and applied. The book aims to show:

- the commercial or other purpose the law is trying to achieve;

- how effectively the law achieves that purpose;

- who benefits and suffers from the law as it stands at present;

- what might, if anything, be done to improve the present law.

Given that this book is a textbook, the reader should note the following:

1. As it is designed primarily for students, it will cover what a student needs to know in order to have a reasonable understanding of what the law is. It also covers those areas where the law is unclear, inconsistent or in need of reform. Such areas commonly form the subject-matter for dissertations or more searching examination questions.

2. Most company law textbooks for students are written primarily from the point of view of English law, which is understandable, but is not always very convenient for those whose professional examinations or future careers take place in Scotland or Northern Ireland. This book takes account of national differences where they are significant.

3. Company law is a very pragmatic subject. It is designed to promote trade and enterprise within a legally regulated framework. Its reason for existence is the encouragement of commerce and the minimisation of the opportunities for fraud. This book seeks to highlight this approach.

4. Company law is not an easy subject to study in isolation. To have a good understanding of company law it is helpful to know a certain amount about contract law, bankruptcy law, conveyancing law, banking law and commercial law generally. It is difficult to understand any one part of company law without reference to another part. Only when you have studied a certain amount of the subject will you begin to see the whole jigsaw beginning to fit together.

5. One of the best ways of understanding company law is to consider why the law on any particular part of company law is as it is. Company law has been

continually updated over its history and on the way there have been some false starts, some great improvements, and some disasters. Most of the changes have been for some reason which seemed appropriate at the time. Some of those reasons are no longer valid or the changes failed to remedy the problem that needed attention. However, if you can understand *why* it was necessary to change the existing law, you are more likely to understand the current law.

6. Company law is primarily statutory, which means that amendments to existing company law statutes are only brought in from time to time as Parliament finds the opportunity. Nowadays the burden of work on Members of Parliament means that legislation is not always being scrutinised as closely as it might be, and accordingly faulty draftsmanship may find its way onto the statute book. This leads to further areas of uncertainty within the law which can only be resolved by further Acts of Parliament or by test cases, neither of which solutions are quick or cheap.

7. Increasingly, British company law is being influenced by European Community law, particularly with respect to public companies. From time to time the EC promulgates a new directive on company law, and while some directives have not been accepted, mainly for political or practical reasons, the less contentious directives have ensured a certain uniformity of company law within Europe.

This book could not have been written without the support and encouragement of my wife, Jean: to her I owe a deep debt of gratitude. I should also like to express my thanks to my editors at Wiley, David Wilson and Susie Hamblin, for bearing with me over the many months it took to write this. My colleagues and fellow solicitors, Josephine Bisacre, Stuart Duncan and John Harding Edgar have been a constant source of good advice.

For those parts of the text that relate exclusively to English law and to Northern Irish law I am indebted to Stephen Griffin, of the University of Wales, Aberystwyth and David Capper, of Queen's University, Belfast respectively for their valuable comments.

Any errors and omissions are and will remain my own responsibility.

Nicholas Grier
Napier University, Edinburgh

Tables

Cases

Legislation

Statutory Instruments

1. WHY DO COMPANIES EXIST?

The usefulness of a separate legal personality – corporations – methods of incorporation – the quest for the avoidance of personal liability – the advantages and disadvantages of limited ability – sources of law – UK legislation – EU legislation – common law – types of trading organisations – sole traders, partnerships and companies – summary of advantages and disadvantages of incorporation – limited partnerships

The usefulness of a separate legal personality

The essential point about any company is that it has a legal existence in its own right. By law a company is treated as an artificial person which can do most things that a person can do in terms of business. Obviously there are certain things a company could never do, such as marry, commit the crime of rape, or leave a will, but most commercial activities that a person could do, a company can also do.

Unlike a human being, however, a company has no natural life span. It can continue in existence even though its original owners may have died or sold up, its managers retired and its business completely altered. This is because the company is not the same thing as its owners or its managers. Although the owners of a company own the shares in the company, and though its directors manage it, the company is still a legal entity distinct from its owners and managers. If a company owns an asset, the asset does not belong to the owners of the company. If the company sues someone for a debt, the company, not its managers, gets the benefit of the court judgment or decree in its favour.

Equally the owners' and managers' personal domestic and business affairs are nothing to do with the company, and the company bears no responsibility for them.

This concept is known as a company's separate legal personality.

Separate legal personality only arises because the company is a corporation. In English law, there are two types of corporation, the corporation sole and the corporation aggregate.

The corporation sole

The corporation sole is used mainly for ecclesiastical posts such as the Archbishop of Canterbury, and arises out of the complexities of ownership of church lands. There is also at least one statutory corporation sole, the Public

Trustee under the Public Trustee Act 1906. There are no corporations sole in Scotland. While the individual representative of the corporation sole may die or retire, the corporation continues in existence with the next incumbent taking the departing incumbent's place. Company law does not apply to corporations sole.

The corporation aggregate

This is the normal type of corporation to which company law does apply. A corporation aggregate is an association of persons or other corporations constituting a legal entity by means of one of the recognised methods of incorporation. Corporations aggregate include charities and municipal bodies not founded by statute and companies. The definition is inherently circular because broadly speaking a corporation only exists because it was founded by one of the methods whereby corporations are founded.

Methods of incorporation

At present there are three recognised methods whereby corporations have been created. The oldest is by use of a Royal Charter.

Royal Charter

Royal Charters used to be granted for certain educational or clerical establishments, such as colleges at Oxford and Cambridge. A Royal Charter protected the college and lent it dignity. Soon the concept was extended to other associations of individuals, such as guilds, groups of merchants or professional bodies. The Stuart monarchs used to "ring-fence" certain monopolies by means of a Royal Charter, and extract a large sum for the Treasury from whichever group of merchants had obtained the monopoly. The group of merchants would thus be incorporated as a company. It is unlikely such a method would be used nowadays.

Act of Parliament

As an alternative to the Crown granting a charter to a company, Parliament could grant a charter to a company, thus giving the company existence: for example, the Bank of Scotland was set up by an Act of the Scots Parliament in 1695. Towards the end of the 19th century the first major railway companies were set up. As the companies had to acquire such enormous quantities of land on which to build their railways and stations, the companies obtained Acts of

Parliament setting out the charters of the companies and their powers to buy land. Similarly some of the public utility companies were set up by Acts of Parliament.

Clearly not every group of merchants, investors or entrepreneurs had the connections to obtain a Royal Charter or could afford to obtain an Act of Parliament. Accordingly there were various unsatisfactory attempts to create companies by means of deeds of settlement, most of which involved the extensive use of trusts in an attempt to insulate the investors from their companies' debts. It was difficult to sue such companies and even more difficult for the companies themselves to sue.

Despite the problems associated with companies generally in the 18th and early 19th centuries, some companies were very successful, notably the East India Company, which proved so lucrative that it could afford its own standing army which conquered much of India and Ceylon. The company also obtained the aristocratic privilege of being known as "Honourable".

Nowadays it would be possible but unusual for companies to be set up by an Act of Parliament.

Registration with the Registrar of Companies

In 1844 Parliament passed the Joint Stock Companies Act which set up a mechanism for the registration of companies. Although there have been many changes in procedure since that date, nearly all incorporated companies still have to be registered with a Registrar of Companies following procedures laid down in the Companies Act 1985. The procedure for this is explained in greater detail in Chapter 3. There are separate Registrars for England and Wales and Scotland, and offices in Cardiff, London, Glasgow and Edinburgh. There is also one in Belfast for Northern Irish companies. The Channel Islands and the Isle of Man have their own similar systems of registration.

Certain corporations not governed by the Companies Act 1985, such as building societies, friendly societies and European economic interest groupings have their own methods of registration which will not be discussed in this book.

Internationally, most countries, and certainly all European countries, have adopted similar registration systems. Some countries, notably Liechtenstein, are said to have more registered companies than inhabitants. The state of Delaware, in the United States, has adopted particularly undemanding registration requirements, to the extent that company registration and incorporation fees are a major source of income for that state (see Chapter 23).

The quest for the avoidance of personal liability for a company's debts

Historically merchants have always sought methods of minimising their risk, not least because in the Middle Ages non-payment of debts could result in imprisonment or slavery. One method is to share the risk amongst partners; another is to offer creditors a high share of the profits if the enterprise prospers, but no recompense if it fails. Alternatively merchants can insure against the risk of loss. In countries where bankruptcy laws are honoured, merchants can threaten bankruptcy if their creditors press them too hard. Once a merchant is bankrupt no creditor is likely to get much.

By these and other methods at least some of the risk of any enterprise was passed to the creditors.

Passing the risk to the creditors

Passing the risk to the creditors means that instead of the controllers of a business taking the risk if the business fails, the business's creditors take the risk that the business may go bankrupt and that they may lose their money.

To put this in context, no transaction is entirely without risk. If you trade with a sole trader he may disappear with your money before he supplies you with your goods. If you trade with a limited company, you will be aware that the company's resources are normally restricted to the net assets (in other words, its assets less its liabilities) – though this may not in practice always amount to much. However, because of the registration requirements for companies, and, in Britain at least, because of the requirement for most companies to publish their accounts annually, you can inspect the past financial progress of the company to gain some idea of its past net asset position. This is no guarantee that the company will honour its debts, but you are in a better informed position than you might have been otherwise. If you visit the Registrar of Companies, and inspect the company's previous accounts, you can see if its assets are minimal and debts high. You may well then choose not to deal with that company. But if you were dealing with a sole trader, you might find it difficult to obtain such information on which to base your decision as to whether or not to deal with that trader.

A further issue in connection with passing the risk to creditors is that broadly speaking many small creditors can bear a little loss more easily than one entrepreneur can bear one large loss. The risk of dealing with a limited liability company is spread out amongst all the creditors rather than one person being liable for all his business's debts, perhaps resulting in his being financially crippled for a long time.

The South Sea Bubble

Sadly, the desire to pass risk to creditors leads on all too easily to the desire to defraud creditors and investors generally. One of the reasons Britain was slow to develop the concept of limited liability was because of the scandal surrounding the South Sea Bubble in 1720. By the use of bribes and share-rigging, the lawyer and financier John Blunt and his "Company of Merchants of Great Britain trading in the South Seas" successfully talked up the value of shares in his company so much that at one stage it was even considering buying the National Debt. Notwithstanding that few investors were sure where exactly the South Seas were, and that few ships were properly completed to sail there, speculation fever seized the country. People who should have known better bought shares in the South Sea Company, or shares in companies that had acquired large blocks of South Sea Company shares, or even shares in companies that had acquired shares in companies that had large blocks of shares in the South Sea Company. When the share price was high enough, and the Prince Regent and prominent politicians had made their profits, the directors, including Blunt, sold their shares and decamped to Paris. Meanwhile other entrepreneurs had discovered the public's enthusiasm for idiotic speculation and were promoting companies for such useful purposes as the fattening of elephants and the solidification of mercury.

The creation of the limited liability company

Once the South Sea Company's directors had disappeared, and once the company's true financial position was revealed, the shareholders tried to sell their shares and found that no one was willing to buy them. Many gullible investors lost a great deal of money. As with certain other great financial collapses, such as the Wall Street Crash in 1929, or the Lloyd's insurance scandal in Britain in the 1990s, it was realised that existing safeguards were not good enough. The Government passed the Bubble Act (6 Geo 1, c. 18) which effectively prohibited the formation of any companies other than companies incorporated by Act of Parliament or Royal Charter. Although there were many ingenious methods of evading the Act none of the methods was very satisfactory. It also soon became apparent that the Act was actually hindering commerce. Accordingly the Bubble Act was repealed in 1825 and the Joint Stock Companies Act 1844 was passed in order to allow the creation of registered companies. In 1855 the Limited Liability Act permitted limited liability to become a legitimate feature of companies. The main impetus for limited liability arose from the fact that the French and Americans had created such forms of companies, and British entrepreneurs were actively seeking incorporation of their businesses under French and American law precisely to obtain the benefit of limited liability.

Advantages and disadvantages of limited liability companies

The arguments for and against the creation of limited liability companies are as valid now as they were in 1855.

Arguments in favour of limited liability

1. *The promotion of commerce*

   If a businessman knows that his maximum liability to his creditors is the amount he has agreed to invest by way of capital in his company and no more, he is more likely to take a risk and set up a business. Without the reassurance of limited liability, he might not bother at all. This would affect his prosperity, result in lowered employment opportunities for everybody, and, if enough people followed his example, result in the impoverishment of the country.

2. *Size of enterprise*

   Some enterprises, such as the building of canals and railways, required an enormous amount of capital, and hence a very large number of investors. Trying to run a large commercial enterprise in the name of several thousand investors is impractical when one body can do it instead. Furthermore, without the benefit of limited liability, investors might not choose to be involved in large enterprises and major commercial opportunities might be missed.

3. *Economies of scale*

   A company with a predetermined amount of capital, fixed and not easily withdrawn by its members, was in some ways a better commercial risk than an unincorporated association of individuals. A supplier or a bank might be more willing to give cheaper credit to a company whose accounts it could inspect than to a collection of private individuals, and suing one company is a good deal easier than suing a multiplicity of partners.

4. *The promotion of investment*

   The absence of limited liability meant that neither small investors nor prudent investors used their capital to their best advantage or to the nation's best advantage. Without limited liability only the foolish, the prodigal, or the already wealthy would invest.

5. *The disclosure principle*

   In order to have the privilege of limited liability, companies must publish sufficient details about their accounts and their management to enable creditors and other people dealing with those companies to have some idea of the companies' financial position. Creditors and outsiders thus have some, albeit not very much, opportunity to come to an informed opinion about the trustworthiness of the companies with which they are dealing.

The arguments against limited liability

1. *The passing of risk to creditors*
   From the creditors' point of view, limited liability is inevitably unsatisfactory. Some creditors can of course incorporate themselves, but inevitably there are some creditors who cannot, such as, for example, doctors and architects. Creditors can occasionally insure against default by their customers, but premiums can be expensive. Otherwise, creditors just have to take their chance that whatever their misgivings about a company with which they have been dealing, or indeed its management, there may be nothing that can be done about the risk of dealing with that company. It is for this reason that banks sometimes insist upon personal guarantees from the directors of a company before the bank will lend that company money.

2. *The danger of fraud*
   It is also inevitable that limited liability is convenient for fraudsters, or those who, if not actually positively fraudulent, are somewhat less than scrupulous. Such people know very well that their behaviour is sometimes not actually illegal but merely immoral. The law is often powerless to deal with such people. Equally, limited liability can mean that companies will sometimes be wound up rather than fulfil obligations they ought to fulfil, such as paying damages in a court action, completing unrewarding contracts, or paying their employees their wages. Although there are rules to prevent such fraudulent or dishonourable activities (see IA 1986 s 212–216), there is inevitably a gap between what the law presupposes should happen and what actually happens.

3. *The danger of speculation*
   As with the South Sea Bubble, unrestricted dealing in publicly traded securities can lead to a form of gambling which some may consider both unwise and indeed immoral, and which can lead to people losing money through a combination of greed, folly and naivety. During the Wall Street Collapse in 1929 many investors, particularly those who were trading in securities using borrowed funds, committed suicide rather than meet their debts or face the ignominy of explaining to their families how they had lost all the family savings. Although nowadays press comments on and analysts' study of companies prevent some of the wilder excesses of earlier in this century, "playing the stock market" can still be a gamble and is not to be lightly undertaken.

4. Limited liability can lead to lowered standards of professionalism

When a person is personally liable for his business's debts, he is more likely to carry out work for other people accurately and carefully. If certain lawyers had limited liability, it is conceivable that they might not take so much trouble to win their cases or carry out their work properly. Limited liability is therefore not advisable, from a consumer point of view, if you wish professional standards to remain high. Or to put it more crudely, would you trust a doctor who limited his own liability?

As a matter of practice, most professional people who cannot at present obtain limited liability (such as doctors, lawyers etc.) are required to take out professional indemnity insurance which will, if necessary, meet the cost of claims against those professionals. However, it is anticipated that the size of some claims against professionals, particularly in the USA, will soon be so great that it may not be possible to insure against them. This would result in a reluctance by professionals to carry out high risk activities, such as auditing, or alternatively, result in increased costs to cover the risk to the professionals. Furthermore if such claims are successful, and there is a shortfall in insurance cover, professionals may choose to become bankrupt – thus ensuring that the claims will not be paid in full.

Notwithstanding the arguments against limited liability, the limited liability company won the day, as it inevitably would, given that most other Western countries were developing limited liability companies and were gaining a commercial advantage from so doing. The Government recognised that such an important issue as companies must be regulated by statute, and statute remains the most important source of company law. Nowadays statute is strongly influenced by the requirements of European Community law as well.

Sources of company law

Principal UK statutes

The principal UK statutes applying to company law are:

- Business Names Act 1985

- Companies Act 1985 ("CA 1985")

- Company Directors Disqualification Act 1986 ("CDDA 1986")

- Criminal Justice Act 1993 ("CJA 1993")

- Financial Services Act 1986 ("FSA 1986")

- Insolvency Act 1986 ("IA 1986")

- Companies Act 1989.

The Companies Act 1985 was a consolidating statute that gathered together and rationalised a number of other company law measures. It took account of certain European directives and at the time of writing is the main company law statute. It was amended, and added to, in certain respects by the Companies Act 1989. This Act sought to introduce a number of radical changes, some of which, such as the changes to the law on the registration of charges, turned out to be so difficult to implement that the Government has thus far declined to introduce them.

The Company Directors Disqualification Act 1986 was introduced as a method of prohibiting certain persons, within one distinct Act, from being company directors, or holding office in a company, on account of their previous unsatisfactory behaviour as a person involved in the management of a company. The maximum prohibition is 15 years.

The Criminal Justice Act 1993 Part V is a restatement of the law on insider dealing (sometimes known as insider trading). At the time of writing it has not been in operation long enough to ascertain whether or not it is any more successful than the previous law on insider dealing (Company Securities (Insider Dealing) Act 1985).

The Financial Services Act 1986 regulates the operation of much of Britain's financial services industry. A vastly complicated Act, it set up the framework for the regulation of the insurance industry, the securities markets, the stock markets and the provision of financial services generally.

The Insolvency Act 1986 regulates personal bankruptcy in England and Wales and corporate insolvency and receivership in England, Wales and Scotland.

In Northern Ireland, the Companies Act 1985 and much of the Companies Act 1989 do not in general apply, though the equivalent Northern Irish legislation is very similar. Neither the Insolvency Act 1986 (except in certain specific areas, such as s 73, winding-up orders in Northern Ireland) nor the Company Directors Disqualification Act 1986 apply in Northern Ireland. The Criminal Justice Act 1993 Part V does apply. The principal legislation applicable to company law in Northern Ireland is as follows:

(a) Business Names (Northern Ireland) Order 1986 (SI 1986/1033 (NI 7))
(b) Companies (Northern Ireland) Order 1986 (SI 1986/1032 (NI 6))
(c) Companies (Northern Ireland) Order 1989 (SI 1989/2404 (NI 18))
(d) Insolvency (Northern Ireland) Order 1989 (SI 1989/2405 (NI 19))
(e) Companies (Northern Ireland) Order 1990 (SI 1990/593 (NI 5))
(f) Companies (No 2) (Northern Ireland) Order 1990 (SI 1990/1504 (NI 10)).

Broadly speaking, (a) is equivalent to the Business Names Act 1985; (b) is equivalent to the Companies Act 1985; (e) and (f) are equivalent to the Companies Act 1989; (c) is equivalent to the Company Directors Disqualification Act 1986 (as amended by subsequent legislation); and (d) is equivalent to the Insolvency Act 1986.

European Union legislation

European directives

European Community law ("EC law") has various types of legislation of which the commonest as far as company law is concerned is the directive. A directive is addressed to Member States of the EU, and it tells the Member States what result is expected to be achieved by the directive. It is then up to each State to devise laws to implement the directive into its own legislation. Some directives leave a good deal of discretion to the Member State, but others are very detailed. A directive has an end-date by which the directive must have been adopted. If the end-date passes without the directive having been implemented, or if it has been implemented but in a defective manner, the directive is enforceable against the Member State or bodies substantially controlled by the Member State, but not against private individuals or corporations by the state, or by private individuals or corporations against each other.

The European Union sees as one of its aims the harmonisation of company law rules, so that broadly speaking the company law rules throughout Europe should eventually be much the same. To a certain extent this aim has been achieved, particularly as far as public companies are concerned, and particularly where there are no political implications. This topic, including a discussion of the relevant directives and draft directives, is considered in greater detail in Chapter 23. The following directives have been implemented:

- First Directive (68/151): this substantially amended the *ultra vires* rules (see Chapter 4).

- Second Directive (77/910): this dealt with the reclassification of public companies (see Chapter 3), the raising of capital (see Chapter 7) and the maintenance of capital rules on payment of dividends (see Chapter 10).

- Third Directive (78/855): this deals with mergers and reconstructions of public companies and in particular where assets of a target company are acquired by a takeover company (see Chapter 19).

- Fourth Directive (78/660): this prescribes the formats for accounts to be presented to shareholders (see Chapter 10). It also created the concepts of small and medium sized companies (see Chapter 2).

- Fifth Directive (82/891): this deals with the opposite situation to that in the Third Directive: it refers to the division of a public company's assets between various other companies in exchange for new shares in the other companies for the public company's former shareholders.

- Seventh Directive (83/349): this prescribes the format of consolidated accounts and group accounts.

- Eighth Directive (84/253): this specifies the qualifications and supervision necessary for auditors.

- Twelfth Directive (89/667): this outlines provisions for single member private limited companies.

Company legislation generally

Company legislation, along with tax legislation, is renowned for its complexity. Although it is the aim of the Department of Trade and Industry ("DTI") to ratio-nalise and simplify company legislation where it can, Parliamentary time is pre-cious and the reform of company legislation is not always seen as an urgent priority. It is probably true too that company law is seen as an unglamorous area for an MP to specialise in. Inevitably, therefore, some company law statutes are not all they might be.

In particular, company law statutes suffer from an inherent problem: what happens when the statute is badly worded or is silent on a particular issue? EC law, in general, works on a purposive basis, which means that even if the exact wording of the directive is not very well expressed or is silent on a particular matter, the important issue is the desired end result, and much EC law can be interpreted so as to give effect to that end result. EC law, accordingly, does not suffer as much as English law from the problem of badly worded legislation or legislation that omits something that perhaps ideally ought to be there.

However, English law, and to a lesser extent Scots law based on statute, nor-mally finds this concept very difficult to cope with. The view was often taken that if the legislation was unclear, there should be a test case (usually at vast expense) to clarify the issue. Equally if the legislation was silent, then if a cer-tain action had not positively been prohibited, it was presumably permissible, since Parliament could have chosen to prohibit that action if it wished to. The fact that the problem might never have crossed Parliament's collective mind is thereby ignored.

However, on a recent occasion when a statute was unclear (*Pepper* v *Hart* [1992] 3 WLR 1032), the House of Lords looked at the records of what took place in Parliament at the time that the Government was trying to pass the statute in the hope that *Hansard* – (the record of Parliamentary proceedings) would make clear what the Government was trying to do. The House of Lords accordingly effectively applied a purposive interpretation of the statute to the particular legal issue in doubt. It remains to be seen whether this principle will be extended to all areas of statute law and company law in particular.

Notwithstanding this recent development, it is generally the case that case law steps in where legislation is unclear or where it is missing. Case law is the decision of judges on similar issues and the British legal system works on the principle that the higher the court, the greater the significance given to the court's decision. This principle is known as judicial precedent. A decision from a higher court is binding on all lower courts and remains in place until over-turned by the decision of a yet higher court, or is overturned by a new piece of legislation. Some further case law develops out of what is known as common law, which effectively fills in the gaps left by statute, or sometimes provides an additional set of remedies to the statutory remedies.

In England and Wales company law cases are dealt with by the Chancery Division of the High Court. In Northern Ireland the relevant court is the same. In Scotland, there is a new Commercial Court to deal with commercial and corporate matters, though the Commercial Court does not oust the jurisdiction of the other courts.

A decision of an English court on a company law matter is not binding on a Scottish or Northern Irish court, just as a decision of a Scottish or Northern Irish court is not binding on an English court. Nonetheless a decision in one juris-diction is often considered highly persuasive in another, particularly if the deci-sion comes from the House of Lords which sits in all three jurisdictions. As Canada, Hong Kong, New Zealand and Australia have, or had, especially through the Privy Council (formerly the ultimate court of appeal for those coun-tries), similar judicial arrangements with English law, considerable attention is paid to decisions coming from those courts too, though their decisions are not binding on British courts. However increasingly nowadays Britain is turning towards Europe for its decisions.

Different types of trading organisation

The three main types of trading organisation within the United Kingdom are sole traders, partnerships and limited companies.

1.   Sole traders

(a)   A sole trader is a person who runs a small business on his own account. Nobody else has an interest in his business, and the only people who see his accounts are the Inland Revenue and the Customs and Excise if he is registered for value added tax. Although certain types of business require licences to operate, depending on local regulations, there are very few formalities required for a sole trader to set up in business.

(b) If a sole trader uses a business name different from his own name the business name must conform to the requirements of the Business Names Act 1985, in that the business name must not suggest a connection with the Government or any local authority or certain professional occupations unless the requisite approval has been given. Accountants and lawyers who set up on their own as sole traders are sometimes inaccurately known as sole partners or single partner firms. They should in fact be known as "sole practitioners". Common examples of sole traders are small shops, businesses or occupations such as newsagents, plumbers, cobblers, specialist consultants, authors, freelance musicians etc.

2. Partnerships

Partnerships are regulated by the Partnership Act 1890 ("PA 1890"). Any two or more persons operating a business together with a view to profit constitute a partnership in the eyes of the law. A group of people who are not together for the purpose of profit do not constitute a partnership, so a bowling club, or a trust run by trustees, does not constitute a partnership. It is possible for two or more companies to band together as a partnership. The PA 1890 is designed to give ground rules for the establishment of partnerships in the absence of any particular agreement. In an ideal world, partners would always regulate their affairs by means of a written agreement, known variously as a "deed of partnership", "contract of co-partnery", "partnership agreement" or "articles of partnership", but in practice many people never get round to doing this. Where any agreement fails to cover a particular point, or where there is no written agreement, the PA 1890 steps in to provide rules for the partnership to follow. A partnership is commonly also known as a "firm".

The main legal points about partnerships generally are:

(a) There is no requirement for a special formal written document to constitute a partnership, though it is nonetheless a good idea.

(b) A partnership in England and Northern Ireland has no separate legal identity in its own right, though for administrative convenience it is treated as a legal identity so that it can sue and be sued in the firm's name. However, any property of any nature held to the partnership account is owned jointly for the partnership by the partners in terms of their partnership agreement, and likewise the debts of the partnership are normally borne by the partnership but the partners are jointly liable for those debts. In

Scotland a partnership does have a separate legal identity (PA 1890 s 4). This means that a Scottish partnership can enter contracts and can own its own property, other than land and buildings (known as "heritage") which can only be owned by the partners as trustees for the partnership (PA 1890 s 20). As in England, the partnership can sue and be sued in the firm name. From a practical point of view the difference between English and Scottish law on this matter is not great because the debts of the partnership are still ultimately borne by the partners. However, in Scotland, unlike in England, partners may be debtors or creditors of the partnership.

(c) Subject to many exceptions, a partnership may not have more than 20 partners (CA 1985 s 716). If it does, it must incorporate as a company, and if it refuses to incorporate it cannot enforce any contracts it makes because it has no legal standing and is merely an association. However, if it does make such a contract in the course of a business with a view to profit, the other party to the contract can enforce the contract against the members of the association personally provided that the other party is unaware that the association has over 20 members (*Greenberg* v *Cooperstein* [1926] 1 Ch 657). The exceptions to the above rule apply to a large number of professions, including solicitors, accountants, actuaries, estate agents, surveyors and others approved by the DTI. At the time of writing there is much debate about the continuing viability of accountancy and legal firms remaining partnerships in the light of potential negligence claims, and this rule may at some stage be changed.

(d) Subject to the terms of the partnership agreement, all partners theoretically have the right to have a say in the management of the partnership (PA 1890 s 24(5)). In practice the partners with the most capital in the partnership are those likely to have the loudest say.

(e) Any partner can bind the partnership in a contract, even if the other partners neither approve nor authorise the contract, provided the partner was acting within his ostensible authority. This means that the partner was acting within the realm of activities within which a partner in a partnership might normally be expected to act. This does not apply if the other party to the contract knew (PA 1890 s 5), or ought to have known by reasons of the surrounding circumstances (PA 1890 s 7), that the partner was not authorised to act in the way he was acting.

(f) Partners have unlimited liability for their firm's debts. A creditor can elect to sue the partnership, and can exhaust the partnership's assets in settlement of his debt. If his debt is still unsatisfied, he can proceed against the partners personally and, if necessary, make each of them bankrupt. In England if one partner cannot pay his debt, the other partners must pay his share between them (PA 1890 s 9). However, if the creditor obtains a decree in Scotland against the partnership he can also claim against any individual partner for the full amount if he chooses (PA 1890 s 9); that partner can then seek recompense from his other partners or the firm (PA 1890 s 4(2)).

(g) Partners can deal in whatever form of trade they wish, subject to the terms of their partnership agreement.

(h) If a partnership wishes to borrow money against the value of any assets it owns, as a matter of practice the lender will usually want the individual partners to grant security to the lender over their own assets before the loan is made available. The lender may take a security over the partnership premises if they are such that a security can be granted over them. But if the partnership wishes to grant a security over assets of the partnership which may in the course of time be constantly changing as they are bought, sold, added to, or processed, there is no wholly satisfactory mechanism to allow this.

(i) A partnership is under no obligation to publish accounts or any other details of the partnership, except to the Inland Revenue, the Customs and Excise for value added tax, and anyone else the partnership agrees to present its accounts to, such as landlords. The accounts need not be audited, but if they are not audited, they are less likely to be taken seriously by those wishing to rely on them.

3. Registered companies

(a) All these points can be compared with similar points for companies. There are considerable formalities involved in the formation of companies. As will be seen in Chapter 6, certain forms must be lodged with the Registrar of Companies before a company comes into existence. Accounts and an annual return also need to be regularly lodged with the Registrar or the company will be removed from the register.

(b) A company has a separate legal existence because company law gives it one. Therefore the company's debts are not the members' debts, nor are its assets the members' assets.

(c) There is no restriction on the maximum number of members a company may have, though a public company may not have fewer than two members, and a private limited company must also have at least two members unless it has taken the relevant steps to designate itself as a single member private limited company (see Chapter 6).

(d) The management of the company is usually delegated to the directors, subject to certain matters which must have the approval of the members, either under statute or under the company's own constitution. For example, changing the name of a company requires the consent of 75% of the members who are entitled to vote voting in its favour. This is not a matter that can be left in the hands of the directors alone. However, if the directors are in favour, the resolution is more likely to be passed, and particularly so if the directors constitute a majority of the voting members.

(e) Any partner in a firm binds his fellow partners when he enters a contract on behalf of the partnership, unless there is something manifestly unusual about the contract. However, it is not always clear who can bind the company in a contract. Normally anyone properly authorised can bind the company, but, just as you would not expect a bank teller to give authority for a £2 million loan to a customer, so not every employee or indeed director of a company has authority to make his company enter any contract. This is a matter which is looked at in more detail in Chapter 4.

(f) In a limited liability company, the members are not liable to the company for its debts except to the amount they have agreed to contribute to the company by way of share capital. So if the members have each agreed to buy 100 shares with a nominal value of £1.00 each, provided each member has contributed his £100 to the share capital, he has no further liability. However, if the member has contracted to pay a premium for the share (in other words, he has paid an amount in excess of the nominal value because he is so keen to buy the shares, or because the directors who set the share price knew that people would be prepared to pay well above the nominal value for the shares) he will have to pay the premium as well.

If the shares are partly paid, the member may be asked to pay up the outstanding amount by the directors if they consider the company needs the money, or by the liquidator if the company is insolvent.

A member can be liable for the company's debts if the member is unwise enough to guarantee the company's debts. This is not uncommon if a bank is lending a company money, for many banks will be unwilling to lend a company money unless the loans are guaranteed and preferably backed by a security over the guarantor's personal property.

(g) The pay-off for limited liability is that the company must publish its accounts and reveal certain other details of its share ownership and directors etc. This is not always welcome to those who run companies, as it can mean that competitors can see if a company has a weak trading position, and trade creditors may inspect the company's published accounts and decide that the company is a bad risk. Potential investors may come to the same conclusion and therefore decline to buy further shares in the company. To prevent companies deliberately delaying the publication of their accounts so that the accounts can be of no interest to competitors because they are so out of date, there are substantial fines for delay in lodging accounts and annual returns.

(h) Theoretically a company is supposed to trade only in the area of business specified in the objects clause in the memorandum of association. This is discussed at greater length in Chapter 4. Although historically deviation from the terms of the objects clause was a ground for winding up the company, it is extremely unlikely that this would be the case nowadays. If the company embarks upon a contract that is not covered by the objects clause, there is an opportunity for a member to go to court to prevent the company taking the contract any further, but if the contract is already in operation or rights have already been given to the other party in the contract, there is little the objecting member can do about it (CA 1985 s 35(2)) other than prevent the repetition of the action which is objected to, unless that other party to the contract is a director of the company (CA 1985 s 322A). This is also discussed further in Chapter 4.

(i) A company can only be terminated in accordance with procedures laid down in the Companies Acts. There are three methods:

   (i)   following a liquidation, the liquidator can ask the Registrar of Companies to remove the company from the Register of Companies (IA 1986 ss 201–205);

   (ii) the directors write to the Registrar indicating that they wish the company to be removed from the register (CA 1985 s 652A);

   (iii) the Registrar himself may write to the company asking if it is still carrying on in business, and if no answer is received, then, providing the procedure under CA s 652 has been followed, the company will be struck off the register.

This is more fully dealt with in Chapter 21.

(j) If a partnership gets into financial difficulties, the worst that can happen to a non-fraudulent partner is that he can be made bankrupt. However, in the case of a company director, if his company has been wound up and his conduct, even if not fraudulent, falls short of the standard expected of a responsible and honest director, in terms of IA 1986 ss 212–216, he may be found liable for the debts of the company and forbidden to be a company director for a number of years under the CDDA 1986.

(k) If a company wishes to offer security for, say, a loan, not only can it grant a mortgage over any land and buildings it owns, as indeed can a partnership, but it can also offer by way of security a floating charge. A floating charge is more fully discussed in Chapter 17, but is in effect a type of mortgage over the company's assets, assets which may be constantly changing in the course of the company's business. The ability to grant such security means that if a company suddenly obtains a business opportunity, it can quickly take advantage of the opportunity by borrowing money from a lender. The lender can secure his loan relatively quickly and easily by means of a floating charge. A partnership would be unable to do this.

(l) A successful public limited company ("plc") can be admitted to the Stock Exchange for a "listing" or have its shares traded on the Alternative

Investment Market. This can result in great wealth for the original share-holders if the public is very enthusiastic about buying the company's shares.
(m) Some people believe that there is a certain status in being a company director.

A summary of the advantages and disadvantages of incorporation

The principal advantages of incorporation in essence are as follows:

1. the limited liability of the company's members;

2. the separate legal personality of the company, so that its liabilities are not the members' liabilities, and its assets are not the members' assets;

3. even if the membership changes, and the directors all change, the company continues to own its own assets;

4. the ability of a company to grant a floating charge means that a company, even if it owns no land and buildings, can still obtain finance on the strength of the value of its moveable assets and any other assets it has not already secured elsewhere;

5. only by means of incorporation can an entrepreneur float his company, once it has become a plc, on the Stock Exchange or the Alternative Investment Market, where, if the shares of his company are seen as desirable, his shares will suddenly become very much in demand and he will make a great deal of money;

6. some people enjoy the status of being a company director.

The principal advantages of being a partnership are:

1. privacy: only the Inland Revenue and Customs and Excise normally inspect your accounts; competitors cannot;

2. some customers may believe that your services will be better performed because you stand to lose everything if you do not carry them out well;

3. setting up a partnership need not cost anything and there are no special for-malities. Even a written agreement, although a good idea, is not obligatory.

The principal disadvantages of being a company are:

1. the public disclosure of accounts and other details, without which limited liability would be unavailable;

2. the cost and inconvenience of incorporation and compliance with all the rules for companies as specified in the Companies Acts and various tax statutes;

3. the expense of an annual audit – though certain small companies do not have to comply with those rules;

4. it is difficult to withdraw capital unless you can sell your shares which, in a small private company, may not be possible;

5. directors sometimes believe that the principle of limited liability will always protect them. However, under certain circumstances under both statute law and common law, directors and occasionally members can be liable for their companies' debts;

6. in practice anyone lending to a private company will almost certainly demand personal guarantees from the directors, thus making the directors personally liable for the company's debts.

The principal disadvantages of being a partnership are that:

1. the partners are personally liable for the partnership's debts;

2. a partnership is generally unable to borrow large sums of money on the strength of the value of items not already charged elsewhere.

It is commonly said that one of the advantages of incorporation is that a company has perpetual existence. This is true, at least in the United Kingdom: by contrast, France limits its companies to an existence of 99 years. Theoretically a British company could last forever, and that suggests that an asset could remain in the hands of the company forever too. By implication it is suggested that a partnership is inferior because it does not have perpetual existence. It is true that some partnerships have to be re-formed each time a partner dies or retires, or a new partner is adopted. This can involve revaluation of assets and a transfer of property to the new partnership. However, in practice, large partnerships set up a management company to hold the major partnership assets, and in addition a well-drafted partnership agreement allows for the continued existence of the partnership, and of the ownership of the partnership assets, even though the individual partners change from time to time. The advantage of a company's perpetual existence (sometimes known as perpetual succession) is therefore somewhat illusory.

It is sometimes also said that taxation consequences favour incorporation. Although this book does not address taxation matters, at the time of writing, there is no significant taxation advantage in being either a partnership or a corporation, depending on the level of salary and/or dividends one is obtaining. A partner is treated as self-employed and therefore has to pay different national insurance contributions from the national insurance contributions that a director employed by the company of which he is the major shareholder suffers. When taxation rates, both for capital and income taxes, were much higher, as they were in Britain in the 1970s, there was an advantage in being a partner, but the advantages have now largely evened out.

Limited partnerships

A limited partnership is a hybrid of a limited company and a partnership. Limited partnerships are regulated by the Limited Partnership Act 1907 and must, like companies, be registered with the Registrar of Companies. In a limited partnership there is at least one "limited partner" who contributes capital which is used by the firm. Commonly the limited partner is a limited company. The limited partner must take no part in the management of the company. If he does take part in the management of the firm, he becomes liable for the firm's debts during the period of his management. Assuming the limited partner does take no part in the management of the firm, if the firm gets into financial difficulties, the limited partner's liability is restricted to the amount he has contributed. There is also at least one "general partner" who is liable for the debts of the firm. There is usually a partnership agreement regulating the positions of the partners, and if such an agreement exists, it must be registered, along with various other particulars such as the names of the partners, the firm name and its place of business.

Limited partnerships are rarely used, mainly because there are few benefits from them that cannot be more easily achieved by means of a limited company. Limited partnerships are sometimes used by venture capitalists as a tax vehicle. Curiously, there is a number of limited partnerships in existence in agricultural areas of Scotland, farming apparently being considered suitable for limited partnerships. The landowner commonly is the limited partner and leases the farmland to the limited partnership. His children are the general partners and their profits rise or fall according to their efforts. The landowner's investment is therefore relatively secure provided he restrains himself, no doubt occasionally with some difficulty, from interfering. Another use of limited partnerships in farming arises where the landowner (the limited partner) lets the land to the limited partnership. The general partner, who would formerly have been the landlord's tenant, ceases to be a tenant and has no statutory security of tenure – which makes it easier for the landlord to sell the land with vacant possession.

Summary

1. A company has a separate legal personality, distinct from its owners and its managers.

2. Most companies are nowadays incorporated by registration under the CA 1985.

3. Limited liability means that the owners of the company are not responsible for the company's debts beyond the amount they have undertaken to pay for their shares or the amount they have guaranteed they will pay in the event of the company's insolvency. The risk of trading with the company passes to the company's creditors. The "pay-off" for limited liability is disclosure by the company of its financial position, its ownership and its management.

4. Advantages of limited liability comprise:

   (a) the promotion of commerce;
   (b) the fact that it is easier to deal with one company than with a large number of separate investors;
   (c) the fact that investors are more likely to invest generally if they know their potential losses are limited. This makes capital easier to obtain;
   (d) disclosure means that it becomes possible to compare companies and to see how reliable they are to trade with or to invest in.

5. Disadvantages of limited liability comprise:

   (a) the risk passing to the creditors, not all of whom can pass the risk elsewhere;
   (b) the opportunities for fraud;
   (c) the danger of imprudent speculation;
   (d) the fact that if someone knows he will not be liable for his business's debts, he may be less scrupulous in his business dealings.

6. The main sources of company law are statutes, in particular the Companies Act 1985 and the Insolvency Act 1986. European directives are also a major source of company law. Case law fills in the gaps in the legislation.

7. The main types of trading organisation in the UK are:

   - sole traders;
   - partnerships;
   - limited liability companies;
   - limited partnerships.

8. *Sole traders* are responsible for their own debts, and need not disclose their accounts to anyone save the Inland Revenue and Customs and Excise.

9. Similarly, partnerships are responsible for their own debts, though the partners are responsible for each other's debts in respect of the partnership business. There is no disclosure of their accounts save to the Inland Revenue and Customs and Excise. In addition:

- it is common but not obligatory to have a partnership agreement;
- partnerships are regulated by the Partnership Act 1890;
- with certain exceptions for professional firms, there may not be more than 20 partners in a partnership;
- each partner is an agent for the partnership;
- a partnership in England and Wales and Northern Ireland has no legal personality, but in Scotland a partnership does have legal personality;
- all partners have an equal say in the management of the partnership unless their partnership agreement says otherwise;
- a partnership can generally only grant security over the immovable or (in Scotland) heritable assets (*i.e.* land and buildings);
- a partnership can be terminated at will or in accordance with the terms of its partnership agreement.

10. A company's members are not normally responsible for its debts unless they choose to honour them or grant guarantees for them. All limited companies' accounts are available for inspection at the Register of Companies. In addition, there are other significant features of companies:

- there are considerable formalities in the incorporation of a company;
- a company has a legal personality separate from its controllers or managers;
- there is no maximum number of members which a company may have;
- the management of the company is delegated to the directors, although some powers, including the right to dismiss directors, are retained by the members;
- companies are expected but no longer obliged to adhere to the purposes for which they were incorporated;
- a company can only be wound up or dissolved in accordance with the CA 1985 and IA 1986;
- because of the privilege of limited liability, there are penalties, both civil and criminal, for directors who abuse that privilege;
- a company can grant a floating charge, thus enabling it to borrow against the value of its moveable assets. In turn this allows a company to use the borrowed funds to take advantage of commercial opportunities;
- a successful company can offer its shares to the public, thus potentially making its owners wealthy.

11. Limited partnerships are fairly rare. A limited partnership has a general partner who takes all the decisions, has unlimited liability, takes most of the

risk and obtains most of the rewards. There is no reason why the general partner should not be a limited company. The other partner is known as the limited partner, who takes no part in the management, has limited liability, generally contributes much of the capital and has very little risk. It is usual for a limited partnership to have a limited partnership agreement. Particulars of the limited partnership must be registered with the Registrar of Companies.

2. THE CORPORATE IDENTITY

Challenging the corporate status – lifting the veil of incorporation – non-statutory lifting of the veil – statutory lifting of the veil – criminal liability of companies

The previous chapter outlined the commercial significance of the separate legal personality of the company. This chapter shows how the principle of separate legal personality was and continues to be upheld as a matter of law and practice, as well as showing the occasions when the courts have refused to apply this principle.

Challenging the corporate status

The concept of incorporation implies a separate legal personality, as was described in the previous chapter. However, from time to time, there have been occasions when creditors or other interested parties have attempted to challenge the corporate status of a company. The courts have been asked to rule, not on whether the company was validly incorporated or not, but on whether in the interests of justice (or for any other reason) the separate legal personality of the company should be ignored. This could make members and/or officers of the company liable for the company's debts, or conversely that a debt due to the company should be paid to its members. Alternatively the courts have been known to treat a group of nominally separate companies as an economic entity, so that a benefit due or a claim against one member of the group can be treated as being available to, or as the case may be, suffered by other members of the group or the group as a whole.

Normally the courts will not allow the separate legal personality to be ignored. There are three well-known cases establishing this:

Salomon v A Salomon & Co Ltd (1987) AC 22

Salomon, a boot-maker, for many years ran a business with the help of his wife and his five children. In 1892 he created a limited company, A Salomon & Co Ltd. He and his family all became shareholders, although he held the vast majority of the shares. He sold the boot-making business to the company for £39,000. As the company could not immediately pay him that amount of money, he took his payment in the form of 20,000 shares of £1.00 each, some cash, and the remainder of the money due to him (£10,000) he lent back to the company. He let the company have the loan because the company had insufficient funds with which to pay him. The company acknowledged the loan by means of some debentures. As Salomon was worried that the company might not at some future date be able to repay his loan, he secured the debentures by means of a floating charge. A floating charge, which is rather like a mortgage, gives the charge holder (in this case, Salomon) on liquidation a prior right to the proceeds of sale of the secured assets of the company. This meant that only after the charge holder's loan had been repaid would the ordinary creditors get their money back – if there were any left over for them. For further information generally about floating charges, see Chapter 17.

Within a year of incorporation, the company suffered financial difficulties. Consequently Salomon transferred his debentures to a Mr Broderip in exchange for £5,000 which Salomon lent to the company. The company failed to pay the interest on the debentures to Broderip who accordingly appointed a receiver over the assets of the company. The receiver sold the assets and this in turn led to the liquidation of the company. Broderip received the monies due to him but there was nothing left over for unsecured creditors. So indignant were the unsecured creditors at what they saw as a dubious or even fraudulent arrangement originally designed to protect Salomon at their expense that the liquidator raised an action against Salomon. The liquidator disputed the validity of the debentures and the validity of the contract for the sale of Salomon's business to the company. In the lower courts it was held that Salomon was the principal and the company his agent (because Salomon had effective control of the company), that in effect Salomon and the company should be treated as the same person, and that the company had a right of indemnity against Salomon for all the company's debts. When Salomon appealed to the House of Lords it was held that because the company had been properly constituted in accordance with the Companies Act 1862;

(i)   Salomon was not the same legal person as his company and there was therefore no reason why he could not contract with the company to sell his business to the company and to have the benefit of the debentures;
(ii) the suggestion that the company was the agent of Salomon was incorrect because even if Salomon did control the company, he and the company were still two legally separate bodies;
(iii) the separate legal identity of the company meant that the company was responsible for its own debts. Salomon was not responsible for its debts and was not required to pay the unsecured creditors.

Accordingly Salomon was not required to indemnify the liquidator for any sums he had received from the company. He and the company were separate legal entities entitled to contract with each other. This decision may at first glance seem unfair on the unsecured creditors. However, if a creditor trades with any company, he must take the risk that that company will not pay its debts and that he may well have no recourse against the company's shareholders or directors.

Lee v Lee's Air Farming Ltd (1961) AC 12

In 1954 Mr Lee, who was a New Zealand aerial crop sprayer, formed a company for the business of spraying crops. He held 2,999 of its shares and his wife held one. He was also the managing director. The company employed him as its chief and indeed only pilot, and took out employee insurance in terms of the New Zealand Workers' Compensation Act 1922. Mr Lee was killed in an air crash while crop spraying. His widow sought compensation on the grounds that her husband had been in the course of his employment at the time of his death. The Privy Council, the ultimate court of appeal for certain Commonwealth countries and consisting of House of Lords appeal court judges, decided that on the principle of *Salomon*, it was perfectly legitimate for Mr Lee's company to have a contract of employment with Mr Lee, and that his widow was entitled to her compensation. This decision confirmed that it is acceptable for a majority member or director to have a contract of employment (or indeed any other legal contract) with what is effectively his own company.

Macaura v Northern Assurance Company Ltd (1925) AC 619

Macaura owned land in Northern Ireland and grew timber on it. He formed a company and transferred the ownership of the timber to the company. He then insured the timber in his own name rather than in the company's name. He was the principal shareholder of the company. A month after taking out the insurance most of the timber was destroyed in a fire. The insurance companies refused to pay out to Macaura personally. The House of Lords held that the insurers were not obliged to do so. Macaura had no insurable interest as a member of the company that owned the timber. The company's assets were not Macaura's assets.

This is often seen as a rather harsh application of the separate legal personality rule, but it is possible that the courts were influenced by the various allegations of fraud that were made about Macaura's conduct and the suspicious nature of the fire.

Although these cases give a very clear indication of the distinction between a company, its members, its directors and employees, the courts have been willing to make exceptions to the principle of separate legal personality.

Lifting the veil of incorporation

Using an uncharacteristically poetic image, company law describes the imaginary barrier between the members or officers of the company and the company itself as the veil of incorporation. On occasion the veil can be either "lifted" or "pierced" which suggests that one can see the true control or ownership of the company. If there is a difference between the two terms it is best described as one of degree rather than form: lifting is in effect the entire removal of the veil whereas piercing suggests that the veil is still in place though not in all respects. Generally speaking, where the veil has been lifted, the company ceases to have a separate legal personality and the members or officers become responsible for the company's debts, become entitled to what otherwise might have been the company's assets, or the company is disbarred from entitlement to an asset because of who the shareholders are (as in *Daimler Company Ltd* v *Continental Tyre and Rubber Company (Great Britain) Ltd* [1916] 2 AC 307, discussed later). Where the veil is pierced, the courts do not necessarily attribute liability to anyone, but may restore the members' position to what it was prior to incorporation (as in *Ebrahimi* v *Westbourne Galleries Ltd* [1973] AC 360, discussed later). However, as the generic term for both lifting and piercing the veil is "lifting the veil", and the distinction more academic than practical, the term "lifting the veil" will be generally used hereafter.

There are two ways in which the veil can be lifted. One is non-statutory and arises where the courts have been persuaded to lift the veil, and on a precedental basis may be prepared to do so again; and the other is where statute expressly permits or demands lifting of the veil.

Non-statutory lifting of the veil

Many judges and academic legal writers have tried unsuccessfully to find a coherent policy behind the non-statutory occasions where the veil has been lifted. In practice the cases on this matter stand on their own particular circumstances, and it is impossible and probably pointless trying to discern a logical and rational policy. If there is a policy at all it is that the courts are in general unwilling to lift the veil but can on occasion be flexible. As will be seen shortly, the courts have sometimes lifted the veil where it seemed the right thing to do in the interests of justice. However, even that can be negated: "The court is not free to disregard the principle of *Salomon* v *Salomon & Co Ltd* [1897] AC 22 merely because it considers that justice so requires." (*Adams* v *Cape Industries plc* [1990] Ch 433 at 536).

Lifting the veil in the interests of justice

Despite the Court of Appeal's pronouncement above, the courts have been known to lift the veil where it would cause an injustice not to do so. This is particularly so where a company is being used, not necessarily fraudulently, as a cover for conduct that would otherwise be contrary to the spirit of an existing agreement.

Gilford Motor Co Ltd v *Horne* [1933] Ch 935. Horne had a service contract with his then employers, Gilford, which stated that after he left their employment he was not to solicit Gilford's customers. After Horne left Gilford's employment he arranged for his wife to set up a company which competed with Gilford's business, and through which Horne approached Gilford's customers. Gilford successfully obtained an injunction (*i.e.* a court order) against both Horne and his company for this: Horne's company was described as "a device, a sham".

Jones v *Lipman* [1962] 1 WLR 832. Lipman had agreed to sell land to Jones, but changed his mind at the last minute. Instead he sold the land to a company of which he was principal shareholder and director, and thus claimed he was unable to carry out the sale. Jones was successfully able to persuade the court to force Lipman and his company to complete the sale to Jones.

The case of *Creasey* v *Breachwood Motors Ltd* [1992] BCC 638 was for some years seen as a good example of lifting the veil in the interests of justice. Following a dispute with his employers Creasey raised an action against his employers for wrongful dismissal. His employers, Breachwood (Welwyn) Ltd, realising that he might be at least partially successful in his claim, transferred the assets of that company to a different company, Breachwood Motors Ltd. When Creasey duly won his employment claim, he found that the defendants had no assets to satisfy the judgment in his favour. The court gave him leave to transfer his claim to Breachwood Motors Ltd. This decision has been expressly overruled in *Ord* v *Belhaven Pubs Ltd* (Court of Appeal, 13 Feb 1998 as yet unreported), a case with broadly similar circumstances to *Creasey*. Hobhouse LJ held that lifting of the veil should only occur where there is evidence of impropriety (as per *Adams* v *Cape Industries plc* [1990] BCC 786). In neither *Creasey* nor in *Ord* was there evidence of impropriety. Accordingly future attempts to lift the veil in the interests of justice are only likely to be successful where there is clear evidence of impropriety.

Lifting the veil in the interests of public policy

Sometimes the courts have lifted the veil in the interests of public or national policy. In the 1950s there were tax incentives for making films in the UK. These incentives could be abused.

Re FG (Films) Ltd [1953] 1 WLR 483. The courts held that a film company, which was British in registration but American in every other respect, was merely an agent to attract a tax incentive and should be taxed as if it were the agent for the American company which controlled it.

Unit Construction Company Ltd v *Bullock (Inspector of Taxes)* [1960] AC 351. The courts looked behind the apparent structure of three companies apparently under Kenyan management in order to establish whether or not the company was liable to tax in the UK. It was decided that as all the decisions about the companies were taken in the UK the business should be taxed in the UK.

Re H. and Others [1996] 2 All ER 391. The defendants were involved in substantial evasion of excise duty leviable on a chocolate alcoholic drink. They carried out their evasion of duty through the medium of two limited companies. It was held that Customs and Excise were entitled to treat the companies' stock as personal assets of the defenders, and entitled to seize the stock in payment of the sums due.

The following case is an extreme example of national policy dictating the law.

Daimler Company Ltd v *Continental Tyre and Rubber Company (Great Britain) Ltd* [1916] 2 AC 307. This case arose during the First World War, when Britain was at war with Germany. Daimler, as a British company, did not see why it should help the Germans by paying a debt to the Continental Tyre and Rubber Company Ltd which, although British registered, was predominantly German-owned and run by Germans. The courts upheld Daimler's view. It is not perhaps very likely that such a situation would arise again, unless a country against which there were international sanctions were trying to sue for payment in the UK.

Lifting the veil using the economic entity theory

Normally a holding company (a company that owns the majority of shares in any other company, known as a subsidiary) is not liable for the debts of its subsidiary. Equally a subsidiary is not responsible for the debts of its holding company, or indeed any other company, unless there is a specific contractual relationship between the companies to that effect. Commonly a bank, when lending to a subsidiary, will insist on a guarantee from its holding company for the subsidiary's debts. But without that guarantee, there would normally be no liability.

However, there have been attempts to suggest that where a group of companies is very closely connected it really forms one commercial unit or economic entity. This is known as the economic entity theory. Accordingly any one member company of the economic entity could be liable for the debts of any other member company in the economic entity; but equally, a benefit technically due to any one member company could be treated as due to another member company.

DHN Food Distributors Ltd v *Tower Hamlets Borough Council* [1976] 3 All ER 462. DHN Food Distributors Ltd ("DHN") and two wholly owned subsidiaries together ran a grocery business. Tower Hamlets Borough Council wished to acquire the premises from which DHN traded but which were in fact owned by one of the subsidiaries. Under s 5 of the Land Compensation Act 1961 that subsidiary was entitled to the value of the land. Had the same subsidiary also been trading from those premises, the Council would also have had to pay compensation for disturbance to trade. DHN had no other premises from which to trade and it was not apparently entitled to compensation for the disturbance, according to the Lands Tribunal to which the matter was referred. On appeal to the Court of Appeal, it was held that the companies could all be treated as one economic entity since it would have been a mere matter of paperwork for DHN as the holding company to have transferred the ownership of property to itself and thus to have obtained the available compensation.

It is significant that the companies in this case were wholly owned subsidiaries. The Court of Appeal was also careful not to extend this particular lifting of the corporate veil to every group of companies. Furthermore the decision was never further appealed to the House of Lords which might have decided differently. It can thus be contrasted with the Scottish case of *Woolfson and another* v *Strathclyde Regional Council*, 1978 SC (HL) 90. Campbell Ltd (C Ltd) were retailers of nuptial wear and leased three shops owned by Woolfson and two shops owned by Solfred Ltd (S Ltd). Woolfson owned all but one share in C Ltd, the remaining share being held by his wife, and both he and his wife were the sole shareholders in S Ltd. C Ltd was registered in the valuation roll as the occupier of the various premises. The Council acquired the premises and was due to pay compensation for disturbance to the occupier or an owner–occupier, but not to a non-occupying owner. Woolfson and S Ltd, realising that as non-occupying owners they might not be able to claim compensation for disturbance, sued the Council on the grounds that the companies should all be treated as one economic entity. On appeal to the House of Lords it was held that C Ltd alone had a right to compensation for disturbance. The *DHN Food Distributors* case was not relevant to the *Woolfson* case, because the presence of his wife's share in C Ltd and his wife's one-third shareholding in S Ltd meant that there was no question of either C Ltd or S Ltd being a wholly owned subsidiary, and furthermore, C Ltd had no control over the owners of the land, (Woolfson and S Ltd). The position might have been different if Woolfson's wife's share in C Ltd had been a nominee shareholding (in other words, she was holding the share on Woolfson's behalf) but this was not in fact the case. The question of an economic entity did not arise and the corporate veil was not to be lifted to make Woolfson the true owner of Campbell's business or the assets of S Ltd. The corporate veil was only to be lifted, in Lord Keith's judgment, "where special circumstances exist indicating that it is a mere facade concealing the true facts."

The approach in *Woolfson* of treating companies as separate, unless there are compelling reasons to do otherwise, was subsequently approved in the English cases of *National Dock Labour Board* v *Pinn and Wheeler Ltd* [1989] BCLC 647 and *Adams* v *Cape Industries* plc [1990] CH 433. In the latter case the judge favourably reviewed *Gilford Motor Co Ltd* v *Horne* [1933] Ch 935 and *Jones* v *Lipman* [1962] 1 WLR 832 as each being an example of a "facade". It is therefore probably the case that for the time being the economic entity theory is in abeyance, though if the once proposed Ninth Directive on European law is ever adopted the theory may well resurface (see Chapter 23).

Statutory lifting of the veil

There is a number of occasions where statute specifically lifts the veil of incorporation. The reasons for these are generally in the interests of fairness, to promote the observance of company law or to prevent frauds.

The quasi-partnership company

One of the saddest of the cases involving the statutory lifting of the veil arises in the case of *Ebrahimi* v *Westbourne Galleries Ltd* [1973] AC 360. Ebrahimi and his partner, Nazar, had run a carpet-selling business together for many years. Finally they decided it would be a good idea to incorporate. Ebrahimi and Nazar became directors of and equal shareholders in Westbourne Galleries Ltd. Nazar's son wanted to join in the business, so Ebrahimi and Nazar arranged that the son should receive some shares. Nazar and his son subsequently decided that with their combined shareholding they were in a position to vote Ebrahimi off the board of directors. Ebrahimi, understandably, was distressed at this betrayal, particularly because the terms of the Articles of Association made it impossible for Ebrahimi to sell his shares without the consent of Nazar and his son – and they refused to consent to this. Ebrahimi petitioned for various orders including the winding-up of the company on "just and equitable grounds" under s 222(f) of the Companies Act 1948 (now IA 1986 s 122(1)(g)). The House of Lords held that the company could be wound up. The House of Lords stated that it could take account of the fact that individuals within the company had rights, expectations and obligations between themselves which predated the incorporation of the company and which were not extinguished by the company's incorporation. The House of Lords was clearly applying equitable considerations to the fact that Nazar and his son were carrying out a lawful act (the removal of Ebrahimi from the board) but in an inequitable way.

Westbourne Galleries Ltd could thus be termed a quasi-partnership company, because it is as if the ethos of the partnership still continued, or should have continued into the company after its incorporation. The veil of incorporation was pierced to allow the underlying partnership's principles – including joint management – to be reasserted.

Nowadays, were Ebrahimi's circumstances to be repeated, it is likely he would be able to obtain a far more satisfactory remedy under the minority protection measures of the CA 1985 s 459 (see Chapter 13). Because of the restrictive nature of the wording of the then equivalent of s 459, s 210 of the Companies Act 1948, such a remedy was not available to Ebrahimi at the time.

Absence of trading certificate under the CA 1985 s 117

Where a public limited company is incorporated as such, it is not wise for the directors to let it trade until it has received a trading certificate under the CA 1985 s 117. The certificate will only be issued by the Registrar of Companies once the Registrar is satisfied that the nominal value of the company's shares is not less than £50,000, each of which shares must be paid to the extent of one-quarter plus any premium on the share. In order to satisfy the Registrar, a director or the company secretary must sign a statutory declaration confirming this. As with all statutory declarations, the signatory is personally liable if he knowingly makes an untrue declaration. Although it is possible for the company to trade without a trading certificate, if the company fails to honour any contract within 21 days of being asked to do so, the directors of the company are jointly and severally along with the company personally liable to the other party to the contract. As a matter of practice this does not often arise, mainly because few people normally want to start a business using a plc. Most people are more likely to start trading with a private limited company, which does not require a trading certificate, and convert to a plc later on – in which case trading certificates are not necessary. This is discussed in greater detail in Chapter 3.

Inaccuracy of company name under the CA 1985 s 349

A company must clearly display its name on, amongst other things, all bills of exchange, promissory notes, endorsements, cheques and orders for money or goods purporting to be signed by or on behalf of the company. Failure to do this renders the defaulting officer personally liable to the holder of the bill of exchange, promissory note, cheque or other order unless it is paid by the company.

This can mean that a simple oversight, such as the failure to write the word "limited" on a company cheque, can make the signatory liable. The original reason for this rule was a third party (*i.e.* the recipient of the cheque or a creditor) should know whether he was dealing with a limited company or an unlimited enterprise such as a partnership. If a company omits the word "limited" a creditor might be under the belief that he was dealing with a partnership, whose partners would be obliged to meet the company's debts – as a result of which the creditor might be more willing to lend the money. Despite the fact that there is no evidence nowadays that the omission of the word "limited" makes an impression on creditors, the rule still stands.

Penrose v *Martyr* [1858] 120 ER 595. A company secretary accepted on behalf of his company a bill of exchange drawn on his company. He unfortunately omitted the word "limited" when inserting his company's name on the bill of exchange. The company defaulted and the company secretary was therefore held personally liable.

Rafsanjan Pistachio Producers Ltd v *Reiss* [1990] BCC 730. Rafsanjan Pistachio Producers Ltd ("RPP") sued a company called Firegreen Ltd, of which Mrs Reiss was a director. RPP settled with Firegreen Ltd that it would provide five cheques of US$100,000, each of which would be postdated. Mrs Reiss did not have a proper cheque-book for the company, and in order to pay the cheques, used special temporary cheques supplied by the bank. These cheques did not state the full company name (as most cheques do) though they did have the company number. Mrs Reiss signed the five cheques but without stating the capacity in which she was signing, as required by the CA 1985 s 394(4). The first three cheques were honoured and the money was safely drawn from Firegreen Ltd's account. The two remaining cheques were not honoured. Mrs Reiss was held to be personally liable for the two outstanding payments.

Had Mrs Reiss had the cheques printed with the name "Firegreen Ltd" and signed "Mrs Reiss, for and on behalf of Firegreen Ltd" she would have saved herself a very great deal of money. It is therefore extremely important that the word "limited" be included. In *Blum* v *OCP Repartion SA* [1988] BCLC 170, Blum, as director of his company, had dealt with OCP by using cheques designated "Bomore Medical Supplies". When his company went into liquidation he was found personally liable for his company's dishonoured cheques, even though all the previous cheques with that name had satisfied OCP. His only opportunity for redress was a possible claim against his bankers for letting his company have cheques that omitted the word "limited". The simple insertion of the word "limited" on each cheque would have saved him £80,000.

Public companies with only one member under the CA 1985 s 24

If a public company carries on business for a period of six months with only one shareholder, (perhaps because the only other shareholder has died leaving his share to the surviving shareholder) and the surviving shareholder is aware that he is the only shareholder, on the expiry of the six-month period, the surviving member becomes jointly and severally liable with the company for the debts of the company. This is designed to encourage public companies either to convert to private companies, which are permitted to have only one member, or to find new shareholders.

Until the advent of the single member private limited company in 1992 this rule also used to apply to private companies, as is seen in the following case where Shepherd ingeniously tried to use a questionable share transfer as a method of avoiding the entire liability for his company's debts.

Nisbet v *Shepherd* [1994] 1 BCLC 300. Shepherd and a friend were the only members of a company. Shepherd bought his friend's shares and purported to execute a stock transfer form transferring all his friend's shares to himself, thus making himself the sole shareholder. Some time later the company went into liquidation and the liquidator sought a declarator that Shepherd was liable for the debts of the company after the expiry of the six-month period. Shepherd had failed to use a normal stock transfer form, and it was arguable that the transfer was void because of this. If the transfer was void, Shepherd could not be the sole shareholder, and could not be liable for the company's debts after the six-month period. It was held that although the stock transfer was not ideal it still could have been stamped. Accordingly there was a proper transfer and Shepherd was found liable.

Fraudulent and wrongful trading under the IA 1986 ss 213, 214

This topic is more fully discussed in Chapter 21 but, briefly, if in the course of a winding-up of a company it appears that the business of the company has been carried on with the deliberate intention of defrauding creditors of the company, any other creditors, or any fraudulent purpose generally, those knowingly responsible, whether they be members, directors or employees, are liable to make such contribution to the company's assets as the courts think appropriate (IA 1986 s 213). Under the wrongful trading provisions (IA 1986 s 21) (also discussed in Chapter 21) directors may also be liable for such amount as the court sees fit if they have traded while the company was insolvent. Likewise under the IA 1986 s 216 directors can be liable for the debts of a phoenix company, which is a company wrongfully reusing the name of a company that recently went into insolvent liquidation. Furthermore, under the misfeasance provisions of the IA 1986 s 212 if a director has misappropriated company assets, or otherwise been in breach of his fiduciary duties to his company and the company has thereafter gone into insolvent liquidation, the director may be personally liable to recompense the company for any loss it may have suffered.

Criminal liability of a company

The question of whether, or to what extent, a company could be convicted for certain offences is at present a very vexed matter. The essential problem is that a company is not itself a human individual, capable of evil or reckless acts such as are required for the perpetration of crimes other than strict liability crimes. For an ordinary human to commit a crime, the human must have the *mens rea* (the guilty or wicked intention) to commit a crime, or failing the deliberate guilty or wicked intention, to have such a reckless disregard for the effects of his actions as to be tantamount to a guilty or wicked intention. It is difficult to prove that a company has *mens rea* since a guilty or wicked intention is something only human beings can have.

Irrespective of the need for *mens rea*, it is obviously physically impossible for a company to commit certain crimes such as rape or bigamy since those are crimes that require a very definite *mens rea* and, in addition, a human involvement. But with crimes that do not so obviously involve a specifically human action, it is difficult to say whether or not a company could have the requisite *mens rea*, since a company, other than a very small company dominated by one or two individuals, could scarcely be said to have a directing mind capable of *mens rea*.

When the cross-channel ferry, the *Herald of Free Enterprise*, sank off Zeebrugge, many passengers died. There were moves to prosecute P & O, the ship's owners, for manslaughter on the grounds that the ship's safety procedures were slack. As it happened the case failed on the merits of the action (*P & O European Ferries Ltd* (1990) 93 Cr App R 72), though it was held that it might have been possible to say that the company could be guilty of manslaughter. In the Lyme Bay canoeing disaster in 1993, the DPP successfully prosecuted OLL Ltd, the company that ran the canoeing expeditions, for manslaughter. In that case the company was run single-handedly by its director/owner, Mr Kite, who was also successfully prosecuted for manslaughter. It was relatively easy to say that the company had a *mens rea* since the company was directed entirely by Mr Kite. In addition Mr Kite pleaded guilty, thus rendering unnecessary the requirement to prove the *mens rea* of the company.

However, it is a different matter trying to prosecute a large listed company such as P & O, the directors of whom cannot have close working knowledge of all their company's actions, and may indeed be completely unaware of them. After all, it would hardly be company policy to commit manslaughter though there have been occasions when companies, through their directors, have quite deliberately sought to carry out some other illegal acts such as tax evasion or setting up cartels. In the case of *Tesco Supermarkets Ltd* v *Nattrass* [1972] AC 153, Tesco successfully pleaded that their failure to adhere to certain trading standards was not for lack of training or direction by the company but was lack of diligence by an individual manager. The company was not held to be criminally responsible for the manager's actions. This can be contrasted with the following, more recent case: *Re Supply of Ready Mixed Concrete (No 2)* [1995] 1 AC 456. The company had given an undertaking to the Restrictive Practices Court not to operate a restrictive practice. Despite this, senior employees continued to operate the forbidden restrictive practice, even though their actions were contrary to the instructions of the board of directors. The company was duly prosecuted and found guilty. The rationale behind this is that without a conviction the undertaking would have been meaningless and would have sent a signal to other manufacturers that such undertakings were worthless. In addition there is the practical point that it is the directors' job to know what is going on and to be responsible for their company's activities. Without such responsibility, it would be tempting for employees to tell their directors only what the directors wanted to hear, on the principle that if the director was not told about something he could honestly claim his ignorance of its existence. By convicting the company the directors are encouraged to ensure that undertakings are properly adhered to.

At present it appears that one of the few other ways in which companies can be satisfactorily prosecuted is where statute provides for "strict liability", which means that irrespective of the reasons for the offence, the fact that the offence occurred makes the company liable. The standard example is pollution offences: British Nuclear is regularly fined for unauthorised and illegal radioactive emissions.

There is an argument that prosecuting companies and fining them is not a very effective sanction. Prosecuting the directors might well have a salutary effect, particularly if the directors were imprisoned, but since one cannot imprison a company, one can only fine or perhaps forbid it to carry out certain activities. Fining a company, particularly a large one, only hurts the shareholders' dividends, and only if it is a massive fine would it have any effect. But even so, why should the innocent shareholders be punished?

The (English) Law Commission and the Government are reviewing the law on this whole area at the time of writing, in view of the obvious defects in the law, and on the law of corporate manslaughter in particular.

It should be emphasised that despite the difficulties involved in prosecuting companies, there are far fewer difficulties involved in the prosecution of officers of a company (*i.e.* its directors, company secretary and auditors) and many sections of the CA 1985 and IA 1986 provide criminal sanctions against errant officers. The liability of directors, both civil and criminal, will be considered more fully in Chapters 14 and 15.

Summary

1. Normally the courts will treat each company as having a separate legal personality, as is seen in:

   - *Salomon* v *A Salomon & Co Ltd* [1987] AC 22
   - *Lee* v *Lee's Air Farming Ltd* [1961] AC 12
   - *Macaura* v *Northern Assurance Company Ltd* [1925] AC 619.

2. Despite the normal rule of the company being separate from its members, on certain occasions the company and its members are treated as one unit. This means that the members or officers can be liable for the company's obligations or, less commonly, the members can receive a benefit otherwise due to the company. This identification of the company with its members is known as "lifting" or "piercing the veil of incorporation". It can also occur when the courts consider it fair under the circumstances (*Ebrahimi* v *Westbourne Galleries Ltd* [1973] AC 360).

3. Lifting the veil takes place under common law and under statute. The common law occasions where the veil has been lifted do not form a consistent body of law, but generally arise where a company is being used as a cloak to hide the true situation (see *Gilford Motor Co Ltd* v *Horne* [1933] Ch 935). Other grounds for lifting the veil are to establish the true domicile of a company (usually for tax purposes) or to treat a company as an enemy alien in time of war.

4. Within the context of the common law occasions where the veil of incorporation is lifted, there has been an attempt to suggest an economic entity theory, whereby a benefit payable to one member of a group can become a benefit to another part of the group. This was advanced in *DHN Food Distributors Ltd* v *Tower Hamlets Borough Council* [1976] 3 All ER 462 but disregarded in the later case of *Woolfson and another* v *Strathclyde Regional Council*, 1978 SC (HL) 90.

5. Of the statutory occasions where the veil of incorporation has been lifted, one should remember:

   - the absence of a trading certificate for a public limited company incorporated as such (CA 1985 s 117);
   - incorrect name of company on bills of exchange, cheques etc. (CA 1985 s 349) (*Rafsanjan Pistachio Producers Ltd* v *Reiss* [1990] BCC 730);
   - public companies with only one member (CA 1985 s 24);
   - fraudulent trading under the IA 1986 s 213, wrongful trading under the IA 1986 s 214, liability for the reuse of the name of a company in insolvent liquidation (IA 1986 s 216), and misfeasance proceedings under the IA 1986 s 212.

On such occasions directors and company secretaries may be liable for the company's debts, and in the case of fraudulent trading, members can be liable as well if they are involved in the fraud.

6. Although there are certain criminal offences involving strict liability, such as pollution offences, for which companies can be successfully convicted, the law has not found it easy to deal with offences carried out by employees of companies, with or without directors' approval. While conviction for certain non-physical crimes may not be too contentious, it is not clear whether or not it is possible or indeed useful to convict companies of physical crimes such as manslaughter, though has been done in the case of the Lyme Regis canoeing disaster. Punishing companies is of limited benefit: imprisonment is not an option and a fine only hurts the shareholders.

3. CLASSIFICATION AND INCORPORATION OF COMPANIES

Types of company: public companies and private companies – dormant, sub-sidiary and foreign companies – single member private limited companies – registration requirements – the disclosure principle – rules for conversion of companies

This chapter outlines all the different types of company, the statutory require-ments for the incorporation of a company, and the methods of converting one type of company to another.

Types of company

There are basically two types of companies: public companies and private companies.

Public companies

A public company has the following characteristics:

1. It must state in its name that it is a public limited company ("plc").

2. A public company must have been incorporated as a company limited by shares.

3. As such, it is potentially able to offer its securities (shares or debentures [a type of loan to a company] or options and warrants to acquire shares or debentures) to the public, though as a matter of practice many plcs do not do so. For more details on different types of security, see Chapter 7.

4. It must have a minimum issued nominal share capital of £50,000 (CA 1985 s 118), and each share must be paid up to the extent of at least one-quarter of the nominal value of each share plus any premium thereon (CA 1985 s 101(1)). The issued nominal share capital of a company is the nominal value of each share (*i.e.* the amount that must be paid on each share to make it fully paid-up) multiplied by the number of shares that the company has actually issued to shareholders. A premium is the amount that an investor will pay in excess of the nominal value in order to buy the share. The premium reflects the desirability of the share.

Suppose a plc has shares of nominal value of £10 each. Each share must then be paid for at least to the extent of £2.50, with the balance of £7.50 on each share being due to the company either when the directors ask the members for it or when the company goes into insolvent liquidation.

If the nominal value of each share is £10, there must be at least 5,000 shares in existence. This is because the nominal value of each share multiplied by the number of shares in existence would then amount to £10 × 5,000, in other words the required minimum of £50,000.

In addition, on commencing trading as a plc, the company should have at least £12,500 (*i.e.* £2.50 × 5,000) in its bank account (or have assets equivalent in value to that figure) because each of the 5,000 shares must be paid up to the extent of one-quarter (£2.50) of its nominal value (£10). If the shares were likely to be very popular, the directors could insist subscribers for the shares should pay a premium of, say, £1.00 for each share. In that case the company's bank account would show at least £12,500 plus £5,000, being £17,500. In the company's accounts, the £12,500 would be credited to the share capital account and the £5,000 would be credited to the share premium account.

5. A plc, *but only if it is incorporated as a plc and not initially as a private company*, is unwise to commence trading or to borrow money unless it has a s 117 trading certificate. This is a certificate issued by the Registrar of Companies permitting the company to trade or borrow.

The reason for this is that a plc can potentially offer its securities to the public. It therefore has to be seen to have greater capital than a private company. In theory, if not necessarily in practice, this makes it safer to invest in and to trade with. Accordingly it would be improper for a company to claim the status and apparent financial solidity of a plc when in fact it did not meet the minimum capital requirements of a plc. The trading certificate is only granted by the Registrar once he has received a statutory declaration from the directors that the company has the required minimum capital (CA 1985 s 117(2)). If the directors have been making the company trade or borrow without a trading certificate and the company fails to pay any debts, the directors will be jointly and severally liable for their company's debts if the company fails to pay those debts within 21 days of being called upon to do so (CA 1985 s 117(8)). A plc that started life as a private company need not obtain a trading certificate under s 117. As a matter of practice most plcs begin as private companies and thus avoid the inconvenience of obtaining the trading certificate.

When a company converts from being a private company to a plc it has to send audited accounts and other documentation to the Registrar of Companies. This is to confirm that its capital position meets the minimum capital requirements of paragraph 3 above (CA 1985 s 45).

6. A plc must have at least two directors (CA 1985 s 292) who may not be over the age of 70 except where the members have approved this (CA 1985 s 293). A plc must also have a suitably qualified or experienced company secretary (CA 1985 s 268(1)). When voting on the appointment of directors, each director of a plc must be approved separately unless the shareholders have previously passed an ordinary resolution to permit voting on the appointment of two or more directors in the one resolution (CA 1985 s 292(1)). This is to ensure that every director is individually approved. Without this, an unpopular or unsatisfactory director could be included within a group of other more satisfactory directors whose joint appointment was being voted upon. The shareholders might then have to accept the unsatisfactory director as the price to be paid for the other directors.

7. Only a public company may have its securities traded on the Official List of the Stock Exchange (in which case the company is said to be "listed"), on the Alternative Investment Market, or any other approved security-dealing markets such as Tradepoint and Ofex. These different market-places for the sale and trading of securities are discussed more fully in Chapter 8. Insider dealing, which is the illicit dealing in securities using secret information denied to most other investors (see Chapter 12), is not possible, at least in the UK, in private companies as their securities are not publicly traded. It should be emphasised that while only public companies can have their shares traded in a recognised investment market, not all public companies choose to do this. There are many public companies whose securities are not publicly traded.

8. On the allotment of shares in a plc, the shares must be fully subscribed for (CA 1985 s 84). This means that when a plc offers and then issues its shares to new and existing investors, all the shares must be acquired by the investors and the offer fully accepted. In addition pre-emption rights will be deemed to apply (CA 1985 s 89) unless they have been specifically waived by the members either by resolution or by consent (CA 1985 s 95). A pre-emption right is a prior right given to existing shareholders to acquire shares before any new investors are given their chance to buy shares (see Chapter 7).

9. It is normal for companies to offer their shares to investors in exchange for cash. However an investor might wish to offer non-cash consideration (see paragraph 11 below) instead, so that the investor could pay for his shares by transferring to the company a building or a business, or by doing some work for the company and receiving his fee in the form of shares. However, a plc may not accept as payment for shares an undertaking to carry out work or perform services for the company (CA 1985 s 99(2)). If the

investor does attempt to purchase shares by means of an undertaking to carry out work or perform services, he will find that he still has to pay cash for the shares plus any interest due (CA 1985 s 99(3)). This is to prevent the company being swindled by people who promise to carry out work for the company but never do, despite having received their shares.

10. A plc may not accept as payment for shares an undertaking to be performed in over five years' time, such as the transfer of a property (CA 1985 s 102(1)). If the undertaking does not take place within the five-year period, the allottee will have to pay for the shares together with any interest due (CA 1985 s 102(2)). This is also to prevent the company being defrauded and to give a truer indication of its net asset position. It can be distinguished from paragraph 9 above because paragraph 9 refers only to the carrying out of work or performing of services for the company, while this paragraph is concerned with any form of undertaking, whether it be the transfer of an asset or the provision of services, which would not take place for at least five years.

11. Any non-cash consideration (in other words, payment for shares by means of something other than money, such as a building or a right to a copyright) given in exchange for shares in a plc must be independently valued before the shares are allotted (CA 1985 s 103). This is to prevent assets being sold to a plc at an inflated price. There are provisions for the auditor and the allottee to check the valuation.

12. Anyone holding 3% or more of the shares in a plc has to inform the company of his holding and of any changes to his holding (CA 1985 s 198). This also applies to those with whom he is connected, such as his family and his other companies (CA 1985 s 203). This is to alert the company to takeover bids by the person holding 3% of the company's shares.

13. Plcs must publish their accounts within seven months of their accounting year (CA 1985 s 244) and the accounts must be tabled at a general meeting (CA 1985 s 241).

14. A plc may only pay a dividend provided the payment of the dividend does not reduce the net asset figure to below the aggregate value of its called-up share capital and undistributable reserves (CA 1985 s 264). The net asset figure is the total value of the company's assets less the total value of its liabilities. The called-up share capital is the amount of the nominal value of each share that has already been asked for by the directors. For a plc the called-up share capital will be at least one-quarter of each share. The undistributable reserves are the reserves of capital that a company, either by its own constitution, or by legislation, is not allowed to distribute by way of

dividend. For example, a share premium account cannot be distributed by way of dividend. This rule ensures that a plc does not pay out so much by way of dividends that the shareholders might not get back what they have paid for their shares in the event of a subsequent liquidation. It also helps reassure creditors of the company that there ought to be funds (to the extent of the called-up share capital and the undistributable reserves) to meet their claims against the company, and that the directors have not distributed all the company's assets by way of dividends. This is discussed in greater detail in Chapter 10.

15. A listed plc (*i.e.* a company whose shares are listed on the Official List of the Stock Exchange) may provide for its members a summary financial statement (CA 1985 s 251). This is because it became apparent after the first major UK privatisations that most shareholders had no idea what to do with the copy of the accounts and directors' report that they were sent annually. As it was costing the companies a great deal to send out these largely unread documents, the CA 1985 s 251 now permits listed plcs to send abbreviated versions of their accounts instead, though the full version is also available for those who want it.

16. A plc may provide financial assistance for the purchase of its own shares only under very restricted circumstances (CA 1985 s 154) (see Chapter 9).

17. A plc may not use capital for the purchase of its own shares (CA 1985 s 171). When it does purchase its own shares, it has a maximum period of 18 months from the date of the relevant members' resolution in which to do so (CA 1985 s 164(4)) (see Chapter 9).

18. A proxy (a personal representative) may not speak at a general meeting of a plc (CA 1985 s 372). The intention behind this is to prevent obstreperous shareholders hiring barristers to represent them at meetings in order to harangue the directors or otherwise impede the proceedings (see Chapter 18).

19. A plc may not have a lien (a right of retention, preventing the owner from selling his shares) over its own fully paid shares (CA 1985 s 150). Were this permitted, it might restrict the marketability of shares which should normally be able to be bought and sold freely.

20. If a plc receives its own forfeited or surrendered shares, they must be either cancelled or reissued within three years or the date of forfeit or surrender (CA 1985 s 146).

21. If the net asset position of a plc drops below half of the value of its called-up share capital, the directors are required to call an extraordinary general meeting to consider what to do about it (CA 1985 s 142).

22. A plc must hold an annual general meeting and cannot pass resolutions by means of written resolutions. In addition, it cannot pass elective resolutions.

Perhaps the most important point about plcs is that they are potentially able to offer their securities to the public. As this is a great opportunity for a company to attract capital and wealth, the following rules apply to afford protection to the investing public and creditors.

1. There must be, at least on incorporation as a plc, or on reincorporation as a plc, a minimum of £12,500 worth of assets. Plcs are seen as being more prestigious than private companies, but the corollary of that is that more information must be disclosed and more capital must be present, at least initially. If there is more capital available, creditors are, in theory, more likely to deal with the company, confident that there ought to be more assets in the company than might be found in a private company, and confident that the company is a better financial risk because of the initial capital contribution. However, as a plc can suffer financial hardship just as easily as a private company can, it is probably the case that a trader does not, in practice, choose to trade with a plc in preference to a private company purely because of a plc's greater initial capital value or its greater level of disclosure. However, because a plc has to publish more of its accounts than private companies, some traders may be keener to trade with plcs than with private companies.

2. Not all plcs wish to have their securities traded publicly. But *only* plcs can have their securities traded publicly, and to do so, they must comply with the requirements of the relevant securities market where their securities are traded (see paragraph 7 above). Publicly offering the shares of a private company is a criminal offence (CA 1985 s 81).

Private companies

A private company is any type of company that is not a public company. There are several different types of private company.

Unlimited companies

The members of these companies are liable for their companies' debts once the companies' funds are exhausted. An unlimited company's name does not include the word "limited". Such companies do not normally need to produce annual accounts (CA 1985 s 254). Unlimited companies are not common, but they are sometimes used where the members wish for some reason to distance themselves from their ownership of a particular asset. Sometimes doctors and solicitors own their own premises by means of an unlimited company.

Stockbrokers trade through the medium of an unlimited company as they are not allowed to have limited liability. The disadvantage of an unlimited company is that the members are responsible for the company's debts, but the advantages are that the company has a separate legal personality and that its accounts remain private to its members. In addition, many of the other disclosure requirements of a limited liability company are not applicable to unlimited companies.

Companies limited by guarantee
A company limited by guarantee normally has members rather than shareholders. This is because normally there are no shares in a company limited by guarantee. In companies limited by guarantee, instead of shareholders being required to pay to their company the nominal value of their shares, members agree in the memorandum of association to pay a fixed amount to the company or liquidator, depending on the circumstances and the wording of the memorandum. This amount is each member's guarantee. There is no statutory minimum or maximum guarantee, though each member has to pay the same amount.

Formerly a company could be limited both by guarantee and by shares. There are a very few of such companies still in existence, but it has not been possible to register any companies limited both by shares and by guarantee since 1980 (CA 1985 s 1(4)).

It is not possible to transfer membership of a shareless guarantee company. Instead a member resigns and is replaced by another. No stock transfer form is required as no shares are transferred. Guarantee companies are often used for charitable purposes, and it is common to find in guarantee companies a requirement that on dissolution, the assets of the company are transferred to another company with a similar charitable purpose. The profits of a guarantee company usually may only be used to further the purposes for which the company was set up.

Private companies limited by shares
These are by far the commonest type of company. Private limited companies have all the benefits of incorporation but do not have the onerous duties of plcs in terms of accounts, meetings and capital requirements. In many respects a private company has advantages over a public company. It can do various things a public company cannot. These include:

1. By elective resolutions it can dispense with:

   - annual general meetings ("AGMs") (CA 1985 s 366A);
   - the requirement to table annual accounts and the directors' report at a general meeting (CA 1985 s 252(1)); and
   - the requirement to appoint auditors annually at a general meeting (CA 1985 s 386). This is because the DTI discovered that many small private

companies either did not understand, ignored or did not see the point of having meetings when the members and directors were all the same people. The AGM and all its concomitant requirements were seen as a mere time-wasting formality of little benefit to anyone except the lawyers who had to be paid to draft the correct paperwork and the auditors who checked it afterwards.

2. By elective resolution a private company can dispense with the requirement that directors may not have the authority to allot the company's shares over a period in excess of five years (CA 1985 s 80A). This is because the DTI discovered that the rule that prevents directors allotting shares over a period in excess of five years was widely ignored by private companies, and indeed served little useful purpose. Furthermore many private companies' records were so poor that they could not recall what had happened five years ago anyway.

3. By elective resolution it can dispense with the rule that the majority required to have short notice of an extraordinary general meeting is reduced from 95% to 90% (CA 1985 ss 378(3) and 369(4)). This minimal reduction is not generally seen as being significantly useful.

4. Private companies do not always need to give such detailed accounts as do public companies. In turn small companies and medium-sized companies do not need to reveal as much detail as other private limited companies do.
   A small company has the following characteristics (CA 1985 s 247(3)):

   - Turnover – not more than £2,800,000
   - Balance sheet total – not more than £1,400,000
   - Number of employees – not more than 50.

   A medium-sized company has the following characteristics (CA 1985 s 247(3)):

   - Turnover – not more than £11,200,000
   - Balance sheet total – not more than £5,600,000
   - Number of employees – not more than 250.

Small companies need only provide an abbreviated version of their full balance sheet and neither a profit and loss account nor the directors' report need to be delivered to the Registrar of Companies (CA 1985 Schedule 8 Part I). For a medium-sized company, a profit and loss account should be delivered, but the directors need only provide an overall figure for the gross profit or loss, without breaking that information down into further detail. Particulars of turnover also need not be given (CA 1985 Schedule 8 Part 2).

The purpose of these exemptions is to protect competitors finding out too much about the company's financial position. This is an example of the compromise effected where companies' natural desire for confidentiality (so as not to give an advantage to competitors) conflicts with the general aim of company law, which is to encourage openness in the presentation of accounts.

5. Certain eligible small private companies with a turnover up to £350,000 need not have their accounts audited at all (CA 1985 s 249A), Although this is meant to relieve the burden of administration on small companies and to save them the expense of auditors' fees, it will only be of use to companies that have little or no borrowing, as it is improbable that a bank would lend to a company unless its accounts had been properly audited first. For more details on this, see Chapter 11.

6. A private company can use capital for the acquisition of its own shares if necessary (CA 1985 s 172) and can fairly easily provide financial assistance for the purchase of its own shares (CA 1985 s 155).

7. A private company can have written resolutions, except for resolutions to dismiss directors or auditors (CA 1985 s 381A).

8. A private company can be a single member company (CA 1985 s 352A), in which case it need only have one member, one director and a separate company secretary.

9. A private company may provide in its articles that the right of pre-emption (the prior entitlement for existing shareholders to buy more shares) on allotment of shares shall not apply (CA 1985 s 91).

10. When a private company allots shares, it can do so without needing to have any non-cash consideration independently valued first (unlike a plc) – provided there is no fraud involved (*Re Wragg Ltd* [1897] 1 Ch 796) – though as a matter of prudence it is sensible to get any non-cash consideration valued first in order to allay existing shareholders' concerns. Unlike public companies it is also permissible to allot shares in consideration of services to be subsequently performed, or actions to be carried out at any stage in the future. Such flexibility may be useful but is, of course, unlikely to impress other shareholders or anyone considering lending money to the company.

11. When a private company pays dividends, it does not have to comply with the net asset rule. Broadly speaking, provided there are more accumulated realised profits than accumulated realised losses, a private company can pay dividends (CA 1985 s 263(3)).

Dormant, subsidiary and foreign companies

Dormant companies

A dormant company is one that has had no material accounting transaction during its financial year. Such companies, provided the requisite special resolution has been passed, need not have their accounts audited nor have an annual general meeting (CA 1985 s 250). Only private companies can be dormant companies. They are commonly used to retain a company name that might be useful later, perhaps because you do not want a competitor to register a company with a name similar to your own company's name, thus causing confusion in the minds of your customers. But you might wish to use a dormant company for other purposes: for example, there is the following doubtless apocryphal story: an Irish solicitor discovered earlier in the century that many of the major American manufacturing and food businesses would in general expand into the UK after they had made their market in the US and Canada. After the UK the senior executives of the American businesses would look elsewhere to expand. Ireland was always their next choice on the grounds that it was predominantly English-speaking and accessible from the UK. The American businesses would then start to set up Irish subsidiaries to market their cars, tyres, breakfast cereals, vacuum cleaners and other products. However, the American executives would find that prior to their arrival at the Dublin Registrar of Companies, the solicitor, having kept a close eye on the UK market, had already registered dormant companies in the Irish Register of Companies with the names of the American businesses. This made it impossible for the subsidiaries to be registered in those names. The impasse could only be resolved by the payment of a large sum of money to the Irish solicitor. He would then sell the dormant companies and more importantly their names to the American companies. It is said he died a very wealthy man.

Dormant companies are sometimes also used to retain ownership of an asset which is not being sold and does not require any money to be spent on it, such as a work of art, a copyright or a piece of jewellery.

Subsidiary companies

A subsidiary company is a company that is either owned, partly owned, or controlled by another company. The other company is generally known as a holding or parent company. Many large companies have a number of subsidiaries through which various parts of the large companies' business is carried out. This has the advantage that if a subsidiary is not profitable, it can be closed down relatively easily without loss to the holding company (unless the holding company has guaranteed its debts). Subsidiaries can also be useful as a means of grooming future directors of the holding company: an up and coming executive can cut his teeth on the subsidiary to give him experience.

Before the creation of single member private limited companies (see later in this chapter), it was common to find wholly owned subsidiaries with two shareholders, one being the holding company, and the other being a director, holding a share as nominee and in trust for the holding company. Since the introduction of the single member company, wholly owned subsidiaries tend to have only one shareholder, which is the holding company. It is possible for a subsidiary company to have subsidiaries of its own. Subsidiary companies may not own shares in their holding companies except as nominees for someone else (CA 1985 s 144). For example, the department of a bank that deals with customers' wills may operate through a subsidiary of the bank. If a deceased customer had shares in the bank, the bank itself could not hold its own shares but the subsidiary could, provided it was doing so on the customer's behalf.

There are two definitions of subsidiary in the Companies Act 1985. For the sake of convenience they can be divided into what might loosely be called the legal definition and the accounting definition.

The legal definition

The CA 1985 s 736(1) defines a subsidiary by reference to a holding company. A holding company is one which:

(i)   holds a majority of the voting rights in the subsidiary; or
(ii) is a member of the subsidiary and has the right to appoint or remove a majority of its board or directors; or
(iii) is a member of the subsidiary and controls alone, in terms of an agreement with other shareholders or members, a majority of the voting rights in the subsidiary.

A subsidiary of a subsidiary is treated as a subsidiary of the holding company.

These definitions need some explanation. In (i), it must be remembered that in some companies not all shares carry voting rights, or some shares may have weighted voting rights (for further information on voting rights see Chapter 18). But provided the holding company has a majority by whatever means, the subsidiary will legally be its subsidiary.

Point (ii) is designed to cover the position where the holding company may not necessarily have a majority of the voting rights, but nonetheless, perhaps due to some carefully drafted provision in the Articles, has the right to dictate who will be directors, either by appointing more directors in order to swell the number of directors supporting the holding company, or by dismissing directors who together form a majority on the board of directors sufficient to oppose the holding company's views.

Point (iii) covers the position where the shareholders or members draw up a shareholders' or members' contract and agree to vote in the way the holding company wants, or not to vote at all, thus allowing the holding company's views to prevail.

The rationale for the legal definition

The legal definition is necessary because there are many occasions in the CA 1985 where some prohibition is levied upon a plc and its legal subsidiaries. For example, stringent rules about loans from their companies apply to directors of a plc and to the directors of its legal subsidiaries (CA 1985 s 330). Financial assistance for the purchase of a company's own shares is normally possible for a private company, but not if that private company is a legal subsidiary of a plc (CA 1985 s 155(3)).

The accounting definition

This definition occurs solely in the context of the preparation of consolidated accounts. It was introduced following the implementation of the Seventh Directive (EC Council Directive 83/349) by means of the CA 1989. The definitions are to be found in the CA 1985 ss 258–260 which refer to subsidiary undertakings and parent undertakings rather than companies.

A parent undertaking relative to a subsidiary undertaking is one which in terms of the CA 1985 s 258(2) the parent undertaking:

(i)   holds a majority of the voting rights in the subsidiary;
(ii) is a member of the subsidiary and has the right to appoint or remove a majority of its board of directors;
(iii) has the right to exercise a "dominant influence" over the subsidiary
      (a) by means or provisions contained in the subsidiary's memorandum or articles; or
      (b) by virtue of a "control contract"; or
      (c) because it is a member of the subsidiary and controls alone, in terms of an agreement with other shareholders or members, a majority of the voting rights in the subsidiary.

A subsidiary of a subsidiary is still treated as a subsidiary of the parent undertaking (CA 1985 s 258(5)).

In the context of these particular sections of the CA 1985, "undertaking" means a company registered under the CA 1985, a partnership or an incorporated association carrying on a business, even if it is not necessarily trading for profit (CA 1985 s 259(1)).

A "right to exercise a dominant interest" means that the parent undertaking has the right to give directions to the subsidiary with regards to the subsidiary's operating and financial policies, and the further right to insist that the directors follow those policies whether or not the policies are for the benefit of the subsidiary (CA 1985 Schedule 10 s 4(1)).

A "control contract" is a written contract which is authorised by the memorandum of articles of association of the subsidiary and is permitted by the law of the country under which the subsidiary is established. These do not generally exist in UK law but are relatively common under German law. Effectively the subsidiary does what the parent says, but the parent in so doing accepts some liability for its subsidiary.

There is a further "catch-all" provision (CA 1985 s 258(4)) to the effect that a subsidiary is deemed to be a subsidiary of a parent undertaking if the parent undertaking has a participating interest (*i.e.* has 20% or more shares in the subsidiary as a long-term investment (CA 1985 s 260(1) and (2))) and in reality:

- actually exercises a dominant influence (this is to be contrasted with the previously mentioned *right* to exercise a dominant influence, so that the catch-all provision applies to the company where there is in reality a dominant influence even where no specific right to that influence has been granted by any means) (CA 1985 s 258(4)(a)), or

- the parent and the subsidiary are managed "on a unified basis" (CA 1985 s 258(4)(b)). The term "unified basis" comes from the Seventh Directive and has been left undefined precisely because detailed definition would only encourage people to find loopholes in the definition and thus evade the purpose of the legislation. This is particularly apposite for off-balance sheet subsidiaries (see below).

The rationale for the accounting definition

The main reason the accounting definition exists, even though in some respects it duplicates the legal definition, is because it is nowadays a requirement of company law that a company with subsidiaries should consolidate its accounts to produce group accounts, featuring a consolidated balance sheet and a profit and loss account (CA 1985 s 227) in terms of Schedule 4 to the CA 1985. It would be difficult to obtain a true understanding of the financial standing of a business unless all the accounts of the business are amalgamated. This includes both incorporated and unincorporated businesses. There are exemptions from the preparation of group accounts where the parent company is a small or medium-sized company (CA 1985 s 248) or if the parent is in itself a subsidiary of another parent whose group accounts are being prepared (CA 1985 s 228(2)).

A further reason the accounting definition exists is in effect an anti-fraud measure. Sometimes a company will acquire assets or incur liabilities which it might not want its shareholders or creditors to see. These assets or liabilities can, by means of ingenious asset transfers, be parked in a company which is not a "legal" subsidiary in the sense that its shares are all or mostly held by the parent company. Such a subsidiary, commonly known as an "off-balance sheet

subsidiary" might be controlled and owned by persons who are apparently completely independent of the parent company but in reality are nominees of the
managing director of the parent company and only act on his instructions.
Without the "accounting definition" of subsidiary such assets or liabilities
might not be brought into the accounts. Not only would this give a false picture
of the true state of the company's finances but the fact of the deception might
lead to a general lack of confidence in the company's management. This in turn
would affect the value of the securities.

Foreign companies

Many companies, registered abroad, have a place of business in the UK. The
advantage of doing this is that it will help establish their credibility in the UK
market. Many business people are suspicious of foreign-registered companies
doing business in the UK on the grounds that if, say, a contract went wrong,
suing the foreign-registered company in the UK might be a waste of time
because it might have few assets in the UK with which to satisfy any judgment
or decree. To sue such a company in its own country of registration might be
time-consuming, expensive, and in certain countries whose legal systems are
not well established or independent, not necessarily productive of justice.

However, it is possible for oversea companies (as they are known) to be registered in terms of the CA 1985 Part XXIII. There are provisions to allow such
companies to grant registered charges and to publish their accounts in much the
same manner as UK companies. Without the publication of such accounts and
other information, business people might be reluctant to trade with oversea
companies.

Another option for foreign companies is to set up a UK subsidiary.

Single member private limited companies

Single member private limited companies were introduced by means of SI
1992/1699 which in turn was implementing the Twelfth Council Directive
89/667 on single member private limited companies. Hitherto all companies
had to have at least two members, even though only one person need actually
have been involved in the running of the company. This rule had been anachro-
nistic for some time, and had some curious results. For example, a wholly
owned subsidiary would have one shareholder which was its holding company,
and a second shareholder who was, say, the company secretary of the holding
company, acting as nominee for the holding company. The rule generated
paperwork without providing any substantial benefit to anyone.

It is now possible for someone to set up a company and for him to be the sole
director and sole shareholder. He must not, however, be the company secretary

if he is the sole director (CA 1985 s 283(2)). In addition, he may not set up a second company to act as the first company's company secretary if he is the sole director of the second company (CA 1985 s 283(4)(a)). Although it may seem odd that the legislation permits only one shareholder but does not permit only one officer of the company, it is believed that the external involvement of at least one other individual will perhaps ensure that company records are properly kept and that the benefit of limited liability is not overly abused.

Although it may also seem odd that a single member company needs to have general meetings consisting of the one individual member, if a meeting is held, the company secretary is apparently expected to attend (see *Re Neptune (Vehicle Washing Equipment) Ltd* [1995] BCC 474 discussed in Chapter 15). Failing that, it is common for single member companies to pass any necessary resolutions by means of written resolutions. In any event the CA 1985 s 382B insists on proper written recording of any resolutions that would normally be passed at a general meeting. This is designed to prevent the sole member claiming that he had passed resolutions when in fact he had not bothered to do so. A similar anti-fraud requirement is that contracts between the single member company and a director who is also the sole member must be properly recorded in writing (CA 1985 s 322B(1)) unless the contract is in the ordinary course of business (CA 1985 s 322B(2)). This can be an issue in the liquidation of a company where the sole director is claiming arrears of salary as a debt against the company. Were the liquidator to allow such claims, there would be less money available for other creditors. The requirement that the contract be in writing reduces the opportunities for spurious claims by directors (again see *Re Neptune (Vehicles Washing Equipment) Ltd* [1995] BCC 474).

The quorum in a general meeting of a single member company is one member (CA 1985 s 370A).

A former multi-shareholder company can become a single member company by all the other members transferring their shares to the one shareholder. That shareholder must, however, enter a statement in the company's register of members that the company is a single member company from the date when all the shares were transferred to the one member (CA 1985 s 352A(1)).

Initial registration requirements

To set up a company is not in principle difficult and is discussed in more detail in Chapter 6. You must send the Registrar of Companies in Cardiff, Edinburgh or Belfast as the case may be (or any of their outstations in London, Glasgow and elsewhere) the following documents:

- Form 10: statement of first directors, company secretary, address of registered office, company name, initial subscribers;

- Form 12: statutory declaration by a solicitor, or a director or the company secretary of the new company, confirming that the requirements of the CA 1985 have been complied with;

- The Memorandum of Association (which we shall look at more closely in the next chapter);

- The Articles of Association (which we shall look at more closely in Chapter 5);

- The statutory fee, at present £20.

If the company is a plc, it is unwise for it to trade until it has applied for and obtained a s 117 trading certificate. This is obtained by sending the Registrar of Companies a statutory declaration (CA 1985 s 117(2)) confirming that the company has a nominal issued share capital of £50,000, that the shares therefore have been paid up to the extent of at least one-quarter plus any premium, the amount of the company's preliminary expenses and to whom those expenses have been payable, and any benefit paid to any promoter of the company (CA 1985 s 117(3)).

If the company is not a plc, the Registrar will, once he has received and checked the incorporation documents, issue a certificate of registration. The company does not exist as a legal entity until the day the certificate is signed. The certificate is conclusive evidence that the requirements of the CA 1985 as regards registration have been fulfilled and that the company is properly registered (CA 1985 s 13). Companies are deemed to come into existence from midnight on the day of incorporation.

Although it is extremely rare for the Registrar of Companies to make a mistake, it has happened at least once: *Re Baby Moon (UK) Ltd* (1985) 1 BCC 99 at 298. The Registrar of Companies in England registered a company with its registered office in Livingston in West Lothian, Scotland as an English company. The question arose as to whether it should be wound up by a Scottish court or an English court. It was held that it should be wound up in England because the certificate stating that the company was registered in England was conclusive.

Just because the company has been incorporated and the certificate of incorporation supplied does not mean that the company's incorporation is beyond challenge, not least by the Crown: *R v Registrar of Companies, ex parte Attorney-General* [1991] BCLC 476. Miss Lindi St Claire, better known as Miss Whiplash, an attention-loving prostitute, set up a company. Her initial choices of name were Prostitute Ltd, Hookers Ltd and Lindi St Claire (French Lessons) Ltd. These names were rejected by the Registrar. However, Lindi St Claire (Personal Services) Ltd was considered acceptable by the Registrar, who curiously had no objection to the objects clause of the company. This was stated to be "the business of prostitution". Miss St Claire's occupation on the Form 10 was stated as "prostitute". Following a judicial review of the Registrar's registration of the company, it was held that the Registrar had erred in law in that he had allowed a company to be set up for an unlawful purpose. The CA 1985 s 1 requires that a company may only be set up for a lawful purpose: it was contrary to public policy that prostitution should be held to be a lawful purpose.

Fuller details of the procedure for preparing incorporation documents and the conversion of partnerships and sole traders into limited companies will be found in Chapter 6.

The disclosure principle

In order for a company to obtain the benefit of limited liability and to have a separate legal personality it must be registered under the Companies Acts with one of the Registrars of Companies. This means that any member of the public is entitled to obtain a microfiche of the information recorded in the relevant Companies House about that company. The cost of the microfiche is at present £3.50 and each Companies House contains fiche readers and a computerised indexing system to enable inquirers to look up the current name of a company using the company's registration number, to find out the names of its directors and to consult the register of disqualified directors. Every single company registered in England and Wales is registered in Cardiff, every one in Scotland in Edinburgh, and every one in Northern Ireland in Belfast.

In order to provide the public with information about each company there is a large number of special forms relating to such matters as the allotment of shares, the provision of financial assistance, the registration of charges, etc., all of which must be completed properly and signed, usually by a director or company secretary. There are mechanisms available which allow for the delivery of the information in an electronic format. The forms and other documents sent to the Registrar of Companies are photographed and a microfiche is prepared for each company. If the forms sent to the Registrar are wrongly completed (as is very common) the form is returned for correction. As a rule the Registrar does not interpret the law so that if a document appears to be accurate he will accept it. If it turns out to be inaccurate there may be action taken against those who prepared the documents that were sent in, but the Registrar does not pretend to hold himself responsible for the contents of the forms or the other documents. If certain forms are not sent in on time, such as annual accounts and the annual return, the Registrar will write a reminder and a warning letter to the directors of the company. If that has no effect, he will instruct proceedings to be taken against the company and its directors if necessary. The fines for delay are considerable. A conviction for persistent failure to deliver the requisite documents, such as accounts, to the Registrar is grounds for disqualification as a director under the Company Directors Disqualification Act 1986 s 3.

The system of access to information about companies is known as the disclosure principle. There are, however, different levels of disclosure.

1. *Information available at Companies House*
   Companies House only displays a certain amount of information about any company, though occasionally Companies House will accept information that is not strictly necessary under the Companies Acts if the company, for some reason, wishes it to be displayed. The information that can be found at Companies House about any company includes the following:

   - incorporation documents (Forms 10, 12, memorandum and articles) and any new memoranda and articles of association (CA 1985 s 18);
   - certificate of incorporation;
   - details of the allotment of shares (CA 1985 s 88) (see Chapter 7);
   - any special, extraordinary, elective and certain ordinary resolutions, together with any resolutions that the company's own articles insist on being recorded (CA 1985 s 380) (see Chapter 18);
   - register of registrable charges (CA 1985 s 401 and (for Scotland) s 417) (see Chapter 17);
   - notices of receivership (CA 1985 s 405 and for Scotland IA 1986 s 53(5)), liquidation (Insolvency Rules 1986 r 4.106(4), Insolvency (Scotland) Rules 1986 r 4.2(1), 4.18(4)) and administration (Insolvency Rules 1985 r 2.10(3)(d) and I(S)R 1986 r 2.2(1)(e)) (see Chapters 20, 21 and 22);
   - various forms and documents in connection with alteration (CA 1985 s 122), increase (CA 1985 s 123) or reduction (CA 1985 s 138) of capital, purchase or redemption (CA 1986 ss 169, 173) of a company's own shares and financial assistance (CA 1985 s 156(5)) (see Chapter 9);
   - the directors' report (except for small companies) CA 1985 ss 242 and 702 (oversea companies));
   - the annual accounts (CA 1985 s 242 and s 702 (oversea companies));
   - change in accounting reference date (CA 1985 s 225);
   - the annual return (a document stating the current directors, company secretary, registered office and list of members as at the date of the annual return (CA 1985 s 363)). Its use is limited since the list is only accurate for that date: the following day all the shares might have been sold;
   - appointments and retirals of directors and company secretary together with information about directors' other directorships (CA 1985 s 288);
   - change in registered office (CA 1985 s 287);
   - location of register of members if it is not the same place as the registered office (CA 1985 s 353), and likewise register of debenture-holders (CA 1985 s 190(5));
   - location of register of directors' interests if it is not held at the company's registered office (CA 1985 s 325);

- the prospectus of quoted companies or other companies whose shares are traded publicly (CA 1985 s 640) (see Chapter 8);
- for companies on the Official List, listing particulars (Financial Services Act 1986 s 149) (see Chapter 8).

People who might wish to consult Companies House to find out this information might include:

- researchers;
- financial journalists;
- trade creditors;
- potential investors;
- people wondering whether or not to do business with the company;
- lawyers and accountants checking that their clients' records are up to date;
- inquiry agents in divorce suits or other litigation;
- Customs and Excise and the Inland Revenue;
- local councils;
- people trying to find the registered office of the company in order to serve court documents upon the company;
- people checking up on the directors to see what other businesses the directors may be running or may have run. If a director has been or is a director of a number of unsuccessful companies it suggests that he might be best avoided.

2. *Information generally available at the company's registered office*
   Information (usually available at the company's registered office or at some other designated place) to any person, generally free to members and on payment of a fee if a non-member, includes all the information in 1. above, plus:

   - a copy of any contract (or memorandum) for the purchase of a plc's own shares (CA 1985 s 169);
   - copies of a company's charges in its own register of charges to be kept at its registered office. This, incidentally, is also free to a creditor (CA 1985 s 407(2) and (for Scotland) s 423);
   - any register of debenture-holders (CA 1985 s 191). This information may be kept at another office if appropriate intimation has been made to the Registrar of Companies (CA 1985 s 190(5)). The keeping of a register is not obligatory as the CA 1985 does not specifically demand it;
   - the register of members. Anyone can inspect the index of members at any time (CA 1985 s 356(1)) provided the register is not closed, but of course the index does not always provide addresses. If you wish to obtain a copy of the register (with addresses) you can do so, but the company has 10 days from the day after your request to send the list out to you (CA 1985

s 356(3)). Consequently by the time you get it it may well be out of date. This section is thus of minimal use to inquisitive shareholders.

The register may be kept at a professional registrar's office (CA 1985 s 353). Many of the leading banks have departments which act as professional registrars, particularly for listed or quoted companies (CA 1985 s 353). The register may be closed for up to 30 days each year (this was designed for the updating of records in pre-computerised age) provided the company or the registrar gives notice of the closure in a newspaper circulating in the district of the company's registered office – even if the register of members is elsewhere (CA 1985 s 358). The company is not obliged to break down the list of members into those living in a particular area, holding more than a certain number of shares or any other category (SI 1991/1998, reg 4(2), (3)). Such a rule is perhaps surprising given that most share registries are computerised and the abstraction of such information would not be difficult;

- in a plc, a register of substantial (*i.e.* over 3% of the issued share capital) interests (CA 1985 s 211(1)), is kept at the same place as the register of directors' interests (usually the company's registered office, but this can be elsewhere (CA 1985 Schedule 13 s 27)). If there has been an investigation by the company into the true ownership of any substantial interests under the CA 1985 s 212, this must be disclosed on the register too. This section is used by companies to ascertain who may be behind the apparent ownership of its shares, because a takeover bidder might well be amassing shares under various company names with a view to gathering enough shares to mount a successful takeover. Although there is an obligation on a plc shareholder to inform the company when he has over 3% of the company's share capital (CA 1985 ss 198–199), not every shareholder sees fit to do this, and some shareholders disguise their ownership by means of nominee companies;

- in any company, the register of directors' interests (CA 1985 s 325) is to be kept at the company's registered office or any other place properly intimated to the Registrar of Companies (CA 1985 Schedule 13 s 27). Directors' interests are securities of the company owned by the directors or their immediate family. It is useful to know if directors and their families are buying or selling shares, because the extent of their holding to some extent demonstrates their commitment to the company's success;

- in any company, the register of directors and secretaries (CA 1985 s 288(3)).

3. *Information at the company's registered office but only available to members and certain others*

Certain additional information at the company's registered office is only available to the members of the company, the directors, the company secretary and the auditors and includes:

- minutes of general meetings (CA 1985 s 383) and class meetings, though only officers of the company and the members of the class itself are entitled to see the minutes of the class meetings, unless the articles say otherwise;
- the terms of the directors' service contracts (CA 1985 s 318);
- in a private company, the terms (or memorandum of terms) applying to the purchase by a company of its own shares (CA 1985 s 164(4) and (5)(a));
- in a private company, the records of all written resolutions, including the members' signatures (CA 1985 ss 382A and 383);
- items required under the company's articles or statute to be available to the members' inspection, such as, for a small company, the directors' report.

4. *Items not generally available to the members*
There are some items that unless the articles say otherwise are not generally available to the members. These include:

- board minutes and accounting records (CA 1985 s 222), which are normally privy to the directors, company secretary and auditors alone, because there is no requirement under the CA 1985 to make them available to the members;
- the company's contracts generally, including non-directorial employees' employment contracts.

5. *Further levels of disclosure for listed companies and quoted companies*

Listed and quoted companies must comply with the requirements of the Stock Exchange in respect of releasing price-sensitive information as soon as possible in order to minimise the opportunities for insider dealing. They must also be prepared to co-operate with continuing Stock Exchange rules such as providing cash-flow statements and other accounts not normally required of private companies. Stock Exchange companies and other companies whose securities are publicly traded must also expect a high level of journalistic interest. Journalists may obtain information leaked to them from employees or customers or competitors.

Disclosure in the Gazette

The London Gazette, the Edinburgh Gazette and the Belfast Gazette are Government publications which are the formal notice of the events narrated therein. Once a notice has been published in the Gazette the world at large is deemed to be aware of the notice. Statute prescribes a large number of items which must be published in the Gazette, of which from a company law point of view, the most important are the appointment of liquidators, receivers and administrators. While much of this information is published in the paper version of the Gazette which is inspected regularly in places such as banks, insurance companies, law courts, etc., further more detailed information is published in a microfiche version of the Gazette by the Registrar of Companies in accordance with the provisions of the CA 1985 s 711(1).

Any information about a company which requires to be sent to the Registrar of Companies for publication in the Gazette must be sent by the company to the Registrar of Companies as soon as possible or within the various time limits specified in the CA 1985. Failure by the company to send the information on time may mean that a third party is not bound by the altered circumstances which should have been sent to the Registrar on time (CA 1985 s 42). However, as the section is designed to protect third parties rather than the company, a company cannot rely on the fact that it did send the information to the Registrar of Companies on time as a way of avoiding any liability to the third party. In any event the items referred to in the CA 1985 s 42 refer only to the following matters:

(i)   the making of a winding-up order or appointment of a liquidator in a voluntary winding-up;
(ii) any alteration in the company's memorandum or articles;
(iii) any change in the company's directors;
(iv) any change in the company's registered office.

So any matter published in the Gazette which is not (i), (ii), (iii) or (iv) above probably does not protect the third party. The position is however not clear. As a practical matter, the Gazette is not widely read and its effectiveness as a matter of communicating information to the general public is very limited.

The rationale behind public disclosure

The intention behind these various levels of disclosure is to provide a reasonable compromise between the need for commercial secrecy and discretion and the need for investor and creditor protection. Some companies have a culture of extreme secrecy, never revealing any more information than necessary in order to maintain a commercial edge and sometimes to prevent employees having a true understanding of the company's financial position. Others have a policy of extreme openness particularly if all the employees are also shareholders. If listed companies are too secretive with their information, financial analysts and the market may, in the long term, lose interest in the company, its share price will decline and it may find itself suffering an unwelcome takeover bid. If companies are too selective in their information, always seeking to highlight the good news and play down the bad, analysts and the market may well learn to distrust the company and sell the company's shares, leading again to a potential takeover bid. If companies are too generous with their information, competitors may take advantage of it. Generally a policy of cautious openness is the best approach.

Reregistration of companies

Reregistration is the process whereby a company is converted from one type of company to another. The following commentary outlines the various procedures and the reasons for such conversions.

Part II of the CA 1985 provides for the following types or reregistration:

- private to public;

- limited to unlimited;

- unlimited to limited;

- public to private.

It is not possible to convert from a private company limited by shares to one limited by guarantee though a public company may do so (CA 1985 s 53(3)). A guarantee company could convert into an unlimited company (CA 1985 s 49).

Reregistration of a private limited company as a plc (CA 1985 ss 43–48)

This requires the following:

1. The company must not have previously been unlimited and reregistered as limited (CA 1985 s 43(1)). If the company has previously been unlimited and subsequently reregistered as limited it is prohibited from reregistering as a plc;

2. The company must pass a special resolution to reregister the company as a plc (CA 1985 s 43(1)(a)) and to alter the memorandum so that the company is to be a plc (CA 1985 s 43(2)(a)), and to make any other necessary changes to the company's name (by the use of the words "public limited company"), the memorandum (CA 1985 s 43(2)(b)) and the articles to allow its securities to be traded publicly (CA 1985 s 43(2)(c));

3. Under the CA 1985 s 43(1)(b) the company must send to the Registrar of Companies:

(i)   the new memorandum and articles of association (CA 1985 s 43(3)(a));

(ii) a balance sheet prepared not more than seven months prior to the application for reregistration, together with an unqualified report (or if qualified, not materially qualified) on the balance sheet by the company's auditors (CA 1985 s 43(3)(c));

(iii) a written statement from the auditors confirming that the balance sheet shows that at the balance sheet date the company's net assets were not less than the total of its called-up share capital and undistributable reserves (CA 1985 s 43(3)(b));

(iv) if any shares have been allotted for a non-cash consideration (*i.e.* in exchange for assets of any sort other than money) at any time between the balance sheet date and the date of the special resolution, an independent valuation report on the non-cash consideration to ensure that the assets transferred have not been overpriced (CA 1985 s 43(3)(d));

(v)   a statutory declaration by a director or the company secretary confirming:

(a) that the special resolution was duly passed;

(b) that between the balance sheet date and the date of application there has been no change in the company's financial position so that its net assets are worth less than the total of its called-up share capital and undistributable reserves (CA 1985 s 43(3)(e)(ii));

(c) that if any shares were issued in the intervening period of up to seven months between the balance sheet date and the application to convert to plc status, and those shares were issued in exchange for non-cash consideration, the non-cash consideration has been independently valued (CA 1985 s 43(3)(e)(i)); and

(d) that if any shares were issued in the intervening period as in (c) above, and the consideration for those shares was work or the provision of services for the company, that work or those services have already been carried out or performed (CA 1985 s 43(3)(e)(i)); or

(e) that if any shares were issued in the intervening period as in (c) above and the consideration for those shares was an undertaking to be performed, that undertaking has already been performed or will be performed within five years in terms of the contract for the undertaking (CA 1985 s 43(3)(e)(i));

(vi) a certified copy of the special resolution altering the company's name and its memorandum and articles of association (CA 1985 s 43(1)).

4. In order to obtain reregistration, the company's authorised share capital must be at least £50,000 (CA 1985 s 45(2)). If the company's previous authorised share capital was less than that, the company will need to pass an ordinary resolution under the CA 1985 s 121 increasing the authorised capital at least to that figure. If the nominal issued share capital is less than that figure, the

company will need to issue more shares to attain that figure. This in turn may mean that the directors must obtain authority from the members, by means of an ordinary resolution, to allot shares under the CA 1985 s 80. Any shares so allotted must be paid up to the extent of at least one-quarter plus any premium and the Registrar of Companies must be informed of the allotment (CA 1985 s 88).

The consideration for the shares may be in the form of work or the provision of services, but only if the work has already been carried out or the services have already been provided (CA 1985 s 45(3)). In this context work and services are such things as the provision of accountancy or legal advice. Future work or services are therefore unacceptable. If the consideration for the shares is in the form of an undertaking, that undertaking must either have taken place or there must be a contract in connection with the undertaking ensuring that the undertaking will be completed within five years (CA 1985 s 45(4)). An undertaking in this context might be a contract to transfer a building to a company once the building has been completed. An undertaking to take place more than five years in the future is therefore unacceptable.

In any event, any non-cash consideration offered for shares between the date of the above balance sheet and the application for reregistration must be independently reported on as being properly valued (CA 1985 s 44(2)). This will ensure that on the date of application the company will have a minimum nominal issued share capital of £50,000 and assets of at least £12,500. This will also be confirmed by the auditors in their report on the balance sheet, and if there has been a gap (of up to seven months) between the balance sheet date and the application to convert the company, the directors' statutory declaration will make the directors personally accountable should the non-cash consideration not be as valuable as indicated.

Assuming all these matters have been complied with, the Registrar of Companies will issue a certificate of reregistration of the company as a plc. The certificate is conclusive evidence of the fulfilment of the requirements of the CA 1985 as regards reregistration as a plc.

Reasons for conversion to a plc

The above procedure may seem cumbersome and expensive, given that auditors' fees will be required, resolutions drafted, a meeting held to approve the resolution and paperwork to be completed. Nonetheless, the procedure is the price that must be paid if the company wishes to have the status of being a plc. While it is arguable that being a plc is of no great advantage on many occasions, if a company wishes ultimately to have its shares traded, if it wishes to be able to obtain capital well beyond the resources of a private company, and if its directors wish to have the status of being directors of a major listed company, at some stage the private company with which the directors first started business will need to become a plc. A further reasons for being a plc is that the letters "plc" at the end of the company name are believed to look more impressive than the mere word "limited". Some directors may even feel personally gratified at describing themselves as directors of a plc. They are playing on the fact that many members of the public are unaware that there is a difference between a plc that has its securities traded on an official market and is thereby a substantial company, and a plc that used the initials "plc" to boost its corporate image while actually none of its securities are traded publicly at all.

Limited company becoming unlimited (CA 1985 ss 49–50)

A plc cannot become an unlimited company (CA 1985 s 49(2),(3)). A company which was unlimited and then becomes limited cannot revert to being unlimited (CA 1985 s 49(2)). A limited company wishing to become unlimited should send to the Registrar of Companies the following:

(i)   amended memorandum and articles to take account of the fact that members' liability henceforth will be limited (CA 1985 s 49(4),(5),(8)(c) and (d));

(ii)   a form of assent signed by every member of the company approving of the change of status to unlimited (CA 1985 s 48(8)(a));

(iii) a statutory declaration by a director or company secretary confirming that all the members or their agents validly signed the form of assent (CA 1985 s 48(8)(b)).

On receipt of the statutory relevant documents, the Registrar will issue a conclusive certificate of reregistration as an unlimited company (CA 1985 s 50).

The important part of this procedure is that every member must sign, since every member is now becoming personally liable for the debts of the company. Each member's signature is evidence that he accepts liability.

Reasons for conversion to unlimited status

The primary reason for conversion is that the members are willing to accept liability for the company's debts but wish to retain the benefit of a separate legal ownership of the company's assets, and the members do not wish the general public to be able to inspect the unlimited company's accounts.

Unlimited company becoming limited (CA 1985 ss 51–52)

It is not possible to convert from being an unlimited company to a plc, nor from a limited company to an unlimited and back again (CA 1985 s 51(2)).

The company must pass a special resolution approving the conversion altering the memorandum and articles (CA 1985 s 51) and those three documents must be sent to the Registrar of Companies within 15 days. The Registrar of Companies will, in due course, furnish the company with a conclusive certificate of reregistration as a limited company (CA 1985 ss 51 and 52).

Reasons for conversion to limited status
In this case, the members will believe that the requirement to publish accounts is a price worth paying for the benefit of limited liability for the members personally.

Public company becoming private (CA 1985 ss 53–55)

A plc can become a private company provided:

(i) the company passes a special resolution (CA 1985 s 53(1)(a)) (altering the company's status and changing the memorandum and articles to those suitable for a private company (such as removing the clauses permitting the offer of securities to the company) (CA 1985 s 53(2));

(ii) a director or secretary has signed the prescribed form and sent it, together with the copy resolution, the new memorandum and the new articles to the Registrar of Companies (CA 1985 s 53(1)(b));

(iii) there has been no successful application to the court for the cancellation of the resolution under the CA 1985 s 54.

Under the CA 1985 s 54 it is open to:

- holders of 5% of the company's issued share capital or of any class thereof (CA 1985 s 54(2)(a)); or

- in the case of a company without share capital, at least 5% of the members (CA 1985 s 54(2)(b)); or

- not less than 50 members (CA 1985 s 54(2)(c))

apply to the court within 28 days of the passing of the resolution for cancellation of the resolution – though an applicant who has previously voted in favour of the change is not to be counted as falling within any of the above three categories of applicants (CA 1985 s 54(2)). A reason that the minority may object is that if the minority's shares are being publicly traded, those shares will become unmarketable because a private company cannot have its securities publicly traded. If a share cannot be traded, it becomes less desirable and may lose some of its value. If, however, the shares are not being traded publicly, reregistration as a private company is unlikely to make any difference at all. In any event, if the shares used to be traded publicly, the company is likely to have suffered severe difficulties if it is reduced to becoming a private company.

The court, having heard the application, can make any order it sees fit, such as adjourning the proceedings to arrange a settlement, ordering the majority shareholders to buy out the minority at a reasonable price, or dismissing the application if it is not well founded (CA 1985 s 54(5),(6)). The court may also insist on alterations to the memorandum and articles of association (CA 1985 s 54(6)) or insist on their not being altered (CA 1985 s 54(8)). If the application is unsuccessful, or there is no application, the Registrar will furnish the company with a conclusive certificate of reregistration.

Reasons for conversion

- The additional disclosure requirements for a public company may prove irksome to the company.

- The company may have shrunk and no longer need the benefit of being a plc in terms of enhanced status.

- The company may find that the legal restrictions on plcs, such as the prohibition on certain types of loans to directors, the net asset rule for dividends and other matters relating to the capital of the company are more trouble than they are worth.

- A large company might be in the process of hiving off its unwanted subsidiaries: a private company would be able to take advantage of the opportunities for financial assistance for the purchase of its own shares, and it might be worth reregistering the former plc as a private company prior to its hiving-off in order to allow its new owners to obtain financial assistance for the purchase of their own shares once it had ceased to be a subsidiary of the large company.

Summary

1. There are two main types of company: public and private. Public companies:
    - have the words "public limited company" or "plc" in their name;
    - potentially can offer their securities to the public (although many choose not to do so);
    - must have a minimum paid-up issued share capital of £50,000 (CA 1985 s 118), of which one-quarter plus any premium must be paid-up (CA 1985 s 101(1));

- if incorporated as plcs (as opposed to converting into plcs) need a s 117 trading certificate before they can commence business (CA 1985 s 117);
- must each have at least two directors (CA 1985 s 292) and a suitably qualified company secretary (CA 1985 s 263(1));
- normally must take into account pre-emption rights on allotment of shares (CA 1985 s 89), must have the consideration for their shares independently valued if not paid in cash (CA 1985 s 103(1)), must not allot shares for work or services to be performed (CA 1985 s 99(2)), nor allot shares for an undertaking to be performed in more than five years' time (CA 1985 s 102(1));
- must be informed whenever anyone acquires more than 3% of the share capital (CA 1985 s 203);
- must publish their accounts within seven months of the end of their financial year (CA 1985 s 244) and have the accounts tabled at a general meeting (CA 1985 s 241);
- when paying dividends may not cause the net assets to be reduced below the aggregate value of the called-up share capital and any undistributable reserves (the "net asset rule") (CA 1985 s 264);
- may provide for their members summary financial statements (CA 1985 s 251);
- may provide financial assistance for the acquisition of their own shares only in very limited circumstances (CA 1985 s 154);
- may not use capital for the acquisition or redemption of their own shares (CA 1985 s 171) and even when using distributable profits must acquire the shares within 18 months of obtaining approval for the acquisition (CA 1985 s 164(4));
- may not have proxies speaking at their general meetings (CA 1985 s 372);
- may not permit liens over their fully paid shares (CA 1985 s 150);
- must cancel or reissue any forfeited or surrendered shares within three years of forfeit or surrender;
- must call an extraordinary general meeting if the net asset position falls below half of the value of its paid-up share capital (CA 1985 s 142).

2. Only plcs can trade their securities publicly, and only those plcs which are listed on the Official List, the Alternative Investment Market or certain other recognised investment markets and who have a broker willing to make a market in their securities can offer their securities to the public.

3. Private companies can be divided into unlimited companies, guarantee companies and private companies limited by shares. Unlike public companies, private companies can:

- dispense by elective resolution (CA 1985 s 379A) with annual general meetings (CA 1985 s 366A), the need to table annual accounts at a general meeting (CA 1985 s 252(1)), and the need to appoint auditors annually (CA 1985 s 286), dispense with the five-year authority to directors for allotment of shares (CA 1985 s 80A)), and reduce the majority required for short notice of an extraordinary general meeting to 90% (CA 1985 s 369(4) and s 378(3));
- be small companies or medium-sized companies in which case less stringent accounting requirements apply (CA 1985 Schedule 8);
- use capital to acquire or redeem their own shares (CA 1985 s 172);
- provide financial assistance for the acquisition of their shares by means of the gateway procedure (CA 1985 s 155);
- can use written resolutions (CA 1985 s 381);
- can be single-member companies (CA 1985 s 352A);
- can state in their articles that pre-emption rights do not apply (CA 1985 s 91);
- may not offer their shares to the public (CA 1985 s 81);
- on allotment need not have any non-cash consideration independently valued, and may accept future services as consideration;
- if small enough, and eligible, will not need an audit (CA 1985 s 249A).

4. A dormant company is one that has had no accounting transaction during its financial year (CA 1985 s 250(1)).

5. There are two definitions for a subsidiary company, depending on the context. Broadly speaking the legal definition of a subsidiary is a company predominantly controlled by its holding company (CA 1985 s 726(1)). If that holding company is a public limited company, the rules that apply to it will apply to its private subsidiaries. The accounting definition is designed to ensure that when companies prepare consolidated accounts all companies connected with the "parent undertaking" (CA 1985 s 258(2)) (*i.e.* the equivalent of a holding company) have their accounts consolidated with the parent company's accounts. This is to prevent parent companies offloading their liabilities into companies that appear not to be connected with the parent company.

6. To incorporate a company one needs a Form 10, Form 12, the memorandum of association, the articles of association and the statutory fee. The company's name must not already be held by any other company or be otherwise unsuitable.

7. Any member of the public is able to obtain information about the company shown on the company fiche at Companies House. Although much information about a company must be sent to and is held at Companies House,

further information is only available to members of the company at the company's registered office or some other designated office. Some information about the company, such as minutes of board meetings, is not even available to members, being restricted to company officers and the auditors instead. Companies whose shares are quoted must disclose further information according to the market where their shares are traded.

8. Further information about companies, in particular receivership, administration and liquidation, must also be published in the Gazette.

9. It is possible to convert a private limited company to a public limited company, or public to a private, or a limited to an unlimited, or an unlimited to a limited. It is not possible to convert a private company limited by shares to a private company limited by guarantee.

10. Of these conversions, the commonest in practice is from a private limited company to a public limited company (CA 1985 ss 43–48). This requires the following:

- special resolution altering name, memorandum and articles;
- an unqualified audited balance sheet prepared within the previous seven months;
- confirmation from the auditors that the net assets are not less than the aggregate of the issued share capital and undistributable reserves;
- independent valuation of any non-cash consideration for shares issued since the balance sheet date;
- a statutory declaration from the directors confirming that the company's financial position has not deteriorated since the balance sheet date, that any non-cash consideration for shares issued since the balance sheet date in exchange has indeed been independently valued, and that no shares have been issued for future work or services or for an undertaking to be performed in more than five years' time;
- a minimum authorised share capital of £50,000 of which one-quarter plus any premium must be paid-up.

4. CONSTITUTION OF THE COMPANY (PART I)

Name – memorandum and its clauses – ultra vires rule and objects clauses – charities

Just as every amateur dramatic society, tennis club, church vestry or other voluntary organisation has a constitution to regulate such matters as the appointment of office bearers, methods for increasing the subscription and maintaining a register of club members, so does a company need its own constitution. This and the next chapter detail the law relating to a company's constitution. There are two parts to a company's constitution, the memorandum of association (commonly just called the memorandum) and the articles of association (commonly just called the articles). Broadly speaking, the memorandum is designed to tell the world at large what the company is and what it does; the articles are more for the benefit of the members of the company. It shows how the internal arrangements of the company operate.

The first item to be dealt with within any company's constitution will be the company's name.

Name

It is not open to a company to have any name it chooses. There is a number of restrictions under statute as to the type of name allowed.

Choice of name

1. Limited and unlimited
If a company is a plc, it must say so in its name (CA 1985 s 25(1)). Welsh companies may say so in Welsh. There are as yet no provisions for companies in Scotland to use (Scots) Gaelic.

If a company is limited by share or guarantee, it must include the word "limited" (or the Welsh equivalent) in its name (CA 1985 s 25(2)) unless it is exempt from this requirement under CA 1985 s 30. Section 30 states that guarantee companies and certain companies, limited by shares and licensed under the Companies Act 1948 s 19, can dispense with the word "limited", provided that the companies' objects clauses state the companies are set up for the promotion of commerce, art, science, education, charity or any profession. These

particular companies must also, in their memorandum and articles of association, require that:

(i)   any profits must be used for the promotion of these objects;
(ii) there must be no dividend payments to their members; and
(iii) on winding-up the assets of the companies must not be handed over to
      their members but transferred to other companies with objects and policies
      similar to their own.

The retention of this rule for a small number of companies is because of their
quasi-charitable status.

  Unlimited companies do not need to include the word "unlimited" in their
name. This is because nearly all limited companies must have "limited" as part
of their name (CA 1985 s 25) but no mention is made of the word "unlimited".

2. Each company name must be different

No company may have the same name as any other company in the index held by
the Registrar of Companies. Leaving aside such minor differences such as
capital letters, "&" and "and", "Co" and "Company", (permitted under CA 1985
s 26(3)) any substantive difference in the spelling of a company name will be
enough to indicate that a different company is being referred to. So "John Smith
and Co (1995) Ltd" is different from "John Smyth and Co (1995) Ltd". The same
principle applies to numbers: "John Smith and Co (1995) Ltd" is different from
"John Smith and Co (1996) Ltd". It is permissible to have a British company with
the same name as a company registered under another country's jurisdiction.

3. Offensive or forbidden names

A company may not have a name which would in the opinion of the Secretary
of State for Trade and Industry be offensive (CA 1985 s 26(1)). A company with
a blasphemous name would probably be prohibited. Certain names are exclusively reserved to certain charities (e.g. The National Society for the Prevention
of Cruelty to Children). A company cannot include in its name the word "Bank"
(in the sense of a financial institution) or "Building Society" without being
authorised under the Banking Act 1987 or the Building Society Act 1986.

4. Approval from the Secretary of State

Certain names need the approval of the Secretary of State. These include names
that convey the impression that the company is connected with the Government
or a local council (CA 1985 s 26(2)). The Company and Business Names
Regulations 1981 (SI 1981/1685) (as amended by the Companies and
Business Names (Amendment) Regulations 1982 (SI 1982/1653) and 1992 (SI
1992/1196)) lists names which require either the approval of the appropriate

Government department (so that, for example, any company including the word "abortion" in its name requires the approval of the Department of Health) or some supervisory body. As a further example, if you wished to use the word "dentistry" in your company's name, you would need the approval of the General Dental Council. Permission is also needed for words like "England", "Scotland", "chartered" and many other words. Generally, permission will not be given for geographical names unless there is some good reason for it. Under the CA 1985 s 29(2) if you wish to have a name that requires approval under the legislation you have to ask permission from the relevant Government department or supervisory body.

5. Change of name

A company can change its name by special resolution. It obviously cannot change its name to a name that would not be acceptable, and if it is not acceptable, the Secretary of State can insist that it be changed (CA 1985 s 28(2)).

As an example of this, in 1994 a small ski and business travel company called First Choice Tours ("FCT") discovered that Owners Abroad, Britain's third largest tour operator, had changed its name in a blaze of publicity to First Choice. Owners Abroad had taken the advice of leading London lawyers, who had established that there were over 130 companies with the words "first choice" in their name. Because of this, it was thought that no one would object to the new name. From the date of the change of name of Owners Abroad, FCT was besieged by telephone calls for First Choice. Amidst mounting confusion it transpired that Owners Abroad had not published its telephone number on its new brochures and Directory Enquiries were re-routing all calls for First Choice to FCT. The directors of FCT objected to the DTI which on 4 November 1994 upheld their claim. First Choice was given 12 weeks in which to rename themselves (source: *The Independent*, 6 November 1994).

If a company has given misleading information in connection with the registration of a particular name, or if the company has given unfulfilled undertakings or assurances in connection with the name, the Secretary of State has five years from the date of registration of the name to compel the company to change its name (CA 1985 s 28(3)). The change of name does not change the company's registered number nor any right or duties attaching to the company. Changes of name are sometimes used by unscrupulous business people to make it slightly harder for creditors to keep track of their companies, but more often they are used when converting an "off the shelf" (*i.e.* a ready made up) company into a company tailored to suit a director's requirements (see Chapter 6).

If the members of a company wish to change their company's name, they must, as previously stated, pass a special resolution to approve the change (CA 1985 s 28(1)). A copy of the resolution must be sent to the Registrar of Companies together with the requisite fee. In due course a certificate of change of name will be issued.

6. Harmful or misleading names

If a company is registered with a name that, in the opinion of the Secretary of State, is likely to cause harm to the public, the Secretary of State can insist on the name being changed (CA 1985 s 32). It is not clear what is meant by "harm to the public".

If someone trades under the name "limited" without in fact being a properly incorporated company, he commits a criminal offence (CA 1985 s 34), and a plc commits a criminal offence if it gives the impression that it is a private company when it is not (CA 1985 s 33).

7. Business name different from the company's name

If a company trades under a name that is not the name by which it is registered, then in order to comply with the Business Names Act 1985 ("BNA"), the business name must comply with the same regulations as those applying to company names as stated in paragraph 3 and 4 above (BNA ss 2,3). If a company conducts business under a trading name, the true name and address of the company must be stated legibly on all business letters, orders, invoices, receipts and demands for payment (BNA s 4). The CA 1985 s 349 supplements this by demanding the company name on all the above documents and also on any financial instruments, such as cheques and promissory notes. The company name, number and registered office number must be on all order forms and correspondence of the company (CA 1985 s 351). At the place of business there must also be a notice stating where the company's registered office is (BNA s 4(1)(b)). If this information is not provided, an action raised by the company against a defendant or, in Scotland, defender will be dismissed if the defendant/defender can prove that he was unable to assert any claim he might have had against the company, or that he suffered financial loss, because of the company's failure to provide the correct name or address – unless the court decides that it would be just and equitable for the proceedings to continue (BNA s 5).

8. Restriction on reuse of liquidated company's own name or business name

It is not permissible for a director to set up a company using the name or the business name or any name similar to the company's name or the business name of a company of which he was a director or a shadow director and which has gone into insolvent liquidation within the 12 months prior to liquidation (IA 1986 s 216). This prohibition extends for five years from the date of liquidation of the insolvent company, unless the court can be persuaded otherwise.

Re Bonus Breaks Ltd [1991] BCC 546. A director of a liquidated company called "Bonus Breaks Ltd" appealed to the court for leave under the IA 1986 s 216 for permission to use the name "Bonus Breaks Promotions Ltd". There was evidence that although the liquidated company had been insolvent for two years prior to liquidation, the directors had taken advice from the company's bank manager and auditors, had kept the company's accounts properly and that the applicant had lost a good deal of her own money. Various creditors supported the application, no doubt hoping that the new company would make good the losses they had incurred with the liquidated company. The application was successful, subject to various undertakings granted by the applicants in connection with the maintenance of the company's share capital.

The purpose of the IA 1986 s 216 to prevent the "phoenix" syndrome, whereby on the analogy of the mythical bird that arose out of the ashes of its own immolation, a new company arises out of an old one. The common example is of a company that has been trading under one name, collapsing, and then being discreetly put into liquidation. Soon afterwards the directors start trading again with another company from the same address with the same business name or a very similar company name. By this simple ruse creditors and customers would be deceived. Creditors of the first company would find that they had no redress either against the directors or the later company. Prior to the enactment of the IA 1986 s 216 such creditors often discovered that the same company directors had behaved in this way several times and no one appeared able to stop them.

To counter this abuse by directors, directors can now be personally liable for the new company's debts if there is evidence of the above actions (IA 1986 s 217). There are also criminal sanctions against such directors.

9. Passing off

Passing off is the unauthorised use of the name of an established enterprise with the effect of depriving the established enterprise of either the goodwill attached to its name or some or all of its business. It leads to a right of action under common law. There is no criminal liability, and accordingly it is not possible for a person to be "guilty" of passing off. Any trading enterprise can be involved in or be a victim of passing off. It is not restricted to companies.

In order to establish a claim of passing off, factors that would be taken into account may include most, if not necessarily all at once, of the following:

- the unauthorised name need not be exactly the same as the established enterprise's name, but it must be sufficiently similar as to be likely to mislead or confuse the public;

- the person using the unauthorised name must be running, or proposing to run, an enterprise in much the same line of business as the established enterprise;

- the person using the unauthorised name must be running, or proposing to run, his enterprise in the same geographical area as the established business;

- the person using the unauthorised name is using the name with the deliberate intention of attracting business to himself as the expense of the established enterprise;

- the established enterprise has suffered, or may suffer, economic loss as a result of the use of the unauthorised name;

- the fact that on a balance of convenience and fairness it would be unreasonable to make an established enterprise change its existing name.

Possible defences include:

- a proprietor is allowed to use his own name for his business, provided there is nothing to suggest dishonesty, as in *Wright, Layman and Unmey Ltd* v *Wright* (1949) 66 RPC 149, CA, where it was held that Wright was entitled to use his own name, but when he started calling his business "Wright's Chemical Co" he committed the tort of passing off. The entitlement to use one's own name does not extend to the use of a nickname, as in *Biba Group Ltd* v *Biba Boutique* [1990] RPC 413 where a proprietor who had been known by the nickname of "Biba" since childhood was not permitted to use that name in competition with the fashion company of that name;

- a company cannot lay claim through its name to the exclusive use of a word in common speech. In *Aerators Ltd* v *Tollit* [1902] 2 Ch 319, Aerators Ltd tried to obtain an injunction against Tollit to prevent him calling his company "Automatic Aerator Patents Ltd". Aerators Ltd made a type of aerator for use in siphons, whereas Mr Tollit's company used a device for aerating beer in public houses. There was no likelihood or intention of confusion; each business had different customers; and Aerators Ltd could not claim the sole use of the word "aerator" just because it happened to have that word as its name.

The remedies for the aggrieved established enterprise include:

- damages;

- recovery of profits from the person carrying out the passing-off;

- a court order to prevent the passing-off continuing. Such an order would be known as an injunction in England, Wales and Northern Ireland, and an interdict in Scotland;

- a requirement that the passing-off company change its name to a less contentious name.

The leading case on passing off is *Ewing* v *Buttercup Margarine Company Ltd* [1917] 2 Ch 1. Ewing operated a chain of shops and warehouses in Scotland and the north of England under the name of the Buttercup Dairy Co, and popularly as "Buttercup". His business was based in Leith, near Edinburgh. In those days Leith was an important whaling centre, and he used whale blubber to make his principal product, margarine. He also sold other dairy products and tea. He had plans for setting up more shops in the south of England. Having been trading successfully for 12 years, he found that a company calling itself the Buttercup Margarine Company Ltd had been set up and was proposing to manufacture margarine for wholesale in the south of England. Ewing obtained an injunction to prevent the new company using the word "Buttercup". The defendants appealed.

Amongst the ground of their appeal was the fact that the name "Buttercup" was used by three other companies in England; that the defendants were operating in the south of England whereas Ewing's business was mostly in the north and in Scotland; and that there was no bar to the use of a name unless there was evidence of a desire to deceive customers into thinking that they were dealing with Ewing's business when in fact they were dealing with the Buttercup Margarine Company Ltd. Finally the defendants asserted that as they were wholesalers, not retailers like Ewing, there could be no confusion in the eyes of the public.

These somewhat specious arguments were disregarded by the Master of the Rolls, Lord Cozens-Hardy, who said that if the defendants had been honest business people they should have changed their name once they realised that an existing business was objecting to their choice of name.

The practicalities of choosing a name

Given the legislation and common law attaching to the choice of name, it is prudent to choose an uncontentious name. Commonly company agents will telephone the Registrar of Companies to check whether or not a proposed name will be available. The Registrar of Companies has lists of extant and all defunct companies and can advise whether or not any particular name has already been used. Choosing an unsuitable name may lead to litigation or delay in the incorporation of the company while the suitability of the name is checked.

Memorandum of association and its clauses

Clearly a company needs a name so that you know what it is called; it needs a registered number to distinguish it from any other company; but it also needs documentation, by way of the memorandum, to tell everyone what it does.

In order to help company practitioners, the Companies (Tables A to F) Regulations 1985 (SI 1985/805) lays out "styles" or standard models for the wording and order of the clauses suitable for different types of company:

- Table A is the articles of association suitable for an ordinary company limited by shares.

- Table B is the memorandum for the same.

- Table C is the memorandum and articles of association for a guarantee company without a share capital.

- Table D is the memoranda for both a public and a private guarantee company with a share capital.

- Table E is the memorandum and articles for an unlimited company with a share capital.

- Table F is the memorandum for a plc.

Table A is the basic model for all articles of association, and all the other tables featuring articles are variations of it.

The memorandum and articles of association that a company adopts on its incorporation remain the company's memorandum and articles (even though there may have been substantial changes in the law since that date) until such time as the company validly alters its memorandum or articles. Because of this, companies which have not altered their memoranda and articles since the passing of the Companies Act 1948, using the then equivalents of Table A and Table B, may well find that those memoranda and articles prohibit certain activities which might be advantageous to the company, and which would be permitted under the 1985 Tables A–F. It is therefore common and prudent for companies to update their memoranda and articles regularly to take advantage of changes in the law.

It would be possible to set up a company that used Table A in its entirety for its articles, and Table B for the memorandum. However, this would be unusual. What happens is that while many companies have Tables A and B as their models, the terms and wording are varied to suit the individual requirements of each company. So a common first clause of a company's articles are "The provisions of Table A apply except to the extent that they are deleted or amended hereby". The articles will then go on to say which parts of Table A are to be discarded and which new clauses should be inserted in their places.

Table B for the memorandum is very brief and is generally followed by companies, except for the objects clause. We shall look at that in greater detail later. Table B's objects clause is three lines long. Until recently it was common to find objects clauses that were eight pages long, though there is now a move to shorten them.

As laid down in Table B, the memorandum of association has five clauses. These consist of:

- the name;

- the country of registration;

- the objects clause;

- the limited liability clause;

- the authorised capital clause.

At the end of the memorandum there is space for the first subscribers (or subscriber) to sign and date their confirmation that they are taking the first shares in the company. This is known as the association clause and is witnessed. The subscribers are the very first members of the company. The subscribers must be legal personae, in other words they must be human beings, limited companies, or, but in Scotland only, partnerships.

Table B above applies to private companies. Table F applies to plcs, and is similar to Table B save that there is an extra clause stating that the company is a public company and the capital clause has to show a minimum authorised capital of £50,000.

Of the five normal clauses, the objects clause is the most problematic. We shall therefore deal with the other ones first, with the exception of the name, which has already been dealt with.

The country of registration

If a company is incorporated in one country it cannot transfer its nationality to another country. Effectively the clause is unalterable. If you have a company registered in Scotland and you wish to alter its country of registration to England it cannot be done. What you would need to do is to set up an English company. You would then arrange with both the English and Scottish Registrars of Companies that on a prearranged date, the Scottish company would take the English name, the English company would take the Scottish name, and by means of an asset transfer agreement, the entire assets and undertaking of the Scottish company would be paid over to the English company. You might do this if a Scottish company no longer wished to use its registered office in Scotland, since its principal business was in England, but wished to retain the goodwill of the Scottish name.

The registered office must be a real address, though unscrupulous companies have been known to use fictitious addresses or post office boxes. It would be difficult for such companies to comply with the requirements to keep their registers of members in an accessible place, and the service of court documents would be problematic. It is a criminal offence not to keep the requisite registers at the registered office, unless the Registrar of Companies has been told that they are to be found elsewhere, and it is also an offence not to mention the registered office on all company correspondence (CA 1985 s 351).

The registered office itself is not stated on the memorandum though it is required on Form 10 and any changes must be intimated to the Registrar of Companies on Form 287. A board resolution will suffice to change the registered office.

The limited liability clause

This normally reads: "The liability of the members is limited." If the company is unlimited the clause is omitted. If the company is a guarantee company, the clause still stands, but is followed by another clause stating that each member undertakes to pay a pre-specified sum, the guarantee, to the company, in the event of its being wound up. There is no minimum requirement under statute as the amount to be paid by way of guarantee. The limited liability clause would be deleted if the company were reregistering from a limited company to an unlimited company (see Chapter 3).

The capital clause

Neither an unlimited company without share capital nor a guarantee company without share capital needs a capital clause. Every other company does, and it will commonly be stated as follows: "The company's share capital is £20,000 divided into 20,000 shares of £1 each". This is known as the company's authorised share capital. A plc must have an authorised share capital of at least £50,000. The share capital of any company other than a plc could theoretically be as low as one penny. The shares could be of any value that seems appropriate: they could be £100 shares or 5p shares. Historically the share capital was significant, because, as now, certain companies had to have a minimum share capital, but it was not to be too large, because, particularly in the USA, there was a fear of "big business". By imposing limits on the size of share capital, it was believed that large enterprises would not be able to build up commanding positions in the American economy.

The authorised share capital is now of much less political significance, but you cannot issue shares in excess of the authorised share capital without amending the share capital clause. Some investors like companies to be restrained by their authorised share capital clause. It prevents the directors being tempted to issue too many shares which, if pre-emption rights proved too expensive to take up, might alter the balance of power between the shareholders. It is possible to increase the authorised share capital or to alter the denomination of the shares under the CA 1985 s 121. The shares can be subdivided, consolidated, converted into stock (or stock can be converted into shares) and shares that have not been taken up and for which no monies have been paid can be cancelled. The Registrar of Companies must be informed on the appropriate form (CA 1985 ss 122, 123), and the memorandum and (if necessary) articles altered appropriately. This is discussed in greater detail in Chapter 7.

Other clauses in the memorandum

It is possible to insert other clauses if you wish. If the company is a plc, it must have a clause saying so in the memorandum. As is explained above, guarantee clauses appear in guarantee companies. Charitable companies often have clauses directing the companies' assets to be paid over to other charities if for some reason the charitable companies have to be wound up.

Occasionally, if the founders of a company felt strongly about a particular issue, they would insert it in the memorandum. For example, the founders might insist that the company was always to trade in a particular locality. Formerly it used to be difficult to change anything in the memorandum, whereas it was reasonably easy to change the articles. So if the clause was placed in the memorandum, the company would have to follow it. Some founders would therefore deliberately put clauses they felt strongly about into the memorandum. But as this could lead to difficulties, the CA 1985 s 17 states that if the relevant clause could have been put in the articles, it is still alterable by means of a special resolution. If the memorandum lays down a particular procedure for alteration of a certain clause, the terms of that procedure must be followed (CA 1985 s 17(2)(b)).

There is an exception to this rule when dealing with class rights. Some companies have different types of shares in addition to the normal "ordinary" shares. Such other types of shares are usually known as "classes" of shares, and typical examples are redeemable shares or preference shares. Any class of shares must have the rights relating to that class ("the class rights") spelt out in the articles and/or memorandum of association. If the class rights for a particular class of shares are spelt out in the memorandum, and variation of those class rights is prohibited or there is no authority for variation of those class rights, the class rights can in fact be varied (at great expense) by means of a scheme of arrangement under the CA 1985 s 425, or by means of every single member voting in favour of the variation (CA 1985 s 125(5)). If the class rights do not prohibit alteration, and the class rights could equally well have been inserted in the articles, the class rights are alterable by special resolution subject to various exceptions:

- holders of 15% of the company's issued share capital, or 15% of the members of the class, can object to the alteration by means of an application to the courts under the CA 1985 ss 5 and 6;

- a minority can apply to the court to cancel the alteration under the CA 1985 s 459;

- the alteration cannot compel a member to buy more shares or pay more for his existing shares without his consent (CA 1985 ss 16 and 17(1));

- if the memorandum itself provides for a special procedure for alteration, that procedure must be followed, except where it conflicts with any of the above exceptions (CA 1985 s 17(2)(b)) or certain rules relating to directors' authority to allot shares under the CA 1985 s 80 and reduction of share capital under the CA 1985 s 135.

The rules relating to the alteration of class rights will be discussed more fully in Chapter 7.

Nowadays it is rare that companies build in complicated extra clauses into the memorandum. This is because while any attempts to make clauses in a company's memorandum unalterable may be successful in the short term, in the long term, when the original founders are dead, the restriction may become commercially pointless. Complicated clauses are likely to lead to disputes and restrict the free transferability of the company's shares. Few investors would be willing to buy the shares of a company where alteration of the memorandum was impossible, or if not impossible, at least inconvenient. In any event, under the CA 1985 s 35(1), to be discussed shortly, the objects clause of the memorandum, which used to be very difficult to alter, is now relatively easy to alter and attempts to prevent its alteration are probably futile.

Ultra vires rule and the objects clause

The *ultra vires* rule, which relates to the operation of the objects clause, has kept lawyers in business and academics in their posts more efficiently than any other part of company law. It is an area full of contradictory judgments, incomprehensible cases and poorly drafted legislation. "*Ultra vires*" means "beyond the powers" and its opposite is *intra vires*. An act that is *ultra vires* the company's constitution is one that is not permitted by the company's constitution, as it is in theory beyond the company's power to carry it out. Although it is over 150 years after the first Act of Parliament relating to companies introduced the objects clause, the problems thrown up by the *ultra vires* rule have not entirely been resolved, except perhaps with regard to the rights of third parties.

In Table B, the draftsman provided an example of what an objects clause might be:

"The company's objects are the carriage of passengers and goods in motor vehicles between such places as the company may from time to time determine and the doing of all such things as are incidental or conducive to the attainment of that object."

The object, in other words, the trade that the company proposes to carry out, is the haulage of goods and the bussing of people, and anything connected with those two activities. This is what the company was set up to do.

Several questions immediately arise:

- is that the only thing the company can do?

- can the investors demand that the company do that and nothing else?

- what happens if the company does something else and most of the investors don't mind but some do?

- what happens if the company does something else, decides or realises that it is not supposed to, and then tells all those it has been dealing with that it must cancel their contracts as it should not have entered into those contracts to begin with?

- what happens if the company does something it is actually allowed to do, but for an improper purpose arranged by the directors?

- what if the company does do something else when perhaps it shouldn't, and the other party to the contract is a director of the company?

- should it make any difference if the company is a charity?

These unanswered questions highlight the shortcomings of what appears to be a simple statement, and underlie the following discussion about the objects clause.

The rationale for objects clauses

Originally the objects clause was a very simple concept. Just as with a village amateur dramatic society, the principal purpose of which is the amateur production of plays, so a company exists to carry out a particular function. However, if a village dramatic society were to renounce the presentation of plays and started instead concentrating its efforts on hunt sabotage, some members of the society would perhaps ask for the refund of their membership dues if they felt their monies were being used for something unconnected with plays; or they might choose to expel those who had steered the society away from the production of plays; or if enough members approved of hunt sabotage and had lost interest in plays, they might make the society adopt a new name and constitution and devote its energies instead to hunt sabotage. Or the society could wind itself up.

But with a company it is more difficult.

Since company law to a certain extent evolved out of the voluntary association or society, in the early days of company law if a company did something that was not permitted in terms of the objects clause, there were various surprising results. The first of these is that following a breach of the objects clause it was considered acceptable to wind up the company.

Re German Date Coffee Co [1882] 20 Ch 169. This company was set up primarily to obtain a German patent and with it to make coffee out of dates. The company did not buy a German patent and obtained a Swedish one instead. The company set up business in Hamburg and proceeded to make date coffee. One-quarter of the members of the company were so disgusted by the fact that the company was not using a German patent that they sold their shares. The majority did not mind whose patent it was. The company was solvent. Nonetheless, two shareholders petitioned for the winding-up of the company on the grounds that it was just and equitable to do so because the company had not fulfilled the terms of the principal part of the objects clause. Although there were parts of the objects clause that allowed for the purchase of other patents, those parts were not deemed to be as important as the principal part of the objects clause in which the German patent was mentioned. Although it may seem surprising to us over 100 years later, the petition was granted. One reason was that the absence of a German patent clearly was seen by investors at the time as significant. Another reason was that there were at the time no satisfactory provisions under company law for minority shareholders to receive redress, as is now possible under the CA 1985 s 459. A third reason was the then view that if you invested your money in a company so that your company could use your money for a particular purpose, you were entitled to demand that the company, through the medium of the directors, used your money for that purpose and no other. A fourth reason was the then difficulty of altering objects clauses.

From a present day viewpoint it is hard to see why the nationality of a patent should matter provided the company is profitable. Nonetheless it is possible to argue that if the patent had come from a particularly tyrannical government, shareholders might not consider it acceptable to deal with that country: for example, there have, at the time of writing, been instances of ethical investment companies selling their shares in oil companies in protest at the oil companies' poor environmental record. But at the time of the *German Date Coffee Co* there appears to have been no question that there was anything particularly sinister about Sweden that might alarm shareholders.

It also seems unreasonable that the majority of shareholders, who did not mind that the wrong patent had been obtained, should find that the company was to be wound up.

The decision in this case has never been overruled, though it is likely that were similar circumstances to arise nowadays the decision would be different. The courts would be more likely to insist that the company convene a general meeting to let the members of the company vote on the matter.

The second surprising result arising from the company's failure to adhere to the terms of the objects clause is that the objects clause itself could deprive third parties of rights which they would normally expect to have been able to exercise.

Ashbury Railway Carriage and Iron Co v *Riche* (1875) LR 7 HL 653. The company contracted with Riche for him to build a railway line from Antwerp to Tournai. The company paid him some money and then ran into financial difficulties. It was decided that to resolve the company's problems the directors in their personal capacity should take over the contract with Riche. Accordingly the company repudiated the contract with Riche whereupon he upset their plans by suing the company for breach of contract. The company's defence was that the original contract was void anyway because such a contract was not permissible in terms of the precise wording of the objects clause – which on a close reading was indeed the case. Accordingly the company was able to win the case because it should never have entered the contract to begin with.

The reasoning of the case was mainly to protect the original investors, though at the time little thought seems to have been given to the unfortunate Riche, or to the wider issue of whether the court's decision would promote trade or good business practice. At the time it was probably expected that Riche should have inspected the company's memorandum himself to see whether or not he was running any risk by accepting the contract. He might have then asked the company to create a subsidiary which would permit the building of railways and the entering of contracts with railway builders such as Riche.

This case also illustrates the substratum rule, whereby the company is required to adhere to the underlying purpose for which the company was founded and which is shown in the first part of the objects clause. Much then depends on the specificity of the first part of the objects clause. The more precise the substratum, the less opportunity there is for the company to do anything other than adhere to that substratum.

The conflict between the commercial approach to the objects clause and the judicial approach.

As a result of the above decisions, the directors of companies, and sometimes the companies' creditors, found that they could be in a difficult position if those companies' activities strayed from the principal part of the objects clause, even for the most sensible and commercial of reasons. The drafting of objects clauses became an art form, as promoters and directors strove to allow companies the maximum breadth of trading activities, while the courts strove to limit the activities of the company to the very first part of the objects clause. This was because judges in general believed that the real objects of the company should be made intelligible to the public, and the courts were adamant that investors should be protected from the wiles of unscrupulous promoters and directors. The next case illustrates one ingenious method to get round the rules.

Cotman v *Brougham* [1918] AC 514, HL (E). The objects clause of a company was drafted with great care to allow the company to do almost anything. The last sub-clause of the objects clause stated that every single sub-clause was to be treated as a substantive clause and could not be restricted by any other sub-clause, and, furthermore, that all the sub-clauses were to be treated as equal and as important as the first sub-clause (the principal objects clause) which referred to the acquisition of tobacco and rubber plantations.

The House of Lords, with extreme reluctance, found that the clever wording could not be faulted because the Registrar of Companies had already granted the company a certificate of incorporation. Under the then equivalent of the CA 1985 s 13 (7) the certificate was conclusive evidence of the registration of the company, and could not be set aside. Because the memorandum as it stood had been accepted by the Registrar the courts could not reject it. Lord Wrenbury described the whole practice of multiple objects clauses as "pernicious" and the Lord Chancellor, Lord Finlay, said that the Companies Act should be amended to prevent such abuses of the legislation.

The contemptuous attitude displayed by the House of Lords was not highly regarded by practising company lawyers. Practitioners of company law took the view that if you became a shareholder you did so on the terms and conditions of the memorandum and articles. There was no obligation to become a shareholder: if you did not like the breadth of a company's objects clause, you should not buy its shares. Those who inherited such companies' shares could sell them. Furthermore, it was not necessarily the case that because a company had a wide objects clause the shares would be less valuable. Good directors could take advantage of wide objects clauses to make the most of commercial opportunities. As regards proposed creditors of the company, they were at liberty to inspect the company's memorandum and articles to see whether or not they wished to trade with the company.

The effect of *Cotman* v *Brougham* was that nothing was *ultra vires* that company, and indeed, soon after that, many other companies started to adapt their objects clauses to follow the *Cotman* v *Brougham* wording. Indeed it is rare to find a company, even nowadays, that does not have a *Cotman* v *Brougham* clause.

The use of the ultra vires *clause to protect the company*
The disadvantage (from a company's point of view) of the *Cotman* v *Brougham* wording was that as nothing was *ultra vires*, the company could not avoid liability for any debts incurred in the running of any part of its business. It used to be possible for a company to avoid honouring certain contracts by saying that the contract out of which the debt arose was *ultra vires* and that accordingly they were unable to honour it – as happened in *Ashbury Railway Carriage and Iron Co* v *Riche* above. This could be very useful, particularly for unscrupulous companies, and could also be useful for liquidators of insolvent companies. Sometimes a liquidator would argue that as a particular contract, entered into by the company prior to liquidation, was *ultra vires* the objects clause, he had no responsibility to include the other contracting party amongst his list of creditors.

Re Introductions Ltd [1970] Ch 199, CA. The company was set up to promote exhibitions at the time of the Festival of Britain and to provide hospitality for overseas visitors to the Festival. Once the Festival was over it moved into pig-farming. It did not see fit to change its objects clause. It borrowed money from the bank for its pigs and supplied the bank with a copy of its memorandum and articles of association. The objects clause of the memorandum stated that the company had power to borrow. On the strength of this, the bank lent the company money in return for the grant of a debenture. On the company's insolvency the validity of the debenture was questioned. It was held that borrowing could only have been in connection with hospitality and not with pig-farming, since pigs were not part of the objects clause. It was true that although there was a general *power* to borrow, this was not the same as an *object*, and the power could only be used for the specific object of hospitality to overseas visitors. The bank was therefore not able to claim under the debenture.

It seems unfair that the bank had to suffer because of the niceties of the drafting of the objects clause. But there have been occasions when a debtor owing money to a company refused to pay, asserting that the particular grounds for payment were *ultra vires* that company. The debtor in the case below had studied the company's memorandum and believed that the company's claim to recover its money was *ultra vires* the company.

Bell Houses Ltd v *City Wall Properties Ltd* [1966] 2 All ER 674. City Wall Properties Ltd ("CWP"), the debtor in this case, refused to pay Bell Houses Ltd ("Bell") commission for Bell's introduction to CWP of a Swiss bank that provided CWP with finance. CWP contended that it was *ultra vires* Bell's objects clause to seek commission for finance broking. The third part of Bell's objects clause allowed the company to "carry on any other trade or business whatsoever which can, in the opinion of the directors, be carried on by the company in connection with or as ancillary to any of the businesses or the general business of the company". The court held that this wording was quite sufficient to include obtaining commission for acting as a broker, especially when read in the light of other sub-clauses. CWP was therefore obliged to pay the commission.

In effect, CWP were hoping to avoid paying their debt by relying on the possible limitations of Bell's own objects clause. Nonetheless, it was commercially unsatisfactory that either a company could potentially avoid liability to a creditor, or a debtor avoid liability to a company, by claiming an act was *ultra vires* the company's own objects clause. The reliance on the usefulness of the *ultra vires* rule was turning it into a fraudster's charter. The courts gradually came round to a more pragmatic view.

Re New Finance and Mortgage Co Ltd (in liquidation) [1975] 1 Ch 420. The objects clause of this company was widely drafted, and allowed the company to trade in a wide variety of occupations, ending in the catch-all words "merchants generally". The company ran a petrol station and Total had supplied fuel to the station. The liquidator refused to include Total in the list of creditors, on the grounds that "merchants generally" did not include the retail of petrol and accordingly buying petrol from Total was *ultra vires*. The courts dismissed the liquidator's arguments on the grounds that the world "merchants" had wide applicability.

The effect of joining the EEC on the ultra vires doctrine

When Britain joined the EEC in 1972, s 9 of the European Communities Act 1972 implemented Article 9 of the First Directive (68/151). This provided that a company could be bound by acts beyond the scope of its objects clause provided the other party to the contract did not know that the act was beyond the scope of the objects clause. For example, if a company had a restrictive objects clause that permitted it only to deal in certain goods, a person buying other goods from that company without knowledge of the terms of its objects clause would be protected. From 1972 on, the *ultra vires* rule started to diminish in importance.

The reasoning behind the EEC rule was that the *ultra vires* rule could be used to prejudice consumers. The average consumer would have no knowledge of objects clauses and it was unreasonable to expect him to have such knowledge.

Distinction between objects and powers

The position was, however, complicated by the problem that for many years the courts felt that there ought to be a distinction between the objects of a company, and the powers that could be used to further or attain the objects. In addition, there was a distinction between substantive (or express) powers and ancillary ones. Sometimes there was a further distinction between acts that were beyond the powers of the company and acts that were beyond the powers of the directors. These matters all came to a head in the case of *Rolled Steel Products (Holdings) Ltd* v *British Steel Corporation* [1982] Ch 478. The directors of

Rolled Steel had arranged that Rolled Steel should grant a guarantee in favour of British Steel to cover any losses to British Steel incurred by a sister company to Rolled Steel. The directors had a personal interest in both Rolled Steel and the sister company, and one director had also personally guaranteed the sister company's debt to British Steel. There was no commercial benefit to Rolled Steel in granting the guarantee, but British Steel were well aware of that fact. Underlying the case are suspicions that the directors were not acting in good faith because of their personal interest and that British Steel had condoned certain actions which perhaps should not have been condoned. Both Rolled Steel and the sister company went into liquidation. British Steel then claimed against the liquidator for the sums potentially due under the guarantee for the sister company.

The Court of Appeal refused British Steel's claim on the grounds that although the granting of guarantees by the company was not in itself *ultra vires*, given the wording of Rolled Steel's object clause, the directors had improperly exercised their power to make the company grant guarantees since ultimately the grant of the guarantee was to spare the directors from being personally liable for the sister company's debt. Normally, because of s 9 of the European Communities Act referred to above, this would have made no difference to British Steel, and they would be able to claim against the liquidator since they were not expected to know the contents of Rolled Steel's objects clause or that the guarantee had been granted for an improper purpose. But as British Steel did know about the improper purpose and the abuse of the directors' powers they could not claim under the guarantee.

These difficult distinctions between objects, directors' powers and what was or was not improper use of those powers were so confusing to non-lawyers that business people were left no wiser as to what was acceptable and what was not. A practical solution was needed. It was clear that one way of avoiding the difficulties of ascertaining what was or was not acceptable in terms of the objects clause was to ensure that the objects clause of a company would cover every eventuality. If, for example, a company was set up to run a hotel, the first part of the objects clause might read as follows:

"The objects for which the company is established are to carry on in such place or places as the Directors deem appropriate the business of hoteliers, restaurateurs, publicans, caterers, licensed premises managers, travel agents, letting agents, caravan hirers, dance-hall and discotheque managers, entertainers, orchestral agents, variety performers, property managers, off-licence retailers, warehousers, hairdressers, newsagents, ostlers and livery managers, fishing tackle retailers, haberdashers, tailors, couturiers, car-hire agents, golf-course proprietors, fishery managers, booksellers and merchants generally."

As can be seen, what started off in a fairly sensible way referring to hotels gradually expanded into anything that remotely might be connected with hotels and with what their guests might need. This sub-clause would be followed by at least a dozen supplementary sub-clauses permitting the company to buy, lease and mortgage property, to borrow and give security for money, to grant guarantees irrespective of benefit to the company, to invest the company's assets, buy and sell them for the company, set up subsidiaries, buy other companies, pay pensions and a host of other activities. At the end there would be a *Cotman* v *Brougham* sub-clause stating that all the specified objects were independent objects, that they were not limited in any way by any of the other photographs, that they were all to be treated as equally important, and that the directors were given all the powers necessary to pursue any of those objects. It may seem absurdly unnecessary that all this should be laboriously transcribed, but lawyers take the cautious view that it is better to have all those sub-clauses spelt out rather than omit something and make their clients the subject of a court case.

Fortunately Parliament eventually realised that these interminable objects clauses were a waste of paper serving little useful purpose. In the Companies Act 1989, Parliament made certain attempts to improve the situation. The first of these was to permit a company to adopt a new kind of objects clause, known as a general trading clause (CA 1985 s 3A).

The second was to clarify the *ultra vires* rule (CA 1985 ss 35, 35A and 35B).

The general trading clause

The CA 1985 s 3A states:

"Where the company's memorandum states that the object of the company is to carry on business as a general commercial company

(a) the object of the company is to carry on any trade or business whatsoever, and
(b) the company has the power to do all things as are incidental or conducive to the carrying on of any trade or business by it."

This is a permissive section, in that companies are not compelled to become general commercial companies or adopt clauses suitable for such companies. If a company does have an objects clause allowing the company to carry on business as a general commercial company, the relevant clause is sometimes known as a "general trading clause".

One might think that the terms of the general trading clause are so liberal that companies would be very keen to adopt new objects clauses that both permit such freedom and reduce the amount of paperwork. Curiously, however, this has not happened. Lawyers have again been wary of doing anything that might involve their clients in unnecessary litigation. If the above hotel company were to incorporate today, it would probably have the same specific hotel-keeping objects clause as was shown above, a general trading clause, the dozen or so clauses that were also referred to above, and conclude with the *Cotman* v *Brougham* clause, stating that all clauses were equal in importance and all simultaneously the principal objects clause. It might not be entirely satisfactory but it would probably work. However, no paper would have been saved and the documentation would be as long as ever.

There are various reasons for this:

(i)   Lawyers by nature are cautious. They are in general not convinced that a short general trading clause would cover every eventuality. If the clause is proved to be deficient in some way, the dissatisfied company clients might sue the lawyers for their poor advice in not drafting the wording of the clause better.

(ii) It is arguable that the wording is deficient. The wording of the CA 1985 s 3A does not specifically allow for the sale of a company's business. The wording allows the carrying on of a trade or business, and anything incidental or conducive to that. But does that permit the disposal of the company's business so that it no longer had a trade or business to carry on?

(iii) The wording does not cover the making of charitable or political donations. Are these conducive to the carrying on of a business?

(iv) If the wording is adopted without qualification, it does potentially give a great deal of latitude to the directors. The directors could then make the company carry on any form of business, even if the directors had no great experience of the proposed trade or business. Investors might have invested their money in the company with the intention that the directors should use their special expertise, not dally in any trade that catches the directors' collective fancy.

The counter-arguments to this particular objection are that:

● in a small company with very few shareholders who all know each other, or are all directors, the objects clause may not matter much anyway;

● restraining the directors by the objects clause is not the most efficient way of doing it. It would be easier to give the directors service contracts which prohibited the directors from carrying on the company's business outside certain well-defined limits without consulting the members first. This could also be included in the company's articles;

● if the directors are majority shareholders and are acting in good faith in the best interests of the company as a whole, they could probably change the wording of the memorandum anyway to allow for any new venture the directors thought appropriate.

(v) The wording is inappropriate for dormant companies and guarantee companies which do not trade.

(vi) The wording does not cover the grant of cross-guarantees and security for loans to subsidiary, holding or sister companies.

(vii) The wording is "Where the company's memorandum states that *the* object of the company is to carry on business as a general commercial company". Is the word "the" before the word "object" exclusive? Could you use this wording if being a general commercial company was merely *an* object of the company?

So, to be on the safe side, at present those who draft memoranda often supplement the general trading clause with a specific main trading sub-clause and a host of subsidiary sub-clauses. As yet there have been no significant reported cases on the use of the general trading clause, so there has been no judicial guidance on the matter. It is also likely that gradually as people become more used to the concept of the general trading clause it will become increasingly common and long objects clauses will disappear.

Clarification of the ultra vires rule (CA 1985 ss 35, 35A and 35B)

The need for reform of the ultra vires *rule*
As has been discussed above, the problem with the *ultra vires* rule was that companies could escape liability for their actions by saying that the actions were *ultra vires*. This was unfair on innocent third parties who did not see why a company, which often knew perfectly well that an act it had carried out was *ultra vires*, should be able to avoid liability for something it apparently should not have done. The *ultra vires* rule depended to a certain extent on the fact that earlier in this century and at the end of the last century, judicial attitudes tended to favour the investor at the expense of the third party. Third parties were deemed to have constructive knowledge of the objects clause and to be aware of its terms, because the memorandum was available for inspection at Companies House. Even if you lived in the Shetlands or Cornwall you were somehow expected to go to the Registrar of Companies, read and be deemed to understand the objects clause of any company you were trading with. With the rise of consumer consciousness and assertion of consumer rights this attitude became increasingly less tenable, especially after the UK entered the EC.

In the Companies Act 1989, which inserted new sections 35, 35A and 35B into the CA 1985, Parliament tried to deal with five problems connected with this matter:

- how to protect innocent third parties;

- how to allow members the right to object to the directors making the company embark upon *ultra vires* acts;

- how to deal with directors who made the companies of which they were directors act *ultra vires* in a contract with the directors personally;

- how to deal with a company whose memorandum or articles imposed limits on the authority of the directors, or those whom they had authorised ("authorisees"), to make the company enter into contracts;

- how to deal with third parties who knew perfectly well that an act by a company was either *ultra vires* the company or *ultra vires* the powers of the directors or authorisees.

The way Parliament chose to deal with these conflicting aims was:

(a) subject to (c) below, to maintain the underlying *ultra vires* rule but to use statute to override it on most occasions ("the overriding statute");
(b) to have an internal policy, by which shareholders could control directors who are making the company act *ultra vires* ("the internal policy rule");
(c) to have an external policy, for the protection of third parties ("the external policy rule").

The overriding statute

A company's capacity to carry out any act is not now limited by its memorandum. This is because of the CA 1985 s 35(1) which states:

"The validity of an act done by a company shall not be called into question on the ground of lack of capacity by reason of anything in the company's memorandum."

This means that the restrictive wording of the memorandum cannot be used as an excuse for saying that a company did not have the legal capacity to carry out any particular act. The company cannot evade liability for an act even if it is *ultra vires*. Equally, it is probably the case that a third party could not use the fact that a company's act was *ultra vires* as an excuse to avoid fulfilling his part in the act. However, it would require a test case to be sure of this point.

It is worth noting the two words "act" and "memorandum". "Act" is a global term, and covers transactions, gifts, contracts, guarantees and anything else that a company might wish to do. "Memorandum" is used to limit the permissive nature of s 35(1) to the memorandum alone: the permission is not extended to the articles. The word "memorandum" was also used because if the legislation had said "objects clause" companies might have inserted an extra clause in the memorandum and claimed that that clause was not the objects clause.

The internal policy rule

The CA 1985 s 35(2) qualifies s 35(1):

"A member of a company may bring proceedings to restrain the doing of an act which but for subsection (1) would be beyond the company's capacity; but no such proceedings shall lie in respect of an act to be done in fulfilment of a legal obligation arising from a previous act of the company."

This is the internal policy in operation. If a company does an act which would be *ultra vires*, any member (and it need only be one member) can petition the court to prevent the act taking place. However that member's right is restricted because if the company has committed itself to fulfilling a legal obligation (a contract, for example) the company must still fulfil that contract and the member cannot stop it. The third party cannot be prejudiced (*i.e.* have his rights curtailed) just because one member says the contract is *ultra vires*.

Consequently, in practice all that a member can do is to obtain an injunction, or in Scotland an interdict, to prevent the repetition of the *ultra vires* act. The principal problem with this is that in many companies a company will have embarked upon an action before a member hears about it. It will often be too late for the member to stop the *ultra vires* act. Ingenious directors could also construct long-running contracts which would effectively deny the member the chance to object.

However, the directors are still supposed to make the company act within the confines of the objects clause or any other part of the memorandum, though they are given an opportunity to overcome any objections to the *ultra vires* act by means of s 35(3):

"It remains the duty of the directors to observe any limitations on their powers flowing from the company's memorandum; and action by the directors which but for subsection (1) would be beyond the company's capacity may only be ratified by the company by special resolution. A resolution ratifying such action shall not affect any liability incurred by the directors or any other person; relief from any such liability must be agreed to separately by special resolution."

From this it can be seen that directors should make the company act within the limits imposed by the memorandum. If they do not, they should convene a general meeting so that the members can pass a special resolution to approve or ratify their *ultra vires* act. The effect of this is to rewrite the memorandum for one particular act, since it also requires a special resolution to alter the objects clause of the memorandum. One could therefore have the process of a company considering entering into an *ultra vires* act, and then being prohibited by injunction or interdict from entering into that act by a member. To the member's vexation, however, he might find that following a special resolution his objection is overruled. The company could then proceed with the *ultra vires* act.

The second sentence of s 35(3) permits the members, if they wish, to pass a second special resolution absolving the directors, or anyone else involved, of any potential liability for making the company embark upon the *ultra vires* act. The reason that a second resolution is required is because it is possible that the members might be prepared to approve an *ultra vires* contract to prevent other members taking out injunctions or interdicts to prevent the contract in question or to avoid losing the goodwill of the other party to the contract, but might wish to punish the director for landing the company in such an awkward position anyway. Under such circumstances, the second resolution to waive the director's liability would not succeed.

Realistically, the opportunity for the objecting member to achieve his aim is limited. Nonetheless the right exists, and if a large company with, say, professed ethical or environmental concerns or worthy employment policies in its objects clause failed to live up to its duties due to unscrupulous directors, incompetence or some other reason, the embarrassing publicity of the injunction and the expense of convening a general meeting might concentrate the directors' minds on the suitability of the act in question.

Exceptions to the internal policy rules
There are two further qualifications yet: s 35(4) states that there are special rules applying to charities (discussed at the end of this chapter); and s 322A applies to directors acting in their own interest. An example of a director acting in his own interests is where he personally enters into a contract with the company, perhaps to supply certain goods or services. If the objects clause of the company forbids the supply of those goods or services, he will be making the company act *ultra vires*, and in addition the forbidden contract advances his own interests. As a director he ought to know better than most what is *ultra vires* the company and what is not, and while it is generally his duty to ensure that the company does not act *ultra vires* (although, as stated above, the members may decide that they do not mind), it is particularly his duty to ensure that the company does not act *ultra vires* where he has a personal interest in the *ultra vires* act.

Under the CA 1985 s 322A, if a transaction involving a director of a company or its holding company, or any person or associate connected with the director, together with the board of directors, exceeds any limitations under the company's constitution, the director or the associate may find that the transaction is voidable at the instance of the company (in other words, the company could, if it wished, renounce the contract, and the director or his associate would have no claim against the company), and he would have to account for any gain he receives from the company (CA 1985 s 322A(3)(a)). He might also have to indemnify the company against any loss (CA 1985 s 322A(3)(b)).

In this context "transaction" means any act of the company, and "constitution" means the memorandum, articles, any resolutions of the members of the company and any shareholders' agreements. The transaction will not be voidable if:

- the director or the associate has indemnified the company for any loss or damage (CA 1985 s 322A(5)(b));

- if the transaction is ratified by an ordinary or special resolution (CA 1985 s 322A(5)(d));

- if the subject-matter of the resolution has been used up or disappeared so that its restitution to the company is not possible (CA 1985 s 322A(5)(a));

- if a third party has acquired rights in the subject-matter, having acted in good faith, without having been made aware that the director in question had exceeded the limitations imposed by the company's constitution, and having paid a reasonable price (CA 1985 s 322A(5)(c)).

This in effect means that the *ultra vires* rules still apply to *ultra vires* transactions between the company and its directors (and their associates) in their personal capacities. This is not unreasonable, as they should be best placed to know what the company can and cannot do. However, under the CA 1985 s 322A(5)(d) a special resolution by the members could serve to ratify an *ultra vires* act involving a director.

The external policy rules

Powers of directors to bind the company

The internal policy rules operate to give members the right to object to what the directors were making the company do. The external policy rules operate:

- to protect those dealing with the company, and

- in particular, to reassure them that notwithstanding the lack of authority on the part of certain directors or employees of the company to make the company enter into certain transactions, those transactions will still be binding on the company.

The wording of the relevant section (CA 1985 s 35A(1)) is as follows:

"In favour of a person dealing with a company in good faith, the power of the board of directors to bind the company, or authorise others to do so, shall be deemed to be free of any limitation under the company's constitution."

The external policy, as stated above, applies where directors (or people, usually employees, authorised by them) have exceeded the authority given to them under the constitution of the company. In this context "constitution" again means memorandum, articles, members' resolutions and shareholders' agreements. If the directors or their authorisees act beyond their authority, a third party, who is unaware of this, probably can assume that the directors and authorisees have no restrictions on their authority to make the company enter into a transaction (here probably meaning a contract) or be party to an act (meaning any form of contract, donation, guarantee or anything else) even if in reality there are restrictions imposed by the company's constitution.

Problems with s 35A

There is some doubt as to the exact meaning of s 35A(1). It was designed to replace and has much of the same wording as the European Communities Act 1972 s 9(1), discussed in the case of *TCB Ltd* v *Gray* [1986] Ch 621. In this case s 9(1) was interpreted generously, to the effect that provided a third party acts in good faith, he is not required to establish whether or not a company representative who signed a contract with him was in fact properly authorised to do so: the third party can assume that the representative was authorised to do so. When s 35A(1) was being discussed in Parliament it was clear that the general intention was to protect the third party who was dealing with a company in good faith. As there has been no reported case on s 35A(1) it remains uncertain whether or not the generous interpretation of *TCB Ltd* v *Gray* will be followed, and to what extent a third party can realistically assume that any authorisee is genuinely authorised to act on behalf of the company.

   One view of s 35A(1) is that it is entirely supportive of the third party who is not expected to worry about anything under the company's constitution and can therefore safely contract with anyone apparently representing the company. Another view is that irrespective of the company's constitution, a third party should still be prudent in his dealings with any representative of a company and be aware of the extent of that representative's actual or ostensible authority, as will be discussed further shortly.

The good faith requirement

There is a qualification to this permissive nature of s 35A(1). The third party must be acting in good faith. This means that if he knows that the directors' action in making the company enter a contract with him would be strictly prohibited, because, for example, an inducement was being paid or some illicit favour was being returned, the third party cannot rely on the protection of s 35A(1). But as there is no specific explanation in the CA 1985 of what is meant by "good faith" in this context, all we can do is speculate how heinous the act must be to constitute lack of good faith.

What the CA 1985 s 35A(2)(b) does instead say is that a third party is not considered to be acting in *bad* faith if he knows that an act is beyond the directors' powers under the constitution. So even if the third party has examined the company's memorandum, articles, resolutions and shareholders' agreements and knows that the directors should not be entering into a transaction with him, he is still deemed not to be acting in "bad faith". What the CA 1985 s 35A(2)(c) says is that a third party is presumed to be acting in good faith unless the contrary is proved.

The doctrine of constructive notice

What this section is touching on is the doctrine of constructive knowledge of a company's constitution. It used to be the case, as stated earlier, that anyone dealing with a company was deemed to know the contents of the company's memorandum, articles of association, resolutions and other matters recorded on the company's file with the Registrar of Companies. Despite the apparent impracticalities of this doctrine, and the fact that most consumers had no understanding of these complex areas of company law, this doctrine was upheld for a long time and indeed lay behind the decisions upholding the substratum rule referred to earlier. The logic of the rule stated that as anyone could inspect the company's file, everyone was deemed to be aware of the contents of the file, and therefore could not object if (a) the company refused to carry out an action which was *ultra vires* or (b) an action by the directors of the company turned out to be unauthorised under the company's constitution.

The indoor management rule

This increasingly unrealistic doctrine was mitigated by the effect of the rule sometimes known as the "indoor management rule", exemplified in *Royal British Bank* v *Turquand* (1856) 6 E & B 327 (Exchequer Chambers). This stated that in the absence of anything to excite suspicion, a third party was entitled to assume that all internal procedures in a company were properly followed, directors validly appointed, and decisions passed at quorate meetings. The indoor management rule coexisted with the doctrine of constructive notice, so that although a third party was expected to be aware of the information on the company's file, he was not normally required to investigate any further in order to establish if directors' acts or authorisees' acts had in fact been properly authorised.

When the indoor management rule and the doctrine of constructive notice are combined with s 35A it would appear to be the case that if a third party deals with a company and the company, through its directors or authorisees, performs an act that is unauthorised or *ultra vires*, the third party:

- would not be acting in bad faith if he knew from a perusal of the company's file in Companies House that the act was *ultra vires* (CA 1985 s 35A(1));

- is entitled to assume, under the indoor management rule, that all internal procedures such as the granting of authority at a quorate meeting have been followed (even if they have not in fact been so followed) unless there is something that should excite his suspicion; and

- is entitled to assume that the company's act is authorised unless the third party is himself acting in bad faith because, say, he has secretly paid an inducement to the directors to approve an otherwise unauthorisable act (CA 1985 s 35A(2)(c).

The proposed abolition of the doctrine of constructive notice
The intention of the legislation was to further clarify this obscure area by introducing a rule to abolish the doctrine of constructive notice (CA 1985 s 711A). This stated that no one was any longer deemed to have notice of the contents of any company file kept at Companies House (CA 1985 s 711A(1)). However, confusingly, the CA 1985 s 711A(2) then stated:

"This does not affect the question whether a person is affected by notice of any matter by reason of a failure to make such inquiries as ought reasonably to be made."

It is not immediately apparent what this means, but it appears to suggest that even though a third party is not expected to know the contents of the company file, he may still be expected to make any reasonable enquiries about a company's acts or decisions if he becomes aware of some matter that should excite his suspicions. The CA 1985 s 711A(2) may not have been intended to contradict s 711A(1) but that is certainly one interpretation. Section 711A(2) may have been designed to maintain the notion that if a third party suspects that some company procedural matter is not entirely in order it is up to him to investigate the matter before continuing to deal with the company.

In any event the vagueness of the wording of s 711A defeated Parliament and it has not so far brought this section into force, so in theory the doctrine of constructive notice is still extant.

Practical aspects arising out of the CA 1985 s 35A

There are various matters worth considering here:

- The protection works in favour of the third party, not in favour of the company. So if the company directors or their authorisees knew very well that they were acting beyond their authority, they could not force the innocent third party to honour his part of the transaction. As their act would be beyond their powers, the directors would have to ratify it first before the company could take action against the third party.

- There may be a gap between dealing in good faith, and not acting in bad faith. It is up to the company to prove that the third party was acting in anything other than good faith. As this may not be easy to establish we may have to await a decision of the courts to clarify how this could be done.

- The wording of s 35A refers to the power of the *board* of directors to bind the company. What then happens when one director does something that is not authorised by the board, even though it is the type of act a director would normally carry out? Is the company bound by his act? What happens if a board of directors is inquorate (*i.e.* two few directors present to make their decisions valid) but it still authorises a certain transaction?

- How would one know whether a relatively humble employee actually had the authority of the board of directors to make the company a party to a transaction? What would happen if a disgruntled senior employee, working his notice before his compulsory redundancy, used his ostensible authority (*i.e.* the typical authority of someone in his senior position) to make the company enter into a contract wildly against its interests?

Agency and authority

These problems are as much to do with agency as with company law. The law of agency states that a principal, in this case, a company, is not bound by the unauthorised acts of its agent unless those acts were the sort of acts that such an agent for such a principal might reasonably be expected to do. This is the principle of ostensible authority (sometimes also known as apparent authority). So, for example, if you went to a bank to borrow £500,000, you might expect that the bank manager would be authorised to lend you that amount of money, but a teller at the counter would not. It would not be realistic of you to take the teller's word that the bank would lend you that amount of money. A bank manager has the ostensible authority; a teller does not.

This approach works very well at a common-sense level. It is flexible, it can take account of circumstances and it assumes all parties in a dispute should be behaving as prudent men of business. The practical solution for the queries raised above from the point of view of the third party is to ask the director or authorisee to obtain a board minute signed by the managing director confirming the board's authority to enter into the contract. This may cause some social offence, but it puts the matter beyond doubt. There is, however, a further complication. Even though the managing director might issue a board minute confirming that a certain action was approved by the directors, it does not necessarily mean that that action is one which the directors ought to be authorising. The directors might conceivably authorise an act that was technically *ultra vires*. However, s 35B states:

"A party to a transaction with a company is not bound to enquire as to whether it is permitted by the company's memorandum or as to any limitation on the powers of the board of directors to bind the company or authorise others to do so."

This means that a third party is not expected to look up the company's memorandum at Companies House, and his ignorance of the terms of the memorandum will not be held against him. Likewise a third party is not expected to have taken notice of any other restrictions on the directors' or authorisees' ability to make the company enter contracts. By virtue of this section, a third party ought, at least to some extent, be protected if it turns out that the board should not have made the company enter into the contract with the third party. Equally, however, just because the third party is not bound to enquire as to what is permitted in the memorandum, he is probably not relieved of the requirement to exercise prudence in his dealings with directors or authorisees. A director or authorisee who was manifestly acting far beyond his ostensible authority should excite the third party's suspicion. A board minute may not therefore be necessary, but it may be a prudent course of action where a director or an authorisee is purporting to make the company perform an act that in the normal course of events it would be unusual for that director or authorisee to carry out. Like so much involving ss 35, 35A and 35B, we shall have to wait for the test cases to tell us.

The CA 1985 ss 35, 35A and 35B have occasioned a great deal of academic comment because of their awkward wording. It is clear that the intention was to protect third parties dealing with companies, because that is the underlying thrust of the First Directive on Company Law (68/151). It is suspected that pressure on Parliamentary time prevented the exact wording of these clauses being debated as fully as it might have been. It is generally agreed that the wording of these clauses is not all it might be, but equally it has not been completely impossible to live with the legislation, because there have been no cases on the exact interpretation of ss 35, 35A and 35B yet. This is partly because objects clauses are not treated with the reverence they once were, and also because company lawyers know that this is an arcane issue over which much money could be spent to little benefit – except to the lawyers arguing in court.

Members' rights when directors act in excess of their powers under s 35A

The CA 1985 s 35A(4) is similar to s 35(2) in that it deals with a member's right to obtain an injunction or an interdict where the directors are acting beyond their given powers. The difference is that while s 35(2) is permissive, s 35A(4) merely says that nothing should prevent the member's right to apply to the court, and furthermore, any injunction or interdict would be to prevent the doing of an act beyond the power of the directors as distinct from beyond the capacity of the company. This distinction would need to be closely followed by those preparing the pleadings for an application to court. As in s 35(2), third party rights are protected (CA 1985 s 35A(4)), but directors could still be found liable for exceeding their powers (CA 1985 s 35A(5)).

Alterations to the objects clause

Although formerly it was difficult to alter the objects clause, and companies instead either had to set up subsidiaries if they wished to carry out an activity not mentioned in the objects clause, or conform to a limited number of permitted reasons for alterations, it is now relatively easy. You need a special resolution (CA 1985 s 4(1)) and the amended memorandum must be sent to the Registrar of Companies. In order to protect any minority that may object to the alteration, the CA 1985 s 5 provides that 15% of the members, or 15% of any class of shares, may apply to the court within 21 days of the passing of the special resolution altering the memorandum. The objectors must not, however, include anyone who previously voted in favour of the alteration. The court has wide discretion to deal with the objectors, but it is envisaged that the common remedy will be for the company or the other members to buy the objectors' shares from the objectors. Applications under this section are rare.

Charitable companies

A special regime applies to charitable companies. A charitable company's objects clause must clearly state that it is a charity and it is not allowed to do anything that is not connected with the provision of charity. This is because some time before the passing of the Companies Act 1989 Parliament became aware that some companies were professing to be charities but were abusing their charitable status. They did this in order to pay reduced rates and were really businesses in disguise. Simultaneously the powers of the Charity Commissioners in England, Wales and Northern Ireland, and the equivalent body in Scotland, were strengthened. Charitable companies, if they wish to remain charitable companies, may not alter their objects clause in such a way as to prevent the donation of their property or income to the recipients of the charity (Charities Act 1960 s 30A(1)); and any alteration must receive the prior written approval of the Charity Commissioners (Charities Act 1960 s 30A(2)). Charitable companies must act within the terms of their objects clauses, and the latitude extended to other companies and their objects clauses is not available to them.

There are, however, exceptions to this rule. The CA 1985 ss 35 and 35A, which do not normally apply to charitable companies, do apply to the acts of a charitable company in favour of a person who:

- did not know that the charitable company was acting beyond its capacity or the directors' powers; and

- had paid a proper price in connection with those acts; or

- did not know that the company was a charity.

A purchaser in good faith having paid full consideration and without notice of the invalidity of the act beyond the company's capacity or the directors' powers will still obtain good title to the assets he acquires (Charities Act 1960 s 30B(2)).

There are similar provisions for Scotland under the Companies Act 1989 s 112.

In Northern Ireland the relevant legislation is the Charities (Northern Ireland) Order 1987 (SI 1987/2048 (N119) art 9) as amended by the Companies (No. 2) (NI) Order 1990 art 47, which operates in the same manner as the English and Scottish legislation. The relevant prior written approval for any alteration of the objects clause must be obtained from the Department of Finance and Personnel.

Summary

1. Limited companies must state the word "limited" in their name unless they are charitable or non-profit-making companies under the CA 1985 s 30.

2. No company may have the same name as any other company within England, Wales, Northern Ireland or Scotland. Some names may be

prohibited by the DTI if deemed to be offensive (CA 1985 s 26(1)) and others require approval from the Secretary of State (CA 1985 s 29). Names can be changed by special resolution (CA 1985 s 28(1)). Under certain circumstances the Secretary of State can insist on a company name being changed (CA 1985 ss 28(3) and 32).

3. Business names must comply with the Business Names Act 1985, and where a company trades under a business name that differs from the company name this must be made clear on all company documentation (CA 1985 s 351). The names of companies which have gone into insolvent liquidation can only be reused with the court's approval (IA 1986 s 216) (*Re Bonus Breaks Ltd* [1991] BCC 546).

4. Under common law a company may not pass off another company's business name as its own (*Ewing* v *Buttercup Margarine Company Ltd* [1917] 2 Ch 1) though no company has a sole right to the use of a word in common parlance (*Aerators Ltd* v *Tollit* [1902] 2 Ch 319).

5. The memorandum of association of a private company tells the public:

   - its name;
   - its country of registration;
   - its objects or trading purpose;
   - that the liability of the members is limited (if applicable);
   - its authorised capital clause;
   - the names of the first subscribers.

   Although there are various standard styles of memorandum available, the most commonly used is Table B, which is adapted to suit each individual company.

6. A company cannot change its country of registration.

7. The limited liability clause must be present if the members are to avoid personal liability for the company's debts.

8. The authorised capital clause indicates how many shares, and up to what amount, the company could issue shares if it wished to do so. It cannot issue shares in excess of the authorised capital.

9. Further clauses may be inserted in the memorandum if necessary but it is not generally wise to make such clauses immutable.

10. The objects clause was designed to reassure investors that their funds would be used for the purpose stated in the objects clause: anything else would be *ultra vires* the company and would entitle the members to have the company wound up (*Re German Date Coffee Co Ltd* [1882] 20 Ch

169). Ingenious lawyers drafted the multiple and equal objects clause (*Cotman* v *Brougham* [1918] AC 514) so that nothing could be *ultra vires*. After many years of wrangling the CA 1989 suggested that companies may use a general trading clause (CA 1985 s 3A).

11. A general trading clause is not without its problems. The suggested wording may not cover every eventuality; it does not necessarily permit the sale of a company's business; and it gives a great deal of discretion to the directors. It also is unsuitable for dormant companies and it is not clear if it permits companies to make gifts, guarantees or grant security to subsidiaries.

12. The *ultra vires* rule has been substantially modified by the CA 1985 s 35(1) to prevent company contracts automatically being void because they were *ultra vires*. Any member of the company is, however, entitled to prevent the company entering into or repeating an *ultra vires* act but where the contract has already given the other party to the contract rights against the company the other party is protected (CA 1985 s 35(2)). Even where a member has successfully restrained the company from entering into or repeating an *ultra vires* act the members could vote by special resolution to ratify the *ultra vires* act (CA 1985 s 35(3)) and also to exonerate the directors as well if necessary (CA 1985 s 35(3)).

13. However the *ultra vires* rule continues in full existence where directors in their private capacity are contracting with the company (CA 1985 s 322A).

14. People contracting with directors who are acting on behalf of their company do not need to check to see if the directors really have the authority to make the company enter into their contracts unless they themselves are acting in bad faith (CA 1985 s 35A). The position is less clear with lesser employees who may or may not have been authorised by the directors to make the company enter into certain transactions.

15. People contracting with the company are not expected to be aware of the contents of its memorandum or of any restrictions on the directors' powers (CA 1985 s 35B).

16. Charitable companies must adhere to the charitable purpose stated in the objects clause, although third parties, unaware of a charitable company's *ultra vires* act will still be protected (Charities Act 1960 s 30B, in Scotland CA 1989 s 112 and in Northern Ireland, Charities (NI) Order 1987).

5. CONSTITUTION OF THE COMPANY (PART II)

Articles – Table A and variations thereto – alterations to the articles

In the last chapter we looked at the memorandum. The memorandum of a company tells the world at large:

- what its name and country of legislation is;
- what business it undertakes;
- whether it is public or private, limited or unlimited;
- what its authorised capital is.

This information is primarily for creditors and those doing business with the company. With the exception of the objects clause, it is not predominantly for the investors. The information relevant to the investors is in the articles.

The articles

As explained in Chapter 4, there is a standard model set of articles which can be used as a template for all companies. It is known as Table A, and it may be amended to suit an individual company's needs. It is almost unheard of for a company to adopt Table A in its entirety, as there are nearly always parts in it which are unsuitable, and any public company that wishes to issue its shares to the public must vary Table A because Table A contains no provision for the public issue of shares. The commonest occurrence of an unamended Table A is in students' examination questions. Table A can be found in SI 1985/805. The wording of a company's articles are subject to any contrary provision within the legislation applicable to companies generally or to the specific terms of the company's memorandum. An example of this is regulation 2 of Table A, which states:

"Subject to the Provisions of the Act, [CA 1985] shares may be issued which are to be redeemed or are to be liable to be redeemed at the option of the company or the holder on such terms and in such manner as may be provided by the articles."

In other words, a company's articles may prescribe the company's own rules relating to the issue of redeemable shares, but anything in the articles which contradicts the CA 1985 will be inoperative. However, provided the minimum requirements of the CA 1985 are satisfied, a company may issue redeemable shares on such other terms as it sees fit.

Principal features of Table A

Share capital
The company can issue different types of shares with broadly whatever rights or restrictions it sees fit (reg 2). Commission, in the form of shares or cash or both, may be paid to those who find subscribers for the company (reg 4). It can also alter or cancel its share capital (reg 32) and can alter or buy back its share capital subject to the relevant provisions of the CA 1985 (see Chapter 9).

Share certificates
Each member is entitled to a share certificate for each class of his shares (reg 6).

Lien, calls and forfeiture
If a member has partly paid shares, and a call has been made upon that member to pay outstanding money due to the company on those shares, the company has a lien over those shares (reg 8). A lien is a right of retention, in this case a right to prevent the owner of the shares transferring the shares to anyone else until the money due or the share is paid. As a further part of this right, the company can also force a sale of those shares in settlement of the outstanding amount due to the company (reg 9).

A call by the directors is a demand by the directors that the shareholders pay up such amount of the unpaid part of their shares as the directors request (reg 12).

Forfeiture may take place when the shareholder who has received a call refuses or is unable to meet the call (regs 18,19). The directors are then entitled to sell the shares, the shareholder loses his interest in the shares and may find that he is still liable for the unpaid amount of the shares if the sale proceeds of the shares were inadequate to pay the amount of the call. Forfeiture is more drastic (from the shareholder's point of view) than a lien. Neither lien nor forfeiture is much used nowadays.

Transfer of shares (regs 23–28) and transmission of shares (regs 29–31)
These are dealt with more fully in Chapter 7. Transfer is the gift or sale of shares, whereas transmission is the passing of shares to someone who holds the shares on someone else's behalf, such as a trustee for a bankrupt or an executor for a deceased person.

Meetings

There are extensive provisions applying to the holding of meetings (regs 36–63). This is dealt with more fully in Chapter 18.

Directors

There are extensive provisions applying to the appointment, retiral and removal of directors, their powers, their meetings and their duties (regs 64–98). These are dealt with more fully in Chapters 14 and 15.

Dividends, bonus issues

Companies may pay both final dividends and interim dividends (regs 102–108) and may convert undistributed profits into further shares (bonus issue) (reg 110). Dividends are dealt with more fully in Chapter 10 and capitalisations in Chapter 9.

Winding up

If the members of a company choose to wind the company up while it is still solvent, the liquidator they appoint is not obliged to sell all the company's assets and in so doing turn them into cash (reg 117): he can, if appropriate, physically hand over the company's tangible assets to the members in settlement of sums due to them, rather than going to the trouble of selling the assets first and giving the cash to the members later. Equally, and for the same purposed, intangible assets can be transferred by their normal means of delivery.

Indemnity

If an officer of the company is alleged to have acted negligently but it transpires, following legal proceedings, that this is not in fact the case, that officer is entitled to have his expenses paid to him out of the company's assets (reg 118).

Common amendments to Table A

As stated earlier, it is often found that Table A is not appropriate for every company. Some rules are too complicated for a small private family company: for example, the rule in Table A applying to the rotation of directors, whereby one-third of the directors are supposed to retire each year and put themselves up for reappointment has commonly been found to be pointless when there are only a few members and directors. Some directors do not see why they should have to resign anyway, and many forget whose turn it is to retire and to stand for reappointment.

Share capital

If a company has more than one class of shares, the rules applying to each class will need to be set out clearly in the articles to avoid any confusion as to their various rights. This will also be done at the time of issue of any new class of shares, on which occasion the articles will be amended to show the rights attaching to the new class of shares. For further information on this, see Chapter 7. If the company is a plc, and proposes to offer its shares to the public, there must be a clause in the articles permitting such an offer.

Shares held on someone else's behalf
English law will not permit the interest of a trust to be disclosed on a company's register of members (CA 1985 s 360). A trust is a non-incorporated legal entity designed to hold assets for the benefit of someone entitled to the proceeds of those assets (the beneficiary), under the care and management of custodians known as trustees, all acting under the instructions of a legal document known as a trust deed. Any trust holding shares in an English company has, in practice, to show the name of the first named trustee or trustees as a personal holders, his true status as trustee being a matter between the trustees and the beneficiaries. By contrast, companies registered in Scotland can show a trust as the registered owner of shares as the CA 1985 s 360 does not apply in Scotland. Table A is accordingly commonly modified in Scotland to take account of this.

Lien
Table A reg 8 states that the company has a right of lien over sums due to the company by way of unpaid share capital. But some companies provide for a right of lien over the shares in respect of any money due to the company from a member, whether it is in respect of unpaid share capital or anything else.

Transfer of shares
Many companies restrict the transfer of shares to a limited number of people, such as immediate family, existing shareholders, or to pre-specified trusts or holding companies. This is deliberately to prevent the shares getting into the hands of those the directors might consider unsuitable. Some articles give the directors unlimited powers to refuse the transfer of shares to an unsuitable transferee. Some articles contain detailed rules for the valuing of shares when shares are transferred within the terms of the articles.

Meetings
Although the procedure of meetings is not usually substantially altered, it may be that certain classes of shares attract weighted voting rights. This means that under certain circumstances, such as a threat to remove a directorship from a member, that member's votes count for, say, 10 times their normal number, thus allowing him to outvote everyone else. This is permissible if the articles allow it, as was shown in the case *Bushell* v *Faith* [1970] AC 1099, discussed more fully later in this chapter.

Quorum

It is possible to draft articles that state that a meeting is inquorate (*i.e.* without the necessary number of persons being present to allow decisions to be validly made) without a certain individual being present, or to state that a meeting is only quorate if, say, six people were present. Table A has a quorum of two. This is also discussed more fully later in this chapter.

Casting vote

Table A provides that the chairman should have a casting vote, but some companies choose to disapply this rule.

Polls

A poll is where each member votes according to the number of shares he owns or represents. If, following a show of hands, there is doubt about the extent of the approval for a particular resolution, it is common for the chairman to call for a poll. If the chairman does not call for a poll, under Table A, reg 46 two voting members, or members representing one-tenth of the voting rights or one-tenth of the paid-up share capital can call for a poll. Some companies choose to have articles that make it even easier than the already simple rules that exist under Table A for members to call for a poll.

Directors

As stated above, the rule relating to the rotation of directors is commonly dispensed with in small private companies, though it is often retained for listed companies. This is because it prevents directors becoming complacent if they regularly have to persuade the shareholders that they should be re-elected.

Some companies' articles specifically name certain directors. Such articles will need to be well drafted to take account of what will happen if the directors in question are incapacitated or die.

Seal

Many companies have a company seal which is impressed on important documents such as share certificates and major contracts. Some companies also have a separate seal for us in executing foreign contracts in order to satisfy the requirements of other countries' laws. Since the passing of the CA 1989 it is no longer necessary to use a seal within Britain, the Government believing that the abolition of the requirement for a company seal would be a substantial lifting of a bureaucratic burden on companies. If a seal is used, the articles usually state who has authority to use it.

Stock Exchange requirements

Before a listed company's shares can be traded on the Stock Exchange, the company has to comply with a large number of provisions laid down by the

Stock Exchange in their book "Admission of Securities to Listing" more commonly known as "The Yellow Book". One of the rules is that listed companies should adopt articles of association which conform to the requirements of the Yellow Book. Amongst other things, these articles generally require that nothing should impede the easy purchase and sale of the company's shares. This Stock Exchange requirement is not as demanding as it seems, because a company which places unwelcome restrictions on the transfer of its shares will find that as the shares are less marketable, so is the company less able to attract the capital it seeks. This is discussed more fully in Chapter 7. Companies listed on AIM and elsewhere have similar, though less demanding rules applicable to them.

Interaction of statute and articles

Unacceptable articles

Sometimes draftsmen of articles try to insert an article in the articles which is contrary to the law. For example, a draftsman might try to insert an article saying that the company can reduce its capital merely by passing an ordinary resolution. This would not be acceptable because the rules for reduction of capital are clearly laid out in the CA 1985 s 130 *et seq*. This states that reduction of capital requires a special resolution and it is not permissible to draft articles to avoid this rule. Such an article would have no effect.

Permissible but regulated articles

Where articles have omitted matters which ought to have been included, statute will sometimes lay down rules which apply where the articles are silent. For example, a company might state in its articles that directors must hold some shares in the company if they wish to be directors. Such shares are known as qualification shares. If the articles prescribe a time limit less than two months within which the qualification shares must be acquired, then the directors must obey the articles. But if the articles are silent as to the time limit within which the qualification shares must be acquired, the CA 1985 s 291(1) says that such shares must be acquired within two months of appointment as a director. Any longer period would be forbidden. There is no obligation for all companies to have qualification shares, but for those that do, the above rule is applicable.

The need to update articles

It is good practice for company secretaries to check their companies' articles every few years to take account of current best practice. A company whose articles were drafted in 1950 might well find that it was unnecessarily restricted by its articles from doing some of the things it might do with a more recent set of articles. A company has to live with its current set of articles until such time as the articles are updated. If the articles contain named individuals who have died or left the company, the company could find itself tied to uncongenial articles that could restrict it in its operations. All that is required to alter and update the articles is the passing of a special resolution (CA 1989 s 9).

The need for clarity in the drafting of articles

When you become a member of a company you undertake to adhere to the terms and conditions specified in the memorandum and articles (CA 1985 s 14). This does not necessarily mean that the memorandum and articles cannot be changed. Unless there is a shareholders' contract to the contrary, or some other ingenious method of preventing the articles being changed, such as weighted voting, you must accept the possibility that the members may cause the articles to be changed from time to time (CA 1985 s 9). If you do not like the terms of the original articles, or, as the case may be, any changes to the articles, you should:

- not become a member to begin with;

- dispose of your membership interest;

- resign in a non-share company such as a guarantee company;

- combine with enough others to pass a special resolution to alter the articles.

On the other hand, being a member means that you may be able to sue in your capacity as a member (but in no other capacity) to enforce the terms of the articles, particularly with regard to the assertion of your own personal rights in your capacity as a member.

Rayfield v *Hands and others* [1960] 1 Ch 1. The articles of the company of which Rayfield was a shareholder and Hands and his colleagues were directors and shareholders contained a provision that if a shareholder wished to dispose of his shares, he had to tell the directors first and the directors would buy the shares from the shareholder at a fair value. Rayfield wished to sell his shares, but Hands and his fellow directors refused to buy Rayfield's shares, claiming that the provision did not apply to them. This was mainly because the relevant term of the articles was not as clear as it might have been, but also because the directors in their capacity as members did not want to buy the shares. Rayfield therefore raised an action against Hands and the others to force them to adhere to the terms of the articles. The judge in this case took a robust view. He said that in this case the directors would be buying the shares as members and were therefore required to buy the shares from Rayfield exactly as the articles directed.

As can be seen from the above case it is very important that the member/ company relationship is clearly expressed. The CA 1985 s 14 states that:

"The memorandum and articles . . . bind the company and its members to the same extent as if they respectively had been signed and sealed by each member, and contained covenants on the part of each member to observe all the provisions of the memorandum and articles."

Unfortunately the wording of this section, which was presumably supposed to lay down the rights of the members as regards the company, is somewhat ambiguous, it not being clear:

- whether the members are covenanting with each other or with the company or both;

- whether the members can sue each other for a failure on the company's part as a whole to adhere to the memorandum and articles, or whether a member can sue only the company to assert his rights;

- whether a member can sue to assert a third party's rights given to that third party under the memorandum and articles;

- whether a member can sue the directors to make them adhere to the terms of the memorandum and articles.

Because of this uncertainty, some other countries, such as Australia, which initially adopted similar wording to the CA 1985 s 14 in their own companies legislation, have amended the wording to bring officers (*i.e.* directors, the company secretary and auditors) of the company into the terms of their equivalents of s 14. This has the merit of setting up a relationship between the members, the company and the officers of the company where each is obliged to respect the rights of the others. This leaves unresolved the question of third party rights, but arguably clarifies the quasi-contractual relationship between members, officers and the company.

In addition to the statutory ambiguity, many of the earlier cases about articles relate to the precise legal interpretation of the wording of the articles. In the early days of drafting articles some of the draftsmen did not always know what they were doing, or overlooked some vital matter which in retrospect should have been inserted. Vague draftsmanship could lead to expensive disputes that ended up in the courts.

Re British Iron Co, ex parte Beckwith [1898] 1 Ch 324. The articles of the company said that the directors' total remuneration should be £1,000. Directors were duly appointed but the precise amount due to each director was never clarified before the company went into liquidation. The liquidator claimed that as there was no specific contract he was not obliged to include the directors' claim as creditors of the company. The court held that while the liquidator was right in that there was no contract, it was at least apparent from the articles what was the total amount that the directors could collectively claim from the liquidator.

Although on the facts given and on the wording of the articles as they stood, the overall sum payable to the directors was apparent, it would have saved the directors considerable inconvenience if the articles had been more specific. The articles did not make it clear how much each individual director was able to claim: instead the articles might have specified how much each director could claim, or set out a mechanism for assessing each individual director's claim in accordance with the terms of his service contract.

Generally the courts try to be pragmatic about such cases and to try to produce a workable interpretation. This is because the courts cannot normally rewrite the articles – though occasionally the courts will declare a particular article void, as happened in the case of *St Johnstone Football Club Ltd* v *Scottish Football Association Ltd*, 1965 SLT 171. In that case one of the company's articles stated that no member might take legal proceedings against the company. The court held that such an article was contrary to public policy and non-enforceable. If there is a conflict between the memorandum and the articles the memorandum prevails (CA 1985 s 9). If there is an inconsistency between different clauses in the articles, it can be very difficult to find a solution, and each case will depend on the precise wording of the actual clauses.

Members' compliance with the terms of the articles

Where the drafting of the articles is clear, the general rule is that members must adhere to the terms of the articles.

Hickman v *Kent or Romney Marsh Sheepbreeders Association* [1915] 1 Ch 881. The articles of the defendant association provided that in the event of a dispute between a member and the association, the dispute must be settled by arbitration. The association tried to expel Hickman, so he took the association to court. His action failed, because the articles already provided a method of resolving the dispute which overrode the court's jurisdiction – in effect when he became a member, he had contracted to accept arbitration in the event of a dispute.

However, just because a company's articles require arbitration in the event of a dispute does not mean that arbitration is always the correct solution, especially when the issue is not actually a member/company dispute.

Beattie v *E and F Beattie Ltd* [1938] Ch 708, CA. Beattie was the managing director of E and F Beattie Ltd. The company sued him to recover monies that had been paid to him rather than the company. The company's articles provided that any disputes between the members and the company should be dealt with by arbitration. Beattie tried to say that a court action against him by the company was incompetent because the matter ought instead to go to arbitration. The court disagreed, saying that the action against him was an action against him in his capacity as a director refusing to account for company money, not a dispute with him in his capacity as a member.

Arbitration only applies to a member/company dispute; the claim against Beattie was not a member/company dispute; the company could therefore sue him in the courts.

It is accordingly important to make sure that when a member sues to make the company adhere to the terms of the articles, he sues in his capacity as a member and for his personal benefit as a member and not for his personal benefit in some other capacity. This is exemplified by the following case:

Eley v The Positive Government Security Life Assurance Company Ltd (1876) 1 Ex D 88, CA. Eley was a solicitor who lent £200 to the defendant company to cover the costs of formation, on condition that he became it permanent solicitor. He proceeded to draft the articles himself, and one of the terms of the articles stated that he should be the company's solicitor. He was given 200 shares in the company, but did not become the company's solicitor. At no stage had there been a board resolution to appoint him as the company's solicitor. Nor was there a contract between him and the company appointing him solicitor. When the company refused his services as a solicitor, he sued for breach of contract. He lost (a) because he was trying to enforce his rights as an outsider to the company (*i.e.* in his capacity as a solicitor and not as a member) and (b) because the courts were very suspicious of the original arrangements which they felt had not been adequately disclosed to the shareholders.

Given that Eley drafted the articles himself, one begins to see why the company might well have decided to use other firms of solicitors. What he should have done was to have a proper contract between the company and himself, regulating the terms of his employment. He thought his own drafting of the articles was sufficient; but it was not. The decision leaves open the question whether or not Eley in his capacity as member could have sued to make the company use him as its solicitor in accordance with the terms of the articles. Equally it is open to question whether or not some other member of the company could have sued the company to insist that Eley be used as the company's solicitor. The question of the ability of the members to assert third party rights in terms of the articles is left unresolved.

Cases, such as *Eley*, concerning the right to sue as a member but not as an outsider, derive from the English law doctrine of privity of contract. Under English law, very broadly speaking, only the parties to a contract have the right to sue under a contract, and it is not possible in a contract between two parties to confer a benefit to an outsider, unless that outsider is brought into the contract and/or confers a benefits upon the company/members.

One might think, in view of the number of cases caused by faulty draftsmanship, wilful refusal to accept the terms of the articles or a lack of fore-
thought by the participants, that nowadays cases on the precise interpretation of
articles are rare, as draftsmen would have learnt from others' mistakes. And
indeed on the whole such cases are rare, partly because of the enormous cost of
litigation and partly because of the ambiguity of the CA 1985 s 14 which makes
it difficult to predict what the outcome of any litigation on this matter might be.
But cases still arise.

Re William Stewart (Holdings) Ltd [1994] BCC 284. The directors of the
company were entitled under one of the company's own articles to refuse to
register transfers of shares except for transfers to "privileged relations", a term
defined in the articles and which included spouses. Another article stated that
directors had the right to demand that an executor of a deceased shareholder
should serve a transfer notice on the company indicating to whom the executor
was going to transfer the shares. The articles had a further clause which stated
that all the provisions applying to transfers generally should apply to transfers
by executors. The executor of a deceased member gave notice to the directors
that he wished to transfer the deceased's shares to the deceased's widow, but the
directors refused to register the transfer. Thereupon the executor took the directors to court where it was held that he was perfectly entitled to have the
deceased's shares registered in the widow's name. One wonders quite why the
directors were so obtuse about the matter, but the problem might have been
resolved if in the drafting of the first article it had clearly included transfer by
executors to privileged relations as a further exception to the directors' general
right of refusal.

Alteration of the articles

As stated earlier, the method of altering a company's articles is by special resolution under the CA 1985 s 9. When you become a member of a company you
must accept the fact that articles are intrinsically alterable, and indeed it is not
generally wise for a company to have articles that are very difficult to alter. Just
as with a memorandum designed to be difficult to alter, what may have seemed
very important to the directors who designed their company's unalterable articles may seem very much less important to a later generation. Inflexible articles
become out of date and can restrict the marketability of the shares. Nonetheless,
some people setting up a company sometimes try very hard to make either the
entire articles or certain articles impossible to alter. The following methods will
not work:

- stating that a particular article is unalterable – this is because the CA 1985 s
  9 overrules it;

- inserting a clause stating that the articles are unalterable – this is also prohibited under the CA 1985 s 9;

- making the company enter into a contract stating that it will not alter its own articles – this is because the CA 1985 s 9 still permits the company to alter the articles though it may run the risk of an action for breach of contract if it does alter the articles. Even if it has to pay damages the company can still alter its articles. However, it is an open question whether or not it would be possible for the other party to a contract with a company to obtain an injunction (in Scotland, interdict) to prevent a company from altering its articles.

Southern Foundries (1926) Ltd v *Shirlaw* [1940] AC 701. The managing director of Southern Foundries, Shirlaw, had a service contract that said he would be managing director for 10 years. It also said that if he ceased to be a director he would lose his position as managing director. In the course of his managing directorship, the articles were altered to give the principal shareholder the power to remove directors. The principal shareholder duly removed Shirlaw's directorship, thereby depriving him of his managing directorship as well. Shirlaw promptly sued the company. The House of Lords said that Shirlaw was entitled to damages for the breach of his service contract, but that the company was still entitled to alter its articles. In the course of his judgment Lord Porter said that the courts would not grant an injunction to forbid the alteration of the articles. Unfortunately this remark was made *obiter* (*i.e.* it did not form the main part of the overall judgment).

Lord Porter's views were followed in the case of *Cumbrian Newspapers Group Ltd* v *Cumberland & Westmoreland Herald Newspaper & Printing Company Ltd* [1987] Ch 1, and were possibly influenced by an earlier case, *Punt* v *Symons & Co Ltd* [1903] 2 Ch 506 where the judge had clearly said that no injunction could be granted. But there is previous Court of Appeal authority in the case of *Bally* v *British Equitable Assurance Company* [1904] 1 Ch 374, and the subsequent case, *British Murac Syndicate Ltd* v *Alperton Rubber Co Ltd* [1915] 2 Ch 186, to the effect that an injunction can be granted. There have been a few recent cases on the matter. This is because lawyers, seeing the lack of clear authority, now advise any client who wishes his company's articles to remain unaltered to make his fellow shareholders enter a personal contract with him not to vote in such a way as to permit the articles to be altered. This still allows the company to alter its articles, but an injunction (or interdict in Scotland) could be taken out against each member who proposes to vote in favour of altering the articles. The matter is not without significance because it is quite common in loan agreements between a company and a bank that the company undertakes not to change its articles nor to increase or reduce its capital without the consent of the bank. Technically the company cannot give such an undertaking; only the shareholders can. This issue arose in the case of *Russell* v *Northern Bank Development Corporation* [1992] 1 WLR 588, where the House of Lords, sitting in a Northern Irish case, held that that part of a shareholders' agreement which fettered a company's ability to increase its share capital was invalid. The shareholders could lawfully contract not to pass a resolution to increase the share capital, but the company could not give such an undertaking. Using the same principle, a company cannot itself contract not to alter its articles.

- *insisting that more than 75% of the votes are required to permit the articles to be altered* – this is again prohibited because of the CA 1985 s 9 which specifically says that a company may by special resolution alter its articles.

There are a few ways in which a company can make a particular provision in the articles effectively unalterable if it is determined to do so:

- *inserting a clause in the articles saying that unless a named shareholder is present any meeting is inquorate* – a quorum is the minimum number of persons who require to be present at a meeting to make decisions passed at that meeting valid. If there are too few people present the meeting is said to be inquorate and no decisions can be taken. In a company with the above clause, any resolutions passed at a meeting where the named shareholder is not present are invalid. This could be useful if a particularly "hands-on" controlling shareholder was determined always to get his own way. If he disapproved of any matters on the agenda of a meeting he would merely need to stay away to ensure that the items on the agenda could never be approved. However, such a clause does lead to difficulties in the event of that shareholder's absence, illness or death unless there is provision for alternates. It also can lead to ill-feeling against the named shareholder. New shareholders would be reluctant to join such a company. A refinement of that clause is to allow certain non-contentious resolutions to be passed in the absence of the named shareholder. Under such circumstances a resolution proposing the alteration of the articles would not be non-contentious.

- *inserting a clause in the articles permitting weighted voting* – weighted voting is an ingenious device whereby the shareholder who has the benefit of the weighted voting can always outvote the other shareholders. For example, a company's articles might have a clause stating that a named shareholder is entitled to 10 times his normal votes in the event of a disagreement between the shareholders on certain specified points, one of which invariably is a resolution to alter the articles. This procedure was permitted in the case of *Bushell* v *Faith* [1970] AC 1099. Bushell and Faith were both directors of a private company, and each held 100 £1 shares in the company. Bushell was Faith's sister. A further sister held another 100 £1 shares. The two sisters were unhappy with the way that their brother, Faith, was managing the company. They convened an extraordinary general meeting and purported to dismiss Faith as a director by means of an ordinary resolution under the then equivalent of the CA 1985 s 303, their 200 votes being greater than his 100 votes. Faith however relied on article 9 of the company's articles, which stated that whenever there was a vote to unseat a director, that director's votes would be three times his normal number of votes. Accordingly Faith claimed that he had 300 votes while his sisters only had 200 between them. The House of Lords agreed with him, saying that although an ordinary resolution was sufficient to dismiss a director, the Companies Acts did not forbid a company granting its members such rights as Faith was enjoying.

Similar clauses to this are found quite frequently in small companies where there is a substantial outside investor who does not wish to lose his seat as a director, or a controlling shareholder who does not wish ever to be outvoted on significant matters. As with the clause with the named individual in a quorum, a weighted voting clause can deter future shareholders and can lead to ill-feeling amongst the shareholders.

There are restrictions on the general power to alter the articles. The main restrictions are as follows:

- A member cannot be forced by the alteration of the articles to subscribe for more shares or to have to pay more for his existing shares – unless he agrees to do so (CA 1985 s 16).

- If the alteration means that there is a conflict with the memorandum, the memorandum prevails and the alteration is void (CA 1985 s 9).

- If the alteration means that there is a conflict with an existing article and the new article, the courts will try to read the two articles together to give a rational and workable solution which may amount to less than the altered article had appeared to offer.

- If the alteration is in conflict with the CA 1985 or some other statute, for example a company might pass a resolution altering the articles to limit the involvement of the company's auditors in checking the company's accounts. Such an alteration would be void.

- A company can alter its articles but not with retrospective effect (as was decided in *Swabey* v *Port Darwin Gold Mining Company* [1889] 1 Meg 385).

- Altering the articles in such a way as to deprive a class of shares of its rights.

Normally the rights of a class of shareholders can only be altered if the members of the class itself agree to have their rights altered. This is done usually by members of the class passing an extraordinary resolution to that effect, followed by a special resolution passed by the members of the company as a whole (CA 1985 s 125). Some companies have their own procedures for varying a class's rights. Sometimes these procedures are contained in the memorandum, though they are more generally found in the articles. Only if the correct variation procedure has been followed may the class rights be varied, and even then, under the CA 1985 s 127(2) holders of more than 15% of the issued shares of the class in question can apply to the court to have the variation cancelled. However, if they wish to do this, they must:

(i) not have voted in favour of the variation beforehand;
(ii) apply within 21 days of the passing of the class resolution or the granting of consent.

It is important to appreciate that it is unacceptable to alter the articles to *deprive* a class of its rights. However, if the class's rights are unaltered, but the members of another class vary their own rights, and then succeed in passing a special resolution to alter the articles to their benefit, it could be that the first class is not deprived of its rights at all; but what has happened is that the other class has increased or improved its rights relative to the first class. This is more fully discussed later in this chapter under the requirement that alterations be made in good faith for the benefit of the company as a whole.

There is a simple method of preventing the above situation happening. In the rights attaching to the first class of shares there should be a clause stating that any variation of the rights attaching to any other class of share is deemed to be a variation of the rights attached to the first class of shares. This means that if the other class of shares wished to alter its rights, say, by giving itself extra votes per shares, or increasing its preference dividend, it will have to wait until the first class agrees to that variation. Naturally the first class is unlikely to agree to any variation of another class's rights if in any way the variation is going to prejudice its own rights.

• An alteration to the articles may cause a director's contract to be terminated, which may result in a claim against the company for damages, as in the case of *Southern Foundries (1926) Ltd* v *Shirlaw* [1940] AC 701 above.

• Altering an article may lead to a minority having grounds for claiming unfair prejudice.

As this last topic was, at least historically, a matter of considerable importance, it requires separate treatment. It should, however, be noted that since the development of the remedies under the CA 1985 s 459 (see Chapter 13) whereby minority shareholders can obtain redress where they can show that they have suffered unfair prejudice at the hands of the majority, many of the former difficulties with this matter are nowadays less significant. Until remedies under the CA 1985 s 459 became available, it was very difficult for a prejudiced, formerly "oppressed" minority to obtain redress through the courts. If the majority used their greater voting power to alter the articles in such a way as to affect a minority of the shareholders for the worse, it was normally acceptable to do so provided that it could be shown that the majority were altering the articles in good faith in the belief that they were acting in the best interests of the company as a whole. This position was outlined in the case of *Greenhalgh* v *Arderne Cinemas Ltd* [1950] Ch 286. Greenhalgh was a minority shareholder in Arderne Cinemas Ltd. Most of the other shares were held by the Mallard family. Greenhalgh and the Mallards did not get on well with each other. The Mallards wished to sell their shares to someone who was not already a shareholder. However, the articles said that members who wished to sell their shares had first to offer them to existing shareholders – and the main existing shareholder was Greenhalgh. As the Mallards did not wish to sell to Greenhalgh, they used their majority voting power to have the company pass a special resolution altering the articles. The alteration stated that an existing member's pre-emptive right to a selling member's shares would not apply if the members passed an ordinary resolution to that effect first. Greenhalgh was unable to block ordinary resolutions because he had too few shares. Greenhalgh was unhappy about this and claimed that his minority interest had deliberately been ignored by the interests of the majority. It was held that after the alteration Greenhalgh was actually in no better or worse a situation than any other shareholder. The new arrangements applied as much to any Mallard shareholder as it did to him. In the course of his judgement, Evershed MR laid down the rules stated above, namely that the alteration must be made in good faith for the benefit of the company as a whole. The company as a whole means the overall body of shareholders. Any alteration must be to their collective benefit. Lord Evershed stated that on this occasion the alteration was for the collective benefit of all the members.

What is for the collective benefit of the company as a whole is likely to vary from case to case. Furthermore, what may be to the commercial benefit of the company as a whole may well not be to the benefit of the minority shareholder in his capacity as a director – as in *Shuttleworth* v *Cox Bros Co Maidenhead Ltd* [1927] 2 KB 9. Shuttleworth was a director of the defendant company. He and other directors were directors for life unless disqualified for certain specified reasons. Over a period of time Shuttleworth retained money which should have been paid to the company, so the shareholders passed a special resolution altering the articles to create a new method of disqualification. The new method stated that if the other directors requested a director to resign, that director was thereby disqualified. Despite his own dubious practice with the company's

money, Shuttleworth objected to the alteration on the grounds that he had contractual rights in the original articles. The court did not agree. This is because
articles are inherently alterable (CA 1985 s 9), and the alteration was made in
the best interests of the company as a whole.

In retrospect, Shuttleworth might have protected himself with a separate
service contract. A further advantage of a service contract is that it will provide
for compensation for early termination of the contract by the company.
Accordingly it is rare nowadays for a director to try to safeguard his contractual rights purely by having himself named in the articles. Any prudent director would also have a service contract.

Further cases illustrating the good faith or "benefit to the company as a
whole" requirement include:

- *Brown* v *British Abrasive Wheel Co* [1919] 1 Ch 290. The majority of shareholders in British Abrasive Wheel Co were willing to invest more money
  into the company provided the articles were altered to allow the majority to
  buy out the minority. This was held not to be acting in good faith – since the
  real intention was to drive out the minority – even though the extra capital
  might well have been for the benefit of the company as a whole.

- *Sidebotham* v *Kershaw, Leese & Co Ltd* [1920] 1 Ch 154, CA. The majority
  shareholders in Kershaw, Leese and Co Ltd disapproved of a shareholder
  whose own business was in competition with the company. They proposed to
  alter the articles to allow for the compulsory purchase at a fair price of the
  shares of any member competing with the company's business. This was held
  to be acceptable.

The decisions above suggest that the courts take a pragmatic and commercial
approach to these matters. Deliberate oppression of a minority is clearly unacceptable, but articles can justifiably be altered to a minority shareholder's detriment particularly where that minority may not have been acting in the best
interests of the company. The relative absence of recent cases on alteration of
articles to the detriment of a minority suggest:

(i)   that nowadays any such cases are likely to be pleaded using the statutory
      provisions of the CA 1985 s 459, or in extreme situations, trying to obtain
      an order for winding-up under Insolvency Act 1986 s 122(1)(g);
(ii) that directors, who formerly used to rely on the articles to act as their con-
      tracts of employment, are seeking the more sure protection of proper
      contracts of employment entirely separate from the articles;
(iii) that as a company may now buy back its own shares from its members,
      companies are more likely to buy back a minority shareholder's shares

than alter the articles just to try, possibly unsuccessfully, to force a minority shareholder out;

(iv) minority shareholders are protecting their position by means of artful drafting of their class rights, in particular stating that any variation of the rights attaching to any other class of shares is a variation of their own rights and must be approved by them first; or by the use of weighted voting for certain matters.

Summary

1. The articles of a company provide the investors or members with the internal constitution of the company. Most articles are in the form of variants of Table A.

   Although originally it was intended that Table A should be a standard for most companies to follow, many of its provisions are either out of date or too complicated to follow. It is therefore common for most companies to make substantial amendments to Table A when preparing their own articles of association.

2. Companies listed on the Stock Exchange have to adopt articles that follow the Stock Exchange's own recommendations for what should be in articles as laid out in the "Admission of Securities to Listing" ("Yellow Book"). Similar rules apply to companies quoted on the AIM.

3. Statute can on certain occasions override any contrary provisions in the articles.

4. When a member of a company is suing that company for enforcement of terms of the articles, it is important to sue as a member rather than in any other capacity.

5. Articles are inherently alterable under the CA 1985 s 9 and it is uncommercial to try to make them unalterable. But there are methods of making it very difficult to alter them in practice:

   - inserting a clause in the articles saying that unless a named shareholder is present the meeting is inquorate;
   - weighted voting (*Bushell* v *Faith* [1970] AC 1099);
   - having a shareholders' agreement not to alter the articles.

   To alter articles the company must pass a special resolution.

6. It is not possible to alter the articles so that they permit something which is forbidden by statute, such as requiring members to subscribe for more shares or pay more for each share (CA 1985 s 16). In the event of inconsistency with the memorandum, the memorandum prevails (CA 1985 s 9). Articles

cannot be altered retrospectively, and alterations which prejudice a minority may be struck down under the CA 1985 s 459. Alterations must be made in good faith for the benefit of the company as a whole (*Greenhalgh* v *Arderne Cinemas Ltd* [1950] Ch 286, *Brown* v *British Abrasive Wheel Co* [1919] 1 Ch 290).

7. Better draftsmanship, the use of service contracts for directors, the ability of companies to buy back their own shares, and the use of the minority protection provisions of the CA 1985 s 459 have reduced the incidence of cases referring to alteration of articles not in good faith and not for the benefit of the company as a whole.

6. THE PRACTICALITIES OF INCORPORATING A LIMITED COMPANY

"Off the shelf" and "tailor-made" companies – incorporation documents – first general and board meetings – practical considerations – taking over an existing business – pre-incorporation contracts – execution of contracts

This chapter explains:

(i) how one sets up a company;
(ii) what is required for a company to begin trading;
(iii) how a company can take over an existing business; and
(iv) what practical matters need to be addressed in doing this.

"Off the shelf" and "tailor-made" companies

If you are a solicitor, company agent or an accountant, and a client asks you for a company as soon as possible so that he can set up a new business, you have a choice. You can either:

(i) take an existing pre-formed company, known as an "off the shelf" company, and alter it to the client's requirements, or
(ii) you can incorporate a brand new company, designed specifically to the client's requirements (a "tailor-made" company).

Firms of solicitors, accountants and company agents (people whose main business is the setting up of new companies) are all normally able to produce both types of company for their clients at reasonably short notice. With notice, some such firms can also use their links with company formation agents abroad to set up or obtain foreign-registered companies for their clients. Britain's best known firm of company agents is Jordan's, which has branches all over the country. Many company agents advertise their services in the back pages of the financial sections of the Sunday newspapers.

Throughout the rest of this chapter, lawyers, accountants and company agents who set up companies for their clients will be known as "company formation agents".

The off the shelf company

In an off the shelf company, the directors, company secretary and shareholders/ members will often be employees or members of the company formation agents. Some company formation agents have in-house companies which exist purely for the purpose of acting as the first directors, secretaries and members of the agents' off the shelf companies.

Few off the shelf companies will be likely to fit the client's requirements, so the memorandum and articles of the off the shelf company will normally need to be altered to the client's specification. Thereupon the off the shelf directors and secretaries all resign, having appointed the client and his colleagues in their places, and the off the shelf shareholders transfer their shares to the client and his colleagues. The procedure for this is outlined later in this chapter. In a company where there are no shares, as can happen in a company limited by guarantee, the off the shelf members resign their memberships and new members, being the client and his colleagues, take their places. In a single member company, the same practice, suitably adapted, is followed.

The main advantage of an off the shelf company is that a client can use it immediately, even if all the necessary paperwork for transferring the company into his hands is incomplete. The disadvantage is that, compared to a tailor-made company, slightly more paperwork is required to change the company to a client's specifications.

The tailor-made company

A tailor-made company is a company made to the client's specification without using an off the shelf company. The advantages of doing this are as follows:

- there is no need to pay the Registrar of Companies a fee to change an existing company's name to the name the client wishes his company to bear;

- the necessary forms can be filled in directly by the client without the need for subsequent transfers of shares or appointments and resignations of directors and company secretary, as would be the case with an off the shelf company. This may marginally reduce the cost to the client;

- the client can give his instructions for the memorandum and articles and there is no need to convene an extraordinary general meeting to pass a special resolution to alter an off the shelf company's memorandum and articles, as there is when an off the shelf company is used. The memorandum and articles can be drafted directly to suit the client's requirements.

The disadvantages of doing this are as follows:

- the financial savings of incorporating directly without using an off the shelf company are unlikely to be substantial;

- although a tailor-made company normally only takes a few days to be registered by the Registrar of Companies following receipt by him of all the correctly completed forms, the client still cannot commence trading as a company until the Registrar of Companies has issued the certificate of incorporation for the tailor-made company. In the case of a plc, the client should also obtain a trading certificate under the CA 1985 s 117 (discussed later) since without it the directors are potentially personally liable for the company's losses if the company fails to honour its obligations. Therefore if the client is eager to start trading, an off the shelf company is probably more use to him since it is already incorporated;

- it is in practice no more inconvenient to alter an off the shelf company's memorandum and articles than it is to design your client's memorandum and articles "from scratch" to suit your client's wishes. This is because most company formation agents work from their own in-house sets of standard or "style" memorandum and articles which are amended as required. The style articles are based, as all articles are, on Table A, but will have been drafted in such a way as to suit most clients' requirements.

The types of style articles that you would expect company formation agents to have available would include the following:

- simple trading company with the Table A rules about rotation of directors removed;

- small family company with restriction on transfer of shares to those who are not immediate family;

- company with preference shares attracting a fixed dividend;

- company with deadlock provision, suitable for a joint venture, whereby two or more equal classes of members have to agree on all important matters or face liquidation;

- plc with or without a clause entitling the company to issue its shares to the public;

- company limited by guarantee, suitable for charities;

- plc with clauses which conform to the normal Stock Exchange requirements for listed companies.

It is not obligatory to use a company formation agent to set up a British company. It is perfectly possible for anyone to set up a British company, though a solicitor, notary public, commissioner for oaths or a Justice of the Peace must sign the "Form 12". This is a form which must be sent to the Registrar of Companies as part of the procedure for incorporating a company. Form 12 is discussed later in this chapter. Although it may be cheap to set up a company on one's own, the disadvantage of doing this is that if one makes a mistake it may be expensive to pay someone else to put it right. It may therefore be wiser to pay a company formation agent to do it properly.

Incorporation documents

All companies have to be created in the same way, whether they are put into immediate use as tailor-made companies or sit on the shelf waiting for a client.
   In order to incorporate a company, the following forms must be sent to the Registrar of Companies along with the statutory fee:

- Form 10

- Form 12

- the memorandum of association

- the articles of association.

The number of the form corresponds to the relevant section of the CA 1985.

Form 10

Form 10 contains the following information:

- the proposed name of the company. As discussed in Chapter 4, it is important that the client uses a name that no one else is already using, or is not so similar to an existing company name and its business as to risk an action of passing off or risk being compelled by the Registrar of Companies to change its name. Company formation agents generally check at Companies House to ensure that the proposed name is available (as discussed in Chapter 4);

- the registered office on incorporation (CA 1985 s 10(6));

- the full name and address of any company formation agents, acting for the subscriber or subscribers to the memorandum (CA 1985 s 10(4));

- the name and address (or registered office) of the company secretary, together with the written consent of the company secretary (CA 1985 s 10(2)(b)). The company secretary can be a company in its own right, in which case a director or the company secretary of that company will have to sign for that company. If the company secretary is a company in its own right and has only one director, that director cannot sign on behalf of his company if he is simultaneously the director of the company that is about to be formed (CA 1985 s 283(4)(a)). In Scotland a partnership may act as the company secretary (CA 1985 Schedule 1 s 3(1)(b)), though in England, Wales and Northern Ireland a partnership would have to act as joint secretaries. Joint secretaries which compromise all the partners of a partnership do not need to provide the entire details of every single partner – the firm's name and address will suffice (CA 1985 Schedule 1 s 3(2));

- the full name, address (or registered office), date of birth and occupation of all directors, together with a list of all directorships held by each director within the last five years with the exception of:

  (i)   directorships of dormant companies;
  (ii) parent companies owning the subsidiary which is being incorporated; and
  (iii) other wholly owned subsidiaries of the parent company owning the company being incorporated (CA 1985 Schedule 1 ss 1–2).

Directors which are companies in their own right (which is perfectly permissible) do not have a date of birth or an occupation. In addition, if the sole director of a newly formed company ("A Ltd") is a company ("B Ltd"), and the sole director of B Ltd is an individual ("C"), C cannot be the company secretary of A Ltd (CA 1985 s 284(4)(b)). The commonest occupation stated on Form 10 is "company director".

- the signature of the agent(s) acting for the subscriber(s) to the memorandum and articles, or the signature of each subscriber or someone authorised to sign on each subscriber's behalf.

There are good reasons for the disclosure of the information on Form 10 about the directors. These are:

- Directors over the age of 70 are not permitted to be directors of plcs (CA 1985 s 293(2)) unless the members, having been given special notice, are prepared to re-elect them by means of an ordinary resolution (CA 1985 s 293(5)). The purpose of this rule is to prevent elderly directors who are no longer in their prime staying on the board indefinitely.

- By examining the directors' lists of other directorships, it is possible to obtain from the Registrar of Companies microfiches for the other companies in which they hold directorships. If the published accounts of those other companies indicate that those other companies are not prospering, it may say something about the competence of the directors.

- The Form 10 gives the address of each director so that anyone who needs to serve a court document on the director should in theory know where to send it.

- CA 1985 s 13(5) states that the first directors and secretary named in the Form 10 are the company's first directors and secretary, irrespective of any provision to the contrary in the company's memorandum and articles.

Form 12

Form 12 is a statutory declaration by either a solicitor involved in the incorporation of the company, or a director of the company or its company secretary. The declaration is to the effect that everything which should have been done for the incorporation of the company has in fact been done. The person making the declaration ("the declarant") is supposed to do so conscientiously believing it to be true (Statutory Declarations Act 1835). The point of this Act is that if a declarant makes a statutory declaration without belief in its truth, he can be prosecuted. In order to make the declaration more significant, the declaration must be in the presence of a justice for the peace (*i.e.* a magistrate), a solicitor, a commissioner for oaths or a notary public, the last two of which will usually be practising solicitors.

It is arguable that the Form 12 serves little useful purpose. Although a justice of the peace or any of the other witnesses to the declaration is supposed to be sure of the identity of the declarant, in practice this tends to be a formality. In any event, if the declarant is a fraudster, the threat of prosecution may make very little difference to him.

Memorandum and articles of association

The memorandum and articles have been discussed in Chapters 4 and 5 respectively. They must both be signed on the back page by the subscribers. These people will be the first members of the company and the memorandum will also detail the number of subscriber shares they have been allotted. Both documents must also be witnessed by one witness and be dated.

Statutory fee and accounting reference date

The statutory fee is at present £20, but may be changed from time to time. Some companies also include with their incorporation documents a Form 224. This is used to alter the date for a company's accounting year end, generally known as its accounting reference date. In the absence of sending in a Form 224, the company's accounting reference date will be the last day of the month in which the anniversary of its incorporation falls (CA 1985 s 224(3)). The Form 224 must be sent to the Registrar of Companies within nine months of the company's incorporation (CA 1985 s 224(2)). The company's first accounting reference period must cover more than six months but not more than 18 months, beginning with the date of incorporation and ending on the selected accounting reference date (CA 1985 s 224(4)). This means that the first accounts for the company could extend to the first 18 months' worth of trading.

Reasons that a company might wish not to have as its accounting reference date the last day of the month in which the anniversary of its incorporation falls include the following:

- it might wish to tie its accounting reference date to another company of which it was perhaps a subsidiary or holding company, so that the accounts can be more easily consolidated;

- if the directors know that a particularly lucrative transaction was to be realised after the company's initial 12 months, it may be worth altering its accounting reference date to after the anticipated date of completion of the transaction but before the 18-month period expires. Its first set of accounts would therefore take account of the transaction. This ought to mean that in due course the company's first published accounts will look more impressive than they may otherwise have done;

- the initial extended period of 18 months may give the company the temporary opportunity to hide some unexpectedly good results (or possible unexpectedly bad results) which it may not wish its competitors to know about.

Assuming all these documents are in order, correctly signed and dated, the Registrar of Companies will issue a signed certificate of incorporation stating the company's registered number, its name, its date of incorporation and its country of registration. This certificate is conclusive of the information contained thereon, as stated in Chapter 3.

Further requirements for plcs

A plc being created as such is unwise to start trading or borrowing any money unless it has first been granted a trading certificate under the CA 1985 s 117. It obtains this by providing the Registrar of Companies with a statutory declaration signed by a director or the company secretary stating:

- that the nominal value of the company's share capital is not less than the authorised minimum, currently £50,000;

- that of the £50,000 nominal value of shares, at least one-quarter plus any premium has been paid up on each share;

- the amount or estimated amount of the company's preliminary expenses together with information as to who pays or would pay those expenses;

- the amount or benefit, if any, paid or given to any promoter of the company, with an indication of what he did for the company to obtain such payment or benefit.

A promoter is any person who sets up a company. Promoters commonly have a personal stake in the company and historically there were many fraudulent promoters persuading gullible investors to buy shares in their companies. This was so that the promoters could sell their own shares and disappear rapidly with the proceeds. Promoters are discussed in greater detail in Chapter 8.

In order for the director or secretary to make the statutory declaration, the memorandum would need to state that its authorised share capital is £50,000. The subscribers should have been allotted their shares, having paid cash for them (CA 1985 s 106).

Assuming the statutory declaration satisfies the Registrar of Companies, he will issue a s 117 trading certificate and the company can begin trading. Without it, the company and its officers could be fined, but since that rarely happens, there is a greater sanction under the CA 1985 s 117(7). If the company embarks upon a transaction without a trading certificate, the transaction will still be valid. However, if the company fails to carry out its obligations under the transaction within 21 days of being asked to do so by the other contracting party, the directors of the company become jointly and severally liable with the company to indemnify the other party for any loss or damage that the other party suffers through the company's failure to carry out its obligations. In practice this rarely happens, not least because most plcs begin life as private limited companies and later convert to plc status.

First board meetings and general meetings

Following the successful incorporation of the company, it is good practice to hold the first board meeting. The items to be discussed depend on the type of company.

The off the shelf company

Once a client has obtained an off the shelf company, it will need to be amended to suit the client's requirements. Some of these changes will need to be done by passing resolutions either at a general meeting or by the use of a written resolution, and some can be done at a board meeting. A private company, if it wishes, is able to dispense with holding a general meeting if it passes written resolutions by means of the written resolution procedure under the CA 1985 ss 381A, 381B and 381C. This means that instead of convening a meeting, which may be inconvenient, the members of the company must all sign a document, or copies thereof, each of which bears the text of the resolutions to be passed. The passing of resolutions is discussed more fully in Chapter 18. Formerly written resolutions needed to be approved by the company's auditors first to see if there was anything in the resolutions that concerned them as auditors. Following SI 1996/1471 this practice is no longer necessary. In any case at this stage in a company's existence it would be very unusual for a company to have auditors since the company formation agents would not normally have been informed of their client's choice of auditors for the new company.

This written resolution procedure is unavailable to plcs: they must hold a general meeting to pass the requisite resolutions.

Amending the off the shelf company

If an off the shelf company is to be amended, it is common for the *members* of the off the shelf company (*i.e.* the company formation agents) to first hold a general meeting (or pass written resolutions) to pass the undernoted resolutions to alter the company's name, memorandum, etc., to suit the client's wishes. If a general meeting has to be held, it may be held at less than the usual notice of 21 days (CA 1985 s 369(2)) by means of the short notice procedure (CA 1985 s 369(4)). More details of how meetings are held and written resolutions are passed may be found in Chapter 18. The resolutions to be passed by the members would normally include the following:

(i)   a special resolution to amend the company's name under the CA 1985 s 28;

(ii)   a special resolution to amend the memorandum of association, together with the new text thereof. The new memorandum would probably be in the form referred to in Chapter 4, with a specific objects clause, a general trading clause and a host of ancillary clauses, all as permitted under the CA 1985 s 4;

(iii) a special resolution to amend the articles under the CA 1985 s 9, together with the new text thereof. The new articles might need to take account of any special requirements of the client, such as special share transfer requirements, or special pre-emption provisions.

In addition the following resolutions would be required if the company were to issue shares:

(iv) an ordinary resolution increasing the authorised share capital under the CA 1985 s 121 if the off the shelf company's initial authorised share capital was likely to be insufficient for the number of shares to be issued;

(v) an ordinary resolution under the CA 1985 s 80 giving the directors authority to allot shares for up to five years up to a specified amount;

(vi) alternatively to (v), for a private company only, an elective resolution under the CA 1985 s 80A waiving the five-year rule and permitting the directors to allot shares up to a specified amount without necessarily restricting to five years the period during which that authority may be exercised.

The issue of shares is discussed in greater detail in Chapter 7.

Once the matters discussed above have been dealt with by the members, the directors deal with the other outstanding matters at the first meeting of the board of directors. On that occasion it would be common for the chairman to:

- table the original certificate of incorporation, note the date of incorporation and table the certificate of change of name and note its date;

- table the amended memorandum and articles;

- table the letters of resignation of the off the shelf directors and company secretary;

- table the acceptance by the new directors (*i.e.* the clients) of their new positions as directors;

- table the acceptance of the new company secretary;

- table the stock transfer forms indicating the transfer of shares from the off the shelf members to the new members (*i.e.* the clients) and directing the company secretary to register the transfers and to have the transfers stamped at the Stamp Office;

- direct the company secretary to register in the company books (see under "The tailor-made company") all the new directors' details such as their interest in the company's securities, their service contracts, their other directorships within the last five years, and to make all necessary returns to the Registrar of Companies, such as:

    (i)   Form 288 (change of directors and company secretary);
    (ii) Form 287 (change of registered office);
    (iii) Form 123 (increase of authorised capital);
    (iv) Form 224 (alteration of accounting reference date);
    (v)   the new memorandum and articles of association;

(vi)   a certified copy of the resolution under ss 80 or 80A authorising the directors to allot shares;

(vii) certified copy resolutions for (iii) and (v) and the resolution for the change of name.

Some companies may hold more elaborate first board and general meetings, but most will have to deal with most of the above matters.

The tailor-made company

A tailor-made company should already have the company name, registered office, individually drafted memorandum and articles of association, directors and secretary all in accordance with its owners' wishes. There need be no changes. But if the company is to trade, as opposed to remaining a dormant company, it would be sensible to have a board meeting to have a formal record, through the minutes (the written record of the proceedings at the meeting) of the following matters:

(i)   the formal noting of the certificate and date of incorporation of the company;

(ii)   the formal appointment of the first directors and company secretary back-dated to the date of incorporation of the company;

(iii) the formal noting of the company's accounting reference date;

(iv)   the instruction of the company secretary to insert the subscribers' names in the register of members, to complete the company books, and to issue any share certificates. The register of members is one of a number of registers which make up the documents known as the "company books". These are kept in the company's registered office and maintained by the company secretary. The company books are not the accounts of the company, but a series of registers, commonly held in a loose-leaf binder, which show such information as:

   (a)   the register of directors and their interests and the register of secretaries;

   (b)   the list of past and present members and their past and present shareholdings;

   (c)   the register of the company's charges and copies thereof;

   (d)   the registers of allotments and of transfers;

   (e)   the minutes of general meetings and board meetings;

   (f)   the principal sets of signed accounts.

   Often the company books, especially for a private company, come in a specially made box with preprinted pages for all these registers, together with blank share certificates. The auditors usually inspect the company books as part of their audit. Off the shelf companies need to have properly maintained company books as well.

Amendments to off the shelf plcs

It is not very common to incorporate off the shelf plcs as plcs, it being more usual for private limited companies to convert to plcs. But if a client obtains an off the shelf plc, he may wish to amend it both so that it suits his requirements and so that it can commence trading. A plc cannot pass written resolutions, nor pass elective resolutions. To pass the necessary resolutions, there would have to be a general meeting.

Even when a plc has been amended in this way, it will still not be able to trade until it has received the trading certificate under the CA 1985 s 117, referred to above.

Practical considerations following incorporation

Once a company has been incorporated to the client's satisfaction, he will need to consider the following matters:

1. All company stationery should be printed with the company's name, registered office, registration number and trading name, if any, clearly on it, all in terms of the CA 1985 s 351. There is no requirement to include directors' names on the company stationery, but if one of the directors' names is mentioned on the stationery, all the directors' names should be on it (CA 1985 s 305).

2. The company should apply to Customs and Excise for a VAT registration number unless it is not registered for VAT.

3. There should be a nameplate outside the company's registered office.

4. The company secretary, or someone appointed by him, should ensure that the company books are properly completed.

5. The company should obtain its own bank account and cheque-book and ensure that it follows its own guidelines on signatories. The company's bank will probably want a certified copy board minute confirming the banking arrangements.

6. The company's auditors should be appointed and their confirmation of acceptance noted.

7. The company should issue share certificates to any new shareholders.

Taking over an existing business

It is very common for a company to be formed expressly to take over the existing business of a partnership or sole trader, so that the former partners or sole trader can obtain the benefit of limited liability. The former partners or sole trader will become the directors and shareholders of the new company. For the purposes of this chapter we will assume that a company ("AB Ltd") is taking over a partnership ("the AB Partnership") of whom the partners are A and B. The usual reasons for transferring a business to a company have been outlined in Chapter 1. In order for the transfer to take place AB Ltd must already be in existence and A and B appointed directors and company secretary. A and B should also hold a token number of shares in the company. A and B should have instructed the company formation agents to draw up or amend the objects clause of the memorandum so that it is appropriately drafted for the business AB Ltd will be undertaking. Likewise the articles will have been drawn up or amended to A's and B's requirements. Advice should be taken from A's and B's accountant as to the best time for transferring the AB Partnership business to AB Ltd, taking into account any taxation considerations, in particular capital gains tax, roll-over relief and VAT.

Certain items attract stamp duty when they are transferred from a partnership to a company. Land and buildings attract stamp duty at the rate of 1% of the value of the land and buildings, although land and buildings worth in aggregate less than £60,000 do not attract stamp duty on transfer. Other items that attract stamp duty, although at the rate of 0.5%, include book debts (sometimes known as receivables, broadly speaking being money due from those who owe the business money in respect of loans, goods or services supplied by the business), goodwill (the monetary value that reflects the desirability to the purchaser of the asset which attracts the goodwill, sometimes calculated by reference to the difference between the base cost of an asset and the price someone would pay to acquire that asset), securities (effectively shares and debentures) and deposit accounts.

As a ruse to avoid paying stamp duty, just before the transfer of a partnership business to a company, it is possible to sell the partnership's book debts for cash to a factoring agent. A factoring agent is someone who buys debts from, say, a supplier who is owed money by his customers. The factoring agent will pay the supplier a discounted cash sum for the debts which the supplier was due. The factoring agent then pursues the debtors, while the supplier has money in his hands and does not need to waste his time pursuing his debtors. The cash from the factoring agent is then placed in a current account. A further ruse is to place all sums held on deposit accounts into a current account. Cash and sums held on current accounts do not attract stamp duty.

The sale and purchase agreement

The terms of the sale of the business by the partnership to the company are encapsulated in a contract known as a sale and purchase agreement, sometimes also known as an acquisition agreement. This should deal, *inter alia*, with the following matters:

- what the consideration (the price, whether in cash or shares or a combination of the two) for the business is and how it is to be paid;

- the date of settlement of the sale and purchase;

- what assets and liabilities are being transferred from the partnership to the company;

- what employees are being taken on by the new company;

- a requirement that if the partnership receives any debts due to the business it is to act as trustee for the company and to hand the money from the debts over to the company.

Practical matters relating to the sale and purchase agreement

The sale and purchase agreement is not the only paperwork required for the transfer of a business from a partnership. Other documentation is required as well.

The value of the business

The business's accountants will need to draw up a balance sheet for the value of the business as at the date of the transfer of the business. The balance sheet may be annexed to the sale and purchase agreement.

Approval of the board of directors to the acquisition

The company's directors will need to hold a board meeting to approve the terms of the sale and purchase agreement, and to approve the execution (signing) of the agreement after the passing by the shareholders of the s 320 resolution referred to shortly. If the former partners, now in their capacity as shareholders, receive shares as their consideration (payment) for transferring the business to the company, the directors will need to approve the creation and issue of those shares and will need to instruct the company secretary to issue share certificates and to send the Form 88(2) to the Registrar of Companies. The procedure for the issue of shares is dealt with further in Chapter 7.

Approval by the members of the purchase by the company of assets belonging to the directors

Under the CA 1985 s 320, when a company acquires substantial assets from the directors personally, the members (even though they may in reality be the same persons as the directors) must formally approve the purchase in a general meeting. Under the CA 1985 s 320(2) "substantial" in this context means assets worth in excess of the lesser of 10% of the company's net asset value or £100,000. However, if the assets being transferred by the directors are worth less than £2,000, the CA 1985 s 320 does not apply. The company will need either to hold an EGM to pass an ordinary resolution, thus permitting the company to acquire substantial assets from the company's directors, or (providing the company is a private company) to sign a written resolution to the same effect (CA 1985 s 320(1)). If the directors do not already have the authority to allot shares, the EGM may be an opportunity to pass a resolution under the CA 1985 s 80 to ensure that they have such authority so that they can issue shares to themselves in their other capacity as shareholders. A s 80 resolution may also be passed by written resolution if the company is a private company.

Transfers of property

If there is any real or (in Scotland) heritable property (*i.e.* effectively land and buildings) being transferred from the partnership to the company, the necessary deeds conveying the property will need to be executed and registered or recorded in the appropriate registers of land ownership for each country and county. Any existing mortgages (in England, Wales and Northern Ireland) and standard securities (in Scotland) over the property and in the name of the partnership will need to be discharged and new ones taken out in the name of the company and registered or recorded in the appropriate registers for land ownership. Any new mortgages or (in Scotland) standard securities will also need to be registered with the Registrar of Companies. All this area is dealt with in greater detail in Chapter 17.

The discharge of existing mortgages and standard securities and the creation of new ones will involve the consent and co-operation of any lender who has a mortgage or standard security over the property. Lenders may well use the occasion to demand extra security from the company's directors by way of personal guarantees. This is because once the borrower is a company, there is less incentive for the directors to ensure the company honours its obligations to the lender than when the borrower was a partnership and the partners were personally liable to the lender in the event of default by the partnership.

If the business was being run from a leasehold property, the lease would need to be transferred from the partnership to the company. The landlord in such a case might well charge a premium for consenting to the transfer of the lease, and might also demand personal guarantees from the directors as a condition of allowing the new lease to be granted. He would also expect his legal fees to be paid by the company. Such practices would, of course, depend on the economic bargaining positions of both landlord and tenant.

Stamp duty on the transfer
The sale and purchase agreement, plus any deeds conveying the property to the company will need to be sent to the Stamp Office (the part of the Inland Revenue that deals with stamp duty) for adjudication. Adjudication is the process whereby the Inland Revenue assesses the amount of stamp duty payable on the value of those items that attract stamp duty. The company will be expected to pay the stamp duty.

Other administrative matters
From a practical point of view, on the transfer of the business from the partnership to the company, many administrative matters will need to be attended to. These include:

- transfer of insurances to the company;

- making any new necessary banking arrangements;

- discharging any existing hire purchase agreements and creating new ones in the name of the company;

- registering vehicles in the name of the company;

- telling creditors and debtors that the company has replaced the partnership;

- assigning contracts from the partnership to the company following intimation to and consent from the other parties to the contracts;

- printing new business stationery, invoices, etc.

Pre-incorporation contracts

A pre-incorporation contract is a contract purportedly made on behalf of a company at a time when it has not yet been formed. Under the CA 1985 s 36C the person who is acting for an as yet unformed company, or as its agent, is personally liable under that contract. This means that even if the person draws up the contract between the as yet unformed company and the other party to the contract, and signs on behalf of his as yet unformed company, the contract is in effect with that person. If the as yet unformed company defaults on its obligations, that person has to make good any loss to the other party. The only exception to that would be if the other party to the contract waived the personal liability of the person acting on behalf of the as yet unformed company (CA 1985 s 36C). Such generosity is unlikely, since no one would then be liable under the contract.

Since the CA 1985 s 36C was enacted there have been no significant cases on this matter, although the issue was touched upon in a case where someone purported to make a contract on behalf of a company which used to exist but by the time of the putative contract had been struck off the register of companies (*Cotronic (UK) Ltd* v *Dezonie* [1991] BCLC 721). A few years later the person purporting to act for the non-existent company realised it was non-existent and created a new company with the same name. The question here was whether there was a contract with a company at a time when both parties thought they were making one, but where the company had no legal existence because it had been struck off. It was held that the person purporting to act on behalf of the non-existent company was entitled to be paid by the other party to the contract on a *quantum meruit* basis (*i.e.* he should be paid the amount his labours would ordinarily have been worth), but that there was no contract between the non-existent company and the other party – because the company did not exist. It was also held that s 36C and the creation of the new company with the same name as the non-existent company were not relevant to the issue. The CA 1985 s 36C refers to pre-incorporation contracts, when what was at issue in this case was a post-dissolution contract to which s 36C cannot apply. Prior to the enactment of the CA 1985 s 36C there were various cases on this matter, of which the most memorable is *Phonogram Ltd* v *Lane* [1982] QB 938. Lane borrowed £6,000 from the recording company, Phonogram, to be used for a company to be called "Fragile Management Ltd". At the time of the loan the company was not formed, but he signed for the loan "for and on behalf of Fragile Management Ltd". He was to use the money to promote a pop group called "Cheap, Mean and Nasty". He never got round to forming the company and failed to repay the money when he was asked to do so. Phonogram sued him personally and won, as he purported to act on behalf of a non-existent company.

The problem still arises, however, of how a company can, at a later date, adopt a contract formed on its behalf at a time when it was not in existence. At present there is no very satisfactory solution to this problem, though one relatively safe method is for the person who acts on behalf of the as yet unformed company to obtain an existing off the shelf company quickly and take the contract in the name of that company, thus obviating the problem. A pre-incorporation contract can however be novated. This means that the contract between an as yet unformed company and another party could effectively be torn up, and a new one produced in identical terms to the previous contract, save that the company would genuinely be in existence at the time of the execution of the novated contract. Novation only is possible with the goodwill of the other contracting party, and if a dispute has arisen, the other contracting party is unlikely to be prepared to novate the contract and lose the advantage of making the person acting on the company's behalf personally liable for his company.

Pre-incorporation expenses

It is possible for a company to incur pre-incorporation expenses but arguably only in Scotland because of the requirement in England for present rather than future consideration (*i.e.* payment at the time of the contract, not at some unspecified date in the future). In *Park Business Interiors Ltd* v *Park*, 1991 SLT 818 the company raised an action against Park for his apparent failure to provide proper consideration for shares allotted to him. Park claimed that the consideration for the shares was the pre-incorporation expenses he had borne on behalf of the company. He was able to prove that the expenses had been included in the accounts of the company as a debt due by the company to him, and that they had not been objected to by the members of the company at the time of the incurring of the expenses. It was held that while a company is not automatically liable for pre-incorporation expenses, provided the expenses are reasonable and made in good faith, the company can agree to accept them. The members' treatment of Park's expenses indicated that this had indeed happened.

Execution of documents

Execution is the legal term for the signing of documents to make them legally valid. Formerly all companies had to have a seal which would be impressed on all legal documents to make them valid. Many companies still use a seal. Some companies need seals for executing contracts abroad where seals are still part of the method of executing documents in other jurisdictions.

In England and Wales and Northern Ireland documents are executed by the signing of the document by the director and company secretary, or by two directors, stating that they are signing for the company (CA 1985 s 36A(4)). A document intended to be a deed (which means that it is a particular type of legal document which does not expire through lapse of time and is particularly necessary for transferring rights in lands and buildings) and which makes it clear that it is meant to be a deed, will be treated as a deed. Delivery of the deed, which is required under the law of England, Wales and Northern Ireland, is deemed to have taken place upon the execution of the deed (CA 1985 s 36A(5)). Furthermore, a purchaser who has been given a document which appears to have been signed by the same persons as above is entitled to rely on the document's apparent validity, provided he has bought the property which is referred to in the document, and has bought it in good faith for a proper price (CA 1985 s 36A(6)). Lesser documents can be signed by a director or secretary on behalf of the company.

In Scotland, documents which need to be authenticated can be subscribed (*i.e.* signed) on behalf of the company by two directors, a director and company secretary, or two persons authorised to sign on behalf of the company all in accordance with the Requirements of Writing (Scotland) Act 1995 s 3. This brings the authentication requirements for important documents into line with English practice, save that it is Scottish practice to refer to any ancillary documents (such as maps, certified accounts, etc.) in the "testing clause" which is the clause at the end which narrates the date and place of execution of the document by the company. Neither witnesses nor the seal are required any longer. Authentication is primarily necessary for documents transferring interests in land. Any other documents may be executed by a director, or the company secretary, or someone authorised by the company to sign on its behalf (Requirements of Writing (Scotland) Act 1995 Schedule 2 s 3).

Summary

1. Off the shelf companies are existing companies waiting to be used by a client and subsequently altered to suit his requirements. Tailor-made companies are companies which are incorporated from scratch to suit the client's requirements.

2. To incorporate a company you need:

   - Form 10;
   - Form 12;
   - the memorandum of association;
   - the articles of association;
   - the statutory fee.

3. The Form 10 details:

   - the name;
   - the registered office;
   - the full name and address of any agents for the subscribers or members;
   - the name and address of the company secretary;
   - the name, address and previous relevant directorships of the directors.

   The Form 10 is also signed by the subscriber, subscribers or his or their agents.

4. The Form 12 is a statutory declaration that all the requirements for the incorporation of a company have been properly complied with.

5. A plc incorporated as such needs a s 117 trading certificate before it starts trading. Without it the directors may be personally liable for the company's

debts. This is, however, very rare, as most plcs being their corporate existence as private companies and convert to plc status later. In that event a s 117 trading certificate is not necessary.

6. An off the shelf company will require substantial alteration to suit the client's requirements. The alterations are likely to affect:

   - the name;
   - the memorandum and articles of association;
   - the registered office;
   - the directors and the company secretary;
   - the shareholders;
   - the accounting reference date.

7. Transfer of an existing business to a company requires consideration of:

   - the exact assets and liabilities to be transferred;
   - tax matters;
   - conveyancing and other property matters;
   - the optimum time from an accounting or tax angle for the transfer;
   - the value of the consideration;
   - the passing by the members of an ordinary resolution under the CA 1985 s 320 permitting the sale of a business from partners to a company of which those partners are directors;
   - consent of any lenders, landlords or lessors, some or all of which may demand guarantees from the directors personally.

8. Pre-incorporation contracts make the person purporting to act for the as yet unformed company personally liable for his company's debts arising under the contract unless the other party to the contract agrees otherwise (CA 1985 s 36C and *Phonogram Ltd* v *Lane* [1982] QB 938).

9. Most important company documents need to be executed, by being signed by two directors or a director and a secretary. Lesser documents require less formality in execution.

7. SECURITIES

Types of securities – allotment and issue of shares – registration requirements – share certificates – mortgages of shares – lien and forfeiture of shares – transfer and transmission of shares

Types of securities

Securities is a global term that can encompass shares, debentures, options to subscribe for shares or debentures, share warrants and convertibles. Convertibles are securities that can change from one type of share into another, from shares into debentures, or debentures into shares.

In different contexts the word "securities" can have different meanings. Later in this chapter it has a very limited meaning in respect of the allotment of shares, but in terms of the provisions of the Criminal Justice Act 1993 referring to insider dealing, securities can include not only the above types of security but also Government stocks. This meaning of security is discussed in Chapter 12.

Confusingly, security is also the term for the collateral to a loan. If a company borrows money from you, you want the company to give you "security". This means that it deposits an asset with you, or gives you rights over that asset, so that you can keep or sell the asset if the company does not pay you back. This particular meaning of security will not be discussed in this chapter, although it is discussed in Chapter 17.

Shares

A share was defined by Farwell J in *Borland's Trustee* v *Steel Brothers & Co Ltd* [1901] 1 Ch 279:

"A share is the interest of a shareholder in the company measured by a sum of money, for the purpose of liability in the first place, and of interest in the second, but also consisting of a series of mutual covenants entered into by all the shareholders *inter se* in accordance with s 16 of the Companies Act 1852 (now CA 1985 s 14)."

The liability in the first place is the amount of money the shareholder has to pay to acquire the share, this being in the case of share for which he has subscribed, the nominal value plus any premium (the meaning of premium is discussed below). The nominal value of the share is the value given to the share for the purpose of ascertaining the minimum amount that needs to be paid to the company in order to say that it is fully paid. If a share is fully paid up to its nominal value the shareholder never has to pay the company any more for that share unless he is required to do so by paying a premium. For example, if a company issues the shareholder with a £1.00 nominal value share, with no premium required, once he has paid the full nominal value of £1.00, his liability to the company is extinguished, even it if subsequently goes into liquidation. He might, however, choose or be obliged to pay more than nominal value of the share because of the competitiveness of the share issue. The extra amount he chooses to pay (or sometimes is asked to pay) is known as the premium, and it reflects the desirability of the share. The money paid by way of premiums is credited to a special capital account known as the share premium account. Once credited there, its use is severely restricted. This is dealt with more fully in Chapter 9.

If a shareholder has not paid the full £1.00 for his £1.00 nominal value share, and has only paid, say, 40p, the outstanding amount of 60p remains a debt due by him to the company. The directors may ask or "call" upon him at any time to pay some or all of the outstanding amount to the company, and in the event of the company's liquidation, the liquidator will ask him to pay the outstanding amount to the company. But once the outstanding amount is paid, his liability to the company in respect of his share is extinguished.

The authorised capital of a company is the total nominal value of all the shares it could issue if it wished to. This figure has to be stated in the memorandum (CA 1985 s 2(5)(a)). The authorised capital is sometimes also known as the "registered capital" (CA 1985 s 123(1)). It is not possible for a company to issue shares which cause the total nominal value of the issued shares to exceed the authorised capital. However the authorised capital can be increased by means of an ordinary resolution (CA 1985 s 121(2)(a) and s 121(4)).

The authorised share capital should be contrasted with the called-up share capital, which is the total amount of share capital paid by the shareholders to the company to date, plus any further amount that the directors have called upon the shareholders to pay even if the shareholders have not actually yet paid it (CA 1985 s 737(1)).

The paid-up share capital is the total amount paid to the company by way of share capital to date, but excluding any premiums and excluding any calls made but not yet paid.

It is very common for shares in private companies to be given a nominal value of £1.00, but there is no reason why shares should not have a nominal value of 5p or £500 or any figure the company thinks suitable. It is generally agreed that to have shares in units that are too large is psychologically off-putting to investors, but there are no real logical grounds for this belief. Not all shares in a company need have the same nominal value: some companies have different classes of shares each with a different nominal value. If a share is issued at par value, it means that the shareholder pays its full nominal value to acquire it. Some countries, notably the USA, consider that shares do not need to have a nominal value, and shares can be issued on a no-par value basis. By doing this the concept of a partly paid share becomes meaningless because there will be no liability on the share anyway, though equally there is no share capital for creditors to fall back on, and thus less reassurance for creditors that the company is worth trading with. The only value a no-par value share has is its market value, and for an unsophisticated investor this approach has some merit because it is simple to understand.

In countries such as the UK where shares do have nominal value, there is often no correlation between the nominal value of the share and its market value. This does not mean that the concept of nominal value is pointless. If shares are paid up to their nominal value, or could at short notice be paid up to the nominal value, a creditor will be reassured that there will be, or ought to be, some capital in the company with which to meet his claims, not least because shares may not generally be issued at a discount to their nominal value (CA 1985 s 100) except to the extent of payment of underwriting commission and brokerage under the CA 1985 s 97. The no-discount rule is discussed later in this chapter. The principle that the existence of share capital provides comfort to creditors is however open to question in the light of the fact that:

(a) for private companies the total nominal value of issued shares may be in excess of the value of any non-cash assets given to the company in exchange for those shares (discussed later in this chapter) and
(b) the total nominal value of the issued shares may not be very great anyway, particularly in, say, the common situation of a company with an issued share capital of £100.

The interest in the second place (referred to in *Borland's Trustee*) is the benefits that normally arise from being a shareholder. These may include:

(a) the right to a dividend when and if declared;
(b) the right to vote; and
(c) the right to a return of capital in the event of a solvent liquidation of the company.

These three benefits may be restricted or indeed added to according to the company's practices: for example, as an additional benefit of being a shareholder in the shipping company P & O, you can obtain reduced ferry travel costs on their ships.

The mutual covenants are the articles themselves, and to a lesser extent nowadays, the memorandum, which together delineate the terms and conditions on which, under the CA 1985 s 14, a person becomes a member in a company, and accepts what the articles and memorandum state concerning the relationship of the members to the company.

When a company creates a share, a person buying the share from the company is known as a subscriber. Confusingly, a subscriber share is slightly different: a subscriber share is normally one issued to a person who subscribes, or signs, the memorandum at the inception of the company. In a company with no shares, a person who signs the memorandum as its first member, or one of its first members, is also known as a subscriber. (In the following context the term *subscriber* means a person buying a newly created share from the company.) If a subscriber subscribes for shares, he is making an offer to the company to buy its shares. Assuming his offer is accepted by the company, and the company has correctly followed the procedures (detailed later in this chapter), he will be allotted a share, which means that he obtains an unconditional right to be entered into the register of members (CA 1985 s 738(1)). When his name is entered into the register of members he becomes a member of the company (CA 1985 s 22) and at that stage the subscriber is said to have been issued his shares, as was decided in *National Westminster Bank plc* v *Inland Revenue Commissioners* [1994] 3 All ER 1.

There are various different types of share, and it is possible to combine the different types of share in whatever way seems appropriate under the circumstances.

Ordinary shares
Ordinary shares will have whatever rights that are given to them under the articles, and in the absence of any express conditions given to them under a company's articles, will have the rights set out in Table A. Ordinary shares will normally entitle the shareholder to vote, to receive dividends, to have a return on capital on solvent liquidation and will normally rank behind preference shares both as to dividends and return of capital. Ordinary shares are commonly said to be participating, in that they participate in the profits of the company on such basis as is recommended by the directors and approved by the members generally, but only after the preference shareholders have received their payments first. Unless the articles say otherwise, ordinary shares may not be converted into other types of shares, are not issued on the assumption that they will be redeemed on specified terms at a later date, and have no special rights. However, it is possible to have different types of ordinary shares. For example, it is not uncommon to have two types of ordinary shares, equivalent in every way, save that one set of ordinary shares, called, perhaps, the "A" ordinary shares will be held by one shareholder and another set, the "B" ordinary shares will be held by another. Typically, in a deadlock management company, there are as many "A" ordinary shares as "B" ordinary shares and both the A ordinary shareholders and B ordinary shareholders must agree on all decisions.

Preference shares

Preference shares are shares that normally attract a fixed or otherwise predetermined rate of dividend and a prior right to a return of capital on liquidation. Commonly they do not carry voting rights except under certain specified circumstances, such as variation of the rights attaching to the preference shares or resolutions for winding up the company. Preference shares are not generally participating and therefore cannot enjoy any further profits that the company may make. However, it is possible to draft articles for participating preference shares that allow a right of participation in either some or all of the profits that remain after the preference shares have taken their portion. This is usually expressed on the basis of an arithmetical formula specified in the articles.

Preference shares are deemed to be cumulative. This means that if no dividend is paid in one year because there were no profits, the following year, when there are profits, the preference shareholder will be entitled to the arrears which ought to have been available the previous year had the company been profitable plus the dividend for the current year. Failure to pay a dividend may trigger action by the investor, particularly if the investor is also a lender to the company. Non-payment of a dividend may be an event of default entitling the lender/investor to appoint a receiver. Although it is not strictly speaking necessary to state that a preference share is cumulative, it is common nonetheless to say that is it cumulative. Equally it is possible to have a non-cumulative preference share, though it is unlikely that any investor would want such a share.

Normally dividends can only be paid following the recommendation of the directors that dividends should be paid. It might therefore be tempting for unscrupulous directors to pay themselves large salaries, pension contributions and expenses in order to ensure that there are no profits available to be paid out by way of dividends on the preference shares or indeed any other shares.

Astute preference shareholders pre-empt this ruse by stating in the articles that dividends will be deemed to be declared if profits are above a certain figure, and that profits will be defined by a carefully worked-out formula which specifies the acceptable level of directors' remuneration, pension contributions, expenses, etc., so that the directors cannot avoid paying dividends whether they make a recommendation to pay dividends or not.

In many respects preference shares are similar to debentures (discussed below) except that:

● the dividend for a preference share is only payable out of distributable profits – if there are any;

● the dividend is not an allowable deduction against the company's corporation tax liability as is the interest arising from a debenture;

- a preference share is not capable of being secured over an asset, whereas a debenture holder can have the security of a charge with which to protect his loan.

Accordingly preference shares are not often seen as being an attractive alternative to debentures. However, much will depend on the rate of interest being offered on either. The cash flow from preference shares is less reliable than from debentures and there is less likelihood of the capital being returned to the preference shareholder. A secured debenture holder at least has rights over secured assets in the event of the company's default.

Redeemable shares
These are shares that are issued in the expectation that they will be brought back (redeemed) by the company at a later date, at the option of either the company or the shareholder. They can only be issued if the articles permit it (CA 1985 s 159(1)) if the company has other non-redeemable shares in existence (CA 1985 s 159(2)), and the terms of the redemption are spelt out in the articles (CA 1985 s 160(3)). The reason that there must be other non-redeemable shares in existence at the time of issue is because without that provision it might be possible for a company to issue only redeemable shares, buy them back and find itself in the position of having no shareholders at all. Curiously, the wording of s 159(2) does not state that there have to be non-redeemable shares in existence at the time of redemption, so that it still might be possible to redeem the shares and have a shareless company. This is, however, unlikely. Redeemable shares must be fully paid-up before they are redeemed (CA 1985 s 159(3)), as without that the company would be making a present of its capital to the redeeming shareholders. The redemption can be at the option of either the shareholder or the company (CA 1985 s 159(1)). It is possible for the selling shareholder to be paid a premium on the occasion of the redemption. This means that not only does the former shareholder get the nominal value of his shares back, but he also gets a further sum, the amount of which will have been stated in the articles or share issue, sometimes by means of an arithmetical formula to reflect any increase in value in the company at the times of the redemption. The question of how the premium and the redemption monies are paid for is dealt with in Chapter 9. Once the shares are redeemed they are treated as cancelled but the authorised capital is not thereby diminished (CA 1985 s 160(4)). New shares may be issued to replace the cancelled shares. Some reasons that a company might issue redeemable shares are as follows:

- A small family company with no non-family investors might wish to appoint an outside manager and sell him or give him as part of his remuneration package some shares so that he can participate in the profits of the company.

This ought to encourage him to work harder for the company. However, shares in a small private company will not normally be easily transferable. The directors would be unlikely to wish non-family members (other than the manager) to hold shares in the company and accordingly it might be difficult for the manager to find a ready buyer for his shares. If the manager's shares are redeemable, he knows that the company will buy back his shares at a pre-determined price on a predetermined date, so that he has a market for his shares. The price might be higher if he achieves certain targets for the company. The members of the family would be content with such an arrangement because after the redemption has taken place there will be no non-family members to interfere in the company's business. A further benefit to the family members is that they personally do not have to buy the manager's shares as the company is buying the shares.

- Investors cannot always be sure that a company is going to be successful, and particularly in a small company whose shares are not traded publicly, it is difficult for an investor to sell his shares. Redeemable shares provide a better chance that the investor can get his money back since the company, assuming it has distributable profits or can make a new issue of shares, ought to be able to buy his shares from him. He is thus given some reassurance that he will get his capital back within a reasonable period of time. This is not quite as secure as having a secured debenture, but equally with the greater risk comes greater rewards: the dividend may be greater, and if the wording of the redeemable shares is careful enough, the same shares would be convertible into ordinary shares on the occasion of the public sale of the shares.

- An ingenious ruse has been devised to avoid paying stamp duty by using redeemable shares. When a lead investor takes a large investment in a company, he may wish to syndicate (*i.e.* sell on) part or all of his investment to other investors as a way of spreading his risk, just as a bank may syndicate part or all of a loan to other banks as a way of reducing its exposure but still picking up some of the interest on the loan and the fees for setting up the loan. Normally a lead investor would sell his shares to the syndicate members. But selling the shares would attract stamp duty at the rate of 0.5% on the value of the consideration for the transfer. Instead the lead investor subscribes for a large number of redeemable shares. Having found members for his syndicate, he makes the company redeem the shares, perhaps a mere matter of weeks after issue, and the company then pays the lead investor the value of the redeemed shares. At the same time, the company issues an equal number of new shares to the syndicate member, who thereby contributes capital to the company equal in value to the amount that was paid to the lead investor, thus ensuring that the company maintains its capital position, that the lead investor gets his money, and that no stamp duty is paid.

Convertible shares

These are shares that can be converted into debentures or into another type of share. The terms of conversion must be clearly stated in the articles. Conversion into debentures may be useful where the investor is concerned about the risk factor of his investment. A debenture can be secured by means of a charge, thus ensuring that the debenture holder has security over the company's assets in the event of the company's liquidation. This is inherently less risky than having a share. The terms of the articles can provide that in the event of some lapse on the company's part, such as the failure to maintain a predetermined level of profits, the shares will convert into debentures.

Convertible shares could also be preference shares which automatically convert to ordinary shares on the occasion of the public sale of the company's shares. If a company were to obtain an official listing on the Stock Exchange, the preference shareholders could then, if the demand were great enough, immediately sell their shares to the public at a large profit. Venture capital fund investors often hope that their investment of artfully worded convertible shares will achieve this result. With convertible redeemable shares, the investor or the company can specify that the shares can be redeemed or converted into ordinary shares depending on what will be most advantageous. As a convertible share is inherently more flexible than an ordinary share, particularly if it is both redeemable and preferential, investors may be prepared to pay more for those shares than they would for ordinary shares. The issue of such shares could thus benefit a company's capital position, and because such shares are not loans they will not adversely affect the level of borrowing.

Deferred shares

These are rare nowadays. Formerly promoters, who were people who set up companies and thereafter encouraged members of the public to invest in those companies, used to demonstrate their belief in the viability of their companies by having shares that would only take a dividend after the ordinary shareholders had received at least a predetermined minimum dividend. Such shares are sometimes known as "Founders' shares".

Non-voting shares

It is possible to issue ordinary shares that do not carry any voting rights. The Stock Exchange does not approve of such shares. This is because they deny the shareholders any opportunity to call the directors to account. However some investors may be content to have non-voting shares if other matters, such as the dividend or the capital appreciation of the shares, are otherwise to their satisfaction.

Some capitalists, however, prefer not to buy shares in a company, but to lend money to the company in the form of debentures.

Debentures

A debenture is another word for a loan to a company, the terms of which are usually evidenced in writing. The terms will generally include the duration of the loan, the rate of interest payable and the right of the lender to be kept informed of the company's progress. The loan may be secured in which case the lender has rights over certain assets of the company in the event of the company's default, or unsecured, which gives fewer rights but generally speaking a higher rate of interest. The significance of secured loans is dealt with more fully in Chapter 17.

Junk bonds and mezzanine finance

High risk, high interest unsecured debentures are sometimes known as junk bonds because a "bond" is the US word for a debenture, and "junk" describes the value of the bond if the company defaults on its undertaking. Junk bonds were often used to finance a takeover bid by one company for another: the takeover bidder would borrow a large amount of money from junk bond-holders in order to pay for the takeover. Once the takeover was complete, the successful company that had completed the takeover would repay the junk bond-holders by selling the assets of the company that had been taken over. The practice attracted a certain amount of opprobrium because it tended to lead to the break up of businesses, and to put employees out of work.

There is no exact equivalent of junk bonds in the UK but unsecured debentures ranking below secured debentures but above shareholders' capital in terms of repayment on liquidation are sometimes known as mezzanine finance. This is by way of an analogy with a mezzanine floor which is a floor in a building half way between the ground floor (the share capital) and the first floor (the secured loans).

Debenture stock and debenture trust deeds

A series of debentures issued together on identical terms is sometimes known as debenture stock. Debenture stock is often issued in such large amounts that it needs someone to look after the interests of the debenture-holders. In such a case a debenture trust deed is set up, with a trustee:

(i)   to monitor the company's observance of the conditions attaching to the debentures;
(ii) to look after the interests of the debenture-holders and
(iii) if necessary, to deal with the transfer of debenture stock between sellers and buyers.

This is obligatory for listed companies (*Admission of Securities to Listing*, Chapter 2, section 9). The debenture trust deed is the document that lays down the terms under which the trustee must act. The trustee is commonly an insurance company or a registrar's department of a bank. If the company defaults on its obligations, the trustee can take such measures as are open to him under the debenture which regulates the terms on which the debenture-holders lend their money to the company. A common measure is the appointment of a receiver (see Chapter 20).

Convertible debentures

It is possible for a company to issue debentures that have the right to convert into shares. If a lender lends a company money at a fixed rate of interest under the terms of a debenture, he may find that the interest on his loan is not as good as the return shareholders are receiving on their shares. In that case, a right to convert his debenture into a share may be very useful. Convertible debentures, if issued by a company listed on the Stock Exchange, must have the details of the conversion rights, and at whose option they can be converted, clearly stated on the debenture certificate.

Market value of debentures

The market value of marketable debentures is related to the interest (sometimes known as "coupon") the debentures pay and to the date of repaying of the loan in full or with an additional premium. If a debenture pays interest at the rate of 7% and the current market rate of interest is 4%, the debenture will be very desirable. Accordingly its price will rise. The price is also affected by the date when the loan has to be repaid by the company because there may be opportunities for capital gain if one buys a debenture priced low because of its poor rate of interest. If a debenture has a market value of 40p and an interest rate of 1.5% (compared to a current market rate of interest of 7%) but a maturity value a few years later of £1.00, a lender may be able to buy his debenture cheaply at that price and make a substantial capital gain when the debenture matures. However, if there is doubt as to whether or not the company will be able to repay the loan when it says it will, the price of the debenture will fall.

Redemption of debentures

There are various methods of redeeming debentures. The simple method is to repay the debenture-holders all their money on the expiry of the loan. But as repayment of a large sum of money may pose cash-flow difficulties for a company, a company may arrange to repay the loan in instalments if the terms of the debentures permit this. Alternatively, the company may have to set aside a certain amount every year into a special account known as a sinking fund. Money deposited in the sinking fund may only be used to repay or buy back the debentures. Unless the company has sufficient money available to redeem the debentures it may be necessary to pay for the redemption by means of a fresh issue of debentures. It is permissible to use capital in the share premium account to pay for any premium payable on the redemption of debentures (CA 1985 s 130(2)).

Irredeemable debentures
It is possible to have irredeemable debentures (CA 1985 s 193), but it is very unlikely that anyone would wish to buy them (except possibly as part of a tax minimisation scheme), since the company might never see fit to repay the loan. In any event the value of the loan would probably be reduced over the years because of inflation.

Bearer debentures and Eurobonds
It is also possible to have bearer debentures (more commonly known as bearer bonds), which do not contain the name of the debenture-holder. As with all bearer documents, such debentures are open to fraud, theft and forgery, though they have the advantages of informality of transfer and anonymity. A Eurobond is a type of bearer debenture issued by a reputable company which wishes to borrow money using the market set up by the Association of International Bond Dealers. Eurobonds entitle the holder to interest from time to time and to repayment of the nominal value of the loan at a predetermined time. A Eurobond is usually denominated in a non-sterling currency. This permits the company and those who deal in the bonds to juggle with the rate of interest the bond attracts (if any), the capital gain on redemption, and the strength of the currency in which the bond is denominated.

The issue of debentures
The public issue of debentures will be dealt with in Chapter 8. If a private company were to issue debentures privately, it would not be required to follow any special procedure laid down in either the CA 1985 or the Financial Services Act 1986. It is nonetheless prudent to keep a register of debenture-holders. There is, however, a requirement that where there is a registered charge given by the company as security for the issue of a series of debentures, each debenture or certificate of debenture stock must have a copy of the certificate of registration of that charge endorsed on the debenture document (CA 1985 s 402). This provision does not apply in Scotland.

Other rights attaching to debentures
Debentures do not normally carry voting rights, except where the articles provide for it. However, the courts may take account of debenture-holders' views on such occasions as rearrangements under the CA 1985 s 425, or proposals by liquidators to sell a business as a going concern to the possible prejudice of the debenture-holders – as was indeed the case on the occasion in Spring 1995

when Barings Bank was sold to the Dutch banking group ING. The debenture-holders were allowed to have a say in the sale of the business although as a matter of fact their objections were overruled by the judge in the greater interests of the company as a whole.

Options

An option is a right to subscribe for or sell a share or a debenture, (though more commonly a share) at a predetermined date and a predetermined price. A call option gives the purchaser the right to buy the security: a put option gives the right to sell the security. There is a market in such call and put options relative to the securities of listed companies and such options are known as traded options. They are discussed in Chapter 8. Traded options are to be distinguished from a different type of option, which allows a person, generally a director, to be allotted shares at a particular price on a particular date or period of time. The price will generally be less than the current market price of the shares. This means that once the allotment has taken place, the allottee can sell his shares for a considerable profit. The terms of the option, including any consideration for the option itself, are usually expressed in a contract between the company and the allottee.

Such options are used extensively as part of the remuneration packages for directors of listed companies. It is believed that they form an incentive to make the directors make the company more profitable which in turn will cause the company's share price to rise. If the share price does indeed rise, the directors may be able to exercise their options most advantageously. This method of rewarding directors has been strongly criticised by, amongst others, the Greenbury Committee (see Chapter 15) both because of the inordinate gains that some directors appear to have made, and also because a rise in the company's share price is not necessarily a reflection of a director's skill: it could just reflect a general upturn in the country's economy. It can be argued, however, that although share options do enable a director to obtain a great number of shares in his company at a cheap price, it is not always easy for directors to sell those shares without either transgressing the Model Code for securities dealings for directors, as stated in the Rules of the London Stock Exchange, or the rules on insider dealing contained in the Criminal Justice Act 1993. There are only limited opportunities for directors to sell their own shares, and even if the directors do sell their shares, such sales inevitably attract criticism from shareholders who wonder why directors do not apparently wish to retain their companies' shares – could it be that the directors know something about the company that nobody else does?

Share warrants

These are not very common in the UK although they are popular in Europe. A share warrant is an entitlement to the shares specified in the warrant. A company can only issue share warrants if its articles permit it to do so. The articles may also prescribe the procedure for the issue of the share warrants. Table A contains no provisions for share warrants. Share warrants are only available for fully paid-up shares (CA 1985 s 188) and they can be traded by delivery. They are made out to "bearer". This means that whoever is holding the share warrants at the time is entitled to go to the issuing company to ask for the cancellation of the warrants and to be issued with the shares specified in the warrants. On the issue of shares the warrant-holder becomes a member of the company (CA 1985 s 32(2)). The articles of the company may prescribe the procedure and the consideration (if any) for the cancellation of the warrants and the issue of the shares. Share warrants are not commonly used because for many years they were prohibited under exchange control rules. Exchange control rules were Government regulations designed to prevent people taking capital out of the country except under restricted circumstances. Without the exchange control rules it might have been possible to sell the share warrants abroad and thus obtain capital abroad instead of keeping the capital in the UK. Share warrants may be easily forged or stolen and in any event, companies generally like to know who their shareholders are. Curiously, these problems do not appear to vex European investors.

So far we have described the main types of security. We shall now look in detail at the procedure for an allotment of shares to investors. There is one set of rules for all companies and in addition, a further set of rules that apply to companies whose shares are to be traded publicly on a recognised market. This further set or rules will be examined in Chapter 8.

Allotment and issue of shares

The allotment and issue of a company's shares is a complex matter. The procedural steps required to be undertaken by any company allotting its shares can be summarised as follows:

1. increase in authorised capital if necessary;

2. authority to the directors to allot shares (if not already granted);

3. pre-emption rights to be determined;

4. payment for the shares;

5. allotment of the shares;

6. issue of the shares;

7. registration.

Increase in authorised capital

When a small private company is incorporated, it normally has an authorised capital of some figure such as £1,000. This means that the maximum nominal value of the shares it can issue must amount to that figure but no more. So if the company had an authorised capital of £1,000, and had already issued 500 shares of £1.00 each, the company would not be able to issue a further 750 shares as that would bring the total issued share capital to £1,250 which is in excess of the authorised limit.

Accordingly whenever a company issues shares, it must make sure that the existing authorised share capital is large enough to accommodate the proposed issue of shares. If it is not, the members will need to pass an ordinary resolution (in terms of CA 1985 s 121) to increase the authorised share capital. A copy of the resolution will need to be sent to the Registrar of Companies (CA 1985 s 123(1)) along with the relevant Form 123, and the company will need to update its memorandum. It will do this by making an addendum to the capital clause in the memorandum stating that as from the requisite date the company's share capital has been increased. The addendum should also state the extent of the increase, and the number, denomination and nominal value of the new shares.

If the proposed issue of shares will not cause the total issued share capital to exceed the authorised share capital, there will be no need to increase the authorised share capital. The same principle of sufficient authorised share capital applies to plcs. If in the process of increasing the authorised share capital the company is also creating a new class of shares, the articles will need to be amended to show the terms attaching to the new class of shares. This will require a special resolution which will need to be sent to the Registrar of Companies along with a copy of the amended articles (CA 1985 s 18).

The members would pass these two resolutions at a general meeting. Alternatively, in the case of a private company only, the resolutions could be passed by a written resolution in terms of the CA 1985 s 381A.

Authority to the directors to allot shares

Before the directors allot shares, they must be granted authority to do this (CA 1985 s 80). The authority may be stated in the articles, or may be granted by an ordinary resolution (CA 1985 s 80(1)). Normally the maximum period for which directors can be granted such authority is five years, though it may be less. The number of the shares which they will have authority to allot will be limited to such figure as is stated in the articles or in the wording of the resolution (CA 1985 s 80(4)) and cannot, when added to the existing number of shares in issue, be greater than the authorised capital. The articles or the resolution may also impose conditions which will need to be satisfied before the directors may proceed to allot shares (CA 1985 s 80(3)). In the case of authority under the articles, the period of five years (or such lesser figure as is stated in the articles) runs from the date of incorporation (CA 1985 s 80(4)(a)). In the case of authority deriving from an ordinary resolution, the period of five years (or such lesser period as may be specified) runs from the date of the resolution (CA 1985 s 80(4)(b)). Once the initial period of five years (or such lesser period as may be specified in the articles or the resolution) has expired, the directors will need to obtain fresh authority to allot shares. Likewise, if the directors issue all the shares specified in the articles or the resolution before the expiry of the relevant period, the directors will need to obtain fresh authority to allot more shares (CA 1985 s 80(5)). The type of shares to which these rules apply are all shares with the exception of shares which are:

- subscriber shares (being the shares allotted to the subscribers to the memorandum); or

- shares allotted in connection with an employee share scheme (CA 1985 s 80(2)).

In addition these rules apply to rights to subscribe for shares, or rights to convert any security into a share other than the two exceptions above (CA 1985 s 80(2)). The reason, particularly as regards larger companies, for the existence of the five-year rule and the cap on the number of shares they may issue is that it is sometimes advisable to restrict the directors' authority to allot shares. Unscrupulous directors might see fit to allot a large number of shares and thus upset any previous balance of voting power. Although pre-emption rights (see later) are designed to ensure that current members always have the opportunity to maintain their current voting power, if directors choose to allot sufficient shares, some members may not be able to afford to exercise their pre-emption rights fully. This would mean that they do not buy their full entitlement. In turn this would mean that the proportion of voting control that those members had previously enjoyed might be diminished – as might well have been the directors' intention.

The terms of any given authority may be altered or revoked but not in excess of the period specified in the articles or the authorising resolution. To revoke or alter the authority requires an ordinary resolution (CA 1985 s 80(8)). The ordinary resolution can, in the case of a private company only, be passed by means of a written resolution.

Waiver of the five-year rule for private companies
Inevitably, a rule that requires directors to check what they were authorised to do up to five years ago is bound to be widely overlooked in practice by busy company directors more concerned with present activities than past history. This is particularly true of a small company, where the directors are the only shareholders, and where the directors, in their capacity as shareholders, are unlikely to mind whether they have been granted the s 80 authority or not. The DTI, having researched the matter, concluded that the rule was widely ignored without any significant consequent difficulties arising. Accordingly Parliament included in the Companies Act 1989 a measure to alleviate the provisions of s 80. A private company (but not a plc) may choose to waive the provisions of s 80 by passing an elective resolution to dispense with the five-year rule (CA 1985 s 80A). A private company may pass a resolution stating that the directors have either indefinite authority to allot shares, or authority to allot shares for any period up to any date the company chooses. The requirement that there is a cap on the number of shares that the directors may allot still stands (CA 1985 s 80A(6)). The authority can be renewed or revoked or varied as the company sees fit. For the details of the passing of elective resolutions, see Chapter 18.

Pre-emption rights

A right of pre-emption is the right given to a member of a company to have the option to buy any newly created shares before any outsider is given the opportunity to buy those shares. When the directors propose to allot more shares, normally under the CA 1985 s 89 they must offer the newly created shares to the existing shareholders first. The existing shareholders normally can acquire the proportion of the newly created shares that corresponds to the proportion of shares they already hold in the company. So if a shareholder owns 25% of the company's shares, he must be offered 25% of any newly created shares.

The terms of the pre-emption offer to existing shareholders must be the same as or more favourable than the terms offered to outsiders (CA 1985 s 89(1)), and the existing shareholders have 21 days in which to accept or decline the offer (CA 1985 s 90(6)). It is not obligatory for all shareholders to accept or decline the offer: it is perfectly acceptable for some shareholders to accept the offer and others to decline it. Equally a shareholder need not accept all the shares offered to him. If a shareholder wishes to decline all the offer, he can either do nothing and let the offer lapse through time, or he can write to the company intimating his refusal. Equally, if he only wishes to accept part of the offer, he must intimate to the company that he will be making a partial acceptance. The shares that are not taken up by the existing shareholders will then normally be offered to outsiders. Some articles, however, provide that there is a second round, whereby those shares that are not taken up in the first offer can be offered to any existing shareholders who may wish to purchase them.

Consequences of failure to communicate the offer to existing shareholders
If the directors fail to make the pre-emptive offers to the existing shareholders, the existing shareholders may demand compensation for any loss, costs or expenses they may have incurred as a result of their being deprived of the opportunity to acquire the newly created shares. However, any aggrieved shareholder must make his claim for compensation within two years of the allotment or his claim will be time-barred (CA 1985 s 92).

Shares to which pre-emption rights do not apply
It should be noted that under the CA 1985 s 94 these pre-emption rules do not automatically apply to the following types of share:

- subscriber shares (as described above);

- bonus shares (*i.e.* retained undistributed profits converted into shares);

- employee share scheme shares;

- shares attracting a fixed dividend and a fixed return of capital (*i.e.* preference shares).

This means that when a company creates some new preference shares, the existing ordinary shareholders are not automatically entitled to the preference shares unless the articles permit this.

The non-cash consideration exemption from pre-emption rights
If the company wishes to allot equity shares to someone without troubling itself about pre-emption rights for existing shareholders, one method of doing this is by persuading the allottee to pay for the shares either wholly or partly by means of a non-cash consideration (*i.e.* payment in some form other than money) (CA 1985 s 89(4)). So if a company wants, for example, to buy a particular building, it could offer the seller shares in the company in order to pay for the building; and pre-emption rights would not apply. But if the seller sold his building to the company for cash, and subsequently used the cash to buy shares in the company, pre-emption rights would apply as regards the other shareholders. The non-cash consideration disapplication of pre-emption rights can seriously alter the balance of voting control within a company, but well drafted articles may prevent this.

The wording of the CA 1985 s 89(4) means that the outsider could pay for his shares mostly in cash, but with the balance being paid in, say, turnips, thus avoiding the pre-emption rights. Surprisingly there is no element of proportionality in the rules to the effect that pre-emption rights only apply to that part of the consideration which is paid for in cash. Pre-emption rights are designed to protect the voting power of existing shareholders, but it is submitted that this aim is not entirely satisfactorily achieved. This issue is discussed further in Chapter 8 in the context of pre-emption rights, listed companies and wider share ownership.

Other occasions when s 89 pre-emption rights either do not apply or are varied

A private company can choose to disapply its pre-emption rights or vary those rights indefinitely, or at least until the disapplication or variation is revoked. The disapplication or variation must be stated in its memorandum or articles (CA 1985 s 91).

Both private and public companies can disapply the pre-emption rights under certain circumstances. Under the CA 1985 s 95(1) any company can, in conjunction with a general grant of directors' authority under the CA 1985 s 80, disapply or vary the pre-emption rights generally but only for the duration of the s 80 authority (up to five years), either through the company's articles or by means of a special resolution. Alternatively, if the directors have been given specific authority under s 80 to allot a specific number of shares and wish the pre-emption rights to be disapplied or varied on a one-off basis in respect of that allotment, a special resolution is needed to permit the disapplication or variation (CA 1985 s 95(2)). Under either s 95(1) or s 95(2) the disapplication or variation of the pre-emption rights need not be total: the disapplication or variation could be subject to such modifications as are appropriate.

If a special resolution under s 95(2) is used, the directors must have recommended the disapplication first, preferably at a board meeting. Next the directors must have distributed a circular to the members of the company prior to the meeting at which the resolution was to be passed. The circular must have been written by the directors and stated the reasons for recommending the disapplication of the pre-emption rights, the amount to be paid to the company in respect of the equity securities to be allotted and the directors' justification of that amount (CA 1985 s 95(5)). Where a private company wishes to pass a special resolution under s 95(2) by means of a written resolution, under the CA 1985 Schedule 15A para 3 the circular can be supplied to each member at the same time as the member is given the written resolution for him to sign.

The reason pre-emption rights exist is to allow shareholders the chance to maintain their voting power before and after the allotment. A 26% shareholder, who is in the position of being able to block any special resolution, would normally always wish to remain in that position and would therefore be likely to take up his entitlement under his pre-emption rights. Where pre-emption rights are not so effective is where the cost of taking up the pre-emptive entitlement is too great for the shareholder. Directors have been known to make a rights issue, where shareholders are offered the opportunity to buy shares in proportion to their existing shareholdings (*e.g.* for every three shares you own, you get the right to buy a further six) knowing very well that some members cannot afford to buy the shares. This means that those who can afford to take up their entitlement increase their voting power at the expense of those who cannot. Under such circumstances one remedy for the impoverished shareholders might be a petition to the court under the minority protection provisions under the CA 1985 s 459. This is discussed further in Chapter 13. Alternatively the impoverished shareholders could raise an action against the directors for breach of their fiduciary duty to the company, as discussed further in Chapter 15.

Listed companies must comply with a Stock Exchange rule stating that the maximum period of disapplication of pre-emption rights is limited to 15 months (*Admission of Securities to Listing*, Chapter 2, section 1, para 18). This means in practice that if the directors wish to disapply the pre-emption rights they must request permission from the shareholders annually, usually at the AGM. This enables the investors to check whether or not the directors have been using the powers to allot shares on a non-pre-emptive basis wisely. It is thought that an unlimited disapplication may give the directors too much latitude. Certain investors, particularly those within the Association of British Insurers and National Association of Pension Funds, take this approach further and have stated that as a policy they would oppose disapplication of pre-emption rights generally in companies in which they were investing unless the disapplication was limited to an amount equal to or less than 5% of the current issued share capital. In addition over any period of three successive years the total amount must not exceed 7.5%.

Some private companies have articles that substantially vary the pre-emption rights, and in some companies pre-emption rights apply to transfers of shares as well as to allotments.

Payment for the shares

This is normally done in cash, but as described above can be done by the transfer to the company of a non-cash asset, such as physical assets, a business, shares, goodwill or by an agreement not to demand payment of a debt. If the payment is made wholly or partly by a non-cash asset, pre-emption rights in respect of equity securities do not apply (CA 1985 s 89(4)). Subscribers to the memorandum must pay for the subscription shares in cash (CA 1985 s 106).

It is always possible that the value of assets transferred to a company may not be as high as the seller maintains they are. The early history of company law is full of cases of promoters selling personal assets to companies at inflated prices in exchange for shares. Nowadays, particularly in respect of plcs, there are strict rules to prevent such abuses.

1. Under the CA 1985 s 90(2) a plc may not accept as consideration for shares an undertaking by the would-be shareholder to carry out work or perform services either for the plc or for someone else. If a plc does accept such an undertaking contrary to the CA 1985 s 90(2), the would-be shareholder will have to pay for the shares plus interest on the outstanding price.

2. Under the CA 1985 s 102 a plc may not allot shares if the consideration for the allotment is an undertaking that will be or may be performed more than five years after the allotment. So if a would-be shareholder states in a contract that he will transfer an asset to the company at some date in the future, but receives shares in the plc prior to the date of the transfer of the asset, he will be safe (assuming the asset is independently valued in terms of the CA 1985 s 103, as discussed later) provided he transfers the asset within five years from the date of the allotment of the shares. He will not be required to pay the proper cash price of his shares plus any interest (CA 1985 s 102(2)). If the contract for the undertaking requires performance within a period of less than 5 years, and the undertaking is not performed within that period, the would-be shareholder again has to pay the proper price for the shares plus any interest (CA 1985 s 102(5), (6)).

3. Under the CA 1985 s 103 if a non-cash consideration is given for the allotment of shares in a plc, the asset must be independently valued to make sure that the value of the asset is at least worth the nominal value of the shares the proposed allottee will be getting (CA 1985 s 109). The valuation is in the hands of the company's auditor or someone who could be appointed as the company's auditor ("the valuer") (CA 1985 s 108(1)).

   However, as not all auditors are in the position to value all types of assets, the valuer can appoint a specialist valuer, such as a surveyor or other reputable independent person who can value the asset instead (CA 1985 s 108(2)). The valuer, or where appropriate the specialist valuer, is entitled to full disclosure of all information about the asset (CA 1985 s 110). The valuer or specialist valuer prepares a report in terms of the CA 1985 s 108. Section 108 closely lays down what information must be included in the report. The report must state whether or not the consideration is sufficient given the value of the shares to be allotted to the proposed allottee as consideration for the asset (CA 1985 s 109(2)). The proposed allottee is entitled to see a copy of the report (CA 1985 s 103(1)(b)) and the report must have been prepared within the period of six months preceding the allotment (CA 1985 s 103(1)(b)).

The valuation rules do not apply where:

- a plc buys all or some of the shares of another company, or of a class of shares of another company, as long as it:

  (i)   offers its own shares as consideration for the other company's shares or class of shares in that company, and
  (ii) makes its offer to all the shareholders of that other company or all the shareholders of that class of the other company's shares, whether or not the offer is taken up (CA 1985 s 103(3));

- a plc is proposing to merge with another company, whereby one company offers shares in itself to the members of the other company as consideration for acquiring the entire assets and liabilities of the other company (CA 1985 s 103(5)).

No valuation is required in the above takeover and merger because the price the acquiring company will pay for the shares or the assets and liabilities ought to be the market price anyway.

If a company has allotted shares in the absence of any valuation, or if there is some other contravention of s 103 or s 108 which the allottee should have known about, the allottee will have to pay the proper price for the shares together with any premium thereon plus any interest (CA 1985 ss 103(6) and 105).

By putting the responsibility in each case on the allottee to ensure that services are not offered contrary to the CA 1985 s 99, and that ss 102, 103 and 109 are complied with, the allottee is likely to take steps to ensure that the plc receives adequate consideration for his allotment of its shares. If he does not comply with these rules, he suffers by having to make proper payment, and the company may benefit from any interest he is required to pay to it.

In the first two years of a plc's existence, either from the date of issue of a s 117 trading certificate (CA 1985 s 104(2)) or the date of reregistration as a plc (CA 1985 s 104(3)), a plc may not enter into a contract for the transfer to the plc of a non-cash asset in consideration of the allotment of shares in the plc if:

(i)   the proposed allottee is either a subscriber to the company's memorandum, and
(ii) the consideration will be equal in value to one-tenth of the company's nominal share capital at the time of the contract,

unless certain conditions are met (CA 1985 s 104(1)). These conditions are as follows:

- the non-cash asset must have been independently valued as above;

- the terms of the contract must have been approved by an ordinary resolution of the company, having been circulated to the members of the company beforehand (CA 1985 s 104(6)).

Contravention of this section means that the company can recover any consideration from the contravenor, or if shares have been issued, can claim the proper price of the shares from the contravenor plus any interest. The purpose of this clause is to prevent promoters or those setting up a plc making the company pay them (by way of shares) inflated prices for assets which they are personally transferring to the plc.

The interest payable in all the above situations is currently 5% (CA 1985 s 107) but the Secretary of State may change it from time to time by statutory instrument.

As far as private companies are concerned none of the above rules apply. There are no statutory rules on this matter, although there are some common law cases that are relevant.

Re Wragg Ltd [1897] 1 Ch 795, CA. Two businessmen sold their business to a company which they founded. The price the company paid for the business was £46,300 and had been ascertained by an expert valuer. When the company went into liquidation shortly thereafter, the liquidator contended that the value of some of the business's assets had been overstated and that there had been inadequate consideration for the businessmen's shares. The Court of Appeal held that provided there was no evidence of fraud there was no reason to set aside the allotment of the shares to the businessmen. Companies must make such bargains as they see fit.

This decision is partly explained by the well-known reluctance of courts to sit in judgment on commercial decisions and partly by the fact that in many matters it would be extremely difficult to assess what would be a proper value for an asset. Even the rules applying to plcs do not expect the valuer to state what the true value of an asset is: the valuer merely has to state that the asset is at least adequate consideration for the shares to be allotted (CA 1985 s 109(2)(d)). Returning to the position on private companies, the courts did set aside a secondary allotment of shares in the following case.

Hong Kong & China Gas Co Ltd v *Glen* [1914] 1 Ch 527. Mr Glen had sold the company the concession to supply gas to a part of Hong Kong. In exchange he received 400 £10 shares paid up in full, and an undertaking from the company that whenever the company increased its share capital it would allot him further fully paid-up shares without the requirement that he do anything or provide anything further for the company. This was held to be effectively issuing fully paid shares at a discount to their true value and therefore void. The objection the courts had was not to the original allotment but to the continuing nature of the allotment of fully paid shares without any present consideration at all.

Partly paid shares and payment of shares by instalments

Shares may be partly paid, in which case the shareholders may have to pay the outstanding amount if called upon to do so by the directors following a "call". The liquidator can also call upon the members to pay up the outstanding balance on their shares at the time of liquidation. It is possible for the members to pass a special resolution requiring them to pay an outstanding amount only on liquidation. In this case the outstanding amount is known as a reserve liability.

Failure to pay the call may, depending on the articles, result in the company having a lien over the shares or alternatively it can make the member forfeit his shares. Both these terms are explained later in this chapter. Commonly, partly paid shares only receive a proportion of the dividend corresponding to the extent to which their shares are paid up (Table A art 104) though in the recent major UK privatisation issues, one of the attractions of the shares on offer is that commonly a full dividend has been payable on a share on which instalments may still be due. Indeed, some shareholders used their dividends to help fund the payment of their next instalment. However, in plcs, the share must be paid up to the extent of at least one-quarter plus any premium thereon (CA 1985 s 101(1)). This rule does not apply to employee share scheme shares (CA 1985 s 101(2)).

Prohibition against allotting shares at a discount

As has been stated in Chapter 6, it is not possible to allot shares at a discount (CA 1985 s 100(1)). If shares are allotted at a discount to their nominal value the allottee has to pay the company the amount of the discount plus interest at 5%. This serves as an effective disincentive to buy discounted shares. It is, however, permissible to deduct from the total monies from allottees underwriting commission and brokerage (CA 1985 s 97). Underwriting commission is payable to someone (commonly an underwriting firm, merchant bank or firm of stockbrokers) who commits himself to buying such of those shares as are not bought by subscribers when the offer is made. The commission must not exceed 10% of the price at which the shares are issued, and there must be full disclosure of the extent of the commission (CA 1985 s 97(2)). Often the underwriters hope to sell on the shares later. However, by taking up the unpurchased shares in a company whose shares are offered to the public, they ensure that the minimum subscription is received as is required under the CA 1985 s 83.

Brokerage is a fee for finding persons willing to buy shares in a company. It is commonly paid to stockbrokers who canvass their clients to see if any of them would like to invest in a company seeking to raise more capital. If the brokers' clients subscribe for enough shares from the company, the brokers will receive their fee.

Allotment of shares

Assuming the consideration for the shares is acceptable, the shares will need to be allotted. Commonly this is authorised at a board meeting. The allottees' cheques or cash will be banked. The allottees will then be informed that they have been allotted their shares. If there is non-cash consideration, a copy of the contract for the transfer of the non-cash consideration to the company in exchange for shares will need to be exhibited to the Stamp Office (as detailed in Chapter 6) to ensure that proper payment of the stamp duty on any stampable assets is made. If there is no such contract in writing, sufficient details must be given to the Stamp Office to enable the Inland Revenue to make an assessment of the stamp duty payable. The company secretary informs the Registrar of Companies on a Form 88(2) and, if necessary, Form 88(3) (used where there is no written contract for the purchase of the shares) who the new allottees are. The forms provide details of the shares that have been allotted, the consideration for the shares, and the names of the new allottees. The Form 88(2) is not particularly useful, however, because in the time between the allotment and the sending of the form to the Registrar some allottees might already have transferred their shares to other people.

Within two months of allotment of the shares the company must issue share certificates for the shares that have been allotted (CA 1985 s 185). Share certificates are discussed in greater detail later in this chapter.

It sometimes happens that an allottee is induced to enter into a contract with a company to subscribe for shares on the basis of information in a prospectus. A prospectus is a document outlining all the important facts about the company and inviting investors to invest in the company. Plcs whose shares are traded publicly are nowadays obliged to use a prospectus to seek subscribers. If there are material inaccuracies in those prospectuses, compensation is available to allottees under statutory rules (discussed in Chapter 8).

As regards private companies or plcs whose shares are not being issued to the public, where no prospectus has been used, and where an investor has unwisely been persuaded to buy shares in such companies, the aggrieved investor has to rely on the ordinary rules of contract and tort (in Scotland, delict) to seek a remedy. If there has been misrepresentation by the company or its agents, the allottee is entitled to ask the courts to rescind or overturn the contract. Where possible the company returns whatever it may have received from the allottee, and the allottee returns his shares which must subsequently be cancelled. However, the inaccurate information or misstatement which constitutes the misrepresentation must be materially inaccurate, so that a trivial error would not normally be grounds for rescinding a contract. Under common law the courts will not rescind a contract where it is impossible to make the parties revert to their original positions before they entered into the contract, as might happen when the company goes into liquidation. In such an event the allottee only has a claim against the liquidator of the company for the value of his subscription monies. Where rescission is impossible, an allottee may instead be able to claim damages under (in England and Wales) the Misrepresentation Act 1967 s 2, (in Northern Ireland) the Misrepresentation Act (Northern Ireland) 1967 s 2, or (in Scotland) the Law Reform (Miscellaneous Provisions) (Scotland) Act 1985 s 10(1) if there is negligent misrepresentation by the company or its agents. This is to compensate the allottee for his loss where he has been induced by the misrepresentation to subscribe for shares. Where there has been fraudulent misrepresentation which induced a subscriber to subscribe for shares, the contract may be rescinded and those responsible may in addition be liable in damages.

Issue of shares

You only become a member of a company when your name is entered into the Register of Members kept by the company. This is usually kept at the company's registered office, but occasionally it may be kept at a professional registry.

Registration requirements

Register of members

The word "member" means a subscriber to the memorandum and every other person who agrees to become a member and whose name is entered in the register of members (CA 1985 s 22). The first entries in the register of members will be the names of the subscribers to the memorandum. Thereafter the register will contain a list of all those who have been issued their shares, those to whom shares have been transferred, and past shareholders (CA 1985 s 355). In companies without shares, there is still a list of past and present members but there are no details of shares to be recorded. The register states the name, address, date of registration, date of cessation of being a member, and where the company has a share capital, the extent of the shareholding and the amount paid up on each share (CA 1985 s 352). Although there are five ways of becoming a shareholder:

(i) by agreeing to take shares in terms of the memorandum;
(ii) by being allotted shares in exchange for contributed capital;
(iii) by having shares transferred either on sale or gift or as trustee;
(iv) by virtue of being given employee shares;
(v) by operation of law (as when a bankrupt's shares are vested in his trustee or a deceased person's shares on his personal representatives or executors)

the register is not obliged to note the provenance of the shares – though many companies do, in practice, record such information in case the information might be queried at a later date. The register is normally kept at the registered office but may be kept elsewhere in the same country provided you intimate to the Registrar of Companies where the register is being kept (CA 1985 s 353). If the company has more than 50 members there must be an index to the register so that members' interests in the register can be easily noted (CA 1985 s 354). If the company has only one member, the register must contain a note of the date when the company became a single member company and a statement that the company has become a single member company. Equally, if the membership increases, there must be a statement confirming that the company has ceased to be a single member company and a note indicating the date when the change occurred (CA 1985 s 352A).

Inspection rights to the register are discussed in Chapter 3.

Inaccuracies in the register of members

If the register is inaccurate in any respect, it is possible to apply to the courts to rectify the inaccuracy under the CA 1985 s 359. The court has wide powers to assert the right of an applicant to have his name entered in the register or have names deleted from the register: *Re Data Express Ltd, The Times*, 27 April 1987. The register of members of the above company was unfortunately thrown into a skip as part of an office clear-out, and was never seen again. The register was deemed to be blank and therefore incorrect, and the company was allowed to rectify it by creating a new register.

Re Thundercrest Ltd [1994] BCC 855. The company proposed to allot 10,000 shares to each of its three members. One of the members, Murray, claimed that he never received the recorded delivery letter offering him his 10,000 shares. The offer letter contained a clause saying that unless the offer was taken up within a very short period the offer was to lapse. As the offer was not taken up within the period the two remaining members in their capacity as directors allotted themselves the 10,000 shares that Murray would otherwise have acquired. Murray sought an order from the courts declaring the allotment to the two other shareholders void and rectifying the register under the CA 1985 s 359, on the grounds that he had never received the offer to begin with and secondly that the time period within which he was to accept the offer was less than 21 days, contrary to the requirements of the CA 1985 s 90(6). The order in his favour was duly granted and the register of members duly rectified to delete the allotment of the 10,000 shares to the other members.

In the absence of rectification, you can assume that the register is correct. The CA 1985 s 361 states: "the register of members is prima facie evidence of any matters which are by the Act affected or authorised to be inserted in it."

Interests of third parties in the register of members

The position in England, Wales and Northern Ireland

Companies registered in England and Wales may not enter in their registers of members notices of any type of third party interest (CA 1985 s 360). In England and Wales (but not in Scotland) it is possible to have an equitable interest in a share. An example of an equitable interest is when a borrower deposits his shares with a bank as security for a loan, but does not actually transfer his shares to the bank for the duration of the loan. This is known as an equitable mortgage. The bank might wish to have its interest noted on the register of members to prevent the borrower attempting to sell the shares in the bank's possession. However, if every time an equitable interest was created in a company's shares that company had to note the interest in the register of members, it might involve the company in a great deal of burdensome and probably unremunerative work. By virtue of the CA 1985 s 360 the company does not need to enter the equitable interest or any other form of third party interest.

Although in the above situation it would not be possible for the bank to have its interest noted in the register of members, it is possible in practice for a bank or other interested third party in England and Wales to obtain some protection. This protection is available to anyone who has an interest in the shares. On application to the High Court, the bank could obtain a stop notice under the Charging Orders Act 1979 s 5(2)(b) and the Rules of the Supreme Court 1965, Ord 50, r 12. A stop notice forbids the company whose shares are in question from registering a transfer of the shares or from paying any dividend without first sending a notice to the bank about the proposed transfer or proposed payment of dividend. The bank has 14 days in which to respond, during which time no doubt the shareholder will be urgently contacting the bank to persuade it to drop the stop notice so that the shares can be transferred or the dividend paid. If the bank does nothing within 14 days the transfer or payment of dividend can take place anyway.

In Northern Ireland the equivalent of CA 1985 s 360 is Companies (Northern Ireland) Order 1986 art 368. However the Charging Orders Act 1979 does not apply in Northern Ireland and there is no equivalent of the Rules of the Supreme Court Ord 50, r 12 stop order. Equitable deposits of share certificates are possible but, apart from seeking an injunction, there would appear to be no satisfactory method for the bank to seek protection.

One purpose of the stop order is to prevent unscrupulous shareholders who have mortgaged their shares from selling their shares without first repaying the loan for which the mortgage was granted. A second purpose arises where a beneficiary under a trust is unsure about the probity of his trustee whose name is registered as the shareholder. This would mean that the trustee could not transfer the share without the approval of the beneficiary. A third purpose might arise in a matrimonial dispute, where a spouse considers that the other spouse might be trying to dispose of his assets by selling all his shares. A variant of a stop notice is a stop order (Charging Orders Act 1979 s 5(2)(a); Rules of the Supreme Court 1955, Ord 50, r 15). This is like a stop notice but without the 14-day period during which the company must await the command of the person who obtained the notice. A stop order forbids transfer or payment of dividend until such time as the order is lifted.

If a member of a company has failed to pay a debt and following an action in the High Court or the County Court a charging order has been made against the debtor–member under the Rules of the Supreme Court 1965, Ord 50, r 5 or the County Court Rules 1981, Ord 31, r 2(3), the company may neither register a transfer of the debtor–member's shares nor pay him a dividend without the approval of the court. In Northern Ireland the same principles apply, but the relevant legislation may be found in the Judgments Enforcement (Northern Ireland) Order 1981 (SI 1981/226 (N16)) art 66 under which the Enforcement of Judgment Office can make a restraining order prohibiting the company from paying dividends or otherwise dealing with the shares without the leave of the Office.

The position in Scotland
None of the above rules apply to Scotland. There are no changing orders or stop notices in Scotland, but the interests of third parties can be noted in Scottish registered companies using Scots law. Trusts can be registered as members of companies in Scotland. In place of charging orders or stop notices, the above circumstance, the court could be asked to grant an interdict (the Scottish equivalent of an injunction) to prevent the transfer of shares. Dividends could be seized by arrestment on the part of the creditor or person having an interest in the shares in question.

Other registers where membership will be noted

These are discussed in Chapter 3, but may briefly be summarised as:

- register of debenture-holders; this is not obligatory but useful (CA 1985 s 190);

- register of substantial interests in shares in a plc under the CA 1985 s 211;

- register of directors' interests in securities under the CA 1985 s 325.

The latter two registers are particularly useful because in a plc you may wish to know who is building up a sizeable stake in the company. From the size of the stake it may be possible to see if a takeover bid is to be mounted. If a share-holder acquires more than 3% of the nominal value of a plc's issued share cap-ital he is said to have a "notifiable interest" (CA 1985 s 199). The notifiable interest must be notified to the company within two days after the interest arises (CA 1985 s 202(1)). Alterations to the extent of the shareholding must also be intimated to the company and registered. If a shareholder is disguising his interest by means of nominees or acting as part of a "concert party" (when a group of investors purchases shares simultaneously, acting together but each just below the notifiable percentage of 3%) there are methods of ascertaining the true ownership of the shares by means of an order under the CA 1985 s 212. A s 212 order requires the shareholder to disclose who the beneficial (*i.e.* under-lying) owner of any shares is; and if the shareholder refuses to comply, the com-pany is entitled to refuse to transfer shares, to permit the shareholder to vote, to pay dividends or to repay the shareholder's capital in a liquidation (CA 1985 s 454(1)). Since a share is effectively useless without any of these entitlements, the nominee shareholders generally eventually provide the required informa-tion. Under certain circumstances the Secretary of State can also prevent the transfer of shares or payments of dividends, but only as regards plcs (CA 1985 s 216) and only in connection with the following matters:

- failure by a member to disclose a notifiable interest in terms of Part VI of the CA 1985. This part is designed to prevent a member and those connected with him and his or their nominees from building up a substantial stake in a plc without disclosing that interest;

- refusal by members of a company to co-operate with inspectors appointed by the Secretary of State to investigate such matters as the true ownership of shares (CA 1985 s 445) and insider dealing (Financial Services Act 1986 s 177).

The register of directors' interests is useful because from it you can see if the company's directors are buying or selling their securities in the company. Directors who are confident of the success of their companies will not wish to sell their shares. If they are buying shares in their companies, it suggests that the shares are undervalued – unless they are trying to prop up a falling share price or the company is short of capital. If they are selling shares in their com-panies, it suggests that they suspect the company's prospects are gloomy, and are selling while the price is still high; or to put it in a more cynical light, they know something the ordinary shareholders do not.

In addition to the 3% rule for an individual shareholder, there is a minimum notifiable threshold of 10% of the shares held by an aggregate shareholder (CA 1985 s 202). An aggregate shareholder is one who controls, not just in his own personal right, shares held in such corporate bodies as unit trusts, investment companies and the like (CA 1985 s 199(2A)).

Share certificates and debenture certificates

Each shareholder should receive a share certificate which indicates the size of his shareholding, his name and address, the name of the company whose shares he owns, and for listed companies, the date of issue. The share certificate is usually signed by a director, the company secretary or some other person authorised under the articles to sign share certificates. If the shares are fully paid and rank equally in all respects with other shares of the same company or class of shares, the distinguishing numbers of the shares do not need to be stated (CA 1985 s 182(2)). At present share certificates are still sometimes issued on paper, but it is expected, as far as listed companies are concerned, that now that the CREST system of share dealing on the Stock Exchange is fully operational, paper certificates will gradually cease to be so important and may ultimately be replaced by computer records. There is a certain amount of consumer resistance to this, as ordinary shareholders feel their paper certificates give a proper sense of ownership. There is also the concern that any form of electronic recording system for share ownership is open to problems such as computer viruses, power failures, illegal hacking and computer fraud. Private companies will probably continue to use paper certificates.

A company must issue a member with his share or debenture certificate within two months of the allotment or transfer of its shares or debentures to him (CA 1985 s 185(1)). If a member wishes to sell his shares or debentures he will have to produce his share or debenture certificate as evidence that he owns the shares or debentures he is trying to sell. Most companies' articles will have provisions to deal with lost or destroyed share or debenture certificates. Generally the company will seek an indemnity from a member if he has lost his certificate. This means that if his certificate turns up in someone else's possession and the company incurs loss through dealing with the shares or debentures shown on the "lost" certificate, it can claim back from him the extent of their loss.

If a company issues a share or debenture certificate the company is making a representation to all the world that the certificate gives the holder a prima facie (*i.e.* on the face of it) title to the securities (CA 1985 s 186). If it turns out that the certificate was wrongly issued, the company is precluded from saying that it was wrongly issued and from claiming that it was therefore invalid. The company is estopped (in England, Wales and Northern Ireland) or in Scotland personally barred (*i.e.* precluded) from asserting that the true state of affairs is different from that which the company had stated on the certificate which the company had issued. Although this may seem harsh for a company that may have been duped into issuing a certificate to someone who obtained it through fraudulent means, the rationale behind the rule is that it is easier to assume that all certificates are valid and make companies bear the occasional loss (which they generally insure against) than to make every transferor of a share prove that he has title to the securities stated in the certificate. If every transferor had to prove his ownership of every security certificate, he would have to carry around a bundle of documents to prove its provenance. The principle of estoppel or personal bar is shown in the following cases.

Re Bahia & San Francisco Railway Co Ltd (1868) LR 3 QB 584. The railway company was estopped from saying that two fraudulent transferors, who had induced the company to make out a share certificate in their name, were not the true owners of the shares. The transferors had forged in their own favour a transfer of shares from an unwitting client of theirs. The company registered the transfer and issued the fraudulent transferors with a share certificate. The transferors then sold the shares to two purchasers who bought the shares in good faith, relying on the share certificate's validity. At this point the original owner discovered that her signature had been forged on the original transfer. As it was a forgery, it was not a valid transfer and she was entitled to be reregistered as a member. The company then refused to register the two purchasers. The purchasers then claimed damages from the company for the value of their shares, or failing damages, they sought to be registered as shareholders. It was held that the company had to pay them damages as the purchasers had relied on the share certificate which the company had issued to the fraudulent transferors. Presumably if the company had been able to find the two transferors it could have in turn claimed damages from them.

Bloomenthal v *Ford* [1897] AC 156. A share certificate erroneously stated that shares were fully paid-up. In fact the shares were not fully paid-up, and the liquidator attempted to recover the outstanding amount from the shareholder. The shareholder successfully contended that the company was estopped by its own assertion on the share certificate that the shares were fully paid-up.

There is a case contrary to the outcome reached in the above decisions: *Ruben* v *Great Fingal Consolidated* [1906] AC 439. The company secretary of a company forged a transfer and then forged the directors' signature on a share certificate which he used as security for a loan. The company avoided liability because it was held that the certificate was not a certificate that the company had issued.

It is unlikely that if these circumstances arose nowadays the decision would be as it was then, especially in the light of the role of company secretaries as seen in the case of *Panorama Developments (Guildford) Ltd* v *Fidelis Furnishings Fabrics Ltd* [1971] 2 QB 711 (discussed in Chapter 16). The company nowadays would almost certainly be bound by the actions of its secretary, not least because of the statutory provisions of the CA 1985 s 35A.

There are no significant modern cases on share certificates, mainly because nowadays nearly all share transfers are accompanied by a stock transfer form. The additional scrutiny of having the stock transfer form stamped by the Inland Revenue generally ensures that most of the circumstances of the cases described above are unlikely to arise. Transfer of shares is discussed in greater detail later in this chapter. The question of the ownership of the actual certificates arose in the case of *Re Baku Consolidated Oilfields Ltd*, [1993] BCC 653. The above company's assets were seized without compensation by the Bolsheviks in Russia in 1920. In 1994 the Russian Government agreed to pay compensation to those who had lost their investment. As many of the original shareholders had long since given up any hope of getting their money back, some had sold the share certificates to scripophilists (*i.e.* collectors of interesting old papers). The certificates themselves were highly decorated and ornate; but were the people who owned the certificates the people who could claim a share of the compensation? Chadwick J held that only those who were the original shareholders at the time of the seizure (1920), their trustees and executors, and those to whom the shares had been properly transferred, were able to claim: the scripophilists were not true members, being merely collectors of documents, and were not entitled to compensation since it was the share certificate documents and not the actual shares that had been transferred.

Mortgages of shares

It is possible to raise a loan against the value of one's shares. While this is not generally feasible in the case of a private company or a plc whose shares are not publicly traded, it is certainly possible for companies whose shares are publicly traded. A private company is not normally able to find a market for its shares, and so a lender may be reluctant to use them as security. There are various methods of mortgaging shares. In England, Wales and Northern Ireland (but not Scotland) it is possible to have an equitable mortgage over the shares, as discussed earlier in this chapter. An equitable mortgage might happen when a member deposits his share certificates with the bank as security for a loan. He cannot easily sell his shares without the certificates, unless he can fraudulently persuade the company to issue him with replacement ones, or he has a very gullible purchaser. The bank is unlikely to release the certificates until he has repaid the loan or provided adequate alternative security. If the bank is concerned about the risk of the member somehow selling his shares, it can obtain a stop notice (as described above) or injunction in Northern Ireland. If he defaults on the loan, the bank can apply to court for permission to sell the shares. Alternatively, the bank may make the member execute a blank stock transfer form which will be used if he defaults. Once the form has been stamped, the bank can then transfer the shares to itself and sell them to repay the loan. The advantage of the equitable mortgage is that it is cheap, convenient, simple and informal.

An equitable mortgage of this nature is alien to Scots law, although as a matter of practice friendly banks may sometimes ask for a deposit of a member's shares as security for a loan. However, all they can do is inconvenience the member by holding on to the share certificates until he repays the loan. This would prevent him selling the shares unless he was unscrupulous enough to obtain replacement share certificates. The bank would have no right to insist on the transfer of the shares to themselves unless the member had contracted to do so on the fulfilment of a certain event.

A further type of mortgage of shares in England, Wales and Northern Ireland is the legal mortgage. This is where the mortgagor (a borrower) borrows the money from the mortgagee (usually a bank) and transfers his shares to the mortgagee by means of a stock transfer form. The mortgagee is registered by the company as the holder of the shares. The borrower contracts to pay the interest on the loan and to repay the capital on the expiry of the loan. In return the mortgagee contracts to transfer the shares back to the borrower on the repayment of the loan and the interest. On the expiry of the loan and fulfilment of all the borrower's obligations the borrower is reregistered as the holder of the shares. The borrower and mortgagee agree between themselves what should happen with regard to such matters as voting rights and payment of dividends. If the borrower defaults the mortgagee is already in a position to sell the shares to cover its loss.

The same method is available in Scotland. It is the only successful way at present in Scotland for natural persons (*i.e.* not companies) to grant security over shares. A company can grant security over any shares it owns by means of a floating charge, as shares form part of the moveable assets of a company which can be secured by a floating charge. If a company wished to grant a fixed charge over shares, it would have to follow the procedure for the legal mortgage. Such a charge is not at present registrable under the CA 1985 ss 395 or 410. The charge would have to be registered in the company's own register of charges (CA 1985 ss 407 and 411), although it is arguable whether or not a transfer with an undertaking to redeliver on expiry of the loan is in fact a charge in the normal sense of the word. Since the scandal surrounding the death of the British publisher Robert Maxwell and the defrauding of his employees' pension scheme, companies' lenders are becoming more cautious about lending against the value of shares. In the case of the Maxwell employees' pension scheme companies, not only is it alleged that Maxwell engineered the mortgaging of shares which were not his to mortgage, as they belonged to the pension schemes, but it is alleged that he managed to mortgage some of the same shares to two different banks at the same time, giving each bank the impression that it had an unfettered right to the shares.

Lien and forfeiture

A lien is a charge over the shares of a member who has not paid the full amount due on his shares despite being called upon to do so. Under Table A arts 8–11 if payment is not made within 14 days of notice being given to the shareholder that it must be paid, the company can sell the shares. It does this by authorising a company official to execute a stock transfer form on behalf of the shareholder and sell the shares. Private companies can extend the lien to cover not just sums outstanding on shares but also any sums, however incurred, due to the company from the shareholder. Plcs are not permitted to extend the lien in this way except where it takes place in the ordinary course of business of a money-lending or hire-purchase company (CA 1985 s 150). So a bank could lend a customer some money under a normal commercial loan. The customer could use part of the loan to buy shares in the bank. If the customer failed to repay the money due to the bank, the bank could have a lien over its own shares in respect of the debt due to the bank; but this would still be acceptable.

As a matter or practice, liens do not arise very much nowadays because shares tend to be fully paid. As many companies' articles state that a company will only pay a full dividend in respect of a fully paid share, and as shareholders do not want the unwelcome shock of unexpectedly having to pay up the outstanding amount on their shares, shares generally tend to be fully paid and liens of little significance.

Forfeiture is a more drastic remedy than a lien. If a company calls upon a shareholder to pay the outstanding amount on his partly paid shares, the shareholder normally has 14 days in which to pay the call. If it remains unpaid, the directors may warn the shareholder that if it is not paid his shares will be forfeited. This means that he will lose his entitlement to the shares and to any dividends due. If forfeiture then takes place, the shareholder ceases to be a member, he loses what monies he has already paid, and he is required to surrender his share certificate. Under Table A art 21 he will still be liable for the outstanding amount on his shares. Other articles may be more generous. A plc must reissue the forfeited or cancelled shares within three years (CA 1985 s 146): a private company is not required to do this.

Surrender of shares occurs when a member voluntarily hands back his shares to the company because he cannot pay the outstanding amount on the shares. The rules for plcs in respect of surrendered shares are the same as for forfeited shares (CA 1985 s 146).

Transfer and transmission of shares

One of the virtues of shares is that generally they are transferable, subject to the provisions of the articles. Normally in the event of a sale of shares in a private company, the seller approaches the purchaser, the terms of the sale are agreed, the seller signs a stock transfer form (discussed later), the purchase has it stamped and takes the signed and stamped form with the seller's share certificate to the company. The company retains the stock transfer form for its records, destroys the seller's share certificate and issues the purchaser with a new certificate.

The same procedure applies with a gift, though there may be no stamp duty payable.

If only part of a seller's shareholding is being sold, the seller will send his certificate to the company, and on the company's being presented with the stamped stock transfer form, the company will issue one certificate to the purchaser for his shares, and one to the seller for the shares he is retaining.

Some companies' articles deliberately restrict the transferability of shares. This is very common in small family companies where the directors may not wish the shares to escape into the hands of those who are not close family members. Whatever the articles say about the restrictions must be closely followed and if the articles are not followed and transfers are not accepted as they should be, the transferee can apply to court for rectification of the register of members under the CA 1985 s 404. Many small companies' articles state that directors have a right to refuse any transfers of which they do not approve, and they are not required to give reasons for their disapproval. Some companies build in pre-emption rights so that retiring members can only sell their shares to existing members, usually at a fair price but on terms specified in the articles.

Listed companies are not generally allowed to have transfer restrictions in their articles (Admissions of Securities to Listing, s 9, Ch 1, para 1.2) except in respect of partly paid shares and shares in certain communications and broadcasting companies.

The transfer of securities of companies listed on the Stock Exchange takes place in a number of different ways. Companies within the FTSE 100 index (being the major companies in the stock market) have their shares bought and sold by the new Stock Exchange Electronic Trading Service ("SETS"), sometimes known as order-driven trading. This is however only applicable for orders of over 1,000 shares, or 500 if the share price is over £5, on standard settlement terms. Unlike the old quote-driven system (to be discussed shortly) with SETS a seller orders a broker to offer the seller's shares to the market. This can be done in four ways. A *limit order* is when the broker announces the price at which the shares will be sold. The seller then waits until the market moves in the direction of the price, and when the market price hits the sale price the sale takes place. A *fill* or *kill order* is when a sale order is executed immediately if it matches a purchase order already in the market. An *execute* or *eliminate order* is similar to a fire or kill order, save that the execution need not be of the entire amount to be sold: there can be a partial sale, and the part of offered shares that are not purchased will be withdrawn from offer (i.e. deleted). An *at best offer* is when the seller specifies the number of shares on offer and will take the best price available. This last type can lead to market manipulation, particularly at the end of the day or on early trading when there are few deals taking place and it would be possible to engineer an artificial price. At the time of writing this is one of the problems with SETS that is still being sorted out. The above four types of order work on the same basis when a purchaser of shares wishes to buy, though with the position of seller and purchaser reversed. As SETS is relatively new, there are still matters that need to be resolved within its operation, but there are safeguards to protect investors, such as halting of deals where there is a "disorderly market", as, say, where there is a suspicion that insider dealing is taking place, or where the share price moves by 10% or more.

The advantage of SETS is that it ought to reduce dealing costs, and bring trading more into line with the methods used in other international stock exchanges. It ought to be cheaper than quote driven trading, because market makers are no longer putting their own capital at risk when they are dealing for their clients. There are long term plans to extend the range of order–driven dealing to shares on the FTSE 250 index.

Not all deals in the FTSE 100 index will go through SETS. Small deals and deals on non-standard terms will be done in the old quote-driven manner, whereby a seller asks his broker to sell his shares to a market maker, or conversely a purchaser asks his broker to obtain shares from a market maker. A market maker is a firm, commonly part of a merchant bank or stockbroking business, which "makes a market" in the securities, in other words, offers to buy and sell on its own account securities that investors either wish to sell or acquire. The market maker makes its profit on the difference between the price it quotes to sell a security and the price it quotes to buy, and it puts its own capital at risk as it does so. Market makers need to be registered to deal in certain securities, and popular securities will have many market makers dealing in those securities, thus encouraging competition and keen pricing. The new name for market makers is "retail service providers" though no doubt they will continue to be called market makers for some time. It is not known how long this form of dealing will continue in the face of the competition from order–driven dealing.

Listed securities outside the FTSE 100 index are dealt with in the quote driven system narrated above.

Shares quoted on AIM have their shares dealt with through a nominated broker who acts as a market maker in the shares.

The former TALISMAN system for the transfer of shares no longer exists. It has been replaced by CREST. CREST is a system for the electronic registration of the ownership and transfer of securities. Formerly investors were issued with paper certificates indicating the number of securities they held. These are still in use, particularly with private investors, but for major investors there was little point in having paper certificates when securities were being bought and sold so frequently. CREST was devised as a method of holding securities in special electronic files. An investor can either:

(i)   continue to use paper certificates, or
(ii) be a sponsored member of CREST, which means that he both remains a registered holder of securities and can transfer securities through his normal broker, which will "sponsor" or otherwise be responsible for his dealing, or
(iii) can transfer his shares to a nominee company operated by a full CREST member, usually a bank, firm of stockbrokers or solicitors, which will hold the securities on his behalf, act on his instructions and be able to obtain rapid settlement for the investor, or
(iv) become a full CREST member – this only being suitable for institutional investors who can be directly computer-linked to the stock exchange and their brokers, thus saving paperwork and money.

CREST is designed to save paperwork and time, and no doubt in the long run will do so. The implementation of CREST has thrown up some problems which are still being resolved, amongst them being:

(i)   if a private investor puts his shares into a nominee account, he will have to rely on the nominee-account-holder to pass on his copies of the annual accounts, directors' reports, notices of general meetings and other information which would in the first instance be sent to the nominee-account-holder;
(ii) likewise a nominee-account-holder would have to pass on (and there would need to be easy mechanisms to allow this) any perquisites arising from share-ownership. For example, some brewery companies allow their shareholders reduced rates at certain hotels. But if the brewery company merely has many nominee shareholders, it may be difficult to pass on the perquisite to the person who has the beneficial interest in the shares;
(iii) it may be difficult for a shareholder to grant a mortgage over his shares if he does not have a paper certificate;
(iv) companies trying to establish who owns their shares by means of a s 212 enquiry may find it difficult to do so because of the prevalence of nominee shareholdings.

These difficulties will probably be resolved in the course of the next few years.
    It is permissible for shares in a quoted company to be traded by a private bargain between two contracting persons, thus avoiding the use of stockbrokers. Stamp duty will still need to be paid and a stock transfer form executed.

As stated above, whenever a transferor wishes to transfer a share, he must sign a stock transfer form indicating the transferee. The transferee normally has to pay stamp duty at a rate of 0.5% on the transfer, though certain transfers, such as transfers to charities, are exempt and certain other categories of transfer, such as the transfer of a beneficial interest in a share, are subject to a duty of 50p. If a stock transfer form is not stamped when it should be, and the company registers it, the company may be fined (Stamp Act 1891 s 17). Furthermore, in the event of a dispute about the transfer between the transferor, transferee and/or the company, the courts will not entertain the dispute if the stock transfer form is not duly stamped.

One advantage of the current system for the Government is that the stamp duty of 0.5% on every chargeable transfer nets the Government a very great deal of money with very little effort. It was formerly expected that when CREST was fully implemented the Government would dispense with stamp duty as part of its attempt to keep the British financial services industry competitive relative to other financial centres. However, for the time being, stamp duty remains in place.

Other regulated markets are being developed in addition to the main Stock Exchange or the Alternative Investment Market. As yet these are fairly small though it is expected that they will increase in number and size over the years.

Transmission of shares occurs where a shareholder is no longer legally able to hold the shares and the shares pass to his personal representative, such as a trustee in bankruptcy or an executor (on the death of the shareholder). Under Table A regs. 29–31 such a personal representative can elect either to become the holder of the shares or to nominate a transferee. In the case of a bankruptcy the shares may be sold to a willing buyer (subject to any restrictions to the contrary in the articles), and in the case of an executry the shares will be passed to the beneficiary under the deceased person's will. In each case the personal representative will be able to sign the stock transfer form in favour of the transferee, who then becomes the shareholder.

Under Table A reg 31 a personal representative is entitled to all the rights attaching to the share as if he were a shareholder, with the exception that he cannot vote at meetings.

Summary

1. The term securities covers shares, debentures, options, warrants and convertibles. Shares normally require payment of the nominal value but entitle the owner to votes, dividends and a right to the return of capital and any surplus on solvent liquidation. A debenture is a loan to a company, rarely entitling the owner to vote but entitling the owner to the return of his loan.

Options are the opportunity under limited conditions to buy other securities. Convertibles are securities that convert into other types of security.

2. Once a shareholder has paid the nominal value of a share he cannot be forced to pay any more in respect of that share unless he contracts to do so. The nominal value of a share may bear no relation to its market value: it is merely an arbitrary amount, decided upon by the directors, for the purpose of assessing how much capital the company needs and how many investors may be needed to produce that capital. The nominal value is significant for the investor because having paid the nominal value for each share, he has limited his liability to the company to the amount of the nominal value multiplied by the number of shares he has acquired. Even if the company goes into insolvent liquidation, he cannot be asked to contribute any further to the company's funds.

3. The authorised capital is the maximum number of shares the company could issue if it wished to do so. The called-up share capital is the total amount of capital the shareholders have paid and have been asked to pay to date. The paid-up share capital is the amount that has been paid to date.

4. Shares may not be issued at a discount to their nominal value (CA 1985 s 100) except for to the extent of deductions for commission and brokerage (CA 1985 s 97).

5. The premium is the monetary value afforded to the desirability of a share on allotment. Premiums must be credited to a share premium account.

6. Allotment is the unconditional right given to an allottee to have his name entered into the register of members. Membership takes place when the allottee's name is entered into the register of members, and on that occasion he is said to have been issued his shares.

7. Preference shares attract a prior and usually fixed dividend before other shareholders receive their dividends. Preference shares are usually cumulative, in that if the dividend is not paid one year, next year the shareholder receives both the current dividend and the arrears.

    Participating shares are normally shares that participate in any available distributable profits instead of being limited, as are preference shares, to a fixed amount. Redeemable shares are shares that will be bought back at a future date and price (specified in the articles) out of the company's distributable profits or, exceptionally, out of capital. They are used:

    (a) to ensure that voting control returns to the existing shareholders once the redeemable shares have been redeemed;

(b) to reassure an investor that he will receive his capital back at the end of a predetermined period because the company serves as a guaranteed market for those shares;

(c) to reassure existing shareholders that they will not personally need to buy the redeemable shares back, the purchase being carried out by the company instead.

Convertible shares are shares that convert into other types of shares or debentures.

8. A debenture is the written acknowledgement of a loan. A lender may make a one-off loan or he may choose to make many individual small loans, some of which he could resell at a later date. The term "debenture" covers both types of loan. If a company wishes to borrow money from many lenders, it can offer the lenders debenture stock, which is effectively units of the total loan given by the lenders collectively to the company. This will be organised collectively for all the individual lenders in terms of a debenture trust deed, managed by a trustee who acts on behalf of all the lenders or debenture-holders.

9. When a company allots shares it must complete the following procedure:

(a) if necessary, increase the company's authorised share capital by ordinary resolution (CA 1985 s 121) and inform the Registrar of Companies; if a new class of shares is being created, a special resolution is required for amending the articles (CA 1985 s 16), which will also need to be sent to the Registrar of Companies;

(b) if authority is not already available under a previous resolution or the articles, by means of an ordinary resolution, give the directors authority under the CA 1985 s 80 to allot shares for up to five years or, in the case of a private company, indefinitely under the CA 1985 s 80A by means of an elective resolution up to a predetermined amount not in excess of the authorised capital;

(c) take account of any existing pre-emption rights under the CA 1985 s 89 unless such rights are disapplied, waived or unnecessary because of the type of share (being subscriber, bonus, employee share scheme or preference), or because there is non-cash consideration;

(d) ensure payment of the consideration for the shares. Private companies need not have the consideration independently valued (*Re Wragg Ltd* [1897] 1 Ch 796); plcs have extensive rules preventing fraudulent or excessive consideration;

(e) convene a board meeting to allot shares to any new shareholders and to existing shareholders taking up any applicable pre-emption rights;

(f) enter shareholders' names in the register of members;

(g) inform the Registrar of Companies of the allotment (CA 1985 s 88) and, if necessary, pay any stamp duty on the transfer of stampable assets to the company.

10. The register of members is deemed to be accurate until proved otherwise (CA 1985 s 361). Third parties may not have their interest noted in the register in England and Wales (CA 1985 s 360) and in Northern Ireland under the Companies (Northern Ireland) Order 1986 art 368 but can in Scotland.

11. A shareholder with more than 3% of a plc, and each time he increases his holding by a further 1%, must inform the company of his ownership of his stake, or the increase in his stake, in the company (CA 1985 s 211). The true ownership of a disguised holding may be discoverable under the CA 1985 s 212.

12. Directors' interests must be declared to the company under the CA 1985 s 325. This is so that you can see if the directors are buying or selling shares in their own companies.

13. Share certificates are prima facie evidence of the information contained on them (*Re Bahia & San Francisco Railway Co Ltd* (1868) LR 3 QB 584).

14. Equitable mortgages of shares occur in England, Wales and Northern Ireland when shares are deposited in someone's hands as security, usually for a loan. The shares are returned when the loan is repaid. The lender can protect its position by a stop notice or, in Northern Ireland, by an injunction. A legal mortgage involves the transfer of the shares to the security holder, with an undertaking by the security-holder to return the shares to the original owner on the fulfilment of the obligation. This method is available also in Scotland although it is not called a legal mortgage. In Scotland it is known as a charge over shares.

15. Lien is a right of retention and sale of a member's partly-paid shares pending paying of sums due on the shares. Forfeiture of shares occurs when a shareholder fails to pay a call on shares. The shares are then cancelled (not sold) and depending on the terms of the articles the shareholder can lose whatever he may have paid to date to the company.

16. Transfer of shares may be restricted by a company's articles. Transmission occurs when shares pass into the custody of another, commonly a trustee for the former owner who may be bankrupt or deceased. Most transfers of securities are taxed at the rate of 0.5% on the consideration paid for the security.

17. Securities on the Stock Market and AIM are sold through the CREST system. There are other regulated markets for certain securities, though these at present are small.

8. OFFERING SECURITIES TO THE PUBLIC

Need for public and regulated markets for sale of securities – Offers to the public – Stock Exchange requirements – Official List Requirements and other securities markets requirements – Alternative Investment Market requirements – Rights of investors under the Financial Services Act 1986 and the Companies Acts 1985 and 1989 – Promoters

The previous chapter explained what securities are in general, how they are issued and transferred. This chapter concentrates exclusively on the issue of securities to the public.

The need for public and regulated markets for sale of securities

Stock exchanges were set up in the 17th and 18th centuries in most European trading cities to serve as market-places for people to buy and sell securities. Merchants who wished to sell their securities in a company would meet in a designated hall, coffee-house or inn to find people who were willing to buy their securities. If they could not find buyers immediately, they would employ stockbrokers to find buyers for them – for a commission. Honest reliable stockbrokers who dealt only in securities in worthwhile companies would tend, in the long run, to attract the better sort of business. Indeed the whole system depended on honesty. This is reflected in the motto of the London Stock Exchange, "*Verbum meum pactum*" (My word is my bond). Despite many regrettable lapses from this high standard, much of the trading on the Stock Exchange in the UK still aims to work on this principle.

Over the years the system of trading shares became institutionalised, refined and improved. Only reputable companies with properly drawn up accounts could have their securities traded. Rogue directors were blacklisted. Proper records were kept. Stock exchanges, designated buildings where security trading took place, became reputable places in which a business could obtain capital without having to borrow it from a bank. The existence of an honest, efficient, well-established stock market designed for dealing in companies' securities meant that any company which needed funds could issue shares and immediately sell them in that market-place to the public. With its new capital, the company could expand, its investors could start to receive good dividends on their investment, and the value of the securities would rise. However,

investors would be more likely to buy the securities if there were a mechanism
for selling those securities should they wish to dispose of them once the price
had risen, or before it fell.

The problem of lack of liquidity

If there were no market where existing securities could be sold, few people
would ever wish to buy securities. The few rash investors who bought securities would have to hope that one day they might meet someone who would buy
the securities or that the dividends would always be so good that they would
never wish to sell the securities. Such inability to make the securities liquid (*i.e.*
easily bought and sold) would mean that the company would never obtain the
investment it wanted unless it could provide some other attractions. As an
example of this, the author has seen the prospectus of a company known as
Classic Bloodstock plc, whose securities are relatively illiquid. This is because
there is no market-place for the trading of its shares. The company invests in
racehorses. Amongst the attractions it can offer to shareholders to compensate
for a potential lack of liquidity in its shares is a distribution of retained profits
on the solvent winding-up of the company once the horses have been sold, an
opportunity to go to the paddocks and watch the training of the horses, the use
of a cottage at the stud-farm where the horses are reared, and an information
hot-line for tips to use at the bookmakers.

Nowadays companies such as the above must make it very clear to investors:

• that there may only be a very limited market in their shares, and

• that therefore it may be very difficult to sell the shares.

Furthermore it may be difficult to agree a price for those shares.

By contrast, it will always be easy to find a value for shares which are regularly quoted in a recognised market-place, not least because the prices are
quoted in newspapers or displayed on computer screens. In the UK the main
recognised market-place for the trading of securities is the International Stock
Exchange of the United Kingdom and the Republic of Ireland Limited ("the
Stock Exchange"), though other markets are being developed.

Market-makers and quotations

Historically, stockbrokers, who merely put buyers and sellers in touch and
obtained a commission from the sale, were known as matching brokers. By contrast, a market-maker (formerly known as a jobber) was and still is someone
who does not just try to find a buyer or seller but actually will buy or sell the

security himself whenever he is asked to do so. If a market-maker is willing to buy or sell a security, that security immediately is more marketable than one which a matching-broker will only try to sell. This is because once a market-maker has committed himself to deal in a particular security he has no choice but to deal whenever he is asked to do so, whereas a matching-broker might never achieve a deal. On the other hand, market-makers will only be willing to commit themselves to deal in securities that are desirable, since they do not wish to be struck with unsellable securities. Nowadays market-makers must be registered to deal in particular securities, and if a market-maker is registered to deal in a particular security, it means that he must produce, on request, a quotation (a firm and binding offer) for the prices at which he will buy or sell that security. The securities in a company for which market-makers given quotations on the Stock Exchange in this manner are said to be quoted on the Stock Exchange. Some companies' securities are so little in demand that there may be only one or two market-makers prepared to quote for that company, or even none at all. The lack of enthusiasm for those securities will generally be reflected in the low price the market-maker will pay to buy them from an investor. By contrast, other companies' securities may be so desirable that market-makers will wish to make a market in those securities, and the market-makers in those companies' securities will be competing with each other to produce the keenest quotations.

Following the reorganisation of the Stock Exchange on 27 October 1986, a day commonly known as "Big Bang", most of the former divisions between jobbers, stockbrokers and market-makers were swept away. Instead, many of them amalgamated, became Stock Exchange member firms and now act in all three capacities. With the advent of the Stock Exchange Automated Quotations ("SEAQ") computer link-up with the Stock Exchange, firms no longer need to be based in London, the old open outcry system of dealing (when jobbers stood in a special hall shouting out prices at each other and harassed officials scribbled figures up on blackboards) gave way to telephone dealing, and major investors were able to break away from standard fixed commissions to negotiated commission rates. The division between stockbrokers and market-makers still continues, in that stockbrokers deal more with clients while market-makers do the actual trading and offering of quotations; but there is no reason why a Stock Exchange member firm, or individuals within a firm, cannot do both and many do. For further details about order-driven trading, see Chapter 7.

Primary markets and secondary markets
The market for existing securities, being traded by existing investors, is known as the secondary market, and may be contrasted with the market for shares being offered on the market for the first time, known as the primary market. The secondary market price serves as a marker for the primary market.

Offers of shares on the stock market

There are five main ways in which a company raises capital on the stock market. These are:

1. offer for subscription

2. offer for sale

3. placings

4. rights issues

5. open issues.

Offer for subscription

This takes place when a company offers its own shares directly to the public. Those who buy the shares are known as subscribers. Some companies are able to do the marketing themselves because they have the in-house capacity. This is rare because marketing of shares is usually done by merchant banks or "issuing houses" experienced in the procedure of a stock market flotation.

Should some of the offered shares fail to find subscribers, under the CA 1985 s 84(1)(a) the company should not allot any of the offered shares unless:

- the terms of the offer permit the allotment anyway, or

- certain pre-specified conditions have already been fulfilled (CA 1985 s 84(1)(b))

though as a matter of practice companies generally take the precaution of using underwriters to take up any unpurchased shares. The underwriters may be paid a fee of not more than 10% of the issue price of the shares or such lesser rate as is permitted by the company's articles (CA 1985 s 97(2)(a)). The pricing of shares offered by subscription is described in the next paragraph.

Offer for sale

When a company offers its shares to the public, the company's existing shareholders often offer some of their shares to the public at the same time. Such an offer by existing shareholders cannot be called an offer for subscription because new shares are not being sold. It is therefore known as an "offer for sale" and those who buy the shares are purchasers not subscribers. Offers for sale are very common, and sometimes on a flotation there is a combined offer for subscription and offer for sale. The company issues its own shares and uses the funds realised to repay borrowing or to pay for new capital items. Simultaneously the members sell their own shares in the hope of obtaining a profit. Commonly a company (and the members if appropriate) will sell its shares to an issuing house which will then offer the shares to the public. The advantage to the company of a sale to an issuing house is that it is assured of the sale of all the shares, and it will get all the money it wants, less the issuing house's fees: the advantage to the issuing house is that if it has judged matters well, it should be able to sell the shares for more than the cost of acquiring them from the company – though it will have to arrange all the marketing and compliance with the Stock Exchange regulations. With either an offer for subscription or an offer for sale, the price the public will pay may be either a fixed price or a tendered price. With a fixed price the company ideally should pitch the price slightly below the price for similar existing securities for similar companies with a similar amount of capital and similar prospects. If the price is pitched too low, speculators get the benefit: if the price is pitched too high, the offer will be undersubscribed, and the underwriters will earn their commission at the company's expense. If the offer is greatly oversubscribed, investors may only receive a proportion of what they sought – as in the major UK privatisation issues. With a tender offer the seller asks each investor what price he will tender (offer to pay) for each share above a certain minimum figure, and how many shares the investor will buy. The company then ascertains the highest price at which all the available shares will be sold. This price is known as the striking price. Although there are many variants of this, broadly speaking if an investor has tendered a price higher than the striking price he only has to pay the striking price but he must buy the number of shares he asked for. A variation of a sale by tender is to dispense with a striking price; the investor then pays exactly what he stated he would pay per share, multiplied by the number of shares he wants to acquire. Those who tendered below the level at which the shares would all be sold get nothing. The skill for the investor is estimating what the striking price is, or the minimum price at which he will obtain his shares.

When an investor fills in an application form to buy some shares he is making an offer to the company to buy the shares and it is not bound to accept his offer. If his offer is accepted he will be sent a renounceable letter of acceptance, valid usually for two or three months. This means that if he changes his mind, he can sell his entitlement to another person who can ultimately be registered as the shareholder instead. There is no stamp duty on the transfer of a letter of acceptance. If the investor does not change his mind he will be registered as the shareholder on the expiry of the time-limit.

Placing
Offers for subscription and sale are expensive and time-consuming. By using a placing, a broker will find purchasers for the company's shares. The broker does this by tapping his network of clients. Such clients will need to be prepared to take a gamble on the shares. Each client will be expected to buy a

substantial number of the shares. If the shares increase in value, the client will prosper; but this cannot be guaranteed. The Stock Exchange does not entirely approve of placings since a placing does not spread the shares over the market-place and may therefore affect their liquidity. There is also the bad publicity arising from "city fat cats", as they may be perceived by the general public, giving themselves excellent investment opportunities denied to the rest of the investing public. The Stock Exchange therefore imposes rules on placing to prevent too many shares being released into too few hands (see the *Admissions of Securities to Listing*, Chapter 3, section 1).

Rights issue

A rights issue is one where the company makes an issue of its shares to the existing shareholders on a proportional basis. So, for example, a three for one rights issue would entitle a member to apply for three new shares for every one he already holds. The entitlement comes usually in the form of a renounceable letter of allotment. If the member does not wish to take up his entitlement he can sell it to someone who will. No stamp duty or broker's fee is payable on the transfer of the renounceable letter of allotment. A rights issue requires that the company applies the normal rights of pre-emption under the CA 1985 s 89 unless the company has already disapplied them under the CA 1985 s 89. A rights issue is seen as an expensive way of obtaining more capital but the CA 1985 s 89 usually precludes any other option. On a rights issue the shares are generally sold at a discount to the market price in order to ensure that the shares are all taken up.

Open issue

This is an offer for subscription only open to existing members on a non-proportional basis. An existing member can therefore apply for as many shares as he wishes.

The procedure for the transfer of shares on the stock market

This is discussed in Chapter 7.

What influences the price of securities?

Although the answer to this question belongs to economics and possibly to psy-chology, there are certain fairly obvious influences, of which the principal one is supply and demand. If demand for a particular security is high, the supply becomes restricted and the price goes up; alternatively, if demand for the secu-rity is low, the price goes down.

What influences investors' decisions to buy or sell?
The more rational reasons for buying include:

- the expectation that the price of the security will rise because of a company's previous good financial results and skilled management;

- a company's successful development and production of new and desirable products;

- a company's successful cost-cutting and efficiency measures;

- the winning or advantageous settlement by a company of court cases: this will mean either that the company becomes entitled to disputed funds or assets, or that the company's liability to creditors or potential creditors is reduced or eliminated;

- more favourable taxation treatment which may stimulate demand for the company's products or services;

- a better political climate both at home and in any countries to which the company exports or where its products are made;

- if a company has been doing badly the belief that the worst has been weathered;

- the possibility of a successful takeover bid;

- the dismissal of a large number of employees;

- the likelihood of the award of major contracts for the company;

- the decline of a competitor.

For selling well-known reasons include:

- the expectation that the price will fall as a result of incompetent management or previous poor performance;

- bad weather affecting the company's products or services, particularly in anything related to agriculture, tourism or leisure pursuits;

- political instability in countries where the company's products are exported or made;

- unfavourable change in Government attitudes or regulatory legislation;

- less favourable taxation treatment resulting in a decline in the demand for the company's products or services;

- bad publicity for the company;

- substantial litigation against the company which may result in enormous claims against the company – for example cigarette-manufacturing companies becoming liable for smokers' illnesses;

- the dubious public reputation of the company's managing director;

- the collapse of a takeover bid;

- if the company has been doing well, the belief that it is unlikely to do any better;

- distaste for the company's environmental record or business practices;

- loss of the company's markets.

Reasons that can affect the price either way depending on the circumstances and the type of company:

- strength or weakness of the currency markets;

- interest rates;

- new management;

- proposed capital expenditure;

- the number of market-makers willing to make a market in the securities in question.

Some investment companies, particularly in the USA, have, or used to have, automatic computer-triggered policies of selling when the price of their investments fell below certain predetermined levels. As many of the investment companies have similar investments and similar policies this can cause a wave of selling of securities, throwing the stock markets into panic.

As investing on the stock market is a form of gambling, there are various irrational reasons why people buy or sell shares and these include:

- persuasive advertising techniques, particularly for privatisations;

- boredom with some investments as not being speculative enough;

- fashion: from time to time certain types of shares are in favour and then fall out of favour again.

It is often said that, if you ask some of the very keenest investors how they have been successful, their general reply is that they take a long-term view, they are unsentimental about their investments, and they have a "sixth sense" about when to buy or when to sell.

Bestial imagery in the stock market

A bull market is one where shares are generally rising. A bull is an investor who buys shares in the expectation that they will rise, whereupon he will sell them. A bear market is one where shares are generally falling. A bear is an investor who sells shares in the expectation that the price will fall. Bull and bear markets used to be particularly facilitated by the practice in the Stock Exchange of having 14-day account periods. A bull who bought on day one and sold on day 13 at a profit would receive a cheque from his stockbrokers, as would a bear who sold at a high price and bought at a low one. Under the new CREST system the 14-day account period will ultimately, it is hoped, shorten to three days. Bulls and bears will therefore have to be quick off the mark.

A stag is an investor who sells his shares the moment he acquires them in the hope of making an instant profit.

Who are the major investors in quoted UK companies nowadays?

In the UK the major investors in quoted companies are the "Institutions" sometimes also known as the "Institutional shareholders". They comprise major insurance companies, pension funds, investment management companies (such as those managing unit trusts and investment trusts), banks and building societies. The Institutions hold shares on behalf of people who have pension policies, life assurance policies, managed savings accounts or who have otherwise delegated the management of their financial affairs to others. The Institutions hold about 70% of all quoted securities in the UK. Consequently they are treated with considerable respect by the companies in which they have invested. If an Institution sells a major shareholding in a company, it is a very strong indication that that company may be a poor investment and as a consequence of such a sale it is likely that its share price will fall severely.

Ordinary members of the public in the UK hold only about 15% of all quoted securities. The Conservative Government of the last decade tried to encourage wider share ownership amongst the British public. Reasons for this include the following:

1. The Government hoped to establish a more entrepreneurial and financially aware society.

2. In the case of the privatisation of utilities that were formerly publicly owned, the Government could claim that the ownership was at least genuinely offered to the public.

3. If there is wider share ownership, it was believed that there would be more shareholders anxious to protect their wealth, and therefore be more likely to

vote Conservative given previous perceptions about Labour government's attitude to private investors and wealth generally.

4. With Western Governments increasingly wondering how they are going to finance long-term welfare benefits such as pensions and health care, the Government was trying to encourage people to create wealth and save for their own retirement. To this end, the Government devised certain tax-efficient schemes such as personal equity plans and business expansion schemes to encourage wider ownership of securities.

It is arguable how successful the Government was in its objective. More people are now willing to consider investing generally in shares, but there is little evidence to suggest that many went on to become investors on a grander scale. Many investors have been known to stag the major privatisation issues. Their shares were then bought by institutions which were expressly not allowed initially to buy major holdings in the privatisation issues. Stagging enabled many investors to make a certain amount of money for a relatively small and risk-free outlay, but has not necessarily encouraged those investors to buy other shares.

There are various other reasons for the reluctance of the British public to buy securities:

1. With every fresh scandal emerging from the City, for example Guinness, Polly Peck, BCCI, Maxwell Communications, Lloyd's and Barings, many investors may take the view that those who work in the City are either crooks or incompetent; and either way are not to be trusted with investors' money.

2. Dealing in securities is seen as speculative, and investors do not wish to lose their hard earned money in a time of recession; deposit accounts in building societies and high street banks may be dull but at least they are safe. It is also often said that you should only invest on the stock market what you can afford to lose. Such an attitude does not encourage the small investor.

3. Many investors cannot be bothered with the paperwork involved in owning shares: they have to keep records of when they bought the shares; they may have to declare the sale proceeds or dividends in their tax returns; and from time to time the companies send investors documents called annual reports and accounts which to a very large number of non-professional investors are unintelligible. To many people, company accounts are meaningless: the only figure they look at is the dividend.

4. Stockbrokers' fees are perceived to be high. Stockbrokers commonly charge a minimum flat fee commission plus a percentage commission. The percentage varies according to the amount of business the investor does with them. In addition, purchasers of shares have to pay stamp duty at 0.5%. This

means that small transactions are not always worthwhile. It is only worth dealing in shares if the investors' profits exceed their stockbrokers' fees. This means that only those with a substantial amount of capital are ever willing to invest.

5. As the business of investment is generally seen as perplexing, there is a suspicion amongst many potential investors that the City is full of sharks keen to take advantage of the public's ignorance of matters financial.

6. For a long period until the mid-1980s most forms of investment were taxed very highly in the UK. At one stage it was possible to be taxed at a rate of 98% on one's investment income. Under those circumstances there was no incentive ever to save or to have investments. Although recent governments encourage saving more than some of their predecessors did, there is always the fear that a later government may bring back high taxation levels on investments.

7. Many benefits that UK citizens enjoy are only available if following means-testing one's assets are sufficiently low. Provident people who had saved or invested their money found that they were barred from receiving benefits that others less careful were receiving. This served as an incentive to spend rather than save or invest.

Despite this, there can be few people in work in the UK who do not hold investments, albeit indirectly. Anyone who has a savings bond, life assurance policy or belongs to a pension scheme indirectly owns shares, although the shares are managed for that person by the insurance company or pension funds managers. Many investors take the view that it is better to let the professionals in reputable financial services firms control their investments. This is because the professionals will have arranged lower transactions costs and because they ought to have a good understanding of the movements of the market-place. Furthermore, the major insurance firms are conscious of their public image and their need for continued probity and efficiency.

Regulation of the Stock Exchange

If the public is to be persuaded to invest in securities, it must be assured that the business of buying and selling securities is efficiently and honestly run. To achieve this, the Financial Services Act 1986 (FSA) was passed to set up systems to improve the entire financial services industry. At the time of the passing of the FSA it was apparent that investors were not always been well served by the financial services industry. The FSA set up various regulatory authorities for bodies providing financial services, all ultimately under the supervision of the Financial Services Authority and Investments Board (SIB), a board set up under the FSA and receiving delegated authority from the Secretary of State. Amongst its other tasks the Authority supervises investment exchanges (FSA s 37). An investment exchange is effectively a market-place for the trading of investments as defined in the FSA Schedule 1 Part 1. These cover:

- stocks and shares;
- debentures;
- warrants;
- depository receipts;
- Government and local authority bonds;
- options in investments, currencies or certain precious metals;
- futures contracts;
- long-term insurance contracts;
- rights in any of the above.

Each investment exchange where a market is made in the above investments needs to be recognised by the Authority. The Stock Exchange is a recognised investment exchange for markets in UK and foreign shares and debentures. Under the terms of its recognition by the Authority, the Stock Exchange is expected to regulate itself, and provided it does so successfully, it is not expected that the Government will interfere. In addition the Stock Exchange has been nominated by the Government as the competent authority to deal with the trading of securities in companies admitted to the Official List (see later) in terms of the three European Community Council Directives, the Admission Directive (79/297), the Interim Reports Directive (82/121) and the Listing Particulars Directive (80/390). The terms of these Directives now constitute Part IV of the FSA. The Stock Exchange has, in turn, delegated its authority to the Committee on Quotations and the Quotations Department of the Stock Exchange.

Regulation by the Stock Exchange

For a company and its securities to be admitted to the Stock Exchange, the company has to comply with a large number of disclosure requirements (to be discussed later) and to adhere to a number of continuing regulations promulgated by the Committee of Quotations and the directors of the Stock Exchange in their rule book, *Admission of Securities to Listing*. The regulations prescribe what information must be given in the company's accounts and directors' reports. Failure to adhere to the regulations generally results in bad publicity, investigation by the relevant regulatory committee and ultimately suspension or removal of the company's securities from being traded on the Stock Exchange. The regulations which quoted companies must follow are unlike the regulations to be found in Government statutes. In Government statutes the letter of the law is, on the whole, what is followed. Generally, if something is not expressly forbidden under an Act of Parliament, and there is no common law rule preventing it, it is permissible. By contrast, the regulations of the Stock Exchange work on the basis that it is the spirit of the law that matters. The regulations are designed to promote honesty and fair dealing and any derogation from that may result in sanctions. However, the Stock Exchange rarely imposes very severe sanctions, normally giving the offending company the opportunity to mend its ways. While cynics may say that the gentle approach of the regulators in the Stock Exchange displays a fear of "making waves" and establishing possible unwelcome precedents, others may say that the regulations are unnecessarily complex, fussy or obscure.

The advantages and disadvantages of a quotation

So far we have examined why stock exchanges exist and why they need to be regulated. But why should companies wish to be admitted to the Stock Exchange?

There are four main reasons:

1. By issuing its shares to the public, a company will obtain more capital and thus may be able to expand and take advantage of commercial opportunities. This will create wealth for the investors.

2. On flotation of a company on the Stock Exchange, the founder members of the company can sell some of their securities hopefully at a profit, and existing debt may be repaid out of proceeds of the issue of securities.

3. A quoted company has a higher profile than an unquoted company. It is thus likely to attract more business. The directors' own status may, in some eyes, be increased by being a director of a quoted company.

4. When one company takes over another company, it can offer its own shares as the consideration for the target company's shares. If the takeover company is prospering, its shares may prove better value than merely receiving cash.

However, there are certain aspects of being quoted which are not always found to be attractive by companies or their directors. These include the following:

1. Any quoted company has to comply with the Stock Exchange's stringent requirements or face unwelcome publicity.

2. The financial press may criticise the management of the company if they feel that matters are being hidden from shareholders.

3. At annual general meetings shareholders may ask awkward questions or call the directors' judgment into question.

4. As a quoted company's shares are generally freely purchased, the company may, at any time, be the victim of a takeover bid.

5. Some quoted companies have been known to complain that the City takes a short-term view of investments and does not appreciate long-term investment strategies, being interested solely in short-term profits.

6. Flotation on the Stock Exchange is a very expensive process which does not necessarily guarantee that the desired extra capital will be raised.

7. The success of a flotation and the quotation of the company on the Stock Exchange have been known to go to founding directors' heads, so that they lose their entrepreneurial or commercial edge.

A well-known example of a company that found being quoted was more trouble than it was worth was Virgin. Richard Branson reacquired all the shares that the public had bought following the flotation of Virgin, and took the shares back into his own and his immediate colleagues' hands. He claimed at the time that the City failed to understand his business and was too short-term in its appreciation of what he was trying to achieve.

Stock exchange requirements

No private company's securities may be offered to the public (CA 1985 s 81) although it is possible to prepare a prospectus for a private company provided the only investors who see it are the existing members and their families, employees and their families, employee share schemes, and existing debenture-holders (CA 1985 s 60).

Only the securities of plcs which have satisfied the Stock Exchange's requirements may be traded in the Stock Exchange. The requirements vary according to the particular market within the Stock Exchange where the company's securities will be quoted. At the time of writing, the Stock Exchange has two markets, the Official List, which is generally for larger, more prosperous and well established companies, and the Alternative Investment Market ("AIM") which is for less well established, more speculative companies. It came into being on 19 June 1995 and replaces the former Unlisted Securities Market. Other markets, such as Tradepoint, exist for dealing in securities, though only a limited number of companies' securities are traded on this particular exchange. Such other markets are not part of the Stock Exchange, though the same companies' securities may be quoted on both exchanges. As the Stock Exchange is the largest securities market in the UK, we shall concentrate on its requirements.

Official List requirements

Under Part IV of the FSA, the Stock Exchange was appointed the appropriate authority to regulate the Official List. It does this by requiring any company which wishes to have its securities listed to comply with its rule book, whose formal title is *Admission of Securities to Listing* but whose informal title is the "Yellow Book" because of its yellow plastic cover. The Yellow Book specifies a number of requirements that must be fulfilled before a listing can be granted, and also specifies a number of continuing obligations with which the company must comply. Failure to do so can mean the suspension or cancellation of trading of the company's securities, in addition to bad publicity.

The import of the Yellow Book is that a listed company must at all times disclose all relevant and necessary information about the company to its investors. This is to protect its investors and prevent runs on the company's shares. In particular it must provide reasons for any derogations from the Cadbury Code and Hampel Code (see Chapter 14) and present its accounts in accordance with current best professional practice. As can be imagined, there is sometimes a gap between the professed intention of the Yellow Book and the actual practice. Directors of a listed company often wish their accounts to be presented in the most favourable light, notwithstanding the true position of the company, and a substantial part of the investment analysis industry is devoted to rewriting listed company accounts. Companies engineering their accounts in this way comply with the letter of the Yellow Book, if not entirely with its spirit. This is contrary to the general intention of the Yellow Book. However, word quickly goes round the financial community and the financial press if a company is being cavalier in its presentation of its accounts and directors' report.

For a new admission to listing, a company must obtain a sponsor, being a member firm of the Stock Exchange. The sponsor deals with all the paperwork demanded by the Stock Exchange and its quotations department. The sponsor must be sure that the company is suitable for admission to listing and that its directors are able to cope with the additional pressures of being a listed company. The Stock Exchange expects sponsors to exercise their duties with the highest standards and care, and sponsors who bring clearly unsuitable companies to the stock market are viewed with great disfavour. Even if the sponsor is satisfied that the company is suitable for listing, the Stock Exchange may still refuse a company's application if it considers that "it would be detrimental to the interests of investors" (FSA s 144(3)(a)) or if in any other country in the European Community the company has failed to comply with any regulations in respect of listing in that country (FSA s 14(3)(b)).

Companies already listed on another EC Stock Exchange may apply for listing "by introduction" from the other country. As the rules of listing are broadly the same throughout the EC the entry requirements are broadly compatible.

Listing particulars

Part of the procedure for application is the preparation and publication of the listing particulars. The rules applying to this may be found in the FSA ss 146–157. In essence, listing particulars must contain all the financial and other information that an investor could reasonably want in order for him to decide whether to invest or not. This means that not every trivial detail need be included (*Admission of Securities to Listing*, section 3, Chapter 1, para 1.5), nor need matters that would generally be known by sensible investors and their advisers be included (FSA s 146). There are very few occasions when exemptions for otherwise useful detail is permitted. These are:

1. when disclosure might not be in the public interest (FSA s 148(1)(a)) as certified, if necessary, by the Secretary of State or the Treasury (FSA s 148(3));

2. when disclosure might be seriously detrimental to the company (FSA s 14(1)(b)) as in the case of, say, details of certain contracts entered into by an armaments manufacturing company seeking listing. This is subject to a proviso that authority for the exemption would not be given if the non-disclosure of the information might cause a potential investor to be misled.

If, at any time, the listing particulars provide significantly incorrect or are significantly superseded by events which the company knows about, the company must produce supplementary listing particulars (FSA s 147). Genuine ignorance of the error or alteration of circumstances will, however, be treated as a fair excuse for not producing supplementary particulars (FSA s 147(3)), though it it unlikely to lend credibility to the company or encourage people to buy its shares. Listing particulars must be published at the Registrar of Companies (FSA s 149) and must be available free at the company's own registered office and at the Stock Exchange. They may also be published in newspapers. The question of compensation for loss following inaccurate listing particulars is dealt with later in this chapter. A prospectus is required for any new company being listed for the first time (FSA s 144(2)) and on each occasion when a company makes a further issue of shares to the pubic (*Admission of Securities to Listing*, section 3, Chapter 1, para 1.1). However, this rule does not apply to a bonus issue to existing shareholders (*ibid*, section 3, Chapter 1, para 5.3), to the increase of a class of shares by 10% or shares being allotted to employees (*ibid*, section 3, Chapter 1, para 5.4).

Listing particulars are notoriously scrupulously examined. The Stock Exchange demands proof of just about every fact, and someone, whether he be a director, an auditor, the company secretary, or one of the company's lawyers, must be prepared to vouch for every statement. If necessary, that person will have to sign a form to show that he approved the particular statement. This makes blame very easy to apportion should things go wrong, and ensures very high standards of accuracy. It also means that listing particulars are very carefully written. These high standards of accuracy are required because:

1. If London is to maintain its reputation as one of the financial centres of the world, it must be seen to be policing the securities being traded on its Stock Exchange.

2. In the 19th century and at the beginning of the 20th century, little was required for a company to be admitted to the Stock Exchange, and many investors were badly swindled. A common trick for promoters of a company (see the end of this chapter) was to invite the public to subscribe for shares in a company to be admitted to the Stock Exchange. The promoters would then sell an asset to the company at a wildly inflated price, giving themselves many shares in the company in return. These shares would be sold in the market and the promoters would then disappear with the proceeds. The remaining investors would then realise how they had been duped. Nowadays such practices would be difficult to carry out, not least because of the requirement for independent valuation of assets and the rules, known as the Model Code, preventing directors disposing of their shares except under permitted circumstances. Although the Stock Exchange cannot guard against every eventuality, it can minimise the opportunities for fraud. By being seen to be an honest and reputable market, it will in the long run attract the better sort of business.

Eligibility for admission to the Official List

In order for a company to be admitted to the Official List:

- it must have an established three-year trading record;

- the securities about to be listed must have a market value of at least £700,000;

- the company must offer at least 25% of its equity to the public.

Another way of explaining the final criterion is that the founder-members of the company may retain as much as 75% of the company's equity in their hands. However, were a company to do this, it is likely that few investors would be willing to buy securities in that company unless the price of the securities was very good and the dividends high. This is because even if all the non-founder members agreed together to vote in a particular way at a general meeting, they still would not be able to block a special resolution. The investors would then always be at the whim of the majority shareholders over whom they would have little control.

Alternative Investment Market (AIM)

This market has been set up to meet the so-called Equity Gap. This is the problem that afflicts some small expanding companies. If a company needs more capital, it has various options such as:

(i)   further investment from the current shareholders;
(ii)   borrowing from a bank;
(iii) investment by a venture capital fund; or
(iv)   obtaining a full listing.

If the founder-members do not have the funds themselves, the company may have to borrow from a bank. But banks may be unwilling to lend to the company: its track record may not be long enough, the security it could grant inadequate, the amount of money it wants to borrow too great.

Venture capital funds often inject capital into a new company but they are generally exacting in their terms. This may not suit the company. So if the company has a desirable product, but lacks the funds to pay for the cost of making the product, it needs investors who are willing to take a risk – which not many investors are keen to do.

Alternatively, it could raise the funds by means of a full listing. This could be very expensive and cumbersome. To raise £20 million might cost as much as £800,000, and there may need to be a wait of several years for the company to establish its financial credibility. The AIM hopes to fill this gap between bank borrowing, venture capital funds and a full listing, by appealing to investors willing to take some degree of risk. AIM has been set up with the hope that its existence will encourage smaller businesses and enable them to maximise their opportunities.

The following are the requirements for a company to be admitted to AIM:

1. a nominated adviser (to help the company comply with the AIM regulations) and broker (who may be the same firm as the adviser) who will match buyers and sellers of the company's shares;

2. incorporation as a plc;

3. accounts that conform with best current professional practice;

4. freely transferable shares;

5. adoption by board resolution of the Model Code for directors' and employees' dealings in the company's shares. The Model Code is a code of conduct to be adopted by all companies whose shares are publicly traded, and it limits directors' and employee's opportunities for dealing in their own companies' shares. It is designed to lessen the opportunities both for insider dealing and for dealing which falls short of insider dealing in terms of the Criminal Justice Act 1993 but which raises doubts in shareholders' minds about directors' and employee's integrity;

6. a prospectus. An AIM company prospectus requires more information about the directors than listing particulars do. In particular it requires directors to reveal past bankruptcies, receiverships and liquidations which either they or their companies have been involved in. Unlike Official List documents, however, the Stock Exchange will not scrutinise the prospectus. It is up to the advisers and the directors to get it correct. The rules relating to AIM prospectuses can be found in the Public Offer of Securities Regulations (SI 1995/1537) ("POSR") and the wording of the rules is deliberately similar to the rules relating to listed companies under the FSA Part IV. Liability for statements made in a prospectus is discussed later in this chapter.

As with the Official List there are ongoing obligations with which the company must comply.

Information about the company will be available through the Stock Exchange Alternative Trading Service (known as SEATS PLUS) which will also display current prices for the company's securities.

There is no minimum market capitalisation, no minimum length of previous trading and no minimum requirement for the number of shares in public hands.

The regulations applying to AIM are to be found in the POSR and the Traded Securities (Disclosure) Regulations 1994 (SI 1994/188). The market in AIM shares will be monitored by the Stock Exchange's Market Supervision and Surveillance Team. AIM is designed to be cheap and uncomplicated and is seen as suitable for:

- young and start-up businesses;

- management buy-outs and buy-ins;

- family-owned businesses.

Typical investors are seen to be funds specialising in smaller companies and experienced investors. AIM is not for amateurs: it is recognised that because of the relative lack of scrutiny there may well be some highly speculative companies, not to mention some dubious ones.

Advisers will need to advise a proposed AIM company of the requirements of the AIM rules and to help it comply with those rules. If an adviser is unhappy about one of its AIM companies' conduct, it can resign from being an adviser. The shares are then suspended, thus completely stranding shareholders, until a replacement adviser is found. Since the advisers are likely to be the ones who attract most criticism if an AIM company turns out to be a fraud, they will need to be well insured against a successful claim for negligence, and they may exact high fees to take account of the risk they may be running. Furthermore, since it is possible to be an adviser and a limited company, there is always the danger that an adviser acts negligently, is under-insured, suffers a claim which it cannot meet and goes into liquidation.

Investors' rights to compensation under the FSA and the Public Offer of Securities Regulations 1995

There is a general requirement that those who prepare listing particulars and prospectuses should include all such information as may be useful or necessary to a potential investor and which he would reasonably expect to be informed of before he made his investment (FSA s 146 and POSR reg 9). If a company produces listing particulars or a prospectus which contains false or misleading information, anyone who was responsible for its preparation under the FSA s 152 or POSR reg 13 is liable to pay compensation (FSA s 150 and POSR reg 14) to anyone who:

- acquired the securities in question;

- suffered loss in respect of them; and

- did so because of an untrue or misleading statement or omission of necessary information as specified in the FSA ss 146, 147 and POSR regs 9, 10 in the listing particulars and prospectus respectively.

There are various points to be noted from this:

1. Formerly it was not absolutely clear whether this rule only applies to those who subscribe directly for shares in reliance of the listing particulars, as opposed to those who buy them "second-hand" from a regulated securities market. In the case of *Peek* v *Gurney* [1861–73] All ER Rep 116, this issue in general was considered, although the matter was not then on a statutory basis. There it was held that only subscribers could claim compensation. Ordinary subsequent acquirers had no claim. If it seems harsh that only the original allottees/subscribers could claim, the reason for the decision to exclude further purchasers was because if the directors could suffer a claim against any purchaser suffering loss and relying on the prospectus, there might be no end to claims. This view has now been superseded by the FSA s 150(1) and (3) and POSR reg 14(1) and (3). Now even someone buying from a source other than the original company but relying on the listing particulars or the prospectus can claim compensation from those responsible for its preparation provided he has suffered loss as a result of that reliance.

2. There are exemptions from liability for compensation if the person making the misstatement or omission reasonably believed that the misstatement were true or the omission not misleading or properly omitted (FSA s 151(1) and POSR reg 15(1)) and:

   - he continued in that belief until the securities were acquired; or
   - the securities were acquired before he could reasonably and practicably bring the correction to the attention of potential buyers of the securities; or
   - he did all he reasonably could to bring any correction to potential buyers' attention; or
   - he ought reasonably to be excused given the length of time the securities had been held following their acquisition.

   This and the following paragraph ensure that negligent and fraudulent misrepresentations attract compensation, but innocent ones do not. The import of the wording is close to that of the Misrepresentation Act 1967 s 2(1) and Misrepresentation (Northern Ireland) 1967 s 2(1). In Scotland the relevant equivalent is the Law Reform (Miscellaneous Provisions) Act 1985 s 10(1).

3. There are further exemptions from liability for those preparing the listing particulars if they are reasonably relying on statements from an expert (FSA

s 151(2) and POSR reg 15(2)). The expert must have given his consent to his statement being used in the listing particulars, and the persons preparing the listing particulars or prospectus ("the responsible persons") must have reasonably believed the expert to be an expert and competent to make or authorise his statement. The exemptions in paragraph 2 above apply to the responsible persons' continuing belief in the expert's statement (FSA s 151(2) and POSR reg 152)). Experts will be liable for their own mistakes and omissions provided they have authorised the publication of their own statements (FSA s 152(1)(d) and (e) and POSR reg 13(1)(d) and (g)).

4. If the listing particulars include statements made from official sources those preparing the prospectus are not liable for those statements (FSA s 151(4) and POSR reg 15(4)).

5. People who acquired the securities knowing that there was a misstatement or omission cannot claim compensation (FSA s 151(5) and POSR reg 15(5)).

6. Experts and others in their positions are only liable for the matters for which they accepted responsibility and the publication of which they authorised in a form and context which has met their agreement (FSA s 152(3) and POSR reg 13(3)).

7. People whose statements were published without their authority (FSA s 152(2) and POSR reg 13(2)), such as experts who declined to have their statements included, are not liable for such unauthorised statements provided that on becoming aware of the publication they give reasonable public notice that the statements were published without their consent or knowledge.

8. There have in fact been few recent cases where compensation has been claimed by aggrieved purchasers. This is partly because all advertisements in connection with listing particulars have to be approved or authorised by the Stock Exchange or other regulatory body charged with ensuring high standards (FSA s154) and so far little significant has slipped through the net as sponsors and the Stock Exchange authorities are so strict. Those responsible for listing particulars are defined in the FSA s 152, and include:

- the company issuing the securities;

- each director of the company;

- anyone accepting responsibility for the listing particulars; and

- anyone not within the above categories but who authorised the contents of the listing particulars.

The sponsors themselves are not responsible for the contents of the listing particulars unless they agree otherwise. As regards AIM companies, as AIM has not been in existence for very long there has been little opportunity so far for the issue of compensation for an inaccurate prospectus to be dealt with. However, given the more speculative nature of companies on AIM, it is possible that a claim for compensation may one day have to be considered.

Investors' rights under common law

We have already seen the rights available to purchasing investors relying on listing particulars/prospectuses and suffering loss. These are the statutory rights which, as stated above, have on the whole proved effective by making listing particulars/prospectuses much more honest about the companies than historically was the case.

However, as stated in the previous chapter, a purchasing investor can also sue under the common law if a misrepresentation induced him to purchase shares in a company. He can ask for rescission of the contract of purchase whether the misrepresentation was fraudulent, negligent or innocent, and the normal rules of contract law apply in that a claimant:

• must sue the person responsible for the misrepresentation;

• must not have unduly delayed in seeking his remedy;

• must not have lost his claim because the company has gone into liquidation or a bona fide purchaser for value received has already obtained rights in the securities in question;

• will only be able to claim consequential losses if they are reasonably foreseeable.

As a matter of practice, anyone suffering loss as a result of acquiring shares on the strength of listing particulars or a prospectus would almost certainly claim for compensation under the statutory provisions in the FSA or POSR. However the common law is also useful where there is no prospectus. In *Smith New Court Securities Ltd* v *Citibank* [1996] 3 WLR 1051 an employee in Citibank induced Smith New Court to acquire shares in Ferranti, and represented to Smith New Court that there were two other bidders for the Ferranti shares. He later indicated that the two other bidders had actually made bids. This was not in fact true, and as a result of these assertions, Smith New Court bid for the Ferranti shares at a higher price than they would have done otherwise, and even retained the shares in the expectation that the price would rise. Meanwhile, unbeknown to all the parties, a major fraud had been perpetrated on Ferranti, and when the fraud came to light, the Ferranti share price was depressed and Smith New Court lost substantial sums. Smith New Court claimed against

Citibank for fraudulent misrepresentation and was able to claim its entire loss from the transaction.

Notwithstanding the above case, on the whole standards in the City are now very high, and any sharp practice swiftly leads to public criticism and possible loss of future business for any issuing house involved. In addition, as listing particulars and prospectuses are very carefully written, not to mention being long and complex, it is not hard to see why it may be difficult to claim that there has been misrepresentation.

Criminal penalties

In addition to the civil remedies under the FSA there are criminal sanctions under the FSA s 47 and CA 1985 s 70 which refer to penalties for making misleading statements which induce people to make investments. In Northern Ireland, the equivalent legislation is to be found in FSA s 47 and in the Companies (Northern Ireland) Order 1986 art 80. In England the Theft Act 1968 may be applicable as well: it specifically deals with false accounting, false statements by company directors and suppression of documents. These latter charges regularly surface in the wake of collapsing listed companies, but are rare in the context of listing particulars and prospectuses. In Scotland the common law offence of fraud would serve to catch any such criminal activity not already punishable under statute.

In Northern Ireland the relevant legislation would be the Theft Act (Northern Ireland) 1969.

Promoters

Promoters are included in this chapter because historically promoters were persons who assisted in the creation of a company, organised its first contracts, issued and printed the prospectus and arranged all matters in connection with the flotation of a company on the Stock Exchange. Often they held shares in the company itself and stood to make a substantial profit on the sale of their shares on the Stock Exchange. During the latter half of the 19th century and the earlier part of the 20th century promoters occupied the position now taken by issuing houses. Unfortunately, in those unregulated times, there was a number of massive swindles by promoters which led to increasing judicial and statutory attention.

Erlanger and others v *The New Sombrero Phosphate Co and others* (1878) 3 AC 1218. Erlanger, a banker in Paris, was the organiser of a syndicate which for £55,000 acquired the lease of the island of Sombrero in the West Indies. The island supposedly contained valuable phosphate deposits. Erlanger promoted a company to buy the lease from the syndicate and appointed the directors of the company. The directors approved the purchase of the lease from the syndicate without any proper enquiry into the true value of the lease, the quality of the phosphate, or who was benefiting from the sale. The price the company paid the syndicate for the lease was £110,000. Although a prospectus was prepared, Erlanger did not reveal that he was the organiser of the syndicate. When it was discovered that the phosphate was non-existent the company collapsed, Erlanger's nominated directors were dismissed and the company tried to rescind the contract with the syndicate. The House of Lords found in favour of the company and stated that the promoters, including Erlanger, of a company were in a fiduciary relationship with the company. The promoters were required to carry out their actions in the utmost good faith and to disclose all necessary information to the members and independent directors of the company.

Although promoters scarcely exist in their former form nowadays, the CA 1985 and FSA 1986 frequently refer to promoters in order to impose upon them many of the same duties and responsibilities of directors and thereby prevent their former opportunities for fraud. Furthermore, nowadays it is rare to find a promoter who is not a director of the company he is trying to promote, and accordingly he is automatically subject to the fiduciary and other duties expected of directors all as detailed in Chapter 15. The work that promoters used to do is now generally done by issuing houses or sponsors in conjunction with lawyers, accountants and professional company secretaries, all of whom, acting in their professional capacities, would not normally be thought of as promoters. Issuing houses, acting as sponsors, gradually took business from promoters on the grounds of their greater expertise, higher professional standards and their probity. Too many promoters had turned out to be little more than confidence tricksters. As promoters have all but died out, there is little recent case law on promoters and their practice. However, the old case law and the statutory requirements remain valid pending the greater significance of the promoter should issuing houses become too expensive or grand to deal with small businesses wishing to come to the Stock Exchange or any of the other recognised investment exchanges.

Although it might appear that the AIM might provide opportunities for promoters in the 19th century mould, the Stock Exchange has tried to pre-empt that concern by requiring proper training and qualification for AIM advisers, proper authorisation from the Stock Exchange and continual scrutiny by the Stock Exchange.

Summary

1. Stock markets or stock exchanges are places where companies can raise funds by selling securities. Such markets need to be orderly, honest and

accessible. The markets must not only permit the sale of securities for the first time (the primary market) but also provide a continual market for the sale by existing security-holders of their investments to new security-holders (the secondary market). Without the possibility of selling and buying securities a company's securities would be illiquid – which means that no one would buy them.

2. Although theoretically anyone can buy and sell securities on a stock market, in practice most securities are bought by and sold to institutional investors, with private investors making up only a small part of the market.

3. The main stock market in the UK is the Stock Exchange which is authorised by the Financial Services Authority to regulate the dealing in securities generally. Companies that wish to be admitted to the Official List of the Stock Exchange and have their securities traded there are expected to comply with the Stock Exchange's rule book, *Admission of Securities to Listing*, commonly known as the Yellow Book. The Yellow Book rules operate on a purposive basis, not a literal basis. Contravention of the spirit of the rules is as heinous as contravention of the precise wording of the rules.

4. Reasons for having a company's securities quoted on a stock market include:

   (a) access to capital (which can sometimes be used to repay borrowings);
   (b) the founder members can sell their shares in the hope of profit;
   (c) the company's public profile increases, as indeed may the directors' profiles;
   (d) the company's own shares can be used as consideration for taking over other companies.

5. Disadvantages of quotation include:

   (a) the requirement to adhere to the Stock Exchange rules, not all of which may be welcome because of stringent disclosure requirements;
   (b) the financial press may criticise the directors and their activities;
   (c) directors have their management at large general meetings;
   (d) quoted companies are at risk of a takeover;
   (e) investors may only be interested in short-term profit so financial stability is not assured;
   (f) flotation of a company is very expensive and time-consuming and there is no guarantee of success;
   (g) success may not be good for the company or its directors.

6. The principle behind the Yellow Book is of full and open disclosure on every occasion that securities are made available to the public. Generally speaking, standards of disclosure are high. To be admitted to the Official List, a

company must have an established three-year trading record, a market value for its securities of at least £700,000 and must offer at least 25% of its equity to the public.

7. The principle behind the Alternative Investment Market ("AIM") is to allow smaller companies with little or no track record to attract outside investment where the so-called equity gap is a problem. The equity gap is the difficulty some small companies have in attracting capital when the banks refuse to lend and when the company is too small or too young to be listed. AIM is for hardy investors and is inherently very speculative. Its standards of scrutiny are not quite as high as the Official List. Investors investing there must therefore be on their guard.

8. Those who prepare inaccurate listing particulars can be liable for any loss occasioned by investors under the FSA 1986 s 152 if the investors acquired the securities and suffered loss in respect of their securities as a result of misleading information in the listing particulars. Similar rules apply to prospectuses for AIM companies under POSR reg 14.

9. The position of promoters has increasingly been taken over by merchant banks/issuing houses and directors, but historically promoters were involved in many swindles, such as *Erlanger and others* v *The New Sombrero Phosphate Co and others* (1878) 3 AC 1218. Consequently the legislation needs to refer to promoters in case they reappear and try to carry out their former swindles. Promoters must exercise a fiduciary duty towards their companies and disclose any interest they may have in companies offering their shares to the public.

9. THE COMPANY'S CAPITAL

The principle of capital maintenance – reduction of capital – share premium accounts – acquisition and redemption of a company's own shares – financial assistance for private and public companies – capitalisation and bonus issues

In the previous chapter we looked at how a company attracts funds through offering shares to the public; in this chapter we look at what is done with the funds that are brought into the company by the shareholders (the "capital"), and what restrictions are placed upon the use of that capital.

The principle of capital maintenance

Once a shareholder has paid for his shares, in cash, in services or by transferring assets to a company, it is difficult for him ever to take his cash, or cash representing the value of his services or assets, back except by:

- selling his shares to the company;

- a reduction of capital properly made; or

- selling his shares either to an existing shareholder or to someone else.

The third option is usually the easiest, particularly in the case of companies whose shares are easily traded through a recognised investment exchange such as the Stock Exchange. But it may be, particularly in the case of smaller companies, that the articles restrict the sale of shares, or no one is willing to buy the shares. In that event, the shareholder must use one of the first two options by asking or requiring the company to buy his shares, or persuading the company to reduce its capital and give him back his money.

Company law makes it deliberately awkward for a company to buy back shares or reduce its capital. This is because of the fundamental principle of company law known as maintenance of capital. Maintenance of capital means that the capital paid into the company by its subscribers ("contributed share capital") must never be diminished except under special circumstances or through trading losses, although it may be increased from its original level. The sale of shares from one shareholder to another does not alter the contributed share capital of the shares; it merely transfers from one shareholder to another the entitlement to a repayment of contributed share capital on a solvent winding-up.

Creditors wishing to do business with the company are able to see from the company's accounts available at the Registrar of Companies the amount of contributed share capital the company has. Depending on the size of that amount, creditors may choose to do business with that company, on the basis that, at least on each occasion that shares were issued (even if not for very long after that) the company ought to have sufficient funds to make it safe for the creditors to transact business with that company. Accordingly the contributed share capital is sometimes known as the creditors' buffer. That is because if the company is unsuccessful, the contributed share capital will be used by the liquidator primarily to repay creditors; and only once the creditors have been repaid will the shareholders be repaid their funds. The buffer, therefore, protects the creditors.

Even if the shareholders have not paid for their shares in full, the principle still applies, because the liquidator can still ask the holders of partly paid shares to pay the outstanding amount on their shares. He can then use these funds to repay the creditors.

The reality behind the creditors' buffer

Although the term "creditors' buffer" sounds impressive, in that it conveys the impression of a large amount of money available to meet creditors' bills, the reality is actually slightly different. This is because the UK does not require a minimum amount of contributed share capital, except in the case of plcs.

Minimum capital requirements for plcs

Under the CA 1985 ss 117 and 45(2)(a) a plc must have a minimum authorised capital and a minimum nominal value of allotted share capital of £50,000. In addition, each share must be paid up to at least the extent of one-quarter plus any premium (CA 1985 s 45(2)(b)). This means that in theory the paid-up share capital of a plc ought to be at least £12,500, with the promise of a further £37,500 being available if the members are called upon to produce it. This effective guarantee is meant to serve as reassurance for creditors that the plc has funds with which to meet its bills.

Capital requirements for private companies

There are no specified minimum capital requirements for private companies, though there must be shares in existence with a nominal value even if that value is only one penny. As a matter of practice many private companies have an issued share capital of only £100. This figure could be greater or smaller at the company's discretion. It means that on incorporation the company may have only £100 sitting in its bank account or have assets worth only £100. To have so little tends not to inspire creditors with confidence in the company. That is why the directors of small under-funded companies are often required to produce personal guarantees for their companies' loans or leases. To have a small issued share capital is, however, good news for the shareholders, who, provided they have paid up the full nominal value of their shares and have been prudent enough to avoid giving personal guarantees, will have no further liability to the company. It is possible, but rare, to have shares in a private company with a nominal value but with nothing paid up on them at all. Off the shelf companies are occasionally incorporated in this manner. One of the first acts of the new shareholders who purchase such an off the shelf company should be to pay up the shares.

The UK position can be contrasted with other countries' positions. In Germany, all companies are required to have a minimum contributed share capital. This serves to create confidence in the company amongst those who wish to trade with the company. By contrast, in Canada, some companies do not need to have any contributed share capital at all. The shares can be issued at no-par value, which means that there is not even a nominal value which the shareholders must at some stage pay. Accordingly there may be no contributed share capital in the company's bank account. Consequently creditors are very chary of dealing with such companies until they have an established trading record.

Dissipation of the company's share capital

There is a second reason for the illusory nature of the creditors' buffer. This is because although the share capital may have been contributed on the first day of the company's existence, or on any subsequent occasion when further shares are issued, there is nothing in practice to prevent the capital subsequently being spent on creditors' bills. Although spending all the capital in this way would tend to mean that the company was insolvent, the insolvency might not be immediately apparent from an inspection of the company's details with the Registrar of Companies, not least because of the delay in lodging accounts. Furthermore, as will be shown shortly, while capital maintenance rules prevent the payment of dividends beyond certain limits (see Chapter 10), there is nothing to prevent the directors paying themselves large salaries or fees, or holding companies levying high administration charges on their subsidiaries.

Alteration of capital

Increase, subdivision and consolidation

If a company wishes to increase its authorised share capital, it can do so under the CA 1985 s 121(2)(a), provided there is the power to do so under the articles. Table A art 32 provides such a power, and it would be unusual for a company not to have this power. If there is no such power, the articles will need to be altered to be given that power. Alteration of the articles will require a special resolution. If the wording of article 32 is used, an ordinary resolution is required to increase the authorised share capital. One must then supply the Registrar of Companies with a further copy of the company's memorandum of association with the capital clause amended to show that from the date of the resolution the authorised capital was increased to its present figure (CA 1985 s 123).

The reason a company would wish to increase its authorised share capital is if the directors wished to allot more shares and the new allotment would bring the total number of shares to more than the existing authorised amount. It is also possible to decrease the company's authorised share capital under the CA 1985 s 121(2)(e). This means that unallotted shares are cancelled and cannot be issued.

If the company's shares are being subdivided or consolidated, or shares that were to be issued are cancelled, the same procedure must be followed: an ordinary resolution is again necessary, and the Registrar of Companies must be informed (CA 1985 s 122).

The reason a company might wish to subdivide its shares is because there is a perception that shares of a high denomination are less marketable than ones of a lower value. Subdivision may also give more votes to those shareholders whose shares have been subdivided.

Consolidation bundles together shares in larger units. This may be useful administratively.

Under the CA 1985 s 121(2)(c) shares can be converted into stock and stock converted into shares. Stock is effectively a bundle of fully paid shares, transferred in units commonly of £100. Formerly stock was useful because it could be dealt with in fractions and, unlike shares, the company did not need to keep track of the individual shares being transferred. However, as the smallest unit of stock was usually stated in the articles to be a round number for ease of administration, and fully paid shares nowadays do not need to be numbered (CA 1985 s 182(2)) there are no real advantages in using stock and this section of the CA 1985 is rarely used. A few old established companies, such as the Bank of Scotland plc, refer to their shares as stock, more out of tradition than commercial need. Confusingly traded loans to a company are sometimes known as debenture stock. The CA 1985 s 121(2)(c) is not concerned with debenture stock.

Reduction of capital

The term "reduction of capital" refers to the reduction of the share capital paid by the members or, in the case of partly paid shares, due to be paid to the company by the members.

Formerly reduction of capital was illegal (*Trevor* v *Whitworth* (1887) 12 App Case 409) since it depletes the creditors' buffer. However, strict adherence to this rule created commercial hardship without necessarily improving creditors' positions. This is because there were sometimes genuine occasions where the inability to reduce the company's capital prevented the company from ever finding its financial feet as instead of writing off a loss the company had either to be wound up or spend many years trying to re-establish its former financial position. It is now therefore permitted under statute, subject to certain procedures. The main statutory rules for reduction of capital are to be found in the CA 1985 Chapter IV (ss 135–141) which will be examined shortly. However, there are other occasions when share capital is reduced:

- when a private company redeems or buys back its own shares out of capital in accordance with the provisions of the CA 1985 ss 171–175 (to be discussed later in this chapter);

- when a court orders a company to buy back a member's or members' shares as a result of a successful objection to some action of the company's, such as the alteration of the memorandum under the CA 1985 s 5, or following a successful application by a minority of the members of the company under the CA 1985 s 459 (see Chapter 13);

- when a member surrenders, gives or forfeits his own shares to the company (see Chapter 7).

Under these three above circumstances, the normal procedure for reduction of capital (CA 1985 ss 135–141) does not apply.

Reduction of capital under the CA 1985 s 135

There are three main reasons why a company might wish to reduce its share capital:

1. The nominal value of the share capital is greater than the value of the company's assets.

2. The company might wish to get rid of a particular shareholder or class of shareholders.

3. The company might have more working capital than it needs and sees fit to return the excess to its members.

These reasons are placed in order of frequency.

The nominal value of the share capital is greater than the value of the company's assets
If a company has a share capital that is stated in its accounts to be greater than the value of its net assets, perhaps because the company has recently lost money

in some unsuccessful venture, the normal process is for the company to retain all its future earnings until such time as the company's assets are greater than its liabilities. Another way of saying the same thing is that accrued losses must be made good. Normally only once they have been made good may the company start paying dividends again. This is because of the rule (to be looked at in Chapter 10) which says that a company may only pay dividends if it has sufficient distributable profits to do so (CA 1985 s 263(3)). Public companies have an additional rule, known as the net assets test, also discussed in Chapter 10, which states that not only must there be distributable profits, but any distribution must not reduce the company's net asset position to less than the aggregate of its share capital and its undistributable reserves (CA 1985 s 264).

If a company cannot pay a dividend it becomes an unattractive investment for present or new investors. The share price, if a quoted company, will drop. The company may then be more likely to be taken over. Furthermore, it cannot offer its own shares to another company's investors if it attempts a takeover of that other company, because the value of its own shares will be low, reflecting the fact that it cannot pay a dividend.

However, a company can reduce its capital, providing the company jumps through the statutory hoops outlined in the CA 1985 ss 135–141. If reduction takes place, the company's capital is reduced to a position where the share capital more accurately reflects the company's net asset position: the company can then start paying dividends again, and confidence in the company will be restored. The procedure in effect ratifies the write-off of the company's funds.

The company might wish to get rid of a particular shareholder or class of shareholders

Normally if a company agrees to buy shares from a willing shareholder, terms will have to be agreed and the provisions of the CA 1985 ss 161–181 (a company buying back its own shares) will apply (as will be explained later in this chapter). If, however, the company wishes to get rid of unwilling shareholders, there may be problems. If the unwilling shareholders refuse to agree terms, perhaps because they have been enjoying a high rate of dividend as preference shareholders, it may be that the only way the company can expel the unwilling preference shareholders is by fully returning the preference shareholders' capital to them by means of a reduction of capital. Under such circumstances the preference shareholders are likely to object. The point arose in *House of Fraser v AGCE Investments Ltd* [1987] AC 387. The ordinary shareholders passed a special resolution to have the preference shares paid off. The preference shareholders objected, stating that under the terms of the company's articles, the preference shareholders' rights could only be altered with their consent. However, Lord Keith in the House of Lords stated:

(i)   that repayment was not an alteration of the preference shareholders' class rights;

(ii) that the preference shareholders were being repaid strictly in terms of the articles in the same manner as if the company were being wound up with the preference shareholders being repaid in priority to the ordinary shareholders; and

(iii) that being a shareholder inevitably involves the risk that the company may go into liquidation or your shares may be repaid.

This can be contrasted with the case of *Northern Engineering Industrial plc* [1993] BCC 267. A preference shareholder successfully objected that its rights had been varied by a proposed reduction under the CA 1985 s 135. The reduction was designed to repay an institutional preference shareholder its share capital because its charges were very high relative to the benefit to the company of having its investment. The preference shareholder was able to rely on the precise wording of the articles which governed the preference shareholders' rights: the articles in this case stated that reduction of capital was a matter which required the prior consent of the class of preference shareholders; and no such consent had been obtained.

Accordingly if a preference shareholder wishes to protect his position against a reduction of share capital, he should insist that the articles and the rights attaching to his class of shares prevent the majority of shareholders unilaterally reducing the capital and repaying his capital. Reduction of capital by means of repaying the preference shareholders could then only be done with the consent of the class of preference shareholders. Alternatively the preference shareholders can rely on the minority rights under the CA 1985 s 459 (see Chapter 13), though it is clearly better to safeguard preference shareholders' positions by means of well-worded articles and/or a shareholders' agreement.

The company might have more working capital than it needs and wishes to return the excess to its members
This situation does not occur very often. Most companies with excess capital find something to invest the spare funds in. However, if a company wishes to reduce its activities and believes that members' capital could be put to better use in their own hands, it could reduce its capital by repaying members some of their capital. Reduction of capital in this manner took place following the post-war nationalisation of the UK coal industry: some mining companies were paid substantial compensation by the Government, and the members then took the opportunity to take their capital out of their now non-trading companies.

Types of reduction of capital

The CA 1985 s 135(1) and (2) permit reduction of a company's capital if:

- it is authorised under its articles (art 34 of Table A permits it);

- a special resolution is passed; and

- the court confirms the reduction.

The types of reduction are as follows:

1. the extinction or reduction of liability on any of the company's shares in respect of share capital not paid up;

2. the cancellation of any paid-up share capital which is lost or unrepresented by available assets;

3. the paying off of any paid-up share capital in excess of the company's needs.

Although these three methods are the commonest, the legislation does not preclude reduction by other methods if they receive court approval. For example, in *Re Ratners Group plc* [1988] BCLC 685, the share premium account (to which the reduction of capital rules also apply) was cancelled in order to produce funds which could be set off against the cost of goodwill purchased from a company that Ratners had taken over.

Extinction or reduction of liability on any of the company's shares in respect of share capital not paid up (CA 1985 s 135(2)(a))
This means that if a share is only partly paid up, the shareholder never has to pay up the balance owed to the company – or only has to pay a portion of the balance. For example, if a company had £1.00 nominal value shares, each of which was only paid up to the extent of 60p, the company could write off the outstanding 40p, thus relieving the shareholders of ever having to contribute a further 40p per share to the company at some later date. In effect, this turns partly paid £1.00 nominal value shares into fully paid 60p nominal value shares.

As partly paid shares are not as common as they used to be, this occurs infrequently.

The cancellation of any paid-up share capital which is lost or unrepresented by available assets (CA 1985 s 135(2)(b))
This is the corollary of the reduction of share capital where the net assets are no longer represented by available assets, perhaps because of poor trading or a collapse in property prices. Where the share capital suggests that the nominal value per share is, say, £1.00, the reality may be that the actual asset value per share is only 50p. By reducing the nominal value of the share, the issued share capital may amount to a figure equal to or less than the net asset value, which

will allow dividends to be paid again. Shareholders will have lost a good deal of their investment, which is unfortunate, but at least after the reduction they can start to receive dividends again.

It is important for this method of reduction that the capital genuinely is lost. However, there appears to be a conflict of opinions on what should be done if the loss does not remain permanent. If the capital is not lost permanently, the company might get its money back after the reduction and then be tempted to use that money to pay dividends – which would be a form of paying capital to the shareholders by way of dividends. This, in turn, could mean that creditors had been or would be prejudiced.

Re Jupiter House Investments (Cambridge) Ltd [1985] 1 WLR 975. The company had developed a property which turned out to have a number of faults within it. This meant that the value of the building, and of the company, was severely reduced, and the company sought to reduce the share capital to reflect its true financial position. However, there was evidence that the company would be successful in an action for damages for the faults. The judge, in confirming the reduction, said that loss in general had to be permanent, but as it was not possible to establish that the loss was permanent, he was willing to permit the reduction after receiving an undertaking that if the damages claim were successful, the funds received would not be distributed as dividends.

Quayle Munro Ltd, Petitioners, 1993 SLT 723. The company wished to cancel a share premium account and to turn the funds that had been in it into a special reserve. This was to be used to write off a deficit on the profit and loss account. The company gave an undertaking that while there were any outstanding creditors the reserve would not be distributed by way of dividend, but could be used to repay two classes of preference shareholders and to write off future as well as current losses. What is unusual about this case is that whereas a past loss can often, with some confidence, be said to be permanently lost, it is difficult to see how permanently lost a future loss might be.

Re Grosvenor Press plc [1985] 1 WLR 980. The court saw no need for a company to provide any such undertakings, as in the *Quayle Munro* case above, to maintain a reserve for funds which might turn out to be permanently lost. It was held that the creation of the reserve was unnecessary as there was adequate protection for creditors and shareholders in the form of the publicity for the reduction and in the publication of the company's accounts.

In considering the above three cases it is perhaps worth remembering that provided all creditors are fully repaid, or arrangements set up to ensure that their claims can be fully met, it is difficult to see how the creditors might be prejudiced. The position, however, may be different where creditors have been persuaded to settle for less than their full claim and the creditors have consented to the reduction of capital as a better alternative to the company's liquidation.

The paying off of any share capital in excess of the company's needs (CA 1985 s 135(2)(c))
This involves the repayment of capital to the shareholders, and may be done either on a selective basis or on a general basis, depending on the terms of the reduction. It is rare, except in the context of getting rid of unwelcome shareholders.

Procedure for reduction of capital

The following procedure applies not only to share capital, but also to share premium accounts (CA 1985 s 130(3)) and to capital redemption reserves (CA 1985 s 170(4)).

Special resolution
The company must have the authority to reduce its capital under the articles (CA 1985 s 135(1)). If it does not, it must amend the articles. Assuming the company does have authority under the articles, the company must pass a special resolution permitting the reduction (CA 1985 s 135(1)). This will need to be passed at a general meeting unless the company is private, whereupon it may be passed by means of a written resolution (CA 1985 s 381A).

Confirmation by the court
Although the CA 1985 s 136(1) states that the company may then apply to the court for confirmation that the reduction may proceed, in practice it would appear that the company must make an application to the court if the reduction is to be successful. The court is involved in order to protect the interests of creditors.

This is because reducing the capital might mean that there was less cash available with which to pay creditors' bills. Accordingly where the reduction involves:

- the diminution in the amount of unpaid share capital due to be paid to the company, or

- the payment to the company of any paid-up share capital, or

- in any other case where the court so directs,

creditors have to be given the chance to object, if they wish, to the terms of the reduction (CA 1985 s 136(3)).

A court-approved list of all the creditors is prepared and each creditor is told of the reduction. This is normally done by advertisement in a newspaper or by writing to every known and every potential creditor detailing the date by which objections must be received. The creditors then have the opportunity to object, but their objections will not be entertained by the court if:

- the debt is paid;

- the company provides for the debt, either by guarantee or security, or in the event of a disputed or contingent debt, by lodging a sum of money or an insurance bond with the court, sufficient to meet the debt (CA 1985 s 136(5)(a)).

If the company refuses to admit a debt or will not provide funds for it, the court will state the amount that must be set aside to meet the debt (CA 1985 s 136(5)(b)).

The problem with advertising a reduction of capital in a newspaper is that the terms of the advertisement may be misunderstood. Creditors unlearned in company law may erroneously believe that reduction of capital is something to do with liquidation and may cease trading with the company. The advertisement may attract unwelcome publicity. For that reason the court has a commonly used discretion to dispense with the advertisement if it sees fit (CA 1985 s 136(6)). However, this dispensation is not available when the company is reducing its capital by cancelling any paid-up share capital which is lost or unrepresented by assets. This is because this type of reduction is not mentioned in the CA 1985 s 136(2) whereas the two other types of reduction are specifically mentioned.

As a matter of practice, most reductions of capital are agreed by all parties long before the courts are asked to confirm the reduction. The judge's role is to ensure that creditors are not prejudiced in any way, and provided there is no prejudice, the reduction may take place. The judge is not obliged to consider any other issues save, where appropriate, the question of shareholders' rights, of which more later.

If the court grants the order for reduction, the court will issue a minute confirming the details of the reduction. This is sent to the Registrar of Companies who registers it and certifies it. This has the effect of altering the memorandum in terms of the reduction (CA 1985 s 138). The court has the discretion to demand that the company publish its reasons for the reduction of its capital (CA 1985 s 137(2)(b)) and to insist that the company add the words "And reduced" after its name (CA 1985 s 137(2)(a)).

One wonders how many company directors would care to have their company's notepaper headed "John Bloggs and Co Limited and reduced".

Although the court is under a duty to protect the interest of creditors, it is still open to a shareholder to apply to the courts for an injunction or (in Scotland) an interdict to prevent the reduction taking place. This might occur where:

1. a class of shareholders believes that the company has ignored or overlooked rights attaching to the class's shares;

2. shareholders who did not vote in favour of the reduction may continue to feel that the reduction is unfair or inequitable;

3. shareholders may believe that by making life difficult for the company by opposing a reduction, their own shares may be bought out by the company at a price higher than they might have been able to obtain otherwise;

4. some shareholders may believe that the company is acting unwisely even though a special resolution has been passed to approve the reduction.

As regards point 1, the issue has been dealt with above. In principle, the court looks at what the articles say with regard to liquidation; and if the repayment on reduction follows what would have happened anyway in a liquidation, the shareholders can have no grounds for complaint (*Scottish Insurance Corporation Ltd* v *Wilsons and Clyde Company Ltd* [1949] AC 462). However, well drafted articles should adequately protect any class of shareholder against any oversight by the company.

As regards point 2, minority shareholders may raise an action under the minority oppression rules under the CA 1985 s 459 or any of the other minority protection remedies available (see Chapter 13).

As regards 3, the cost in management time may well make it worthwhile settling a court action raised by dissenting shareholders on terms advantageous to the dissenters.

As regards 4, the courts are notoriously reluctant to intervene in matters of commercial judgment. Judges are there to interpret the law, not to decide what commercial actions a company should take.

If, in the process of reduction of capital, a public company's share capital dips below the minimum authorised for a plc (£50,000), the company must either apply to the court for reregistration as a private company as one of the terms of the reduction (CA 1985 s 139(3)), or the company must itself register as a private company under the provisions of the CA 1985 s 53.

Share premium accounts

If a company were to issue shares with a nominal value of £1.00 each and at a price of £1.00, the shares would be said to be issued at par value, and the nominal value of £1.00 per share would be credited to the share capital account. If the same shares were to be offered at a price of £1.20, the nominal value of £1.00 would be credited to the share capital account and the difference of 20p credited to the share premium account. The premium reflects the desirability of the share. Once the premium is in the share premium account it is difficult to get it out again. Like share capital, company law rules make it deliberately difficult to take the premium out of the company. If the share premium account is to be extinguished or reduced, the preceding procedure for reduction of capital must be followed (CA 1985 s 130(3)).

A share premium account may be used for the following purposes under the CA 1985 s 130(2):

- creating bonus shares;

- paying for the company's preliminary expenses, such as the cost of incorporation;

- paying the expenses of any issue of shares or debentures, including the cost of any commission or discount;

- paying a premium on the redemption of debentures of the company

and under the CA 1985 s 160(2) sums held in the share premium account may be used under restricted circumstances indirectly to provide funds for the premium payable on redeemable shares themselves issued at a premium. It is worth noting that the use of share premium account to create bonus shares is in fact a method of enabling shareholders to get cash since the bonus shares could be sold by those entitled to them. However, from an accounting point of view the changing of share premium into share capital merely represents the transfer from one capital account to another, and the overall capital position does not change; and thereby creditors are not prejudiced.

There is no general obligation on the directors to obtain the maximum possible premium (*Hilder* v *Dexter* [1902] AC 474) and indeed it is quite common, especially on the occasion of a rights issue, not to seek the maximum premium since the price must be sufficiently low in a rights issue to attract further investment.

Historically, when one company acquired another (the "target company") and:

(a) the target company's shareholders were allotted shares in the acquiring company's shares as consideration for selling the target company's shares, and

(b) the assets in the target company turned out to be greater in value than the value of the shares in the acquiring company which were used as the consideration for the purchase of the target company's shares,

the difference in value between:

(i) the total nominal value of the shares in the acquiring company's shares given by way of consideration to the target company's shareholders, and

(ii) the actual value of the assets of the acquiring company (once the target company had been taken over)

was credited to the share premium account of the acquiring company. Once there it became undistributable. This occasionally had the benefit that it could not be taxed, but it primarily meant that there was little incentive to take companies over if the target companies' profits were going to be locked in to the acquiring company.

As this was clearly unsatisfactory, merger relief rules were introduced (CA 1985 ss 131–134). Under s 131 if the acquiring company acquires over 90% of the target company's shares and allots the target shareholders shares in the acquiring company as consideration for the target shares, the difference between:

(i) the total nominal value of the newly enlarged acquiring company's shares and
(ii) the total asset value of the newly enlarged acquiring company

need no longer be credited to the share premium account. This means that the target company's funds or assets can be used for distribution.

Acquisition and redemption of a company's shares

For many years, companies were not permitted to buy back their own shares. This was because unscrupulous directors used to perpetrate a simple but effective fraud. Directors of a company whose shares were traded publicly, and who wished to make a great deal of money quickly, quietly used to buy shares in their own company. They would then arrange for a nominee of the company, or a subsidiary, to buy shares in the company on the Stock Exchange. The demand for shares would cause the price of the shares to rise. This was known as "talking the price up". When the price was high enough, the directors would sell all their own shares and decamp for sunny climes. In the meantime, the other shareholders would find that the company's own money or assets had been used to buy the shares and the company's coffers were empty.

It is still generally the case that companies, or their subsidiaries, may not own their own shares (CA 1985 s 143(1)). However, a company may receive a gift of its own shares (CA 1985 s 143(3)), and a company may acquire its own shares:

● under the procedures outlined in the CA 1985 ss 159–181 (to be examined shortly) (CA 1985 s 143(3)(a));

● following a reduction of capital under the procedures outlined in the CA 1985 ss 135–141 (as stated above) CA 1985 s 143(3)(b);

- if ordered to do so by the court following:

    (i)   a successful objection to the alteration of a company's objects under the CA 1985 s 5;
    (ii)   a successful objection to the reregistration of a public company as private under the CA 1985 s 54; or
    (iii) a successful petition under the minority protection rules at the CA 1985 ss 459–461 (see Chapter 13) (CA 1985 s 143(3)(c));

- the forfeiture of shares (see Chapter 7) (CA 1985 s 143(3)(d));

- the surrender of shares in terms of the company's articles (see Chapter 7 (CA 1985 s 143(3)(d)).

Occasionally a company inadvertently does find that a subsidiary owns shares in its holding company. For example, a bank might have a subsidiary whose task is to manage clients' portfolios of investments. Amongst those investments might be shares in the bank itself. This is acceptable, despite the apparent contravention of the general rule, because the beneficial interest (*i.e.* the underlying ownership) of the shares is not with the bank but with the client (CA 1985 ss 144(1) and 145(2)).

If a public limited company acquires shares in which it has a beneficial interest, or a member's shares are surrendered or forfeited to the company, those shares must be cancelled or reissued within three years (CA 1985 s 146(3)(a)), unless the company provided financial assistance to a person to enable him to buy shares in the company and the company has a beneficial interest in the shares. In that case the time-limit is 12 months (CA 1985 s 146(3)(b)). If, in the process, the cancellation of the shares causes the company's issued share capital to fall below £50,000, the company must reregister as a private company (CA 1985 s 146(2)(b)). During the time the company is holding the shares, neither it, the nominee nor the person holding shares for the company may exercise the voting rights in respect of those shares (CA 1985 s 146(4)).

The above rules do not apply to unlimited companies (CA 1985 s 143(1)) because creditors will always be able to have recourse to the members of the company in event of the company's failure to adhere to the capital maintenance rules; and in any event, there are no unlimited companies with shares being traded on a recognised UK investment market.

Companies may now buy back their own shares, but to do so they must closely follow the procedure laid down in statute. The procedure for the financing of a company's acquisition of its own shares is almost the same as the procedure for redemption of redeemable shares.

Why would a company wish to acquire its own shares?

A company might wish to acquire its own shares for the following reasons:

1. The company might wish to be rid of a particular shareholder and be willing to pay him to go away.

2. The shareholders of a company might not personally have funds to buy out a particular shareholder, but the company, being cash-rich, can. In addition, the other shareholders might be anxious that the particular shareholder does not sell his shares to someone they might find uncongenial. The company's purchase of the shares can also help existing shareholders to retain control.

3. The company might be potentially a target for a takeover bid. By buying the shares itself, it makes it more difficult and expensive for the takeover-bidder to take over the company.

4. Buying back the shares may increase the asset value per share even though the company may have had to spend some money buying back the shares. This is particularly significant for property and investment companies if the market price per share is actually below the net assets per share. Buying back some shares can increase the market value of the remaining shares.

5. Buying back some shares can also increase the earnings per share if the company buys back the shares when the ratio of price to earnings is less than the ratio of the company's surplus cash on deposit to the interest earned on that deposit. An increase in earnings per share will increase the market value of the company's shares. A shareholder who has some of his shares bought from him by the company can have a double benefit in that he receives cash for his purchased shares while his remaining shares increase in value.

6. A company may have more cash than it needs, and by buying back its members' shares, it is effectively returning the members' cash to them. Formerly there were tax advantages, particularly for pension funds, in doing this.

7. A company may wish to buy back an employee's shares which he has obtained through being a member of the company's employee share scheme.

8. Shareholders may welcome the fact that surplus capital is going to a safe haven, namely themselves, rather than being used to acquire potentially risky investments.

9. If it is cheaper to fund the company's operations through borrowing than to provide high dividends on shareholders' capital, it makes sense to repay shares and increase debt – particularly if interest rates are low.

The redemption of redeemable shares

Chapter 7 examined redeemable shares and the reasons for and provisions applying to their creation.

When a company redeems redeemable shares, it does not need to pay stamp duty. Provided the company follows the rules specified in the CA 1985 s 160 (financing of redemption) no further procedure is necessary. Once redeemed, the shares cease to exist, though the company may issue new shares to replace them. The share certificates for the redeemed shares should be destroyed or otherwise made invalid.

The rules for the financing of the acquisition of a company's own shares and for the redemption of shares are virtually identical (CA 1985 s 162(2)), and will be discussed in the context of the acquisition by a company of its own shares.

Procedure for the acquisition of a company's own shares

If a company wishes to acquire its own shares, included redeemable ones, it must first have the power to do so under the articles (CA 1985 s 162(1)). Table A art 35, provides for this, and it would be unusual for a company not to have such a clause.

There are two methods of purchase: off-market and market.

Off-market purchase

This takes place where a company buys its own shares privately, *i.e.* not through a recognised investment exchange such as the stock market or the AIM (CA 1985 s 163(1)(a)). It therefore applies to all purchases of shares in private companies and plcs whose shares are not traded publicly. It also applies where a listed company buys its own shares in a private deal with one of its own members without going through the Stock Exchange (CA 1985 s 163(1)(b)) – though the Stock Exchange would still need to be notified.

There are various steps that must be followed:

1. The company and the selling member must draw up a contract for the sale of the shares (CA 1985 s 164(1)). Ideally the contract should be in writing: if it is not, a memorandum of its terms must be prepared, and either the contract or the memorandum should be available for inspection by the members for at least 15 days before the passing of the special resolution referred to in step 2 below (CA 1985 s 164(6)(a)). This is to enable members to peruse the terms of the contract and to consult their professional advisers.

2. The company must be given authority to enter into the contract (CA 1985 s 164(2)). This is done by means of a special resolution of the company. A special resolution requires 75% approval of votes cast. If the company is

private the resolution could be passed by the written resolution procedure (CA 1985 s 381A).

3. The authority granted by the resolution can endure indefinitely for a private company, but for a public company the authority must be given for a period not more than 18 months after the passing of the resolution (CA 1985 s 164(4)). The authority can be revoked, varied or renewed from time to time (CA 1985 s 164(3)), although for plcs, the renewal cannot be for a period greater than 18 months (CA 1985 s 164(4)).

4. Ideally the member selling the shares should not use the votes attached to the shares that he is proposing to sell to the company. Under the CA 1985 s 164(5) the resolution is ineffective if without the selling member's votes in respect of the shares to be sold the resolution would not have been passed.

5. After the passing of the resolution, a copy of the contract, or a memorandum of its terms, must be kept at the registered office of the company for 10 years (CA 1985 s 169(4)) and must be available for inspection by any member or, in the case of a plc, by anyone.

It is possible for a company to enter into a contingent purchase contract. This is effectively an option for the company to buy shares from a member, or an undertaking by the company that it will purchase the shares on the fulfilment of an uncertain event. If the company wishes to do this, the above procedure must be followed in respect of the contingent purchase contract (CA 1985 s 165(2)). If the company makes a payment to obtain the option, that payment must come from distributable profits (CA 1985 s 168(1)(a)).

Market purchases
Market purchases are those conducted on the Stock Exchange or any other recognised investment exchange, such as AIM.

As with off-market purchases, there must be authority under the articles (CA 1985 s 162(1)), though it would be unusual to find a listed or quoted company without such authority. In a market purchase no contract is necessary because the shares are being bought on the open market and from market-makers or from investors generally. It would be impossible to have separate contracts with each seller individually.

There are various matters that need to be addressed:

1. The company must seek authority for the purchase from the members by means of an ordinary resolution (CA 1985 s 166(1)). The authority may be for a one-off purchase, may be general or limited to a particular class, and may be conditional or unconditional (CA 1985 s 166(2)). However, the authority must state the maximum number of shares to be acquired

(normally expressed as a percentage of the issued share capital), and the maximum and minimum prices which it will pay for those shares (CA 1985 s 166(3)). This may also be done by specifying the total sum to be spent on acquiring the shares, or by producing a formula for the company to follow (CA 1985 s 166(6)). The resolution must also state the date of expiry of the authority (CA 1985 s 166(3)). This date must not be more than 18 months from the date of the resolution (CA 1985 s 166(4)), and the 18-month rule applies to any variation of renewal of authority (CA 1985 s 166(4)).

2. The Stock Exchange must receive a copy of the draft resolution for approval. It is also common to produce a circular outlining the reasons for the acquisition.

3. The company must keep the Stock Exchange informed of its purchases, not least because the purchases themselves may well have the effect of driving up the price of the shares.

4. It is possible that the directors of the company might be tempted to use the information about a forthcoming acquisition of the company's shares in order to carry out some insider dealing. This is dealt with in Chapter 12.

Matters that apply to both off-market and market purchases
1. It is not normally possible to assign the company's right to acquire the shares to somebody else (CA 1985 s 167(1)). If a company wishes to do this, it would have to obtain a special resolution to renounce its rights under the contract (CA 1985 s 167(2)) and then persuade the selling member to offer his shares to the would-be assignee.

2. Every company buying its own shares must send a copy of the resolution approving the purchase to the Registrar of Companies within 15 days under the CA 1985 s 380(4)(a) for off-market purchase companies' special resolutions, and under the CA 1985 s 380(4)(h) for market purchase companies' ordinary resolutions.

3. Every company buying back its own shares must inform the Registrar of Companies of the number of shares purchased, their nominal value and the date or dates of purchase (CA 1985 s 169(1)). Public companies must also state the sums spent overall in purchasing the shares and the maximum and minimum prices that were paid for the shares (CA 1985 s 169(2)).

4. Unless the payment for the purchase is made entirely out of the proceeds of a new issue of shares, the company must set up a capital redemption reserve equal in value to the nominal value of the shares that have been acquired (CA 1985 s 170). The capital redemption reserve will be discussed later in this chapter in the context of the financing of the acquisition.

5. The acquired shares must be cancelled by the company on acquisition (CA 1985 s 160(4)).

6. If the company is unable to buy back shares that are due to be bought back on the predetermined date, the seller is not permitted to sue the company for damages for failure to perform the contract (CA 1985 s 178(2)). Although other remedies may be open to the seller, it is also not possible for the seller of shares to raise an action for specific performance by the company if the company shows that it is unable to pay the seller out of distributable profits (CA 1985 s 178(3)).

Items 3, 4, 5 and 6 apply to redeemable shares as well.

The financing of redemption and acquisition

Payment of the nominal value of the shares to be redeemed or acquired
When a company redeems or acquires its own shares, under the CA 1985 s 160(1) it repays the *nominal value* of the redeemed or purchased shares out of:

- distributable profits,

- the proceeds of a new issue of shares made for the purpose of the redemption or acquisition, or

- a combination of these two sources.

Distributable profits are defined in the CA 1985 s 263(3) and effectively are the company's net realised and accumulated profits. For further details of this definition see Chapter 10.

The proceeds of a new issue of shares made for the purchase of the redemption or acquisition means the amount of money raised by the company from subscribers for new shares in the company, less the costs of offering the shares to the subscribers. The new shares must have been issued expressly to raise funds for the redemption or acquisition. Under certain circumstances private companies may pay for the shares out of capital (CA 1985 ss 171–177). This will be considered later.

Payment of any premium on the occasion of the redemption or acquisition
If the redeemed or acquired shares are going to be redeemed or acquired at a *premium* (*i.e.* at greater than their nominal value) the premium must come from distributable profits (CA 1985 s 160(1)(b)), unless the shares about to be redeemed or acquired themselves were themselves issued at a premium (*i.e.* subscribers paid more than the nominal value to buy the shares when the shares

were originally issued). In that event, under the CA 1985 s 160(2), the premium payable on redemption or acquisition may instead be paid out of the proceeds of a new issue of shares made for the purpose of the redemption or acquisition.

However, the actual amount that may be taken out of those proceeds to pay for the premium on redemption or acquisition is restricted to the lesser of:

(i) the total premiums that the company received when the shares to be redeemed or acquired were first issued (CA 1985 s 160(2)(a)), or
(ii) the amount that happens to be in the company's share premium account at the time of the redemption or acquisition, inclusive of any new premiums credited to the share premium account in respect of the new shares issued for the purpose of the redemption or acquisition (CA 1985 s 160 (2)(b)).

Various points arise from this:

1. The company is not obliged to pay for the premium on redemption or acquisition entirely out of the proceeds of a new issue up to the value of the lesser of (i) or (ii) above. It would be possible to pay most of the premium out of distributable profits and the balance out of the proceeds of a new issue of shares. But whatever is taken out of those proceeds must not exceed in value the lesser of (i) and (ii) above.

2. The above rule states that if sums are paid out of the proceeds of the new issue of shares to pay for the premium on redemption or acquisition, the proceeds of the new issue will be depleted by the amount of the payment. Under certain circumstances this could have the effect of reducing the company's share capital as there is no unequivocal requirement to make good the depletion which the proceeds of the new issue will have suffered. The legislation is silent as to whether or not the depletion of the share capital needs to be remedied by adding to the capital redemption reserve (to be discussed shortly) an amount equal to the extent of the depletion of the proceeds of new issue of shares. This appears to be a legislative oversight which remains unresolved.

An example may help. Albert is allotted 2,000 redeemable shares each with a nominal value of £1.00 in Bump Limited. He pays Bump Ltd £1.25 for each share, making a total of £2,500. Of the figure of £2,500, £2,000 goes into the share capital account and £500 into the share premium account.

Five years later, Albert's shares are to be redeemed at a premium of 50p per share. This means that he expects to receive from Bump Ltd his original nominal value of £2,000 plus 2,000 × 50p, making a total of £3,000.

Bump Ltd would pay for the nominal value of the shares (£2,000) out of distributable profits or out of the proceeds of a new issue of shares to fund the redemption of Albert's shares (CA 1985 s 160(1)(a)) or a combination of these two methods.

Bump Ltd could pay the premium of £1,000 out of distributable profits (CA 1985 s 160(1)(b)), but as Albert's shares were issued at a premium originally, the premium of £1,000 could be paid out of the proceeds of a new issue of shares to fund the redemption of Albert's shares (CA 1985 s 160(2)).

However, the amount that can be taken from those proceeds is restricted to the figure representing the lesser of:

(i) Albert's original premiums (£500), or
(ii) whatever may be in the share premium account at the time of redemption.

If since Albert's original investment the share premium account had increased because there had been an issue of 1,000 ordinary shares of £1.00 nominal value to Clare, who paid a premium of 80p per share, the total amount of the share premium account would be £500 + £800, being £1,300. In those circum-stances only the lesser figure of £500 in (i) could be drawn from the proceeds of the new issue of shares, and given to Albert as payment of part of his £1,000 premium on redemption. The rest of the payment for Albert's premium would have to come from distributable profits.

The capital redemption reserve

When shares are redeemed or acquired by the company, the company pays the shareholder the nominal value of the shares plus any premium on redemption or acquisition, and the shares are cancelled. The shares then cease to exist. On the fact of it, this would mean that the share capital had diminished by the amount of the payment.

Were this to happen, however, the share capital would have been reduced without the views of the creditors being taken into account. If this were per-mitted, an unscrupulous company might well be tempted to acquire all its direc-tors' shares in order to repay them their investment before they disappeared with the money at the expense of other shareholders and the creditors.

In order to prevent this, and to adhere to the principle of capital maintenance, when shares are redeemed or acquired wholly out of distributable profits (as opposed to the proceeds of a new issue of shares) a special capital fund is created, called the capital redemption reserve (CA 1985 s 170(1)). Into the capi-tal redemption reserve is placed a sum of money equalling exactly the nominal value of the cancelled shares. This means that after the redemption or acquisition the total capital of the company remains the same as before, albeit that the share capital is reduced by the amount of the cancelled redeemable or acquired shares, and a capital redemption reserve is created equal in value to the amount of those cancelled shares.

An example may help:

ABC Ltd
Balance sheet as at 31 December 19X1.

	£	£
Fixed assets		£100,000
Current assets (excluding cash)	45,000	
Creditors	(21,000)	
		24,000
Cash in bank		35,000
		159,000
Financed by		
80,000 ordinary £1.00 shares fully paid		80,000
30,000 redeemable £1.00 shares fully paid		30,000
Profit		49,000
		159,000

On 1 January 19X2 20,000 redeemable shares are redeemed at a premium of 10% (*i.e.* £2,000). This is the new balance sheet:

ABC Ltd
Balance sheet as at 1 January 19X2.

	£	£
Fixed assets		£100,000
Current assets (excluding cash)	45,000	
Creditors	(21,000)	
		24,000
Cash (35,000 – 20,000 – 2,000)		13,000
		137,000
Financed by		
80,000 ordinary £1.00 shares fully paid		80,000
10,000 redeemable £1.00 shares fully paid		10,000
Capital redemption reserve		20,000
Profit (49,000 – 20,000 – 2,000)		27,000
		137,000

As shown above, the capital redemption reserve is created equal in value to the nominal value of the redeemed shares. The profit figure is reduced and there are fewer funds available with which to pay a dividend. The overall capital position remains the same.

If the payment for the shares to be redeemed or acquired is paid for:

(i)   wholly out of the proceeds of a new issue of shares;
(ii) made to provide funds for the redemption or acquisition;
(iii) and those proceeds equal to or exceed the nominal value of the shares to be redeemed or acquired,

the incoming proceeds replace the outgoing payment, and at no stage do the shares to be redeemed or acquired coexist with the newly issued shares (CA 1985 s 160(5).

If the payment for the shares to be redeemed or acquired is:

(i) wholly or partly out of the proceeds of a new issue of shares, and
(ii) the proceeds of the new issue of shares is less than the nominal value of all the shares to be redeemed or acquired,

the difference between the total proceeds and the total nominal value of the redeemed or acquired shares is transferred to the capital redemption reserve (CA 1985 s 170(2)). Without this provision, it would be impossible for the company to keep the overall capital position the same as it was before the redemption or acquisition. There would be a gap representing the difference between the nominal value of the cancelled redeemable or acquired shares and the sums received from the proceeds of the new issue of shares. That gap would need to be plugged by distributable profits or conceivably some other source, such as a gift.

The main effect of creating a capital redemption reserve, apart from protecting the creditors' buffer, is to reduce the amount of money available with which to pay dividends. This is because the capital redemption reserve is created out of funds taken out of distributable profits.

The capital redemption reserve can only be reduced by means of the reduction or capital procedures outlined earlier in this chapter, but it may be used to pay up bonus shares (CA 1985 s 170(4)).

Redemption or purchase of own shares out of capital

It is possible for private companies, but not public ones, to pay for the redemption or acquisition of their own shares out of capital under the CA 1985 ss

171–177. It is a permitted form of reduction of capital, although the procedure is carefully designed to ensure that members or creditors have the opportunity to object if they believe that their interests are being threatened.

The procedure is as follows:

1. The company must have power under its articles to reduce its capital. Table A art 34 provides for this, and art 35 allows a company to purchase or redeem its own shares out of funds other than distributable profits or the new issue or shares – in other words, capital. Most private companies are likely to have these terms.

2. The directors must first make a statutory declaration on a Form 173 under the CA 1985 s 173(3) stating:

   (i) that having investigated the company's business and prospects they are of the view that at the date the proposed payment out of capital is to take place there will be no grounds on which the company would be unable to pay its debts, and

   (ii) that for the period of 12 months following that date, the company will be able to carry on business as a going concern and be able to pay its debts as they fall due.

   "Debts" in this context means prospective debts (*i.e.* likely debts) and contingent (*i.e.* potential debts, such as a liability under a disputed claim for damages) as well as actual debts (CA 1985 s 173(4)). The company's inability to pay its debts as they fall due is to be ascertained by the same criteria as are used when a company is compulsorily wound up by the courts on the grounds of inability to pay debts as they fall due in terms of the Insolvency Act 1986 s 122. The definition of the inability to pay debts as they fall due is further explained in Chapter 21.

   The significance of the directors' statutory declaration is emphasised by the Insolvency Act 1986 s 76 where it states that where:

   (i)   a company is wound up;

   (ii) the company had made a payment out of capital in respect of the redemption or acquisition of its own shares;

   (iii) the company's net assets are less than its liabilities; and

   (iv) the company went into liquidation within a year of the date of the payment

   the person from whom the shares were redeemed or acquired and the directors who signed the statutory declaration without reasonable grounds for doing so are jointly and severally liable to contribute to the company's funds to the extent of the capital payment.

A director who makes the statutory declaration without reasonable grounds for doing so is also liable to a fine or imprisonment under the CA 1985 s 173(6).

3. As the law does not trust the directors necessarily to be the best judges of whether or not the company is solvent and likely to remain so for the following year, the company's auditors are required to submit to the Registrar of Companies a report addressed to the directors stating that they:

   (i)   have looked at the company's financial standing;
   (ii) have checked the calculation of the permissive capital payment (to be discussed shortly); and
   (iii) are unaware of anything to suggest that the directors' belief in the company's current and continuing solvency is unreasonable (CA 1985 s 173(5)).

4. The payment out of capital must be approved by a special resolution of the company (CA 1985 s 173(2)). The resolution may be passed by means of the written resolution procedure. The resolution must be passed within seven days after the date of the directors' statutory declaration (CA 1985 s 174(1)). As with the special resolution for a company acquiring a member's shares, the votes representing the shares that are to be bought by the company may not be counted if without them the resolution would not have been passed (CA 1985 s 174(2)). At the time of the voting on the resolution the statutory declaration and the auditors' report must be available for inspection by the members (CA 1985 s 174(4)).

5. Within a week of the resolution the company must arrange for the Gazette and a suitable national newspaper to publish a notice under the CA 1985 s 175(1) stating:

   (i)   that the company has approved a payment of capital in order to redeem or purchase its own shares;
   (ii) the amount of the permissible capital payment;
   (iii) that the statutory declaration and the auditors' statement may be inspected at the company's registered office; and
   (iv) that any creditor or a dissenting member (see 7 below) may apply to the courts within a period of five weeks beginning on the date of the resolution to object to the payment out of capital.

Given the complexity of the concept of the permissible capital payment (to be discussed shortly), it is curious that the legislation requires the notice to state the figure for the permissible capital payment. Without an understanding of the accounts of the company in question, stating the amount of the permissible capital payment is unlikely to be of much use to an objecting creditor.

6. The company must send the Registrar of Companies a certified copy of the special resolution and copies of the directors' statutory declaration and the auditors' report (CA 1985 s 175(5)). Those documents must also remain available for inspection at the company's registered office from the earlier of the date of the notice in the Gazette, or the date of the notice in the other newspapers, until five weeks after the date of the resolution (CA 1985 s 175(6)(a)).

7. During the period of five weeks from the date of the resolution any member of the company who has not previously voted in favour of the resolution approving the payment out of capital, or any creditor, can apply to the court to have the resolution cancelled (CA 1985 s 176). The company must then tell the Registrar of Companies (CA 1985 s 176(3)). The court can then, as it sees fit, under the terms of the CA 1985 s 177:

    (i)   approve the application by the member or the creditor;
    (ii)   set up arrangements for the buy-out of dissentient shareholders or the protection of creditors;
    (iii) confirm or cancel the resolution;
    (iv)   make such alterations in the company's memorandum and articles of association as it sees fit, or make an order preventing any alteration of the memorandum of articles of association.

8. If there is no objection, the payment out of capital must take place within a period of two weeks beginning five weeks after the date of the special resolution (CA 1985 s 174(1)).

The permissible capital payment

When a company redeems or acquires its own shares, it normally pays for them out of distributable profits. The shares representing the redeemed or acquired shares are cancelled, but a capital redemption account is set up with funds in it equal to the nominal value of the redeemed or acquired shares. The company's capital is thus maintained at its previous level. Alternatively, new shares are issued, and the proceeds thereof are used to make the payment to the member whose shares are being redeemed or acquired. However, if the company follows the procedure outlined above, the company need not pay for the redemption or acquisition entirely out of distributable profits or the proceeds of a new issue of shares. It may, in addition, be able to use the company's own capital to make that payment, thereby writing off or reducing some of its own capital. The permissible capital payment ("PCP") is a method for calculating the actual amount of money which can be taken out of capital to help pay for redeemed or acquired shares. A company would only need to use such capital if it had already exhausted both:

(i)   whatever distributable profits were available; and

(ii) the proceeds of a new issue of shares made specially for the purpose of the redemption or acquisition (CA 1985 s 171(3)).

If there is no new issue at all, then the company merely has to have exhausted the distributable profits (if any).

One of the common difficulties in understanding the PCP is that it is not always realised that the PCP is not the actual amount of money that is paid out of capital to the member redeeming or selling his shares to the company, but a formula for calculating by how much the company's total capital accounts and revaluation reserve may be reduced.

The PCP is expressed thus:

Price of redeeming or acquiring the shares (*i.e.* the nominal value plus any premium or less any discount) – available profits – proceeds of new issue = PCP

For example: A company might have to pay £1,000 to redeem A's 1,000 £1.00 shares. If its available profits amount to £500, and the company has just issued some new shares which only brought in £300, the PCP would be £1,000 less £500 less £300 = £200. If the PCP plus the proceeds of any new issue is *greater* than the nominal value of the shares being redeemed or acquired, the difference may be taken from any of:

• the fully paid share capital;

• the capital redemption reserve;

• the share premium account;

• revaluation reserve (CA 1985 s 171(5)).

What this means in practice is that in addition to the reduction of the company's share capital caused by the cancellation of the shares being redeemed or acquired, one of the above capital accounts or revaluation reserve is debited with a further sum representing the difference between (a) the total of the PCP and the proceeds of the new issue, and (b) the nominal value of the shares being redeemed or acquired.

For example: If Bee Ltd is required to redeem C's 1,000 preference £1.00 shares at a premium of 20p per share (*i.e.* £1,200), has only £150 available profit and issued 800 £1,000 shares to help pay for the redemption of C's shares, the PCP would be (£1,000 + £200) less £150 less £800 = £250.

Is the PCP + the proceeds greater than the nominal value of C's shares? Is £250 + £800 greater than £1,000? Yes. Under the CA 1985 s 171(5) the balance of £50 may be taken from any of the capital accounts or the revaluation reserve above. Let us assume it is taken from the share premium account.

The actual payment to C of £1,200 would be reflected in the balance sheet by the reduction of the net assets by £400 (*i.e.* £1,200 – £800). The share capital would be reduced by £200 (*i.e.* £1,000 – £800). The profit figure of £150 would be extinguished. The share premium account would be reduced by £50.

As can be seen, the occasions when the additional amount is going to be taken out of a capital account or a revaluation reserve are likely to arise when:

(i)   the price of redemption or acquisition is high;
(ii) distributable profits are low; and
(iii) the proceeds of a new issue of shares made to replace the redeemed or acquired shares are low also.

If the PCP plus the proceeds of the new issue are *less* than the nominal value of the repurchased or redeemed shares, the difference is transferred from distributable profits to the capital redemption reserve (CA 1985 s 171(4)). This is to partially maintain the creditors' buffer referred to earlier in this chapter. The share capital may be reduced by the redeemed or acquired shares which are cancelled, but the company's overall capital position is to some extent restored by the creation of the capital redemption reserve.

For example: If D Ltd, with a share capital of £10,000, is to buy back E's 1,000 ordinary £1.00 shares at par, has distributable profits of £600 and was only able to obtain proceeds of £300 by way of a new issue of shares made to replace E's shares, the PCP would be £1,000 – £600 – £300 = £100.

Is the PCP + proceeds of new issue less than nominal value of E's shares? Is £100 + £300 less than £1,000? Yes. The difference is £600 and the capital redemption reserve is credited with £600.

The actual payment of £1,000 to E would be reflected in the balance sheet by the reduction of net assets by £700 (*i.e.* E's £1,000 less the new issue of shares for £300). The share capital would be reduced to £9,300 (*i.e.* £10,000 – £1,000 + £300) since E's shares would no longer exist. The former profit figure of £600 would be extinguished as the £600 is credited to the capital redemption reserve. The capital redemption reserve in this instance goes some way to maintaining the creditors' buffer notwithstanding that £100 of the company's total capital has effectively been written off. The company's total capital position would be £9,900 (*i.e.* £10,000 – £1,000 + £300 + £600).

In order to be able to calculate the PCP it is necessary to know what the distributable profits are. These are calculated in terms of the CA 1985 s 263 and are discussed in Chapter 10. The accounts used for this purpose must relate to a period ending not more than three months prior to the date of the directors' statutory declaration (CA 1985 s 172(6)). The available distributable profits must also take account of any lawful distributions since that date and up to the time of the declaration (CA 1985 s 172(4)), lawful distribution in this context meaning such payments as lawfully given financial assistance (CA 1985 s 172(5)(a)) or any payment for shares acquired by the company under a court order (CA 1985 s 172(5)(b)).

Financial assistance by a company for the purchase of its own shares

The original prohibition on companies buying their own shares arose because of the fear that companies would use their own funds to buy shares in the market in order to give a good impression of the company's viability. One method that was designed to get round this prohibition, or to disguise the purchase of a company's own shares, was for the company to lend money to a favoured individual who would buy the shares instead, usually in return for some other favour received at a later date. Such an activity was clearly unacceptable as well.

This practice is known as financial assistance. In general, it is prohibited under the CA 1985 ss 151–158, which follows Article 23 of the Second European Directive on Company Law (77/91/EEC). It is also indirectly prohibited in the *Admission of Securities to Listing*, Chapter 9, section 16. The CA 1985 s 151(1) prohibits direct or indirect financial assistance to a person acquiring, or proposing to acquire shares in the company, either before or at the same time as the acquisition. To put it more simply, the company may not help an investor buy its own shares. The CA 1985 s 151(2) covers the position where a person acquires shares in a company and a liability has been incurred (which for most practical purposes will mean that the person has borrowed money with which to fund the purchase of the shares), and the company then provides financial assistance directly or indirectly for the purpose of reducing or discharging the liability (*i.e.* the company then directly or indirectly repays the borrowed money even though it was not a party to the original loan).

Financial assistance is widely defined in the CA 1985 s 152(1) and covers virtually any form of gift, loan, guarantee, or indemnity by the company whereby the investor is enabled to buy shares in the company more easily than he might otherwise have done. There is a sweep-up sub-clause saying that financial assistance is any form of assistance by the company to a favoured investor which has the effect of reducing the company's net assets to a material extent. There are, however, certain exceptions which will be looked at later.

At one time the penalty when a company or its directors were convicted of financial assistance was so small it was considered a price that was worth paying. This flouting of the rules permitted various well-known abuses:

1. A takeover bidder would borrow money to take over a company. Once he had won control of a majority of the votes, he would make the company guarantee his loan and then sell off its assets. The company would then pay the takeover bidder substantial dividends which he would use to repay the loan. The company thereby effectively underwrote the provision of funds to help the bidder buy the shares. This deprived the other shareholders of value.

2. A company would lend money to a favoured bidder in order to enable him to buy the company rather than let anyone else do so, thus rigging the market and not necessarily being the best use of shareholders' funds.

3. A company ("the takeover bidder") involved in taking over another company ("the target company"), and offering its own shares as consideration, would have an interest in keeping its own share price as high as possible in order to encourage the target company shareholders to exchange their shares for the takeover bidder's shares. In order to keep the takeover bidder's share price high and its shares desirable, the takeover bidder would lend money to certain favoured investors to enable them to buy its shares, as part of what is known as a share support scheme. Buying the shares would indicate demand and the share price would therefore rise or remain high, thereby making the takeover bidder's shares more attractive to the target company's shareholders. The takeover bidder would give the favoured investors indemnities in case the share price fell and the favoured investor lost money. As a loan might be all too obvious in the accounts, some of the favoured investors would fund the purchase themselves, but later render the company an invoice, the terms of which might be sufficiently innocuous to fail to excite the notice of an auditor. The invoice would be the fee for the investor having carried out his instructions to buy shares in order to keep the share price high and to reimburse the favoured investor for any loss he might have suffered. One such spurious invoice used in the Guinness scandal read as follows: "Consultancy services re acquisitions and commercial services in Europe."

   A variation of this is instead of the share price supporter being paid a fee for bolstering the share price, the supporter asks for a particular contract or some other commercial opportunity in return.

4. A company would lend money to an investor to enable him to buy shares, create demand, and at the critical moment when the share price was as high as it was likely to go, he would sell all his shares and pocket the profit, having repaid the company.

   In all of these above situations, there is always the danger that the borrower would default and refuse to repay the loan, thus depriving the company of funds and technically reducing the company's capital.

The harm that the legislation seeks to prevent

The principal harm adduced by the above activities is that the market is misled or rigged in favour of a few selected individuals. In the Guinness affair certain shareholders were treated more favourably than others and were in the happy position of knowing that if they bought shares they could not lose – even if the market altered against them. This was not an option open to all the other shareholders.

A further consequence of unfair financial assistance is that if a particular benefit is conferred to a shareholder as his price for supporting the share price, he is probably effectively obtaining a gift from the company to the detriment of the shareholders. It is an inefficient use of company resources. In the Guinness affair, one of the Americans involved in the share support scheme was offered the franchise for the distribution of certain of Distillers products (assuming the takeover went ahead) in return for buying shares in Guinness in order to keep the Guinness share price high. Because of the selective offer of the franchise, the franchise was not, as it normally would have been, put out to tender. Guinness was thereby potentially deprived of the possibility of obtaining a better price for the tender.

A third harm is that financial assistance in the hands of the unscrupulous can lead to asset-stripping. Asset-stripping in itself is not illegal, despite its social consequences from the point of view of employment. It is legitimate for one company to take over another and then to sell off the assets of the target company, but it is not legitimate to do so on the basis of a loan taken out by the takeover bidder which is repaid out of the assets of the target (CA 1985 s 151(2)) – unless the takeover company is a private company, in which case the law does not operate to prevent the financial assistance. Where a public company is involved, the takeover company must fund the takeover out of its own resources.

Non-contentious financial assistance

Although it is entirely proper that the legislation should seek to outlaw the dubious practices outlined above, there are occasions when financial assistance might take place without any sinister motive. Such occasions occur when:

(i)   the members are content that their company provides the financial assistance;
(ii) financially assisting an investor to buy shares in the company is the only alternative to the collapse of the company;
(iii) the company is being restructured (*i.e.* its finances are being reorganised) and financial assistance is part of the overall plan for improving the finances of the company;
(iv) there is a management buy-out or buy-in and some form of financial assistance is an important part of the funding of the operation;

(v) where the net assets are not significantly reduced by the financial assistance.

What a "significant" reduction might be would depend on the individual circumstances of each company.

The legislation has therefore to prevent the abuses described above but to permit innocuous or non-contentious financial assistance. Given the need to satisfy both the requirement to outlaw fraudulent practices and permit innocent ones, it is not surprising that the legislation is not to everyone's satisfaction. In particular, the drafting of the legislation has thrown up queries as to whether or not a particular matter is financial assistance. Some of these matters are:

- arrangement fees: a company pays stockbrokers a fee for finding an investor who provides more capital;

- legal fees: a venture capital company invests in a new company and has its legal fees paid for by the company in which it has just invested;

- a company has a floating charge in favour of a lender. One of the terms of the charge states that all subsidiaries must also grant floating charges to the lender as well. The company, in the normal course of its borrowing from the lender, uses funds from the lender to take over another company. That company is then required to grant a floating charge in favour of the lender;

- during a takeover bid, there may conceivably be those who are being financially assisted by the company who are thus being given an advantage by the company. But what about those who are "piggybacking" on the advantaged investors without knowing the details of the financial assistance, but who just happen to suspect that some discreet financial assistance is taking place? Are the piggybackers to be penalised as well?

In order to get round some of these difficulties and to comply with the EC Directive on Financial Assistance, the legislation permits certain specific exemptions for both private and public companies and permits the *gateway* procedure for private companies.

The specific exemptions: the purpose exception and the good faith exception
Under the CA 1985 s 153(1) a company may give financial assistance for the purpose of an acquisition of shares in it or its holding company if:

(i) the company's principal purpose in giving that assistance is not to give it for the purpose of any such acquisition, or the giving of the assistance for that purpose is but an incidental part of some larger purpose of the company, and

(ii) the assistance is given in good faith in the interests of the company.

These two exceptions are known respectively as the "purpose exception" and the "good faith exception".

This subsection corresponds with the CA 1985 s 151(1), this being the prohibition on direct or indirect financial assistance to a person acquiring or proposing to acquire shares in the company.

There is a similar subsection (CA 1985 s 153(2)) which corresponds with the CA 1985 s 151(2) and refers to indirect assistance by a company towards helping a person repay a loan which had been taken out in order to buy shares in the company. The CA 1985 s 153(2) permits a company to reduce a person's liability (such as, say, a loan from a bank used to help the person buy the company's shares) where the reduction of liability is not the company's principal purpose and is but an incidental part of some larger purpose of the company. The good faith provision is also repeated.

These two subsections have over the years attracted a great deal of debate. This is partly because they are not immediately intelligible, and partly because company lawyers were waiting for a test case to clarify them. The subsections were inserted to deal with problems that arose in the two undernoted cases, both of which were decided under the terms of the Companies Act 1948 s 54. The Companies Act 1948 prohibited any form of financial assistance.

Belmont Finance Corporation v *Williams Furniture Ltd (No 2)* [1980] 1 All ER 393. Company A sold goods to company B. Company A then used the proceeds of sale to buy shares in company B. The question arose as to whether or not this was financial assistance. Buckley LJ said that where the sale and purchase was a normal commercial transaction, there was no financial assistance; but where the sale and purchase was collusive with the express purpose of putting company A in funds to buy shares in company B, that was financial assistance. This immediately led to questions about the difficulty of proving collusion, and to questions as to what the law was where there was both a commercial transaction and collusion: how could the two be realistically separated?

It is because of the difficulties caused by the *Belmont* case that the purpose exception was produced. If financial assistance takes place, either inadvertently or only as a relatively insignificant issue within a greater plan, the purpose exception ought to render it non-criminal.

The second problem related to the use of financial assistance for a questionable purpose: *Armour Hick Northern Ltd* v *Whitehouse* [1980] 3 All ER 833. A subsidiary of a company made a payment to a shareholder in its holding company in order to encourage him to sell his shares in the holding company. He duly sold his shares for their proper price. The financial assistance was therefore made to a seller not a buyer of shares and thereby was not a breach of the Companies Act 1948 s 54.

Accordingly the blanket prohibition on financial assistance had to be amended, and the good faith principle was introduced to catch any collusion. The result is s 152(3) and (4).

The purpose exception and the good faith exemption came before the courts in the case of *Brady* v *Brady* [1989] AC 755 (HL). Two brothers both ran a group of companies specialising in haulage and drinks. The two brothers quarrelled, and after a first sortie to the courts agreed terms on how to divide up the business between themselves. At the last minute, one brother decided that the division was not to his liking, so he refused to complete the transaction. His brother then sued for specific performance, to be met by the counterclaim that the division involved financial assistance and was therefore illegal.

The case finally reached the House of Lords where Lord Oliver said that the undoubted financial assistance was not an incidental part of some larger purpose. On the contrary: there was nothing incidental about the financial assistance; the entire purpose of the financial assistance was to enable one brother to buy shares in the company assisting his purchase. Lord Oliver expressly drew a distinction between the reasons for which a company might provide financial assistance to a shareholder, and the purpose for which the financial assistance was given. In this case the reasons for the financial assistance were to enable the division of the businesses to take place in a satisfactory manner, to keep the companies going as opposed to collapsing into liquidation and to end the management deadlock. While these were excellent reasons for providing financial assistance, they were not the purpose of the financial assistance, which was to enable the brother to buy the shares. Lord Oliver was keen to give meaning to the distinction between purpose and reason, and to ensure that s 151 served as a sieve through which legitimate financial assistance which was indeed a small and insignificant part of some greater corporate purpose could pass, while other financial assistance could not. He therefore held that the financial assistance in this case was not an incidental part of some larger purpose; it was an essential part of the acquisition of the shares by the brother. However, he then directed that an order for specific performance could nevertheless be made because the companies involved were private companies anyway and could have followed the gateway procedure.

This decision has been criticised by some, mostly by business people, on the grounds that the distinction between purpose and reason is too fine for most people to understand readily. In terms of the CA 1985 s 151 it may well be logically correct, but ignores the commercial reality that without the division, the business might well have collapsed while the brothers argued.

As for the question of good faith, the Court of Appeal said that the financial assistance had not given in good faith, while the House of Lords said that it had. Either way it does not lead to confidence in what is meant in this context by "good faith".

There is a particular irony in the *Brady* case in that, as Lord Oliver pointed out, as the companies were private anyway, they could have done as much financial assistance as they liked, provided they had followed the gateway procedure. Quite why this obvious point was not noticed earlier is not clear, but it does not entirely reflect well on the Bradys' advisers. The *Brady* decision was approved in *Plaut* v *Steiner* (1989) 5 BCC 352, where the judge held that the financial assistance was designed not to help carry out the division of the company but to make the proposed terms of a deal between the parties more attractive. In this case the company providing the assistance became insolvent because of the difficulties of providing the assistance: it was held that the financial assistance could not therefore have been given in the best interests of the company.

In these two cases the judges were circumscribed by the wording of the statute. In the *Brady* case Lord Oliver confessed that he was not entirely clear as to what was meant by "larger purpose" and in order to give it meaning at all, gave it the restrictive meaning he did. It is arguable that the *Brady* decision leaves something to be desired on commercial grounds, and this problem, and various suggested remedies, is extensively discussed in a DTI Consultation Paper (October 1993) on financial assistance. One of the DTI recommendations is expressly to overturn the *Brady* decision in order to permit financial assistance given in good faith for the benefit of the company. Another is to permit financial assistance where the assistance does not materially reduce the net assets of the company.

The case of *Barclays Bank plc* v *British and Commonwealth Holdings plc* [1996] BCLC 1 may however suggest a movement away from the strict rule in *Brady*.

Caledonia Investments plc did not wish to realise all its investment in the defendant ("B & C") by means of a straight sale in the market since that would have depressed the price it might otherwise have achieved for its shares. It therefore arranged to have its investment changed into redeemable preference shares. If B & C failed to redeem those shares, Caledonia had a right under an option agreement to make a further company, Tindalk Ltd, which was financed by Barclays and other banks, buy the shares. Tindalk, as the new owner of the shares, would then require B & C to redeem the shares. In order to persuade the banks to enter into this transaction, B & C covenanted to maintain certain asset ratios.

Tindalk duly was required to buy the shares. B & C was unable to maintain its covenant and failed to redeem the shares. The banks sued B & C for damages for breach of covenant. As a claim for damages ranks higher in a liquidator's order of repayment of debts than the payment of redemption monies to a shareholder, the banks, as they were probably well aware, were better off with a claim for damages than with a right to the redemption monies.

It is arguable that this arrangement is quite close to financial assistance, in that without the covenants the banks would not have entered into the transaction in the first place. However Aldous L J stated that the arrangement was "reassurance" rather than financial assistance. Since the arrangement did not constitute indirect financial assistance, B & C could not avoid liability under the covenants on the grounds of the illegality of any potential financial assistance.

It is at least arguable that if one borrows Lord Oliver's distinction in *Brady*, the whole purpose of the covenants was to induce Tindalk to buy the shares, even if the reason was to maximise Caledonia's chances of getting a good price for its shares. But the Court of Appeal appears to have drawn back from the distinction. Had it done so, it would have prevented Barclays' claim, or, to look at it another way, allowed B & C to avoid liability on the grounds of the illegality of financial assistance to which it had been a willing party.

As the issue remains unclear, it is to be hoped that if ever there is an opportunity in the Government's legislative timetable for an Act amending parts of the current Companies Acts 1985 and 1989, space will be found for revision of the rules applying to financial assistance. It is important that revision takes place, because at the moment, a breach of financial assistance is a criminal offence both for the company and the officers of the company who authorised it (CA 1985 s 151(3)). There are various points that arise because of this:

1. It is curious that the legislation seeks to penalise the company for something which its shareholders and many employees may not have known anything about. Financial assistance, where it has taken place and been subsequently discovered, is usually organised in secret by the directors. While there may be some merit in penalising directors who are failing to comply with the law, it seems odd to fine the company – and thereby indirectly punish the shareholders – if they had no knowledge of what was taking place.

2. There is concern that the finer points of the financial details of financial assistance may well be beyond the ability of certain juries to cope with. It has been suggested that the reason the prosecution in the Guinness case dropped the charges of financial assistance was because of the difficulties of explaining to a jury what exactly is the difference between the "larger purpose" and a "reason" in terms of Lord Oliver's judgment in the *Brady* case.

3. The sanctions might be more effective if those who obtained the financial assistance were required to indemnify the company for any loss or hand over any profit made out of the assistance.

4. One consequence of the unlawfulness of illegal financial assistance is that if the initial assistance was illegal, everything derived from it is void. It might be wise to have an amendment to the CA 1985, protecting third parties acquiring rights under contracts which turn out to be void.

5. Financial assistance provided by a foreign subsidiary does not fall within the ambit of the legislation (*Arab Bank plc* v *Mercantile Holdings Ltd* [1994] 2 All ER 74). This suggests that all a financially assisting company needs to do is set up a foreign subsidiary. The subsidiary can use its money to assist the person who wishes to buy shares in the holding company.

6. Finally, if the purpose of penalising financial assistance is to ensure that it does not take place, it has not been very successful. In retrospect, it is apparent that at the time of the Guinness scandal, financial assistance and share support schemes were not unknown, even if people kept fairly quiet about them: it does not at the time seem to have been seen either as a criminal matter or as a matter that should excite the concern of those shareholders not being provided with assistance. This may have been because the excitement of carrying out a takeover meant that certain details were overlooked, or that the fees at stake caused the merchant banks which arranged the financial assistance to be less punctilious than they might have been. Furthermore, the prohibition did not stop Robert Maxwell, who, having removed shares from his employees' pension fund, pledged them as collateral to banks for borrowings by his private companies. He then used the borrowed money to buy shares in his main company which was in major financial difficulties. By buying his company's shares, the share price rose, and the banks then pressed him a little less urgently about the loans to other parts of his empire.

The specific exceptions: the "for the avoidance of doubt" exceptions

The undernoted exceptions have all been stated in the CA 1985 because for some time there was doubt as to whether or not they counted as financial assistance. They are to be found at CA 1985 s 153(3):

(a) dividends;
(b) bonus shares;
(c) a court-approved reduction of capital;
(d) a redemption or purchase of shares as described earlier in this chapter;
(e) anything done under a CA 1985 s 425 scheme of arrangement (see Chapter 19);
(f) anything done under an Insolvency Act 1986 s 110 arrangement (see Chapter 21);
(g) anything done under a company voluntary arrangement under the Insolvency Act 1986 ss 1–7.

Dividends are specifically mentioned because it is not unknown for shareholders in a company to invest their funds in the company in the form of partly paid shares. They then use their dividends to fully pay up the shares (assuming the articles permit the payment of a full dividend on a partly paid share).

The specific exemptions: moneylenders and employees

Following representations from the finance industry and from those seeking to encourage employees to invest in their own companies, further exemptions were introduced and are to be found at CA 1985 s 153(4). These include:

(a) the lending of money by a company in its ordinary course of business to a customer who proceeds to use that money to buy shares in the company – as might well happen with someone borrowing money from a bank who happens to use his borrowed funds to invest in that bank;
(b) the provision of financial assistance (in various forms) by the company to an employees' share scheme or for its employees or their dependents to enable them to obtain shares in the company.

As stated above, all these exceptions apply to both private and public companies. However, if a public company wishes to provide financial assistance for the lending of money in the normal course of business, or to provide financial assistance to its employees, their dependents, or their employee share scheme, the financial assistance is only permissible if the company's net assets are not reduced as a result of the assistance. This means that, for example, any loan to an employee for him to buy shares must require a rate of interest on the loan that covers the company's costs. By this means the net assets would not be diminished. As even a low-cost loan to an employee might well prove to be small incentive to an employee to buy shares in his employer's company, there is a proviso to the rule that net assets may not be diminished. The proviso states that the net assets may be diminished if the assistance is provided out of distributable profits (CA s 154(1)) – in other words, not out of capital, undistributable reserves or the proceeds of a new issue of shares. Slightly oddly, s 154(2) proceeds to define net assets and liabilities for the purpose of s 154(1) in a different way from the definition of the same terms in s 152(2).

If you discount the "for the avoidance of doubt" exceptions, the moneylending loan exception and the employee financial assistance exceptions, it is in general extremely difficult for a public company to provide any form of financial assistance. As has been seen already, the "purpose" exception is very tightly restricted, though curiously, should a public company be able to use that particular exemption, there is no requirement that the net assets should not be materially reduced. A non-quoted public company might therefore be tempted to become private again if it wished to provide financial assistance. This is because private companies can adopt the gateway procedure to permit the financial assistance.

The gateway procedure

The gateway procedure, whereby a private company may provide financial assistance, is in many ways similar to the procedure for a private company redeeming or acquiring its own shares out of capital. However, there are significant differences which must be detailed.

The assistance must be provided out of distributable profits (not capital or the new issue of shares) if it is to be provided at all (CA 1985 s 155(2)) and if the company providing the assistance is a subsidiary of a public company, it is prohibited from providing the assistance because of its connection with the public company (CA 1985 s 155(3)). But if there is a private holding company in existence, and a subsidiary company is providing financial assistance for the purchase of shares in the holding company, both the subsidiary and the holding company must approve the financial assistance (CA 1985 s 155(5)).

Approval is given by means of a special resolution unless the company providing the assistance is a wholly owned subsidiary (CA 1985 s 155(4)). This is because there would be little point in holding a meeting if the entire votes were going to be cast in the way the holding company wished. The special resolution must take place within a week of the directors' statutory declaration (CA 1985 s 157(1)).

The directors of the company making the financial assistance, and the directors of a holding company if the financial assistance for the purchase of shares in the holding company is to come from a subsidiary (CA 1985 s 155(6)), must make a statutory declaration. The statutory declaration is in much the same terms as the one for payments out of capital referred to earlier. However, unlike the redemption or acquisition of shares out of capital, there is no reference in the Insolvency Act 1986 s 76 to directors or shareholders being required to repay sums to the company if the company is wound up within 12 months of the date of payment.

An auditors' report, confirming the directors' views, is required (CA 1985 s 156(4)), and it, the special resolution(s) and the directors' statutory declaration(s) all must be sent to the Registrar of Companies within 15 days of the date of the resolution(s) (CA 1985 s 156(5)). At the time when each resolution is passed, members must have been able to inspect the terms of the resolution, the statutory declaration(s) and the auditors' report. Once the company has passed the resolution, it must wait a period of 28 days (CA 1985 s 157(3)) during which period shareholders representing 10% or more of the company's share capital or any class of it, or in an unlimited company, 10% of the company's members, but not, curiously, the company's creditors, may apply to the court for cancellation of the resolution (CA 1985 s 157). Members who have already voted in favour of the resolution may not change their minds (CA 1985 s 157(2)).

Assuming the resolution is passed and there are no objections, the payment itself may take place within eight weeks of the date of the (last declared) statutory declaration unless the court orders otherwise (CA 1985 s 158(4)).

Capitalisation and bonus issues

Capitalisation is the process of turning undistributed profit into capital, either by putting it into a non-distributable reserve, such as a capital redemption reserve, or into share capital, in which case it is turned into shares known as bonus shares and allotted to the members in proportion to their existing holdings in the company. The term "bonus" implies that the shares are free. This is not the case, though they can be a reward for loyalty, as when a shareholder in a privatisation issue is encouraged to hold his shares for a certain length of time in order to obtain more shares without having to pay for them. The other term for an allotment of bonus shares is a scrip issue.

Following a bonus issue, the asset value per share diminishes, since the total assets are spread out over a greater number of shares, but each shareholder's overall shareholding is worth as much before as after. Sometimes, however, a bonus issue is seen as a sign of confidence by a company, and the shares rise in price accordingly.

Once a bonus share has been issued, it cannot be turned back into distributable profit. The issue of bonus shares normally requires an ordinary resolution of the members (Table A art 110).

Sometimes shareholders elect to take their dividends in the form of shares, thus capitalising their profits. This is useful for shareholders who do not need income but want capital growth, and it avoids stockbrokers' fees. Income tax is still payable on the dividend, even though the dividend is paid in the form of shares.

It is possible to create bonus shares not only from profits but from the share premium account or the capital redemption reserve. If so, they must be allotted fully paid (CA 1985 ss 130(2) and 170(4)).

Whenever a company issues bonus shares, it should ensure that its authorised share capital is sufficiently large enough to accommodate all the new shares.

Summary

1. The principle of capital maintenance is that once capital is paid to the company it is there for the benefit of the creditors, not for the members. If the members wish to get their investment back, they must:

   - sell or redeem their shares if they can; or

- persuade the company to buy back their shares; or
- persuade the company to reduce its capital and return capital to the members.

2. The monies the investors contribute to the company is sometimes known as the creditors' buffer. But the creditors' buffer in practice may not amount to very much, because the share capital may not be large or because it has already been used up settling other debts.

3. Companies can increase or reduce the authorised share capital (CA 1985 s 121), and can subdivide or consolidate their shares (CA 1985 s 122).

4. Reduction of capital under the CA 1985 s 135 may be necessary where:

- the nominal value of the company's share capital is greater than the value of the company's net assets;
- the company wishes to be rid of a particular shareholder or class of shareholders;
- the company has capital in excess of its needs.

5. Reduction is only possible where:

- the company's articles permit it (CA 1985 s 135(1));
- the company passes a special resolution to approve the reduction (CA 1985 s 135(1));
- the court confirms the reduction (CA 1985 s 136).

After reduction has been confirmed, the Registrar of Companies is informed and the company's capital is duly reduced.

6. Under the CA 1985 s 135 the types of reduction are:

- the extinction or reduction of liability on any of the company's shares in respect of capital not paid up;
- the cancellation of any paid-up share capital which is lost or unrepresented by assets;
- the paying back of any share capital in excess of the company's needs.

7. The court's involvement is necessary to protect the interests of creditors, who either must be told of the reduction and given the chance to object, or must have their debts settled or provided for first. Shareholders may wish to object as well though their rights to object may well be limited by the articles. If the company has fully complied with the terms of the articles, an objecting shareholder may have no valid grounds for objecting (*Scottish Insurance Corporation Ltd* v *Wilsons and Clyde Company Ltd* [1949] AC 462).

8. Share premium accounts are where share premiums are credited to. The same rules that apply to reduction of share capital apply to share premium

accounts. There is no obligation on the company's directors to obtain the maximum premium on the issue of shares (*Hilder* v *Dexter* [1902] AC 474).

9. Under the merger relief rules of the CA 1985 ss 131–134, the difference in value of newly allotted shares used as consideration for the purchase of another company and the value of the net assets of that other company need not be credited to the share premium account. This means that the acquired company's funds can be used to pay dividends to all shareholders of the newly merged company.

10. A company may acquire its own shares:

   - under the normal acquisition procedures (CA 1985 ss 159–181);
   - under the reduction of capital rules above;
   - if ordered to do so by the court;
   - if the shares are forfeited or surrendered.

11. Why would a company buy its own shares?

   - to get rid of a particular shareholder;
   - because even if the members cannot afford to do so, the company can;
   - to prevent a takeover bid;
   - to increase the asset value per share;
   - to increase the earnings per share (occasionally);
   - because the company has too much cash;
   - to buy back the employee's shares.

12. The two main methods of acquisition of a company's shares are off-market and market (CA 1985 s 163). Market acquisitions are those conducted through the stock market. Off-market are all others.

13. Under the CA 1985 s 164 the procedure for an off-market acquisition is as follows:

   - there must be authority under the articles;
   - preparation of a contract or memorandum for the acquisition. This has to be available for inspection 15 days before;
   - the passing of a special resolution for the acquisition, which in the case of a plc permits the acquisition to take place within the next 18 months only.

   The contract must be retained at the registered office for a period of 10 years after the acquisition.

14. Under the CA 1985 s 166 the procedure for a market acquisition is as follows:

- there must be authority under the articles;
- the passing of an ordinary resolution limiting the extent of the acquisition and the duration of the authority of the resolution (no more than 18 months);
- intimation to the Stock Exchange.

15. In each case under the CA 1985 s 169 the Registrar of Companies must be informed of the acquisition, and a capital redemption fund, equal in value to the nominal value of the acquired shares, must be set up (CA 1985 s 170). The acquired shares must be cancelled or reissued.

16. The financing of the acquisition of shares is virtually identical to the financing of the redemption of redeemable shares.

17. The nominal value of such acquired or redeemed shares is paid out of distributable profits and/or the proceeds of a new issue of shares to replace the acquired or redeemed shares (CA 1985 s 160(1)).

   Any premium or acquisition or redemption must come from distributable profits (CA 1985 s 160(1)(b)) unless the original shares were issued at a premium in which case they can be paid out of the proceeds of a new issue of shares (CA 1985 s 160(2)) but only to the extent of the lesser of the total premiums when the shares were originally issued (CA 1985 s 160(2)(a)) or whatever happens to be in the share premium account at the time of acquisition or redemption (CA 1985 s 160(2)(b)).

18. Private companies can pay for the acquisition or redemption of their shares out of capital (CA 1985 ss 171–177). To do this:

- the company must have the requisite power under the articles;
- the directors must have made the necessary statutory declaration under the CA 1985 s 173(3) concerning the continued solvency of the company on pain of personal liability for the directors;
- there must be an auditor's report to confirm the statutory declaration (CA 1985 s 173(5));
- the payment out of capital must be approved by special resolution (CA 1985 s 173(2));
- a notice about the payment out of capital must be inserted in the Gazette (CA 1985 s 175);
- the company must wait for a period of five weeks for any objections to the payment (CA 1985 s 176);
- the company must make the payment within two weeks of the end of the five-week period (CA 1985 s 174(1)).

19. The Permissible Capital Payment is the price of acquisition/redemption of the shares less the available profits less the proceeds of any new issue of

shares. This figure is used to calculate how much money, if any, may be taken out of capital to fund the acquisition or redemption.

20. The provision by a company of financial assistance for the acquisition of its own shares is generally prohibited except in limited circumstances. The main exceptions are:

   - the purpose exception (CA 1985 s 153(1)), which means that the assistance is a small part of some greater operation and the assistance is given in good faith (*Brady* v *Brady* [1989] AC 755, HL);
   - exemptions for moneylending companies (CA 1985 s 153(4)(a));
   - exemptions for employees buying shares in their own companies (CA 1985 s 153(4)(b), (bb) and (c));
   - for private companies only, the gateway procedure.

   Public companies may provide financial assistance but only within the limits of the above exceptions and only where the company's net assets are not diminished, unless the assistance comes from distributable profits (CA 1985 s 154), or where the company is relying on the purpose exception.

21. The gateway procedure is broadly similar to the procedure for acquisition/redemption of shares out of capital (see 18 above). It is only available to private companies (CA 1985 ss 155–158).

22. Financial assistance is well recognised as being an unsatisfactory area of law and in need of improvement.

23. Capitalisation is the turning of undistributed reserves into bonus shares.

10. COMPANY DISTRIBUTIONS

Profits available for distribution – realised profits and realised losses – relevant accounts – distribution rules for public companies – rules for investment companies – payment of dividends – liability for improper distributions

In the previous chapter we discussed the important principle of maintenance of capital. Part of the way that this operated was by permitting the redemption or purchase of a company's own shares to take place only if the company used distributable profits or the proceeds of a new issue of shares made specially for the purpose to fund the redemption or acquisition. Even though private companies may exceptionally use capital to fund redemption or acquisition, this is only possible if available distributable profits or the proceeds of the new issue of shares have been used up first.

Distributable profits are what dividends are paid out of, and statute has set up a number of rules designed to outlaw the more dubious practices that used to exist in relation to dividends, such as:

- paying dividends out of unrealised profits arising out of the revaluation of assets;

- ignoring depreciation; or

- paying dividends out of capital.

Profits available for distribution

It is important to understand what is meant by profits available for distribution or "distributable profits".

Distributable profits as a term is defined in the CA 1985 in three places, one being specifically in the context of financial assistance (CA 1985 s 152(2)), another for the purposes of redemption or purchase of a company's own shares (CA 1985 s 181(a)) and the third and most important in this context at CA 1985 s 263(3):

> "For the purposes of this Part (of CA 1985), a company's profits available for distribution are its accumulated, realised profits, so far as not previously utilised by distribution or capitalisation, less its accumulated, realised losses, so far as not previously written off in a reduction or reorganisation of capital duly made."

Most of the terms here need explanation.

- Capitalisation in this context means the conversion of retained and current net profits into bonus shares.

- Written off means treated as no longer present in the accounts either as an asset or a liability.

- Reduction means reduction in terms of the CA 1985 s 135 (see Chapter 9) or any other permitted reduction such as the redemption or repurchase of a private company's own shares out of capital (see also Chapter 9).

- Reorganisation means any valid form of rearrangement of capital such as:

  (i)   the swapping of shares for debentures,
  (ii) a scheme or arrangement under the CA 1985 s 425 (see Chapter 19), or
  (iii) a reorganisation following, for example, a successful minority petition under the CA 1985 s 459 (see Chapter 13).

Distribution

Under the CA 1985 s 263, distribution means any method of handing back the company's assets to the members, whether in cash or in the form of any other assets of the company, with the exception of the following:

- an issue of partly or fully paid bonus shares (CA 1985 s 263(2)(a)) (see also Chapter 9);

- the redemption or purchase of any of the company's own shares out of capital (including the proceeds of any new issue of shares) or out of unrealised profits (CA 1985 s 263(2)(b)) (see also later);

- the reduction of share capital in terms of the CA 1985 s 135(2)(a) or (c) (extinction or reduction of shareholders' liability in respect of share capital not fully paid up, or the repayment to shareholders of paid-up share capital) (CA 1985 s 263(2)(c));

- a distribution of assets on winding up (CA 1985 s 263(2)(d)).

These exemptions are specified because without them there might be confusion as to what exactly was meant by a distribution.

A bonus issue in the context of distributable profits is the conversion of funds that would otherwise be available for distribution as cash into shares. Once converted into shares, they cannot be turned back into funds available for distribution since by then they have become part of the company's share capital.

The redemption or purchase of shares out of capital is by definition a payment out of capital and not out of funds available for distribution. Reduction of capital involves the return of capital to members without touching the funds available for distribution.

A distribution on winding up is a distribution, in that assets are handed over to the members, but special insolvency rules apply to such distributions. Such distributions are not seen purely as the distribution of distributable profits since there may be a return of capital as well.

One way of thinking of the distributable profits is to see them as the net profits (*i.e.* profits after deduction of all overheads) available for the payment of dividends to the members, whether in cash or in the form of any other asset of the company. The dividend is the amount of profit per share that the directors consider appropriate or is required (depending on the articles) to pay out of the company's distributable profits to the shareholders. Not all the profits of a company are usually paid out in dividends: what is not paid out is known as "retained profit" or 'undistributed reserves". A prudent company always keeps enough retained profit to meet any unexpected liabilities, but not so much that the members claim that there is a poor income arising from their investment.

Furthermore, no distribution can be made except out of profits available for the purpose (CA 1985 s 263(1)). Two points arise from this:

1. A company cannot invite subscriptions for new shares, and use the newly contributed share capital to pay dividends to the existing shareholders. This is a well-recognised type of fraud, known as a Ponzi scheme (named after its original perpetrator), common in poorly regulated stock markets and popular with confidence tricksters. A recent example was in 1994 when a Mr Mavrodi in Russia set up a company called MMM operating on precisely this principle. Such was the gullible public's faith in his abilities that even when first, his company collapsed, leaving investors with worthless shares, and secondly, he was imprisoned for tax evasion, he still managed to be elected an MP. Such frauds only last while there is a pool of willing investors, but as with all pyramid sales, eventually there are no more investors to buy the shares, and no money with which to pay the dividends. Similar schemes afflicted Albania in 1996.

2. A company must not use its existing capital to pay dividends, as that offends the principle of capital maintenance. The capital exists for the benefit of those who trade with the company. Directors who knowingly permit the payment of capital as dividend will be personally liable for the loss to the company and potentially to the company's creditors (see end of chapter).

Accumulated

"Accumulated" means that previous year's profits, if they are still in the hands of the company and have not been used for any other purpose, are amalgamated with the current year's profits and treated as a global figure, known as the accumulated profits. The same principle applies to losses. It used to be the case that if a company had suffered losses for several years and then made a profit, it was allowed to distribute that profit in the form of dividend. This is not now possible because of the use of the word "accumulated" in s 263(3) in respect of both profits and losses. In other words, a company must make good its accumulated losses out of subsequent profits before it starts to pay dividends – unless it reduces its capital in terms of the CA 1985 s 135.

Realised profits and realised losses

These terms are defined in the CA 1985 s 262(3) and are such profits and losses as:

> "fall to be treated as realised in accordance with principles generally accepted, at the time when the accounts are prepared, with respect to the determination for accounting purposes of realised profits or losses.
>   This is without prejudice to –
> (a) the construction of any other expression (where appropriate) by reference to accepted accounting principles or practice, or
> (b) any specific provision for the treatment of profits or losses of any description as realised."

Some of these phrases need clarification.

The profit must actually have been realised

The important issue is that the profits must actually have arisen by the balance sheet date (CA 1985 Schedule 4 r 12(a)). When an asset is sold at a profit, the profit will be recorded as a profit on the day it is sold. However, if it is sold on credit, it is not treated as realised until payment has been made.

Equally, if a company has an asset which is revalued upwards, the increase in value cannot be treated as a realised profit until the day it is sold. This is because the profit is only realised on sale. No sale means no realisation. The revaluation of an asset is not a sale. The increase in value of an asset following an upwards revaluation cannot be stated in the accounts as a realised profit and cannot be used as part of the distributable profits. The increase in value is instead credited to a revaluation reserve. This is in accordance with the CA

1985 Schedule 4, Part II of which lays out extensive accounting principles and rules to be followed when drawing up companies' accounts.

Principles generally accepted

The phrase "principles generally accepted", which is referred to above in the context of ascertaining what is a profit or a loss, suffers from a certain vagueness which has often been criticised. At the same time it is difficult to find a more satisfactory definition which would not have provided loopholes through which ingenious lawyers and accountants could put their companies' accounts. Leaving the issue vague and relying on current accounting standards may in fact encourage companies to use best practice wherever possible – in order to be on the safe side. Best practice in accounting is something that changes regularly, but there are two main sets of guidelines, these being Statements of Standard Accounting Practice ("SSAPs"), issued by the Accounting Standards Committee, and Financial Reporting Standards ("FRSs"), issued by the Accounting Standards Board. The FRSs are gradually replacing the SSAPs. When directors are preparing their companies' accounts, they have to state that the accounts have been prepared in accordance with applicable accounting standards (*i.e.* SSAPs and FRSs) and any material departures from those standards must be explained (CA 1985 Schedule 4 para 36A). In *Lloyd Cheytham & Co Ltd* v *Littlejohn & Co* [1987] BCLC 303 the judge stated that SSAPs are "very strong evidence as to what is the proper standard to which should be adopted and unless there is some justification, a departure from this will be regarded as constituting a breach of duty." Although this case actually concerned the liability of auditors, it is significant that judicial approval was thus given to SSAPs and by extension to FRSs.

Unrealised losses

Although unrealised profits are not treated as realised profits, unrealised losses will sometimes be treated as realised losses.

Although a realised profit must actually have taken place, a realised loss does not always have to do so: on occasion the law will treat an unrealised loss as a realised loss as part of a prudent accounting policy. For example, under the CA 1985 s 275(1) a provision, which under the CA 1985 Schedule 4 para 89 is a future liability uncertain as to amount or the date on which it may be due, such as a claim for damages following a negligence claim against the company, is treated as a realised loss. Although the company might ultimately win the case, the company's accounts should in the meantime be drawn up on the assumption that the claim against the company will be successful. Another way of saying this is that the company should normally take account of all potential losses whether or not the loss actually takes place, but is not allowed to take account of any potential gains until they actually take place.

Revaluation of fixed assets

There is a proviso to the above rule concerning the unrealised losses provisions in the CA 1985 s 275(1), namely, if:

(i) there is a revaluation of all the fixed assets of the company, or all the fixed assets save goodwill, and
(ii) the revaluation indicates that an unrealised profit overall in respect of all the revalued fixed assets (with or without goodwill) has been made,

any one fixed asset which:

(i) has in fact diminished in value, and
(ii) whose diminution in value would normally be treated therefore as a provision,

need not have its diminution in value treated as a provision or as a realised loss. It can therefore be set against the unrealised profits of the rest of the revalued assets (CA 1985 s 275(1)).

This takes account of the realistic view that if all but one of a company's assets have gone up in value it is not unreasonable to set the diminished value of the one fixed asset that has not gone against the general upwards revaluation. So the overall effect is that the revaluation reserve is not as high as it might be, but the realised losses are not as low as they might be either. It might be argued that this exemption for one asset is satisfactory, provided that the asset itself has not greatly diminished in value and provided the other assets have genuinely increased in value, but equally, an unscrupulous company might be tempted to offset a large loss in value of one significant asset against a collective small increase in value of all the other assets elsewhere, and thereby create a misleading set of accounts.

The impact of this is in some ways diminished, because assets are normally entered into the accounts at their historic cost, and any increase on revaluation merely goes into a revaluation reserve, the contents of which are not available anyway to shareholders except by issuing bonus shares (fully or partly paid) (CA 1985 Schedule 4, para 34). In addition, the auditors might well comment on the wisdom of any questionable set-off against the revaluation reserve.

Deemed revaluation

As for how the revaluation takes place, the CA 1985 gives a surprising amount of discretion to the directors. If this seems odd, it must be remembered that the rules as drafted apply to all companies, but, as will be seen shortly, public limited companies have more stringent rules for distributions generally, and furthermore, creditors and shareholders would begin to distrust directors if revaluations began to be too suspiciously attractive. The auditors also might have their misgivings. The CA 1985 s 275(4) states that any consideration (in this context this means "considered view", not "price") by the directors, however informal, of the value of a fixed asset, is treated as equivalent to a revaluation of that asset for the purpose of the proviso in the CA 1985 s 275(1). This proviso permits the diminution in value of one fixed asset to be set against the increase in value of all the other fixed assets instead of being taken to profit and loss.

But unless the fixed asset or assets have actually been properly revalued by an independent valuer, as opposed to merely being considered, the directors must have satisfied themselves (generally as evidenced by a board minute) that the overall current value of the assets is greater than the value that is stated for the assets in the company's accounts (CA 1985 s 275(5)). If the directors are satisfied that the revaluation figure for all the fixed assets is greater than the original historic-cost figures stated in the accounts, they must say so in a note to the accounts (CA 1985 s 276(6)). They must also state that they did genuinely consider the value of the assets in question and that their consideration is treated as a revaluation (CA 1985 s 275(6)(a)).

Notwithstanding all the above rules about revaluation, it is unlikely that any prudent investor, creditor or lender to the company would be much impressed with the directors' own consideration of the revalued value of their company's assets. An independent survey or revaluation would considerably enhance the credibility of the view of the directors as to the true value of the revalued assets and consequently the company's ability to pay a dividend.

Revaluation and depreciation

As a further part of the rules on revaluation, the CA 1985 s 275(2) states that if:

(i) any fixed asset is revalued, and
(ii) thereby makes an unrealised profit, and
(iii) on or after the revaluation a sum ("X") is taken off the value of the asset in respect of depreciation for each year (or such other period), and
(iv) prior to the revaluation a sum ("Y") used to be taken off the value of the asset in respect of depreciation,

the difference between X and Y is treated as a realised profit. The reason for this is that if the depreciation is done on a percentage basis, a property that was worth, say, £1,000 and was depreciated at the rate of 10% a year would suffer a realised loss of £100 each year until such time as it written off. The figure of £100 represents Y in the previous paragraph. If that property was revalued and now found to be worth £10,000, the annual depreciation charge would be £1,000. The figure of £1,000 would represent X in the above paragraph. The company might have been able to bear £100 a year as part of its losses, but £1,000 might impose an intolerable strain on its profits, and its profits might all be eaten up by the depreciation charge. What the CA 1985 s 275(2) allows the company to do is to treat £1,000 – £100 (*i.e.* X – Y) = £900 as realised profit.

Another way of saying the same thing is that the company can continue to use the pre-revaluation depreciation charge.

It is arguable that following this procedure can present a rosier view of the company's accounts than is justified. Therefore, although the directors can deal with the depreciation charge in this way, it might be prudent not to do so and to insert a note in the accounts stating why the normal statutory depreciation method has not been followed (CA 1985 Schedule 4 para 36A).

Original value of fixed asset not known

One of the problems with revaluing assets or indeed selling assets is that the company may have lost track of the original value of the asset, thus making it difficult to know how much profit has been made. Under those circumstances, the earliest available recorded figure after the asset's acquisition will be deemed to be its acquisition value (CA 1985 s 275(3)).

Non-cash dividends and revaluations

If any company is making a distribution of a non-cash asset, and that non-cash asset has been revalued so that its book value (and therefore the value being placed on it for the purposes of the distribution) contains an element of unrealised profit (being the difference between its original value and its revalued value), the unrealised profit is deemed to be a realised profit (CA 1985 s 276) and the distribution itself is deemed to be legal – which it might not otherwise be, since normally one cannot distribute any part of an unrealised profit.

Treatment of development expenditure

When a company develops a new product, it may need to spend a good deal of money on researching and developing it. Research and development expenditure can be dealt with in three ways:

(A) The costs can be paid for as they are incurred.

(B) The company may choose to bundle all the development costs together, carry them forward and charge them all against the first year that the company actually starts to sell the new product. This would mean that:
   (i)   the profits for the years while development was taking place would not show the extent of the development costs,
   (ii) the first year of production would be unlikely to show much profit for the new product, but (assuming it was successful)
   (iii) subsequent years might show very good profits.
(C) A further alternative is to save up all the costs until such time as the product is ready, and then set the costs off over a period of years during the time that the product is selling (amortisation).

Under the CA 1985 s 269(1) method A would require the development costs to be treated as a realised loss as they arose.

If the development costs are dealt with as in method B, the development costs are still treated as a realised loss, except where there is an unrealised profit arising out of any revaluation of those costs. The unrealised profit can be set against the realised loss of all the other development costs (CA 1985 s 269(2)).

Method C is possible as well, but there must be special circumstances which justify the directors using this method (CA 1985 s 269(2)(a)). Those circumstances must be explained in the notes to the accounts (CA 1985 s 269(2)(b)).

Relevant accounts

Having ascertained what is acceptable to be treated as realised profit and what is realised loss, subject to any extra provisions in the articles of association one must subtract the accumulated losses from the accumulated profits to calculate the distributable profits. Dividends can only be paid out of distributable profits, and distributable profits can only be calculated by reference to the company's accounts as prepared by the directors. Schedule 4 to the CA 1985 sets out extensive rules for the layout of accounts, the notes to the accounts and many other details. Some of this is discussed more fully in Chapter 11.

In order to calculate the distributable profits, one must refer to the last annual accounts made up to the most recent accounting reference date in respect of which the accounts were prepared (CA 1985 s 270(3)) and tabled at a general meeting under the CA 1985 s 241 or, in the case of private companies which have been exempted from tabling their accounts at a general meeting following an elective resolution to that effect, sent to the members (CA 1985 s 252(3)). These are known as the relevant accounts. Except where the company is exempt from the auditing requirements because of its small size (CA 1985 s 249A) the accounts must be audited, and the auditors must indicate that the accounts give a true and fair view of the balance sheet and the profit and loss account.

The auditors must also state in their report on the accounts whether any qualification they are making to the report is material (*i.e.* significant and worth being concerned about) for determining whether the company would contravene the CA 1985 ss 263–265 by making its proposed distribution. If it is a material qualification, the company should not make the distribution at all, or if it has already been made, it should not have been and may be required to be reimbursed so far as that is feasible. Such a distribution is classed as "unlawful" in terms of the CA 1985 s 277, discussed later in this chapter.

Initial accounts

If the directors wish to declare a dividend before the end of the company's first accounting reference period, it would clearly be impossible to refer to the company's last set of accounts. It is, instead, permissible to refer to initial accounts (CA 1985 s 270(4)(b)), prepared in the same manner as ordinary accounts (CA 1985 s 273(3)). No auditors' certificate for initial accounts is required if the company is a private company, but if it is a public company, an auditors' report is required (CA 1985 s 273(4)). This must state any material qualification which affects the company's ability to make a distribution and which would make the distribution unlawful as above (CA 1985 s 273(5)).

Interim accounts

If a company's last annual accounts would not permit a distribution, but the company has suddenly prospered so that it could pay a dividend, it is possible to pay a dividend on the basis of interim accounts (CA 1985 s 270(4)(a)). These do not need to be audited even in the case of public companies as there is no subsection specifically stating the need for auditing.

Initial and interim accounts for public companies must be filed with the Registrar of Companies (CA 1985 ss 273(6) and 272(4)).

Distribution rules for public limited companies

Although a private company may not pay a dividend unless its accumulated realised profits are greater than its accumulated realised losses, there is a further rule for the payment of dividends that applies to public limited companies. It is known as the net assets rule. It is stated in the CA 1985 s 264(1):

"A public company may only make a distribution at any time –

(a) if at that time the amount of its net assets is not less than the aggregate of its called up share capital and undistributable reserves, and

(b) if, and to the extent that, the distribution does not reduce the amount of those assets to less than that aggregate."

What this means in practice is that before any distribution is made,

(i) the net assets must be greater than the total of the called-up share capital and the undistributable reserves, and
(ii) the proposed distribution must not make the net assets amount to less than the total of the called-up share capital and the undistributable reserves.

So, for example, if a company has net assets of £100,000, share capital of £50,000 and a share premium account of £10,000, the maximum distributable profits that could be distributed by way of dividend is £100,000 − £50,000 − £10,000 = £40,000.

Undistributable reserves is defined in the CA 1985 s 264(3) as any of the following:

- share premium account;

- capital redemption reserve;

- the amount by which the company's accumulated unrealised profits, less any unrealised profits capitalised into bonus shares, exceed its accumulated unrealised losses, in so far as these have not been written off in a reduction of capital. This is effectively the same as the revaluation reserve referred to earlier;

- any other reserve which the company is prohibited from distributing either under statute or under the terms of the company's memorandum or articles.

A public limited company may not treat any uncalled share capital as an asset in terms of the net asset rule (CA 1985 s 264(4)).

Distribution rules for investment companies

Investment companies are public companies that invest in other businesses and make their money through judicious investment by specialist fund managers. Many such companies are also known as investment trusts and have a special exempt status from capital gains tax. If you invest in an investment company, the company uses your funds to invest in a large number of securities, thus spreading the risk. Investment companies must be properly registered as such (CA 1985 s 266(1)) and must not invest more than 15% of the funds under their management in any one company. They may not distribute any capital profit, nor may they retain more than 15% of their income from securities.

An investment company has a net asset rule similar to a public company save that a distribution can only be made provided the company's assets are at least one-and-a-half times its liabilities, and the distribution does not reduce the company's assets so that they become less than one-and-a-half times its liabilities (CA 1985 s 265(1)(a) and (b)).

Payment of dividends

Many private companies do not bother with paying dividends, because the members, who are often the directors, take the profits out of the companies in the form of salaries. One advantage of paying dividends, however, is that unlike salaries, no national insurance is payable on dividends. A disadvantage of dividends is that when a company pays dividends it suffers a considerable outflow of funds. This may have cash flow implications for the company. On the other hand, if a company does not pay dividends regularly it may cease to be an attractive company to invest in and, if quoted, its share price may slip. If too much is kept in reserves instead of being distributed, a company may become a target for a takeover bid, the bidder seeking to unlock the reserves. If too little is taken to reserves, the directors will be accused of being improvident. The directors therefore have to find an acceptable balance between all these competing interests.

Investors generally wish their dividends to gradually increase year by year. Erratic dividend payments suggest unreliability. This is not welcome to the institutional investors who must be seen to be following prudent investment policies. In order to achieve the desired gradual increase in dividends some quoted companies manipulate the presentation of their accounts in such a way as to produce the desired result. The SSAPs and FRSs referred to above are designed to reduce the opportunities for this practice.

It is common for companies to pay final dividends and interim dividends, interim usually being half-yearly. A few companies pay dividends quarterly. How dividends are to be paid is normally stated in the articles, but commonly:

- a full dividend is only payable on a fully paid-up share, partly paid shares attracting only a proportion of the dividend;

- unless the articles say otherwise, there is no automatic right of the members to a dividend. The directors recommend the amount of the dividend to the members at a general meeting. The members then pass an ordinary resolution to approve the level of dividend or reduce it, but not increase it (Table A, art 102);

- dividends are payable in cash or in assets of the company (Table A art 105);

- a dividend is a debt due to the members only once it has been declared. It is a deferred debt in a liquidation, and shareholders will only get their outstanding dividends once preferential and ordinary creditors have been paid (Insolvency Act 1986 s 74(2)(f));

- dividends can be paid in the form of further shares of the company provided there is sufficient authorised capital and unissued share capital to do so, and provided the company's articles permit it;

- dividends suffer advance corporation tax before payment, so that the investor receives his dividend less the tax paid on it, on the investor's behalf, by the company. If the investor has a low income he may be able to reclaim the tax already paid; if he has a high income he may have to pay additional tax later;

- interim dividends do not need the approval of the members in general meeting;

- dividends are normally paid by cheque or paid straight into the shareholder's bank account. In the case of joint ownership of a share, the dividend is normally paid to the first-named holder unless there is written notice otherwise. Unclaimed dividends are normally forfeited after a period of time specified in the articles. Table A provides for 12 years before forfeiture;

- in order to pay the dividends, companies may close their shareholders' registers for a period of time prior to the payment in order to send out the dividend cheques. Alternatively, dividends will be payable to all those registered as members on the date selected by the directors as the date of payment. The purchase price of the share will reflect whether the share is sold with a due dividend (known as *cum*) or if it is sold without (*ex*).

- an investor has a period of up to six years in England and Wales to sue a company for non-payment of a declared dividend (Limitation Act 1980 s 5). In Scotland the period is five years (Prescription and Limitation (Scotland) Act 1973 s 6). In Northern Ireland the period is also six years (Limitation (Northern Ireland) Order 1989 art 4).

Liability for an improper distribution

Under the CA 1985 s 277(1), any member of a company who receives a distribution knowing that the payment of the distribution was in contravention of the CA 1985 ss 263–265 is liable to repay it. This does not preclude any other liability to repay the distribution which might arise, say, through being a company officer (CA 1985 s 277(2)).

Conceivably a member who receives an improper dividend, even if he does not know or has no reason to believe that the dividend is improper, may still be liable under the CA 1985 s 277(2) if, say, there is a clause in the articles specifying this, or if he has at some stage signed a contract specifying that he would repay any improper dividend irrespective of the underlying circumstances. The CA 1985 s 277 also catches members who receive distributions (or other payments that were in essence distributions even if disguised as something else) that are illegal, as in *Aveling Barford Ltd* v *Perion Ltd and others* [1989] BCLC 626, where a subsidiary arranged for an asset to be sold at a gross undervalue to its holding company, thus making what was effectively an illegal return of capital.

As can be seen in the following case, even an affirmative resolution in general meeting by the recipients of the dividend, on this occasion the holding company, will not validate a payment that is illegal.

Precision Dippings Ltd v *Precision Dippings Marketing Ltd* [1986] Ch 447. Precision Dippings Marketing Ltd ("Marketing") received a substantial dividend from its subsidiary, which subsequently went into liquidation. The liquidator claimed that the dividend should not have been paid because the auditors' report had made no mention of the *materiality* of a qualification to the accounts concerning the basis of the valuation of work in progress. After the subsidiary's liquidation, the auditors issued a statement saying that their qualification to the accounts concerning the valuation of the work in progress was not in their view material. Not surprisingly, since they were sitting on the dividend, the members of the subsidiary (*i.e.* Marketing, the holding company) approved the auditors' statement by ordinary resolution. Nonetheless it was held that Marketing knew enough of the circumstances surrounding the payment of the dividend, irrespective of whether or not its directors knew that the materiality of the qualification ought to have been commented upon, to be deemed to have notice of the facts. Furthermore since the materiality of the qualification ought to have commented on, the payment of the dividend was illegal and under the rules then applying, *ultra vires*. Notwithstanding Marketing's efforts to validate the payment, it was still an illegal payment. Marketing was therefore a constructive trustee of the dividend and was required to repay it to the liquidator who used the refunded monies to repay the subsidiary's creditors.

Directors who negligently authorise a payment of a dividend which is improper are under common law jointly and severally liable for the sums paid on the grounds of the breach of their fiduciary duty (*Re Exchange Banking Co (Flitcroft's Case)* (1882) 21 Ch D 519 CA). If they do not know the payment is improper they may be relieved from liability if they can convince the court under the CA 1985 s 727 that they acted reasonably and honestly with regard to all the circumstances. Equally, if the directors relied on accounts that were carelessly drawn up by accountants, or negligently audited, any liability suffered by the directors might then be passed on by them to the accountants or auditors. This, however, would not be a matter of concern to the members of the company or the company itself. This is because it is the directors' duty to ensure that the accounts present a true and fair view of the company's financial state. Directors who cause the company to be wound up because of unjustified distributions might also find that the liquidator could ask the court under the Insolvency Act 1986 s 218 to refer the matter to the prosecuting authorities. The directors might also be disqualified under the Company Directors Disqualification Act 1986.

Members who realise that a dividend is unlawful could obtain an injunction (in Scotland, interdict) to prevent the dividend being paid.

Summary

1. Dividends may only be paid from distributable profits (CA 1985 s 263(1)). Distributable profits are a company's accumulated realised profits less its accumulated realised losses (CA 1985 s 263(3)).

2. Realised profits must genuinely have been realised (CA 1985 Schedule 4 r 12(a)), but for prudent accounting reasons, realised losses includes potential and likely losses ("provisions") even if not already realised (CA 1985 Schedule 4 r 12(b)). In general, upwardly revalued assets cannot be treated as realised profits, though part of the depreciation charge against an upwardly revalued asset is treated as realised profit (CA 1985 s 275(2)).

3. Distributable profits are calculated with reference to relevant accounts. These are in general the annual accounts of the company, representing a true and fair view of the company's financial state, and audited by the company's auditors.

4. Public limited companies must satisfy the net assets rule, whereby the net assets must never be reduced to less than the aggregate of the share capital and undistributable reserves; and no payment of dividend is permissible if the payment would result in the net assets being less than that aggregate figure (CA 1985 s 264(1)).

5. There are similar rules for investment companies. Their net assets must always be one-and-a-half times their liabilities (CA 1985 s 265(1)).

6. Payment of dividends is normally recommended by the directors and approved by the members, who may reduce but not increase the amount of the dividend (unless the articles say otherwise). Dividends are deferred debts, suffer tax before payment and, if the articles so provide, need not be paid in cash.

7. Members who knowingly receive improper dividends will be required to reimburse the company (CA 1985 s 277(1)). Directors who knowingly

authorise improper dividends will have to do the same (*Re Exchange Banking Co (Flitcroft's Case)* (1882) 21 Ch D 519), and may suffer further civil sanctions in the event of the company's insolvency. Innocent members and innocent directors, except perhaps where they should have known better, may escape liability. Where members are found to be constructive trustees of assets properly belonging to the company and improperly distributed as a dividend the members will be required to reimburse the company (*Aveling Barford Ltd* v *Perion Ltd and others* [1989] BCLC 626 and *Precisions Dippings Ltd* v *Precisions Dippings Marketing Ltd* [1986] Ch 447).

11.   COMPANY ACCOUNTS

The rationale for publication of company accounts – accounting records –
approval and publication of accounts and directors' and auditors' reports –
abbreviated and group accounts – revision of defective accounts and reports

The precise principles, formats and mechanisms for preparing company
accounts will not be dealt with in this book. Readers who wish to learn how to
draw up and interpret company accounts should consult an appropriate book on
accountancy. This chapter presents an overview of the legal requirements
for maintaining, publishing and approving a company's accounts and their
ancillary documentation.

The rationale for publication of company accounts

As was stated in Chapter 1, part of the trade-off for limited liability is the
requirement to publish details about a company and its accounts. If an investor
wishes to be protected from liability for his company's debts, he must be prepared to reveal his company's accounts to those who wish to lend money to his
company, trade with his company, or invest in his company. Reluctance to publish company accounts punctually may lead to suspicion about the company's
integrity, on the grounds that the honest company has nothing to hide.

Despite this, most directors feel uneasy about publishing their own company's accounts, particularly if it is a small or family run company.

Publication of a company's accounts may feel like an invasion of one's privacy. Directors may look enviously at partnerships and sole traders, who do not
need to reveal their accounts, except to the Inland Revenue and Customs and
Excise. Publication of a company's accounts could allow its competitors to
undercut the company. Publication of its accounts may tell others, including the
company's employees, how much the directors earn from the company. If that
figure is excessive, it may cause at least embarrassment and at worst strife.
Publication of a company's accounts may also reveal how badly the company
is doing, thus dissuading others from having any further commercial dealings
with the company.

So a compromise has been effected between the need for publicity and the
desire for privacy. Most information about the accounts has to be published, but
smaller companies need reveal less than larger companies, and access to the
accounting records, as opposed to the published accounts, is restricted.

The value of accounts

Although the principle of disclosure of accounts lies at the heart of company law, the decision to lend to, to trade with or to invest in a company depends on many more factors other than the accounts as presented. This is because there is widespread scepticism about the value of published accounts, particularly for quoted companies, some of which have acquired a reputation for "creative accounting", accounting which complies with the relevant rules – but only just. Professional analysts learn which companies have a reputation for less than frank presentation of accounts, and can sometimes tease out what the directors would probably prefer to remain hidden.

Equally, many private companies have a disclaimer in the report prepared by the auditors to the effect that the accounts, *so far as information has been made available to the auditors by the directors*, represent a true and fair view of the company's financial position. Where the directors have not made all the information available, who knows what might be lurking in the company's true accounts?

Some canny company directors conduct their business through a myriad of small companies, some of them offshore, with interlocking shareholdings, nominee directorships and the bare minimum of published information. Even with the benefit of the company accounts, a creditor trying to enforce a court judgment against such a business might well find that it would be extremely difficult to ascertain which company owned which asset. A further issue is that many investors and creditors, other than professional investors and accountants, are unable to understand company accounts with confidence.

Despite these failings, it is still useful to have the accounts: they may not represent the true picture, but they at least provide some information for the lender, the creditor or the investor. And there can be no more obvious proof of a director's incompetence or deceit than the failure of his company to have properly drawn-up accounts.

Accounting records

Under the CA 1985 s 221(1) it is the duty of every company to keep accounting records which:

> "are sufficient to show and explain the company's transactions and are such as to –
> (a) disclose with reasonable accuracy, at any time, the financial position of the company at that time, and
> (b) enable the directors to ensure that any balance sheet and profit and loss account prepared under this Part (VII) complies with the requirements of this Act (CA 1985)."

The contents of the accounts should record all receipts and expenditure and contain a record of the company's assets and liabilities (CA 1985 s 221(2)). If the company deals in goods, the accounting records must contain details of stock held at the end of the financial year (CA 1985 s 221(3)(a)), and, except in the case of ordinary retail traders, details of who bought and sold the company's goods (CA 1985 s 221(3)(c)). The accounting records are thus the ordinary day-to-day record of transactions. Failure by the directors, without good excuse, to adhere to these rules will:

• excite the attention of the Inland Revenue or Customs and Excise;

• be a matter for the court to consider in the context of disqualification of directors in terms of the Company Directors Disqualification Act 1986 Schedule 1;

• be grounds for prosecution under the CA 1985 s 221(5).

Preservation of records

Private companies must keep their records for three years and public companies for six years (CA 1985 s 222(5)). The records are normally to be kept at the company's registered office and are open to inspection by the company's officers at any time. The members themselves do not have such access to the accounting records unless the company's articles permit it. Table A art 109 only permits such access where permitted under statute, or where authorised either by the directors or by the members by means of an ordinary resolution. Without this clause, it could be inconvenient for the company if it had to produce all its accounts whenever a member wished. In any event, a member might be a competitor who might thus be placed in an advantageous position.

Approval and publication of accounts and directors' and auditors' reports

The opportunity most members have to see their company's accounts is when the accounts are sent out to the members prior to the Annual General Meeting ("AGM") at which the accounts and directors' report normally are tabled and approved. For each company, the directors must prepare a balance sheet, made up to the end of the company's financial year, and a profit and loss account for the same period (CA 1985 s 226(1)). These accounts must give a true and fair view of the company's financial position (CA 1985 s 226(2)) and the form and content must comply with the provisions of the CA 1985 Schedule 4.

The true and fair view

What is meant by "a true and fair view" has been the subject of much debate. Under the EC Fourth Directive (78/855) annual accounts are required to give a true and fair view of the company's assets, liabilities, financial position and profit or loss (Art 2(2)), and, as stated above, this phrase occurs in statute (CA 1985 s 226(2)). The consensus seems to be that a true and fair view is that which accountants versed in company accounts consider in the context of company law to be a true and fair view; in other words a circular definition of something that is almost impossible to define except in self-referential terms. SSAPs (Statements of Standard Accounting Practice) and FRSs (Financial Reporting Standards) promulgated by the Accounting Standards Board and its successor the Financial Reporting Council try to maintain common standards in accounting so that accounts can present true and fair views of companies' financial positions. While there is and will always be disagreement about details, it is broadly recognised that "a true and fair view" of a company's accounts is a reasonable level of probity to strive for in the preparation of accounts.

Approval of accounts

The accounts are first approved at a board meeting (CA 1985 s 233(1)) and then signed on the balance sheet (CA 1985 s 233(2)). The normal practice is then that the accounts are considered by the members at the next annual general meeting.

Accounting reference date

The accounts are made up to the end of the company's financial year.

The company's first financial year

A company's first financial year is from the date of its incorporation until its accounting reference date (or up to seven days before or after, at the directors' discretion) (CA 1985 s 223(2)), provided that the period between those two dates may not be less than six months nor greater than 18 months (CA 1985 s 224(4)).

Although a company can change its accounting reference date, in the absence of any change, a company will be deemed to have an accounting reference date which ends on the last day of the month in which the anniversary of its incorporation falls (CA 1985 s 224(3)). If this date is not suitable, the company may, within nine months of its incorporation, alter its accounting reference date by sending the Registrar of Companies a Form 224 altering the date (CA 1985 s 224(2)). A common reason for altering the date is to make a newly created subsidiary company have the same accounting reference date as its parent company.

A company's subsequent financial years

A company's subsequent financial year begins with the day that immediately follows the company's last financial year and ends with the last day of its next accounting period (or up to seven days before or after, at the directors' discretion) (CA 1985 s 223(3)). It will be noticed that a financial year is not necessarily a calendar year, for the company might be changing its accounting reference date to have a financial year shorter or longer than a calendar year. Normally, however, an accounting reference period will be 12 months after the end of the previous one, unless altered by using the requisite form. The period may also be lessened or increased:

- where a company alters its accounting reference date to a date more than nine months after incorporation, using a Form 225(1) (CA 1985 s 225) in respect of a current and future accounting reference periods; or

- where a company alters its accounting reference date retrospectively for a previous accounting period and subsequently for all future accounting reference periods. This is only applicable if the company is altering its date to coincide with a parent's or subsidiary's accounting reference date or if an administration order under Part II of the IA 1986 is in force (CA 1985 s 225(2)). In these events a Form 225(2) is used.

No change in the accounting reference date is possible if it means that an accounting reference period will be longer than 18 months (CA 1985 s 225(6)) or if the company has already extended the accounting reference period within the previous five years (unless the Secretary of State grants a special exemption) (CA 1985 s 225(4)). This five-year rule will not, however, apply if the purpose of the extension is to make the accounting reference dates of parents and subsidiary companies coincide (CA 1985 s 225(4)(a)) or if an administration order under Part II of the IA 1986 is in force (CA 1985 s 225(4)(b)).

Other information relating to accounts

At the end of the accounts are to be found the notes to the accounts. Under the CA 1985 s 231 and Schedule 5 each company must state its interest in other undertakings (*i.e.* other companies in which it has invested money or is a member) whether or not those undertakings are subsidiaries in the strict legal sense of the word. Under the CA 1985 s 232 and Schedule 6 the notes to the accounts must reveal, *inter alia*, the directors' emoluments (*i.e.* fees, wages, salary and pensions), any compensation for loss of office paid to former directors, and loans and transactions involving the directors personally with the company or any of its subsidiaries.

Auditors' report

After the notes to the accounts there will be the auditors' report. The auditors' report must state whether, in the auditors' opinion, the accounts have been properly prepared in accordance with the Companies Acts, and whether a true and fair view has been given of the balance sheet, profit and loss account and of the consolidated accounts in the case of a group (CA 1985 s 235(2)). The auditors' report must be signed by the auditors (CA 1985 s 236(1)) and a copy (usually the one signed by the directors) must be lodged with the Registrar of Companies (CA 1985 s 236(3)). When the auditors are preparing their report, under the CA 1985 s 237 they are required to investigate:

- whether proper accounting records have been kept,

- whether proper returns for the purposes of the audit have been sent from branches of the company which the auditors have not been able to visit,

- whether the company's individual accounts are in agreement with the accounting records and returns.

If the auditors form the view that proper accounts and returns have not been kept or made, or if the auditors fail to obtain the information and explanations necessary for the preparation of the audit, they must say so in their report on the accounts (CA 1985 s 237(2) and (3)). They should also disclose in their report any information about directors' earnings, pensions, compensation or loans which might not otherwise be shown in the accounts (CA 1985 s 237(4)).

Auditors are also required to qualify their report if there are matters which might materially affect the ability of the company to make distributions (CA 1985 s 271(4)). These matters are stated in the CA 1985 s 270(2), being:

- profits,

- losses,

- assets and liabilities,

- provisions (*i.e.* depreciation, diminution in value of assets, retentions for liabilities),

- share capital and

- reserves.

Since 11 August 1994 it has been possible for certain small companies to be exempt from supplying audited accounts. Under such circumstances there is no need for an auditors' report. This will be discussed in the context of small companies later in this chapter.

Dormant companies
Most dormant companies can claim exemption from audit, and consequently will not need to produce an auditors' report (CA 1985 s 250). To become dormant and to claim exemption from audit, the company must first have passed a special resolution to that effect (CA 1985 s 250(1)(b)).

Charities
Small charitable companies can also claim exemption from audit under the same rules as small companies provided their turnover is less than £250,000 (CA 1985 s 249A(5)).

Directors' report
With the accounts there is always a directors' report. This is required under the CA 1985 s 234. It must state who the directors are and have been during the financial year, the principal activities of the company and its subsidiaries and any significant changes from previous years. There is normally a review of the business of the company over the financial year, the forthcoming prospects for the company, and the recommendation of the directors as to the level of dividend. Many reports are accompanies by glossy pictures of the company's products and head office, graphs and pie charts, and pictures of the company's directors. Schedule 7 to the CA 1985, which is referred to in the CA 1985 s 234, requires the directors' report to state:

- general matters, such as changes in the value of the company's assets, directors' shareholdings, political and charitable contributions;

- information concerning the company's acquisition of its own shares or any charges on the company's shares;

- information about the training, employment and advancement of disabled people;

- information about the health, safety and welfare at work of the employees;

- information about the involvement of employees in the "affairs, policy and performance" of the company.

The directors' report must be approved by the board of directors and signed on its behalf by a director or the company secretary (CA 1985 s 234A(1)).

Usually the directors' report, the accounts and the auditors' report (usually in that order) are all in the one document which is sent to all the members. In order to save postage costs many companies also attach a copy of the notice of the AGM at which the accounts are to be approved. A signed copy of each document, signed by a director or secretary as far as the directors' report and accounts are concerned (CA 1985 ss 234A(1) and 233(1)), and by the auditors for their report, must be sent to the Registrar of Companies (CA 1985 s 236(1)). If the auditors are of the view that proper accounting records have not been kept, or they have been unable to verify all necessary information for the performance of their audit, they are to say so in their report (CA 1985 s 273(2)). They must state if there is any qualification to their report on the accounts (CA 1985 s 274(4)). If the matter in respect of which the report is qualified is "material" such that it could affect the legality of a distribution in terms of the CA 1985 ss 263–265, they must state as much (CA 1985 s 273(5)).

Entitlement to the accounts and reports

The following are entitled to receive copies of the accounts and reports under the CA 1985 s 238:

- members;

- debenture-holders;

- all those entitled to receive notice of general meetings, being:

  - directors,
  - the company secretary,
  - the auditors,
  - anyone designated by the company as entitled to see the accounts and reports.

The above must receive their copies of the accounts and reports not less than 21 days before any general meeting at which the accounts and reports are to be laid (CA 1985 s 238). There are exceptions to the 21-day rule:

(i) If the members of the company consent to the holding of the general meeting at shorter than 21 days' notice, the 21-day rule does not apply (CA 1985 s 238(4)).

(ii) Private companies that have passed an elective resolution under the CA 1985 s 252 to dispense with the laying of accounts and reports at general meetings have to send their accounts to their members in accordance with the CA 1985 s 252. Such accounts and reports must be sent out to the members at least 28 days prior to the date when an ordinary private company would have had to lodge the accounts and report (*i.e.* 10 months after the end of the relevant accounting reference period) (CA 1985 s 253(1)(a)). The accounts and reports must be accompanied by a note indicating that if a shareholder wishes the accounts and reports to be laid at a general meeting, he can ask the directors of the company to convene a meeting for this purpose (CA 1985 s 253 (2)).

In respect of (ii) above, if the directors:

- receive a notice from a shareholder indicating that he wishes the meeting to take place;

- ignore or overlook the notice, and thereby

- fail to call such a meeting within 21 days,

the shareholder can convene it himself (CA 1985 s 253(3)). Any reasonable expenses incurred by the shareholder can be recovered by the shareholder from the company which, in turn, will recover the monies from the directors out of their salaries or fees (CA 1985 s 253(5)). The meeting must take place within 28 days of the notice, or the directors will be deemed not to have convened the meeting in time and then become liable to the company (CA 1985 s 253(6)). This is to prevent unscrupulous directors convening a meeting as required, but at a date a long time in the future.

The exemption from tabling accounts at a general meeting was introduced because it was found that many small private companies were ignoring and gaining no benefit from the rules requiring the tabling of accounts at general meetings. In many small companies, there is little need for a general meeting to consider accounts which are well known to everybody present. At the same time, it was necessary to build in a procedure to ensure that even in those companies which had chosen to dispense with the tabling of accounts at a general meeting there was an opportunity to hold a meeting, if a member wanted such a meeting.

Any member or debenture-holder is also entitled to be given a copy of the company's last set of accounts and reports on demand and free of charge (CA 1985 s 239) unless the company is a dormant company (CA 1985 s 250(4)(a)).

Approval of accounts and reports at a general meeting

For those companies which do present their accounts and reports at a general meeting under the CA 1985 s 241, it is worth noting that the general meeting at which the accounts are tabled does not need to be (though it commonly is) an annual general meeting. Any general meeting will do. Furthermore, statute does not specifically say (although a company's articles may) what is to be done with the accounts and reports. It is common for the notice of the meeting to state that the accounts and reports are to be "tabled", "received" or "laid before the members". The accounts and reports are then "considered", "adopted" or "approved". The important point is that there should be an opportunity for the members to look at the accounts and reports, to ask questions about them and to be seen to say that in their collective view the accounts appear to be acceptable.

The reality is, particularly in large companies, that few shareholders can be bothered to turn up, much of the voting is organised in advance and most of the problems in the accounts and reports will already have been ironed out between the major investors and the company. Skillful or stonewalling chairmen can deter many questioners, and some companies' articles forbid the asking of questions on the accounts or reports without extensive prior notice to the board – thus avoiding awkward questions from shareholders at the meeting itself. The conduct of meetings is discussed in greater detail in Chapter 18.

As stated above, under the CA 1985 s 252 private companies can elect not to present their accounts at a general meeting by means of an elective resolution, carried out by means of a unanimous resolution in terms of the CA 1985 s 379A. It is common to combine this elective resolution with elective resolutions to dispense with having annual general meetings under the CA 1985 s 366A and reappointing auditors annually under the CA 1985 ss 384–386.

Time for lodging of accounts and reports

All companies are required to lay the accounts and reports before a general meeting (except those which have elected not to or dormant companies) under the CA 1985 s 241. All companies without exception must deliver a signed copy of their accounts and reports to the Registrar of Companies under the CA 1985 s 242. The time-limits for laying and delivering are as follows:

(a) for a private company, 10 months after the end of its accounting reference period (CA 1985 s 244(1)(a));

(b) for a public company, seven months after the end of its accounting reference period (CA 1985 s 244(1)(b)).

If a company's first accounting reference period is greater than 12 months, the maximum period before laying and delivery is 10 (for a private company) or seven (for a public) months from the first anniversary of the incorporation of the company (CA 1985 s 244(2)(a)); or three months from the end of the accounting reference period (CA 1985 s 244(2)(b)), whichever is the later.

This means that a private company could have up to 22 months before its first accounts had to be laid and delivered, and a public company could have up to 19 months.

Listed companies require the accounts and reports to be laid and delivered within six months of the end of the company's financial year (*Admission of Securities to Listing*, Chapter 12, section 42(e)).

Failure to lay and deliver the accounts is treated very seriously by the Registrar of Companies and incurs substantial penalties (CA 1985 s 242A). The directors can also be personally prosecuted for failure to lodge the accounts in time (CA 1985 s 242(2)). The reason for this was that formerly some companies were taking advantage of the considerable laxity in enforcement of the rules. By delaying publication of their accounts, companies could hide behind old, impressive accounts, while not revealing their more recent unsatisfactory accounts. Furthermore, the fines used to be insignificant. The Registrar of Companies is now very active in chasing companies that fall behind in the publication of the accounts. Tardy directors are regularly prosecuted. Persistent failure to publish accounts in time is a matter which the courts can take into account when considering whether or not to disqualify a director under the Company Directors Disqualification Act 1986 s 3(3).

Unlimited companies

In general, unlimited companies do not need to deliver accounts to the Registrar of Companies (CA 1985 s 254(1)) though the accounts still need to be laid before the members unless there has been an elective resolution to the contrary. However, to prevent unscrupulous companies taking advantage of the dispensation from publishing accounts, if an unlimited company at any stage during its accounting reference period was:

- to its knowledge, a subsidiary of an undertaking which was at the time limited; or

- to its knowledge, subject to the potential or actual exercise of rights held by two or more limited undertakings, which if or when exercised would have made the unlimited company a subsidiary of one of those undertakings; or

- a parent company of a company which was at the time limited; or

- a banking company or the parent company of a banking group; or

- a company which was a promoter of a trading stamp scheme such as the Green Stamp scheme and Red Stamp schemes (popular in the late 1960s)

all under the CA 1985 s 254(2) and (3), its accounts must be delivered.

Summary accounts

Although a listed public company must lay its full accounts before a general meeting, and published those accounts and deliver them to the Registrar of Companies, under the CA 1985 s 251(1) a listed public company may send a summary of its accounts to those members who wish to receive a summary financial statement as opposed to the full accounts and reports. This is because following the privatisation of some of the former nationalised industries, companies found that they had huge numbers of shareholders, each of whom received an expensive set of accounts and reports. Conscious that many of the new shareholders only had very small shareholdings and in any event did not trouble themselves to read the accounts and reports anyway because:

(a) they did not understand them or were bored by them,
(b) their views were insignificant because of their small shareholdings,

listed companies lobbied the Government to be allowed to produce less detailed accounts for those that were prepared to have them. Full accounts are still available if they are requested.

Abbreviated and group accounts
Small and medium-sized private companies

Private companies that fall into the above two categories must present their members with their full accounts in the normal way. However, if they are small or medium-sized they do not need to give the Registrar of Companies all their accounts.

A small company is one that under the CA 1985 s 247(3) in relation to a financial year comes within two or more of the following specifications:

– Turnover: not more than £2,800,000;
– Balance sheet total: not more than £1,400,000;
– Average number of employees per week: not more than 50.

"Balance sheet total" means total assets without deduction of liabilities (CA 1985 s 247(5)).

Under the CA 1985 Schedule 8 paras 1–4 the small company may publish accounts without any:

• profit and loss account (CA 1985 Schedule 8 para 2);

• directors' report (CA 1985 Schedule 8 para 4);

• information about the directors' remuneration (CA 1985 Schedule 8 para 3.3);

- details about the different types of assets and capital (CA 1985 s 246(1)(a)).

The accounts thereby produced are known as an abbreviated balance sheet, and the CA 1985 Schedule 8 states what notes to the accounts need to be given. In essence, the abbreviated balance sheet and the notes thereto provide the bare outlines of the company's financial state, without revealing much detail.

A medium-sized company is one that under the CA 1985 s 247(3) in relation to a financial year comes within two or more of the following specifications:

- Turnover: not more than £11,200,000;
- Balance sheet total: not more than £5,600,000;
- Number of employees: not more than 250.

A medium-sized company is similar to a small company, save that it does have to produce a profit and loss account, although within that account the details of the turnover, cost of sales and other operating income need not be specified, all being lumped together in one figure known as "gross profit or loss" (CA 1985 Schedule 8 para 5). The company does not need to give particulars of the figure for turnover broken down into its different sources. However, in all other respects a medium-sized company must provide full company accounts, notes and reports.

Under the CA 1985 s 246(3) the small or medium-sized company exemption from preparing full accounts is not available to the following if at any stage the company is or was during the financial year to which the accounts relate:

- a public company;

- a banking or insurance company;

- an "authorised person" under the Financial Services Act 1986 (*i.e.* someone professionally involved in the provision of investment, insurance or other finance-related advice or services).

Many companies do take advantage of the opportunity to produce abbreviated accounts, though it is worth observing that the Inland Revenue will still require full accounts and any lender or investor would be likely to insist on seeing detailed accounts before it lent or invested money in the company. Equally, anyone trading with the company might wish to see its accounts before becoming too involved in its business. But for very small companies, particularly those that no longer require an audit, the exemption from providing full accounts for the Registrar of Companies is very useful.

If the directors wish to take advantage of the above exemptions, they must:

- state that they are taking advantage of the exemptions;

- state the grounds for their belief that they are entitled to present such accounts;

- make such a statement on the actual balance sheet just above the directors' signature (CA 1985 Schedule 8 para 7).

These rules also apply to single member companies with only one director. The auditors must also provide a report confirming that the company may claim these exemptions and that the accounts are properly prepared within the terms of the exemptions (CA 1985 Schedule 8 para 8).

Small companies exemption from audit

In addition to the above dispensation for providing full accounts, certain small companies (as defined earlier in this chapter) may be exempted from having their accounts audited, although under the CA 1985 s 249B(1) the exemption does not apply to the following types of company:

- public companies;

- banks, insurance companies and insurance brokers;

- authorised persons and representatives under the Financial Services Act 1986;

- special register bodies and employers' associations under the Trade Union and Labour Relations (Consolidation) Act 1992;

- charities with an income of more than £250,000;

- companies whose article require or whose members demand an audit;

- parent companies or subsidiary undertakings, unless part of a small group and within the terms of the CA 1985 s 249B(1B) and (1C).

Under the CA 1985 s 249(A) (as amended by the Companies Act 1985 (Audit Exemption) (Amendment) Regulations 1997), for a company to be exempt from audit:

(i) its turnover must be less than £350,000;
(ii) there must be a statement by the directors on the company's balance sheet indicating that the company is exempt under the CA 1985 s 249A(1);
(iii) there must be a statement by the directors on the company's balance sheet confirming that the members have not lodged a notice demanding an audit in terms of the CA 1985 s 249B(2). This subsection states that holders of

10% of the company's issued share capital, or 10% of any class of shares, or in a guarantee company, 10% of the members, may require the company to have the accounts audited. If the members wish to demand an audit, they must give written notice to the company at its registered office at least one month before the end of the company's current financial year;

(iv) there must be a statement by the directors acknowledging that they are responsible for:

    (a) ensuring that the company keeps proper accounting records under the CA 1985 s 221;

    (b) preparing accounts which give a true and fair view of the company's financial affairs in accordance with the requirements of the CA 1985 s 226; and

    (c) otherwise complying with any other relevant requirements of the Companies Acts.

Although it would be possible for a small company not to have its accounts audited but still to produce full accounts for the Registrar of Companies, it is more likely that small companies with unaudited accounts will wish to take advantage of the small company exemption from providing full accounts to the Registrar. If so, the balance sheet must, as with all small companies claiming exemptions from providing full accounts, include a statement by the directors stating that the company is taking advantage of the small company exemptions and that the directors consider that the company is entitled to those exemptions on the grounds of it being a small company.

The purpose of these exemptions, both from audit and from providing full accounts, is to make life easier and cheaper for the small company. The directors will still need to prepare their accounts in the normal way and thereafter refer to the exemption from audit under the CA 1985 s 249A(2).

Some companies may need to change their articles of association to permit the accounts not to be audited.

It is arguable how useful the audit exemption will be. Its primary use will be for a small company that wishes to preserve its privacy and has no other need to produce audited accounts. However, any bank lending to such a company, or any creditors considering trading with such a company, might well wish to have the reassurance of having properly audited accounts, since most people will realistically be suspicious of the directors' own version of the accounts, unchecked by anyone. In any case, the Inland Revenue and Customs and Excise may want to see full accounts. The topic of audit-exemption is also addressed in Chapter 16.

Group companies, and small and medium-sized groups

For the distinction between and significance of group companies and subsidiaries see Chapter 3. Under the CA 1985 s 227 the directors of a parent company are obliged to prepare group accounts in addition to the accounts for the parent company itself. Group accounts combine the accounts of a parent company with its subsidiary undertaking companies' accounts and are known as consolidated accounts. These effectively ignore inter-company transfers which might be used to disguise the unsatisfactory financial position of some of the companies within the group. Under the CA 1985 s 228 a parent company is exempt from preparing consolidated accounts in the UK if the parent company itself is part of a group elsewhere in the European Community and that group's consolidated accounts are drawn up and audited in terms of the provisions of the EC Seventh Directive (83/349). This does not apply, however, if the parent company is listed on a stock exchange anywhere in the European Community (CA 1985 s 228(3)).

All subsidiary undertakings' accounts must be included within the consolidated accounts unless the subsidiary undertaking comes within the terms of the exemptions specified in the CA 1985 s 229:

- the inclusion of the subsidiary undertaking's accounts would not be material for the purpose of giving a true and fair view of the consolidated accounts, on the grounds that the subsidiary's transactions, if any, are too insignificant to have any bearing at all on the consolidated accounts (CA 1985 s 229(2));

- the parent company is severely restricted from exercising any rights to the assets or management of the subsidiary undertaking, perhaps because of the terms of a shareholders' agreement (CA 1985 s 229(3)(a));

- the information necessary for the preparation of the group accounts could not be obtained from the subsidiary undertaking without excessive time, trouble and expense (CA 1985 s 229(3)(b));

- the parent company's interest in the subsidiary undertaking is restricted purely to a subsequent sale and at no previous stage have the subsidiary undertaking's accounts been included within the group accounts (CA 1985 s 229(3)(c));

- the activities of a subsidiary undertaking are so very different from all the other undertakings within the group that the inclusion of the subsidiary undertaking's accounts would be incompatible with the need for the accounts to present a true and fair view of the group's financial standing (CA 1985 s 229(4)).

Just as companies can claim exemptions from some of the normal accounts rules requirements if they are small or medium-sized, so small groups and medium-sized groups can do this as well.

A small group is one that under the CA 1985 s 249(3) in relation to a financial year comes within the following specifications:

– Aggregate turnover: not more than £2,800,000 net or £3,360,000 gross;
– Aggregate balance sheet total: not more than £1,400,000 net or £1,680,000 gross;
– Aggregate number of employees: not more than 50.

A medium-sized group is one that under the CA 1985 s 249(3) in relation to a financial year comes within the following specifications:

– Aggregate turnover: not more than £11,200,000 net or £13,440,000 gross;
– Aggregate balance sheet total: not more than £5,600,000 net or £6,720,000 gross;
– Aggregate number of employees: not more than 250.

Under the CA 1985 s 264(4) a group is ineligible for the above exemptions available to small and medium-sized companies if any of its members are:

• a public company

• a banking or insurance company

• an authorised person under the Financial Services Act 1986.

The CA 1985 Schedule 4 A applies to the preparation of group accounts and is broadly in line with Schedule 4 and with the exemptions for small and medium-sized companies save that inter-group transfers are ignored.

A small group may be audit-exempt in the same manner as a small company, but the group's turnover must be greater than £350,000 and the aggregate balance sheet must not be greater than £1,400,000 (CA 1985 s 249B(1c)).

Dormant companies

Dormant companies are also referred to in Chapter 3. As stated above, under the CA 1985 s 250(3), providing there has been no accounting transaction in the company records the company may be treated as dormant and is not required to have an audit. The directors must state that there has been no change in the company's financial position and the dormancy of the company must initially have been approved by the members by a special resolution (CA 1985 s 250(1)). For each year that the company is dormant the directors will prepare their own accounts showing the company's assets (commonly the capital value of just one or two shares) and stating that there has been no change in the company's financial position.

The dormant state of the company stops the moment there is an accounting transaction, and thereafter accounts will need to be prepared in the normal manner.

Revision of defective accounts or reports

If the directors consider that the published accounts or reports are defective, they may prepare revised ones, as permitted by the CA 1985 s 245. If, however, the accounts come to the notice of the Secretary of State as to whether the accounts have been properly prepared within the terms of the Companies Acts, he can ask the directors to explain any non-compliance with the terms of the Companies Acts (CA 1985 s 245A). The Secretary of State, or someone authorised in his place, can apply to court to insist that the accounts be revised (CA 1985 s 245B). At present the Secretary of State delegates his authority in this matter to the Financial Reporting Review Panel Limited, part of the Review Panel, which, in turn, is part of the Financial Reporting Council which advises on Financial Reporting Standards (FRSs). Compulsory revision of accounts has not happened often, although the conglomerate Trafalgar House plc was recently required to rewrite its accounts after questions about the extent of its compliance with the accounting requirements of the Companies Acts has been raised. Court action was not necessary: the potential bad publicity overcame the directors' reluctance to amend the accounts.

Summary

1. Accounts are the normal method of assessing a company's financial viability. Most companies lodge most of their accounts at the Registrar of Companies: there are exemptions for small and medium-sized companies limiting the amount of information that needs to be published (CA 1985 ss 246–249), and groups of companies must provide consolidated accounts (CA 1985 s 227). All members are entitled to see the accounts (CA 1985 s 238).

2. Each company must maintain accounting records, though these are not available to the general public (CA 1985 s 221).

3. Accounts must be made up to the end of the company's financial year, and lodged with the Registrar of Companies within strict time-limits thereafter (CA 1985 s 242). The accounts are prepared by the directors (CA 1985 s 226(1)) and must present a true and fair view of the company's financial position (CA 1985 s 226(2)). The accounts must be audited by auditors (except for certain small companies) (CA 1985 s 235) and there should be explanatory notes to the accounts prepared by the directors (CA 1985 Schedule 5). The directors must also provide a directors' report detailing the progress of the company over the financial year for the accounts in question (CA 1985 ss 234 and 234A).

4. Defective accounts may be revised: if the Secretary of State considers it appropriate, the accounts must be revised (CA 1985 s 245B).

12. INSIDER DEALING

Insider dealing: "The victimless crime" – Criminal Justice Act 1993 – to whom does the Act apply? – investigation of insider dealing – the permitted defences – how insider dealing is dealt with in other jurisdictions – should insider dealing give rise to civil penalties? – is the criminalisation of insider dealing an effective sanction?

Insider dealing: "The victimless crime"

Insider dealing is the use for gain of secret information about publicly traded investments by those who are privy to that information and who should not be taking advantage of their knowledge of that information. The mechanics of insider dealing are best explained by the well-known case of Geoffrey Collier.

R v Collier 1987 (Unreported). Geoffrey Collier was a director of Morgan Grenfell, the merchant bank. While working in one department of the bank, he received secret information from another department about a proposed and hitherto undisclosed takeover of the engineering company, AE. Acting on that information, he telephoned the local agent for his own private company, Pureve Ltd, registered in the Cayman Islands, and instructed the agent to place an order with firms of London stockbrokers to buy shares in AE. The agent did as requested. Shortly after, the news of the takeover of AE became official. The share price of AE soared. When Collier judged that the share price had risen far enough, he telephoned his agent again to arrange for his shares in AE to be sold, netting Collier a healthy profit. The Stock Exchange Surveillance Unit noticed the curious buying and subsequent sale by Pureve Ltd. On investigation, Pureve was found to be registered in the Cayman Islands. On investigation at the Cayman Islands Register of Companies, it was found that Collier and his wife were directors of the company. When challenged about this, Collier admitted that he had been insider dealing. He was tried and convicted. He received a 12-month sentence, suspended for two years, a fine of £25,000 and £7,000 costs. He also lost his job at Morgan Grenfell.

Many people's introduction to insider dealing is through the film, *Wall Street*, starring Michael Douglas, playing the Mephistophelian role of Gordon Gekko, a corporate raider. Gordon Gekko made his own contribution to the world of corporate finance by the two phrases, "Greed is good" and "Lunch is for wimps". Gekko is alleged to be loosely based on the New York arbitrageur, Boesky. Boesky was a renowned insider dealer, with an extraordinary ability both to manipulate his contacts and to control his highly complex financial transactions. Ultimately he was caught, convicted and served two years in an open prison, apparently spending must of his time there playing tennis. Despite the considerable fines and compensation he was required to pay, it is alleged that on his release he was able to return to the large sums of money that he had prudently banked offshore, in non-traceable accounts, prior to his arrest.

The victimless crime

Insider dealing is described sometimes as a victimless crime, because, while it is easy to see who benefits from it, it is harder to see who loses by the crime. However, people do lose by insider dealing. They are those investors who are denied the same opportunities as the insider dealers to make profits because they do not have access to the information which the insider dealer has. Such investors are the victims, though it is difficult to identify them all individually and to assess what their losses are. Their losses are the difference between the profits they made (if any) or the losses they managed to avoid (if any) and the profits they might have made, or the losses they might have avoided, had they had access to the same information as the insider dealer. Producing an accurate figure for the extent of these losses is almost impossible to calculate since it involves so many hypotheticals.

The need for immediate access to information

The significant issue is the access to information. It is in the nature of information that some people will always have it before others, and those who have it first will take advantage of it. Rothschild, the famous 19th century London banker, employed a team of runners to tell him the result of the battle of Waterloo, so that he could be first in London to know who had been victorious. If the British and Prussians had been victorious, any exporting business would be likely to have great opportunities open to it, and the stock of exporting businesses would rise (as indeed they did) once confirmation of victory arrived. Rothschild thus earned himself another fortune. Had Napoleon won the battle, exporting companies' shares would have fallen, and Rothschild would have sold his holdings while he still could.

   The leaking of untrue information may also give rise to the creation of an artificial market in shares. A confidence trickster managed to cheat the London Stock Exchange a few years before Waterloo by claiming to be a senior officer of the British army in Europe who had been sent home with the secret news of Napoleon's death. He explained that the news of the emperor's death was being kept secret by the French Government because the French Government had not had time to decide upon Napoleon's successor. The confidence trickster had bought a large amount of stock in British companies shortly before he made his spurious announcement about Napoleon's death. As the rumour of Napoleon's death spread, so the price of many companies' shares rose because of the likelihood of increased trade with Europe. Once the overall share prices had risen far enough but before the rumour could be proved false, the confidence trickster sold all his newly acquired stock and fled the country with a large fortune.

In order to minimise the opportunities for insider dealing or misleading the financial markets, the Stock Exchange tries to ensure that in the UK all relevant information about securities is made public as soon as possible (*Admission of Securities to Listing*, Chapter 9, sections 1–10). Even so, some people are bound to know about some company information sooner than others. Such people might be the typists who type out the information, the directors who take the decisions, the officials who decide when to release the information. Even a doctor or other professional person who deals with a company director might be in possession of useful information. Although many people working in the financial world have tight confidentiality clauses in their contracts of employment, as a matter of practice gossip is rife in the financial world. It is thus almost impossible to eradicate illicit use of insider information. It is well known that before major takeovers there is often much activity in the securities of the companies concerned. It is even occasionally suggested that directors of listed companies might be trading in shares in their own companies, usually through private offshore registered companies, in advance of publication of their own companies' annual accounts.

The effect of insider dealing on a stock exchange

When insider dealing takes place, it causes investors to lose confidence in the stock market because those "not in the know" feel that not all investors are being treated equally. They feel that the market is rigged in favour of the insider dealer. The market will not be seen to be running smoothly and fairly. "Clean" investors will then go to another stock market abroad, where the market is seen to operate more fairly. Although London and New York and Tokyo are the largest stock exchanges in the world, there are others eager to supplant them, such as Frankfurt, Paris and Singapore. It is therefore in the London Stock Exchange's interest, and indirectly the national interest, to have a market free from insider dealing lest a large amount of capital ceases to be available to British companies.

Arguments in favour of insider dealing

Although the current consensus is that insider dealing is wrong, there are those who claim that as it has always existed, and always will, one may as well accept the fact of its existence. It is true that insider dealing has existed for a long time. Historically, one of the reasons investors used stockbrokers was because stockbrokers were always supposed to keep their ear to the ground. They were thus able to recommend certain investments about which they had inside knowledge. Some stockbrokers took this one stage further. They would buy certain shares in advance of recommending the shares to their clients. The clients would then buy the shares, thus pushing up the share price. When the share price had risen enough, the stockbrokers would then sell their own stock.

The reward for entrepreneurial ability
It is said that insider dealing is one way whereby senior managers (a term which includes all directors and senior executives in a quoted company) can be rewarded for their entrepreneurial skills.

The problem with this argument is that there are other fairer and more accountable methods of ensuring that managers are rewarded for their entrepreneurial skills. Managers could be paid bonuses or high salaries. These methods do not involve taking advantage of information which only the managers have. Managers allowed to reward themselves by means of insider dealing might spend their time seeking the best time to make announcements about their companies, more for the benefit of their own wallets than for the benefit of the shareholders as a whole. While managers are not necessarily obliged to consider the position of individual shareholders who might be deprived of the managers' opportunities to carry out insider deals, the managers would be unwise to alienate all their shareholders by obvious profiteering. There might also be a breach of the fiduciary duty of the managers to act in the best interests of the company as a whole. In any event, under the Model Code for directors of listed companies there are only limited opportunities for directors to acquire or sell securities (see *Admission of Securities to Listing*, Chapter 16 (Appendix)).

Those who support the argument that insider dealing is a fair return for managers' entrepreneurial ability often find their views hard to justify when managers are selling shares in advance of price-sensitive bad news about the company. It is one thing to reward managers by letting them take advantage of good results arising from their hard work or good ideas when the share price rises: it is another to let those same managers be rewarded for knowing about bad news sooner than anyone else – and making a profit out of the fall in their company's share price.

A further reason for managers not to carry out insider dealing is that it is demoralising for employees. If the employees see the senior management apparently taking advantage of the market and the other shareholders (some of whom will often be employees) by insider dealing, it will lead to a lessening of respect for the management. This, in turn, leads to less loyalty and commitment by the company's employees – and consequent lowering of standards. Lowered standards ultimately lead to unprofitability.

Insider dealing helps relay information into the market and thereby makes it efficient

It is said that insider dealers, by their moving before anyone else, ensure that price-sensitive information about the company is not withheld by the company. If a company had poor end of year results, it might wish to delay publishing them for as long as it could get away with it. But the insider dealer would sell his shares while he could. Because he would sell them, other investors would wonder what was behind the inside dealer's move, and raise questions about the company's finances – thus flushing out the unwelcome news about the accounts. Indeed, this is what used to happen. Boesky, mentioned earlier, had such a good net of contacts that whenever he took a stake in a company a number of "piggy-backing" investors used to follow him, not because they knew much about the company, but they knew that he did, and that the relevant information about the company would be bound to come out fairly soon. So, to a certain extent, this argument is valid. However, even if it is valid, it does not mean that it serves as a justification for unfair treatment of shareholders not "in the know". There are fairer ways than insider dealing of relaying information into the market-place. Probably the best way is to ensure that all relevant information is made to the Companies Announcement Office as soon as possible (*Admission of Securities to Listing*, Chapter 9, sections 1–10). In theory this should prevent the insider dealer being able to profit from his insider knowledge.

Criminal Justice Act 1993 ss 52–64

The above legislation contains the current law on insider dealing, and is part of the Criminal Justice Act 1993 ("CJA") because insider dealing is a criminal offence, not a civil offence. There are no sections of the CJA dealing with the civil consequences of insider dealing. Previously the crime of insider dealing had been prohibited under statute in the Company Securities (Insider Dealing) Act 1985. The European Community subsequently produced its Insider Dealing Directive (89/592) which the Government was required to implement in due course. Before doing so the DTI issued a consultative document on the law on insider dealing, and drew on the responses it received to prepare the current Act. The present rules were brought into force on 1 March 1995.

The way that the rules operate is that the offence of insider dealing is defined in terms of the actual dealing by insider dealers within the context of a regulated market. Any act within those parameters is an offence unless it comes within the various permitted defences. What is meant by insider dealing, insider dealers, and regulated markets is carefully explained. Insider dealing, depending on the severity of the offence, can be prosecuted either at summary level (*i.e.* before one judge with a maximum penalty of two years' imprisonment and/or a fine) or on indictment (*i.e.* before a judge and jury, with a maximum penalty of seven years' imprisonment and/or a much greater fine). As an additional penalty, a company director may be disqualified from being a director under the CDDA 1986, as happened in *R* v *Goodman* [1993] 2 All ER 789.

The offence of insider dealing

The offence of insider dealing takes place when an individual (but not a corporate entity) who has insider information (from an inside source) as an insider deals in securities whose price will be affected by that information if and when the information is made public. The dealing must take place on a regulated market, and must be done by the insider or through a professional intermediary or by an insider acting in his capacity as a professional intermediary (CJA s 52(1) and (3)).

In addition, the legislation catches an insider who encourages some other person to deal in securities which are price-affected – irrespective of whether or not the other person knows they are price-affected – while knowing or expecting that dealing would take place on a regulated market, through a professional intermediary, or through the insider acting as a professional intermediary (CJA s 52(2)(a)). This is to outwit astute insider dealers who arrange for others – close relatives, for example – to do the insider dealing either secretly on their own behalf or genuinely to benefit those relatives without the insider dealing being traced back to the insider dealers.

It is furthermore an offence of insider dealing to disclose information which you have as an insider to any other person except in the proper performance of your employment, office, or profession (CJA s 52(2)(b)). This means that if you gave a secret tip to a friend about, say, a proposed takeover, you could still be convicted of insider dealing, even if you did not deal yourself.

There are many definitions required here.

Inside information

This is information about particular securities, or a particular issuer of securities, which is specific to this securities in question. The information must not have been made public, but if it were to be made public it would have a "significant" effect on the price or value of the securities (CJA s 56(1)). "Significant" is not defined in the CJA, so it remains to be seen what is meant by that term. Not all unpublished information is likely to affect the price of securities is specific enough to be inside information. For example, trade with some countries would be profoundly affected by successful assassination attempts on their rulers. These assassinations might not be made public by those countries' governments, but once known would probably affect the securities of all companies trading extensively with those countries. However, information about such events does not relate specifically to a particular company's securities or to one issuer of securities: it would affect all companies trading with those countries. Or to use the historical event referred to above, what Rothschild did in 1815 after Waterloo could not be classed nowadays as insider dealing.

Insider source
Under the CJA s 57(2) a person has information from an inside source if he has that information:

(i)   in his position as a director, employee or shareholder of an issuer of securities, or
(ii) because he has access to the information through his employment, office or profession, or
(iii) because he obtained the information from someone in (i) and (ii) above.

So if you are a banker, lawyer or accountant for a company which is your client and you have inside information about that company and you use it or pass it on to others who use it, you will be an inside source. The previous legislation in a similar context used the word "obtain" rather than the words "has" or "have". The word "obtain" suggested a purposeful seeking out of information, or so the unsuccessful accused argued in *Attorney-General's Reference (No 1 of 1988)* [1989] AC 971. Although the House of Lords gave a wide interpretation to "obtain" in that context, the Parliamentary draftsmen has in the CJA use the more neutral words "has" or "have" to convey the sense of being in possession of the information even if you did not actively try to get hold of that information.

Insider
Under the CJA s 57(1) an insider is someone who:

(i)   has inside information (as opposed to information which he thinks is inside information but actually is public knowledge);
(ii) knows he has inside information;
(iii) has information which he has obtained from an inside source (as opposed to obtaining it from some other method, such as an intelligent guess or by deduction from observing the previous business practice of the company and its directors); and
(iv) knows that it came from an inside source (as opposed to obtaining it from someone who he did not realise was an inside source).

So if an accused can prove that he genuinely did not know his information was inside information and that he did not know it came from an inside source –

neither of which would be easy to prove unless the accused was very naive – he should be able to raise a defence.

Securities
Securities is defined in Schedule 2 to Part V of the CJA and covers:

- shares;

- debt securities, being debentures, bonds, deposit certificates, local authority bonds, treasury bonds ("gilts");

- warrants to subscribe for shares or debt securities;

- depositary receipts

- options to acquire any of the items in Schedule 2;

- futures in respect of shares, debt securities, or depository receipts;

- contracts for differences in respect of the same items as futures.

For the definition of shares, debentures, warrants and options, see Chapter 7.

Gilts are like debentures issued by the Government, paying a fixed return of interest and returning their full value on redemption. They are called "gilts" because they used to be printed with gilt edging on the outside. Depositary receipts are a form of investment comprising a bundle of securities issued by a particular issuer and deposited with a bank. The bank then issues further securities which can then be traded in their own right. They are useful in transnational transactions for British companies wishing to raise capital in the USA. Inside information about the underlying securities will affect the value of the securities issued by the bank.

Futures are contracts which provide for securities to be bought or sold and delivered at a future date at a predetermined price. Contracts for differences are a sophisticated form of gamble on the price movements of share indices (such as the FTSE 100), securities or interest rates.

Public
The CJA clearly did not wish to limit the many potential ways by which information can be made public. It therefore stated that information is made public under the CJA s 58(2) if:

- it is published through the rules of the market in which the securities are being traded;

- it is to be found in records open to the public, such as the registers in Companies House;

- it can be readily acquired by those likely to deal in the securities or with the issuer of the securities;

- it derived from information which is already in the public domain.

Information is still deemed to be public even if it can only be acquired by persons exercising "diligence or expertise", is limited to a few recipients, can only be obtained by observation or requires to be paid for, or is published outside the UK (CJA s 58(3)). This particular exemption is designed to protect investment analysts who study company results and quiz the companies' management on those accounts. It would be iniquitous if perspicacious analysts were to be classed as insider dealers just because they happened to worm out more information than others. These rules are not exhaustive, and other methods of becoming public, such as publication in a newspaper, will be deemed to be public.

Dealing
Dealing is any buying or selling securities as principal or as agent, or the procuring of any buying or selling of any securities by an agent or nominee or someone acting under the dealer's directions (CJA s 55). In this context, buying and selling include agreeing to buy or to sell (CJA s 55(2) and (3)). This is to cover options for purchase or sale.

Regulated market
A regulated market at present means the London Stock Market (both the Official List and the Alternative Investment Market), the London International Financial Futures and Options Exchange and such other markets as the Treasury approves from time to time.

Professional intermediary
A professional intermediary means, in effect, a stockbroker or other broker of securities acting in the course of his regular business. Occasional broking transactions are not deemed to be carrying on a business. (CJA s 59).

Price-affected and price-sensitive
In relation to securities and information respectively, the information about the securities must be likely to have an effect on the securities if the inside information about the securities were made public.

Issuer
An issuer is a company, public sector body or individual which or who issues securities. A public sector body includes the Government, local authorities, international organisations which include the UK or other EC members, the Bank of England or the central bank of any sovereign state (CJA s 60(2) and (3)).

To whom does the CJA apply?

Clearly the CJA applies to insider dealers, but as a matter of practice certain people are more likely to have to be aware of the reach of the CJA than others. These include:

- directors and employees of quoted companies;

- professionals, such as lawyers and accountants, acting for such companies;

- those providing services to such companies, such as bankers or stockbrokers;

- people working in merchant banks advising such companies;

- those working in certain Government departments which have access to confidential matters in connection with such companies, such as the Inland Revenue, Customs and Excise, the DTI, the Monopolies and Mergers Commission;

- those working for the Stock Exchange itself.

This list is not exhaustive. It is now common for bank employees and other persons working in the financial industry to have to report their personal dealings in any investments to an official known as a compliance officer (frequently the same person as the company secretary) whose task is to monitor those dealings and thereby to ensure that no employee is taking advantage of any inside information. If employees unauthorisedly deal in securities in a company for which the bank is acting, they may be dismissed – if they are caught. Some banks are so worried about the possibility of insider dealing that all telephone calls and faxes from and to the bank are logged. This means that insider dealers have to use other non-traceable means of communicating, such as public telephones.

Some insider dealers are ordinary investors with very good or discreet contacts. Boesky (discussed earlier) had very good contacts, and sometimes paid his contacts on a commission basis.

Investigations into insider dealing

In order to prosecute an insider dealer, it is necessary to detect instances of insider dealing and, if necessary, to investigate those instances. Under the Financial Services Act 1986 ss 177–178 ("FSA") the Secretary of State can appoint inspectors to investigate any insider dealing and make a report to him (FSA s 177(4)). The team of inspectors, who usually comprise an accountant and lawyer, can require anyone who knows about the insider dealing to hand over documents (whether in written or computer form) to them, to be examined by them, on oath if necessary, and to assist in the investigation (FSA s 177(3)). It is the duty of that person to comply with these requirements. Any evidence supplied by that person may later be used in evidence against him (FSA s 177(6)) in criminal or civil proceedings. The only exemptions to this arise where legal privilege or banking confidentiality arises (FSA s 177(7) and (8)). If, as a result of any subsequent proceedings arising out of the report by the investigation the accused is convicted, he has the added indignity of having to pay the expense of the investigation (FSA s 177(11)).

Since anyone involved in insider dealing would be understandably reluctant to volunteer information to the inspectors, the FSA s 178 provides means of enforcing compliance. If someone refuses to co-operate or answer questions put to him, the matter can be referred to court. If there is no reasonable excuse for his lack of co-operation or refusal to answer questions he can be punished as if for contempt of court even though he is not technically before a court of law when he is being questioned by the inspectors (FSA s 178(2)). The Secretary of State is also empowered to cancel any authorisation that person may have to carry on investment business (FSA s 178(3)).

How the inspectors are supposed to act in the course of their investigation has been the subject of some discussion, but broadly speaking, the inspectors are there to ascertain facts rather than to establish guilt – though their report may well make recommendation or have findings which are used in subsequent proceedings – but in so doing, the inspectors must act fairly, and allow those likely to be affected by the findings of their report an opportunity to explain their position. There is no right of appeal against the findings of a report, though there might be a judicial review of the manner in which the findings were reached if there were some fundamental unfairness in the way information was obtained.

There are suggestions that the inspectors' powers are excessive, and that the power to compel witnesses to answer on oath is oppressive. After all, if you are alleged to have committed a murder, you are not bound to answer police questions, though the fact of your refusal to answer them may be brought to the attention of the jury. The justification for these powers is said to be that insider dealers are usually crafty enough to route their insider dealing through offshore companies which cannot, by their very nature, testify. Without the power to compel attendance or to give answers under oath, the inspectors might get nowhere. As ever, there is a balance to be found between the need for civil liberties and the need to find out the facts in order to prevent their repetition.

The permitted defences

The burden of proof

Normally in a criminal trial, the burden of proving that the accused committed a crime lies upon the prosecution. If the prosecution cannot prove beyond reasonable doubt that the accused committed the crime, the accused is acquitted.

However, in a trial for insider dealing, the burden of proof lies upon the accused to show that his defence comes within the terms of one or more of the permitted defences (CJA s 53 and Schedule 1). But because the wording of the CJA s 53 and Schedule 1 specifically uses the word "shows", as opposed to "proves", the accused does not have to prove beyond all reasonable doubt that his actions fell within the terms of the permitted defences. It may not always be easy to show that an accused's actions were within the terms of the permitted defences. It is nonetheless considerably easier to *show* that the actions were within the terms of the permitted defences than to have to *prove* that the actions were defensible. Accordingly, although it may seem unjust that the accused has the burden of proof placed upon him to establish his innocence, at least the standard of proof is not as high as it might otherwise be. The standard of proof for the accused is close to that of a civil case (*i.e.* on the balance of probabilities) rather than a criminal case (*i.e.* beyond all reasonable doubt).

Specific defences

Some of the defences involve the lack of a deliberate intention to commit an insider deal. So if someone did not know that certain information was inside information, but it was, and he unexpectedly made a profit because the information turned out to be price-sensitive, he would not be committing a crime (CJA s 53(1)(a)). Likewise if someone had reasonable grounds for believing that information he had was sufficiently well known to ensure that no other investors were prejudiced, although in reality it was inside information, he would have committed no crime (CJA s 53(1)(b)). If someone would have dealt anyway even if he had not had the information, again no crime is committed (CJA s 53(1)(c)). This might happen if someone were required to sell all his investments in a hurry because he had to settle some urgent claim against him.

There are similar defences for those who encourage others to deal in securities (CJA s 53(2)).

For those who disclose inside information, and would normally be guilty of insider dealing under the CJA s 52(2)(b) (disclosing information other than in the proper course of their business), there are two defences.

The first is that they did not expect those who received the information to use it to deal in securities on a regulated market (CJA s 53(3)(a)).

Proving the existence of their lack of expectation of what others might do may in practice be quite difficult.

The other is that while they did expect the recipients of the information to deal on a regulated market, they did not expect that dealing to result in profit because the information unexpectedly turned out to be price-sensitive.

In all these defences, making a profit means both making a profit and avoiding making a loss (CJA s 53(6)).

In addition to the above defences, there is another set of defences, known as "Special Defences". The requirement of the burden of proof on the accused, discussed earlier, applies to these defences as well. The Special Defences are to be found in Schedule 1.

The first of them is designed to protect market-makers who are acting in good faith in the course of business (Schedule 1, para 1). A market-maker might be instructed by a client to buy some shares and sell them again. The market-maker might have his doubts, but if he is acting in the course of his normal business, it is not for him to query the transaction. The Stock Exchange Surveillance Unit will do that.

The second defence is that the insider dealer (or the person encouraged to deal on his behalf) was using "market information" and that it was reasonable for him to have used it as he did. "Market information" has been deliberately left wide, not to say vague, in its meaning. Some examples may help.

1. A company bidding to take over another company (the "target") will naturally wish to build up a stake in the target. The buying of shares to build up that stake will undoubtedly affect the price of the target company's shares. Accordingly anyone in the takeover company or any merchant bank involved in the proposed takeover has the benefit of price-sensitive information but, without this special defence, would be an insider dealer if he used that information as part of the strategy for the takeover.

2. A liquidator might be required to wind up the assets of a company which happens to have investments in another company which that liquidator, in another capacity, might happen to have inside information about.

The third defence is a defence to the effect that you would not be guilty of insider dealing if you were acting in conformity with the price stabilisation rules under the Financial Services Act 1986 s 48(2)(i). These are rules which an authorised body can draw up for the purpose of preventing the price of investments fluctuating wildly. Acting in accordance with the regulations will be a valid defence.

There are further possible defences. Under the CJA s 62 the legislation only applies within the United Kingdom, so insider dealing carried out from abroad will be difficult to prosecute. Insider dealing on another country's stock market is also not a crime justiciable in the UK (CJA s 62(1)(b)). This provision gives effect to the obvious point that the UK authorities could not police insider dealing in another country, and that the authorities are powerless when insider dealing is being carried on in the UK from a source outside the UK. Many insider deals are alleged to be routed through offshore tax havens, particularly if they have laws requiring their banks to retain strict confidentiality. However, if an insider dealer proposes to flee to certain countries with the gains from his insider deals, he should first ensure that he flees only to countries with which the UK does not have an extradition treaty.

Sometimes questions of evidence arise. Although the case is not relevant in England or Northern Ireland, the Scottish case of *HMA* v *Mackie*, 1994 SCCR 277 resulted in an acquittal on appeal because in Scotland corroboration of evidence is required.

Mackie had had a conversation with a Mr Runciman, the chairman of the waste company, Shanks and McEwan plc. Runciman's account of that conversation was that he told Mackie of a forthcoming profits warning which would lead to a drop in the value of the shares. Runciman claimed that he told Mackie not to use this information until the profits warning had been issued. Mackie's understanding of the same conversation was that there was no mention of any profits warning, but that Runciman had said that the financial year they had been discussing had not been a vintage year and that there would be little growth in the earnings per share. Mackie believed that this was information in the public domain. Mackie thereupon advised his clients to sell a small proportion of their shares in Shanks and McEwan while retaining the rest. Since there was no one else present during the conversation, it was a question of Runciman's word against Mackie's. The prosecution had argued that the subsequent sale of the shares was corroboration, and the jury accepted that view – or in other words they believed Runciman more than they believed Mackie. However, the High Court stated that the sale of the shares did not amount to corroboration of Runciman's words and that Mackie should be acquitted. Runciman shortly afterwards retired, and ever since that case, investment analysts have gone around in pairs, taking notes and carefully asking not to be given any inside information.

How insider dealing is dealt with in other jurisdictions

In the United States the Securities Exchange Act 1934 ss 10b–5 and 16(b) and the Insider Trading and Securities Fraud Enforcement Act 1988 apply (as does the common law) to insider dealing. Stockbrokers and other financial services businesses are required to set up systems to prevent insider dealing. There are various sanctions for insider dealers: they may have to pay a fine to the US Treasury of up to three times the amount of the unlawful profits and/or be sent to prison. There are also civil remedies available, provided you can be sure who suffered as a result of the insider deal.

In the Republic of Ireland insider dealing is also a criminal matter, but the law there differs significantly from the British position. Under the Companies Act 1990 financial intermediaries are not to countenance deals if they believe that a deal might be an insider deal, off-market insider deals can be illegal (whereas only deals on a regulated market in the UK are illegal), and there is a civil remedy for insider dealing. Where one party has inside information and the other does not, the party with the inside information must compensate the other for any loss caused by the insider deal. This will only work effectively when the insider is aware who the other parties to the transactions are.

Most developed countries are adopting anti-insider dealing legislation, some more Draconian than others. In some countries it has taken some time for insider dealing to be recognised as unfair, let alone illegal. Insider dealing is obviously easier to carry out where the securities market is not open to public scrutiny and where companies can easily withhold price-sensitive information. Much also depends on how effectively the sanctions against insider dealing can be enforced.

Should insider dealing give rise to civil penalties?

In the case of *Percival* v *Wright* [1902] 2 Ch 421, a shareholder wished to sell his shares. He asked the directors if they could help him find a purchaser. Mindful of the fact that there was a potential takeover offer, some of the directors agreed to acquire the shareholder's shares. They then intended to sell them to the takeover bidder. When the shareholder heard what the directors were proposing to do, he was aggrieved that the directors had withheld the information about the takeover from him. It was held that the directors owed the individual shareholder no duty to disclose to him information that they had obtained in their capacity as directors. The shareholder should have been on his guard when the directors wanted to buy his shares. This decision, which is also of significance in the area of directors' fiduciary duties, perhaps belongs to a time when the courts were less critical of directors' behaviour unless it was positively dishonest. Nonetheless, it, in effect, held that to profit from inside information would not give rise to a civil claim.

This decision has not been overruled, but the principle of no civil liability for insider dealing is not generally regarded nowadays as being entirely fair to the uninformed shareholder. In any event nowadays such behaviour would be a breach of the directors' fiduciary duty to account to the company (not the shareholder) for any unauthorised profits (see *Regal Hastings Ltd* v *Gulliver and others* [1967] 2 AC 134, discussed in Chapter 14).

Some commentators on the law of insider dealing in the UK say that insider dealing should have civil consequences. The threat of having to repay, by way of damages, the amount that others have lost, or failed to gain, might, it is thought, concentrate the insider dealer's mind towards honesty.

The reason that this idea has not been implemented into UK law is that it is difficult under the present arrangements for the sale and purchase of securities on the stock market always to know:

(a) who has suffered loss,
(b) who was the insider dealer, and
(c) how great the loss is.

The insider dealer who buys in the stock market does not generally know who held the shares before he did, and any former shareholder might have been quite happy to sell anyway. The insider dealer who sells shares while they are still high before the announcement of bad news will not generally know who buys his shares once he sells them. A purchaser might have been quite happy to buy at the insider dealer's price anyway. It is thus difficult precisely to identify the aggrieved shareholders who could be plaintiffs (in Scotland, pursuers) in any action for civil damages against an insider dealer.

It is also difficult to devise a scheme whereby compensation was payable to those who were truly the victims of an insider deal, but not to those who would have been dealing anyway. In any event for some smaller shareholders the amount of compensation might be minimal – far less than the administrative cost of giving each shareholder his proportional share of the compensation.

If it is difficult to identify the plaintiff, it can be difficult to identify the defendant (in Scotland, defender). Although the Stock Exchange Surveillance Team may notice insider dealing, it cannot necessarily discover who the insider dealer is if the insider dealer is using an offshore company.

However, in a one-to-one deal, or a deal involving a very small number of easily ascertainable people who are aware how much they lost, it would be relatively easy to identify the defendant.

It is a well known rule of seeking damages that you must be able to quantify your loss. If you sold your shares to an insider dealer, who then watched the share price soar, as he knew it would, you could, in theory, quantify your loss as his profit on his subsequent sale. But he might argue that you had been quite happy to sell at the agreed price anyway: you were under no obligation to sell. He might also say that at the time he bought the shares he did not know when he going to sell them. Furthermore, how could he know that you might have sold them at the same price as he did?

There is a further difficulty with a civil action against an insider dealer – and it is true of a criminal action too – and that is that many insider deals are carried out on the instructions of companies registered offshore. If an action were raised against them, they would have to agree to defend the action in the UK, something which they would be unlikely to do. Even if an undefended action were taken against an insider dealer in the UK, it might not be worth doing so.

The insider dealing offshore company might have no assets in the UK. By the time the judgment or decree was enforced against the insider dealing company in its offshore jurisdiction, any assets it had would have been safely transferred to another company or indeed country. Enforcement procedures could be a waste of time and money.

As a further difficulty, the legislation as it stands at the moment only applies to individuals, not to corporate entities.

One particular solution to the problem of insider dealing generally might be to make stockbrokers responsible for the insider dealing if the clients for whom they were acting were in fact insider dealers. But one cannot see stockbrokers accepting this responsibility willingly. If they did accept it, it would mean that they would have to vet all their clients and all their clients' transactions, which would drive up their costs. This might, in turn, mean that other uninvolved investors would go to a cheaper stock market elsewhere. And the insider dealers would probably move to another less punctilious stock market too. How scrupulous would the vetting have to be to both workable but effective?

While none of these individually are very telling points, cumulatively they make it unlikely that under the present system there will be civil penalties for insider dealing involving publicly quoted shares. It might be possible to permit civil action against insider dealing in unquoted companies but so far this has not taken place in the UK. It is possible in the Republic of Ireland. As most insider dealing laws throughout the developed world are fairly recent, it remains to be seen in practice how effective civil sanctions will be in those countries that have adopted them. At present the most useful civil sanction against insider dealing is that those who are convicted normally lose their jobs and their status. Cynics would also argue that they would lose their credibility: if they cannot even carry out a successful insider deal, they clearly are ineffective operators.

Is the criminalisation of insider dealing an effective sanction?

The short answer to this question is – not very. Insider dealing is widely seen as unfair, bad for any market where it takes place – but not necessarily as dishonest as, say, theft or false accounting. Indeed, in some quarters it is possibly seen as smart if you can get away with it. Unfortunately, it is relatively easy to get away with it. In the UK, between 1980 and the beginning of 1994 there were 33 prosecutions involving 52 accused. Of these 24 were found guilty (House of Lords Deb. col. 858, 24 January 1994). Within the same period the Stock Exchange Surveillance Unit reported 104 cases to the Department of Trade and Industry.

The authorities contend that while the success rate by the prosecution has not been high, the legislation has been effective in that:

(i)   it serves as a deterrent, and

(ii) it changes people's attitudes to something which to a certain extent had
      formerly been seen as one of the prerequisites of working in the City of
      London or in a stockbroker's office.

This is probably true. However, there are several reasons why the legislation to
date has not been very effective:

(i)   The financial world is highly complex and inhabited by some very sophis-
       ticated and secretive investors. Such people will have many ways of cov-
       ering their tracks, so that although the Surveillance Unit can see there has
       been insider dealing, they cannot find out who is behind the company that
       is doing it. One trick is to spread insider deals through a number of differ-
       ent stockbrokers and through a number of different front companies.
       Another is to use front companies that are registered offshore, preferably
       in jurisdictions where you do not need to give more than minimal details
       about directors or shareholders. The simplest of all is to use a false name
       and address.

(ii)   In some countries, banking secrecy laws are strictly enforced. Any
       inquiries from the Surveillance Unit will be ignored. British police war-
       rants may not be recognised. Some countries, such as Turkish-held
       Northern Cyprus, have uncertain and anomalous international recognition.
       Some countries have no extradition treaties with the UK.

(iii) In Scotland, as stated above, there is a requirement of corroboration. When
       there are two people in the room, and two differing accounts of the same
       conversation, whom do you believe?

Finally, the fact remains that insider dealing takes place. Two stories illustrate
this.

     In August 1995 there was an important announcement by the Electricity
Regulator. The day before the announcement, as a matter of courtesy he wrote
to the chairman of all the English electricity companies warning them of the
decision which was to be the subject of his announcement, and warning them
that his announcement was probably going to affect their companies' share
prices. The letter was meant to be for the chairman's eyes only. But all day long
there was substantial trading in electricity shares as leaks burst out and confidentiality requirements were overlooked. The insider dealing laws did not
detain the insider dealers from taking their usual profits.

     In 1992, the American merchant bank, Salomon Brothers, was accused of
trying to rig US Treasury bond auctions. Paul Mozer, one of the bond traders
involved in the fraud, suspected that his dealings on behalf of his firm were
being monitored by Government regulators. Realising that eventually there

would be a scandal which, in turn, would affect the share price of Salomon Brothers securities, he arranged for his broker to sell his entire holding of 46,000 Salomon shares. The scandal duly broke and the share price fell by 30%.

When he was arrested for his part in the rigging of the Treasury bonds, he discovered that he was also to be charged with insider dealing, having, probably uniquely, managed to make an illegal profit out of the likelihood of being caught for his other illegal activities.

Summary

1. Insider dealing is the illegal use of inside information about securities, and the dealing in securities on the basis of that information by those who should not be using it. It is a criminal offence and is regulated by the Criminal Justice Act 1993.

2. There are specified exemptions to cope with the realities of the financial world. Broadly speaking, the exceptions are to accommodate people, such as market-makers, who have the benefit of inside information but are using it innocently.

3. The law on insider dealing is not particularly effective, but serves as a useful deterrent. At present there are no civil penalties for insider dealing.

13. MINORITY PROTECTION

The problems associated with minority protection – the Foss v Harbottle rules and the exceptions thereto – statutory protection under the CA 1985 s 459 – winding up on the "just and equitable" grounds – DTI investigations – judicial factories in Scotland

One of the blessings and perils of living in any democracy is that the majority view prevails. In a company, the majority view is obtained by the counting of votes, with each person (unless the articles say otherwise) having only one vote per share.

Those who have the most shares in a company generally have the most votes and can direct the affairs of the company. The rationale for this is that those who have most shares have contributed the greatest amount of capital in the company. They are therefore entitled to direct the company to use that capital effectively. This is discussed in greater detail in Chapter 18.

The problems associated with minority protection

Since shares mean votes, and votes mean power, and since power often corrupts, sometimes those who have most shares in the company begin to see the company's interests as solely an extension of their own interests. If a majority of shareholders holds the majority of the company's votes, naturally the majority will decide what the company will do and accordingly may ignore the minority shareholders' wishes. If the minority shareholders dislike this, they can:

- sell their shares, if they are able to;
- accept the fact that they are outvoted;
- in limited circumstances raise an action to protect their own interests;
- under certain circumstances ask the DTI to investigate the company;
- in limited circumstances have the company wound up;
- (in Scotland only) have a judicial factor appointed to run the company.

This at least is the current position. But for many years, the courts found it very difficult to cope with the idea of a minority of shareholders have a justified grievance against a majority. There were various reasons for this:

1. When you become a shareholder, under the CA 1985 s 14 (and its predecessors) you become a member on the terms and conditions of the memorandum and articles of association. These make it clear that majority rule prevails: by becoming a shareholder you accept this rule and you accept that sometimes your views and wishes will be overruled.

2. If you, as a minority shareholder, have been treated badly by the majority, what remedy can you seek? Are you seeking a benefit for yourself, or are you seeking a benefit for the company? Or are you doing both? Whom should you be suing? Should you be suing the company, the majority shareholders or the directors?

3. If every disgruntled minority shareholder was entitled to rush to the courts to complain every time the company made a decision with which the minority disagreed, the courts might be full of pointless and expensive actions.

4. The courts are very reluctant to question commercial decisions. When is a resolution passed by the company a commercial decision which is entirely the company's business, and when is it mistreating a minority?

5. There may be no point in the courts protecting a minority by overruling an unauthorised action by the company, even if strictly speaking the company should not have done the action complained of. This is because the company might then convene a general meeting and ratify, perfectly legitimately, the formerly unauthorised action. This particular argument will be referred to hereafter as the "pointless protection" argument.

At the same time, there are occasions when it is clear that a minority is being mistreated by the majority.

1. Majority shareholders may be in a position to change the company's articles in such a way as to disadvantage a minority. For example, the majority might create a new class of shares with enhanced rights for themselves while keeping the minority ordinary shareholders in a lesser position. Another majority ploy might be to award high salaries and pension contributions to themselves as directors while awarding the minority shareholders little or nothing by way of dividends.

2. Majority shareholders are often the directors of a company, and as directors they are not normally obliged to discuss all business and financial matters with the shareholders. The minority might not have much idea what the company is doing and be unable to force the directors to reveal more.

3. If the directors are also the majority shareholders, it becomes impossible for the minority shareholders to dismiss the directors under the CA 1985 s 303.

4. The minority shareholders might find the cost of raising an action against the majority very expensive.

5. Although it is easy to say to a disgruntled minority shareholder that he should sell his shares, in practice in any but a publicly quoted company (and sometimes not even then) it may be difficult to find purchasers for the shares.

6. If the directors are doing something which they should not be doing, the company should raise an action against them. But if those directors are also the majority shareholders, they are not going to vote in favour of an action which might ultimately be to their detriment.

Historically the progress of legal protection for minority shareholders has proceeded as follows:

1. Following the rule in *Foss* v *Harbottle* (1843) 2 Hare 461 (to be discussed below) minority shareholders could not obtain redress against a majority of shareholders unless the company in general meeting authorised action against the majority. Only the company had title to sue.

2. It was soon realised that this was unduly oppressive to minority shareholders who had clearly been treated unfairly. Four categories of unfairness were established, and these act as exceptions to the rule in *Foss* v *Harbottle*.

3. Despite having admitted those categories, the courts were extremely reluctant to use them or to expand them, though the position of directors (who often were the same people as the majority shareholders) was increasingly brought under control by statute (see Chapter 14).

4. The Companies Act 1948 s 210 was designed to protect minority shareholders but was barely effective, partly through poor drafting and partly through judicial reluctance to widen the ambit of minority shareholders' claims. Rather as with the *ultra vires* rule, judges seemed to have been wedded to a legalistic view of company law at odds with the commercial needs of businessmen for certainty and clarity.

5. The Companies Acts 1980, 1985 and 1989 have all improved the position of the minority shareholder significantly. The CA 1985 s 459 (as amended by the CA 1989) contains the current statutory remedy for the minority shareholder. However, there is a growing view that the pendulum has almost swung too far in favour of the minority shareholder. As most companies do not wish to be tied up in litigation, the aggrieved minority shareholder may well effectively have to be paid to go away.

6. Increasingly, minority shareholders are using the statutory remedy of the CA 1985 s 459 and ignoring the exceptions to the rule in *Foss* v *Harbottle*. They

are wise to do this. The four categories of exceptions to the rule in *Foss* v *Harbottle* are procedurally awkward, vexed by inconsistency, or are unlikely to arise because of changes elsewhere in company law and practice. It is significant that there have been very significant recent cases on minority protection using the exceptions to *Foss* v *Harbottle*. A recent reported case is *Barrett* v *Duckett* [1995] 1 BCLC 243, the significance of which lies in the fact that the judge was clearly unimpressed by the use of a derivative action under the exceptions to *Foss* v *Harbottle*, saying that the CA 1985 s 459 was not only an alternative remedy but the "plain and obvious" one. Other countries, such as Australia and Canada, which had initially adopted the exceptions to *Foss* v *Harbottle*, have moved to statutory remedies similar to the CA 1985 s 459. Increasingly, the exceptions will become of historical interest only.

7. There are alternatives to minority protection actions. It is possible to have the company wound up on "just and equitable" grounds under certain limited circumstances.

   It is possible to invite DTI inspectors to investigate the company, or DTI inspectors may be imposed on the company.

   In Scotland only it is possible to have a judicial factor appointed by the courts to take over the affairs of the company.

The *Foss* v *Harbottle* rules and the exceptions thereto

The case of *Foss* v *Harbottle* predates the first Companies Acts but dealt with a very fundamental problem in company law.

Foss and Turton were minority shareholders in a company of which Harbottle and his associates were directors and shareholders. In their personal capacities Harbottle and his associates sold a plot of land to the company at an inflated price. At that time the present rules on fiduciary duties of directors were undeveloped and there was little judicial control over companies. Foss claimed that Harbottle and his associates had defrauded the company. Harbottle replied that as directors they were entitled to decide what price the company should pay for its acquisitions. Foss and the other minority shareholders sued Harbottle and his associates. It was held that it was not for Foss and his fellow minority shareholders to raise an action against the directors for fraud or for making the company lose money on expensive purchases. The proper plaintiff (*i.e.* the person or body who ought to be raising the action) was the company itself, as it was the company as a whole that was being defrauded or mismanaged. As the plaintiffs (Foss and Turton) were not the company (because of the separate legal personality rules – see Chapter 1), the issue of fraud or mismanagement need not be decided upon.

This case is renowned both for its logic and its unfairness. The decision is logical because it is true that the company was the direct victim of the overpriced sale. The company had suffered: Foss had not suffered, except indirectly as his shares were now under-represented by assets. If the company had suffered, it was for the company to raise an action. To do this would need the approval of the members, and Foss and Turton had not sought shareholders' approval for an action against the directors. Had a resolution to this effect been passed, the company could have raised the action against the directors.

The decision is unfair because of the requirement of shareholders' approval for action against the directors. The decision in *Foss* v *Harbottle* took no account of the fact that sometimes the majority shareholders, whose approval would be needed for any action, are directors and the perpetrators of the fraud. They would be most unlikely to vote for an action to be raised against themselves.

Gradually the courts realised that the "proper plaintiff" rule and the pointless protection rule, although not without their merits, did lead to injustice. Four exceptions have been permitted to the rules:

1. *ultra vires* or illegal transaction;

2. failure to follow proper procedure;

3. infringement of the personal rights of the shareholders;

4. fraud on the minority by the majority.

Although separating the exceptions gives the impression that they are all distinct, there is considerable overlap between them. There is also a considerable overlap between them and the fiduciary duties applicable to directors, since majority shareholders commonly are directors. Furthermore, in view of the general practical difficulties in matching the facts of a minority protection action to the terms of these four exceptions, and in view of the relative dearth of new cases using this common law approach to minority protection, the confusion between the exceptions is likely to continue. However, as minority shareholders wishing to assert their claims stand a greater chance of success using the CA 1985 s 459 it may not in the long term matter very much that the common law exceptions are not entirely clear-cut.

Ultra vires or illegal transactions

If a company embarks upon an *ultra vires* transaction, technically the company should not be doing it (see Chapter 4). The company can be restrained from doing it by an injunction (in Scotland, interdict) raised by any shareholder.

While this may have been formerly useful, the CA 1985 s 35(2) (as inserted by the CA 1989 s 108) now states that if the company has entered into a transaction with another party, that transaction cannot normally be terminated just because it is *ultra vires* the company. It can certainly be terminated where the other party to the *ultra vires* transaction is a director of the company (CA 1985 s 322A), since directors are supposed to be fully aware of the *ultra vires* rule.

However, an *ultra vires* transaction may be terminated if the objecting shareholder obtains his injunction or interdict quickly enough:

- to prevent the company entering into the *ultra vires* transaction, or

- to prevent the company entering into future *ultra vires* transactions, even if he cannot stop an *ultra vires* transaction which is already in operation (CA 1985 s 35(2)).

On a practical basis the objecting shareholder has three problems:

(i)   He is unlikely to know about *ultra vires* transactions anyway unless the company is small or he is very well informed about the company's activities. What he is unaware of he will be unable to object to.

(ii) Even if he does obtain an injunction or interdict to prevent the *ultra vires* transaction, the company may under the CA 1985 s 35(3) pass a special resolution to ratify the *ultra vires* transaction. It may also pass a second special resolution to absolve the directors of any liability arising out of the transaction being *ultra vires* (CA 1985 s 35(3)). This would mean that the objecting shareholder's objections would be effectively overturned.

(iii) Many companies' objects clauses nowadays are so broadly drawn it is difficult to say what is *ultra vires* or not: most legitimate activities will be *intra vires*. This will be particularly true if the company has adopted a general trading clause available under the CA 1985 s 3A (see Chapter 4).

An illegal transaction is illegal until such time as the law making the transaction illegal is changed. An illegal transaction cannot be ratified and a member can force the company not to undertake it, or if it is already being carried out, the shareholder can (unlike *ultra vires* transactions) stop any further activity in the illegal transaction. So if a company embarks upon a transaction with a business in a country against which there are sanctions, a shareholder can take out an injunction or interdict to prevent the company entering into or completing any transaction with that business. Equally, if a company decided to give someone financial assistance for the purchase of shares in the company, it would be illegal if the company provided the assistance by any means other than that stated in the CA 1985. No amount of ratification of the improper means would make the assistance legal, and a shareholder who knew about the illegality could obtain an injunction or interdict to prevent it.

Failure to follow proper procedure

If a company's articles state that a particular procedure must be followed for a particular matter, that procedure has to be followed. Although this might seem self-evident, in the case of *Quin and Axtens Ltd* v *Salmon* [1909] AC 442, HL, the company failed to follow its own procedure. Its articles stated that certain transactions required the approval of both managing directors. One of the managing directors would not approve a particular transaction that required joint approval. The shareholders thought they would get round his refusal by passing an ordinary resolution authorising the transaction anyway. This was held to be unacceptable. What the shareholders should have done was to pass a special resolution to rewrite the articles so that joint approval was no longer necessary. If they were unable to pass the special resolution, then no authorisation could take place.

A similar case is *Edwards* v *Halliwell* [1950] 2 All ER 1064. This case involves a trade union, but is significant because the constitution of the trade union was similar to the articles of association of a company. The executive of the trade union decided that members' subscriptions should be increased, but did not first obtain the approval of a two-thirds majority of the members – as was needed under the trade union's constitution. Edwards successfully challenged the executive's authority to increase the subscription without members' approval. The executive was thus obliged to ballot its members.

These two examples should not, in an ideal world, have arisen: a careful reading of the company's articles in the first case, and the trade union's constitution in the second, would have shown what the procedure was and following it would have saved a great deal of trouble and expense.

Infringement of the personal rights of a shareholder

Whereas above the company has failed to follow procedures so that all the members are potentially affected, this exception arises when a particular member is affected but no others are.

Pender v *Lushington* (1877) 6 Ch D 70. A company had unusual articles which stated that for every 10 shares a member had, he was entitled to vote, but that no member could have more than 100 votes irrespective of the number of shares he held. In order to vote, the shares had to have been held for more than three months, and no shares could be held on trust for another member. A member of the company had a large number of shares but was only able to exercise the maximum of 100 votes. That member therefore transferred shares to Pender, the plaintiff, who would then be able to use the shares to obtain a vote. On the occasion of a general meeting, Pender wished to exercise his vote, but the chairman (Lushington) refused to count his votes, saying that Pender's shares were merely a ruse so that the other member could obtain more votes, and that Pender had no beneficial interest in the shares anyway as he was holding them for the other member.

The courts had no difficulty disposing of this argument, because there was nothing in the articles to prohibit the transfer of the shares; the motive for the transfer was irrelevant to the current proceedings; Pender had held the shares for over three months; and there was no evidence that Pender was holding the shares in trust or in a nominee capacity. Pender was therefore entitled to his votes.

In retrospect, this is a bizarre case. Had the chairman studied his company's articles properly, he would have realised that the problem lay in the drafting of the articles. If the articles had wanted to mention the question of motive, they should have said so. As with the second exception above, one must follow the exact wording of the articles; and if the wording of the articles is unacceptable, a special resolution is needed to alter the articles to produce more acceptable wording.

This case is also an example of how not to draw up articles: generally speaking, the more complicated and unorthodox the articles; the more people will try to find loopholes in them and the more the company's members are likely to end up in court.

Fraud on the minority by the majority

For the purposes of this exception it is important that there be a fraud, carried out by the majority, who are commonly also the directors, at the expense of the company as a whole. Although the whole company may suffer as a result of the fraud, in practice the majority shareholders will not be distressed because they will have often received the benefit of the fraud. The minority shareholders will be distressed because, for example, their shares may be worth less than if the fraud had not taken place. The best known case to illustrate this is the Canadian case of *Cook* v *Deeks* [1916] 1 AC 554, PC. Cook, a director and shareholder of the Toronto Construction Company, raised an action against Deeks and two other directors of the same company on the grounds that Deeks and the others had misappropriated a contract that in equity belonged to the company. Deeks and his fellow directors were majority shareholders in the company. The company had obtained a lucrative construction contract. Deeks and his friends decided that it would be better if they took the contract themselves personally rather than divide the profits amongst all the shareholders. As Deeks and his fellow directors commanded a majority of the votes, they passed a resolution making the company renounce its interest in the contract. Deeks and his friends then took the contract for themselves. It was held that this was not only a breach of the directors' fiduciary duty but was also an abuse of the majority voting power. The contract had to be handed back to the company.

The issue here is that what Deeks did was unratifiable because it was plainly fraudulent. Deeks had deliberately intended to deprive the company and the other shareholders of something that rightfully belonged to the company. By contrast, it is possible in general for a majority legitimately to ratify actions, even if the minority are unhappy, provided those actions in themselves do not involve fraud, show evidence of bad faith, or involve directors appropriating assets which belong to the company. This was explored in the case of *Pavlides v Jensen* [1956] Ch 565, where a mine was sold to an outsider at a very low value, due to the incompetence of the directors. The decision to sell was ratified in general meeting, but the minority shareholders objected. It was held that the directors'/majority shareholders' actions may have been negligent but not fraudulent, and that therefore the ratification was acceptable. By contrast, in *Daniels v Daniels* [1978] Ch 406 the directors sold an asset at an undervalue to one of the directors. This was held not to be ratifiable because it was an appropriation of company assets, in other words, a case of self-serving negligence.

Interestingly, no one is sure what the position would be in the UK if a company in general meeting renounced a contract without any suggestion of fraud, and if a director or majority shareholder then approached the other party to the contract to ask if he could take over the contract instead. Presumably provided he declared his interest to the other directors and members there would be no reason in principle why he could not then take the contract. His position would be strengthened if, in any vote on whether or not the company should renounce the contract so that he could get it instead, he abstained from voting. There would then be no question of a conflict of interest affecting his voting. Well drafted articles might well permit this.

Other examples of fraud on the minority might arise where:

- company A is in dispute with company B. B has failed to honour its obligations to A, but the majority of shareholders in B are also a majority in A, and not surprisingly do not wish to litigate contrary to their own interests. A variation of this is where a very generous settlement is reached between the two companies, thus unduly benefiting the majority shareholders in A;

- the directors have authority to allot shares, and use that authority to allot shares to new members, who when voting with the directors in their capacity as shareholders, are able to outvote the previous majority and turn it into a minority (*Hogg v Cramphorn* [1967] Ch 254);

- the directors, or those to whom the minority are objecting, do not actually have a majority of the votes but are in a position of control, usually by relying on shareholder apathy, and are abusing that position. This arose in the case of *Prudential Assurance Co Ltd v Newman Industries Ltd (No 2)* [1980] 2 All ER 841, where the directors had *de facto* control even though they did not have a majority of the votes. By artful practices the directors managed to persuade the company to pass a resolution favourable to themselves. When the minority shareholders realised how they had been hoodwinked by the directors' non-disclosure of an important report on the subject-matter of the resolution, they sued the directors. The directors successfully asserted that what they had done did not come within the terms of the exceptions to the rule in *Foss* v *Harbottle*, except possibly fraud by the majority (as in *Cook* v *Deeks*) – only the directors themselves were not a majority. Therefore the plaintiffs had no case. While this ingenious argument temporarily won the day in court, it did not prevent the company from holding a further general meeting at which the company adopted the minority shareholders' claim, thus negating the directors' victory in court.

The above four categories of exception to the rule in *Foss* v *Harbottle* are still extent and from time to time occasions may arise when a litigant may choose to sue under their restrictive terms. The position of a plaintiff in England and Wales and Northern Ireland is complicated by certain aspects of court procedure. Scottish court procedure makes no distinction between personal and derivative actions (as defined later) and there is no difficulty in making the company a defender in any action involving minority protection.

Procedural aspects under Northern Irish law are the same as in England.

When a shareholder raises an action against a company for some wrong done to him personally, he is said to be raising a personal action. An example might be the refusal of a company to pay a declared dividend. When a shareholder raises an action against a company on behalf of a group of people, including himself, with identical interests, he is said to be raising a representative action. An example might be an action by a class of shareholders against a company for its failure to follow procedural rules set out in the company's articles and designed to protect the class of shareholders.

When a minority shareholder raises an action on behalf of a company and for the benefit of the company, he is said to be raising a derivative action. What happens is that the company is brought into the action as a defendant, even though the company is not itself alleged to have done anything wrong. It is purely a means of getting the company involved in the action. It is necessary to bring the company in as a defendant because generally the majority of members/directors would not, if left to their own devices, let the company raise an action against themselves. However, any damages could still be paid to the company since it is party to the court proceedings. Damages would not be paid to the shareholder who had raised the action since he had not been seeking the benefit of the damages for himself but for the company. He would under limited circumstances be able to claim his expenses back from the company (*Wallersteiner* v *Moir (No 2)* [1975] 1 All ER 849). An example of a derivative action would be an action against majority shareholders who had fraudulently purchased assets from the company at a gross undervalue, even though they had obtained approval from the members by means of an ordinary resolution as required under the CA 1985 s 320. However, even if a plaintiff establishes that his complaint comes within one of the four exceptions to the rule in *Foss* v *Harbottle*, and he is trying to obtain some benefit for the company by means of a derivative action, he still may be prevented from proceeding with his action if, in the opinion of the majority of the shareholders who are not part of the oppressive majority, the action will do more harm than good (*Smith* v *Croft (No 2)* [1988] Ch 114).

Cases such as *Prudential*, where wrongdoers were clearly able to use the deficiencies of the existing minority protection law to their own advantage, and the hurdles imposed by the derivative action, resulted in a demand for better and above all, simpler protection for minorities. This has been provided by the CA 1985 s 459.

Statutory protection under the CA 1985 s 459

The CA 1985 s 459 reads as follows:

> "A member of a company may apply to the court by petition for an order under this Part on the ground that the company's affairs are being or have been conducted in a manner which is unfairly prejudicial to the interests of its members generally or of some part of its members or that any actual or proposed act or omission of the company (including an act or omission on its behalf) is or would be so prejudicial."

There is a number of points to note from this.

A member

There is no minimum shareholding requirement. Any member, however small his interest, may apply. However, he must sue in his capacity as a member, and not as an employee or a director. For the purposes of this part of the CA 1985, member is also deemed to mean those who have shares transferred or transmitted to them by operation of law, such as trustees in bankruptcy or executors under a will (CA 1985 s 459(2)).

Petition

A petition is when you ask the court to grant a particular request. Someone defending a petition in England or Northern Ireland will often ask that the

petition be "struck out" usually on a point of law to see whether or not the petitioner has a claim recognised by law: the facts can be argued about later.

Order

Under the CA 1985 s 461 the courts have wide discretion as to the type of order
that they can grant, and can impose any order that they see fit. The commonest
order is that the company or the majority shareholders buy out the petitioner's
shares at a fair price reflecting the value of his shares prior to the behaviour to
which the petitioner is objecting to took place.

Are being or have been conducted

The use of the present and past tense enables the petitioner to petition in respect
of current mistreatment or of past mistreatment, providing, it would seem, that
he was also a member at the time of the past mistreatment. A past member is
unlikely to be able to petition in respect of his past mistreatment while he was
a member.

A manner that is unfairly prejudicial

This phrase is interpreted to mean what it says: there is a requirement both of
unfairness and of prejudice. For example, in the case of *R A N Noble (Clothing)
Ltd* [1983] BCLC 273 (to be discussed later) the petitioner had indeed suffered
some prejudice, but in view of his own behaviour it could not be said that he
was treated unfairly.

To the interests of the members generally or of some part of the members

This wording was introduced by the Companies Act 1989, and arose because of
the case of *Re Sam Weller Ltd* [1989] 3 WLR 923. In this case the directors/
majority shareholders had not increased the dividend for 37 years, but had used
the company's considerable profits to give themselves excessive salaries and
other benefits. When a minority shareholder complained at the pitiful level of
his dividend, the majority shareholders countered by saying that their dividends
were equally poor too – though of course they had their large salaries to compensate them. They also argued that the then wording of the legislation did not
allow a claim for prejudice to be suffered by all the shareholders. In other
words, where everybody received an inadequate dividend, there was no claim,

though there might have been a claim had only some shareholders received an inadequate dividend.

This ingenious argument failed to win favour with the courts, and in order to put the matter beyond doubt, the legislation introduced by the Companies Act 1989, by the use of the word "generally", allowed a claim to be made even if the entire body of shareholders was unfairly prejudiced.

Actual or proposed

The conduct being complained of need not already have taken place; it is sufficient if the majority are going to do it as evidenced by past conduct or proposed conduct of a similar nature.

Act or omission

By including the word "omission" the legislation catches the failure to carry out a certain act. Failing to do something may be just as prejudicial as deliberately carrying out a prejudicial act.

Statutory protection under the CA 1985 s 460

The Secretary of State is empowered under the CA 1985 to investigate companies for various reasons such as fraud or unfairly prejudicial conduct (CA 1985 s 432(2)). If he has received a report from inspectors confirming the existence of such conduct, he can petition the courts in the same manner as described above. This does not preclude the Secretary of State having the company wound up (CA 1985 s 460).

The court's remedies

The CA 1985 s 461 states: "If the court is satisfied that a petition under this Part is well founded, it may make such order as it thinks fit for giving relief in respect of the matters complained of." This gives the court wide discretion, provided that the court agrees that the complaint is justified. The rest of s 461 gives various specific examples of remedies that the court could grant if it saw fit. In essence they are:

- Ordering the company or the majority shareholders to buy the minority out at a fair price, taking account of the value of the minority shareholding prior to the prejudicial conduct. Ideally the price should be a proportion of the

le piorata

overall value of the company with no discount for the lack of voting power concomitant with a minority interest. In practice the price may be difficult to establish because the valuation of shares is not an exact science and will depend upon the individual circumstances of each case.

- Preventing the company doing something the majority wished it to do, or making the company do something the majority did not wish it to do. This may include instigating litigation on behold of the company despite the contradictory wishes of the majority.

- Altering the memorandum or articles to a particular effect, or insisting that the existing memorandum or articles are not altered, or permitting any subsequent change only with leave of the court.

Where the court orders shares to be bought back by the company, it will be necessary for the company's capital to be reduced as well. This is usually taken account of in the court's judgment or (in Scotland) interlocutor. The price that the shares are bought back is generally speaking the price most favourable to the petitioner with regard to all the circumstances. This might be the value at the date of the petition, the value at the date of the court's decision or the value at the date when the prejudicial conduct took place, depending on what would be fairest.

 These sections have been productive of much case law, much of it illustrating the remarkable high-handedness of majority shareholders. Below are examples of various remedies that have been given over the years.

Purchase of the minority shareholding by the majority at a fair value

Re Bird Precision Bellows Ltd [1984] 2 WLR 869. The petitioner was unhappy with the way the majority shareholder was running the company. The petitioner believed that the majority shareholder in his position as managing director was paying bribes to obtain business opportunities. The minority shareholder asked the DTI to investigate. The DTI declined to do so. By way of retaliation the majority shareholder convened a general meeting at which he was able to use his majority shareholding to dismiss the petitioner from the directorship. The judge held that the petitioner should have his shares bought by the majority shareholder at a price that ignored the discount in value normally attributable to a minority shareholding because of a minority's minimal voting power.

The minority shareholder need not come to the court with clean hands

Re London School of Electronics Ltd [1985] 3 WLR 474. "Coming to the court with clean hands" is a term of law in English law, and means that if you are seeking an equitable remedy, you yourself must not have behaved in an inequitable manner. However, in this case, neither party had behaved honourably. The petitioner was a teacher at the London School of Electronics ("the School"), and was also a shareholder in the company that ran the School. The majority shareholders were two Greek brothers. The two brothers started diverting some of the students to another school they had set up, thus depriving the petitioner of his work. So the petitioner set up a school himself. At that point the Greek brothers convened a meeting at which they dismissed the petitioner from his directorship. When the matter came to court the petitioner obtained an order that the brothers should buy his shareholding. Nourse J, however, held that the value of the shareholding should be assessed on a fair value basis, and on the basis as if the unfair prejudice had never occurred. In addition, the value should be the value of the shareholding as at the date of the presentation of the petition. This was because since the petitioner had left the School, the Greek brothers had successfully built up the business of the School again. It would not have been fair if the petitioner had been able to gain from their industry after he had departed.

The fact that the petitioner had set up his own school was not considered relevant, as there was no requirement under the then equivalent of the CA 1985 s 459 that the petitioner should have "clean hands".

The petitioner must however look after his own interests

R A Noble (Clothing) Ltd [1983] BCLC 273. The petitioner was a director of the above company, but had taken little interest in its affairs. He later complained that he had been excluded from management of the company. It was held that if he had taken the trouble to attend board meetings he would have been able to remedy the situation without recourse to court.

Even if the majority shareholder disposes of his shares, he can still have a complaint raised against him

Re a Company (No 005287 of 1985) [1986] 1 WLR 281. The majority shareholder took all the profits out of the company in the form of management fees and then transferred all his shares to a Gibraltar registered company. He was made to account for the abstracted money even though he was not a shareholder.

The court can give a remedy appropriate to the facts of the case

Re H R Harmer Ltd [1958] 3 All ER 689. This case was decided under previous legislation but is still a good example. At the age of 82 H R Harmer set up a company to acquire and manage his existing stamp selling business. He and his wife were the majority shareholders with 78.6% of the votes, but had contributed only about 10% of the capital, the rest being contributed by Harmer's sons. Harmer and his wife were thus able to direct the management of the company as they pleased, notwithstanding that he and his two sons were stated in the articles to be directors for life. He also had a casting vote as chairman of the board of directors. Harmer was not a man to trouble himself with other people's views and ran the company as if it were his own private empire. In the process he made several unwise investment and personnel decisions. He hired a private detective agency to spy on the staff. His two sons became so vexed by the father's impetuous and ill-considered conduct that they petitioned for relief. By the time of the court case Harmer was deaf, confused and had trouble understanding what the case was about. The kindly and thoughtful judge ordered that Harmer be appointed a consultant to the company, that the articles be amended so that he could no longer be a director for life with a casting vote, that he was not to interfere in the management of the company and that he was to be appointed president of the company but without any duties or rights.

The majority may not use its controlling position to further weaken the position of the minority

Re Cumana Ltd [1986] BCLC 430. The majority and minority shareholder agreed that the company's profits should be divided in three, with the majority shareholder receiving two-thirds. The majority shareholder then started diverting some of the company's business to another company which he controlled, and convened a general meeting at which he ensured by means of his majority shareholding that a resolution giving himself a large bonus and large pension contributions was passed. When the minority shareholder started proceedings under s 459 he convened a meeting to pass a resolution for a rights issue which he knew the minority shareholder could not afford to take up – or if the minority shareholder had taken it up, it would have deprived him of funds with which to continue the s 459 action. The minority shareholder successfully obtained an order preventing the implementation of the large bonus, the pension contributions and the rights issue.

In a plc, any informal arrangements between certain shareholders will be ignored by the courts in the context of a s 459 petition

Re Tottenham Hotspur plc [1994] BCLC 655. As part of the acrimonious dispute between Terry Venables (the minority shareholder) and Alan Sugar, Venables petitioned for relief under s 459 on the grounds that there had been an understanding between him and Sugar that their respective companies would share control and that Venables would be chief executive. It was held that even if there had been some understanding between Venables and Sugar, this was a private matter between the two of them which did not affect any other share-holders' rights. Furthermore it would be a misuse of the company's money to have it involved in what was essentially a private dispute. Relief was not there-fore available under s 459. The court was clearly reluctant to use s 459 as a rem-edy for all private disputes between shareholders in publicly quoted companies which should not be entertaining such private arrangements anyway.

As can be seen from the above examples of cases heard under the CA 1985 s 459, s 459 is being used extensively by minority shareholders seeking redress. There are ever more reported cases on unfairly prejudicial conduct, and the courts are simultaneously trying to remedy unfairly prejudicial conduct where it has occurred while at the same time preventing the use of a s 459 petition as a panacea for all corporate ills. Unfortunately, such is the nature of the wording of s 459 that people can be tempted to raise s 459 petitions where it is hardly cost-effective to do so. An extreme example of this arose in *Re Elgindata Ltd* [1991] BCLC 959. In this case there was a dispute over the value of certain shares originally purchased for £40,000. In the course of the case, which took 43 days and involved substantial trawling over otherwise long since dead issues, the costs amounted to £320,000 and the final figure for the shares was £24,600.

Broadly speaking, the courts are anxious not to widen the gates of litigation to litigants unless s 459 genuinely is the appropriate remedy. The courts are reluctant to be involved in matters of commercial judgment. This is partly because judges do not feel qualified to take commercial decisions but also because there is a recognition that shareholders should sometimes have to accept that there is no unfairness where majority shareholders/directors act in accordance with the articles even though the commercial decisions the directors take may not be to the minority shareholders' liking.

Re Saul Harrison & Sons plc [1994] BCC 475. The petitioner held shares which entitled her to dividends and to capital distributions on a winding-up, but did not permit her to vote. The company had been running at a loss for some time but had substantial assets. The directors, who were also the majority share-holders, having taken professional advice, moved their business premises, paid themselves greater (though not unreasonably so) salaries, and attempted to improve the business generally. The petitioner was of the view that the directors should have the company wound up and a return of capital made to all the members. She sought a petition under s 459 to obtain redress for what she saw as unfairly prejudicial conduct towards herself.

In the light of the evidence it became apparent that the directors' actions were unexceptionable. It was true that there had been some trivial and technical breaches of their duties under the articles, but none of such breaches was enough to constitute unfairly prejudicial conduct towards the petitioner. The important issue was that the directors had not breached their fiduciary duties in the management of the company, and that they had overall conducted themselves in accordance with the articles of association. There was also no element of "self-serving" by the directors/majority shareholders as is found in many other minority protection cases, such as *Re Bird Precisions Bellows*. The court in its judgment introduced the term "legitimate expectations" to describe what the shareholder might hope to receive in her capacity as a shareholder. She was not entitled to expect more that that the directors abided by their fiduciary duties and managed the company within the rights and powers given to them under the company's memorandum and articles. As a shareholder she knew what they were entitled to do in terms of the memorandum and articles, and by being a shareholder she had consented to their management of the company within those parameters. She could not legitimately expect that they should take any further consideration of her particular wishes. As it was apparent that the majority shareholders/directors had not breached their duties, they were entitled to take such commercial decisions as they saw fit, and her petition was refused.

The area of minority protection under the CA 1985 s 459 is a developing area of law, and it is likely that the concept of "legitimate expectation" will be further refined. At the same time it is recognised that s 459 fills a need. Some majority shareholders do behave in a blatantly oppressive way, and the great virtue of s 459 is that gradually it has educated majority shareholders to think twice before commending particularly unfairly prejudicial conduct.

Winding up on the "just and equitable grounds"

Before the existence of the CA 1985 s 459 an unhappy minority shareholder had either to obtain redress through the limited exceptions to *Foss* v *Harbottle* or, in desperation, have the company wound up. Having the company wound up might ensure the return of the shareholder's capital, but in many cases, was a drastic remedy for the particular problem. It could also be unfair on other shareholders who were not involved in the unfairly prejudicial conduct, either as perpetrators or as victims.

The remedy of winding up is available under the Insolvency Act 1986 s 122(1)(g) where it is stated that the court can wind up the company if the court is of the opinion that is just and equitable that the company should be wound up.

The meaning of "just and equitable"

The phrase "just and equitable" is a deliberately loose term which allows the courts considerable discretion. There have been various occasions where the courts have wound companies up on the just and equitable grounds on the basis of a minority shareholder petition. These are as follows.

The quasi-partnership company

Some businesses are formed as partnerships but after some years the partners choose to incorporate. Under certain circumstances the ethos of the partnership, such as equal say in decisions, is deemed to continue even though the company has been incorporated. Such a company is known as a "quasi-partnership", the word "quasi" meaning in Latin "as if", so that the company is to be treated as if it were still really a partnership. This is well illustrated in the case of *Ebrahimi* v *Westbourne Galleries Ltd* [1973] AC 360.

Ebrahimi and Nazar, a partnership, dealt in oriental carpets. After some years they transferred their business to a limited company, of which they were sole shareholders and directors. Nazar's son was introduced to the business and obtained some shares in the company. Nazar and his son together had more shares than Ebrahimi, and following a disagreement they used their majority shareholding to dismiss Ebrahimi as a director of the company. The articles prevented Ebrahimi transferring his shares to anyone other than Nazar and his son, and so Ebrahimi was unable to realise his capital. Ebrahimi accordingly petitioned for relief under the precursor of s 459, or failing that for the winding up of the company on just and equitable grounds. The precursor of s 459 required Ebrahimi to prove that he had been the victim of "oppressive" treatment. This he was unable to prove, but he was able to prove that he had been treated unfairly and convinced the courts that it was just and equitable that the company should be wound up. Had Ebrahimi, Nazar, and Nazar's son been in a partnership together, Ebrahimi would have been able to have the partnership wound up. It was therefore reasonable under the circumstances to have the company wound up, since in spirit, if not in fact, the company was in reality a partnership concern.

Were such a case to come to the courts nowadays, Ebrahimi would have been able to use the CA 1985 s 459, the terms of which are less stringent than its precursor. Quasi-partnership cases are not common now, but in the case *Jesner* v *Jarrad Properties*, 1994 SLT 83, the pursuers sought either relief under the CA

1985 s 459 or a winding-up order under the IA 1986 s 122(1)(g). The pursuers were unable to obtain relief under s 459 because it was not evident that there had been unfair prejudice when the actions of both parties over a number of years were taken into account. However, the pursuers were able to obtain a winding-up order because the company was really a quasi-partnership. The members of the company could not agree how the company should be managed, nor did the pursuers have confidence in the directors' actions. The mutual trust that had formerly characterised the litigants' family company had completely broken down.

The company is set up for a fraudulent or illegal purpose
If a company is set up deliberately to carry out a fraud, the minority shareholders can petition for its winding-up.

Re Thomas Brinsmead & Sons Ltd [1897] 1 Ch 45 and 406. Brinsmead was the name of a well-known piano manufacturer. Some disreputable relatives of his set up a company to cash in on his name. The intention was that members of the public would invest in the company thinking that it was the piano manufacturer's business. The company issued a prospectus which was a masterpiece of inaccuracy. The directors of the company peculated the subscribers' money and Brinsmead himself, when he heard what his deceitful relatives were doing, took out an injunction prohibiting the use of the name "Brinsmead". The minority shareholders successfully petitioned for the winding up of the company on the grounds that it was set up deliberately to carry out a fraud. Given the much greater stringency in the financial world today, it is unlikely that such circumstances would reoccur.

There is deadlock in the management of the company
If the company is unable to operate because of disputes between the members, some of whom may be minority members, the company may be wound up.

Re Yenidje Tobacco Co Ltd [1916] Ch 426. Two tobacconists decided to merge their separate businesses into one company, which turned out to be reasonably profitable. Unfortunately the two tobacconists immediately started to squabble. Although the articles provided for a reference to arbitration, one of the tobacconists would not implement the award against him and sued the other for fraudulent misrepresentation. They were only able to converse by sitting in separate rooms, relaying messages through the company secretary. One of the tobacconists managed to have the company wound up on the grounds that it was just and equitable to do so.

Were this unedifying situation to arise nowadays, it is likely that a company would have well-drafted articles that would provide for means of resolving any disputes in a more sensible manner.

Members are being prohibited from ascertaining the true financial position of the company
Loch v *John Blackwood Ltd* [1924] AC 783. The representative of the majority shareholder deliberately avoided producing accounts for the company or keeping the other members informed. This was so that the minority members would be sufficiently disheartened as to the true value of their shares that in despair they would transfer their shares to the majority shareholder. This plan was not successful and the company was wound up.

This case is significant because it is normally the case that a company can only be wound up by a member of the company on the just and equitable ground if the company is solvent. The IA 1986 s 125(2) states that the court should not make a winding-up order if the petitioner is acting unreasonably in seeking to have the company wound up instead of pursuing some other remedy. Winding up an insolvent company is unreasonable because there would be no point in a member putting a company into liquidation if he was not going to get his money back. However, in the above case, the plaintiff could not know if the company was solvent or not as he had been denied the necessary information. In the UK at least this situation is unlikely to arise again because of the more favourable wording of the CA 1985 s 459 and the greater diligence by the Registrar of Companies in chasing up companies that delay in filing their accounts.

The principal purpose (or substratum) of the company is gone
Re German Date Coffee Co (1882) 20 Ch D 169. The above company was founded to use a German patent for the manufacture of coffee from dates. The company instead used a Swedish patent in Germany. Many shareholders left the company, believing that they had been deceived. Two shareholders successfully petitioned the courts for the just and equitable winding up of the company on the ground that it was not fulfilling its stated object in its object clause and indeed in its name.

Given the change in the law and indeed shareholders' attitudes to objects clauses, it is unlikely such a case would be raised nowadays. Nonetheless it has never been overruled and is still a valid ground for just and equitable winding-up.

Applicable factors when petitioning under the just and equitable grounds

1. A member must be able to convince the court that no other remedy apart from winding up is suitable (IA 1986 s 125(2)). In many cases nowadays a s 459 petition would actually be more useful and would be less unfair on other shareholders who were not party to any dispute.

2. The company must also be solvent, for the reasons stated above, unless there is insufficient information available to ascertain the solvency of the company.

Who can petition under the just and equitable grounds in the context of minority protection?

The IA 1986 s 124 allows the company, its directors, creditors, clerks of magistrates' courts and contributories to petition on the just and equitable grounds. Of these only contributories are relevant in the context of minority protection. A contributory is someone who is liable in certain circumstances to contribute to the assets of the company in the event of its liquidation, as, for example, a shareholder whose shares are only partly paid (IA 1986 s 74). In the context of minority protection, the following type of contributory can petition under the just and equitable grounds:

- current fully paid and partly paid shareholders, who:

    (i)   have been shareholders for at least six out of the previous 18 months, or
    (ii) were originally allotted their shares, or
    (iii) inherited the shares from a former shareholder (IA 1986 s 124(2)(b)).

DTI investigations

The DTI has extensive powers to investigate the affairs of a company. This can be one more weapon in the minority shareholders' armoury. Investigations are carried out by one or more inspectors, usually a lawyer and an accountant working together, and are appointed by the Secretary of State. DTI-appointed inspectors can be asked specifically to investigate majority shareholders' abuse of their majority voting power.

The present law on DTI investigations is contained in the CA 1985 Part XIV.

Who can apply to have a company investigated?

The company can itself apply (CA 1985 s 431(2)(c)). A company with a share capital, 200 or more members, or members holding in total more than one-tenth of the shares issued, can apply (CA 1985 s 431(2)(a)).

In a company without a share capital, a minimum of one-fifth of the members on the company's register of members can apply (CA 1985 s 431(2)(b)). The application must be supported by evidence showing that there is good reason for requiring the investigation (CA 1985 s 431(3)). This imposes a considerable burden on a minority shareholder who may know there is prejudice but cannot obtain the information to prove it – which is why he is asking for the investigation in the first place. Equally the evidence requirement may serve to deter petty-minded applicants seeking to cause trouble for their company.

In order to deter frivolous applications, the Secretary of State may require the applicant to provide security for the costs of the investigation (CA 1985 s 431(4)).

Who can insist that a company be investigated?

If a court by order declares that its affairs ought to be investigated, the Secretary of State must appoint inspectors for the investigation (CA 1985 s 432(1)).

When may a company be investigated?

In addition to investigation following an application by the company or the members as detailed above, the Secretary of State may appoint inspectors on the following grounds under the CA 1985 s 432(2), if it appears to him that:

(a) the company's affairs are being or have been conducted with intent to defraud its creditors or the creditors of any other person, or otherwise for a fraudulent or unlawful purpose, or in a manner which is fairly prejudicial to some part of its members; or

(b) any actual or proposed act or omission of the company (including an act or omission on its behalf) is or would be so prejudicial, or that the company was formed for any fraudulent or unlawful purpose; or

(c) persons concerned with the company's formation or the management of its affairs have in connection therewith been guilty of fraud, misfeasance or other misconduct towards it or towards its members; or

(d) the company's members have not been given all the information with respect to its affairs which they might reasonably expect.

While normally the inspectors publish a report on their investigations, if the inspectors are appointed on any of the above four grounds they may be appointed on the basis that any report they prepare is not for publication (CA 1985 s 432(2A)).

Even if a company is in voluntary liquidation, under the CA 1985 s 432(3) inspectors can be appointed if the court requires it under the CA 1985 s 432(1) or if the Secretary of State considers it appropriate under s 432(2). Where the Secretary of State has ordered the appointment of inspectors, he is not obliged to give his reasons for the appointment provided he has not ordered the investigation for an improper purpose or in the absence of good faith. (*Norwest Holst Ltd* v *Secretary of State for Trade* [1978] Ch 201).

The inspectors have wide powers to interview directors and employees and anyone else connected with the company (including its solicitors, bankers and auditors) under investigation. All such persons have to provide such assistance as they reasonably can, and to produce any relevant documents in their care (CA 1985 s 434(1) and (2)) except where in the case of solicitors they can justifiably claim that they hold privileged information which they would be entitled to refuse to disclose in the High Court or the Court of Session (CA 1985 s 452(1)).

Bankers have a similar privilege except where the bankers' client is the company being investigated, where the company itself consents to disclosure or where the Secretary of State orders the privilege to be overruled (CA 1985 s 452(1A)). The inspectors can demand that the interviewees can be put on oath (CA 1985 s 434(3)), and refusal by the interviewees to comply with the inspectors' requests may result in the matter being reported to the court. The court may then listen to any evidence and has the power to punish the obstructive interviewees for contempt of court.

The inspectors are required to act fairly while remembering that they are not a court of law. This was established by the cases raised by the late Robert Maxwell in *Re Pergamon Press Ltd* [1971] Ch 388 and *Maxwell* v *Department of Trade and Industry* [1974] QB 523), where he attempted to deter or delay the publication of the report into his business affairs.

The inspectors' report

The inspectors compile a report within the terms of the remit given them by the Secretary of State. If the court had ordered the report to be produced, the courts must be given a copy (CA 1985 s 437(2)). If it appears from the report that in the public interest civil proceedings ought to be instituted on the company's behalf, perhaps against errant directors or majority shareholders, the Secretary of State has power to order this to be done (CA 1985 s 438). The report is itself admissible evidence to be used if necessary against any director under the Company Directors Disqualification Act 1986 (CA 1985 s 441) or in any criminal proceedings (CA 1985 s 441). The report can also be used as evidence in any petition brought by the Secretary of State to have the company wound up under the IA 1986 s 124A, or to obtain a remedy for conduct unfairly prejudicial to the company's members (CA 1985 s 460).

Other powers of investigation

The inspectors can be appointed to report on the membership of the company, and in particular the ownership of its shares and debentures, and to ascertain who truly controls the company (CA 1985 s 442). Under the CA 1985 s 442(3) the Secretary of State must appoint inspectors to ascertain the true ownership where requested to do so by the minorities referred to in the CA 1985 s 431(2)(a) and (b), unless he considers that the members' application is vexatious or where it is unreasonable that any or part of the matters to which the minorities are objecting should be investigated (CA 1985 s 442(3A)).

If the Secretary of State wishes he can investigate the ownership of shares or debentures in the company or its members using inspectors (CA 1985 s 444). To refuse to give information or to give false information is an offence.

If members are being obstructive about providing the information to the inspectors or the Secretary of State, the Secretary of State, under the CA 1985 ss 454–457, can prohibit all or any of the following:

- the transfer of any shares;

- the transfer of the right to be issued with new shares and any subsequent issue of those new shares;

- the exercise of any voting rights in respect of shares whose ownership is being investigated;

- the issue of any further shares arising out of the existing ownership of shares (*i.e.* a bonus issue or the exercise of pre-emption rights);

- the repayment of capital or payment of dividends, except in the case of a liquidation.

These sanctions effectively make the shares virtually useless, since you cannot sell them, you cannot vote with them and you cannot make any money out of them.

Investigation of share dealings

Under the CA 1985 s 446 inspectors can be appointed to investigate whether or not directors and their families have been contravening the rules on share options in listed companies under the CA 1985 s 323, or failing to disclose their interests in their companies' securities under the CA 1985 s 324.

Requisition and seizure of books and papers

Appointing inspectors is a very public process and may do the company and innocent shareholders more harm than good. There is a more discreet option available to the Secretary of State, if he thinks there is good reason, to enable to find out what may be taking place within a company, and thereby to ascertain whether a full-scale investigation would be necessary. This is the requisition and seizure of the company's books by personnel within the DTI. Compared to a full-scale investigation, this type of investigation is cheap, and is by far the commonest response by the DTI to any requests for an investigation.

The Secretary of State can require documents to be brought to him (CA 1985 s 447). He can obtain warrants to permit the police to search premises to prevent the destruction or concealment of such documents (CA 1985 s 448). He is only allowed to disclose what information he finds within certain defined circumstances, these being mostly in connection with criminal matters, disciplinary proceedings, or disqualification of company directors.

As a matter of practice, raids on companies generally take place when the company least expects it. This is to prevent the company's directors trying to destroy incriminating documents. This dramatically occurred in the Guinness scandal where the managing director, Ernest Saunders, was said to be tearing pages out of his engagement diary and shredding whatever documents he could find. Mutilating or destroying company documents is an offence (CA 1985 s 450).

Although the retrieval of documents does serve as a useful base from which to decide whether or not to mount a full-scale investigation, it does have the major drawback that any determinedly fraudulent company will keep very few incriminating documents where they might be found. Equally, such a company would retain contentious information in some electronic form with tightly restricted accessibility. As technology increases, search warrants become less effective.

As can be seen, the considerable powers open to the Secretary of State can be used to good advantage to protect minority shareholders suffering unfairly prejudicial conduct, provided, of course, that the Secretary of State is willing to use them. As the whole operation is costly and time-consuming, the Secretary of State is only likely to be involved when it is clearly in the public interest that he should be involved. As a matter of practice, this means that only the major financial scandals are investigated in this way.

Judicial factors in Scotland

The remaining method of minority protection is only available in Scotland. If the directors are at loggerheads or have all resigned, or for any other good reason which is acceptable to the court, it is possible for any shareholder to petition the court for the appointment of a judicial factor to the company. A judicial factor is a court-appointed accountant (usually) who is given the task of acting as a company caretaker and protecting the interests of the shareholders until such time as new and acceptable directors are appointed. This took place in the case of *Weir* v *Rees*, 1991 SLT 345.

Reform

It is recognised that the whole area of minority protection is one that needs to be rationalised and made more "user-friendly" without becoming a mechanism for querying every single managerial decision. There clearly is a balance to be struck between the right of the majority to have the business of the company conducted in the way the majority wishes it to be conducted, and the right of the minority not to be unfairly prejudiced by the majority's decisions. It is arguable that the balance has yet to be found. A pertinent and well informed discussion of this topic is to be found in the Law Commission Consultation Paper No 142, 1996. The Paper provides an overview of the current state of the law together with interesting comparisons with other judicial systems' treatment of the same area of law.

Summary

1. Under the rule in *Foss* v *Harbottle* (1843) 2 Hare 461 only the company itself can raise an action against shareholders alleged to be taking advantage of their position within the company.

2. This rule, while designed to prevent:

    (i)   a multiplicity of actions,
    (ii) the questioning of commercial decisions, or
    (iii) the pointless prohibition of certain acts which the members might subsequently legitimately ratify,

    was seen to be unduly restrictive for minority shareholders, particularly when the majority shareholders were the persons alleged to be causing the harm to which the minority shareholders were objecting.

3. Four common law exceptions were developed to the *Foss* v *Harbottle* rule, these being where the harm being complained of was:

    (i)   an illegal or *ultra vires* act;
    (ii) a failure to follow proper procedure (*Edwards* v *Halliwell* [1950] 2 All ER 1064);
    (iii) a violation of a member's rights (*Pender* v *Lushington* (1877) 6 Ch D 70);
    (iv) the majority perpetrating a fraud on the minority (*Cook* v *Deeks* [1916] 1 AC 554).

4. Even these exceptions proved to be too restrictive. Eventually the CA 1985 s 459 introduced a sensible and operable remedy for unfairly prejudicial conduct suffered by minority shareholders at the hands of majority shareholders,

as may be seen in such cases as *Re Bird Precision Bellows Ltd* [1986] Ch 658 and *Re Cumana Ltd* [1986] BCLC 430). For a remedy to be granted there must be both unfairness and prejudice, not the mere questioning of a commercial judgment. The case of *Re Saul Harrison & Sons plc* [1994] BCC 475 introduced the concept of "legitimate expectations" which may come to be seen as a benchmark against which unfairly prejudicial conduct may be measured.

5. Although the CA 1985 s 459 is generally the most useful remedy for a minority shareholder, a minority shareholder can still have a company wound up on the just and equitable grounds under the IA 1986 s 122(1)(g). This is still valid albeit rare. Successful petitions on these grounds include:

   (i)   breakdown of quasi-partnership (*Ebrahimi* v *Westbourne Galleries* [1973] AC 630);
   (ii)   the company founded for an illegal purpose (*Re Thomas Brinsmead and Son Ltd* [1897] 1 Ch 45 and 406);
   (iii) deadlock in the management of the company (*Re Yenidge Tobacco Company* [1916] 2 Ch 426);
   (iv)   the impossibility of establishing true financial position of the company (*Loch* v *John Blackwood Ltd* [1924] AC 783);
   (v)   the principal purpose of the company is not being achieved (*Re German Date Coffee Company* (1882) 20 Ch D 169).

6. Alternatively, it is possible for minority shareholders to ask that their company be investigated by the DTI. This rarely takes place but is still valid.

7. In Scotland alone, a judicial factor can be appointed to run the company on an interim basis in order to protect the shareholders' interests until new management takes over (*Weir* v *Rees*, 1991 SLT 345).

14. DIRECTORS

What does a director do? – how do the directors manage the company? – what can the members do if they disapprove of what the directors are doing? – types of director – the Cadbury Code – directors' remuneration – the Greenbury Report and the Hampel Report – who can be a director? – appointment of directors – disclosure requirements for directors – termination of office – disqualification under the Company Directors Disqualification Act 1986 – liability of directors under the Insolvency Act 1986 – criminal sanctions against directors.

If the shareholders are the people who control the company, the directors are the people who manage it. They direct such of the company's affairs as do not require approval from the members at a general meeting. When someone becomes a member of a company he accepts that in terms of the CA 1985 s 14:

(i) the directors carry out most of the management of the company on behalf of the members;

(ii) the directors use the members' investment in the company for the benefit of the company as a whole.

The above is subject to certain powers retained under statute or the company's articles permitting members certain rights, such as the right to dismiss the directors or the right to alter the articles. In turn, directors have to accept that their positions are dependent on their ability to make a good return on investors' capital or otherwise preserve the members' willingness to let the company be managed by the directors.

Company law postulates a balance between the desire of the investor to be reassured that the directors are using his capital wisely and running the company properly, and the desire of the director to retain his position and any financial benefits that may accrue to it. The temptation of the investor is to refuse to let the director get on with his job without interference: the temptation of the director is to put his own private interests above those of his company's investors and anyone else who may be affected by his policies, such as employees, creditors or investors.

In many small companies, this conflict does not arise, as the directors are the shareholders. The larger the company, the greater becomes the separation between ownership and control. The opportunities for the directors to take advantage of their position increase, though equally, in a well-run company, the accountability of the directors increases too.

The law applicable to directors assumes that directors will take advantage of the members if they get the chance. While this assumption is unfair on the many honourable and assiduous directors that clearly do exist, it is founded on many years of court cases where directors have attempted to abuse their position at the company's expense. Accordingly there are now complex statutory rules to ensure "fair play", a large body of common law on the duties directors owe to their companies (see next chapter) and specific rules about the eligibility, appointment, dismissal, disqualification and personal liability of directors. We shall shortly be looking at these rules.

What does a director do?

In addition to the general task of managing the company as a member of the board of directors, a director has various statutory and common law functions. Amongst other matters it is his job to:

- prepare and sign the accounts and directors' reports which are sent to the Registrar of Companies (CA 1985 s 242);

- act bona fide in the best interests of the company as a whole;

- sign and take responsibility for any statutory declarations that may be required on such occasions as a company redeeming its own shares out of capital (CA 1985 s 173(3)), providing financial assistance for the purchase of a company's shares (CA 1985 s 155) or asserting the solvency of a company on a members' voluntary winding-up (IA 1986 s 89);

- consider the interests of his company's employees (CA 1985 s 309);

- sign various forms required by the Registrar of Companies such as annual returns (CA 1985 s 363);

- convene general meetings when they are requisitioned by the members (CA 1985 s 368) or in a plc where there is a serious loss of capital (CA 1985 s 142);

- formulate proposals for approval of creditors in a company voluntary arrangement (IA 1986 s 1);

- lay a statement of affairs of the company before the creditors in a creditors' voluntary winding-up (IA 1986 s 99);

- recommend a dividend out of the distributable profits.

From where does a director obtain his authority?

Directors obtain their authority to manage the company from the articles. Table A art 70 states:

"Subject to the provisions of the Act [CA 1985], the memorandum and the articles and to any directions give by special resolution, the business of the company shall be managed by the directors who may exercise all the powers of the company. No alteration of the memorandum or articles and no such direction shall invalidate any prior act of the directors which would have been valid if that alteration had not been made or that direction had not been given. The powers given by this regulation shall not be limited by any special power given to the directors by the articles and a meeting of the directors at which a quorum is present may exercise all powers exercisable by the directors."

While not all companies will adopt the wording of Table A art 70, many will have similar wording which give the directors the authority to carry out their tasks of "exercising all the powers of the company". These powers are the powers that are specified in the memorandum as enabling the fulfilment of the objects clause. Historically, directors were not supposed to exceed those powers. However nowadays many companies have almost unlimited powers and open-ended objects clauses and so there is less likelihood of the directors exceeding those powers. Any decision taken by the directors within those powers will be valid.

However sometimes the memorandum, the articles or special resolutions will state limits on the directors' own powers. Directors may be prohibited from making the company borrow more than a specified sum without obtaining the approval of the members first. This is deliberately to impose prudence upon the directors and to make them justify to the members their proposed actions.

In small companies where all the shareholders are also the directors, there may be no need for such clauses. If the memorandum or articles impose too many restrictions upon the directors, it may be difficult to find directors willing to put up with such restrictions. It may also be inconvenient having to call general meetings regularly to approve matters which are beyond the directors' authority. Furthermore, the directors, and indeed the shareholders, may start ignoring the memorandum or articles. This may not always matter very much if the members sanction the absence of prior approval. The CA 1985 ss 35, 35A and 35B (see Chapter 4) may also be applicable. If a company, through its directors, acts beyond its powers (*ultra vires*), any member can bring proceedings to prevent the company repeating the unauthorised act, but those proceedings will be void where some other person has already been granted contractual rights in respect of the unauthorised act. In any event the members can by special resolution sanction the unauthorised act, thus legitimising it.

How do the directors manage the company?

The directors manage the company through meetings of the board of directors (usually known as board meetings), which deal with matters that do not require the approval of the members. Consequently at board meetings most of the items that are discussed are administrative and commercial. One function of the board is to instruct the company secretary to convene general meetings when members' approval is needed.

Delegation of authority

Sometimes a board of directors can delegate its authority over a certain matter or matters to a committee of the board of the directors or to one particular director, commonly the managing director (Table A art 72). The committee (or director) may be given a remit, on such terms as the board sees fit, and normally is required to report back to the full board from time to time or to seek approval of its or his recommendations from the full board. Each case depends on the precise wording of the articles and the extent to which authority can thereby be delegated to a committee (or director).

Guinness plc v *Saunders and Ward* [1990] 1 All ER 652. During the takeover of Distillers plc by Guinness plc, a committee of the board consisted of Saunders (the managing director), Roux (the finance director) and Ward, who was in charge of tactics for the bid. Between themselves they agreed that Ward should be paid a success fee of 0.2% of the final value of the takeover bid if it were successful. This, not surprisingly, was not disclosed to the full board of directors. The bid was successful and Ward submitted an invoice for £5.2 million which was duly paid by Roux. Following the scandal that surrounded the takeover, the success fee was discovered and Guinness plc sought recovery of the £5.2 million from Ward.

It was held by the House of Lords that Guinness plc's articles did not permit the committee to authorise payments of this nature. The contract was void and the company was entitled to seek repayment.

The practice of board meetings

At board meetings thee will normally be a chairman, who, depending on the articles, may have a casting vote, the managing director (who may be the same person as the chairman), the other directors and the company secretary. The company secretary, who may sometimes also be a director, advises the chairman and deals with procedural matters at the meeting. He also takes the minutes of the meetings. For further details of the duties of the company secretary see Chapter 16.

How the directors regulate their meetings may be specified in the articles or the directors can make their own rules. Normally there is a requirement of a quorum. Table A art 89 states that two is the quorum, except for the purpose of co-opting further directors to the board (art 90). Board meetings normally require reasonable notice (Table A art 88) to allow the board members the opportunity to attend.

Barron v *Potter* [1914] 1 Ch 895. Barron and Potter were the only directors of a dysfunctional company. Potter was chairman and had a casting vote. The quorum at board meetings was two. Barron deliberately ignored board meetings so that Potter could not use his casting vote. One day Potter met Barron as Potter was alighting from a train at Paddington station. Potter immediately called a board meeting and used his casting vote to appoint directors sympathetic to him. Next day there was an extraordinary general meeting at which Barron was able to use his greater shareholding to appoint directors sympathetic to him. Potter claimed that it was for the board to appoint directors. Barron claimed that there had not been a proper board meeting in the absence of reasonable notice and so Potter's directors had not been properly appointed.

It was held that a board meeting requires reasonable notice, that the meeting at the station was not a proper board meeting, the directors ostensibly appointed at the board meeting were not in fact appointed and that the appointment of the directors at the general meeting was valid.

As members who are not directors are not normally present at board meetings, members have no say in how the board meetings are run. In larger companies, the board usually meets once a month. On each occasion the previously circulated minutes of the previous meeting are tabled for approval. If approved by those present at the meeting as being an accurate record of the previous meeting, the minutes are signed by the chairman. The directors deal with matters arising from the minutes, and listen to reports on ongoing matters of board meetings. Certified extracts thereof are normally good evidence that the board has considered the matters and made the decisions stated in the minutes (CA 1985 s 382(2)). If the directors all sign a written resolution, the resolution is as valid as a resolution passed at a board meeting (Table A art 93). Directors are not normally supposed to vote on matters on which they have a material interest (Table A art 94) (see next chapter).

In the case of *In re Neptune (Vehicle Washing Equipment) Ltd* [1995] 1 BCLC 352, it was held that directors of sole director companies are still required to hold board meetings, even though there may only be the one director present, or the one director and the company secretary. This is because under statute there are certain matters which must be raised at board meetings (for example, see CA 1985 s 317, declaration to the board of directors' interests in contracts with the company), so that the interests of directors and shadow directors can be considered. If the director is on his own, the meeting may be silent, in which case the minutes should still record the decisions of the meeting; if with another, such as the company secretary, the meetings should be conducted out loud and the minutes taken therefrom. In the absence of minutes, the testimony of the company secretary would then go some way to ascertaining that the company held a meeting as required by statute.

Only the directors and the auditors can see board minutes, unless a certified excerpt is specially asked for. Companies opening a new bank account are commonly required to provide the bank with an excerpt board minute confirming the opening of the account and the authorised signatories for the cheque-book.

The main advantages of having board meetings are that:

- they are a formal method of stating who has to do what;

- they ensure that matters regularly are followed up and brought to fruition or a decision taken to abandon them;

- they are a formal record of the proceedings;

- they enable the board members to be able to attribute praise for successes and blame for failures;

- it is easier to take unwelcome decisions and to implement them in the name of a committee than it is to take such decisions by oneself.

What can the members do if they disapprove of what the directors are doing?

Providing the directors are acting within the powers given to them under the memorandum, the articles and any special resolutions, the members in theory should have no grounds for complaint and the members cannot normally set aside any decisions the directors may have already made in favour of third parties (CA 1985 s 35A(4)). Nonetheless the directors may still make unpopular if legal decisions. In that event, the members have various options, assuming they have the requisite majorities to pass the appropriate resolutions:

1. They can rewrite the articles or change the objects clause or otherwise give instructions to the directors, all by means of special resolutions. This would prevent the directors repeating the act to which the members object, or force the directors to do something the members particularly want.

2. They could petition the court to wind up the company under the just and equitable grounds (IA 1986 s 122(1)(g)) if the behaviour of the directors in their positions as majority shareholders warranted it.

3. They could dismiss the directors by means of an ordinary resolution with special notice (CA 1985 s 303) (see later).

4. If the articles provide for retirement of directors by rotation, the members could refuse to re-elect the undesirable directors on those directors' retirement.

Types of director

In addition to the general category of director, there are certain commonly recognised types of director:

- managing directors

- executive directors

- non-executive directors

- chairman of the board of directors

- alternate directors

- shadow directors

- *de facto* directors.

Directors (generally)

There are two main methods of being appointed a director. These are the formal and informal methods. Formal methods require a positive act by some organ of the company to appoint the director. For example, the members may vote to appoint a person, a director, or the existing directors may co-opt a new director.

Informal methods require no positive act by the company. A person can be a director if everyone treats him as a director and he holds the position of a director without having formally been appointed to the post or completing the necessary forms of appointment (CA 1985 s 741(1)). This is known as a *de facto* director. He can still be deemed in law to be a director even if the company has conferred on him some other title such as "manager". The other informal method is by being a shadow director, (CA 1985 s 741(2)) of which more later.

The important issue is that whether or not the putative director has been formally appointed as a director, if he acts and is treated as a director, the law will deem him to be a director. This can be significant in the context of disqualification of directors (see later).

Managing directors

No company is obliged to have a managing director, but many do. Each company that has one (it is rare to have more than one, since they would be apt to disagree) must have power to have one under the articles. Table A art 72 provides for such a power. Commonly a managing director is given wide authority, delegated from the board of directors, to allow the company to enter into contracts. He may also be the chairman of the company, but under the Cadbury Code (see later) it is considered unsuitable for the managing director also to be the chairman. This is because a chairman is supposed to be impartial and to be able to take an objective overview for the purposes of company and board meetings. If a company does not formally appoint a managing director, but the other directors treat one particular director as if he were the managing director, and take no steps to correct that impression, that director will be deemed to be the managing director and the company is then responsible for any contracts he enters into as agent for the company (*Freeman & Lockyer* v *Buckhurst Park Properties (Mangal) Ltd* [1964] 2 QB 480).

A managing director will be an employee of a company, and holds the office of managing director on such terms as may be agreed between him and the company in a service contract.

Under Table A art 84, where a director with an executive position, such as a managing director, is dismissed from his directorship, he automatically loses his managing directorship as well. This happened to Shirlaw in *Southern Foundries (1926) Ltd* v *Shirlaw* [1940] AC 701 (see Chapter 5). However, a managing director's service contract should, if well drafted, entitle him to damages for the unexpired portion of his contract. Under Table A art 84 a managing director does not retire by rotation.

Executive directors

An executive director is a director who is an employee of the company, or who holds an executive position within the company. Such positions include managing directors, financial directors or such other positions as companies sees fit. Under Table A art 72 the directors can delegate such powers as they see fit to a director holding executive office, and they can also specify the terms on which he holds that position. Under Table A art 84, an executive director does not retire by rotation. Sometimes the senior director who works full time for his company is known as its "chief executive".

Non-executive directors

A non-executive director is not an employee of the company, but is appointed to the post of director because of special skills or connections he is able to bring to the board of directors. Non-executive directors are meant to furnish an independent viewpoint which a full-time director might not be able to provide. Commonly non-executive directors hold positions in other organisations such as banks, in academia, in politics or in some area of interest to the company. For example, some of the ethical investment management companies have non-executive directors form major charitable or environmental protection bodies. In the Hampel Report (see later) it is recommended that a nominated senior non-executive should be a company "troubleshooter", especially if there are serious concerns about the running of the company.

Chairman of the board of directors

A chairman's functions are primarily concerned with organising board meetings and general meetings. A chairman may be said to be the public face of the company. The company chairman is usually selected from the available directors (Table A art 91) and commonly has a casting vote. Being a chairman requires certain skills: he has to give each speaker his chance but he must not let any speaker dominate the floor; he must be able to read the mood of the meeting and know when to call a vote on matters; he needs considerable tact but firmness; ideally he is meant to act as a disinterested conductor of the meeting. For meetings generally see Chapter 18.

The Cadbury Code (see later) recommends that the post of chairman and managing director should be filled by different persons. The chairman can provide an dispassionate overview of a company's activities and restrain the wider impulses of the managing director or the other directors. Commonly dynamic and self-confident entrepreneurs who are managing authority, even to a chairman. Such persons usually want to be chairmen too – which means there is no one who will dare to call their decisions into question. It also means that when things go wrong there is no one else with whom to share the blame.

A chairman is usually paid a fee for his services and is rarely an employee of his company.

Alternate directors

In a company that has adopted Table A or parts thereof, there is a provision under arts 65–69 for the nomination of an alternate director who stands in at board meetings for a director who is absent on business, ill-health or on vacation. The alternate director can be a specified person or be an existing director who thus can vote once for himself and once as the alternate for the absent director. Alternate directors can be useful where there may be difficulties in obtaining sufficient directors to make up a quorum. However, if an existing director is doubling up as an alternate, he still only counts as one person in a quorum.

Nominee directors

It is commonly a term of the class rights attaching to a class of shares that the class may nominate one or more directors who will have a seat at the board and represent the class's interests. Such a director is known as a nominee director. Nominee directors sometimes represent the interests of debenture-holders, Government bodies or other persons with an external interest in the company.

Shadow directors

Not all those whom the law treats as directors are formally appointed as directors. In addition to *de facto* directors whom the law treats as directors because they hold the position of director (CA 1985 s 741(1)) even if they are called by some other title, someone can be a director if he is a person " in accordance with those directors or instructions the directors or the company are accustomed to act" (CA 1985 s 741(2)).

In this case, the person is known as a shadow director. As with a *de facto* director, his name may not be on the company's headed paper, nor on the necessary appointment forms sent to the Registrar of Companies, but he will still be a director in law. The definition of shadow director is specifically designed to catch those who wish to influence a company's perhaps because they prefer anonymity, or perhaps because the company is carrying on some dubious activity with which they do not publicly wish to be associated. In order for a person to be classed as a shadow director it is important that the whole board of directors should closely follow that person's instructions: merely directing a few nominee directors does not make a person a shadow director (*Kuwait Asia Bank EC* v *National Mutual Life Nominees Ltd* [1990] 3 All ER 404).

The significance of being a director, whether appointed formally or otherwise, is that:

- directors can sometimes on winding-up be liable to contribute funds to their company if they have been making the company trade fraudulently (IA 1986 s 213), wrongfully (IA 1986 s 214), have been guilty of any misfeasance or breached their fiduciary duties to the company (IA 1986 s 212) or been involved in a phoenix company (IA 1986 s 217);

- even when a company is not being wound up, a director can sometimes be required to account to a company for any secret profits or for breaching any fiduciary duty he owes to the company;

- directors are liable to criminal penalties for failure to carry out certain statutory duties such as preparing accounts and filing annual returns;

- directors are subject to extensive disclosure requirements about their interests in their companies and to restrict their duties in connection with loans;

- the Model Code applies to directors of listed companies, whether formally appointed or not.

Although the CA 1985 s 741(2) contains a clause stating that a person is not a shadow director by reason only that the directors of a company act on advice given by him in a professional capacity, there is a genuine fear among some banks, lawyers, accountants or other corporate advisers that if they take too close an interest in a company's affairs, particularly at a difficult time in the company's existence, they may be deemed to be shadow directors. It is important for these people to maintain a certain distance. They should recommend certain courses of action, not direct or dictate them. This means that they will not then be deemed to be shadow directors. The issue of whether a bank then became very closely involved in a company's continued existence could be a shadow director was touched upon in *Re a company (No 005009 of 1987) ex parte Copp* [1989] BCLC 13 but never decided upon. It remains to be seen what may happen on this matter in the future.

It is possible that a holding company could be liable as a shadow director of a subsidiary if the subsidiary went into liquidation and its directors were held liable for its debts. This issue was discussed in *Re Hydroban (Corby) Ltd* [1994] BCLC 161 where the liquidator of Hydroban pleaded that two executive directors of the holding company, Eagle Trust plc, were shadow directors of the subsidiary. The judge suggested that although Eagle Trust plc might have been a shadow director, it did not automatically follow that the directors of Eagle Trust plc were thereby shadow directors of Hydroban. At the same time, if there had been an executive director of Eagle Trust plc who had specifically given directions to Hydroban's board, that executive director might have been a shadow director. Under the CA 1985 s 741(3) a holding company cannot be a shadow director of a subsidiary merely because the directors of the subsidiary are accustomed to act in accordance with the holding company's directions or instructions in the following matters:

- directors' duties to employees (CA 1985 s 309);

- directors' long-term contracts of employment (CA 1985 s 319);

- substantial property transactions involving directors (CA 1985 s 320);

- contracts with sole members who are directors (CA 1985 s 322B);

- the rules applying to loans to directors and other connected persons (CA 1985 ss 330–346).

The Cadbury Code

The Cadbury Committee was set up in May 1991 by the Financial Reporting Council, the Stock Exchange and the major accountancy bodies to provide, amongst other things, a report on:

- the perceived low level of confidence in listed company accounts;

- the perceived inability of auditors to provide the safeguards that those who use listed company accounts might expect auditors to provide;

- the concern over excessive rates of directors' remuneration in listed companies;

- corporate governance of listed companies, in other words the role of the board of directors in setting, implementing and controlling the financial policy of the company, and communicating that to shareholders and other accounts-uses.

In their report published in December 1992 the Cadbury Committee prepared a Code of Best Practice, known as the Cadbury Code (the "Code"), and various recommendations for company directors. The Code was welcomed by the Stock Exchange, which proceeded to insist that listed companies adopt the Code's requirements.

These are as follows:

- companies must be more open and frank in their accounting practice;

- boards of directors must consider all major transactions involving the company. This is both to ensure that they all know what is going on and to pin responsibility on the directors should the company or its directors not be adhering to the Code as it or they should;

- directors must state that their company is a going concern and be able to justify that assertion;

- all listed companies are expected to comply with the terms of the Code;

- listed companies that fail to comply with its terms are required to explain in their accounts and directors' reports why they are not doing so;

- any such explanation must be reviewed by the auditors.

The threat behind non-compliance is that if listed companies are not prepared to regulate themselves by means of a "voluntary" code, the Government may step in to force regulation upon them.

The implementation of the Code is through boards of directors and the auditors. It is ironic that boards should be the bodies charged with the implementation of a policy of greater disclosure, since boards have sometimes been anxious to avoid telling their investors, creditors or the financial press any more than they have to – often for good commercial reasons, sometimes out of fear lest their less reputable practices are brought into the public light.

The Code and the Committee made various recommendations concerning directors:

- the chairman should not be the chief executive/managing director;

- the board should consist of executive directors and at least three non-executives (one of whom may be the chairman), the function of the non-executives being to review the executive management and to prevent, or at least bring to everyone's attention, conflicts of interest between the directors and the company;

- non-executives should be appointed on merit and for a fixed but renewable term; they should receive a fee but neither a salary nor share options should be available to them; they should be genuinely independent and neither they nor any businesses in which they are already involved should be in a commercial relationship with the company;

- directors should undergo some formal training on the rights and duties of being a director, experience having shown that some people have been elevated to the level of director without a real understanding of the legal complexities and responsibilities of the position;

- in the annual report the directors should produce a statement about their responsibility for the accounts, and should include a comment about the effectiveness of the company's own internal control system of accounting;

- listed companies should set up audit committees comprising the finance director, external auditors, internal auditors and the directors, though of the directors the non-executives should be in a majority;

- the non-executive directors should set up a remuneration committee to ensure that directors are taking reasonable, as opposed to excessive reward for their labour.

Few could disagree with the principle of the Cadbury Committee's recommendations:

- that accounts should be more meaningful than hitherto;

- that directors should have greater regard to the good of the company as opposed to the good of themselves; and

- that directors should generally be accountable to the shareholders for the directors' and their company's conduct.

Some directors, especially those whose personal standards did not match those expected by the Committee's recommendations, may have felt uneasy about the Committee's recommendations. However, they were hardly in a position to object since that would have been tantamount to saying that they approved of limited disclosure and limited accountability of directors' actions to shareholders – not a view likely to ensure investor confidence. However, there were criticisms that the Code relied too much on voluntary compliance, and that it lacked teeth.

Particular criticism was reserved for the question of non-executives. It was found that the pool of available and competent non-executives was not perhaps as great as had been imagined, nor were they always as independent as might be thought. This sort of person who had the relevant experience to be a non-executive tended to be an already successful businessman, who often moved in the same business and sometimes social spheres as the executive directors, perhaps compromising the apparent independence of the non-executives. There was the suspicion that certain non-executive positions with the accompanying fees might be awarded by some company directors to their friends on a "you scratch my back, I'll scratch yours later" basis. This is not to deny the genuine contribution made by many diligent non-executives, but as was found with remuneration committees (see below), the genuine independence of view on what directors' salaries ought to be was not often found. If one director has managed to obtain an enormous increase in salary for himself, when he sits as a non-executive director in a remuneration committee on another company he is scarcely likely to recommend a lesser figure for another director's salary which will make his own look greedy.

Directors' remuneration

The reward for being a director is usually money and status. However, just because a person is a director does not mean that he is thereby entitled to remuneration. Table A art 82 permits remuneration for the directors, but it usually must be approved by the members or the full board, and in the absence of approval, no remuneration is due. Ward, the recipient of a success fee of £5.2 million as was revealed in *Guinness plc* v *Saunders and Ward* [1990] 1 All ER 652 tried to claim that he was entitled to this sum *quantum meruit* (*i.e.* because that was what his work was worth) but the courts did not agree. This was because there had been no proper approval of the remuneration for his services.

Under Table A art 83 directors are entitled to their expenses, and under art 84 may be employed by the company in a non-directional capacity on such terms as the other directors may think fit.

Directors in small companies usually take their gain from being a director in the form of salary, in dividends, or in the increasing value of their shares. There may also be other perquisites, such as company cars, the use of certain company accommodation etc. In larger, listed companies, the same methods of remuneration are used, but the scale is much greater, and directors used to be, and in some cases still are, given share options as an incentive. The directors were set targets of profitability for the company to reach: if those targets were met, the directors were able to exercise their share options. These allowed the directors to acquire newly issued shares from the company at a predetermined low price and immediately (if they wished) to sell those shares at the higher price which the ordinary shares were by then trading at. The advantage of this method was that it cost the company virtually nothing; all it had to do was issue the shares at a low price.

Share options as a form of remuneration and incentive have been criticised because it is quite possible that a company's share price has risen, thus triggering the opportunity to exercise the share options, due to factors that were nothing to do with the directors' labours or skills. There might just be a general upturn in the economy, from which the company happens to have benefited. Accordingly, as a method of rewarding directors it has somewhat fallen out of favour recently, long-term incentive plans being used in its place (of which more later).

The controversy over high salaries for directors

The issue of directors' remuneration has attracted a great deal of public criticism within the last few years because of the very large increases some directors have received. This has sometimes been accompanied both by the dismissal of large numbers of other employees and by some directors' poor grasp of public relations.

The justification for the high salaries is said to be that in order to get the best persons to be directors, one must pay them a very great deal since persons of that calibre can often obtain very large salaries elsewhere. This justification is not without substance. Leading directors of major companies elsewhere in the USA and Europe are very well paid. Directors recruited from those areas to jobs within the UK were able to negotiate salaries and terms no less favourable than they had been hitherto enjoying. This had a cumulative effect as British directors generally sought to emulate the salaries that the foreign directors had managed to obtain. At the same time salaries and bonuses within the financial world were generally rising for those who were particularly successful. The general "going rate" for salaries was thus talked up.

The Cadbury Committee recommended that listed companies set up remuneration committees of directors and other directors. Not all of the remuneration committees' recommendations were well received by shareholders, particularly employee–shareholders and small private investors. Directors' pleas that the newly increased salaries had been approved by the remuneration committee inevitably prompted speculation as to what the average salaries for the members of the remuneration committee were.

In fairness to directors, although a very high salary might excite some attention as being overgenerous, paying directors a few hundred thousand pounds more than they used to be paid actually makes very little difference to a major company's financial position, while paying less than the going rate may mean that the company will have trouble filing its senior executive positions with suitably competent directors. Most of the criticism about high salary levels for directors has come from small private shareholders whose shareholdings even collectively do not generally greatly influence the voting control of a major listed company. Generally speaking the major investors, the institutions, do not publicly criticise the level of directors' remuneration. This is partly because they may sometimes believe the directors are doing a good job for the salaries, but mainly because they generally believe that if there are problems with directors it is better that these are sorted out quietly in a private conference with the directors rather than publicly and embarrassingly at a general meeting. At a public meeting any major dispute might alarm the confidence of the market in the company's management and drive down the company's share price.

It is also suggested that one reason the institutions do not question the level of remuneration of the directors is because some of the directors of those institutions themselves have salaries of a similar size.

The Greenbury Report

Consequent to the implementation of the Cadbury Code and the public concern at the high level of directors' remuneration, a new committee, known as the Greenbury Committee, was set up to review the question of corporate governance and directors' remuneration.

The Committee addressed various issues, the most significant being:

- the position of non-executives within remuneration committees;
- the introduction of long-term incentive plans for directors;
- higher levels of disclosure of director's remuneration;
- the duration of directors' service contracts.

The position of non-executives within remuneration committees

As stated earlier, there has been some criticisms of the genuine independence of non-executive directors. The Greenbury Report (1995) sought to deal with this in various ways. It recommended that executive directors should not be allowed to sit on remuneration committees: there had been instances of the executive director sitting on the committee that decided his own pay, a situation that did little to encourage genuine independence of views on the committee. This recommendation has been widely adopted and seen as sensible. However there is still some doubt as to just how independent the non-executives are. It appears to be the case that even when the chief executive no longer sits on the remuneration committee, his influence is still widely felt – as it is not surprising, as a chief executive, all things being equal, will encourage the appointment of non-executives with whom he can work well generally. As the non-executives sit on other committees apart from the remuneration committee, there has to be a degree of co-operation in the other committees which will spill over into the remuneration committee. Furthermore, the non-executives often owe their position as non-executives to the chief executive's recommendation, and will not wish to lose their own fees as non-executives by being awkward to the chief executive who put them there. There are suggestions in the financial press that some chief executives see the use of remuneration committees as a cosmetic exercise designed to palliate vexatious shareholders. While this may overstate the position, it is also possible to argue that genuine independence on the part of remuneration committees is an unrealistic dream unless there is a significant shift in culture amongst those who run major businesses. There is a further, more ruthless, argument, which is that it does not much matter what a remuneration committee does provided the company is profitable.

The introduction of long-term incentive plans for directors

As discussed earlier, rewarding directors by share options which can be exercised at a low price, thus allowing the directors to make an immediate gain if the share price has subsequently risen, was increasingly viewed with disfavour. The Greenbury Report recommended that such share options be replaced by long-term incentive plans, based on "Challenging performance criteria". Broadly speaking, the long-term incentive plans are designed to reward directors who, say, maintain or increase the company's performance within a comparable band of other businesses, or in some other way benefit the company, perhaps by introducing a new production method. Provided the company maintained its position, or the chief executive successfully introduced the new method, the chief executive might be rewarded with a highly motivated bonus. The remuneration committee has to provide the chief executive with sufficient bonus to encourage him, but also sufficient salary to prevent him being lured to another business.

The Greenbury Report suggested that three years was the minimum for such plans, though in practice one year appears to be common. However, the Stock Exchange does now require that all long-term schemes have to be put to the members for their approval, so that members genuinely have the opportunity to see how challenging the performance criteria area. At the same time, there were criticisms of some long-term incentive plans because of their complexity and because members, even with the new disclosure requirements to be outlined shortly, did not have access to all the information on which to see how effective the plans are.

Higher levels of disclosure of directors' remuneration

It was widely agreed that this recommendation, which has been written in to the Stock Exchange rule book, was of greater service to members. Directors of listed companies used to be able to disguise the true level of their salaries by listing their remuneration within bands of tens of thousands of pounds. Now their true salary has to be stated, and members can now see what the directors are earning.

However, such clarity has not yet been extended into companies' pension contributions for their directors: despite the greater disclosure requirements it is by no means easy for most members to work out the level of funding of directors' pensions by the company.

The disclosure of directors' remuneration has also had the unexpected consequence that directors were able to compare their own salaries with those of similar directors in other businesses. Some directors realised that they were being paid less than their peers and insisted on similar rewards – thus increasing the going rate for directors' pay.

The duration of directors' service contracts

The Greenbury Report recommended that directors' service contracts be restricted to one-year rolling contracts. This was to prevent directors being able to claim several years' worth of salary if they were dismissed before the expiry of their term of office. This is a contentious issue, because it is generally agreed that it is difficult to find top class executives who can successfully manage leading businesses. In order to receive their services, they have to be promised considerable rewards, one of which is a certain amount of job security. On the other hand, too secure a job could make the directors complacent, and members would be unhappy about having to pay off an incompetent director with several years' worth of salary. The Greenbury Report contained a let-out clause saying that two-year rolling contracts might sometimes be acceptable, though they were not to be encouraged. As a result, two-year contracts became the norm, though three-year contracts, which formerly were quite common, ceased to be so prevalent.

In addition, there has for some time been a practice of paying directors very large sums of money on their departure, sometimes to the disgust of the private investors. The large pay-offs may be payment for the directors' silence about their companies' difficulties, or may reflect the fact that a dismissed director may find it difficult to obtain another position. However, large pay-offs inevitably lead to the cynical suggestion that some directors might not be averse to being dismissed, and that continuing directors in companies where directors have been handsomely rewarded for their dismissal are setting useful precedents for their own pay-offs in their event of their own dismissal at a later date.

The Hampel Report

The Hampel committee was set up to review the implementation of the Cadbury and Greenbury Reports. In January 1998 the committee issued its own report ("the Hampel Report"). Amongst its findings were the following:

- there should be an updated version of the Cadbury Code, to be known as the "supercode" which would incorporate recommendations from all three reports and that this should be part of the Stock Exchange listing requirement rules;

- companies should be required to explain any departure from best listed company practice;

- a nominated non-executive should be a "troubleshooter" whose job it is to investigate without hindrance from the company any matters that are open to scrutiny as being deviations from good business practice;

- the institutions, whose block votes command much attention at AGMs, should be required to consider carefully the effect of their votes instead of nodding directors' recommendations through;

- directors' remuneration should be clearly and understandably shown in companies' accounts;

- the recommendations about accounts and audit specified in the Cadbury report should be maintained although directors should not have to give an opinion on the effectiveness of internal financial controls.

Matters that were rejected by the Hampel Committee were:

- the adoption of the two-tier managerial system much favoured in Germany (one tier for management, one tier for supervision);

- compulsory voting by the institutions at AGMs;

- approval by shareholders of directors' remuneration;

- a set of rules specifying the numbers of non-executive and executive directors a company ought to have;

- obligatory board representation for stakeholders, these being such interest groups as employees, customers, local environmental organisations etc.;

- the setting up of a permanent committee on corporate governance.

It will be seen that Hampel had to tread a narrow path between the increasing public demands that directors generally become more accountable for their actions, show higher standards of business ethics and bear considerations other than the quest for profit in their corporate deliberations (this being view advanced by the corporate governance lobby) and the interest of many directors in wishing to run their businesses in the best way that they see fit without having to comply with what some might consider as interfering, bureaucratic and uncommercial rules and regulations. The issue of corporate governance is discussed further in Chapter 23 and it is likely that the issues raised by the Hampel Report will continue to be the subject of much debate. The Government's reaction to the report may well arrive in the forthcoming Green Paper on Company Law due to be published in 1998.

Who can be a director?

There are no specific qualifications needed to become a director unless the articles say so. Anyone who is not prohibited from being a director may become a director. A company, limited or unlimited, can be a director, and so can a Scottish partnership. A director which is a company functions through its own directors, and a director that is a Scottish partnership can function through any of the partners.

Sometimes persons in a business are given titles such as "sales director" or "marketing director". This does not mean that they are directors of the company in law. You are only a director if you have been appointed by one of the formal undernoted methods, are a director by virtue of holding the position of a director under the CA 1985 s 741(1) or are a shadow director by virtue of the CA 1985 s 741(2).

The following are prohibited from being directors:

- an undischarged bankrupt without leave of the court under s 11 of the Company Directors Disqualification Act 1986 ("CDDA");

- persons disqualified under other sections within the CDDA, such as having a conviction for running a company for a fraudulent purpose;

- directors over the age of 70 in a public limited company or one of its subsidiaries unless retained in office by the articles (CA 1985 s 293(7)) or unless the members have approved their directorship by means of ordinary resolutions following special notice (CA 1985 s 293(5));

- directors who have failed within the requisite time (normally two months) to obtain the minimum number of shares required for them to be directors in terms of their companies' articles (CA 1985 s 291). These shares are known as qualification shares;

- auditors of the company;

- the secretary of a private company when there are no other directors (CA 1985 s 283(2));

- in a company (A) with only one director (B), a company (C) acting as that director (B), when company C's sole director (D) is the company secretary of a company A (CA 1985 s 283(4)(b)).

Table A art 81 includes several further prohibitions, commonly adopted by many other companies:

- bankrupts even with the leave of the court, or anyone who has had to make any arrangement with their creditors;

- anyone suffering from certifiable mental disorder;

- someone who has absented himself from directors' meetings for six consecutive months without permission.

Bankrupts

The principle behind the prohibition of bankrupts is very clear: no one would wish a person who is unable to look after his own finances to look after a company's. Unfortunately the reality is less simple. A bankrupt is not supposed to be a company director, but a bankrupt director could, if devious enough, invent a new name and address and be appointed to the directorship of a company. Even though directors are supposed to give their national insurance number to the Inland Revenue on the incorporation of a company, the bankrupt could claim to be foreign and not have a national insurance number: there are no nationality restrictions upon company directors.

A second problem in practice is identical names. In a household with two John Smiths it is hard to know which one might be the bankrupt. It is for that reason that the age of the director has to be given. The registers of bankrupts and those disqualified under the CDDA are cross-checked with the Register of Companies to ensure that no bankrupts or other disqualified persons illegally become company directors.

Directors over the age of 70

The principle behind the age requirement, which only applies to plcs and their subsidiaries, is to prevent elderly directors hampering the progress of the company. Occasionally people who run their own companies find it difficult after many years to hand over the reins to others. They may also be unwilling to accept that they may not be as good businessmen as they once were. Once the director reaches the age of 70, the members of the public company will at least have the opportunity to vote him out of office – unless the managing director owns most of the shares or has tailored the articles to his own benefit beforehand.

Qualification shares

Qualification shares exist because it is thought that directors who have a personal stake in a company are more likely to try hard for the overall good of the company.

The sole director is the same person as the company secretary

The rules in the CA 1985 s 283 are designed to prevent a company having effectively a sole director who is simultaneously, either in his own name or through a company, the secretary. This applies to single member companies as well.

Unsuitable company directors

It is possible to appoint a minor as a company director. It would be very unwise to do so, because children below the age of 18 may not necessarily be bound by a contract, even if they are purporting to be acting for a company and in the course of a business. The contract might be put aside by a court if it is not proper for a child to have entered into it.

Sometimes major investors or lenders appoint a representative to be a nominee director. This is usually to protect the investors' or lenders' interests. In each case the representative as a director is supposed to act bona fide in the best interests of the company. This may lead to a conflict of interests when the company is not prospering and the investor or lender wants its money back even though that might not be in the best interests of the company. There is no satisfactory solution to this problem. The best that can be said of it is that while the director is on the board he is at least well aware of what the company is doing. With an extreme conflict of interest the representative director should resign.

Appointment of directors

The first directors are those who sign the Form 10 which is sent to the Registrar of Companies on incorporation. Even if someone else is named in the articles on incorporation as the first director, the first director or directors will be those named in the Form 10 (CA 1985 s 10(5)). Private limited companies need only have one director (CA 1985 s 282(3)), but it is common to have two. Table A requires a minimum of two (art 64). Public companies must have at least two (CA 1985 s 282(1)). A director can simultaneously be company secretary and director, but if so, there must be one other director since the one person cannot act in a dual capacity whenever an act, such as signing certain forms, has to be performed by both a director and the secretary (CA 1985 s 284).

Subsequent directors

The method of appointing further directors is normally stated in the articles. Common methods include:

- appointment by the members at a general meeting;

- appointment by the other directors to fill a vacancy until the next general meeting (Table A art 79);

- appointment of a retiring director in a Table A company, where the retiring director offers himself for re-election and the meeting has not rejected his offer or resolved not to fill the vacancy (art 75);

- co-option by the existing directors.

A new director in a Table A company offering himself for election must:

(i)   have been recommended by the directors;
(ii) have arranged that the members should have been given between 14 and 35 days' notice prior to the meeting when the election will take place of the intention to elect the new director (art 76);
(iii) inform the company of all the details that would need to be entered into the company's own register of directors' interests;
(iv) consent to being a director.

The rules on rotation and appointment of directors under Table A are notoriously difficult to follow and many companies that have Table A style rotation of directors articles ignore them. This was because in small companies directors have no desire to keep resigning and being reappointed, and furthermore, they cannot remember whose turn it is to retire and make himself eligible for re-election. Many small companies nowadays have much simpler articles that dispense entirely with the rotation of directors rules. Despite this, rotation of directors as a principle is not without merit, because:

(i)   every few years there is an opportunity to fail to re-elect directors who might otherwise be there for ever;
(ii) it provides a mechanism for dismissing directors without having to go through the cumbersome and sometimes embarrassing s 303 procedure (see later);
(iii) the knowledge that every three years (or such shorter period as may be demanded by the articles) the directors have to justify their continued directorship to the members can motivate the directors to work harder for the company.

However, determined directors, particularly if they are founder directors, ensure that their companies' articles state that they are to be directors for life, or give themselves weighted voting rights (see *Bushell* v *Faith* [1970] AC 1099, for the facts of which see Chapter 7).

If a public company wishes to appoint several new directors at a general meeting, each director must be separately voted on to the board (CA 1985 s 292(1)). However, if at the meeting there is a preliminary motion asking that two or more directors be appointed all in the one resolution, and that motion is passed without anyone voting against it, it is permissible to vote two or more directors into office without the need for separate resolutions (CA 1985 s 292(1)).

The purpose of this piece of legislation is to prevent an unwelcome director being part of a package with some desirable directors, so that to obtain the desirable directors one has to accept the unwelcome one. This is not permissible (CA 1985 s 292(1)), but because there might be occasions when a public company is appointing many new directors, and it would be tedious to vote on each one separately, the permissive procedure is available (CA 1985 s 292(1)).

Where a new director is being appointed to fill a vacancy, other than a casual (*i.e.* temporary and until the next AGM) vacancy, arising out of the dismissal of a director under the CA 1985 s 303, special notice must be given of the resolution both to dismiss the outgoing director and to appoint the new one (CA 1985 s 303(2)). For the details of special notice and dismissal under the CA 1985 s 303, see later.

What happens if the appointment is defective?

Under Table A art 92 and the CA 1985 s 285 if a director carries out certain acts, either on his own or as part of a board of directors, and it subsequently turns out that at the time he was not formally holding the post of director because of a defective appointment, his acts are still valid. This is because a director might genuinely have believed he was a director; everyone might equally have been of the same belief; and it would be unfair on third parties who had relied on the company's word and his word that he was a director to be told that his acts were invalid and that the third parties' contracts with the company were invalid. Providing all parties have acted in good faith, there should be no difficulties with this. In the case of *Morris* v *Kanssen* [1946] AC 459, a director deliberately used these rules to assert the validity of a bogus appointment but failed. This was because the wording of art 92 and s 285 are designed to protect the inadvertent failure to appoint, not to permit the ignoring or overriding of the substantive provisions relating to such appointment. Directors over the age of 70 in public companies are meant to vacate office at the end of the AGM following their 70th birthday. If by some oversight they fail to vacate office and continue to act, their acts are still valid even if it is afterwards discovered that their appointments as directors have terminated (CA 1985 s 293(3)). This is again to protect those who had the director's word or the company's word that he was still in office. In any event, it is probable, though not certain, that the CA 1985 ss 35, 35A and 35B serve to protect the third party dealing with the company through the defectively appointed director. It is, however, likely that if the third party knew any director was defectively appointed and was taking advantage of that information, the good faith requirement of the CA 1985 s 35A(2)(b) would apply and the third party would not be able to enforce the contract against the company.

Disclosure requirements for directors

On appointment, a new director signs a Form 10 (for the first directors) or a Form 288a. This indicates his consent to the directorship. The forms must be sent to the Registrar of Companies. On these forms he must also indicate his:

- present name;

- any past names;

- usual residential address, or for a company, its registered office, and for a Scottish partnership, its place of business;

- nationality (except for companies and partnerships);

- business occupation (many directors just write "company director");

- particulars of any other directorship held by him or which have been held by him within the last five years, with the exception of dormant companies or other companies within the group of companies of which the present company forms a member (CA s 289(3));

- the date of his birth. This is because directors of public companies and their subsidiaries need approval from the members if they are to remain in office over the age of 70 (CA 1985 s 293)).

The reason for the disclosure of the present and past directorships is to allow investors and creditors the opportunity to see what other companies any director has been involved in. Investors and creditors can then obtain those other companies' accounts from Companies House. They can then ascertain how successful he has been in running them, and decide whether or not they should invest in or trade with any company of which he is a director. With computerisation it will ultimately be easy to check whether or not the director has been entirely truthful in his statement of past and present directorships.

In addition, the director is under an obligation to disclose to the company his interest in any securities and options in the company of which he is now a director. This also applies to any securities in any subsidiary or holding company of that company (CA 1985 s 324). He is obliged to notify the company within five days of any changes to his holdings of these securities (CA 1985 Schedule 13 Part II). These rules apply to:

(i)   the director's spouse and children (CA 1985 s 328);
(ii) companies in which he has more than one-third of the voting control or in which the board of directors acts as he wishes (CA 1985 Schedule 13 Part I para 4(a) and (b));

(iii) any trust in which he has an interest as a beneficiary (CA 1985 Schedule 13 Part I para 2).

The company must keep a register where all these interests are noted (CA 1985 s 325). This information is kept at the company's registered office but is not forwarded to the Registrar of Companies. However, in the case of companies whose securities are listed on a recognised investment exchange, this information must be conveyed to that exchange the day after the company receives the information from the director (CA 1985 s 329(2)). In practice in the UK this is the Stock Exchange. This means that it is possible for ordinary investors to see whether directors are selling their shares or buying them. If the directors are buying the shares, they presumably know something advantageous about the company's prospects that others do not: if they are selling, one may be tempted to assume that bad news lies ahead.

Termination of office

A director's office can be terminated by any of the following methods;

- death;

- expiry of his contract;

- transgression of some term of the articles or of his service contract;

- failure to obtain or retain qualification shares (CA 1985 s 291) if qualification shares are required;

- his bankruptcy;

- under Table A, art 81, certifiable insanity;

- under Table A, art 81, his absence from board meetings for more than six consecutive months without permission and following a vote of dismissal by the other directors;

- his resignation;

- retirement by rotation in those companies that use retirement by rotation;

- dismissal from office under the CA 1985 s 303;

- attainment of the statutory age limit in plcs (CA 1985 s 293);

- disqualification under the Company Directors Disqualification Act 1986.

On termination, the Form 288b must be sent to the Registrar of Companies.

In the event of the termination of a director's contract:

(i)   before its natural expiry,
(ii)   at the instance of the company,
(iii) without breach of the terms of the service contract by the director, or
(iv)   without breach by the director of any other agreement between the company and the director,

the director will normally be entitled to damages for the unexpired part of his contract. Shareholders should consider this when they propose to dismiss a director, since the company will then have to meet his claim for the salary he would have earned had he been employed for his full term. Astute directors have clauses in their contracts saying that if they are forced to resign, or otherwise vacate their offices through no fault of their own, they will receive special dismissal payments ("golden parachutes") in addition to their outstanding salary. Sometimes these can take the form of large pension contributions. Cynics will say that if the "golden parachute" is large enough there will be every incentive for a director to recommend that his company be taken over because then he can be dismissed and claim his golden parachute. Equally if the parachute is large enough, it may discourage a takeover bidder from taking the company over. This is because it will cost too much to get rid of the director. If a director's service contract does not contain a clause dealing with compensation for loss of office, any compensation he receives will need the prior approval of the members. This is dealt with in the next chapter.

Death

A directorship is not an asset that can be passed to an estate on death. Death in service may entitle the deceased director's relict to special pension or lump sum payments, but rights to these would normally arise out of any service contract.

Expiry of his contract

The articles or the director's service contract may prescribe a fixed period for the director's tenure of his office. On its expiry without renewal he will have to leave.

Transgression of some term of the articles or of his service contract

The articles or service contract may impose certain obligations upon the director to carry out his duties in a certain way. If he fails to do so, he may be summarily dismissed by his fellow directors or by the members, according to the terms of the articles or the service contract. He then cannot expect to receive anything more from the company except perhaps a payment to encourage him not to reveal any secrets about the company in public.

Failure to obtain or retain qualification shares

Some companies' articles require the director to hold qualification shares. If the director fails to obtain them, or disposes of them, he ceases to be a director (CA 1985 s 291(3)).

Bankruptcy (sequestration in Scotland)

If a bankrupt is unable to manage his own affairs, it is assumed that he is not fit to manage a company's affairs. Bankruptcy automatically terminates his directorship. The purpose of this rule is to protect the general public from incompetent or deceitful would-be directors. If a director cannot manage his own finances, he certainly should not be let loose on other people's money through the medium of a limited company. It is possible for a bankrupt to petition the courts to be given leave to be a director, but as the petition has to be held in the court that pronounced him bankrupt (CDDA 1986 ss 11 and 13), such petitions have to be well founded.

Insanity

Table A art 81(c) states that if a director is or may be suffering from mental disorder and:

(i) is either admitted into hospital for treatment under the Mental Health Act 1983 or the Mental Health (Scotland) Act 1960, or
(ii) an order is made by a court appointing an official to look after the insane person's affairs and property,

the director ceases to hold his office as director.

Resignation

Under Table A art 81(d) a director can resign his office by notice to the company. This can be done at any time. In boardroom battles directors are generally encouraged to resign quietly rather than be sacked by their fellow directors.

Making a fuss is likely to prejudice that director's chances of being accepted as a director anywhere else, and may lessen his chances for obtaining handsome compensation for loss of office. Some companies have articles that require a director to resign if the other directors ask him to go.

Retirement by rotation

If retirement by rotation takes place in accordance with the rules of Table A, under Table A art 73 at the first AGM all the directors retire and may ask the members to reappoint them. At the next, one-third of the directors retire. Some of those may be re-elected, or the members may choose not to elect them, or not to fill in vacancies. At the following AGM a further third retire and re-elections take place or not as the case may be. At the subsequent AGM, the remaining third retire and are re-elected on the same basis. At each AGM those who have been directors longest are the ones who have to retire.

Directors appointed to fill a casual vacancy retire at the next AGM but are not treated as falling within the retirement by rotation rules (Table A art 79). Managing directors and directors holding any other executive office do not retire by rotation (Table A art 84).

Dismissal from office under the CA 1985 s 303

Despite what may be said in a company's articles, or in a service contract with a director, the members of a company can by ordinary resolution vote to remove a director before the natural expiry of his term of office under the CA 1985 s 303 – though if the members do this contrary to the terms of a shareholders' agreement to which they are parties, they can expect to be sued for breach of the shareholders' agreement.

To dismiss a director under the CA 1985 s 303, the company must be given special notice of the resolution to dismiss the director. Special notice means that those members who wish to move the resolution must give the company at least 28 days' notice of their intention to move the resolution at a forthcoming general meeting (CA 1985 s 379(1)).

The period of 28 days is to allow the company to include the resolution in its notice to the members of the forthcoming meeting. That notice by the company must be sent out, or otherwise intimated by advertisement or other approved method to the members, at least 21 days before the meeting (CA 1985 s 379(2)). On the agenda of the meeting it will be stated that the company has received "special notice" of the resolution to dismiss the director. In the past, companies tried to evade the 28-day rule by bringing forward the date of the meeting and thus making the motion to dismiss the director time-barred. This is not now possible because of the CA 1985 s 379(3) which says that even if a meeting is called for a date within the period of 28 days, the notice by the members proposing to move the resolution for dismissal of a director is still valid.

The problem with these worthy rules is that they presuppose that members know when the next general meeting is going to take place, which unless a notice intimating the date has already been sent out, might not always be the case. On might have to wait nearly a whole year for the next general meeting, on which occasion the resolution to dismiss the director could be moved. If the directors were unwilling to bring forward the next general meeting or were otherwise being obstructive, as well they might, the members might have to requisition a meeting under the CA 1985 s 368. To do this the requisitionists must jointly hold one-tenth of the paid-up share capital or, in a company without share capital, one-tenth of the votes (see Chapter 18). As an alternative to requisitioning a general meeting, the members could insist that the dismissal resolution be dealt with at the next annual general meeting (CA 1985 s 376(1)), provided that the requisitionists hold one-twentieth of the total voting rights or that there are 100 requisitionists who collectively have paid by way of share capital on average at least £100 per member (CA 1985 s 376(2)) (see also Chapter 18). Assuming the special notice has been properly given, the director is told of the resolution, and he is entitled to speak about the resolution at the meeting (CA 1985 s 304(1)). He is also entitled to prepare a statement about his proposed dismissal. The statement must be of a reasonable length and sent to the company in sufficient time for the company to circulate it to the members (CA 1985 s 304(2)). If it is received too late for circulation, or the company is unwilling to circulate it, the director can have it read out at the meeting (CA 1985 s 304(3)). However, the company or any person who is aggrieved by anything in the statement is entitled to apply to the court for an order prohibiting the circulation or the reading-out of the statement if, in the view of the court, the rights of circulation and hearing are being abused "to secure needless publicity for defamatory matter" (CA 1985 s 304(4)). The right of the director to issue a statement saying why he should not be dismissed is commonly known as the right of protest.

The director's protests may be to no avail, because the members may already be determined to pass the ordinary resolution to dismiss him. However, he may be able to bring to the members' attention matters which they had not considered. He also may be able to create some embarrassment if, for example, he blows the whistle on activities that the company might not wish to be made public.

As this procedure is cumbersome, some companies' articles provide that a director can also be dismissed by means of a special resolution without any opportunity for a right of protest. This avoids any awkward publicity. This does not preclude the use of a s 303 dismissal: it is in addition to the rights of the members to use the s 303 procedure to remove a director. It is not possible for a private company to use the written resolution procedure to dismiss a director because that would prejudice his right of protects (CA 1985 Schedule 15A para 1(a)).

Naturally most directors do not wish to be dismissed. Directors can retain their positions by the use of weighted voting, as took place in *Bushell* v *Faith* [1970] AC 1099 (for the facts of which see Chapter 7). If using weighted voting, directors will also need to be allowed to use the weighted voting rights to prevent any alteration of the articles which might adversely affect the directors' weighted voting rights.

Alternatively, as stated above, the directors could protect their position by means of a shareholders' agreement. In such an agreement, all or a majority of the members contract not to vote for the directors' dismissal. If a member does vote for the dismissal of a director, he will be breaching the terms of the agreement and could be liable in damages for that breach.

Attainment of age limit

As stated earlier in this chapter, if a director of a public company, or one of its subsidiaries, reaches the age of 70 and wishes to continue in office, he will find that he is required to vacate his office (CA 1985 s 293(3)) unless the articles say otherwise (CA 1985 s 293(7)). However, if the members wish to keep him in office, or indeed wish to appoint any director over the age of 70, the members or the directors must give the company special notice (under CA 1985 s 379) of the resolution to reappoint or, as the case may be, appoint the director.

As stated above, the purpose of the legislation is to provide an opportunity to make elderly directors relinquish their grasp on the company. However, if an elderly director and his supporters have arranged the articles in their favour, hold a majority of the voting rights, or have the benefit of a shareholders' agreement to keep him in office, the director's position will remain secure.

Disqualification under the Company Directors Disqualification Act 1986 ("CDDA")

The CDDA was introduced to consolidate and expand the legislation dealing with unscrupulous directors who take advantage of the protection a limited company affords its members and directors to defraud creditors and investors. The CDDA does not apply to directors only: under the CDDA s 1(1) it also applies to:

• liquidators;

- administrators;

- receivers or managers of a company's property;

- anyone involved in the promotion, formation or management of a company.

The last category includes shadow directors and those occupying the position of a director without formal appointment, *i.e. de facto* directors. However, for simplicity, in the context of disqualification under the CDDA in this part of the chapter all these above persons will be referred to as "directors".

What the CDDA does is to prevent a person from acting as a director for a specified number of years except by leave of the court. He is still able to trade as a sole trader or in a partnership. Those who are caught being directors while banned are subject to criminal sanctions (see later). There is a number of grounds for disqualification. These are:

- conviction for an indictable offence (CDDA s 2);

- persistent breach of companies legislation (CDDA ss 3 and 5);

- fraud in winding up (CDDA s 4);

- unfitness for being a director (CDDA s 6);

- participation in wrongful trading (CDDA s 10);

- undischarged bankruptcy (CDDA s 11).

Conviction for an indictable offence (CDDA s 2)

If someone has been convicted of an indictable offence (*i.e.* an offence that is sufficiently serious that it could be tried before a jury) in connection with the promotion, formation, management, or liquidation of a company, or the receivership or management of its property, he can be disqualified under the CDDA s 2 for up to five years in a court of summary jurisdiction, and up to 15 years otherwise. These are deliberately wide grounds to catch errant directors. For example, in *R* v *Georgiou* [1988] 4 BCC 322, Georgiou had failed to obtain authorisation under the Insurance Companies Act 1982 to carry on an insurance business through a company. This was an indictable offence in connection with the management of his company. He was disqualified for five years.

Persistent breach of companies legislation (CDDA ss 3 and 5)

If a director persistently fails to return annual returns, accounts or other documents to the Registrar of Companies when he should, he can be disqualified under the CDDA s 3 and s 5. "Persistent" means at least three or more convictions for defaults in the last five years. Mitigating circumstances can, however, be taken into account. In *Re Arctic Engineering Ltd (No 2)* [1986] 2 All ER 346, a liquidator was dealing with 34 companies within a complicated receivership and liquidation. He had a history of supplying the relevant returns just in time after many reminders. He was cautioned rather than disqualified because it was realised that disqualification of the liquidator would cause enormous problems for those companies without particularly protecting the public.

The difference between s 5 and s 3 is that under s 5 the court can simultaneously convict the director for some default (his third in five years) and disqualify, whereas under s 3, there is a specific and separate application to the court for an order for disqualification.

Fraud in winding up

Under the CDDA s 4(1)(a), if someone has been found guilty of fraudulent trading under the CA 1985 s 458, or if any officer of the company has been found guilty of any fraud in connection with the company or any breach of his duty to that company (CDDA s 4(1)(b)), he can be disqualified for up to 15 years.

Unfitness for being a director

Whereas the above grounds give the courts a discretionary power to disqualify, the CDDA s 6 is mandatory. The court *must* disqualify a director if it is satisfied that:

(a) that the director is or has been a director of a company which has at any time become insolvent (whether while he was a director or subsequently), and

(b) that his conduct as a director of that company (either taken alone or taken together with his conduct as a director of any other company or companies) makes him unfit to be concerned in the management of a company).

"Becoming insolvent" in this context means going into insolvent liquidation or the appointment of an administrator or administrative receiver (receiver in Scotland). The significance of this definition is that insolvency does not normally include administrative receivership or a Scottish receivership. If in insolvent liquidation, the company must actually be insolvent: if it is wound up but its assets are greater than its liabilities, the CDDA ss 6 and 7 will not apply.

The Court will make a disqualification order in the public interest where there as been an application by:

- the Secretary of State (CDDA s 7(1)(a));

- the Official Receiver (but only for companies being wound up in England and Wales (CDDA s 7(1)(b)). The Official Receiver may also apply in Northern Ireland (Companies (Northern Ireland) Order 1989 art 10(1)(G)).

Following a report by the Official Receiver, a liquidator, an administrator or an administrative receiver (hereafter known collectively as the "insolvency practitioner") (CDDA s 7(3)). However, except with leave of the court, this must be done within two years beginning on the day when the company became insolvent, the administration order was granted, or the administrative receiver (or Scottish receiver) was appointed (CDDA s 7(2)). Leave of the court has been sparingly granted so far. Before granting or refusing leave to let the petitioner apply to the court late, the court will consider such matters as the length of and reasons for the delay, the prejudice the directors have sufferance by the delay, and the strength of the case against the directors. In *Re Polly Peck International plc (Secretary of State for Trade and Industry* v *Ellis and others)* (No 2) [1993] BCC 890 the court refused to let disqualification proceedings continue against the four respondents, mainly because the grounds for disqualification were so weak.

The report prepared under the CDDA s 7(3) itself is confidential and a director who fears that he may be about to be disqualified cannot apply to court to see what it says in advance of the petition for disqualification (*Secretary of State for Trade and Industry* v *Houston (No 2)*, 1994 GWD 6 361).

If, following a report made by DTI appointed inspectors, the Secretary of State considers it in the public interest that a director should be disqualified, he can apply to the court for a disqualification order. This can apply even in respect of a private company which is not offering its shares to the public. Disqualification will be sought under the CDDA s 8. The Secretary of State can use evidence about the director and his conduct as a director compulsorily obtained by DTI inspectors as part of his grounds for bringing disqualificatory proceedings (*R* v *Secretary of State for the DTI*, ex parte McCormack The Independent 15 Jan 1998).

Re Looe Fish Ltd [1993] BCC 348. The Secretary of State obtained documents under the CA 1985 s 447 and acting on the information he found therein applied for disqualification, under the CDDA s 8, of two directors in the company. They had allotted shares to themselves so that they could retain voting control, but wished to avoid paying any money for those shares. The directors initially paid the subscription money for their new shares, but the company then lent them their subscription money back, and the company finally bought the shares back without following the procedure laid down in the CA 1985 s 135 *et seq*. The company was solvent throughout this operation, but one director was disqualified in the public interest since his behaviour made him unfit to hold the office of director.

The grounds for determining whether or not a director is unfit to be a director are to be found in the CDDA Schedule 1, Parts I and II. Part I refers to unfitness generally, and Part II to unfitness in the context of a company that has become insolvent (CDDA s 9).

The grounds under Part I are:

- misfeasance or breach of fiduciary or other duty by the director in relation to the company;

- misappropriation of the company's assets by the director;

- transactions with the intention of defrauding creditors under the Insolvency Act 1986 Part XVI (only applicable in England and Wales) such as sales by the company at a deliberate undervalue to the director;

- failure to ensure that the company;
  - keeps accounting records in the correct place for the correct length of time;
  - maintains registers of directors, secretaries, and members in the correct place;
  - makes annual returns;
  - registers charges;

- failure to prepare annual accounts and thereafter to approve and sign them.

The grounds under Part II are less specific because of the use of the word "extent". The greater the extent of the director's responsibility, the greater the likelihood of his being disqualified. The grounds are as follows:

- the extent of the director's responsibility for the causes of the company becoming insolvent;

- the extent of the director's responsibility for any failure by the company to supply any goods or services which have been paid for;

- the extent of the director's responsibility for the company entering into any transactions or preferences made after the commencement of winding up, transactions at an undervalue (gratuitous alienations in Scotland) or preferential payments (unfair preferences in Scotland) within the time-limits specified in the Insolvency Act 1986;

- the extent of the director's failure to make the directors honour their duty to call a creditors' meeting in a creditors' voluntary winding-up;

- any failure by the director to comply with the duties imposed by him under the Insolvency Act 1986 in connection with:
  - preparing a statement of affairs in an administration;
  - preparing a statement of affairs to an administrative receiver or a Scottish receiver;
  - preparing a statement of affairs in a creditors' voluntary winding-up and attending and presiding over a meeting of the creditors at which that statement is presented;
  - preparing a statement of affairs in winding up by the court;
  - failure to deliver up to a liquidator, administrative receiver or an administrator any assets or papers that that official is entitled to ask for;
  - failure to co-operate with any liquidator, administrative receiver or administrator when he should.

These categories of unfitness are not exhaustive and it is open to the insolvency practitioner to recommend disqualification for behaviour not included in the above list. Furthermore, the categories apply whether the director being considered unfit is a properly appointed director, a *de facto* director or a shadow director.

Two decided cases give a limited amount of guidance as to what circumstances amount to unfitness.

Re Lo-Line Electric Motors Ltd [1988] Ch 477. Browne-Wilkinson V-C stated that ordinary commercial misjudgment is not itself sufficient to justify disqualification. There must be a lack of commercial probity, though he also felt that an extreme case of gross negligence or total incompetence would merit disqualification.

Re Sevenoaks Stationers (Retail) Ltd [1991] Ch 164. The Court of Appeal declined to give exact guidelines as to what constitutes unfitness, this being a matter of fact in each case, but Dillon LJ observed that incompetence does not need to be "total" (as suggested in *Lo-Line*) and that negligence need not be "gross".

As each case is different, the judges are clearly reluctant to say what is or is not worthy of disqualification. However, there are some common failings or actings which may predispose a judge towards disqualification.

These are:

- trading while knowingly insolvent;

- trading while the director ought to have known that the company was insolvent;

- drawing excessive remuneration while the company could not afford it;

- accepting customers' money while insolvent;

- using money due to the Inland Revenue and VAT for other purposes;

- failure to keep proper accounting records and file returns with the Registrar of Companies;

- confusing companies' funds, their subsidiaries' funds and the owners' funds;

- failing to consider the state of the company's accounts, or to take steps to regularise them, when well qualified to do so.

Although the court must look at past behaviour to assess whether a disqualification order is suitable, it cannot look at subsequent behaviour. For example, in *Re Pamstock Ltd* [1994] BCC 264 Vinelott J disqualified a director for the minimum period of two years, but did so with some reluctance because he was unable to take account of the subsequent steps the director had taken to ensure that the difficulties which had ultimately led to the director's disqualification were not repeated. The director in question was an experienced corporate financier and five years before the application for disqualification had come to court, one of this companies had gone into insolvent liquidation with considerable financial loss to himself. Since that date he had become a director of many other companies and had taken the trouble to ensure adequate financial systems in the companies with which he was associated. The director was also refused leave to apply to the court to be permitted to resume his directorship of all his other (solvent) companies and any new companies he became involved in. This was because it would have been impractical to keep applying to the court for each new company, and because the disqualification was for only two years.

The period of disqualification depends on the section under which the disqualification is being sought. Under summary jurisdiction (CDDA s 23(a) and 5(5)) the period of disqualification is up to five years. In all other cases it is up to 15 years (CDDA ss 2(3)(b), 4(3), 6(4), 8(4) and 10(2)). In respect of disqualification under the CDDA s 6 the minimum disqualification is two years.

Re Sevenoaks Stationers (Retail) Ltd [1991] Ch 164 is the leading case for detailing the duration of the disqualification order. In essence it is:

- 10 years or more for particularly serious cases, as in reoffenders;

- from six to 10 years for serious cases which do not merit the top bracket;

- two to five years for those for whom sentence is mandatory although the offence justifying disqualification is relatively non-serious.

The guidelines set out above are generally followed but there is some discretion given to the court to ban a director generally from being a director for a certain number of years, or under the CDDA s 17 to have the disqualification waived for certain of his directorships if there is good reason to do so. For example, in *Re Gibson Davies Ltd* [1995] BCC 11 the court allowed the director to be a director of one company after he had given undertakings to set up proper financial controls, to limit his own benefits from the company and to make proper returns to the Registrar of Companies.

The courts are conscious that the purpose of disqualification is not just a penalty for the director but also to protect the public. Where the public is unlikely to suffer or where there may be good commercial reasons for permitting the director to remain in office, at least to a certain extent, the courts may take those points into consideration and make a modified order.

Re Godwin Warren Control Systems plc [1993] BCLC 80. In this case two directors were disqualified, the first being a chartered accountant who had quite clearly been deceiving creditors and others. The second director had known of the deceit but had not spoken out when he could have done. Under cross-examination it was apparent that he had been attempting, not very successfully, to deceive the court. The court held although his behaviour was less heinous than the other director nonetheless he should be banned for a period of three years. He could however remain chief executive of one of his companies and could remain a director of his consultancy company, neither of which companies were being run improperly. In addition, the court required to be satisfied that the board of directors of the companies with which he was continuing to be involved should be informed of his disqualification. This lessening of the ban was because, unlike his accountant co-director, he was not deemed to be a risk to the public.

A further issue that is being raised at present is the standard of proof that is required to establish a director's culpability. Should the court use the civil standard of proof, being "on a balance of probabilities", or the criminal standard of proof, "beyond all reasonable doubt"? Sometimes very serious allegations are made about a director's behaviour and personal integrity. If a person is to be disqualified on the basis that he is unfit to be a director, it is perhaps not enough that on a balance of probabilities his behaviour was sufficiently unsatisfactory as to warrant disqualification. This was the approach taken in *Re Living Images Ltd* [1996] 1 BCLC 348 where the judge, while not going so far as adopting the criminal standard of proof, came close to it, stating "The more serious the allegation, the more the court will need the assistance of cogent evidence" (at 355). This is done to protect the reputation of the director, though it may have the opposite effect of allowing directors whose behaviour is questionable, if not overwhelmingly so, to avoid disqualification. There is clearly a balance to be found between the need to treat an errant director fairly and the need to protect the public.

Participation in wrongful trading (CDDA s 10)

Although the CDDA s 10 refers to its title solely to wrongful trading, the wording of the actual section states that where the court has made a declaration under:

(a) the wrongful trading provisions of the IA 1986 s 213 or
(b) the less commonly used fraudulent trading provisions of s 214 (for the details of which see later in this chapter), and
(c) that the responsible directors should contribute to the insolvent company's assets,

it is open to the court to disqualify the responsible directors from being directors for up to 15 years. This disqualification is at the court's discretion.

Undischarged bankrupts (CDDA s 11)

Undischarged bankrupts may not act as directors except with the leave of the court that originally adjudged the bankrupt person bankrupt. "The court" in this context means the level of court (*e.g.* High Court, Sheriff Court) rather than the geographical designation. This section imposes strict liability. In *R* v *Brockely* [1994] 1 BCLC 606 the bankrupt was found to be guilty of acting as a director of a company while bankrupt. His unsuccessful defence was that he did not know he was bankrupt at the time. It was held that irrespective of his ignorance of his continuing bankruptcy, he was not permitted to be a director as the CDDA s 11 imposes strict liability on the bankrupt.

As stated earlier, there is a register of disqualified directors (CDDA s 18), and after a slow start and criticism from the National Audit Office in 1993 the register is now both more accurate and useful than before. There have now been many cases on disqualification of directors and are likely to be many more. Each year about 600 directors are disqualified. Even directors who are resident abroad can be disqualified. (*Re Seagull Manufacturing Co Ltd (No 2)* [1994] 1 BCLC 273), though the disqualification will clearly only affect their ability to set up or run companies within the UK.

It is difficult to say how effective disqualification is. A director who has been disqualified and remains or becomes a director commits a criminal offence and can be both fined and imprisoned for up to two years (CDDA s 13). In addition, such a person will become personally liable for the debts of his company while he was involved with that company. Such a threat is in practice often toothless, as such directors are often insolvent anyway. One main effect of the legislation is to serve as a deterrent, in that all but the most reckless directors will be more likely to consider the wisdom of their actions if it might result in the public humiliation of being disqualified by a judge. The other effect is to protect the public. In some cases this is only too necessary.

Re Moorgate Metals Ltd [1995] BCLC 503. This company was set up by a former bankrupt (A) who asked a friend (B) to join him in a scrap metal business. B had already been bankrupt three times and had not been discharged. As B could not be a director, B's wife became a director and shareholder. In the company's short existence, the company never traded profitably. Most of the metal it dealt in went to one outlet. A had little idea about business, but became aware that they were undercharging the one outlet for their scrap metal. B explained to A that in the scrap metal business it was common to send out one low-priced invoice and then a supplementary one for the difference. However, B intercepted all the supplementary invoices. In the meantime, both A and B paid themselves large salaries, and at the company's expense bought expensive cars and a holiday property in France. A was disqualified for four years, B for 10.

Liability of directors under the Insolvency Act 1986

Under the insolvency Act 1986 ("IA") a director may be required to contribute to the assets of a company on a winding-up if his behaviour falls within the ambit of the IA ss 212, 213, 214 and 217.

Misfeasance proceedings under the IA s 122

Section 122 applies to directors (within the meaning given to directors under the CDDA) who have appropriated or become accountable for any property of the company, or been guilty of any breach of fiduciary duty or misfeasance towards the company. A breach of fiduciary duty is a breach of the duty the director owes to the company as a whole. These duties (which are explored in greater depth in the next chapter) include the duty;

- to act bona fide in the best interests of the company as a whole;

- to safeguard its assets for the benefit of the company;

- to avoid conflicts of interest;

- not to take advantage of the director's position within the company to award himself hidden benefits;

- to account for any funds held by him on behalf of the company;

- to make the company adhere to its memorandum of association;

• to act within the terms of the powers granted to him under the company's memorandum and articles of association.

Misfeasance is the wrongful exercise of lawful authority and to some extent overlaps with breach of fiduciary duty. A well known example before the current legislation was *Re Exchange Banking Co (Flitcroft's Case)* [1882] 21 Ch D 519, CA, which involved the payment of dividends from a source other than distributable profits. This was achieved by the falsification of the company's accounts. The directors were required to reimburse the company for its loss. The directors were lawfully authorised to prepare the accounts and to pay dividends. But they were not allowed to do so by falsifying the accounts.

On the application of the Official Receiver (in England and Wales only), the liquidator, any creditor or contributory, (but not an administrative receiver or a Scottish receiver), the court can examine the director's conduct and require him to repay or account for any property of the company's that he holds (IA s 212(3)(a)) or to contribute such sum to the company's assets by way of compensation in respect of the breach of fiduciary duty of misfeasance as the court sees fit (IA 212(3)(b)).

Bishopsgate Investment Management Ltd (in liquidation) v *Maxwell* [1993] BCLC 1282. Ian Maxwell, son of the late Robert Maxwell, transferred stock belonging to the company (an employee pension fund) to other companies that were privately owned by Robert Maxwell or by his family interests. He did this to diminish borrowings incurred by the Maxwell family interests companies. His brother, Kevin, had also signed the transfers. He and Kevin were both directors of the company. However, he failed to satisfy himself that these transfers were properly authorised by the board of directors or were in the best interests of the company and could thus be subsequently ratified. He was held to be in breach of his fiduciary duty to the company and was required to compensate the company to the extent of £500,000.

Re D'Jan of London Ltd, Copp v D'Jan [1994] 1 BCLC 561. A director of a company employed an insurance broker to deal with insurance matters. The broker asked him to sign an application form for a fire policy. When the company's premises were burnt down, the insurance company refused to pay out, saying that the application form had been incorrectly completed, as was indeed the case. The director said that as he was a busy man, he had not read the form and he had relied on the broker to get it right. It was held that the director had been careless, but that it was not gross carelessness. At the time of the fire the company was still solvent and the only persons who suffered financially were D'Jan and his wife. The judge was able to use the CA 1985 s 727 to relieve the director of some blame. Nonetheless the director was still required to contribute to the company but only to the extent of the outstanding unpaid dividend which he would otherwise have received as an unsecured creditor of the company.

Some directors have sought to avoid misfeasance proceedings by claiming that the members had ratified the alleged misfeasance.

Re DKG Contractors Ltd [1990] BCC 903. The members, who were the director and his wife, ratified the payment of £400,000 to the director in respect of sums owed to the director for work which in effect had been sub-contracted to him by his own company. This took place while the company was insolvent. The liquidator successfully claimed the money back under the IA s 212, because:

(i) the company was insolvent at the time and therefore the creditors were being defrauded;
(ii) no ratification of a fraud validates a fraud.

In principle, ratification of an action that could potentially be seen as misfeasance would be acceptable provided the company is solvent, because no creditors are affected. But with an insolvent company, ratification cannot be used as a means to avoid paying creditors what they are due.

Proceedings for misfeasance are relatively common because some directors are tempted to remove assets from the company and give them to themselves if they think the company is likely to go into liquidation. Another common ploy is for directors to pay themselves unreasonable amounts of remuneration. In such an event the liquidator can sometimes claim compensation from the director if the director is not already bankrupt.

Fraudulent trading under the IA s 213

If a liquidator in a winding-up believes that someone (not just officers of the company) was knowingly involved in running a company, and that company was operated with the intention of defrauding creditors or anyone else, the liquidator can apply to the court to make that person contribute towards the assets of the company. The amount the director will be required to contribute will, in general, be the amount the creditors have lost through his fraudulent trading plus any compensatory amount required by the court. All this will be used to swell the company's assets generally (*Re a Company (No 001418 of 1988)* [1991] BCLC 197). In addition to this civil liability the director may be disqualified under the CDDA ss 3 and/or 6 and/or prosecuted for fraudulent trading under the CA 1985 s 458. Fraudulent trading may be investigated by DTI inspectors whose reports may recommend prosecution. What constitutes fraudulent trading is by no means clear. The extent of the fraudulent trading is not significant: provided at least one transaction by the company was carried out for a fraudulent purpose, s 214 can apply (*Re Gerald Cooper Chemicals Ltd* [1978] Ch 262). The problem lies in the fact that the concept of fraud involves an element of intention or at best recklessness as to the effect of one's actions. How fraudulent does fraudulent trading have to be? How intentionally deceitful does the director have to be? The courts have looked extensively at criminal cases to ascertain this. In *R* v *Grantham* [1984] QB 745 the courts decided that:

- fraud involves (deliberate) deceit and

- the deceit puts the victim in a position where his economic interests may suffer, even though the perpetrator may not have set out to cause any loss.

How far does incurring credit when the company is insolvent come within those terms? A company deliberately obtaining credit without ever expecting to meet the creditors' claims would be fraudulently trading (*Re William C. Leitch Brothers Ltd* [1932] 2 Ch 71). But what happens when a company is having a temporary cash-flow difficulty but expects to be able to meet all payments once, say, a particular contract is fulfilled? In the absence of a deliberate intention to defraud, it becomes hard to say whether s 214 is appropriate. However, in the case *Re a Company (No 001418 of 1988)* [1991] BCLC 197 Judge Bromley QC had no difficulty in disbelieving the assertions of the director/defendant that he did not intend to defraud creditors and did not know about fraudulent trading. Judge Bromley also said that there was "read moral blame" attaching to the director/defendant in the way that he procured the company to trade despite the fact that it could not meet its debts as they fell due. He then found the director personally liable for certain debts of the company.

Another case which partially explains what constitutes fraudulent trading is *Re Sarflax Ltd* [1979] Ch 592. A liquidator tried to obtain contributions from the directors after the company had gone into (solvent) voluntary liquidation after all but one creditor had been paid prior to the liquidation. The outstanding creditor entered his claim after all the assets had been distributed amongst all the other creditors, and the liquidator claimed that by paying the other creditors without making a retention for the outstanding claim, or by failing to pay all creditors on a pari passu basis (on the basis of the proportion of the creditor's debt to the total of all the debts) the company had been carrying on a business with intent to defraud creditors. Oliver J held that although distributing assets could be said to be carrying on a business, the failure to pay on a *pari passu* basis, or to put it another way, paying some creditors in priority to others while solvent, did not amount to fraudulent trading.

It is perhaps worth mentioning that this case was decided when the periods during which antecedent transactions such as unfair preferences can be set aside by the courts were shorter than is at present the case under the IA s 240.

Re Augustus Barnett & Son Ltd [1986] BCLC 170. A holding company provided comfort letters to its subsidiary and had them published in the subsidiary's accounts three years running. The letters stated that the parent company would support the subsidiary. The subsidiary went into liquidation. Hoffmann J stated that the comfort letters could not be used to assert a claim of fraudulent trading The letters were valid at the time; the company was entitled to change its mind; the change of mind did not indicate that there were grounds for a claim for fraudulent trading.

EB Trading Ltd [1986] NI 165. The directors admittedly were slow in paying debts, and paid one creditor in preference to others. But they were unaware that the company was insolvent. It was therefore not possible to accuse them of fraudulent trading.

It appears that while the decided cases give some indication of what does not constitute fraudulent trading, it is less easy to say what does constitute fraudulent trading. Given this uncertainty, and the fact that the liquidator has the difficult task of proving intent to defraud, it is not surprising that there are few recent cases on this area, and that liquidators prefer to avoid proceedings on these grounds. They stand a much greater chance of success on the wrongful trading grounds of the IA s 214, where the onus is on the directors to show that they acted sensibly under the circumstances – not always an easy thing to do for a director whose company has just become insolvent under his management.

Wrongful trading under the IA s 214

As with misfeasance and fraudulent trading, this section only applies in the context of a winding-up. A liquidator can apply to the court to ask that a director (as defined before) be declared liable to contribute to the company's assets as the court thinks proper (IA s 214 (i)).

However, in order that the application can succeed, the following events must have taken place:

- the company must have gone into insolvent liquidation (IA s 214(2)(a));

- at some time before the commencement of the winding-up of the company, the director knew or ought to have concluded that there was no reasonable prospect that the company would avoid going into insolvent liquidation (IA s 214(2)(b)); and

- the director was a director at the time of the relevant transaction which occasioned the wrongful trading (IA s 214(2)(c)).

However, if the director:

(i)   has taken every step that he ought to have taken;

(ii) with a view to minimising the potential loss to the creditors which would result from a liquidation, and

(iii) assuming he was aware that insolvent liquidation was reasonably likely to be the company's fate,

the court will not make the declaration that he should be liable to contribute to the company's assets (IA s 214(3)).

The facts which a director ought to have know, the conclusions which he ought not have reached, and the steps he ought to have taken, should be judged against the standard of a reasonably diligent person have both the general knowledge, skill and experience that could reasonably be expected of someone carrying out the same functions as the director and the general knowledge, skill and experience that the director himself had (IA s 214).

These rules have attracted a certain amount of criticism, of which the most obvious is that while it is easy to judge a person's conduct in hindsight as deficient, it is not so easy at the time. The courts are, in effect, being asked to judge from a position of advantage the wisdom of what at the time may have seemed sensible commercial actions. The wording states that the directors should have taken "every step". This is an inherently unachievable task, though effective from the liquidator's point of view since it will not generally be too difficult to find at least one step a failing director ought not have taken. Furthermore, the legislation assumes the existence of the hypothetical reasonably competent and hard-working director. An under-qualified director will be judged against that hypothetical standard while someone who is of that standard or better will be expected to live up to the standards he already possesses.

The intention of the legislation was to catch directors who knew perfectly well that their company had no chance of ever being solvent again, but were continuing to incur credit, to accept prepayments and to hide behind the corporate veil to avoid being responsible for the debts the company had incurred through their actions. The secondary intention was to protect those directors who had genuinely tried to do something about their companies' parlous state (IA s 214(3)). The legislation hoped to coerce directors into seeking professional advice, such as consulting with their accountants, lawyers and bankers, at an early stage before the problems of the company became too unmanageable. And indeed, a prudent director of an ailing company may well escape liability if board minutes record his concern, and if correspondence and minutes of meetings show active consultation with those professionals. Sadly it is often the case that where a company is heading for financial disaster the directors become more and more indecisive or trust more and more to some miracle that will save the company, rather than seeking professional advice. It is also the case that in such circumstances the professionals often become anxious about payment of their own outstanding fees and may refuse to help until unpaid bills are met. In addition, the provision of too much advice, or wrong advice, from the professionals might make those professionals shadow directors and be responsible for the company's debts as well.

Most of the cases involving wrongful trading reveal the directors making the company continue trading long after the point when it could reasonably be said that the company would ever be solvent again.

Re Produce Marketing Consortium Ltd [1989] BCLC 520. Two directors placed an unrealistic belief in the value of fruit stored in their cold store. They lied about the company's continued viability. They ignored auditors' warnings. One of the directors was primarily concerned with limiting his exposure under a guarantee to a bank for the company's debts. The directors were found liable to contribute personally to the assets of their liquidated company.

Re Purpoint Ltd [1991] BCLC 491. The directors were found liable simultaneously under the misfeasance provisions of s 212 and the wrongful trading provisions of s 214. The amount that the director was required to contribute was the amount that was due or become due to creditors from the date that the director should have realised that the company could not avoid going into insolvent liquidation until the date it was wound up.

One problem that arises from a successful application by the liquidator for compensation is that if the compensation is paid, it may end up benefiting a floating charge-holder rather than the ordinary creditors whose claims the liquidator is trying to meet. The Cork Committee which was responsible for much of the IA had clearly hoped that such compensation would be available for the ordinary creditors, and the judge in *Re Produce Marketing Ltd* indicated that in principle this ought to happen although the legislation is silent on the point. Despite much academic discussion about this issue, it remains at this moment unresolved.

Liability for use of prohibited names under the IA ss 216 and 217

If a director or shadow director sets up a phoenix company trading under the same or similar company name as a previous company which within the last five years has gone into insolvent liquidation, and that company name (or close variants thereof) is thereby prohibited from being reused, he can be jointly and severally liable with the new company under the IA s 217 for the new company's debts unless he has leave of the court under the IA s 216(3) to be permitted to use the otherwise forbidden name. These sections are designed to prevent the old fraud whereby a company would trade unsuccessfully from certain premises under a particular name, and when it found it could no longer pay its creditors, it would be wound up. Having few remaining assets, there would be little or no repayment to creditors. The directors would then set up a similar company with a similar name in the same premises and defraud a new set of creditors.

Criminal liability of directors

There are innumerable instances in the CA 1985, the IA and elsewhere whereby a director who fails to obey certain statutory rules is liable to a fine or imprisonment. The rules that are enforced are generally speaking the ones involving failure to disclose information to the Registrar of Companies in time, offences of dishonesty towards creditors or investors, inadequate maintenance and preservation of company records and accounts, false accounting and tax evasion. This area is more properly addressed in studies of criminal law to which reference should be made.

Summary

1. Directors manage the company through powers granted them in the memorandum, articles and resolutions by the members, and collectively through the board of directors.

2. Different types of directors include executive directors, non-executive directors, managing directors, *de facto* directors and shadow directors.

3. The Cadbury Code, Greenbury Report and Hampel Report recommend certain minimum standards of accountability and competence for boards of directors and best practice for directors to follow.

4. Anyone can be a director provided he is not prohibited by law or by the company's constitution.

5. There are many ways of appointing directors, but all properly appointed directors should intimate their acceptance to the Registrar of Companies, and furnish both the Registrar and the company itself with certain details. Directors are required to disclose their other directorships and any matters involving the company in which they or their connections have a personal interest.

6. Premature termination of a director's term of office may be valid but may trigger a claim for breach of contract. Directors may be dismissed by the members under the CA 1985 s 303. Directors can sometimes protect their position by means of weighted voting (*Bushell* v *Faith* [1970] AC 1099) or by means of a shareholders' agreement.

7. Directors may be disqualified from holding office if disqualified under the Company Directors Disqualification Act 1986.

8. Directors of a company in liquidation may be liable to account to the company for sums or assets in their possession, or to make good any loss to the company, in the event of the director's involvement in misfeasance under the IA s 212, under fraudulent trading under s 213, under wrongful trading under s 214, and phoenix syndrome trading under s 217.

15. DIRECTORS' DUTIES

A: Fiduciary duties – the bona fide rule – the proper purpose rule – ratification – the conflict of interest rule
B: Duties of skill and care – duties owed to the company as a whole – duties to employees – duty to creditors
C: Statutory duties – duties imposed on the directors – duties imposed on the company in connection with its directors – duty not to make certain loans, quasi-loans and credit transactions to a director – relief from liability for company officers

The director's role in a company is to manage it. To this end he is given extensive powers by the company under the memorandum, the articles, any resolutions by the members and by statute.

These powers are not unlimited. He must manage the company within the limits of the powers given to him. If he exceeds those limits, the members may exert some control over him, by dismissing him or by various means by which he may be made accountable to the company. The law is alert to the fact that it is very easy for a director to abuse his powers.

Accordingly the law imposes certain duties on a director. These duties are:

- fiduciary duties;

- the duty to use skill and care;

- statutory duties.

Fiduciary duties

A director is in a similar position to that of a trustee. He is an agent of the company in which he holds office. Like a trustee or an agent he owes fiduciary duties to his principal, and in a director's case, these duties are to his company. In the exercise of his fiduciary duties towards his company he:

- must at all times act bona fide (in good faith) in what he considers to be in the best interest of the company as whole;

- must ensure that any transaction that he enters into on behalf of the company is for a proper purpose and not for some collateral purpose;

- is normally only entitled to his remuneration and expenses for doing his job, as agreed between the company and himself;

- may not treat the company's assets as his own;

- may not take personal advantage of any commercial opportunities which come his way through his position as director;

- may not favour some shareholders over others.

The bona fide rule

When directors consider making their company enter into any transaction, one criterion of the suitability of that transaction should be that they genuinely consider the transaction to be in the best interest of the company as a whole. If the directors are not acting bona fide in what they consider to be in the best interest of the company as a whole, by definition they will be acting in someone else's interests, quite often themselves. This can be seen in the following case.

Alexander v *Automatic Telephone Co* [1990] 2 Ch 56. Each member of the company subscribed 6d per share. The five directors then held a board meeting at which it was decided that all the members, with the exception of the three directors who had the largest shareholdings, should have to pay a further 2s 6d per share. The three non-paying directors justified their non-payment on the grounds that the articles permitted them as directors to issue shares on such terms as were expedient, and to treat some shareholders differently from others. It was held that the three directors had failed to carry out their duty to act in good faith in the best interest of the company as a whole. What the directors ought to have done was to disclose their non-payment to the other shareholders as a whole and obtain the shareholders' consent. The directors had obtained a benefit for themselves at the expense of the other shareholders.

In the unlikely event that the directors had been able to prove that they genuinely believed that their non-payment was in the best interests of the company as a whole, in theory, at least, they would have satisfied the duty to act in good faith. However, a later stream of cases (to be looked at next) illustrate the point that directors can subjectively believe that they are acting in good faith while carrying out an action for an improper purpose.

The proper purpose rule

Any transaction the directors make the company enter into must be pursued for a proper purpose. This means that it is to benefit the company or to help it fulfil the purpose for which the company was set up, as seen from an objective point of view and as evidenced by the objects clause of the memorandum of association or any other direction of the members. This means that the transaction must be *intra vires* and, broadly speaking, the type of transaction or activity the company is authorised to carry out in terms of the company's memorandum of association or any direction of the members. The transaction must be reasonably incidental to the company's business. Historically this was a problematic issue, but the change in the law in relation to *ultra vires* transactions has resulted in most transactions nowadays being considered *intra vires* (CA 1985 s 35(1)), especially if the transaction confers a right on a third party acting in good faith (CA 1985 s 35(2)). Accordingly almost anything can be reasonably incidental to a company's business if the company has a wide enough objects clause. This issue is discussed further in Chapter 4.

What is the position when the directors, acting under authority legitimately given to them by the members or the company's constitution, make the company enter into a transaction:

(a) which the directors genuinely believe will benefit the company, and
(b) is permitted by the company's constitution or by the members, but
(c) which is not the purpose for which the members gave the directors authority to make the company enter into the transaction?

In the following case the directors genuinely believed that they were entitled to allot the shares in the way they did as it was in their view in the best interests of the company.

Hogg v *Cramphorn* [1967] Ch 245. The directors of a company wished to thwart a takeover bid which they genuinely believed would not be good for the company. Using the powers given to them as directors, they arranged that the company should give an interest-free loan to the employee pension fund so that it could subscribe for newly created shares with special voting rights. Those new shares would then be used by the employee pension fund trustees to support the directors – some of whom were on the board of the pension fund anyway – in their attempt to prevent the takeover bid being successful. A minority shareholder objected. It was held that the issue of the new shares with the special voting rights was beyond the powers of the directors (as such shares would have required a special resolution which had not been obtained), and the overall plan to allot shares with special voting rights using an interest-free loan was in breach of the directors' fiduciary duty. This was because the power to allot shares was not purely being used in good faith for the benefit of the company but was instead being used to thwart the takeover bid – and the thwarting of takeover bids was an improper motive for the exercise of the directors' powers.

Howard Smith Ltd v *Ampol Petroleum Ltd* [1974] AC 821. Ampol and another company owned 55% of R W Miller (Holdings) Ltd ("Miller"). Miller received an offer of a takeover from Howard Smith Ltd. The directors of Miller genuinely believed that the takeover bid was a good one, and would be advantageous to the company because it would inject some much-needed capital into the company. Unfortunately, Ampol and the other shareholders who comprised the majority of the shares disapproved of the bid. The directors of Miller had to find a way round their disapproval. As the directors had already been given power by the members to allot shares from time to time, the directors allotted some shares to Howard Smith Ltd. Ampol and the other objecting shareholders then ceased to have a majority and the takeover could then proceed. Ampol objected. It was held that notwithstanding the directors' genuine belief that the allotment of shares to Howard Smith Ltd was for the benefit of the company and to promote its prosperity, the directors were not entitled to use their existing and legitimate authority to allot shares in such a manner as deliberately to destroy the balance of voting power within the company. Such an exercise was an abuse of their fiduciary duty to act bona fide in the best interest of the company as a whole and not for some other collateral purpose.

In the following case, although good faith was not an issue in the decision of the court, the court adhered to the principle of the proper purpose rule outlined in *Howard Smith Ltd*.

Lee Panavision Ltd v *Lee Lighting Ltd* [1992] BCLC 22. The plaintiffs were able to nominate the directors of the defendant company under a management agreement. Just before the management agreement expired, the directors of the defendant company executed a second management agreement. They did this as a method of retaining control of the defendant company in order to ensure that it paid an outstanding debt to another company associated with the plaintiffs. On the expiry of the first management agreement, new shareholders in the defendant company dismissed their company's directors and renounced the second management agreement. The plaintiffs tried to obtain an injunction to make the defendant company retain the management agreement. It was held that it was not constitutional for the former directors of the defendant company to make the company enter into the second management agreement when they knew very well that the new shareholders would not want it. Although the directors had the power to make the company enter into such contracts, they had exercised that power for an improper purpose, this being the payment of the sums due to the company associated with the plaintiffs. In so doing they had breached their fiduciary duty to the company. This case is referred to later in this chapter in the context of directors' duty to disclose their interest in contracts with their company.

The duty to act in the best interests of the company as a whole and not for some other purpose can sometimes lead directors into a difficult position where:

(a) on the one hand they have to use their best efforts for their company, and should therefore be given wide discretion to do anything that may be advantageous for it (as opposed to fettering their discretion, which means that the directors are restricted in the options they can offer the company);

(b) on the other the directors may have made agreements with other persons
concerning what course of action the directors recommend the shareholders
should follow.

This issue arose in the two contrasting cases.

Dawson International plc v *Coats Patons plc and others* [1989] 5 BCC 405.
The board of directors of Dawson claimed that it had come to an understanding
with the board of directors of Coats that the board of Coats would recommend
to Coats's shareholders the terms of a proposed takeover bid from Dawson, and
would not encourage any other bidder. Dawson alleged that subsequent to that
understanding the directors of Coats entertained the attentions of another
takeover bidder, which was eventually successful in taking over Coats. In the
course of the attempted takeover, Dawson had incurred substantial costs, which
it sought to recover from Coats. There was no actual formal contract between
Dawson and the directors of Coats, such agreement as there was being of the
nature of an understanding that the directors of Coats undertook to recommend
the terms of the Dawson takeover to the shareholders. The shareholders were
under no obligation to accept the directors' recommendations, though the fact
that the directors made a particular recommendation might have persuaded
some shareholders which way they should vote. It was held that as a matter of
law Coats's board of directors was entitled to change its mind and reverse its
recommendations, because it had an overriding fiduciary duty (i) to act in the
best interests of the company and (ii) not to fetter its future discretion if doing
so would mean that the best interests of the company would be prejudiced –
even if that meant breaking a prior agreement.

Fulham Football Ltd v *Cabra Estates plc* [1994] 1 BCLC 363. The directors
of the plaintiffs reneged on an agreement with the defendants. They attempted
to justify this on the grounds that their discretion as directors could not be
fettered and that they were entitled to change their minds. This was, they said,
because they were bound by their fiduciary duty as directors of their own company to act in the best interest of their own company, even if that meant that
other agreements were prejudiced. The Court of Appeal held that whether or
not they were entitled to change their minds, they were certainly able to fetter
their future discretion providing they were doing so bona fide and in the best
interests of the company. Having fettered their discretion by choice at the time
they entered into the agreement, and especially if the members at that time also
approved it, it was not permissible for the directors to change their minds at the
time of the implementation of the agreement.

Much depends on the precise nature of the agreement in each case. In the
Dawson case an "understanding" did not necessarily amount to an agreement.
An agreement by the directors that they will recommend a takeover does not
bind the members to that agreement, and it would be foolish of the company

instigating the takeover to think that it would. Even if the directors say they will ignore other offers for a takeover, such an undertaking cannot be binding on the members except where the members and directors are substantially the same persons and the members have assented to the directors' undertaking (as happened in the *Fulham* case).

If directors in general are allowed to renege on previous agreements because the agreement effectively fettered the directors' future discretion, and the members have not specifically approved the agreement, unscrupulous directors could break their word with impunity – as indeed they sometimes do. However, in the *Fulham* case Cabra Estates plc had made a substantial payment to the club, in return for which the club undertook not to oppose a certain planning application. This meant that a proper contract was in existence, and the argument that directors should not fetter their discretion was arguably a somewhat specious attempt by Fulham's directors to justify the proposed breach of that contract.

At the moment there appears to be no satisfactory solution to the problem illustrated in the *Dawson* case. The directors, even if they have agreed to recommend a takeover, cannot force the members to accept a takeover. Equally, if the members insist that they wish to be approached by a rival takeover bidder, the directors who say that they are committed to refusing the rival takeover bidder could be dismissed or overruled by a resolution of the members. The first takeover bidder should be well aware of that. If the other party wishes to ensure that the directors adhere to the terms of their agreement to recommend only their takeover bid and no other, it should make a contract with the directors personally. However, it is unlikely that any director would be rash enough to sign such an agreement.

Ratification

If the directors by approving some transaction of the company have breached their fiduciary duty towards the company, it is sometimes permissible for the company to ratify (*i.e.* retrospectively to approve) the action that was the subject of the breach.

In general, ratification will resolve any breach of the directors' fiduciary duty unless:

● the transaction is inherently fraudulent;

● the transaction is not permitted under company law generally because there are other procedures which must instead be followed (see *Aveling Barford Ltd* v *Perion Ltd and others* [1989] BCLC 626 below);

- the transaction prejudices a minority of the members, in which case the minority might seek redress under the CA 1985 s 459 (see Chapter 13);

- the transaction is illegal anyway (*e.g.* trading with an enemy alien, trying to enforce a prejudicial contract against a minor);

- the transaction by the directors prejudices creditors because the company is insolvent. The directors of an insolvent company are treated as the custodians of the company's assets for the creditors (see *West Mercia Safetywear Ltd v Dodd* [1988] BCLC 250 referred to later in this chapter).

If the breach of the fiduciary duty is impermissible because some other procedure has been omitted or some rule of law transgressed, no amount of ratification can validate the breach.

Aveling Barford Ltd v *Perion Ltd and others* [1989] BCLC 626. Perion's principal shareholders were the principal shareholders in Aveling. Aveling could not pay a dividend because it had insufficient retained profits. So it sold property, which had been valued at £650,000, to Perion for £350,000. Perion paid for this by means of a mortgage raised on the value of the property. Perion subsequently sold the property for £1,526,000. Aveling went into liquidation, and the liquidator claimed from Perion the proceeds of the sale of the property. Perion claimed the members of Aveling had approved the transaction. Hoffmann J held that what had happened was a return of capital by Aveling to Perion. The sale at an undervalue of the asset was not the sale of an asset for value in the ordinary course of business. Since Aveling could not pay a dividend to Perion it was effectively giving away its capital, and capital can only be given back to the members of a company by means of the methods in the CA 1985 s 135 *et seq*. The ratification by Aveling's members of the sale by Aveling to Perion was illegal and of no effect.

Where there is a dispute concerning a director's breach of his fiduciary duty the court may decide that rather than give a judgment which might subsequently be overturned by a decision of the members, the members themselves should decide whether or not to ratify the breach, provided:

(i) all the members are in possession of all the facts of the matters in dispute;
(ii) there is nothing fraudulent about the transaction;
(iii) the directors are acting in good faith in what they genuinely believe to be in the best interests of the company; and (sometimes)
(iv) only those who do not have a conflict of interest may vote.

This means that the members can vote on the merits of the issue, and the majority decision will prevail. If those who have conflicts of interest are expressly forbidden to vote, or abstain, and the remaining members ratify the transaction, an objecting member normally no longer has grounds for objection. In *Hogg* v *Cramphorn* above, the court decided that although the directors' actions were indeed a breach of their fiduciary duty to the company, the members should hold a general meeting at which they could, if they wished, ratify what the directors had done, providing the pension fund trustees did not vote on the matter. The members in due course ratified the issue of the shares, though without the shares' enhanced voting rights.

In the following case the court approved the ratification of a breach of fiduciary duty.

Bamford v *Bamford* [1970] Ch 212. The directors of Bamford Ltd issued shares to a new member purely to prevent a takeover bid. A month later the members ratified the allotment in a general meeting, with the new member abstaining. A minority shareholder objected. It was held that the issue to prevent a takeover bid was a breach of fiduciary duty, but the members' ratification with the new member abstaining had been a valid ratification.

Conflict of interest rule

Conflicts of interest arise when the directors stand to gain personally from a transaction in which the company is involved. A conflict of interest is not strictly speaking considered to be a breach of fiduciary duty, instead being, at least in terms of English law, an equitable rule. Scots law does not have the concept of equity, but the principle remains the same, that a director may not take advantage of his own fiduciary position for his own purposes. He must not without permission enter into transactions in which he has or could have personal interests that conflict with the interests of those whom he is supposed to protect. This is because it is part of a director's job to safeguard the company's assets for the benefit of the company as a whole. It is not his job as director to seek to improve his own personal position, as happened in the following case.

Cook v *Deeks* [1916] AC 554. Deeks and some fellow directors, who together were the majority shareholders, decided that a contract which their company had entered into was far too valuable to be wasted on the company, because that meant that some of the profits it produced would have to be given to the minority shareholders. Deeks and his fellow directors arranged for a resolution to be passed in general meeting to the effect that the company was renouncing its interest in the contract. Deeks and his fellow directors then took the contract for themselves. A minority shareholder successfully petitioned for Deeks and his fellow directors to restore the contract to the company.

If he obtains any benefit from his position, other than that which has been previously agreed or is subsequently ratified, that benefit must be declared to and approved by the company. This includes any commercial opportunities which he hears about through his position as a director. Failure to disclose and obtain approval of any such benefits or opportunities puts the director in breach of his duty to the company, unless the articles permit him to do otherwise. In addition, any contract in which he is personally involved may be voidable at the instance of the company, unless subsequently ratified.

A director might not wish to obtain the approval of the members lest the disclosure of his plans make him lose the commercial opportunity, present him in a bad light, or meet with refusal from the company. He might then be tempted to keep quiet about any personal and unauthorised benefits he was obtaining. But were he to do so and be found out, he would be required to make over any benefit he had obtained thereby to the company.

Boston Deep Sea Fishing Company v *Ansell* (1888) 39 Ch D 339. As the Boston Deep Sea Fishing Company needed a new trawler, Ansell, one of the directors, was sent to a firm of shipwrights to buy one. The firm of shipwrights agreed to pay him personally a commission for bringing them the business. He did not reveal his commission to the company. When it was discovered that he had received it, the company successfully sued him for the commission, since it was an unauthorised secret profit. In addition, Ansell had breached his fiduciary duty to act in the best interests of the company: he had made the company pay an excessive price for the trawler, since the price he should have negotiated should have been without the addition of the commission which went into his pocket.

In the following case, it was agreed that the directors had acted in good faith and that they believed that they were acting in the best interests of the company as a whole. Nevertheless, they took advantage of an opportunity which came to them as directors.

Regal (Hastings) Ltd v *Gulliver* [1967] 2 AC 134. The directors of Regal (Hastings) Ltd ("Regal") were able to take advantage of the fact that by subscribing for shares in a subsidiary of Regal known as Hastings Amalgamated Cinemas Ltd ("Amalgamated") – an opportunity only available to them as directors who knew what was happening – Amalgamated was able to acquire the lease of two cinemas. Subsequently the members of Regal sold their shares in Regal and Amalgamated for a substantial profit. Regal then sued the former directors for the undisclosed profit they had received from the sale of their shares in Amalgamated. The significant issues arising out of the case were:

(i) the opportunity to invest in Amalgamated had come only to the directors instead of anyone else because they were the directors and the first to know about it;

(ii) the directors had breached the equitable rule whereby in the absence of disclosure and approval those who make a profit from their fiduciary position are liable to account for that profit even if there is neither fraud nor absence of good faith involved.

The House of Lords held that those directors who had made secret profits were required to make over their profits to the company. Had the directors revealed to the members of Regal: (a) the information about their subscription for shares in Amalgamated, and (b) the profits arising from those shares, and had the members in general meeting approved the subscription and profit from the sale of the shares, the directors would have escaped liability.

The principle that a director may not take advantage of his fiduciary position and put himself in the position of a conflict of interest with his company can work even on a retrospective basis.

Industrial Development Consultants Ltd v *Cooley* [1972] 2 All ER 163. Cooley was the managing director of the company. The company had recently tendered to be depot manager for a contract with the gas board. The gas board told Cooley that his company would not get the contract, but then told Cooley that if he left his company, the gas board would make him a project manager for the depot-manager's post for which the company had tendered. Cooley then persuaded his company to release him on the grounds of ill-health. He then started work for the gas board. His former company successfully sued him for the profits of the contract. This was on the grounds that he had obtained a secret profit arising from an opportunity which had come to him as a director and which should have been approved first by the members.

If the no-secret profit/conflict of interest rule seems draconian, it must be remembered that it is designed to prevent bribery, improper dealing with the company's assets and fraud. An honest director who is frank with his company has nothing to fear. But where there is any conflict of interest, even in the absence of fraud, or of harm to the company involved, it is possible to have the contract avoided.

Aberdeen Railway Co v *Blaikie* [1854] 1 MacQ 461. The chairman of the railway company was a partner in a firm from which the railway company had ordered certain goods. The railway company refused to accept the goods saying that because of the chairman's conflict of interest the contract was voidable at its option. The refusal was upheld by the courts.

Although this rule is not defunct, it is not very practical, as there inevitably will be occasions when a company will have to contract with a director, not least by means of a service contract. Most companies have articles that permit conflicts of interests provided the relevant rules under statute or the company's articles are followed.

Under statute there is a mechanism for dealing with conflicts of interest in two specific areas. These can be found at the CA 1985 s 317, as regards the disclosure of directors' interests in contracts, and at the CA 1985 s 320 as regards the sale of company assets to directors or purchases by the company of directors' assets. The CA 1985 s 320 is dealt with later in this chapter under the heading of statutory duties.

Under the CA 1985 s 317, if a director finds he has an interest, direct or indirect, in a contract or proposed contract with his company, he has to declare the nature of the interest at the next available meeting of the board of directors.

Statute does not require that the director do anything other than declare his interest. But the articles of most companies insist that more be done. Under Table A art 85, the director must not only declare the nature of his interest (*i.e.* what it is) at a board meeting, but he must declare the extent of his interest (*i.e.* how large it is) and provided he has done so, he will be free from any liability to account to the company for any profits he makes or losses he incurs through the transaction, though under art 94 he may not then vote at the board meeting on the matter which involves any conflict or potential conflict of interest.

These articles are tempered by the fact that the interest in question must be "material". This is because there could be occasions that technically reveal a conflict of interest but the amounts involved are minuscule. For that reason the word "material" is used, both in art 85 and in art 94. However, "material" is a slippery word, and there might be a temptation for directors, who are the ones who decide how material an interest needs to be to be disclosed, to have a self-serving definition of "material". One director might say to another that he would not condemn the other director's interest in a particular transaction as material if the other director would help him on a later occasion.

Some companies have director-friendly articles which permit the directors to vote on these matters.

The need for the actual disclosure under the CA 1985 s 317 was discussed in the undernoted case, but was not decided upon.

Lee Panavision Ltd v *Lee Lighting Ltd* [1992] BCLC 22. The facts are as stated earlier. As regards the issue of non-declaration of interest Dillon LJ would not commit himself to saying that the absence of a formal declaration of interest in terms of the CA 1985 s 317 meant that the adoption of the management agreement was flawed and of no effect. This was because although there was no formal declaration, everyone present at the board meeting shared the same interest in doing the plaintiff's bidding and knew what was happening. A declaration might therefore be unnecessary. The point was left unresolved.

The use of a declaration under the CA 1985 s 317 was also the subject of the following case.

Re Neptune (Vehicle Washing Equipment) Ltd [1995] BCC 474. A sole director was trying to establish that he had a contract with his company. If he did have one, he would be entitled to claim compensation for the cessation of his employment. It was unclear (a) whether or not he had declared his interest in his own contract with the company at a meeting of the board, as normally is required under the CA 1985 s 317, and (b) if he needed to declare his interest given that he was the only director anyway. The liquidator argued that if the director had not declared his interest, the contract would be voidable at the instance of the company. It was held that he ought to have declared his interest at the meeting. This could have been done out loud, if there had been the company secretary or others present at the board meeting, or silently if the director were on his own. Either way it should have been recorded in the minutes. In the absence of minutes, or the testimony of the company secretary, it could not be established that the required declaration of interest had taken place.

This case has a certain unreality about it: the spectacle of the sole director solemnly holding a board meeting all by himself, making a declaration to himself and having (as the judgment quaintly puts it) a statutory pause for thought, invites ridicule. However, the declaration was nonetheless required and its absence was problematic for the director.

Directors as constructive trustees
A constructive trustee is a person in breach of his fiduciary duty to another and who is in the possession of assets which belong to the other person. He may have acted in good faith and from the best of motives for the other person. He may have believed that the assets are his own, or that he is entitled to have them. However, if the court finds that they are not his to keep, but are merely in his hands, he is under an obligation to return them to their true owner and to look after them properly in the meantime. In the context of company law a director may find himself in the position of a constructive trustee for his company. Ward, in *Guinness plc v Saunders and Ward* [1990] 1 All ER 652, asserted that he deserved his success fee of £5.2 million and believed that he was entitled to it. The courts disagreed, and held that as he had not received the proper approval for the level of remuneration he obtained, he was a constructive trustee for the £5.2 million and he was under a duty to return it to the company. Likewise in the previously mentioned case of *Aveling Barford Ltd v Perion Ltd and others* [1989] BCLC 626, Perion was held to be a constructive trustee for the plaintiff and required to hand over the proceeds of sale to the plaintiff.

Any accomplice who knowingly assisted in a director's breach of fiduciary duty may also be treated as a constructive trustee. To make an accomplice liable it was formerly necessary to prove the accomplice's knowing assistance in a *fraudulent* and *dishonest* breach of fiduciary duty by the director. The accomplice had to know that the breach was fraudulent and dishonest, and if it was not fraudulent, the accomplice was not liable (*Baden, Delvaux and Lecuit v Société Generale pour Favoriser le Developpement du Commerce et de l'Industrie en France SA* [1983] BCLC 325).

Recently, following the Privy Council case of *Royal Brunei Airlines Sdn Bhd v Tan* [1995] 3 WLR 64, a new distinction has arisen. In this case, Tan was the controlling director and shareholder of an insolvent company which had held certain monies in trust for the plaintiff. The company was the constructive trustee and Tan the accomplice. Tan's company was not worth suing, but Tan was. Tan had made his company misapply the monies it held on trust. The company carried out the instructions given to it by Tan, but because the company is not a human being, no fraudulent or dishonest intention could be imputed to the company; it was therefore acting innocently. Formerly this might have meant that Tan escaped liability because the constructive trustee (his company) had to have been acting fraudulently, which it was not. However, the Privy Council held that because of Tan's own dishonest involvement in the company's innocent breach of fiduciary duty, Tan could be liable instead. This means that an accomplice, provided he acted fraudulently and dishonestly, can henceforth be treated as a constructive trustee not just where the original director has acted fraudulently in breach of his fiduciary duty, but where the director has acted in breach of his fiduciary duty generally, whether innocently or not.

If a claim is made against a director to the effect that he is a constructive trustee of assets properly belonging to the company, he may be relieved from liability if he is able to convince the court that he had acted honestly and reasonably under the circumstances in terms of the CA 1985 s 727. The CA 1985 s 727 is discussed further later in this chapter.

The director wearing two hats: a conflict of loyalties
A problematic matter in connection with conflicts of interests occurs when a director is a director or representative of two competing companies. It is the director's fiduciary duty to act in the best interest of any company of which he is a director: what should he do when his loyalties to one company conflict with any loyalties he may have to another company? Is the director ever allowed to fetter his fiduciary duty to act in the best interest of one of the companies in which he holds office? As stated above, there is no clear-cut answer to this problem. There are, however, various practical approaches, albeit that they are not entirely satisfactory:

(i)   he should withdraw from any discussion whenever a conflict of interest arises;

(ii) he should tell the other directors of his predicament and seek their views on his proposed course of action;

(iii) he should resign from one or both boards, though it is unlikely that any director would be so eager to give up his director's fees that he would do this as a first course of action;

(iv) if the members recognise in advance that in certain circumstances a director, particularly a director nominated by a lender or a particular investor, will inevitably have a problem of conflicting loyalties, they can then release the director from his normal fiduciary duty to act in the best interests of their company. They should accept that it might even be useful to have a director who is able to put across a differing viewpoint.

One might be able to pre-empt the problem as follows:

(v)   the situation could be prevented from occurring by making it a term of a director's contract of employment that he may not have any significant interest in any business in competition with the company of which he is a director;
(vi) a provision could be placed in the articles to outline exactly what a director should do whenever such a conflict of interest arises.

It is almost impossible to find one clear solution to this problem, mainly because each situation is likely to be different, and no one remedy would suit all circumstances.

Remedies for breach of fiduciary duty
Assuming the members do not choose to ratify any breach by the director, what remedies does a company have against a director who breaches his fiduciary duty or abuses his fiduciary duty not to permit conflicts of interest? The company has a number of remedies. These include:

- restitution to the company of any assets the director has misappropriated from the company (*Cook* v *Deek* [1919] AC 554). If the asset itself is sold or destroyed the value of the asset must be restored to the company. If the asset has been sold on by the director to a purchaser who knew that the director did not have the company's permission to have it, and the sale was at an undervalue, the purchaser would have to return it to the company;

- an accounting by the director to the company for any secret profits the director may have made (*Regal (Hastings) Ltd* v *Gulliver* [1967] 2 AC 134);

- requiring the director to reimburse or indemnify the company for any loss it may have suffered arising from the director's breach (*Boston Deep Sea Fishing Co* v *Ansell* (1888) 39 Ch D 339);

- rescinding of the contract in which the director has an interest (*i.e.* cancelling the contract without any claim for breach of contract by the director) (*Aberdeen Railway Co* v *Blaikie Bros* (1854) 1 MacQ 461);

- injunction (England and Wales and Northern Ireland) or interdict (Scotland) to prevent the director carrying out an action disapproved of by the company.

Duties of skill and care

In addition to their fiduciary duties, directors are expected to carry out their duty of managing their company with due skill and care. This is a common law duty. Failure to do so may result in the company or other aggrieved plaintiff (pursuer in Scotland) raising an action for negligence against the directors.

In order to succeed in any action for negligence, the plaintiff/pursuer must prove all three of the following:

(i)   that the director owed the plaintiff/pursuer a duty to carry out his duties with skill and care;
(ii) that the duty was not exercised; and
(iii) that the plaintiff/pursuer suffered loss.

Historically, the standard of care expected of a director was not very high. The reasons for this are probably more sociological than commercial. The leading cases, dating from the last century and from earlier in this century, were decided upon at a time when little was expected of a director.

Re Brazilian Rubber Plantations and Estates Ltd [1911] 1 Ch 425. The company unwisely ventured upon various unsatisfactory enterprises. There were attempts to hold the directors responsible. One director knew nothing about the business but understood that he could make a certain amount of money from it. Another was aged 75 and deaf and could not usefully participate in board meetings. A third became a director merely because he liked the other directors. Despite their limited business skills, none of the directors was held accountable for the company's failure.

At the time the current view was that it was not fair to expect a director to have to prove his suitability to be a director. The courts were very reluctant to restrain the entrepreneurial activities of directors and if that meant that some directors were less than competent, that was a risk for the shareholders alone. They, after all, had the ability, if they commanded sufficient votes, to dismiss the directors. Furthermore, it was believed that if directors started becoming liable for the company's losses arising from their own negligence, no one would want to become a director and the commercial life of Britain would suffer. Accordingly the directors did not owe the company a duty to carry out their duties with skill and care.

Another reason directors escaped liability was that sometimes their presence on the board was a mere formality, their names adding lustre to the company. Under such circumstances it was unfair to make them accountable for any losses.

Re Cardiff Savings Bank [1892] 2 Ch 100. The Marquess of Bute had substantial interests in Cardiff through his ownership of coal mines in the area. He was also one of the area's principal employers and landowners. He accepted the position of president of the Cardiff Savings Bank, an honorary post for which little application was required. This was just as well, for in 38 years he only attended one meeting. His name, however, conferred respectability upon the company. When an attempt was made to make him bear some responsibility for its losses, it was held that even as director/president there was no requirement that he devote his energies to the company in an effective way.

Again, no duty of skill or care was expected. Interestingly, his continued absence protected him: had he been more involved, he might have been found to be responsible.

In *Re City Equitable Fire Insurance Company Ltd* [1925] Ch 407, the managing director had systematically produced misleading accounts which painted a false picture of the company's finances. He was eventually convicted and imprisoned for this. The Official Receiver tried to make the other directors responsible for the loss suffered by the company. Fortunately for those directors, an articles in the company's articles of association completely exempted the other directors from any liability whatsoever. In addition, the judge stated that it was almost impossible to say what level of competence was required of a director, since it varied so much from company to company. However, he outlined three propositions:

(i)   a director need not exhibit in the performance of his duties a greater degree of skill than may reasonably be expected from a person of his knowledge and experience;
(ii)   a director is not bound to give continuous attention to the affairs of his company;
(iii) in respect of all business that may properly be left to some other official, a director is, in the absence of grounds for suspicion, justified in trusting that official to perform such duties honestly.

These propositions now seem dangerously complacent, especially in the context of a company whose shares are publicly traded. The current position is to be found in the following case, which although it took place in 1977 was not reported until 1989.

Dorchester Finance Co Ltd and another v *Stebbing and others* [1989] BCLC 498. The non-executive directors left the ordinary management of the company to Stebbing, the executive director. All three directors were qualified accountants. For convenience sake, the non-executives adopted the practice of pre-signing blank cheques for Stebbing to use on company business. Stebbing was thus able to misuse the company's funds. The company, when its members realised what had happened, sued all three directors for negligence, Stebbing for his misuse of the company's funds, the other directors for their unprofessional attitude towards running the company's business. All three directors were found liable in damages to the company for their negligence. The judge advanced three standards of duty of skill and care for directors to follow. A director must:

(i)   show such skill and care as may reasonably be expected from a person with his knowledge and experience;

(ii) take such care as an ordinary person might be expected to take of his own affairs;

(iii) exercise any power vested in him in good faith in the best interests of the company.

Of these three standards, possibly the most significant is the second. It suggests that a director must exhibit a certain business prudence, in contrast to the undemanding requirements of the *City Equitable* case.

Duty owed to the company as a whole

Hitherto we have been discussing the director's duty to his company. What is meant by the company as a whole? Does he have any duty to individual members? The answer is that in general he does not, but under certain occasions he may.

The general rule

Directors are certainly required to act in the best interests of the company, but need not concern themselves with the best interests of individual members. There is a practical reason for this: one could not expect every director to be mindful of every member's best interests. The leading case on this matter is *Percival* v *Wright* [1902] 2 Ch 421, referred to also in the context of inside dealing in Chapter 12.

Wright was looking for someone to buy his shares, and approached the directors for help in finding a purchaser at a price that he named. The directors meanwhile were in the process of negotiating with a potential takeover bidder. Without telling Wright of the takeover bidder's interest, the directors approached Wright to see if he would sell his shares to them, so that they could then sell their newly acquired shares to the takeover bidder. The takeover bid never materialised, but Wright was aggrieved at the lack of disclosure on the part of the directors. It was held that the directors were not liable for their lack of disclosure.

This decision has been extensively criticised because it apparently permits the directors:

(i)   to withhold information from the shareholders;

(ii) to profit from inside information unavailable to the shareholders;

(iii) to escape the normal rules applicable to directors of a company not to take advantage of their position to obtain a secret profit.

As regards (iii), it would appear that a director's breach of fiduciary duty to his company is unacceptable, but sharp practice towards a shareholder receives no censure.

It is, however, possible to argue that as the shareholder in this case had sought a buyer at a particular price he could not complain if the directors took him up on his request. Ideally he should have asked the directors to find someone who would give him the best price for his shares. This case is probably best considered as being limited in applicability to the specific facts of the case. Now that insider dealing rules are to be found instead in the Criminal Justice Act 1993, and minority shareholders have remedies under the CA 1985 s 459 and elsewhere, members who feel that they have been mistreated by the directors/majority shareholders have some remedies open to them. A direct claim by members against the directors on the grounds of the directors' negligence in running the company incompetently is unlikely to be entertained. This is because at present a director owes no duty of care to his members. A member who believes that a director is running a company incompetently can either try to get the director dismissed – which may be impossible due to the director's voting control – or seek a remedy under the CA 1985 s 459 if the director's shares constitute a majority of the shares and the directors are conducting the affairs of the company in a manner that unfairly prejudices some or all of the members (see Chapter 13).

Duty to employees

Under common law, directors have no duty of care towards employees, but statute now supplies a carefully worded duty in the CA 1985 s 309:

> (1) The matters to which the directors of a company are to have regard in the performance of their functions include the interests of the company's employees in general as well as the interests of the members.
> (2) Accordingly, the duty imposed by this section on the directors is owed by them to the company (and to the company alone) and is enforceable in the same way as any other fiduciary duty owed to a company by its directors.

This provision was inserted to satisfy criticism that a company should be seen to give some attention to those who labour to produce the dividends that the members receive. There are inevitably various difficulties with the wording:

- the wording does not specifically confer a right upon employees to raise an action against directors in the way that, say, the CA 1985 s 459 specifically confers a right to minority shareholders to petition the court in the event of suffering unfairly prejudicial conduct from majority shareholders. Under s 309, the directors merely have to "have regard", a term which suggests a passing mild concern rather than a positive duty to consider what might genuinely be in the best interests of the employees;

- subsection (2) makes it clear that only the company can raise an action if the directors are not having enough regard for the interests of their employees. So if the members are not minded to make the company raise an action, the employees will obtain no remedy under this section. However, this will be less true in the case of companies where the employees have a substantial stake in the company – their interest will be then less lightly ignored;

- although it might be politically unwise to put it so boldly, it is obvious that a greater concern for the employees may in the short term diminish profits for the members, especially if the concern is realised in the form of higher wages. Except where mistreatment of the employees erupts into strike action which affects the profits of the company, many members are unlikely to trouble themselves about the employees. They are then less likely to put pressure upon the directors to concern themselves about the interests of the employees;

- increased employee benefits may be a cost that lowers the profits and consequently the share price of a company. If a director's remuneration is linked to the attainment of certain high share price targets, or he has share options which are triggered by a rise in the share price, the director may have less incentive to attend to the interests of the employees.

It can therefore be said that though UK law does ostensibly take cognisance of employee interests, the reality is that the relevant section is of little practical use.

A recent attempt by an employee to assert a duty of care against a director failed.

Richardson v *Pitt-Stanley* [1995] 1 All ER 460. An employee was injured at work. At or around the same time, the company went into liquidation. On investigation, it was discovered that the directors whose job it was to insure their employees against work injuries had failed to obtain any such insurance. The company secretary had also failed in this respect. The employee tried to sue the directors and company secretary for negligently failing to insure against employee injury. It was held that notwithstanding the directors' and company secretary's undoubted failure to obtain insurance, which could be the subject of criminal proceedings, any claim the employee had for negligence could only be against the company and not the directors or company secretary personally. As the company was in liquidation, the employee was unable to obtain any compensation from the company.

Duties to creditors

Inherent in the concept of the limited company is the fact that a company's creditors bear the risk attached to the business undertaken by the company. If the company fails, it is the company's creditors who suffer. That is why lenders are always so keen to obtain security, and suppliers to insert retention of title clauses in their contracts. Every business dealing with a company has to assess the risk of dealing with that company. It can assess the risk by looking at the company's past accounts published at the Registrar of Companies. It can obtain trade and bank references. It can approach credit agencies, which hold details of all persons and businesses that have had a court judgment against them for non-payment of a debt. The normal rule is that the creditor should know that he is taking a risk when he deals with a company. As the creditor should be aware of that risk, the directors of the company do not normally have a duty of care to any creditor of that company while the company is solvent. In *Multinational Gas and Petrochemical Co Ltd* v *Multinational Gas and Petrochemical Services Ltd and others* [1983] 1 Ch 258 (a case which involved the alleged mismanagement of a solvent company) Dillon LJ said:

> A company owes no duty of care to future creditors. The directors indeed stand in a fiduciary relationship to the company, as they are appointed to manage the affairs of the company and they owe fiduciary duties to the company though not to its creditors, present or future, or to individual shareholders.

However, there has been an occasion where the courts have considered creditors' interests.

Winkworth v *Edward Baron Development Co Ltd* [1987] 1 All ER 114. The company's two directors/shareholders, who were husband and wife, were divorcing each other. As part of the divorce proceedings, the wife sought to assert her claim to some of the company's assets. While the husband and wife bickered over the division of the company's assets, neither attended to the management of the company. The company ran into financial difficulties. A creditor sued the directors for his loss arising from their failure to manage the company properly. He successfully persuaded the House of Lords that the directors in these circumstances owed a creditor a duty of care.

This is an unusual case and has not so far been generally adopted as establishing a general duty of care to creditors. It remains to be seen whether or not this case will receive judicial approval and general applicability. However, if a company is insolvent, the directors must consider the interests of the creditors. This is because if a company is insolvent, the assets of the company ultimately will be vested in the liquidator who will hold them for the benefit of the creditors. If, prior to liquidation, a director makes an insolvent company satisfy one particular creditor to whom the director had given a personal guarantee (as happened in *West Mercia Safetywear Ltd* v *Dodd* [1988] BCLC 250), he is prejudicing the general body of creditors instead of looking after their interests. To a certain extent this is covered by the law relating to liquidation (see Chapter 21). The liquidator can raise an action against the preferred creditor and seek return of the sums wrongfully paid to the creditor by the director.

To the larger question of whether a liquidator, or any creditor, can make a claim against a director on the grounds of the director's breach of any duty of care to the creditors generally, there is no satisfactory answer, not least because it may be difficult to establish at what point the company may be insolvent and when the creditors' interests may be said to override the members' interests. As a matter of practice, in the above circumstances a liquidator would be better advised to raise proceedings under the wrongful trading provisions of the Insolvency Act 1986 s 214 or under s 239 (adjustment of preferences in England and Wales) or s 243 (adjustment of unfair preferences in Scotland). It might also be possible to make a claim against such a director under the fraudulent trading provisions of the Insolvency Act 1986 s 213 or the misfeasance provisions of s 212.

Statutory duties

We have already examined two statutory duties of directors: CA 1985 s 317 (declarations of interest) and s 309 (duties to employees). There are also statutory duties imposed on directors in connection with the management of the company, such as the duty to convene meetings, sign statutory declarations, deliver accounts and other tasks. The failure to adhere to those statutory requirements may attract criminal penalties. However, what is discussed in this part of this chapter are the duties that deal with the directors' own personal interests in the company.

There are two main types of such duties. The first are duties imposed on the directors: the second are duties imposed on the company in connection with the directors.

Duties imposed on the directors

Duties imposed on the directors include:

- the duty of disclosure on sale of business (CA 1985 s 313) or takeover (CA 1985 s 314);

- the requirement that substantial transactions between directors and their companies should have the approval of the members (CA 1985 s 320);

- the duty to adhere to the objects clause of the company in contracts between directors and their companies (CA 1985 s 322A);

- the duty not to deal in share options (CA 1985 s 323);

- the duty to disclose to the company their own shareholdings, and those of their families, in their companies (CA 1985 s 324);

- duty to take up qualification shares if so required under the articles (CA 1985 s 291);

- duty to disclose their ages because of the age requirement of directors of a public company or its subsidiaries (CA 1985 s 294).

The duty of disclosure on sale of business (CA 1985 s 313) or takeover (CA 1985 s 314)

If company A offers the directors of company B financial compensation for loss of their jobs as directors in connection with the transfer to company A of the whole or part of the business or property of company B, the details of the compensation must be disclosed to and approved by the members of company B (CA 1985 s 313).

If company A is considering acquiring all the shares of company B, the takeover may be contested or amicable. One way of encouraging an amicable takeover is for company A to offer the directors of company B a payment by way of substantial compensation for their loss of office or retiral as directors. Again, any such compensation must be disclosed to and approved by the members of company B (CA 1985 s 314).

Failure to do this is not only a criminal offence (CA 1985 s 314(3)), but it means that the amount of compensation, if paid, is to be held by the directors in trust for the company (CA 1985 ss 313(3), 315(1)). In each of the above cases the disclosure and approval is necessary because the price the company might receive for the transfer of the business or property, or the members for their shares, might actually be greater if the directors were not receiving their compensation. The company or the members, as the case may be, may feel that the directors are benefiting at the expense of the company or members.

The law assumes that any such payments within a period of a year before and two years after the takeover of company B or acquisition of company B's business are compensation to which the above rules apply, unless the directors can convince the courts otherwise (CA 1985 s 316). However, provided the compensation is genuinely damages for breach of a service or other contract, or a bona fide pension payment, the compensation will not be deemed to be held in trust for the members (CA 1985 s 316(3)). What the above statutory rules do not say, but is implicit in their terms, is that if company A pays discreet inducements, or to put it another way, bribes, dressed up as compensation for loss of office, to the directors of company B to ensure that company B's property is sold to company A, or to ensure that company A can buy up all the shares in company B, those inducements have to be revealed to the members. The members would be unlikely to approve such inducements, and the directors of both companies would be reluctant to disclose them. For that reason criminal sanctions to ensure compliance are necessary.

The requirement that substantial transactions involving directors and their companies should receive the approval of the members under the CA 1985 s 320
It is debatable whether the requirement that directors seek approval of their substantial transactions with the company is a duty or merely a prudent course of action, since without it, any such transaction is voidable at the instance of the company. But in view of this contiguity with the succeeding topic it is dealt with at this point. Under the CA 1985 s 320, if a director is selling the company a "substantial asset, or buying from the company a "substantial" asset, the sale or acquisition must first receive the approval of the members by an ordinary resolution passed at a general meeting. The director, if a shareholder, can vote on this occasion. A "substantial" asset is one:

(i)   that is greater than £2,000 in value;
(ii) but exceeds whichever is the lesser of:
      (a) £100,000 or
      (b) 10% of the company's asset value. This issue arises whenever a company buys the business of a partnership run by the directors in their
           personal capacity. The company must convene a general meeting to
           approve the purchase of the partnership business from the directors.

Failure to follow these rules under the CA 1985 s 320 means that the contract is voidable at the instance of the company but not the director. The company can insist that restitution take place, *i.e.* that the transaction be undone and that both the company's and the director's position be restored to what it was before the transaction took place. If that is not possible in practice, because the asset has been sold on to a third party buying in good faith and without notice of the director's transaction, the director will have to account personally to the company under the CA 1985 s 322(3) either by handing over any profit or by indemnifying the company for any loss it may have made. Any other director authorising the voidable transaction will be jointly and severally liable along with the director who bought the asset from or sold the asset to the company (CA 1985 s 322(3)).

The duty to adhere to the objects clause of the company in contracts between the directors and their companies (CA 1985 s 322A)

As has been stated above, substantial contracts between a company and its directors need approval from the members under the CA 1985 s 320. These contracts, and indeed any transactions between a company and one or more of its directors, should be transactions which the company can enter into without exceeding the limitations on the powers of the directors under the company's constitution (CA 1985 s 322A(1)) or any resolutions of the members (CA 1985 s 322A(8)).

So if a transaction between a company and one of its directors is *ultra vires*, the company, through a decision of the members, is entitled at its option to avoid the transaction (CA 1985 s 322A(2)). This means that the director cannot sue to make the company fulfil its side of the transaction. If the transaction is avoided, the director has either to return the asset, or hand over its value to the company, or to reimburse the company for any loss it suffered (CA 1985 s 322A(3)).

This is because the director is deemed to know what is *intra vires* the company's powers and what is not.

However, the company cannot avoid the contract at its option if any of the following events take place:

- restitution of any money or the asset which formed the subject-matter of the transaction is impossible (CA 1985 s 322A(5)(a)). In that case, the transaction still stands but the director has to

    (i)   account to the company for any gain he made on the transaction (CA 1985 s 322A(3)(a)), or
    (ii) indemnify the company for any loss the company made (CA 1985 s 322A(3)(b));

- the company is indemnified for any loss or damage resulting from the transaction (CA 1985 s 322A(5)(b));

- the purchaser who subsequently acquired the asset or other benefit under the transaction did so:

    (i)   in good faith and
    (ii) for fair value
    (iii) without being aware of the fact that the directors had exceeded their powers (CA 1985 s 322A(5)(c)).

Provided that the purchaser was not party to the original transaction between the directors and the company, he is entitled to retain the asset or benefit and the company cannot claim it back. What the company then can do is claim the gain on the transaction back from the directors or demand an indemnity from the director for any loss the company may suffer from the transaction;

• the company ratifies the transaction by means of a resolution of the members at a general meeting, or by means of a written resolution in the case of a private company (CA 1985 s 322A(5)(d)). If the directors who made the company enter into the *ultra vires* transaction are also the majority shareholders, there should be no difficulty in obtaining the majority decision to ratify the offending transaction. However, they should be aware that by doing so, they may incur the risk of a minority protection application to the courts under the CA 1985 s 459 in the event of unfairly prejudicial conduct towards the minority (see Chapter 13).

Duty not to deal in share options

This duty, to be found at the CA 1985 s 323, only applies to options to buy or sell shares and debentures in listed companies, otherwise known as traded options. This practice is forbidden because if a director is allowed to deal in traded options, he may be tempted to manipulate the performance of his company by a form of insider dealing (see Chapter 12). If he knew, through information that only he as a director would be likely to have, that the company was going to prosper in say, six months time, he might be tempted to buy options which would allow him to buy shares on that date at a predetermined low price so that he could instantly sell his newly acquired shares at a high price.

These rules also apply to the director's immediate family (CA 1985 s 327). This prohibition does not apply to the share options (or options to subscribe for shares) that are sometimes granted to directors of companies as part of their remuneration. Such share options are not traded options: they are not capable of being transferred to any one else and there is no market for them, as there is in traded options.

Duty of director to disclose his own and his family's shareholdings in his company

Under the CA 1985 ss 324(1), a director, and members of his immediate family (CA 1985 s 328) are required to inform the company in writing if any of them holds any securities in the company, or has an interest in any securities in the company. Any further acquisitions or disposals of those securities or the rights to acquire to subscribe for securities must be notified as well (CA 1985 s 324(2)). There are extensive provisions under the CA 1985 Schedule 13 to define all circumstances when the directors or their family have an interest in the company. These are discussed shortly in the context of the company's requirement to keep a register of directors' interests in their company's securities.

Duty to take up qualification shares
Under the CA 1985 s 291, if a company's articles require new directors to take up qualification shares, they must do so within two months or such shorter time as is specified under the articles. If he fails to do so, he will lose his position as director, and cannot take it up again until he has acquired the shares. Some companies believe that owning shares in the company is a good thing because it encourages the director to work for his own financial benefit. However, it can also be said that those who do not have shares in the company may have a more objective viewpoint than those who own shares. Having less to lose, they can afford to say what otherwise might be objectionable.

Duty to disclose age
A director of a public company or any of its subsidiaries may not continue in office over the age of 70 without the approval of the company. It is therefore necessary for the director to disclose his age (CA 1985 s 294).

Duties imposed on the company in connection with its directors

Companies have various duties imposed upon them in relation to the directors. In certain cases these duties also apply to those connected to the directors under the CA 1985 s 346. The duties include the following:

- the company must keep a register of its directors (CA 1985 s 288) and of their particulars and interests (CA 1985 s 325);

- prohibition on a company giving tax-free payments to its directors (CA 1985 s 311);

- duty of disclosure of payments to directors for loss of office (CA 1985 s 312);

- duty to make directors' contracts open to inspection (CA 1985 s 318);

- restriction on a company giving a director a contract of employment for more than five years without approval from the members (CA 1985 s 319);

- duty, in the case of single member companies, to ensure that contracts with the sole member/director are properly recorded (CA 1985 s 322B);

- duty not to make certain loans, quasi-loans and credit transactions available to a director (CA 1985 s 330).

Duty of the company to keep a register of its directors (CA 1985 s 288)
Just as a director is required to tell his company of certain particulars about himself (age, address, other relevant directorships, business occupation) so he

is under a duty to keep the company informed of any changes to those particulars. Likewise the company is under a duty to publish those details by sending the directors' particulars regularly to the Registrar of Companies.

Directors may have securities, or interests in securities, in their own companies. These need to be registered in the company's own register of directors' interests (CA 1985 s 325), so that the members, but not the general public, can inspect them. The register of directors' interests shows at any time how many shares or other securities the directors have in their company. The company must insert any changes to that register within three days of intimation by the director (CA 1985 Schedule 13 para 22) and if a member requests a copy or part of the register, the company must send it to him within 10 days (CA 1985 Schedule 13, para 26(2)), usually after payment of a fee. These rules are applicable to the directors' wives' and children's interests as well (CA 2985 s 324). The company, if listed, is also obliged to report all these interests to the Stock Exchange within one working day following intimation by the director or his family (CA 1985 s 329).

Prohibition on a company giving tax-free payments to its directors (CA 1985 s 311)
A company may not pay its directors in such a way that he suffers no liability to tax on the sums that the company pays him. The company can act as a tax collector by remitting to the Inland Revenue any tax that he is due on his remuneration, but the company cannot effectively make him a gift of the tax that he is required to pay. In such an event he would be taxed on the total of the remuneration and of the gift of the tax. This section is generally agreed to be entirely unnecessary.

Duty of disclosure of payments to directors for loss of office (CA 1985 s 312)
If a company is proposing to make a payment to a director by way of compensation for loss of office, it must tell the members and obtain their approval first. This is to prevent a director granting himself an enormous sum by way of compensation, at the expense of the company. However, if sufficient members, including the director himself, approve, such compensation is payable.

Duty of a company to make directors' service contracts open to inspection (CA 1985 s 318)
Directors, if left to their own devices, would probably not generally wish to have their service contracts, and the level of their salaries, open to inspection. Such coyness is prohibited. The service contracts must be available for inspection at the company's registered office or at the place where its register of members is kept. If the director does not have a proper written contract of employment, a written memorandum of the terms of his employment must be

provided and available for inspection instead. No service contract or memorandum is, however, necessary if the unexpired portion of the term for which
the contract is in force is less than 12 months, or if the company can terminate
the contract within the ensuing 12 months without payment of compensation
(CA 1985 s 318(11)).

Restriction on a company giving a director a contract for more than five years
without approval from the members (CA 1985 s 319)
It might be very tempting for a director to have the company award him a service contract of, say, 15 years' duration. This would mean that if the members
ever dismissed him, he would be able to claim compensation for every outstanding year of the contract. This might beggar the company, and would effectively ensure that the members would think twice about dismissing him.

Another temptation open to a director would be to arrange for a service contract which only he could terminate, or which could only be terminated on the
occurrence of events of his choosing.

None of these temptations is permitted, unless the members approve them –
and this they are unlikely to do as such contracts would be weighted too heavily in favour of the director at the expense of the company. Where a director
inserts such clauses in his service contract without obtaining the necessary
approval, the law will override the director's wishes and insert a clause allowing the company to terminate the contract with reasonable notice (CA 1985
s 319(6)).

However, provided the director is willing to have his contract last for no
more than five years, he can impose whatever conditions he wishes. If the members of the company are willing to accede to a director's insistence that:

(i)   he have a contract enduring more than five years,
(ii) only terminable by him, and/or
(iii) terminable only on the occasion of circumstances specified in the contract,

they must approve the relevant terms relating to duration and the specified circumstances by passing an ordinary resolution to that effect (CA 1985 s 319(3)).

Directors, knowing that contracts for less than five years are permitted to
contain terms that (a) permit only the director to terminate the contract, or (b)
specify only a limited number of circumstances justifying termination, might
try to have overlapping five-year contracts containing the same unreasonable
terms. This could mean that the director's employment on the same terms could
continue almost indefinitely, with some compensation always due for the unexpired portion of each contract. This, however, is not possible under the CA 1985
s 319(2), except with members' approval. Subsection 319(2) states that the
period of the new contract is added to the overlapped portion of the previous

contract (unless that portion is less than six months). In most cases that will make the contract more than five years in duration, and the above rules will apply. Overlapping in an attempt to preserve a director's contract of employment indefinitely will not work – unless the members consent to it. The rigour of these provisions is tempered by the fact that there is normally nothing to prevent the director as a shareholder voting on his own contract of employment. If he is the majority shareholder he may therefore dictate his terms.

Duty, in the case of single member companies, to ensure that contracts with sole members/directors are properly recorded (CA 1985 s 322B)
Where a company is a single member private limited company, the company is obliged to record any contract it enters into with its sole member in his capacity as a director either by means of a written memorandum of its terms or by having the contract reported at the first meeting of the directors of the company after the making of the contract. This clause does not apply if the contract is already in writing or is in the ordinary course of business.

This is to prevent the sole member/director claiming that he is employed by his company without there being any written evidence of that contract of employment. It would be very easy for a sole member/director to say that the director of the company (*i.e.* him) had verbally approved it. This might be true but unprovable; a written statement is instead required. It should be emphasised that s 322B refers to the company's duty to note the contract, as opposed to the director's duty under s 317 to obtain shareholders' approval for his contracts.

Duty not to make certain loans, quasi-loans and credit transactions available to a director (CA 1985 ss 330–347)
When a company has spare funds sitting in its bank account, and when a director is temporarily short of cash, it is both very easy and very common for the director to borrow some money from his company. While a small loan to a director might be acceptable, soon the small loan becomes a large one. Shortly afterwards the company is insolvent and so is the director. The law therefore provides extensive and complicated rules to prevent directors abusing their position to give themselves "soft" loans (loans at a less than full interest rate or on otherwise easy repayment terms). Although the duty not to give directors such loans is a duty imposed on the companies, the law recognises that such loans are likely to be at the instigation of the directors rather than at the instigation of the company. Accordingly the criminal sanctions for permitting the loans are aimed (mainly) at the directors who procure the granting of the loans, rather than the companies themselves (CA 1985 s 342).

There are two sets of rules about loans of money by companies to their directors. The first applies to all company loans to and company guarantees for their directors, and the second only to public companies and their subsidiaries. The second set of rules applies only to certain indirect loans known as quasi-loans and credit transactions. Under the CA 1985 Schedule 6, details of all loans, quasi-loans and credit transactions (unless less than £5,000 in total per director or person connected with a director (para 24(1)) must be stated in the notes to the company's accounts.

Loans by companies to their directors
All companies, whether public or private, are restricted in the giving of loans to their directors (CA 1985 s 330(2)(a)). Equally a company may not act as a guarantor for a loan by someone else to a director or provide security for a loan made by someone else to a director (CA 1985 s 330(2)(b)). The rules apply both to directors of the company in question and to the directors of that company's holding company (CA 1985 s 330(2)(a)). However, there are certain noteworthy points about and exceptions to this rule:

- It is not forbidden to grant a loan to a director, but such a loan must not exceed £5,000 (CA 1985 s 334). Any larger loan is forbidden except as specified hereafter.

- A holding company may request and receive a loan from one of its subsidiaries. The subsidiary can also guarantee or provide security for a loan to its holding company (CA 1985 s 336). This section has been inserted because if the holding company, in addition to being the subsidiary's major shareholder, was also one of its directors, the holding company could only receive a loan of up to £5,000. To receive a larger loan, the holding company would have to resign as a director, which might be inconvenient. A similar issue is dealt with in s 333. This permits a member of a group of companies to make a loan to, or guarantee a debt for, or provide security for any other company within that group, even if that other company is a director of the company making the loan or guarantee, or providing the security.

- A company may lend a director funds with which to pay any expenses he incurs in the proper performance of his duty as a director. If this is done, however, the members of the company must give their prior approval (CA 1985 s 337(3)(a)) following disclosure of all the details of the advance and of any liability in connection with the transaction with which the advances of expenses are associated (CA 1985 s 337(4)). If this is not forthcoming, approval must be obtained at the next annual general meeting. If the approval is not given then, the loan for the expenses or any other liability must be repaid within six months of the date of the meeting (CA 1985 s 337(3)(b)). In any event, the advance for expenses must not exceed £20,000 (CA 1985 s 337(3)).

- There are special exemptions for moneylending companies, namely banks and other finance houses (CA 1985 s 338). This was as a result of special lobbying of the Government by banks. This is because banks make their money out of lending money and they did not wish to be prohibited from lending money to their directors generally or providing guarantees for their directors. However, any such loans or guarantees:

    (i)   had to be made in the ordinary course of the moneylending company's business (CA 1985 s 338(3)(a)), and
    (ii) be on terms no more favourable than would be granted to anyone of the same financial standing but unconnected with the company (CA 1985 s 338(3)(b)),
    (iii) subject to the proviso that the amount of the loan to or the guarantee for the director must not be more than £100,000.

    But, as a further proviso still, if the moneylending company in question is a bank, the rule in (ii) above is relaxed to permit a soft loan to a director (or a director of its holding company) provided the loan is used

    (iv) to facilitate the purchase of the director's only or main home and any surrounding land (CA 1985 s 338(6)(a)), or
    (v)   to improve any home and/or surrounding land occupied by the director (CA 1985 s 338(6)(b)),

    and provided

    (vi) soft loans of that type are normally also made available to non-director employees on terms no less favourable than those enjoyed by the directors (CA 1985 s 338(6)).

The effect of all this is that a director of a moneylending company can obtain a loan of up to £100,000 on easy terms (assuming the terms are the same as would be applicable to any other employee of that company) provided he uses the loan by way of a mortgage to help him buy or improve his home. As it is a common perquisite of working for a moneylending company that an employee can obtain a subsidised mortgage, this section ensures that directors can enjoy that particular perquisite too. Without the benefit of s 338(6) bank directors would have been barred from the subsidised mortgages other bank employees enjoy. The relevant section in the CA 1985 was inserted as a result of consultation with leading bankers who not surprisingly wished to retain their subsidised mortgages.

Indirect loans by companies to their directors
There are two types of indirect loan specified in the CA 1985. They are quasi-loans and credit transactions.

A "relevant" company may not make a quasi-loan to a director (CA 1985 s 330(3)). Under the CA 1985 s 331(6) a relevant company is:

(a) a public company;
(b) a subsidiary of a public company;
(c) a subsidiary of a company which has as another subsidiary a public company; or
(d) a subsidiary which is a public company.

A free-standing private company, without any of the above connections to a public company, can therefore make quasi-loans.

A quasi-loan is defined as:

> "a transaction under which one party ('the creditor') agrees to pay, or pays otherwise than in pursuance of an agreement, a sum for another (the borrower) or agrees to reimburse, or reimburses otherwise than in pursuance of an agreement, expenditure incurred by another party for another (the borrower) –
>
> (a) on terms that the borrower (or a person on his behalf) will reimburse the creditor; or
>
> (b) in circumstances giving rise to a liability on the borrower to reimburse the creditor."

As this is not entirely easy to understand, an example may help. A company may issue a credit card to a director for use on company business. The director, being short of cash on holiday with his family, uses it to pay his family's hotel bill. In four months or so the hotel bill appears on the credit card account for payment by the company. During that period of four months, the credit card company will have given a loan to the company. Meanwhile the company will have indirectly given the director a loan for the cost of the hotel bill. The director will presumably need to reimburse the company in due course.

In this example, the company is the "creditor", and the director is the "borrower". The reason that this arrangement is not called a loan is because the credit card company is the lender, as it is lending the company the money used to pay the hotel bill. Had the statute restricted itself to loans, an ingenious director might have been able to argue that there was no loan by the company to him, merely a loan by the credit card company to the company. Quasi-loans are not restricted to credit card companies: it can be any situation where the company on behalf of the director is effectively paying someone else, in anticipation of reimbursement by the director at a later date.

Short-term quasi-loans are permissible, provided that the director is obliged to reimburse the company within two months and the amount of any quasi-loans outstanding at any one time is not greater than £5,000 (CA 1985 s 332).

There are certain matters arising from quasi-loans:

- As with an ordinary loan, a company can make a quasi-loan to its holding company if requested to do so (CA 1985 s 336) or to another company within the group of which it is a member even if that other company is a director of the company making the quasi-loan (CA 1985 s 333). This provision applies to guarantees and security for quasi-loans as well.

- The previously narrated provisions relating to moneylending companies also apply to quasi-loans (CA 1985 s 338(1)). Moneylending companies can accordingly make quasi-loans to their directors provided the sums involved are less than £100,000. However it is not possible for directors of moneylending companies to use a quasi-loan to obtain a cheap mortgage. This is because the relevant part of the statute (CA 1985 s 338(6)) only refers to loans and not to quasi-loans.

A relevant company (as defined above) may not enter into a credit transaction for a director (CA 1985 s 330(4)). Accordingly, a free-standing private company, not connected with a public company, may enter into a credit transaction with a director.

A credit transaction is defined in the CA 1985 s 331(7) as

"a transaction under which one party (the creditor) –

(a) supplies any goods or sells any land under a hire-purchase agreement or a conditional sale agreement;

(b) leases or hires any land or goods in return for periodical payments;

(c) otherwise disposes of land or supplies goods or services on the understanding that payment (whether in a lump sum or instalments or by way of periodical payments or otherwise) is to be deferred."

As this too is difficult to understand, it is worth explaining that the creditor in the above means the company, and the person to whom the goods are supplied or land sold or services rendered is the director.

An example may help to explain it. A director might be able to persuade his company to be the lessee under a hire-purchase agreement. The company then makes the regular payments to the hire purchase company, while letting the director use the hire-purchased item. On the completion of the hire-purchase period, the company makes over the item to the director, and the director repays the company. Until the company is repaid, the company will have paid the monthly instalments, while the director has not had to pay anything until the company has paid for the item.

There is a number of exemptions to the rule concerning credit transactions. They are as follows:

- a company may enter into a credit transaction for a director if the amount is less than £10,000 (CA 1985 s 335(1));

- a company may arrange a credit transaction for a director if:

  (a) it is in the ordinary course of business (CA 1985 s 335(2)(a)), and
  (b) the value of the transaction, and the terms on which it is entered into, are nor more favourable than that which the company would have offered anyone else of the same financial standing but who was not connected with the company (CA 1985 s 335(2)(b);

- a company can arrange a credit transaction whereby it acts as the creditor for its holding company. It can also provide a guarantee or give security for a credit transaction made by anyone for its holding company (CA 1985 s 336(b)).

What happens if a director obtains a prohibited loan, quasi-loan or credit transaction?

There are two formal sanctions, these being the civil sanction and the criminal. There is also the nuisance value of having a qualification to the report on the accounts inserted by the auditors who, if they discover that the directors have been receiving prohibited loans etc., will be required to state as much in their report. While having a qualification to the accounts may not trouble a small private company, it may be a great deal more problematic in a major listed company, and call into doubt the judgment of the directors.

The civil sanctions

If a company enters into one of the above prohibited transactions, the transaction is voidable at the instance of the company (CA 1985 s 341(1)). This means that the company can, at its choice, but not the director's, cancel the loan, quasi-loan or credit transaction. The director will then be obliged to repay any sums for which he has had the benefit up to the date of cancellation.

However, this rule will not apply if:

(i)   restitution by the director of the monies or the assets is no longer possible (CA 1985 s 341(1)(a));
(ii) the company has already been indemnified by the director and anyone else involved for the loss or damage suffered by the company (CA 1985 s 341(1)(a));
(iii) someone else, ignorant of the illegal transaction and acting in good faith, has obtained rights in the monies or assets involved and would be affected by the company's avoidance of the transaction (CA 1985 s 341(1)(b)).

If a transaction is avoided or if (i) and (iii) of the above paragraph apply, then the director in question, or anyone connected with him, or any director who authorised the transaction, is liable:

- to account to the company for any gain he made through the transaction (CA 1985 s 341(2)(a)); or

- jointly and severally with any other person liable, to indemnify the company for any loss or damage the company may have suffered from the transaction (CA 1985 s 341(2)(b)).

There are two exceptions to this liability, the first being where a director is able to show that he took all reasonable steps to ensure the company's compliance with the rules prohibiting these loans (CA 1985 s 341(4)). This is to cover the position of the director who knows that making a large loan to another director is forbidden, and who tries to persuade the company of this, but fails. He could have his objections minuted. He might not then be found liable to contribute to the company's funds in the event of default in repayment of the loan to the director.

The second exception arises where the director who would otherwise be found liable is able to show that at the time of the entering into the transaction he did not know the relevant circumstances which amounted to the infringement (CA 1985 s 341(5)).

The criminal sanctions

Although these are not greatly used, a director who makes a company enter into any of the above illegal transactions can be punished (CA 1985 s 342(1)), as can be a company entering into such a transaction on behalf of one of its directors (CA 1985 s 342(2)) unless it did not know of the relevant circumstances (CA 1985 s 342(5)).

Connected persons

The above rules in connections with directors and loans, quasi-loans and credit transactions also apply to those connected with the directors. Under the CA 1985 s346(2) such persons include:

(a) the director's spouse, child or stepchild;
(b) a company in which the director, and/or the other persons connected with him (in terms of this overall definition) owns or is interested in shares comprising one-fifth of the equity share capital, or in which he has one-fifth of the voting power;
(c) a trustee for a trust the beneficiaries of which include the director, his spouse, his children and stepchildren, a company of which he has one-fifth

of the equity or one-fifth of the voting power (as above), a further trust for the benefit of any of the above;

(d) a person who is a partner of a director, or a partner of the director's spouse, child, stepchild, company (as in (b)) or trustee (as in (c));

(e) a Scottish firm (firm in this sense being a Scottish partnership, which has a legal personality separate from the members thereof) in which:

    (i)   the director is a partner, or

    (ii) in which someone within (a), (b) or (c) above is a partner, or

    (iii) in which one of the partners is another Scottish firm, and of that other firm, the director, or someone within (a), (b) or (c) above is a partner.

In the above context, the references to the words "children" and "stepchildren" include illegitimate children, but not anyone over the age of 18.

Furthermore, the definition of trustee in (c) above does not apply to anyone in his capacity as a trustee for an employees' share scheme or employee pension fund (CA 1985 s 346(3)).

Curiously, none of the above definitions cover such persons as uncles, grandparents, girlfriends, lovers, grandchildren, or nephews and nieces. Whether it would be wise to lend company money to such persons is another matter.

Relief from liability for company officers

Under the CA 1985 s 727, the courts may, if they think fit, relieve a director, company secretary or auditor from the liability to his company that would otherwise attach to him by reason of some branch of duty, breach of trust, fiduciary duty, negligence, or other default towards his company. The relief can be partial or full as the court sees fit. The relief will be available where the court thinks the officer acted reasonably and honestly and that having regard to all the circumstances the officer ought fairly to be excused either in whole or in part, as occurred in *Re D'Jan of London Ltd* [1994] 1 BCLC (see Chapter 14).

Historically, directors used to be able to draw up articles which stated that they would not be liable for any negligence or breach of trust whatsoever. Astonishingly, some such companies managed to find investors despite the directors' complete and unaccountable freedom (see *Re City Equitable Fire Insurance Co* [1925] 1 Ch 407, for the decision of which see earlier in this chapter). However, such latitude is no longer available to directors, the current position being contained in the CA 1985 s 310. Directors and other officers can no longer avoid liability for the consequences of their "negligence, default, breach of duty or breach of trust" by ingenious wording of the articles or by the wording of any contract between the officer and the company (CA 1985 s 310(2)). However, this does not cover conflicts of interest. Conflicts of interest were discussed in *Movitex Ltd* v *Bulfield* [1988] BCLC 104 where Vinelott J held that the rule against directors' conflicts of interests should be seen as a restriction on the conduct of directors acting in their fiduciary position rather than as a duty to which they must adhere. As the rule is not a duty, it is possible to draft articles which permit conflicts of interest while not infringing s 310.

Despite the wording of s 310, there is also a saving provision which states that where an action, either civil or criminal, is raised against the officer in his capacity as an officer of the company but his defence is successful, the company may indemnify him for any liability incurred by him in defending the action. This also applies where the director successfully obtains relief at the court's discretion available under the CA 1985 s 727. In other words, if he wins, the company will bear his legal costs. Table A art 118, is construed in substantially the same terms. The company may also take out insurance for the officer against any liability (CA 1985 s 310(3)(a)).

Summary

1. Directors owe a fiduciary duty towards their company to act in good faith for the benefit of the company as a whole, and not to enter into transactions for an improper purpose. Breach of fiduciary duty may sometimes be ratified by the members (*Bamford* v *Bamford* [1970] Ch 212).

2. Directors are governed by the equitable rules relating to conflicts of interest. Directors must not make secret profits (*Boston Deep Sea Fishing Co* v *Ansell* [1888] 39 Ch D 339) and any personal gains must receive the prior approval of the members (*Regal (Hastings) Ltd* v *Gulliver* [1967] 2 AC 134).

3. If the director has breached his duty to the company, or is in breach of the conflict of interest rule, he must, so far as possible, restore any unlawfully held assets or monies to the company, account for any loss or make over any secret profits. The company can also rescind any *ultra vires* or unapproved contracts with him personally and obtain an injunction or interdict to prevent him breaching his duties to the company.

4. In general a director must not fetter his discretion in the exercise of his duties as a director.

5. A director must exercise duties of skill and care (*Dorchester Finance Company Ltd and another* v *Stebbing and another* [1989] BCLC 498). He must:

   (a) show such skill and care as may reasonably be expected from a person which his knowledge and experience;

   (b) take such care as an ordinary person might be expected to take of his own affairs;

    (c)   exercise any power vested in him in good faith in the best interests of the company.

6. A director does not normally owe a duty of care to the members of his company individually (*Percival* v *Wright* [1902] 32 Ch 421).

7. Under the CA 1985 s 309 a director owes a duty to the company as a whole to consider his company's employees' interests.

8. There is normally no duty to creditors although in the specific circumstances of *Winkworth* v *Edward Baron Development Co Ltd* [1987] 1 All ER 114 the courts accepted that such a duty might exist.

9. There are numerous statutory duties in connection with directors and their companies. These duties are designed to prevent the directors taking advantage of the company. These duties include:

- disclosure and approval of compensation payable on loss of office (CA 1985 ss 312–314);
- requirement that directors adhere to the terms of the company's objects clause in their personal dealings with the company (CA 1985 s 322A);
- prohibition on directors in listed companies dealing in traded options in their companies' securities (CA 1985 s 323);
- disclosure of directors' and their families' interests in their companies (CA 1985 s 324);
- duty to take up qualification shares (CA 1985 s 291);
- duty to disclose age for directors of public companies (CA 1985 s 294);
- prohibition on tax-free payments CA 1985 s 311);
- directors' contracts of employment must be available for inspection and generally should not be over five years in duration (CA 1985 s 318);
- sole directors must record in writing their contracts with their companies (CA 1985 s 322B);
- extensive prohibitions on loans, quasi-loans and credit transactions to directors (CA 1985 ss 330–347). These restrictions apply to those "connected" with the director (*i.e.* close family, partners, other companies of which the director is a director or major shareholder etc.) (CA 1985 s 346).

10. Under the CA 1985 s 727 the courts may grant relief to a director who has committed some breach of his duties to his company but who acted honestly and reasonably under the circumstances.

11. Under the CA 1985 s 310 there cannot be a clause in the company's articles or a director's contract of employment exempting him from any liability arising out of his failure to perform his duties properly, but he can

obtain an indemnity from his company for the cost of any court action raised against him in his capacity as a director in which he was found either not liable or not guilty.

16. COMPANY SECRETARY AND AUDITOR

Role of company secretary – role of auditor – qualifications of auditors – appointment of auditors – removal of auditors – liability of auditors – audit-exempt companies.

Role of company secretary

Historically the company secretary was a glorified clerk. The profession of company secretary gradually received a higher profile, helped by the foundation of the Institute of Chartered Secretaries (later the Institute of Chartered Secretaries and Administrators), of which Winston Churchill's father-in-law was an early and much respected member. The current position of a company secretary is much as described by Lord Denning in *Panorama Developments (Guildford) Ltd* v *Fidelis Furnishing Fabrics Ltd* [1971] 2 QB 711:

> "He is an officer of the company with extensive duties and responsibilities. This appears not only in the modern Companies Acts, but also by the role which he plays in the day-to-day business of companies. He is no longer a mere clerk. He regularly makes representations on behalf of the company and enters into contracts on its behalf which come within the day-to-day running of the company's business. So much so that he may be regarded as held out as having authority to do such things on behalf of the company. He is certainly entitled to sign contracts concerned with the administrative side of a company's affairs, such as employing staff, and ordering cars, and so forth. All such matters come within the ostensible authority of a company's secretary."

As a matter of practice the tasks that the company secretary has to do very much depend on the size of the organisation he works in. In a small company run by, say, a husband and wife, it is common to find both spouses as directors with one of them doubling as company secretary. In slightly larger companies, the company may ask a practising solicitor to be its company secretary. In still larger companies, the company secretary may be a full-time lawyer or accountant with extensive administrative responsibilities: it is his task to ensure that directors' decisions are implemented. For that reason being a company secretary is sometimes seen as a reactive job, rather than a proactive one. It is a post that requires a safe pair of hands rather than entrepreneurial flair. In some institutions the company secretary and his department may be looked down upon because they rarely generate much revenue, and because, being lawyers, they often notice legal problems that stand in the way of a particular transaction. However, a good company secretary is often a very experienced individual, with a wide legal knowledge, a good eye for detail, marked efficiency and a practical commercial attitude to business. A good company secretary can also be a very effective power behind the throne, and may occasionally ascend to the throne itself in due course.

Every company must have a company secretary (CA 1985 s 283). The sole director of a company cannot also be the company secretary (CA 1985 s 283(2)). This applies even if the company is a single member company. The company secretary, if a corporation in its own right, may not have as its sole director the director of the company (CA 1985 s 284(4)(a)). Equally, if a company has a sole director which is a corporation, the company secretary of the corporation must not be the same person as the secretary of the company (CA 1985 s 283(4)(b)).

The details of the first secretary are shown on the Form 10 on incorporation. Subsequent company secretaries need to sign a Form 288a (CA 1985 s 288(2)). A company secretary is not expected to provide as many details about himself as is a director. There is no requirement for a company secretary to disclose to the members or the public any directorships he may have or his interest in any contracts with the company. However, any loans, quasi-loans or credit transactions, in excess of £2,500, granted to the company secretary need to be disclosed in the notes to the accounts (CA 1985 Schedule 6, Part III). His age is not relevant, and as stated above, a company secretary can be a corporation or, in Scotland, a partnership. A company secretary is an officer of the company. This means that those parts of the CA 1985 and IA 1986 which refer to officers of the company will refer to him, as in the IA s 212 (misfeasance by officers of the company). However, a company secretary could be treated as a shadow director if he took too great a role within the company's management (see the discussion on shadow directors in Chapter 14).

A company secretary is an employee of the company and appointed by the directors. He is employed on such terms and to carry out such duties as the company's articles may prescribe, as may be delegated to him by the directors, and his contract of employment may state. On dismissal or retiral he has no right of protest to the members. He may be permitted to delegate some of his task to an assistant company secretary, in which case it is wise to clarify the position of company secretary in the articles so that the assistant may have power to sign important documents in the absence of the company secretary.

Company secretaries of public companies

Under the CA 1985 s 288, only the following are permitted to be company secretaries of public companies:

- persons already practising as company secretaries as at 22 December 1980;
- persons who within the five years preceding appointment have spent at least three years employed as a company secretary of a public company;
- qualified accountants recognised by the major accountancy bodies;
- United Kingdom barristers, advocates or solicitors;
- members of the Institute of Chartered Secretaries and Administrators;
- persons who, in the view of the directors of their companies, appear to be capable of acting as company secretaries because of their previous experience.

The last of these qualifications serves as a "catch-all" for company secretaries who have no formal qualifications but plenty of experience.

Tasks conventionally specific to company secretaries

Meetings

It is commonly the task of the company secretary to organise general meetings, board meetings and class meetings. For each of these the directors usually instruct the company secretary to convene a meeting at the appropriate time and place. This is why on the bottom of the notice of an annual general meeting it often says "By order of the Board" followed by the company secretary's name.

The company secretary organises the booking of the rooms for the meetings and sends out the notice of the meetings with any agendas, ancillary documentation, directors etc.

At the meeting the company secretary normally sits beside the chairman, taking notes, guiding the chairman through the agenda and providing him with guidance and information where necessary. A wise chairman always studies his agenda with his company secretary prior to a meeting, and a good company secretary will have prepared briefing notes for the chairman. After the meeting the company secretary prepares draft minutes which are usually first shown to and if necessary revised by the chairman. The minutes, once finalised, will be tabled at the beginning of the next meeting and if found accurate will be approved. If inaccurate, the company secretary will be required to rewrite the erroneous passages. The writing of company minutes is a specialised skill. As the minutes are often the only evidence that the members or directors, as the case may be, considered the items discussed at the meeting, the wording is very important. In company minutes there can be no room for ambiguity.

Drafting and signing of documents
In many companies the company secretary doubles as an in-house lawyer. Frequently he will be asked at short notice to prepare or revise contracts and other legal documents. The company secretary's scrutiny serves as a final check before the document leaves the office.

The task of countersigning legal documents is usually given to the company secretary. The mode of execution of documents varies according to the matters referred to in the documents and the company's articles. Commonly very important documents require the signature of a director and the company secretary: others may only need the signature for overseas contracts, or may need sealing with the company seal, which often is in the custody of the company secretary.

Sending documents to the Registrar of Companies
Under the CA 1985 many documents have to be sent to the Registrar of Companies, and many of these can be signed by the company secretary. Such documents as the annual return, which details the current list of members, directors and other details about the company, can be completed by the directors but as a matter of convention are normally prepared, signed and delivered by the company secretary.

Statutory registers
Although it is quite common for large companies to delegate the registration of members to professional registrars (commonly banks), most other registers are kept by the company secretary as a matter of convenience. These registers include such registers as the register of directors' interests and the register of charges.

Company secretaries are often charged with the preservation of important documents, whether registrable or not.

General administration
In small companies, the company secretary often deals with such matters as personnel and compliance with employment legislation; tax; insurance; pensions; management of the company's office and computer equipment; and such other administrative tasks as may be agreed. The company secretary may be required to ensure that his company complies with certain duties under the Health and Safety at Work Act 1974 s 2, Environmental Health Act 1990 s 73 and the Data Protection Act 1984 s 20(1).

In listed companies, he may also be the compliance officer, whose job it is to monitor employees' share-dealings to ensure the prevention of, or at least to minimise the opportunities for, insider dealing or other contraventions of stock exchange rules.

The ability of the company secretary to make contracts on behalf of the company

As the above range of tasks make clear, company secretaries have a wide range of duties. The directors may give a company secretary express written authority to carry out these tasks, or implied or ostensible authority, by letting him carry out the normal duties of most company secretaries. Most company secretaries rely on their implied authority, and most people dealing with company secretaries rely on that implied authority too. The CA 1985 s 35A(1) also permits the board of directors to authorise the company secretary to enter into contracts even if those contracts are prohibited under the company's memorandum or articles of association. A company will be bound by such a contract providing the other party to the contract acted in good faith.

What happens when a company secretary exceeds his implied authority or his express authority, and the act is not ratified by his company? It would appear to be the case that if a company secretary is doing the sort of things that a company secretary normally does, even if actually he has no authority for it, and the other party is unaware of the lack of authority, the company will still be responsible for their errant company secretary's actions.

This was discussed in the case of *Panorama Developments (Guildford) Ltd* v *Fidelis Furnishing Fabrics Ltd* [1971] QB 711. The company secretary of Fedelis approached Panorama to hire vehicles from them, allegedly to meet foreign clients at an airport. He signed the documentation in his own name but added "Company Secretary" and told Panorama that he was company secretary of Fedelis. Panorama was under the impression that he was hiring the cars on company business. The company secretary used the car for his own purposes, so Fidelis refused to pay for the car-hire charges, saying that he had not been authorised to use the cars for his own purposes, and that he was acting beyond his authority.

Lord Denning MR was unimpressed by Fidelis's arguments, in effect stating:

(i) the hiring of cars was within the normal duties of company secretaries and hence it was reasonable of Panorama to believe that the company secretary was acting within the terms of his ostensible authority;

(ii) Fidelis had chosen to employ a fraudster as their company secretary, and while that was certainly their problem, there was no reason why it should be Panorama's problem as well. Fidelis should be responsible for their employee's actions in the ostensible course of his business for them.

The issue discussed above can be reduced to that of the ostensible authority of the company secretary to act as agent for the company. The consensus seems to be that while a company secretary restricts himself to administrative matters as narrated above he will be within the terms of his ostensible authority. Actions carried out beyond those matters are more dubious. It would therefore be prudent for anyone who was dealing with a company secretary and apparently acting for his company but in respect of a matter not normally associated with a company secretary's duties, such a major commercial contract, to ask for evidence that the company secretary is empowered to deal with the matter in question. The evidence could be in the form of a board minute signed by the chairman of a letter of approval from the board. While it may be possible for anyone dealing with a company secretary to rely on the CA 1985 35A to protect his position, the wording of this section is not so free from ambiguity that it would be safe to place complete faith in it.

Role of auditors

The auditor looks after the interests of the members. He does this by inspecting the company's accounts to see if the accounts as prepared by the directors give a true view of the financial state of the company in terms of the requirement of the CA 1985 s 235. Auditors have to prepare and sign a report attached to the end of the accounts (CA 1985 s 236). Since many members of a company may have little opportunity of inspecting or indeed understanding the company's accounts, the auditor's unqualified report approving of the accounts is seen as vital reassurance that the investors' funds are being properly used.

Although the auditor is normally only accountable to the company as a whole, other persons may have an interest in his approval of the accounts. Creditors, potential investors, lenders, and the Registrar of Companies all from time to time may look to auditor-approved accounts for reassurance. This is because the auditor is independent of the company, even though the company pays him. If he is not satisfied with a company's accounts, he can state in his report on the accounts what matters appear to him to be unsatisfactory. Such a report is known as a "qualified" report. This means that the accounts are satisfactory subject to the qualifications he mentions. A qualified report may not disturb a small company without borrowings, but has considerable significance for a large and indebted one, as will be shown shortly.

There is a common misconception that auditors check the company's accounts to make sure they are all correct. This is not the case. In most cases it would be quite impossible for auditors to check the financial details of every single transaction to see if the clerks have added up their sums correctly. Auditors see their task as being able to check anything that needs to be checked, with the results that because a company might never know what exactly will be inspected, it is wise to ensure that all the accounts are in order. Auditors see their task as deterring fraud, not preventing it. In a bestial phrase from Lopes LJ in *Re Kingston Cotton Mill (No 2)* [1986] 2 Ch 279 at 288, the auditor "is a watchdog but not a bloodhound".

At the time of writing, auditing is receiving considerable public scrutiny. Certain difficult matters have yet to be resolved. These include:

- The contracts between the public's perception of auditors as fraud detectors and auditors' perception of themselves as fraud deterers.

- The increasing dominance of the six major UK accountancy firms in the market for auditing: small accountancy firms fear that the "big six" may be able to undercut their business or poach their clients.

- The huge liability suits in the USA and elsewhere that could potentially bankrupt accountancy firms because of the principle of joint and several liability. Current practice can mean that a partner in a firm of accountants who has no auditing work at all can be liable for the errors of his auditing partners, despite having no involvement in their work.

- The auditing part of an accountancy business may now be hived off into a separate company with limited liability, in order to protect non-auditing partners. This means that the auditing company has to publish its accounts and indeed have them audited by another firm of accountants. How genuinely independent would such auditing be? How could rival auditors be prevented from poaching auditing companies' clients, having seen the level of fees they were charging their clients?

- The realistic problem that if a company is large enough, or has enough foreign subsidiaries in parts of the wold where accounting standards are not as rigorous as they might be, even armies of auditors could never truly ascertain its true financial position. The best the auditors can do in such circumstances is say that the accounts *as prepared by the directors* present a true and fair view. This leaves open the question of how valid the accounts are.

- If the auditors were to qualify the accounts of a major listed company, it could have major ramifications. In theory banks might cease to lend, the share price might fall, the company might collapse bringing many other businesses down with it and employees could be put out of work. Even more cynically, the auditors would perhaps lose business. In practice, the market generally knows, or is aware of rumours that a company's accounts are to be qualified. In such an event, depending on what matters the auditors have revealed, the markets will probably take account of the qualification before the accounts are published.

- The suspicion that some companies offer accountancy firms lucrative tax and other work provided the accounts are not audited too fiercely.

- The independence of an auditing firm may be called into question when its client, for whom it does the audit, provides too much of the firm's income, or if it is involved in litigation with its own client.

- The perception among some accountants that auditing is dull, unglamorous and not as financially rewarding as, say, management consultancy. Trainee accountants used to be sent in droves to carry out the audit of large companies. The trainees were collectively known as "cannon fodder" or "grunts".

- Recent rules from the DTI have allowed certain small companies to dispense with the need for their accounts to be audited. It remains to be seen how useful this exemption proves to be. The rules regarding dispensation from auditing will be dealt with at the end of the chapter.

Qualification of auditors

Under the CA 1989 ss 24–54 extensive regulations have been set down for the qualifications of auditors.

Auditors must be members of a supervisory body recognised by the DTI. At present the supervisory bodies are:

- the Institute of Chartered Accountants of England and Wales;

- the Institute of Chartered Accountants of Scotland;

- the Institute of Chartered Accountants in Ireland;

- the Chartered Association of Certified Accountants;

- the Association of Authorised Public Accountants.

The rules applying to continuing membership of these supervisory bodies and practising as an auditor while remaining a member of those bodies are generally more stringent than the more general rules that the legislation promulages. There are extensive ethical and other guidelines that members are expected to follow. Derogation from the required standards is viewed most unfavourably and may result in an errant member being barred from membership. The auditor must also be genuinely independent of the company he audits, so that he may not be an officer or employee of the company (CA 1989 s 27(1)(a)), nor in partnership with such a person (CA 1989 s 27(1)(b)). Technically there is no legislation that says an auditor may not be a shareholder in a company he audits, but under the supervisory bodies' own guidelines, being an auditor of a company of which the auditor or close member of the auditor's family are shareholders is unacceptable, except where the articles positively prescribe the acquisition of shares by auditors. In that case only the minimum number of shares required for compliance with the articles may be obtained. If he finds that he has become ineligible for any reason, he must inform the company in writing of the fact and resign his appointment (CA 1989 s 28(2)). If the auditor is found to be ineligible to carry out the audit despite having already done it, the Secretary of State can insist on a second independent audit (CA 1989 s 29(1)) or at the very least have the first audit reviewed to see if a second audit is necessary.

Who can be an auditor?

Formerly auditors needed to be individuals or partnerships. This was because it was seen as desirable that the auditors should be personally responsible to the companies which they audit. If auditors were forbidden to incorporate, they would probably carry out the audit more zealously for fear of being personally liable for any errors. They would also need to carry adequate indemnity insurance.

However, since the implementation of the Companies Act 1989, it has now become possible for a limited company to carry out audits (CA 1989 ss 25(2) and 53(1)). That limited company must in its own right be recognised by the appropriate supervisory body to be an auditor. This gives rise to the interesting possibilities raised earlier of an auditing firm revealing its own accounts to the public and having its own accounts audited. At the time of writing few auditing companies have been set up but it is likely that the major accountancy practices will ultimately incorporate their auditing departments. There are various advantages to this:

- an error by an auditor will not necessarily bankrupt the practice as a whole;

- auditing companies will be able to raise finance perhaps by issuing shares or by borrowing;

- auditing companies might be more prepared to qualify reports to accounts which needed to be qualified: without limited liability the partners might not otherwise have been prepared to take such a risk.

There are some disadvantages to incorporation of auditing firms;

- the audit might not be carried out so scrupulously if the members of the audit company know that they would not be held personally liable, though no doubt professional and reputable auditing practices would not countenance such an attitude;
- major companies, when selecting auditors, might still prefer unincorporated auditors on the grounds of greater personal responsibility.

Whether the auditing is carried out by a partnership or a limited company, control of the partnership or company must be in the hands of qualified persons, in other words persons who in their own right would be qualified to be auditors. "Control" as far as most of the supervisory bodies are concerned, means 75% of the voting rights.

Criminal sanctions

Someone who acts as an auditor, or tries to obtain the position of auditor when in reality he is not appropriately qualified or on the appropriate register of auditors required to be kept under the CA 1989 s 35 commits a criminal offence (CA 1989 s 41(2)). However, it is a valid defence to be able to prove that he took all reasonable precautions and exercised all due diligence to avoid the commission of the offence: in other words if he was omitted from the register and did all he could to be restored to the register he would have a good defence.

Appointment of auditors

It is the prerogative of the members to appoint the auditor (CA 1985 s 385(2)), and the duty of every company except:

- dormant companies (CA 1985 s 388A);
- certain companies with a turnover of less than £350,000 (CA 1985 ss 249A to E)

to have auditors (CA 1985 s 384(1)).
  For companies that have not dispensed with annual appointment, being:

(i) all public companies and
(ii) private companies that have not taken advantage of the available dispensations (see later),

the CA 1985 s 385(2) states that at each general meeting (*i.e.* not necessarily an annual general meeting) at which accounts are laid, new auditors are appointed, or the old auditors reappointed, from the conclusions of the meeting (CA 1985 s 385(2)).

A company's first auditors are appointed by the directors and remain in office until the end of the first meeting at which accounts are tabled (CA 1985 s 385(3)).

The Secretary of State has power to appoint auditors if for some reason the members or directors fail to do so (CA 1985 s 387).

If there is a casual vacancy in the office of director (*i.e.* an auditor unexpectedly dies or resigns) the directors or the members can fill the vacant position, but if the members propose to fill the position by means of a resolution at a general meeting, the company must be given special notice of the resolution for the filling of the vacancy or a resolution to reappoint as auditor a retiring auditor who had been appointed by the directors to fill a casual vacancy. Special notice is intimated to the company by the directors or members, as appropriate, 28 days prior to the meeting at which the resolution to fill the vacancy will be tabled. This is to enable the company to include the matter on the notice of the forthcoming general meeting. The requirement of special notice is supposed to highlight to members the significance of the issue. In practice it is doubtful how much attention members pay to the significance of special notice.

The position of private companies

Private companies (but not public companies) may, if they wish, dispense with the requirement to table accounts at a general meeting under the CA 1985 s 252, and also to dispense with the requirement to appoint auditors annually (CA 1985 s 386). Both these dispensations are available by means of an elective resolution passed by all the members eligible to vote in accordance with the CA 1985 s 279A. Despite these dispensations, the accounts will still need to be audited unless the companies are audit-exempt companies as discussed later.

Companies that have dispensed with the requirement to lodge accounts at a general meeting but are not audit-exempt
The accounts for a non-audit-exempt company need to be considered by the members. In a company that has dispensed with the tabling of accounts at a general meeting, the accounts are instead sent out to the members within 28 days of the expiry of the period of laying and delivery accounts to the Registrar of Companies (CA 1985 s 253(1)(a)) (*i.e.* within 10 months of the end of the company's financial year).

If the company has dispensed with the requirement to table the accounts before the members in a general meeting, the law still has to provide a mechanism to allow for:

(a) the appointment of auditors notwithstanding the fact that accounts will not be tabled at a general meeting;
(b) the appointment of auditors at a general meeting if the members wish to change their minds and have the accounts tabled at a general meeting (CA 1985 s 253). This might occur where the members are seriously concerned about the quality of auditing or the contents of the accounts.

The legislation deals with these problems as follows:

(i) As regards (a) and the first auditors to be appointed after incorporation, the directors can appoint the auditors at any time before the expiry of the period of 28 days commencing on the date of sending out the first annual accounts to the members (CA 1985 s 385A(3)(a)).
(ii) As regards (a) and the appointment of subsequent auditors, the company must hold a general meeting within 28 days of the sending out of the accounts to the members. At that general meeting the auditors must be appointed (CA 1985 s 385A(2)).
(iii) Both for the first auditors or subsequent auditors, (a) is subject to (b), whereby the members decide to exercise their right to demand the tabling of accounts at a general meeting under CA 1985 s 253(2).
(iv) With regard to (b) and the appointment of the first auditors, the directors can appoint the first auditors at any time up to the beginning of the meeting that the members have demanded for the purpose of considering the accounts (CA 1985 s 385A(3)(b)).
(v) With regard to (b) and the appointment of subsequent auditors, the auditors can be appointed before the conclusion of the meeting that the members have demanded (CA 1985 s 385A(3)(b)).

Companies that have dispensed with the requirement to appoint auditors annually
If a private company does not need to table its accounts at a general meeting, perhaps because it believes that the contents of the accounts are already so well known to the members, or of so little interest to the members, and if the company is satisfied with its current auditors, the company may dispense with the formal requirement to appoint auditors annually. This is possible provided the company passes an elective resolution to that effect under the CA 1985 s 386. Under such circumstances the auditors are reappointed annually for each financial year without the need for re-election until such time as the company becomes

audit-exempt or the elective resolution is revoked. As a private company can also dispense with the requirement to hold annual general meetings under the CA 1985 s 366A, a private company can now send in its audited accounts once a year without any meetings or other formalities.

The rights and duties of the duly appointed auditor

Once the auditor has been appointed, he is entitled to access to all the company's papers, books, and accounts and may obtain such information from the directors and company secretary of the company as he sees fit (CA 1985 s 389A(1)). Directors and company secretaries who lie to the auditor may be committing a criminal offence (CA 1985 s 389A(2)).

The auditor is entitled to receive notices of, attend and speak at all general meetings, but not board meetings (CA 1985 s 390(1)).

The auditor is entitled to be paid, and the members of the company approve the entitlement (CA 1985 s 390A). It is common for the members to delegate to the directors the question of how much the auditor should be paid. The amount he is paid needs to be disclosed in the annual accounts (A 1985 s 390A(3)). Any other sums the auditors are paid for non-auditing work must be disclosed in the notes to the accounts (Companies Act 1985 (Disclosure of Remuneration for Non-Audit Work) Regulations 1991). This is to enable members to make their own assessment of the genuine independence of the auditors and their client. If substantial sums are being paid by the company to its auditors for non-audit work, the auditor's independence may be compromised by his reliance on that source of income.

The auditor is under a statutory duty under the CA 1985 s 237 to carry out such investigations as will him to decide whether or not:

(i)   proper accounting records have been kept;
(ii)   proper returns have been received from branches of the company not visited by the auditor;
(iii) the company's internal accounts correspond with the prepared accounts.

Removal of auditors

It is possible to remove the auditor before the expiry of his term of office by means of an ordinary resolution (CA 1985 s 391(1)) provided there has been special notice (CA 1985 s 391A) and intimation to the auditor of the resolution to remove the auditor (CA 1985 s 391A(2)). The auditor who may be about to be removed is given a right of protest, in that he can send to the company written representations (*i.e.* a statement outlining the reasons why he thinks he should not be removed as auditor, or a statement about matters in connection with the audit that he believes the members of the company ought to know) about his removal. The company is then obliged to tell the members that it has received the written representations (CA 1985 s 391A(4)(a)). It must send a copy of the representations to each member (CA 1985 391A(4)(b)) unless the company has received the representations too late to be able to send them out to the members. In that event, or if for some reason the company failed to send out the representations, the auditor can read them out at the meeting where the resolution for his dismissal is to be heard.

If, however, the representations are beyond a reasonable length, the company is not obliged to send them out (CA 1985 s 391A(3)). Equally, if the representations are producing needless publicity for defamatory matter, either the company or anyone referred to in the representations can go to court to obtain an order to prevent the reading out of the representations (CA 1985 s 391A(6)).

These provisions apply both to auditors being removed by their company and to auditors who fail to be reappointed due to the company's desire to have a new auditor (CA 1985 s 391A). The special notice required when it is proposed not to reappoint an existing auditor should draw the members' attention to the fact that the directors do not wish to reappoint the existing auditor.

Where an auditor is removed, the Registrar of Companies must be informed within 15 days (CA 1985 s 391(2)). The auditor may be entitled to compensation for the unexpired portion of his contract with the company (CA 1985 s 391(3)). The removed auditor is still entitled to speak at the meeting at which his term of office would normally have expired or at which someone would be appointed to fill the vacancy caused by his removal (CA 1985 s 391(4)).

The above provisions are designed to deal with two matters. The first is the legitimate desire of a company to remove an incompetent auditor. The second is the desire of an unscrupulous company to remove an auditor who might be asking more questions than the company wished to answer, or who might be proposing to qualify the accounts. The above rules make it still possible to dismiss the auditor, but doing so does not prevent him speaking at a general meeting and if necessary drawing any unwelcome facts to the attention of the members.

It is worth noting that it is the members who pass the resolution to dismiss the auditor. Generally the directors may instigate the removal of an auditor, but the directors have first to convince the members that it is appropriate for the auditor to be removed. This may not always be easy. If, however, the directors are also the majority shareholders it will not be problematic, and any representations made by the outgoing auditor will probably be ignored.

Under the CA 1985 s 394 if the auditor is removed, or fails to be reappointed as above, he is obliged to deposit at the company's registered office a statement of any circumstances, connected with his ceasing to hold office, of which he thinks the members ought to be aware. Even if there are no such circumstances, he must still deposit a statement at the company's registered office stating there are no such circumstances (CA 1985 s 394(1)). The company, on receiving the statement of the circumstances which the auditor believes the members ought to know about, is required to send the statement out to the members (CA 1985 s 394(3)). The auditor must also send a copy of his statement to the Registrar of Companies (CA 1985 s 394(5)).

Resignation of auditors

If an auditor resigns in the course of his appointment, he can do so by written notice to the company (CA 1985 s 392(1)). However, in order for his resignation to be effective, he must provide the company with a statement under the CA 1985 s 394, as stated in the preceding paragraph. Even if there are no such circumstances, he must still supply a statement confirming that there are no such circumstances. The company must then tell the Registrar of Companies (CA 1985 s 392(3)) within 14 days.

If the auditor believes there are circumstances which should be brought to the attention of the members or creditors, he should prepare a statement to that effect and can if necessary requisition a meeting, to be called by the directors, at which he can explain to the members his reasons for resigning (CA 1985 s 392(2)). He can also insist that the company circulate his statement to the members (CA 1985 s 392A(3)). If the directors fail to call the meeting they commit a criminal offence (CA 1985 s 392A(6)). As before, if the auditor's statement contains defamatory material, the statement need not be sent out nor read out at the meeting (CA 1985 s 392A(7)).

An auditor who has resigned can still speak at the next general meeting (CA 1985 s 390) on any matter which concerns him in his position as a former auditor of the company (CA 1985 s 392A(8)).

This section has been inserted because an auditor might be tempted to resign from auditing the company if he discovers something so unsatisfactory that he wants no part in it. Formerly he could just quietly resign and let someone else deal with it. Nowadays, he has the right to call a meeting to explain to the members and creditors why he felt he had to resign about it. He also is under the aforementioned duty to draw the members' attention to any matters of which he thinks they ought to be aware, or if there are no such matters, he should say so (CA 1985 s 394(1)). Silence is now no longer an option for the auditor who wishes to resign quietly, because if there is something suspicious afoot, he would be committing an offence if he failed to do something about it (CA 1985 s 394A(1)).

It is worth noting that it is normal practice for any new auditor to seek the permission of the company to approach the outgoing auditor to see if there is anything he ought to know about. A company which refuses such permission may well have something to hide.

Terminating the appointment of auditors not appointed annually

If a company has passed an elective resolution under the CA 1985 s 386 not to appoint auditors annually, the auditors could theoretically stay in office forever. However, if a member wishes to bring the appointment not an end, he can do so by depositing a notice with the company requiring that the directors convene a general meeting be held to terminate the appointment (CA 1985 s 393(2)). If the directors fail to call a meeting for this purpose the members can (CA 1985 s 393), the expenses thereof being met by the company. The company in turn seeks reimbursement from the directors who failed to convene the meeting (CA 1985 s 393(6)). Under the CA 1985 s 394, auditors whose appointment is terminated in this way still have to provide the company with the necessary statement confirming whether or not there are circumstances which should be drawn to the attention of the members and creditors. He must also send the statement to the Registrar of Companies (CA 1985 s 394(5)).

Liability of auditors

When auditors are appointed to carry out the annual audit of a company, they generally do so in terms of a contract drawn up between the company and the auditors. This will lay down exactly what each party expects of the other, though it will naturally include the minimum requirement that the auditors will carry out the audit in a manner consistent with the requirements of the CA 1985.

The major contentious issue in connection with the liability of auditors is the duty of care that auditors owe to the company. This is separate from any contractual duty, and can arise:

- where there is no contract between the auditors and the company;

- where any contract for the performance of the auditor is silent on the matter of the duty of care; or

- in addition to any contractual duty.

Ideally the contract for the audit spells out exactly what any liability for the duty of care may be.

The duty of care that the auditors owe the company is the duty to take reasonable care in performing the audit of the accounts as prepared by the directors. The auditors must not carry out their duty negligently or carelessly. If they do they will have to pay damages to those to whom they owe the duty of care and who would be reasonably foreseen as relying on the audit. The damages will be the amount of the loss suffered by those relying on the proper performance of the audit.

One might think that the duty of care that the auditors must shown in carrying out the audit was owed to all those who rely on the audited accounts, such as:

- current shareholders;

- creditors;

- future investors;

- in the case of financial service companies, regulatory bodies such as LAUTRO and IMRO;

- Inland Revenue and Customs and Excise;

- the financial press.

However, although all the above might well rely on the auditors' report, auditors, at least at present, do not owe these bodies a duty of care in respect of their report except where there is a special relationship between the auditor and one or more of the above, of which all parties are aware, and where the auditors are aware that their report is being used for a special purpose. In the absence of such relationships and purpose, a duty of care to any or all of the above is not present. This has been well established in the leading case of *Caparo Industries plc v Dickman and Others* [1990] 2 AC 605, often known as the *Caparo* case.

Caparo was a shareholder in Fidelity plc, and accordingly received copies of the accounts duly audited by Dickman and others. On the strength of the audited accounts, Caparo made a takeover bid for Fidelity. On investigation, it turned out that the audit had been incorrectly carried out, so that while the accounts showed a profit there was in reality a considerable loss. Caparo asserted that had it known the true position it would not have made the takeover bid. Caparo sued the auditors for damages for negligently auditing the accounts and for stating that the accounts showed a true and fair view of the company's finances when this was not the case. The issue before the House of Lords was not the accuracy of the accounts, but whether or not the auditors owed a duty of care to the plaintiffs. It was held that the auditors did not owe a duty of care to the plaintiffs. The important question was the purpose for which the audit was carried out. Although the audit was carried out in order to give reassurance to the members of the company generally that the accounts as prepared by the directors showed a true and fair view of the company's finances, it was *not* carried out to serve as information which would be used as the basis for the plaintiff's takeover bid.

While this may seem unfair to Caparo, there are various justifications for the decisions. These are:

1. In the view of tort (or delict in Scotland) the defendant (the auditor) must be aware of the investor's/plaintiff's specific use of the accounts, and there must be a "relationship of proximity" between the plaintiff and the defendant. Each party must be in reasonable contemplation of the former before that relationship exists. When the auditors audited the accounts, Caparo was no more significant to them than any other user of the accounts. There was no specific relationship between the two parties, as might be constituted by contract, by commissioning the audit, or by being put on notice by the company that the plaintiffs would be relying on the audit.

2. If one allowed Caparo's claim, there would be no end to the number of those entitled to claim against the auditors. It could lead to liability for an indeterminate amount to an indeterminate number of claimants. Any other shareholder could also claim. Creditors might claim.

3. The auditors could possibly never be able to insure against such a quantity of claims. Equally, if such liability could be attributed to auditors, auditors might well consider that it was not worthwhile carrying out any audits: the risk of insolvency following an error might be too great.

4. The auditors had been instructed by the company and not by Caparo. Only the company had a claim against the auditors.

This decision was greeted with considerable relief by auditors, and with suspicion by consumer groups, who might have hoped for a wider standard of care. However there have been subsequent cases where litigants other than the company have successfully raised actions against auditors, but only where the auditors have specifically been put on notice by the company that a third party would be relying on the accounts – even though the company had commissioned the accounts. This occurred in *Morgan Crucible Co plc* v *Hill Samuel and Co Ltd and Others* [1991] 1 All ER 148: in this case the auditors were well aware that their accounts were to be relied on by a particular investor and the duty of care normally only available to the commissioning company was extended to that investor.

This can be contrasted with the case of *James McNaughton Paper Group Ltd* v *Hicks Anderson & Co* [1991] 1 All ER 139. Copies of accounts audited in draft were circulated amongst various parties negotiating over an agreed takeover bid. The audit was inaccurate and one of the parties sued the auditors for their negligence. The claim was rejected partly because the audit was only a draft and partly because the auditors were unaware that their draft was being used by the plaintiff. As far as the auditors were concerned, it was not reasonably foreseeable that the plaintiff would be using the draft audited accounts in this way and accordingly the auditors had no duty of care towards the plaintiff.

In *ADT Ltd* v *BDO Binder Hamlyn* [1996] BCC 808, ADT was about to complete the purchase of Britannia Securities Group plc ("BSG"). As the final hurdle before the purchase took place, ADT asked BSG's auditors, Binder Hamlyn, to confirm that the accounts showed a true and fair view of the state of affairs of BSG. ADT made it clear that it was relying on Binder Hamlyn's audit. An audit partner at Binder Hamlyn was summoned at short notice and required to vouch for his firm's report on the accounts. Presumably unwilling to deny the competence of his own firm's audit, he confirmed the report. It subsequently became apparent that the accounts did not reveal a true and fair view and that the audit report should have been heavily qualified. Binder Hamlyn admitted negligence and were to be taken under the circumstances to have a duty of care to ADT, to whom they were accordingly liable.

The limits to the duty of care were further explored in the case of *Anthony and Others* v *Wright and Others*, *The Independent*, 27 September 1994. The plaintiffs were investors in an investment company that subsequently went into liquidation. The directors of the company were later imprisoned for obtaining property by deception. The plaintiff's investment had been held by the investment company in trust for the plaintiff, and to begin with at least, the trust money was kept separate from the other company monies. The plaintiffs sued the company's auditors on the grounds that the auditors owed a duty of care to the investors because of the special relationship between the auditors and the investors as beneficiaries of trusts of the existence of which the auditors were well aware. The plaintiffs claimed that the trust status imposed a duty of care on the auditors. Lightman J held that there was nothing on the auditors' part to suggest that any special relationship existed, and there was no suggestion that the plaintiffs particularly relied on the audit reports. Furthermore he did not see that a trust, just by virtue of being a trust, should be placed in a better position than an individual shareholder to whom auditors normally owe no duty of care.

Although there are clearly practical policy reasons for not extending the auditors' duty of care beyond the company as a whole, the greater issue of the liability of auditors for their negligence remains unresolved. Auditors have never claimed that they can spot ever fraud or pick up every mistake: they claim only to deter fraud and work within the limits of the accounts as presented to them by the directors. Despite that, following the gradual rise in consumer rights and public accountability of professionals, and the fact that in the USA juries are much more prone to take a harsh view of negligence by professionals and will award substantial amounts by way of damages, auditors are under-standably feeling threatened. It is no wonder that frequently negligence cases against auditors are settled out of court and that auditors are considering incor-porating to obtain the benefit of limited liability.

Audit-exempt companies

Subject to certain specified exceptions, there are three types of audit-exempt company;

- dormant companies;

- companies with a turnover of less than £350,000;

- charitable companies with an income of less than £250,000

These companies do not need to have their accounts audited by a qualified audi-tor, though there has to be some scrutiny of their accounts. This is a deregula-tory move by Parliament, designed to remove an unnecessary burden on small businesses. It remains to be seen how effective it is.

Dormant companies

Dormant company accounts
Dormant companies are exempt from the requirement to appoint auditors under the CA 1985 s 388A and, provided a special resolution has been passed, from the requirement to have an audit (CA 1985 s 250). Such exemption is not avail-able to public companies, banks or authorised persons under the Financial Services Act 1986 (CA 1985 s 250(2)).

However, even though a company is dormant and is exempt from audit, it still has to produce accounts. The directors prepare accounts which will nor-mally remain unchanged from year to year until a significant accounting trans-action takes place (CA 1985 s 250 (3)). If an accounting transaction takes place, the dormant company ceases to be dormant and may need to be audited unless it comes within the above categories of audit exempt companies. Accounts for dormant companies commonly show the contributed capital from the share-holders and little else. This is because dormant companies often exist to hold an asset that does not fluctuate in value, a common such asset being the company's own name. Sometimes people set up a dormant company with an interesting name in the hope that someone else will want the name and will buy it from the company for a large sum of money.

The audit requirement on cessation of dormancy
If the dormancy ceases, the directors may appoint auditors at any time until the next meeting when accounts are tabled (CA 1985 s 388A(3)). In the case of a formerly dormant company which now requires an audit, and which has dispensed with the tabling of accounts at a general meeting, the directors can appoint auditors:

(i) at any time before the end of the period of 28 days beginning with the day the accounts are sent out to the members (CA 1985 s 388A(4)(a)), or
(ii) at any time before the beginning of a meeting demanded by the members in order for the accounts to be considered at a general meeting (CA 1985 s 388A(4)(b)).

For further matters in connection with dormant companies and off the self companies, see Chapter 11.

Companies with a turnover of less than £350,000

Companies within this category are "small" companies in terms of the CA 1985 s 247. They are therefore able to deliver to the Registrar of Companies an abbreviated balance sheet with notes to the accounts and no profit and loss account, rather than complete accounts that would otherwise be necessary. The members, however, are entitled to see the full accounts of the company.

Companies with a turnover of less than £350,000 and a balance sheet total of less than £1,400,000 can, if they wish, be audit-exempt.

Companies which cannot be audit-exempt
Under the CA 1985 s 249B(1) exemption from audit is not available to the following types of company even if their turnover is less than £350,000:

● public companies;

● parent companies and subsidiaries, unless the group of parent company and subsidiaries itself qualifies as a "small" group under the CA 1985 s 249(3), not ineligible under any other part of this paragraph, the group's turnover is less than £350,000 and its aggregate balance sheet total is less than £1,400,000 (CA 1985 s 249(1B) and (1C));

● banks, insurance companies and insurance brokers registered under the Insurance Brokers (Registration) Act 1977;

● authorised persons and appointed representatives under the Financial Services Act 1986;

- special register bodies and employers' associations under the Trade Union and Labour Relations (Consolidation) Act 1992.

The following companies are also unable to be audit-exempt:

- charities with a gross income in excess of £250,000 (CA 1985 s 249A(4);
- companies whose members demand an audit (CA 1985 s 249B(3)).

Right of members to demand an audit

If at any stage a member or members holding at least 10% of the company's share capital, or 10% of any class of share, or in the case of a guarantee company, 10% of the members, wish the company to have its accounts audited, those members should send a written notice to that effect to the company at least a month before the end of the company's financial year (CA 1985 s 249B(2)).

This could potentially be awkward for minority shareholders with less than 10% of the issued share capital, and where an audit is demanded, it leaves little time for the appointment of auditors and the preparation of audited accounts. It is curious that there is no preliminary requirement to seek approval of the audit-exempt status from the members. Members could find that their company had become audit-exempt without anyone telling them first.

Directors' statement on audit-exempt companies' balance sheet

If the accounts are to be audit-exempt, the directors need to provide a statement attached to the balance sheet stating the following:

(a) for the financial year in question the company was exempt from the requirement to produce audited accounts (CA 1985 249B(4));
(b) the company has not received notice from members requiring the accounts to be audited (CA 1985 s 249B(4)(b));
(c) the directors acknowledge their duty to ensure that the company keeps proper accounting records in accordance with the CA 1985 s 221 (CA 1985 s 249B(4)(c)(i)), and that the accounts as prepared by the directors give a true and fair view of the financial state of the company in terms of the CA 1985 s 226 and in all other respects comply with the relevant requirements of the CA 1985 (CA 1985 s 249B(4)(c)(ii)).

In addition, under the CA 1985 s 246(1B) the directors will need to produce the usual statements suitable for a company taking advantage of a small company exempt under the CA 1985 Schedule 8 Part III Section A.

The accountant's report

Formerly, audit-exempt companies with a turnover of between £350,000 and £90,000 needed an accountant's report on the accounts as prepared by the directors. However, as from 15 April 1997, companies with a turnover of less than £350,000 and a balance sheet total of £1,400,000 no longer need an accountant's report (The Companies Act 1985 (Audit Exemption) (Amendment) Regulations 1997).

Charities

A charity company can be totally exempt from audit if its gross income is less than £90,000 (CA 1985 s 249A(3)(b)).

If its gross income is more than £90,000 but less than £250,000, it can deliver unaudited accounts provided there is an accountant's report (CA 1985 s 249A(4)(b)).

Advantages of the absence of requirement for audit

The intention of the above deregulatory regime is that the absence of an audit will save money and trouble for small businesses. It is thought that for small solvent companies this may well be true. It may also save some paperwork. Whether in practice there will be a substantial saving for such companies remains to be seen.

Disadvantages of the absence of requirement for audit

Notwithstanding the dispensation granted by the government to small companies, creditors dealing with the company and banks lending to the company will still probably want to see properly audited accounts before they embark on any major transaction with the company. An independent audit provides some reassurance that the accounts are reasonably accurate. Few but the most gullible would merely accept the directors' word that the accounts complied with the requirements of the CA 1985.

Summary

1. The company secretary is commonly the chief administrative officer of the company. He usually organises general and board meetings, takes the minutes of those meetings, and provides legal advice to the company.

2. The auditor acts as a deterrent not as a detective. He is there to provide reassurance to the members and creditors that the accounts as prepared by the directors give a true and fair view of the company's financial state.

3. An auditor must be a properly qualified accountant and be registered with an appropriate supervisory body. Auditors can now be incorporated.

4. The CA 1985 lays down strict rules for appointment, removal and retiral of auditors to ensure that auditors cannot leave a company without the opportunity of bringing unsatisfactory matters to the attention of members.

5. Auditors are normally only liable to the company as a whole in respect of any errors in the performance of the audit.

6. Certain small companies with a turnover of less than £350,000 do not require an audit.

17. CHARGES

Security in general – debentures – companies and security – the usefulness of the floating charge – comparison between fixed and floating charges – why a company has to register charges – charges registrable in England and Wales – charges registrable in Scotland – charges registrable in Northern Ireland – non-registrable charges – registration requirements in England and Wales – registration requirements in Scotland – registration requirements in Northern Ireland – instruments of alteration and deeds of priority – the company's own register of charges – entries of satisfaction and relief – enforcement of rights under a security – problems with charges – proposals for the reform of the law relating to charges

Security in general

Before discussing how a company grants security for a loan, it is perhaps worthwhile clarifying certain issues to do with loans and security generally.

If a bank lends a borrower money, the bank will want to be sure that the borrower can:

(a) repay the loan when required to do so;
(b) pay any interest on the loan.

If there is likely to be any difficulty with either of these tasks, the bank will ask the borrower to provide security or collateral for the loan.

The significance of security

Security or collateral is anything that can be used by the bank to enable the loan to be repaid in the event of the borrower's default. It could be a guarantee from a family friend, a deposit of money or whatever is acceptable to the bank. What is important is that the bank has a right over the secured object or undertaking which will only be removed once the borrower has repaid the loan. When there is such a security over an asset of the borrower's, that asset is said to be "secured" or "charged". The security itself may be known as a charge.

So, for example, a borrower might let the bank retain a valuable painting as security. While the bank holds the painting, the borrower cannot sell it. If he wants to sell the picture to repay his debt, the bank will only release the picture to the purchaser once it knows the loan will be repaid out of the sale proceeds.

For most people, their most valuable possession is their home. It is very common for a bank to make it a condition of any loan that the borrower grant the bank a mortgage over his home. This gives the bank a legal right in his home. He then cannot sell his home without the bank's consent, and under the terms of the mortgage, if the borrower defaults on any payments due to the bank, the bank can repossess his home and throw him out into the street. The bank can then sell his home to repay the debt.

Mortgages and fixed charges in England, Wales and Northern Ireland

There are two closely related types of security that prevent someone disposing of an asset without the lender's consent. In English and Northern Irish law they are known as a mortgage and a fixed charge. A fixed charge is to be contrasted with a floating charge which will be discussed in the context of companies and securities.

There are two types of mortgage over "real property" (*i.e.* land and buildings) in England, Wales and Northern Ireland. The first is known as a charge by way of legal mortgage (sometimes known as a legal charge), and the second is an equitable mortgage. Neither legal mortgages nor equitable mortgages exist in Scotland.

Legal mortgages in England and Wales

A legal mortgage is normally created by means of a deed (a written legal document) which must be stated to be a charge by way of legal mortgage under the Law of Property Act 1925 s 85(1). Legal mortgages need to be registered with the English and Welsh registers of land ownership. In England and Wales legal mortgages over registered land must be registered at the Land Registry (Land Registration Act 1925). Legal mortgages over unregistered land must be registered at the Land Charges Registry (Land Charges Act 1972).

Equitable mortgages in England and Wales

These do not have to be registered in any land register. An equitable mortgage is one created in writing but other than by deed, or one whereby its creation can be established by some act of part performance. A common example of an equitable mortgage is the deposit of title deeds with a bank as security for a loan. The owner of the house cannot sell his house without producing the title deeds, and the bank will not release the title deeds unless it knows its loan will be safely repaid.

Mortgages in Northern Ireland

There is no charge by way of legal mortgage in Northern Ireland. If the land is unregistered a mortgage created by deed should be registered in the Registry of

Deeds under the Registration of Deeds Act (Northern Ireland) 1970. For registered land a mortgage should be registered in the Land Registry under the Land Registration Act (Northern Ireland) 1970.

Equitable mortgages in Northern Ireland

The position of an equitable mortgage in Northern Ireland is identical to that in England and Wales.

Fixed charges

Fixed charges must be distinguished from mortgages. An asset that is subject to a fixed charge:

(a) must be identifiable, and
(b) cannot be sold or otherwise dealt with
(c) without the consent of the person receiving the benefit of the charge.

However, with a mortgage, not only do the above rules relating to a fixed charge apply, but there is a conveyance, or deemed conveyance, of an interest in the asset which forms the subject-matter of the charge. As a matter of practice, the term "mortgage" applies mainly to real property. In terms of English and Northern Irish law only, fixed charges are of an equitable nature.

Fixed charges over property (other than real property) in England, Wales and Northern Ireland

As will be seen shortly, in England, Wales and Northern Ireland companies can grant fixed charges over chattels (tangible moveable assets) and over intangible property. Tangible moveable assets cover such items as stock and equipment that can be physically handled: intangible property covers such items as licences, legal claims, entitlements to payments, copyrights and so on. It is acceptable to grant a fixed charge over future assets such as future book debts.

Standard securities and fixed charges in Scotland

The Scottish term for a security over land and buildings, the equivalent to the English legal mortgage, is a standard security, although in ordinary speech it too is often called a mortgage. Standard securities need to be registered with the Scottish registers of land ownership. For those countries of Scotland where registration of title is operable, the standard security is registered in the (Scottish) Land Register. For the remaining counties of Scotland, the standard security is recorded in the Register of Sasines.

Scots law does not have the concept of an equitable charge. Under the terms of the Conveyancing and Feudal Reform (Scotland) Act 1970 the only types of charge possible over land and buildings (properly known as "heritage") are a standard security and in addition, for companies only, a floating charge. While a deposit of title deeds would undoubtedly inconvenience a borrower, under Scots law it would not give a lender a good security and is not a proper charge.

Scots law accepts fixed charges in a more restrictive manner than English law. Nonetheless, the same basic rule applies, that an asset that is subject to a fixed charge:

(a) must be identifiable, and
(b) cannot be sold or otherwise dealt with
(c) without the consent of the person receiving the benefit of the charge.

In Scotland companies can create fixed charges over corporeal and incorporeal moveable assets. Corporeal is the Scots legal term for tangible, and incorporeal is equivalent to intangible. As discussed later, in Scotland it is not possible to create a fixed charge over moveable assets without delivery of the asset to the chargee (known as pledge), together with, where appropriate, intimation to the debtor, though at the time of writing there are proposals promulgated by the DTI for reform of this rule. The word "chattels" does not apply to property in Scotland, and Scots law does not recognise the term "equitable charge".

Chargor, chargee and other definitions

A company (or person) granting a charge in favour of some other person is known as the "chargor" (sometimes "charger"). If he grants a mortgage he is known as a mortgagor. In the context of secured loan, the chargor is commonly the debtor or borrower.

The person obtaining the benefit of the charge or mortgage is known variously as the "chargee", "mortgagee", "charge-holder" or "mortgage-holder", depending on the type of charge concerned. In the context of a secured loan, the person obtaining the benefit of the charge will be a creditor or lender.

Debentures

A debenture is any document recording the written acknowledgement of a debt, or creating a debt. In terms of company law, a debenture is a document of debt executed by a company in favour of a lender. A company can issue one debenture in exchange, say, for a loan from a bank, or can issue a number of debentures to many different debenture-holders, each of whom lends money to the company.

Features of debentures

(i)   They attract a fixed interest or coupon. The interest is allowable against the taxable profits of the company. Unlike dividends, which depend on the directors' recommendation, the interest on a debenture is certain.

(ii)   Debentures are redeemed (*i.e.* repaid) on terms specified in the debenture deed.

(iii)   Debentures can be redeemed at a premium.

(iv)   Some debentures incorporate a fixed or a floating charge over the company's assets. Such debentures are called secured debentures. If they contain a mortgage over real property, they may be called mortgage debentures.

(v)   Some debentures are convertible. On the fulfilment of a certain event such as the exercise of an option they can be converted into shares.

(vi)   Most companies issuing a number of debentures will keep a register of debenture-holders, and any issue or transfers of debentures will be recorded there.

(vii)   Debentures can be issued in a batch, even if the actual date of issue varies, and treated as ranking equally with each other provided the debentures are stated to be *pari passu* (ranking equal with each other).

(viii) In the United States, and to a certain extent in Scotland, debentures are commonly known as bonds.

(ix)   When share prices tumble on the stock market, the price of debentures/bonds, with their fixed return, their security and promise of repayment, tends to rise. On the other hand, debentures are not so attractive at times of high inflation as the sum paid on redemption tends to lose its value.

Debenture trust deeds and debenture stock

It is possible for a company to issue a large number of debentures to lenders, each debenture being a separate loan and each having a nominal value in the same manner as shares. Since a large number of independent debenture-holders may be administratively inconvenient for the company, it is common for the company and the lenders to set up a debenture trust deed, whereby the company through the medium of one global debenture borrows money from a trust of which the beneficiaries are all the lenders. The lenders are then knows as debenture stockholders.

The trust is administered by a trustee under the terms of the debenture trust deed. The trustee is commonly a bank or insurance company. The trustee usually has the following tasks:

(i)   it makes the company adhere to the terms of the debenture trust deed;

(ii)   it receives the interest from the debenture from the company and dis-
       burses it to the stockholders;
(iii) it pays the stockholders the capital (and any premium) on redemption of
       all or parts of the debenture;
(iv)   it holds any mortgages or other charges the company may have granted
       under the terms of the debenture, and makes the company comply with
       any terms of the charges, such as keeping any charged property well
       maintained and insured;
(v)   it can appoint a receiver under the terms of any floating charges and the
       receiver will safeguard the stockholders' interests;
(vi)   it can deal with the transfer of any debenture stock in the trust deed;
(vii) it organises regular meetings of the stockholders to whom it is account-
       able.

There is a market in debenture stock in listed companies. This is because the
interest rate on a debenture may be advantageous compared with interest rates
generally, and because traded debentures usually undertake to repay the full
loan at a predetermined date. There may also be a discount on issue thus making the interest rate particularly attractive. Traded debenture stock is dealt with
through the transfer systems referred to in Chapter 7. Stamp duty is at present
payable on transfers of both debentures and debenture stock at the rate of 0.5%.
   Debenture stock which is issued to the public must be issued in accordance
with the requirements of the Yellow Book or such other authorised market
where they are traded (see Chapter 8). They are normally issued *pari passu*, in
other words treated as equal in all respects, irrespective of the date of issue.
Debentures, as opposed to debenture stock, issued without the benefit of a *pari
passu* clause, will normally rank in date order.

The advantages of debentures and debenture stock

(a) The interest payable is an allowable deduction against tax on a company's
    profits, thus ensuring that even if the company makes no profits for its
    shareholders, at least the debenture-holders get paid.
(b) If a debenture is secured, a receiver can be appointed on default and the
    debenture-holder stands some chance of getting his money back.
(c) The interest may not be as spectacular as the dividend on shares, but it is
    more likely to be reliable.
(d) If the debenture is issued at a price lower than equivalent interest-bearing
    securities (*e.g.* gilts) it may be possible to obtain a good income flow for
    low capital expenditure.

(e) A professional trustee for a debenture trust deed is generally better placed and more experienced in looking after the interests of the stockholders than many individual debenture-holders would be.

(f) From the point of view of the company, the advantage of issuing debentures is that the shareholders do not relinquish control of the company and the right to profits after payment of interest to the debenture-holders. However, sometimes the terms of debentures allow for the debenture-holders to have rights of management or ownership under such circumstances as the failure to adhere to certain minimum solvency levels.

Companies and security

If a company wishes to borrow money for its business the procedure is much the same as for a natural person. The directors of the company will be required to supply much the same information about their company as a personal borrower would supply about his own business. Furthermore, a company may be asked to grant a security in the same way as a personal borrower. A company, after all, may well have many of the same sort of assets as an individual.

Additional security for lenders' loans

As a matter of practice lenders will often insist that by way of security the company grants whatever charges it can over its assets, and that, particularly in the case of private companies, the directors in their personal capacity grant the lenders security over their own assets – and that includes their homes. Lenders do this because:

(i) it is bad policy to lend money unless there is a good chance of getting it back from any available source, and

(ii) if the directors have granted charges over their own homes in favour of the lenders, they will have an incentive to maintain the interest payments on their company's loan lest their own homes be repossessed.

Furthermore, it is usually the case that the better the security, the lower the interest rate the borrower has to pay on the loan.

When a company grants a charge it can do so in the same manner as a natural person, though it must follow certain additional registration procedures to be discussed later.

Problems with fixed securities for companies

If a chargor grants a fixed security over a moveable asset to a chargee but does not physically hand the asset over to the chargee, there is always the danger that the chargor will:

(a) keep the money that the chargee has advanced on the strength of the value of the charged assets, and
(b) disappear both with the money and the charged assets.

It is therefore tempting for the chargee to insist on delivery and subsequent custody of the asset. However, if the chargee physically controls access to the asset which is being used as security, it means that the chargor often cannot use it. For example, if a bank were granted a charge over a road-building company's earth-moving equipment, it would be no use having the equipment sitting in the bank's vaults. For one thing, the company could not generate any funds from the use of the equipment, and for another, the bank would not want to have to look after the equipment.

English law recognised that this was a problem. Accordingly the law has been developed to make it possible for an English company to retain and use a charged moveable asset, providing the asset is identified and provided the instrument of charge prohibits the disposal of the asset without the consent of the chargee. This is not possible in Scotland, which still adheres to the rule requiring physical delivery (or deemed physical delivery) of the charged asset to the chargee. Consequently Scottish companies sometimes have to set up English subsidiary companies which can grant fixed charges over moveable assets, while letting the companies continue to use the charged assets.

Even though English law does not require delivery of the fixed charged asset to the chargee, before anyone buys that asset from the chargor, the chargee must release the asset from the charge. This can be administratively inconvenient as well as time-consuming. However, despite that inconvenience, the advantage of a fixed charge is that it defeats all other creditors' rights to the charged asset, and thus is excellent security. This means that a chargee will nearly always try to obtain a fixed charge if he possibly can.

The usefulness of the floating charge

To get round the practical difficulty of a chargee being granted possession of the charged asset, English common law developed the concept of the "floating charge". This is an equitable charge over present and future assets belonging to a chargor, and the assets in question may change in the course of business as they are bought and sold, added to, replaced or altered. The chargor is allowed to trade with the charged assets and use or dispose of them freely (unlike a fixed charge), usually provided that at any time the total asset value of the property secured by the floating charge is no less than the amount of the lender's loan to the company. The great virtue of the floating charge is that it strikes a balance between the lender's need for security and the borrower's need to continue trading with the charged assets – which are used to generate enough funds to repay the lender.

In addition, a company that does not own land and buildings (normally the best form of security there is), because it leases its office or factory premises, can borrow on the strength of the security over other assets it does own, such as its stock, its intellectual property, its sums held on deposit in a bank, etc.

Crystallisation of the floating charge under English and Northern Irish law

Crystallisation is the conversion of a floating charge into a fixed charge. Although a well drawn-up instrument creating the charge will usually contain the following events triggering crystallisation, it is well established that crystallisation occurs when:

(a) a receiver is appointed by the court;
(b) an administrative receiver is appointed by the chargee;
(c) a liquidator is appointed;
(d) under the terms of a debenture an event occurs which entitles the chargor to give a notice of conversion of the floating charge into a fixed charge and such a notice is given;
(e) under the terms of a debenture an event occurs which causes automatic crystallisation;
(f) the company ceases to be a going concern.

Receivership
On receivership, the chargor hands over its charged assets to an agent appointed by the chargee, known in England, Wales and Northern Ireland as an administrative receiver (though commonly known as a receiver). The agent must be an insolvency practitioner. The company is thereby prevented from dealing any further with the assets that happen to be secured by the floating charge at the time of crystallisation. Normally only the administrative receiver may then deal with those assets. Subject to various exceptions, the administrative receiver then disposes of the assets for value in order to pay off the chargor's indebtedness to the chargee. Receivership is more fully discussed in Chapter 20.

One way of describing the effect of the appointment of the administrative receiver under the terms of a floating charge is to imagine that while the company is trading, the chargee suspends a net over the assets of the company. While the company trades and pays its interest regularly to the chargee, the net remains suspended over the company. However, if the company fails to pay its interest, or contravenes some other requirement of the floating charge instrument, the chargee drops the net, trapping everything (with certain exceptions, such as preferential debts (IA 1986 Schedule 6)) underneath, so that only the administrative receiver can then deal with the trapped assets. The net will even trap land and buildings not already secured elsewhere, notwithstanding the absence of registration of the floating charge in the land registries. As a matter of strict law, not every asset of the company will always actually be trapped by the net, but it is to be hoped that the image of the net will be seen as a useful metaphor for the effect of crystallisation of a floating charge.

Conversion of a floating charge into a fixed charge
It is possible, and indeed very common, in England, Wales and Northern Ireland to have a composite charge that is partly floating and partly fixed, and possible to have a floating charge that on the occurrence of a pre-specified event automatically converts into a fixed charge without the appointment of an administrative receiver. The wording of a charge document can be crucially important, because a fixed charge always ranks in priority over a floating charge and does not suffer the prior repayment of the preferential debts. Naturally a chargee will always wish to secure his interest with a fixed charge since it gives the chargee better security, but the general rule is that if the chargor can still deal with the charged assets, *i.e.* freely dispose of such assets, then the charge is floating, not fixed. However, where a charge can be converted from a floating charge into a fixed charge on the fulfilment of some event, it places the converting charge-holder in a very advantageous condition relative to any other charge-holders, or indeed creditors generally, who may be unaware of the conversion: such a charge-holder has the best of both worlds. As this can be problematic for other charge-holders, they may try to prevent the creation of prior-ranking fixed charges by means of negative pledge clauses. These are dealt with later in this chapter in the context of problems with charges. As regards ordinary creditors, it is indeed the case that a conversion clause can operate to their disadvantage, because the notice of conversion is not registrable, and a creditor might well advance money to a company unaware that a conversion was about to take place – and thus find that he was subsequently prejudiced. Had the Companies Act 1989 Part IV been brought into force (which it was not) this issue would have been dealt with by the introduction of rules requiring the registration of events causing floating charges to crystallise.

How can one tell, under the law of England, Wales and Northern Ireland, whether a charge is floating or fixed?

The English Registrar of Companies receives something like 1,500 charges a week, and with this sort of volume it is just not possible for the clerks there to assess to what extent each presented charge is fixed or floating. Provided the documentation is on the face of it satisfactory, the clerks will register the charge. If there is doubt about the extent to which a charge is floating or fixed, they take the view that it is for the receiver under the floating charge to assert his claims against any liquidator or creditors, or to let the courts rule on the matter.

In this the courts will be guided by the well-known words of Romer LJ in *Re Yorkshire Woolcombers Association Ltd* [1903] 2 Ch 284 at 295:

> "I certainly think that if a charge has three characteristics that I am about to mention it is a floating charge. (1) If it is a charge on a class of assets of a company present and future; (2) if that class is one which, in the ordinary course of business of the company, would be changing from time to time; and (3) if you find that by the charge it is contemplated that, until some future step is taken by or on behalf of those interested in the charge, the company may carry on its business in the usual way as far as concerns the particular class of assets I am dealing with."

The effect of this judgment, and a large body of case law on this matter, is that, generally, if the chargor can freely deal with the charged assets, it is a floating charge, irrespective of the description of the charge.

The problem of the fixed or floating charge over book debts

Book debts, which, broadly speaking, are the sums due to be paid to the company by its debtors, are a valuable asset of a company. Consequently, lenders may wish to obtain a security over both present and future book debts. From the lender's point of view it is clearly better to have a fixed charge, since then the lender does not have to suffer the extraction of the preferential debts from the sums caught by the charge. In *Siebe Gorman & Co Ltd* v *Barclays Bank Ltd* [1979] 2 Lloyd's Rep 142 it was held that there was no difficulty with a company granting a fixed charge over its present and future book debts. Provided the wording of the charge makes it clear that such book debts are not available to the company to be used by the company, it is perfectly acceptable to grant such a fixed charge. However, in *Re Brightlife Ltd* [1987] Ch 200, the wording of a purported "first specific charge" was not so clearly drafted as to prohibit the company's use of the apparently charged book debts. Accordingly, although the charge appeared to suggest that it was fixed over the company's book debts, it was not in fact a fixed charge.

Much depends on the actual wording of the charges, and draftsmen preparing the wording of charges consequently have to be very careful in their choice of words. In addition, various judicial decisions analysing the wording of different charges suggest that a fixed charge over book debts does not necessarily mean that a company is completely barred in all instances from any dealings with the book debts (*Siebe Gorman*). In *Re New Bullas Trading Ltd* [1994] 1 BCLC 485, the draftsman quite deliberately made book debts subject to a fixed charge while they were uncollected and subject to floating charge once collected and paid into a bank account. The preferential creditors objected to this because it was in their interest to have as much as possible covered by a floating charge out of which the preferential debts could be paid. But it was held that it was acceptable to have such an ingenious charge.

Although one of the terms of the definition of a floating charge in *Re Yorkshire Woolcombers Ltd* was that the company can carry on business with the class of assets until some step is taken by those interested in the charge, in *Re Atlantic Computer Systems plc* [1992] Ch 505, it was held that rental payments paid to the company and used by the company in the ordinary course of business could nevertheless be subject to a fixed charge since the fixed charge did not actually forbid this. The reason for this decision was that the rental payments arose not from the general business the company carried on, but from specific computer leasing agreements. As these were clearly identified, it was held possible under the particular wording and particular circumstances to have such a fixed charge.

As can be seen, this is a developing area of law, as the requirements of commerce demand ever more careful drafting that will stand up to judicial scrutiny.

The meaning of "the whole assets and undertaking" in a floating charge

Most floating charges are described as being over the whole assets and undertaking of the company. While assets means the valuable items that the company owns, the word "undertaking" is significant, because, following the case of *Re Panama, New Zealand and Australian Royal Mail Co* (1870) 5 Ch App 318, "undertaking" includes both present and future property and commonly includes the idea of the business as a commercial whole, inclusive of goodwill and ongoing contracts. As stated above, the agent the chargee appoints to manage those assets and undertakings in the event of crystallisation is known as in England, Wales and Northern Ireland as an administrative receiver. It is, however, possible to have a selective floating charge which floats over only a very few assets of the company. In such cases a receiver or manager is appointed over those few assets rather than an adminsitrative receiver.

Comparison between fixed and floating charges
Advantages of fixed charges
(i)   A company cannot dispose of an asset subject to a fixed charge without the chargee's consent.
(ii) Fixed charges are always over specific assets and the chargee has immediate rights over those items.
(iii) If the chargee validly repossesses and subsequently sells the charged assets, the chargee is not required to pay out of the proceeds of the repossessed assets any sums to anybody else except the chargor which is entitled to any surplus.
(iv) A fixed charge-holder does not have to pay the preferential debts out of the proceeds of the charged assets.
(v)   A fixed charge always ranks in priority to floating charges unless there is some specific agreement between the chargees to the contrary (though this may be subject to the effect of any negative pledges discussed below).

Disadvantages of fixed charges
(i)   A fixed charge over land may involve the chargor or possibly the chargee in expense by way of conveyancing fees.
(ii) Some businesses may have no assets which realistically could be subject to a fixed charge. It is in the nature of some businesses that all their assets are constantly changing and the inconvenience of referring back to the chargee for consent for every sale would outweigh the possible benefit of the fixed charge.
(iii) (Scotland only) It may be logistically awkward for the chargee to look after the charged asset, and inconvenient for the chargor not to be able to use the asset which helps generate the funds to redeem the security.

Advantages of a floating charge
(i)   A floating charge may be the only effective security a business can give, and thus will at least enable a company to be able to borrow to some extent.
(ii) A company can continue to trade with the assets subject to the floating charge, and those assets can change in the course of business.
(iii) A floating charge allows the chargee to appoint an administrative receiver on default of the terms of the charge.

Disadvantages of a floating charge
(i)   Only on crystallisation can the chargee find out what is actually caught in the net of the floating charge. It may be that the chargor has been running down its stock and there are fewer assets than had been thought.

(ii)   On crystallisation the chargee may find that the preferential creditors have extensive rights over the assets caught in the net of the floating charge. The preferential creditors, who are generally, Customs and Excise, Inland Revenue and unpaid employees, may be due so much money that there is little or nothing left over for the floating charge-holder. Judgment creditors in England, Wales and Northern Ireland, or creditors who have effectually executed diligence in Scotland, may also have rights over the assets caught in the net. This is more extensively discussed at the end of this chapter in the section "Problems with charges".

(iii) Fixed charge-holders always rank in priority to the floating-charge holders unless there is some agreement to the contrary (depending on the effect of any negative pledge).

(iv)   Some suppliers may supply their goods to a company under a retention of title agreement and accordingly the net of the floating charge will not be able to trap those goods. This is discussed further in the section "Problems with charges".

(v)   Some floating charges may be invalid if created within certain time-limits prior to the company going into liquidation (IA 1986 s 245).

The need in Scotland for the floating charge

Under Scots law, until 1961, the only type of security that a company could offer was a fixed charge, generally over land and buildings. Under Scots law, with the exception of land and buildings, it was not possible for a company to grant a charge to a chargee without physically delivering the asset to the chargee or at least putting the asset under the control of the chargee. This arose out of the provisions of Roman law from which Scots law is descended (*Traditionibus, non nudis pactis, dominia rerum transferuntur* – by delivery, not by mere agreement, is the title to an asset transferred).

This was obviously inconvenient for everyone, and arguably put Scottish businesses at a disadvantage. Having fewer assets over which securities could be granted, Scottish businesses could not borrow so much money and so could not always take advantage of commercial opportunities. As Scots law, with its Roman law origins, could not readily accommodate the English common law floating charge, statute was used to invent such a charge. Under the Companies (Floating Charges) (Scotland) Act 1961 it became possible for companies to create floating charges in the manner of English companies; and following the Companies (Floating Charges and Receivers) (Scotland) Act 1972 it became possible for charge-holders to appoint receivers, just as in England. Unlike England and Wales, statute governs most aspects of floating charges and receiverships in Scotland.

The nature of the Scottish floating charge

In most respects the Scottish floating charge is effectively similar to the English one. There are six main differences. These are as follows:

(a) Crystallisation is technically referred to in Scotland as "attachment" of the floating charge, although increasingly "crystallisation" is becoming the common term, and will be used in this book.

(b) Administrative receivers are unknown in Scots law. The equivalent agent in Scotland is known as a "receiver" irrespective of the extent of the floating charge.

(c) If at any stage you wish to alter a floating charge in Scotland, you must complete an "instrument of alteration" which must be registered with the Registrar of Companies under the CA 1985 s 466. This procedure is not required in England, apparently because the Registrar of Companies there does not wish to be involved in a matter which is essentially a private matter between charge-holders and the company whose assets are being charged.

(d) Crystallisation takes place in Scotland on the contravention or fulfilment of terms specified in the instrument creating the charge, on the appointment of any receiver over the company's assets or on the appointment of a liquidator. The appointment of a receiver is regulated by the Insolvency Act 1986 s 52 and is discussed further in Chapter 20. In England floating charges are not regulated by statute.

(e) In Scotland if a floating charge contains a term (a negative pledge) stating that no other charge, fixed or floating, may rank in priority to it or *pari passu* with it, as is permitted under the CA 1985 s 464(1)(a), that floating charge will indeed have priority over any subsequent fixed or floating charge (CA 1985 s 464(1A)). This point arose (under the previous legislation then in place) in the case of *AIB Finance Ltd* v *Bank of Scotland* [1994] BCC 184 where a company granted a floating charge to the Bank of Scotland and a standard security to AIB. Normally one would expect the standard security to have been registered with the Registrar of Companies first, and the floating charges afterwards. As it happened, the floating charge was registered first. The floating charge contained a negative pledge. The standard security was held to be postponed to the floating charge, which was possibly not what had been intended by all the parties originally, but which was unexpectedly gratifying for the receiver under the floating charge. His net caught far larger asses than he had expected.

   Although negative pledges exist in English law, they are not regulated by statute. Negative pledges in English law are dealt with in greater detail shortly.

(f) It is not possible in Scots law to grant a charge that is partly floating and partly fixed, and equally it is not possible to grant a charge that converts from a floating charge to a fixed charge. In Scotland a floating charge remains a floating charge until crystallisation. This is because of the underlying Scots law requirement of delivery to the chargee of the charged asset.

Floating charges do not require to be registered in the Scottish land registers (the Register of Sasines and the Land Register) notwithstanding that a floating charge normally does give a receiver rights over land if the land is not already secured elsewhere. As a matter of practice, a seller of land which is subject to a floating charge is usually required to exhibit to the purchaser a letter, sometimes known as a letter of non-crystallisation, from the chargee, confirming that within a specified number of days the chargee does not propose to put the company into receivership. This practice was omitted in the Scottish case of *Sharp* v *Thomson*, 1997 SCLR 328 (HL) as a result of which purchasers unfortunately found themselves in the position of having paid the purchase price to a company for their new home but having their new home seized by the company's receiver. This was because the disposition recording the purchasers' title had not been recorded prior to the receivership. Although the case was finally decided in favour of the purchasers, so that the receiver had to relinquish the house, the issue might not have arisen had the purchasers obtained a letter from the company's lenders confirming that within the next 14 days the company would not be put into receivership. This case, and its implications, are discussed further in Chapter 20.

Floating charges and priority agreements

Most floating charges in all three jurisdictions are worded in such a way as to cover the entire assets of the company. It is, however, possible for a company to grant more than one floating charge, so that one floating charge is over one set of assets, and another floating charge in favour of a different chargee is over another different set of assets. It is also common to have two (or more) floating charges over the same set of assets, in which case, at least as far as England, Wales and Northern Ireland is concerned, and in the absence of a priority agreement to the contrary, the earlier charge, provided it has crystallised first, always has precedence over the later one. In Scotland, the earlier charge, in the absence of a ranking agreement to the contrary, has priority irrespective of the date of crystallisation.

For example, a company might have assets worth £100,000. It grants Bank A a floating charge in return for a loan of £80,000. Later, Bank B, unwisely as it turns out, chooses to lend the company £60,000 on the strength of what it thinks are good prospects for growth. Bank B secures its loan by a floating charge postponed to Bank A's floating charge. The company founders and Bank

A appoints a receiver. The company's total assets turn out to be £90,000. The appointment of Bank A's receiver triggers the appointment of Bank B's receiver. In the absence of any priority agreement or ranking agreement to the contrary, and in the absence of any preferential debts and prior-ranking fixed charges, Bank A will get its £80,000 back but Bank B will only get £10,000.

Under Scots law only, the CA 1985 s 464(5) states that when Bank A hears that Bank B has obtained a postponed charge over the same assets as Bank A, in the absence of a ranking agreement, Bank A's advance (and if necessary sub-sequent claim by its receiver) is forthwith limited to:

(a) what Bank A has already advanced,
(b) what it has undertaken to advance in terms of the floating charge,
(c) interest on all such advances, and
(d) expenses due or to become due for those advances.

In all jurisdictions as a matter of practice it is quite common for lenders and borrowers to agree between themselves what the priority of their respective securities should be. This can be advantageous to the first lender because as the price for permitting an equal ranking second security he might insist that some of his loan might be repaid. Alternatively, he may be glad to have another lender help out a struggling company where he may be reluctant to commit any more funds. If a second floating charge is granted, the arrangements are detailed in a priority agreement (sometimes known as deed of priority (in England and Northern Ireland) or "ranking agreement" (in Scotland).

It is also a common term of such deeds of priority or ranking agreements that all the loans will be treated as having been made at the same time and ranking *pari passu* in all respects except as to the proportion of their loan to the total loans. So, where Bank A lends a company £80,000 and Bank B lends £60,000, in each case secured by *pari passu* ranking floating charges, but the company's assets turn out to be only worth £100,000, on receivership, Bank A will get £80,000 ÷ (80,000 + 60,000) × 100,000, *i.e.* £57,000 and Bank B will get £60,000 ÷ (80,000 + 60,000) × 100,000, *i.e.* £43,000.

In Scotland if the ranking agreement causes the terms of one or more of the already registered floating charges to be altered, the ranking agreement becomes an "instrument of alteration" and needs to be registered under the CA 1985 s 466. Registration requirements are discussed later in this chapter.

No such requirement exists in England. This means that in England and Wales a registered floating charge whose terms may be displayed on the public fiche from the Registrar of Companies may, in practice, be extensively varied without the public being any the wiser.

Ranking of charges in the absence of a priority agreement or ranking agreement

The position is complicated when there are both floating charges and fixed charges in existence. The normal rule in all three jurisdictions is that:

(i)   fixed charges rank in order of priority between themselves according to the date when they were created,
(ii) fixed charges rank in priority to floating charges, and
(iii) floating charges rank in order of priority between themselves according to the date they were created.

This rule is stated in statute in respect of Scotland only (CA 1985 s 464(4)(a) and (b)) unless varied otherwise by the affected parties (CA 1985 s 466(1)). In England, Wales and Northern Ireland the same position applies although it is not stated in statute. The priority position as described above assumes all charges have been duly registered.

The negative pledge in English law

In theory there is nothing to prevent a company granting a floating charge, and subsequently granting a fixed charge at least over some of its assets, as approved in *Re Castell & Brown Ltd* [1898] 1 Ch 315. In this situation the fixed charge would take priority over the floating charge. This would not be well received by the floating charge-holder. He might find to his surprise that his charge was postponed to a subsequent fixed charge of which he might be unaware. This also happened in the case of *Re Woodroffes (Musical Instruments) Ltd* [1986] Ch 366. The company had granted a floating charge to a bank. Subsequently the company granted a second floating charge to a Mrs Woodroffe. The terms of her floating charge permitted her to give a notice to the company converting her floating charge into a fixed charge. It is not clear whether or not the bank was aware of Mrs Woodroffe's right to do this. She gave such a notice on 27 August 1982 and the bank appointed a receiver on 1 September 1982. The question arose as to whether the bank's receivership could be backdated to the date of conversion of Mrs Woodroffe's charge. It was held that in the absence of evidence that the company had ceased trading, it could not. This meant that Mrs Woodroffe's subsequent floating charge had, by means of prior crystallisation, defeated the bank's floating charge at least in respect of those assets secured by her formerly floating, now fixed charge.

No doubt the bank quickly amended the wording of all its standard debenture and floating charge forms to prevent this happening again. Most banks' standard documentation nowadays has wording specifically preventing the company from granting fixed charges, or charges that can become fixed, in priority to the bank's floating charge. Such wording is commonly achieved by means of a negative pledge clause, discussed in the next case.

Griffiths v *Yorkshire Bank plc* [1994] 1 WLR 1427. A company granted fixed and floating charges ("a composite charge") to the Yorkshire Bank, and later on another composite charge to APH Industries Ltd. Unfortunately, there was no deed of priority. APH crystallised its floating charge a day before the Yorkshire Bank crystallised its own charge. Morritt J decided that despite the date order of creation of the two charges, as APH's charge had crystallised first, it had priority over the Yorkshire Bank's charge and over the preferential debts. This was because the resulting fixed charge in favour of APH had priority over a floating charge, and it was certainly unarguable that APH's charge had crystallised first. There was a negative pledge clause in existence in the Yorkshire floating charges. A negative pledge is a term in a floating charge or deed of priority or ranking agreement which prohibits the company from granting a fixed charge which ranks in priority to the existing floating charge, or from granting any charge that ranks *pari passu* with the existing floating charge. The judge held that the effect of a negative pledge clause will only be relevant where a subsequent chargee has actual notice of its contents, and it was not clear that APH did have such actual notice. In the absence of proof of such actual notice, APH was entitled to behave as it did, and to ignore the negative pledge clause.

The arguably unsatisfactory nature of this decision is discussed later in the context of "Problems with charges".

Why does a company have to register its charges?

Under the Companies Act 1985 s 395 and, for Scotland, s 410, for a charge to be given precedence over the claims of creditors, a liquidator or an administrator, it must be properly registered. The Companies Act 1985 ss 395 and 410 state that a charge must be registered within 21 days of its creation. Failure to do this means that the charge is no longer secured and in the case, say, of a secured loan, the lender loses his priority rights over the secured asset.

For example, if a lender advanced monies without the charge being properly registered within the 21-day period, and if the company were put into liquidation on day 22, the liquidator would be entitled to retain the lender's loan to the company, and the lender would merely rank as an unsecured creditor. So instead of the lender expecting his loan to be protected by being secured over assets of the company, the lender could find that it had no protection at all, and was no better off than the ordinary creditors who so frequently get little or nothing when a company goes into liquidation.

It is therefore extremely important that a charge is properly registered within the 21-day period. If a firm of solicitors failed to register a lender's charge in time, and subsequently the company went into liquidation, the lender would almost certainly sue the firm of solicitors for its failure.

A further reason for registering charges generally is that it means that the public, creditors and potential investors can see the extent of the company's charges. If a company has every single asset charged, it means that there would be little left over for unsecured creditors in the event of the company's insolvency. It also means that a new lender might need to seek additional forms of security other than the company's own assets.

Remedies for failure to register the charge in time

The 21-day deadline is virtually immutable. It is, however, possible, if there is sufficient good reason, to apply to the court for permission to lodge the charge after the 21-day period has expired (CA 1985 s 404 and in Scotland s 420). While the courts are not generally sympathetic to such applications, the Act provides that where the failure to lodge arose through accident or inadvertence, and providing that creditors or shareholders are not prejudiced in any way, the register of company charges held for that company by the Registrar of Companies may be rectified.

It is both expensive and embarrassing to have to apply to the courts. One common reason for the non-registration of a charge in time is that the charge is put in a drawer and forgotten about. Another familiar reason is that the company directors who are to sign the charge are either dilatory about returning the charge to their solicitors or accountants for registration, or do not execute it correctly. Sometimes a charge is sent off to the Registrar of Companies in time, but the Registrar notices a mistake or queries a point as a result of which the document is returned. It is the Registrar's practice to amend minor mistakes such as the company number or tiny typing errors himself – with the consent of the presenter of the form – but anything significant will cause the form and the charge to be returned to the presenter. Although the Registrar makes every effort to deal with charges expeditiously, and to return them quickly if wrong, the 21-day period of grace still ticks away even if the Registrar returns the document. Whatever the reason, except perhaps through mishap at the Registrar of Companies office, if the 21-day deadline is missed, the charge is at risk. Furthermore, any loan connected with the security theoretically becomes immediately repayable by the company to the lender if the charge is void for any reason (CA 1985 ss 395(2) and 410(3)).

The registration of charges is therefore generally a matter of considerable anxiety for those whose task it is to register them.

As a matter of practice, if the 21-day deadline is missed, sometimes the only practical thing to do, apart from going to court, is to prepare a new charge and to pray that the company does not go into liquidation or administration before the new charge is registered.

If a company goes into liquidation or administration within the 21-day period from the date of execution, the charge is still a valid charge and will not put the chargee at risk provided the charge is registered in time.

Because of the 21-day rule, some lenders insist that until the charge is registered and a certificate of charge available, they will not release the money for which the charge has been granted. This is extremely awkward for a borrowing company which may need the money desperately. But it is even more awkward for the lender if he discovers that the charge was not properly registered and that the liquidation has "grabbed" the money the lender had hoped was secured.

The procedure for registration of charges is dealt with later in this chapter.

Charges registrable in England and Wales

The charges which may be registrable in terms of the CA 1985 s 396 are:

(a) a charge for the purpose of securing any issue of debentures;
(b) a charge on the uncalled share capital of the company;
(c) a charge created or evidenced by an instrument which, if executed by an individual, would require registration as a bill of sale;
(d) a charge on land (wherever situated) or any interest in it, but not including a charge for any rent or periodical sum issuing out of the land;
(e) a charge on book debts of the company;
(f) a floating charge on the company's undertaking or property;
(g) a charge on calls made but not paid;
(h) a charge on a ship or aircraft or any share in a ship;
(i) a charge on goodwill, on a patent or a licence under a patent, on a trade mark or on a copyright or a licence under a copyright.

These may be explained as follows:

(a) *A charge to secure an issue of debentures.*
    As stated earlier in this chapter, a debenture is a written acknowledgement of a loan to a company. It has never been entirely clear what Parliament meant by the precise wording of "for the purpose of securing any issue of debentures". It is probably intended to mean that when a charge is taken over a corporate asset, the security interest being evidenced as an issue of debentures, the security interest is registrable under s 396. The Companies

Act 1989 s 104 attempted to clarify the point by defining an issue of debentures as a group of debentures or an amount of debenture stock secured by the same charge. As s 104 has yet to be brought into force, and there are no British cases on the point, the point may have to remain unresolved.

It has also been argued, not entirely convincingly, that because the words "issue of debentures" is used, a charge to secure the issue of one debenture would not be registrable. This issue also remains unresolved.

In any event, this particular charge is now very rarely used. There is more on the subject of debentures in Chapter 8.

(b) *A charge on the uncalled share capital of the company.*
As detailed in Chapter 7, it is possible for shares to be partly paid. The amount remaining unpaid is a debt due by the shareholders to the company. Under this sub-clause this debt can effectively be charged provided it is registered.

(c) *A charge created or evidenced by an instrument which, if executed by an individual, would require registration as a bill of sale.*
A bill of sale is a creation of English law designed to allow a private individual to grant security over some asset that he or she owns but which he or she might wish to continue to use. This means that someone who wishes to borrow some money on the strength of the value of, say, his grandfather's pocket watch which he has inherited, can register the fact that he has charged the pocket watch in favour of a lender by means of a proper legal document known as a bill of sale. The bill of sale is registered in a special register. It is only possible to charge non-essential assets, so, for example, a carpenter could not charge the tools of his trade, his bed and other necessary furnishings, but he could charge his golf clubs or his hi-fi system. Bills of sale are nowadays little used mainly because of the inherent difficulties in tracing the borrower if he defaults or if he sells the asset even though it has been charged.

(d) *A charge on land (wherever situated) or any interest in it, but not including a charge for any rent or other periodical sum issuing out of the land.*
This sub-clause requires the registration of all charges over land both in the United Kingdom and abroad, and is used for the registration of legal mortgages and standard securities. There is nothing to prevent a company registering the grant in favour of a third party of a charge over the rents it receives from its own tenants. What a company cannot do is to register a charge in favour of its landlord of the rent it, as a tenant, is due to pay its landlord.

(e) *A charge on book debts of the company.*
Book debts is one of the amorphous phrases used in accounting and in company law without any very satisfactory definition. In essence it means debts

due or to become due to the company and which will usually, though not always, be entered into the company's books. They are sometimes known as "receivables". A company wishing to borrow money from a bank might wish to grant the bank security over all the monies due to be paid to the company by its various present and/or future debtors. If it does so, the charge over the book debts must be registered. The Registrar of Companies appears to take the pragmatic view that provided the charge on the face of it is correctly documented, it is not for him to query whether the debts in question are book debts or not: that is a matter for the courts to decide. The issue of the extent to which charges over book debts can be fixed or floating is discussed earlier in this chapter.

(f) *A floating charge on the company's undertaking or property.*
This has been dealt with above, but the distinction between undertaking and property arises because property denotes assets, tangible or intangible, whereas undertaking suggests the idea of the "business" as a whole, including its future business.

(g) *A charge on calls made but not paid.*
This is a charge on the requested but as yet unpaid amount of the nominal value of issued shares.

(h) *A charge on a ship or aircraft, or any share in a ship.*
If one grants a charge on a ship, generally known as a ship-mortgage, it is necessary to register the charge at the ship's port of registry under the terms of the Merchant Shipping Act 1894. It is also necessary to register the mortgage with the Registrar of Companies. Aircraft mortgages need to be registered with the Register of Aircraft Mortgages kept by the Civil Aviation Authority in terms of the Civil Aviation Act 1982, but they too need to be registered with the Registrar of Companies.

(i) *A charge on goodwill, on a patent or a licence under a patent, on a trade mark or on a copyright or a licence under a copyright.*
Goodwill, like book debts, is a term much used in accounting and company law but is difficult to define. It is perhaps best described as the value attached to a good reputation. It is consequently very hard to quantify, but where it can be valued, a charge can be granted over it.
Chargers over patents and trade marks must also be intimated to the Patents Office.

Charges registrable in Scotland

All the same types of charges are registrable under Scots law under the CA 1985 s 410, with the exception of the charge over assets which could be charged under a bill of sale. This is because bills of sale are not known in Scots law. In Scotland it is not possible to have charges that are both fixed and floating, in other words converting from a floating charge to a fixed charge on the fulfilment of a particular event.

Charges registrable in Northern Ireland

These are exactly the same as those registrable in England and Wales (Companies (Northern Ireland) Order 1986, art 403).

Non-registrable charges

Any charge not mentioned in s 396 or s 410 is by definition a non-registrable charge and therefore need not be registered. Absence of registration does not make the charge invalid. Non-registrable charges, such as a charge over Government loan stocks (gilts), or a charge over another company's shares, do not require to be intimated to the Registrar of Companies. It is difficult to see what the virtue of such deliberate exclusion is, save that it is administratively inconvenient to keep track of large numbers of individual gilts or shares. There are, in any event, methods of taking non-registrable security over gilts and shares, though it is wise for the chargee to retain the actual gilts certificates or share certificates in his hands to prevent unscrupulous chargors trying to charge the same gilts or shares twice over.

Other non-registrable charges include charges that are not created by the company, and the CA 1985 s 395 only applies to charged created by a company. For example, if a company left a car to be repaired at a garage, the garage would not release the car until the repaid bill had been paid. The garage has a lien over the car, but it is the garage that creates the charge, not the company. It is not therefore registrable. Certain other charges arising by operation of law, such as a landlord's right to distrain for rent or in Scotland a landlord's hypothec, are non-registrable, created by a party other than the company. Such charges rank in priority to the receiver's rights under a floating charge, provided the charge is in place before the receiver is appointed.

Registration requirements in England and Wales

The presenter (the person completing the form) must complete a Form M395, specifying the type of charge. The form must be signed by the company secretary or a director of the company. The information contained in the Form M395 must correlate with the actual charge document. If there are significant inconsistencies or inaccuracies, the form will be returned to the presenter.

The chargor has 21 days from the date of execution of the charge to send the original charge and the completed and signed Form M395 to the Registrar of Companies. If the charged property is in Scotland, Northern Ireland or overseas, copy documents of the original charge will be accepted (s 398) although a Form M398a or a Form M398 will be needed as well. This is because in Scotland, Northern Ireland and in some foreign jurisdictions the original charge document usually needs to be registered in some other register which will not accept copies. Any copies of charges that are sent must be clearly indicated as being copies, and the company secretary, a director or someone authorised by the company (a solicitor, for example) should write the words "Certified a true copy" followed by the date and the authority of the person certifying the authenticity of the copy.

If a company acquires property which is subject to an existing charge which would normally be registrable if the company had granted the charge after it had acquired the property, a Form M400 is required with a certified copy of the original charge.

Absence of charge documentation

Sometimes a company grants a charge over some of its property even though there is no charge documentation. This can happen with equitable mortgages. In these circumstances it is possible to send in the Form M395 alone without the accompanying charge documentation.

Most charges, however, are expressed in writing to save any later difficulties as to the exact terms of any charge. If the charge is a legal charge (*i.e.* a mortgage over land and buildings situated in England or Wales) over registered land, the Registrar of Companies will need to inspect the original legal charge before returning it duly stamped to the presenter. The original legal charge will need to be registered, usually by the company's solicitors, with the Land Registry within a period of a month. If the land is unregistered land the charge must be registered with the Land Charges Registry.

The charge certificate

Within a few days of the Form M395 (and where appropriate, Forms M398, M398a or M400) and the charge (if there is a written form of charge) arriving at the Registrar of Companies, and assuming all the documentation is satisfactory, the Registrar will issue a charge certificate confirming that the charge was duly registered on whatever date it arrived (CA 1985 s 401(2)). The charge certificate is conclusive evidence that the charge is registered (CA 1985 s 401(2)(b)), and it effectively guarantees the validity of the registration of the charge. It does not guarantee that it is a good charge, an effective charge or a well-drafted charge. It does not guarantee its priority relative to other charges. What it does guarantee is that the requirements of the Companies Act as regards registration have been satisfied.

The Registrar keeps a file on every company. In each file there is a register of charges, and the Registrar is required to enter into that register all the registrable charges the company grants (s 401). The entry will indicate, amongst other things, the date of creation of the charge, the amount secured by the charge, details of the property that has been charged, and the names of the chargees. All this will be microfilmed and shown on the company's microfiche, thus making it open to public inspection. After microfilming the charging documents, the charging documents and the certificate of registration of charge are returned to the presenter of the documents – commonly the lender's agents, though it is open to the lender, the company itself or any of its agents to lodge the documents with the Registrar of Companies. The certificate and the charging documents, with the exception of legal charges which are to be sent to the Land Registry or the Land Charges Registry, are then usually forwarded to the actual chargee for the chargee's retention. In the event of a court case or the need to appoint a receiver, the original documents would be required. Eventually the Land Registry or the Land Charges Registry will also return the legal charges to the presenter, who, in turn, will forward them to the chargee.

Every company must keep its own register of charges, together with copies of the charging documents (CA 1985 ss 406,407).

The problem of the rejected legal charge

A legal charge may be registered with the Registrar of Companies but subsequently rejected by the Land Registry/Land Charges Registry. It will then be returned to the presenter. This will mean that what had appeared to be a good charge in fact only provides an uncertain security for the chargee.

Under those circumstances, if the presenter can prove that neither creditors nor shareholders have been prejudiced in any way, or that the error or omission was accidental, or that it would be just and equitable under the circumstances, the presenter can then apply to the court under s 404 for rectification of the register of charges to allow a new corrected legal charge to be substituted for the old one. To do this is expensive because of the need to pay court fees and lawyers' bills. Furthermore, if there has been an error or omission for which the presenter was responsible, such an application will be embarrassing and create a poor impression of the presenter's competence.

If the presenter becomes aware of the deficiencies of the legal charge quickly enough, he may be able to ask the Registrar of Companies to withdraw the inaccurate legal charge. The presenter then starts again with a corrected legal charge.

A further, desperate alternative is to ask the chargee to provide a memorandum of satisfaction of the inaccurate charge and then to produce a new legal charge for registration with the Registrar of Companies and subsequently the Land Registry.

Each of these alternatives runs the risk that, between the time that any funds were advanced under the mistaken belief that a legal charge was safely registered and the time that the corrected charge was finally properly registered, the company might go into liquidation or administration or its assets might be seized under a court order obtained by a creditor. If that were to happen, the loan advanced by the would-be chargee might well be taken instead by a liquidator, administrator or creditor as the case may be, and retained by such person to the prejudice of the chargee.

Registration requirements in Scotland

This section does not apply to the registration of standard securities or charges over book debts, though it does apply to floating charges. Floating charges and standard securities are by far the commonest types of charge in Scotland. Standard securities and charges over book debts are dealt with shortly.

According to the CA 1985 s 410, the person presenting the form ("the presenter") should complete a Form M410, specify the type of charge, and have the form signed by the company secretary or a director of the company in question. The information in the Form M410 must correlate with the charge. The Registrar of Companies will return the form if it is incomplete or inaccurate. It is a peculiarity of Scottish company law that the Form M410, unlike its English equivalent, has a box which allows for:

(i)   details of the manner in which the terms of the floating charge restrict the ability of the company to grant charges ranking in priority to, or on the same level of priority as, the floating charge being registered (*i.e.* any negative pledge clause), and

(ii) details of the ranking of the floating charge relative to any other charges over the property covered by the floating charge.

Such information is not required on the English Form M395.

The presenter has 21 days from the date of execution of the charge to send the Form M410 together with a certified copy of the original charge to the Registrar of Companies. A certified copy is effectively a photocopy on which the company secretary, a director, or someone authorised to certify the charge on the company's behalf, writes the words "Certified a true copy" followed by the date and the authority of the person certifying the charge. The date of the execution of the charge is the date that the charge is signed by those authorised by the company to sign on its behalf, usually a director or secretary. The original executed charge is normally sent to the chargee for its records.

Within a few days of the Form 410 and the certified copy charge arriving at the Registrar of Companies, the Registrar will issue a certificate confirming that the charge was duly registered on whatever date it arrived (s 418). The certificate is conclusive evidence of the validity of the registration of the charge though the certificate does not guarantee the accuracy or legality of the contents of the charge. The Registrar makes a copy of the Form M410, a copy of the certified copy charge and a copy of the certificate, and inserts these on the company's microfiche. After microfilming, the certified copy charge and the certificate of registration of charge returned to the presenter – commonly the lender's agents, though it is open to the lender, the company itself or any of its agents to present the documents with the Registrar of Companies. The presenter may then send the certified copy and the certificate to the lender unless there are other instructions. In the event of a court case or the need to appoint a receiver, the original documents would be required. The company itself must keep a copy of the charge and enter it into its own register of charges (CA 1985 ss 421, 422).

The above procedure applies to all the forms of charge mentioned in s 410 with the exception of the registration of standard securities and the registration of assignations of such things as rents or book debts.

If a Scottish company acquires property which is subject to an existing charge which would normally be registrable if the company had granted the charge after it had acquired the property, a Form M416 is required with a certified copy of the original charge.

Registration of standard securities

Standard securities require to be recorded at the Register of Sasines or registered at the Land Register before they can be registered at the Registrar of Companies.

Notwithstanding the actual date of execution by the company granting the standard security, the effective date from the point of view of company law is the date that the standard security arrives at and is subsequently recorded in the Register of Sasines or registered in the Land Register. Although the date of recording or registration is normally the date of presentation at one or other of these Registers, if a standard security subsequently turns out to be invalid for some reason, there will be no date of recording or registration. The date of presentation should be the date of execution or as soon as possible thereafter. Any delay runs the risk that the company might go into liquidation or administration in the meantime.

The date of recording or registration is significant because under s 410(5)(b) the date of creation of a charge which is not a floating charge is defined as "the date on which the right of the person entitled to the benefit of the charge was constituted as a real right". A real right establishes the validity of a charge over property or a right of ownership of property, valid against all–comers, and in the context of land and buildings is obtained by recording or registering the deed in the appropriate Register.

Accordingly the date of recording/registration of the standard security is the date from which the 21-day period runs.

To put this into practice, the presenter should send the Keeper (the official who is in charge of the two Registers):

(i)   the standard security;
(ii) a letter asking the Keeper to confirm the date of presentation of the standard security;
(iii) a certified copy standard security to be stamped as received by the Keeper. The Keeper is generally willing to provide a note of the date of presentation which will be deemed to be the date of recording or registration unless circumstances prove otherwise.

The presenter must then send the Registrar of Companies:

(i)   a completed Form M410;
(ii) the stamped certified copy standard security;
(iii) the note from the Keeper confirming the date of recording or registration as the case may be

all within 21 days of the date of the presentation.

If the presenter misses the 21-day period, the charge is void against any liquidator, administrator or creditor having a valid claim (CA 1985 s 410(2)).

Within a few days of sending the documents to the Registrar of Companies, and assuming there are no difficulties with those documents, the Registrar of Companies will issue a certificate in the same manner as he does with any other charge (CA 1985 s 418). Just as with all the other charge certificates, this certificate is conclusive evidence of the registration of the charge, though the Registrar of Companies takes no responsibility for the effectiveness of the charge. He will return the certified copy standard security with the certificate. The certificate and the certified copy standard security should then be sent to the lender for the lender's safe keeping unless there are instructions to the contrary. The company itself should retain a copy for its own register of charges which it is required to keep (CA 1985 ss 421,422).

The problem of the defective standard security

The above procedure is highly dependent on the standard security being valid. Occasionally a standard security is drafted, executed by the borrower and sent to the Keeper of the Register of Sasines/Land Register; several months later it emerges that there is something wrong with the standard security. The Keeper then generally returns the defective standard security to the firm of solicitors which sent it in. If this happens, it means that the registration of the standard security with the Registrar of Companies is defective as well. Under such circumstances the proper procedure is to petition the court to rectify the register under s 420 and start again with a corrected standard security. This is expensive and embarrassing, and like the English equivalent at s 404 the applicant to the court must prove that there has not been or will be any prejudice to any creditor or shareholder. More commonly, the only thing to do is to have a new correct standard security executed and to record or register that, followed by registration with the Register of Companies. It is also prudent to register a memorandum of satisfaction (under s 419) for the defective standard security. This would prevent the company's charges register apparently having a charge which does not appear in the Register of Sasines of the Land Register.

If the company has gone into liquidation or administration while the defective standard security was making its way through the Register of Sasines/Land Register, the defective standard security will ultimately prohibit the security holder from exercising any rights under the security. Any attempt at repossession might well fail. Under such circumstances the security holder would almost certainly sue the solicitors, or whoever was responsible for dealing with the standard security, for their failure to draw up the standard security properly.

Charges over book debts

Assignation of rents

Sometimes a bank will grant a loan to a property company on condition that the company's tenants pay their rent directly to the bank as a way of servicing the loan. To protect the bank's position the bank will insist that the company assign the rents to the bank and in so doing grant a charge over the rents. This is done by a document known as a deed of assignation. The company executes it. The tenants receive by recorded delivery a copy of the deed with a covering letter instructing the tenants to direct their rental payments to the bank instead of to the company. Telling the tenants about the assignation and asking them to direct the payments to the bank is known as "intimation". The certificate of recorded delivery posting to each tenant is then attached to the Form 410, which together with a further certified copy charge is sent to the Registrar of Companies. As a matter of practice some tenants ignore such letters or do not understand them, though many very properly instruct their own banks to direct their standing orders to the requested account.

This procedure is not limited to rents: it could be used for any type of book debt or payment from a debtor which is assigned in security of some obligation. It commonly arises in the context of life assurance policies, taken out on the managing director's life in favour of his company, and subsequently assigned in favour of a lender. The particular procedure involving recorded delivery certificates only applies in Scotland and arises out of the requirement under Scots law that assignations of debts from one creditor to someone in place of the original creditor must be intimated to the debtor. The debtor formerly paying the debt to the company is supposed to acknowledge the assignation of the debt to the chargee (Transmission of Moveable Property Act 1862). In theory the procedure has the virtue of ensuring that everyone knows who is supposed to be paying whom. In practice the procedure is seen as cumbersome and as far as the debtor is concerned a matter of little interest to him. The DTI is looking into methods of improving this area of the law. In the meantime any such assignations require to be registered with the Registrar of Companies under the CA 1985 s 410(4)(C)(i).

This procedure specifically does not apply to the payment of rent by a company to its landlord (CA 1985 s 410(4)(a)).

Registration requirements in Northern Ireland

The registration requirements for legal charges is essentially the same in Northern Ireland as they are in England and Wales (Companies (Northern Ireland) Order 1986, Part XIII).

Registration of instruments of alteration and deeds of priority

Instruments of alteration (Scotland only)

Sometimes a Scottish company wishes to alter the terms of a charge it has granted. This will generally be because the company has managed to renegotiate the terms of the loan for which the charge forms security. If, in the process of renegotiation the terms of a floating charge are altered, the Registrar of Companies must be informed of the alteration on a Form M466. This procedure only needs to be followed for floating charges.

If there are several floating charges which are to be varied because the parties wish to reorganise the manner in which the various floating charges are ranked, a separate Form M466 must be filled in for each charge that is varied.

It is common to record all the changes in one comprehensive document, commonly called a ranking agreement, but it would be possible to have a separate instrument of alteration for each charge that is altered.

If the instrument also refers to standard securities, it will be common practice for the instrument to be recorded/registered in the Registrar of Sasines and/or the Land Register. There is a school of thought that says such registration in the Register of Sasines/Land Register is unnecessary, but it is certainly the case that any instrument involving the alteration of a floating charge must be registered with the Registrar of Companies (s 466(4)).

No requirement to register deeds of priority in England, Wales and Northern Ireland

In England, Wales and Northern Ireland one is not required to send the Registrar of Companies a special form to show how the floating charges have been varied. So an English company could prepare an instrument varying all its charges substantially without the public being any the wiser.

The company's own register of charges

This applies to all three jurisdictions.

In addition to the Registrar of Companies having a register for each company of all charges which are registrable under the Companies Act, *i.e.* the charges specified in the CA 1985 ss 395, 398, 400, and for Scotland ss 410(4), 411 and 416, each company must also keep its own register of charges for all charges created by the company (CA 1985 s 406 and for Scotland s 422(1)). This applies both to charges registered with the Registrar of Companies under the CA 1985 s 395 and for Scotland s 410 and to charges which cannot be registered with the Registrar of Companies. If they are not registrable, the company must still make an entry in its own register of charges showing the existence of the unregistered charges, what property is charged and the amount of the charge (CA 1985 s 407 and for Scotland s 422(2)). The company's own register of charges, together with the copies of any registrable charges (CA 1985 s 406(1) and for Scotland s 421(1)), is open to inspection during business hours by any creditor or member of the company free of charge (CA 1985 s 408 and for Scotland s 423). Anybody else requires to pay no more than 5p per inspection. The reason for the derisory fee is to discourage companies from charging an outrageous fee merely for allowing someone to inspect its charges.

In Northern Ireland the relevant and equivalent legislation is to be found in the Companies (Northern Ireland) Order 1986, art 415–416.

Entries of satisfaction and relief

Under the CA 1985 s 403 and for Scotland s 419, once a charge is discharged, or partially discharged by the chargee, it is possible to send to the Registrar of Companies Forms M403a, M403b or in Scotland 419a, known as a memorandum of satisfaction. This confirms that the debt for which the charge is given has been discharged, or that all or part of what was formerly charged has now been released.

England and Wales

Under the English practice, the Forms M403a and M403b require a statutory declaration by a director or the chargee's agent that the debt has been paid and/or that all or part of the property which had been charged may now be released from the charge. It is considered good practice to include a certificate from the chargee confirming that details of the memorandum are correct, but there is no statutory requirement for this. The Registrar of Companies will not reject it if it is attached to the statutory declaration.

The reason for bothering with such a certificate is that a statutory declaration by a director, while no doubt an expression of the director's honest belief as evidenced by swearing as much in front of a Justice of the Peace, a notary public or a commissioner for oaths, is only really of any use if either:

(i) the director is worth suing in his personal capacity for his error, or
(ii) the threat of being forbidden to be a director, because of similar transgressions under the Company Directors Disqualification Act 1986, holds any terrors for a deceitful director – an in the case of a director who is a rogue it probably will not.

If the director is a rogue, no amount of swearing will render his statement true. But a certificate from the mortgagee, assuming it is not forged, will put the position beyond doubt.

Scotland

In Scotland, the same statutory declaration is required under s 419(3)(a) using the Form M419. In respect of floating charges only, there is a special box for the chargee or his agent to sign, confirming that the details of the memorandum are correct. If the chargee or his agent is unwilling to do this, the company can, if necessary, obtain an order from the courts forcing the Registrar of Companies to accept the memorandum notwithstanding the absence of the chargee's consent (s 419(3)(b)).

Northern Ireland

In Northern Ireland, the procedure is similar to that in England and Wales, and may be found in the Companies (Northern Ireland) Order 1986, art 411.

Until recently companies tended not to bother with memoranda of satisfaction, mainly because the Companies Act does not oblige companies to notify the Registrar of Companies that their charges have been discharged. However, recently it has increasingly become the case that lenders are insisting that prior to the granting of any new loans all existing charges must be discharged, that memoranda of satisfaction be registered, and that chargees must be seen to have given their consent to the memoranda. While it is not obligatory to discharge charges, it is of course good practice to discharge the charges formally, because an apparently undischarged charge can lead to confusion or delay if company searchers ever come across a charge which does not on the face of it appear to have been discharged.

Enforcement of rights under a security

The whole point of having a charge is that the chargee has rights in the charged property. What those rights are depend on the type of charge, the wording of the charge and the type of property.

As regards a fixed charge over real property and specific property in England, Wales and Northern Ireland, and heritage in Scotland, on the occurrence of a default by the chargor the chargee is normally entitled to repossess the land and buildings subject to the charge. This is sometimes known as foreclosure. The chargee and his possessions will be removed and the land and buildings sold to repay the debt. Any surplus on sale is refunded to the chargor. If the sale fails to bring in enough funds to repay any loan, the chargee keeps what funds it can get and may be entitled to claim against the chargee for any outstanding balance but only on the basis of an unsecured creditor. This can be done by means of an ordinary action for debt. If the company is insolvent, the chargee will have to lodge his claim for the outstanding balance with the liquidator.

Fixed charges over most assets other than land and buildings do not normally pose any problems, because the chargor itself has given a right over the asset to the chargee, albeit on a temporary basis until the charge is discharged. So in the case of a fixed charge over book debts, the chargee continues to receive the book debts until the chargor's obligation is fulfilled. A charge over a copyright is not released until the chargee discharges the charge following, say, payment of all sums due to him.

As regards a floating charge, the chargee may appoint an administrative receiver or, in Scotland, a receiver on the occurrence of the events specified in the floating charge, and additionally in Scotland, on the occurrence of any other circumstances outlined in the IA 1986 s 52. The procedural aspects of the appointment of receivers will be discussed more fully in Chapter 20. The administrative receiver, or receiver as the case may be, will then take such steps as are necessary to realise the property subject to the floating charge. As the appointment of the administrative receiver or receiver effectively turns what had been a floating charge into a fixed charge, the receiver normally needs no further authority (unless the courts direct otherwise) to sell the property in as advantageous a manner as possible. Whatever funds are realised by this will be subject to the requirement that the administrative receiver or receiver deduct the amounts owing to any holders of fixed charges (if they have not already exercised their rights to obtain the sums due to them) and the preferential debts (IA 1986 Schedule 6). Only after the preferential debts have been paid may the balance be paid by the administrative receiver or receiver to the chargee. If there is sufficient to repay the chargee and any preferential debts, the chargee will discharge the receivership and any surplus is returned to the company.

If there is insufficient to repay the chargee, the chargee must obtain the balance from the company if the company is still trading. Given that most floating charges are over the entire assets and undertaking of the company, it is rare for a company to survive receivership; if it does not, it may go into liquidation in which case the liquidator will be asked to entertain a claim from the administrative receiver or receiver for the outstanding balance.

Problems with charges

This section deals with the problems that afflict the extent or the validity of charges. If an adminsitrative receiver, or receiver as the case may be, is appointed under the terms of a floating charge, he may find that he does not have his expected unfettered right to all the company's assets. Other creditors may appear to have a better right to those assets; some of the assets may not be owned by the company at all; the charge may be void for want of registration; or if the company is in liquidation, the charge may be struck down by the liquidator because there are suspicions as to the genuineness of the transaction giving rise to the creation of the floating charge.

Negative pledges

As stated earlier, a lender may wish to ensure that its mortgage/standard security/ floating charge ranks in priority to any other mortgage/standard security/floating charge which the company chooses to grant. One way to do this is to include a provision in any floating charge expressly preventing the company from creating any fixed or floating charge ranking in priority to, or ranking *pari passu* (*i.e.*

equally) with the existing floating charge. In England and Wales and Northern Ireland this is permitted under common law. In Scotland this is available under statute (CA 1985 s 464(1)(a)). In Scotland it can also be done in a ranking agreement/instrument of alteration (CA 1985 s 466(4)) or in England and Wales in a deed of priority. Such a provision is known as a negative pledge clause. The purpose behind the negative pledge clause is to prevent the first lender's prior right to the charged assets being prejudiced by any other chargee.

There is an anomaly in connection with negative pledges clauses. As has been noted earlier, in England and Wales negative pledge clauses do not need to be mentioned in the Form M395 which is sent to the Registrar of Companies showing the creation of the charge. There is no requirement under statute for negative pledges to be shown. As a matter of practice, however, negative pledges are commonly mentioned. However, in Scotland, the equivalent form for Scottish charges, the Form M410, specifically has a box allowing for the mention of negative pledges which prevent the borrowing company from granting any other charge ranking in priority to or equal with the charge in favour of the chargee (CA 1985 s 464(1)(a)). Furthermore, the Scottish Registrar of Companies must include in the company's register of charges the relevant details restricting the granting of other charges or altering the priority of the floating charge (CA 1985 s 464(1)(b)). This is also true of any negative pledge in any instrument of alteration (CA 1985 s 466(4)).

This has the curious result that prospective creditors in England may not necessarily know, on the basis of the information shown at the Registrar of Companies' office, whether a negative pledge exists, whereas in Scotland such information will be apparent.

In all three jurisdictions the common practice is for a potential second charge-holder to check all the company's details and accounts before obtaining the charge from the company. Nonetheless the issue is not merely a matter of checking the fiche, because, as far as England and Wales is concerned, the mention on a Form M395 of the existence of a negative pledge does not automatically mean that the second charge-holder ought to be aware of it. This is because there is no statutory obligation that it be mentioned on the Form M395. On the other hand, it would suggest bad faith on the part of the subsequent chargee if it deliberately ignored a negative pledge clause in a pre-existing charge which was clearly mentioned on the fiche – especially given that normal business practice is to check the fiche. Whilst a subsequent chargee will not be held to have had constructive notice of a negative pledge, (see *Griffiths* v *Yorkshire Bank plc* [1994] 1 WLR 1427), actual notice of the clause may render a subsequent chargee bound by its contents. This could be done in England, Wales and Northern Ireland by all parties signing a deed of priority. It should be noted that a negative pledge clause will create a binding obligation between the company and the first chargee, so that contravention of the contract is

actionable by the first chargee. However, any such action may be futile as far
as the first chargee is concerned, because a claim for damages might well be
pointless in the context of the company's receivership.

The view that actual notice of a negative pledge clause will bind a subsequent chargee is consistent with the Scottish position and makes commercial
sense, in that there is no point in inserting a negative pledge clause in a charge
if it can be freely disregarded on the grounds that the subsequent chargee did
not have "actual" notice of the negative pledge clause despite the fact that it was
shown on a fiche which is freely available for the public or for any potential
chargee to inspect. The position is more complicated where the subsequent
chargee was genuinely unaware of a negative pledge because it was not mentioned on the Form M395, or it was not otherwise brought to his attention. If
the subsequent chargee obtained a legal mortgage from a company that had
overlooked or ignored the existence of a negative pledge clause in a floating
charge, that legal mortgage would rank before the floating charge on the
grounds that a legal mortgage-holder cannot be bound by prior interests which
had not been disclosed to him (*Re Standard Rotary Machine Co Ltd* (1906) 95
LT 829). This is clearly very satisfactory for the legal mortgage-holder and very
unsatisfactory for the floating charge-holder. Even if the floating charge-holder
retaliated by appointing a receiver, the legal mortgage-holder might merely
exercise his rights under his legal mortgage at the expense of the floating
charge-holder. It is not clear what the position of the company in the midst of
all this would be, though there might be some personal liability attaching to a
director or the company secretary if he had personally and negligently vouched
for the freedom of the company to grant the prior-ranking security.

This whole area was one which was to be addressed by reforms introduced
under the Companies Act 1989 s 103. However, the section has not been
brought into force. The procedure in England and Wales would then have followed the Scottish procedure (CA 1985 s 464(1A)) which makes it clear that
any charge with a negative pledge clause ranks above any other subsequent
charge unless the parties agree otherwise. Despite the above, the current position, at least in England and Wales, is as indicated in *Griffiths* v *Yorkshire Bank
plc* [1994] 1 WLR 1427 and casts doubt on the effectiveness of a negative
pledge clause. It is submitted that it cannot be sensible to have different rules
on a common issue depending which side of the Scottish border you are.

Retention of title agreements

A retention of title clause (sometimes known as a *Romalpa* clause after a case
of that name) in a contract of sale entitles the seller to retain ownership of the
item being sold until such time as all monies due by the purchaser to the seller
are paid. Such clauses are commonplace in Europe and the UK.

The advantage to the seller is that in the event of the purchaser becoming insolvent or going into receivership prior to payment the seller can go to the purchaser's premises and take back the item – assuming they are easily identifiable, separable and recoverable.

The disadvantage to the receiver is that when he exercises his rights over assets secured by a floating charge he may find that certain assets are subject to the retention of title agreement and recoverable by the seller. This will reduce the sums available to the floating charge-holder with which to satisfy the debt due to him.

The problem with retention of title clauses is that there are some occasions when a retention of title clause arguably is a charge and should therefore be registered to be effective. As this is rarely done, the retention of title clause may be ineffective.

Over the years there have been many attempts by sellers to safeguard their right to payment by means of retention of title agreements, and some retention of title clauses have been less well drafted than others. Under English law there have been attempts by sellers to make the purchasers bailees for the sellers, and artful arrangements for covering the position where the seller's goods were used and made into different objects. If the retention of title clause was valid, the seller was protected. If the clause was badly drawn up, the clause was invalid and might be, in effect, an attempt to create a charge; and if it was a charge, it needed to be properly registered in favour of the seller. This would often not have taken place because the purchaser would generally be unaware that he was supposed to be creating a charge for the benefit of the seller. The charge would be then void for lack of registration; the seller would lose the right to possess his goods and would in effect be relegated to the standing of an unsecured creditor.

A well-drafted retention of title clause does not allow any ownership to pass to the purchaser until full payment. In addition, if the seller does resell the goods, the contract should make it clear that he does so purely as agent of the seller, and that the resale price which the sub-purchaser pays the purchaser belongs exclusively to the seller. The contract of sale by the seller should retain full ownership at all times: the moment he lessens his ownership right to an equitable claim to the proceeds of sale the purchaser has created a charge in favour of the seller, which should be registered.

Unfortunately, the simple approach runs into difficulties where the product supplied is incorporated within a new product produced by the purchaser. For example, if a supplier supplied paint to a manufacturer he might put a retention of title clause into the supply contract, stating that even if the paint were used in the production of a new product by the purchaser, the supplier would have rights over the proceeds of sale of the product. Unfortunately once paint is applied, so at a practical level the supplier's ownership of the paint is lost and a new object, belonging to the purchaser, is created. If the seller wants the proceeds, he will have to insist in his contract that the purchaser grant him a charge over the new products for the value of the paint that is used in the new products. This is because a right to retain the paint is different from a right to the proceeds of sale of the new products which incorporated the paint. This principle can be seen in the following case: *Re Peachdart Ltd* [1983] 3 All ER 204. The supplier supplied leather to a manufacturer of leather bags. The manufacturer made the leather into bags and added handles and buckles to the leather. The supplier's terms of sale included a retention of title clause over the finished products. This failed for want of registration as a charge under the then equivalent of the CA 1985 s 395 on the grounds that the leather was so altered that it was no longer merely leather but bags, and the bags were truly the property of the purchaser who had not granted a charge in favour of the seller.

In such a situation nowadays, a prudent seller could attempt to ensure that:

(i)   his contract of sale made it clear that he retained ownership at all times until payment;
(ii) until payment his goods were to be kept in such a way as to show that they were identifiably his and easily separable;
(iii) if the purchaser used the seller's goods to make new products the seller was to be the owner of the products and/or that any sub-sale of the new products by the purchaser was done by the purchaser as agent of the seller.

In such circumstances the purchaser would never have any rights of ownership over the goods and so would be in no position to grant a charge over the goods in favour of the seller. The seller might be able to retrieve his goods or obtain the new finished products from the purchaser. He would then have to account to the purchaser for the purchaser's share in the products.

Three problems arise with this:

(a) Any form of production which alters the seller's goods or makes them inseparable from the finished product means that the products are owned by the purchaser and not by the seller even if the contract between them says otherwise (*Ian Chisholm Textiles Ltd* v *Griffiths* [1994] BCC 96).
(b) It would be surprising if any purchaser would be willing to accept such terms since they so clearly favour the seller. Both seller and purchaser would in any case have to be aware of the effect of the Sale of Goods Act 1979 s 25, whereby if a purchaser sub-sells goods:

(i)   over which there is a retention of title clause, and
(ii) the sub-purchaser is unaware of the retention of title clause, and
(iii) buys the goods in good faith for a proper price,

the sub-purchaser is protected from the effects of the retention of title clause by the Sale of Goods Act 1979 s 25. The sub-purchaser would then be able to retain the goods he had acquired.

(c) One solution to the above difficulties would be to have a clause in the supplier's contract insisting that the purchaser grant a charge in favour of the supplier both over the supplier's goods and any products in which the supplier's goods are used, irrespective of any alteration or the separability of those goods. Even this potential solution has its problems because there might be a pre-existing floating charge forbidding the granting of a charge ranking in priority to the pre-existing floating charge.

As the law in England, Wales and Northern Ireland stands at present, retention of title clauses can pose an intractable problem, mainly because it is very difficult to ascertain a general rule applicable to all circumstances, detailing the exact point at which a supplier's goods cease to be his goods and instead merely become one item within new goods created by the purchaser.

In Scotland retention of title clauses are now fully acceptable – historically there had been difficulties with them – provided the goods are unaltered, identifiable and recoverable. With a well drawn-up retention of title clause the seller retains ownership until payment, and because the seller retains ownership, the purchaser is in no position to grant a security of goods he does not own (*Armour* v *Thyssen Edelstahlwerke*, 1990 SLT 891). However, because of Scots law's Roman law origins, the position is less clear:

(i)   where the seller's goods are affixed to some other goods (*accessio*);
(ii)   where a new product is made of goods including the seller's (*specificatio*);
(iii) where solids are mixed together (*commixtio*);
(iv)   and where liquids are mixed (*confusio*).

Under any of these circumstances it is likely that the retention of title clause would not be effective unless the contract of sale could provide for exclusive ownership for the seller of any product arising from one of the above four situations. Failing exclusive ownership, there should be a clause in the contract of sale requiring the purchaser to grant a charge in favour of the seller of the sale proceeds. Even this is not wholly satisfactory, and, for much the same reasons as in English law, the position is unclear. However, as again with English law, the Sale of Goods Act 1979 s 25 (detailed in the English law section above) acts to protect sub-purchasers acting in good faith, paying a proper price for the goods and unaware of the retention of title clause.

That the law on retention of title clauses is unsatisfactory in both England and Scotland is not surprising. This issue poses a problem for any legal system. At what point should a seller have to relinquish his rights in goods he has sold but has not yet been paid for? Most would agree that a sub-purchaser buying in good faith without notice of any retention of title agreement should be protected in the manner of the Sale of Goods Act 1979 s 25. But if almost every supplier had an extended retention of title clause, there might be little left for receivers or liquidators or for those unsecured creditors, such as suppliers of utilities, the nature of whose business precludes retention of title clauses. If receivers found they were losing out, the cost of borrowing might rise.

What often happens in practice is that where there is a retention of title clause that is clearly effective in that the goods are still identifiable, unaltered, separable and recoverable by the seller, most receivers or liquidators would accept that the supplier should recover his goods if he has not been paid. If the goods are not obviously identifiable, unaltered or recoverable, receivers or liquidators may be more prepared to take a commercial view of the strength of the seller's position and the depth of the seller's pockets. A receiver acting for a finance institution could afford to argue about the matter longer than an impoverished supplier. Consequently, the supplier may, as a commercial fact of life, have to settle for less than the full value of his claim because the cost of litigation will be too high.

Preferential creditors

These will be dealt with in greater detail in Chapter 20, but in essence these are debts mainly in respect of taxes and employees' wages which have to be paid to the Inland Revenue and to employees out of the sums gathered in by the receiver appointed by a floating charge-holder. The full list of the preferential creditors is to be found at Schedule 6 to the IA 1986. Only after the preferential creditors have been satisfied can the balance be paid by the receiver to the floating charge-holder. Sometimes the preferential creditors take the major part of the monies otherwise available to the floating charge-holder, much to the dissatisfaction of the floating charge-holder. The presence of extensive preferential debts can make the floating charge-holder's chances of recouping his losses much slimmer. Preferential creditors only have priority over floating charge-holders. If the charge-holder has a fixed charge, he does not need to concern himself about preferential creditors.

In *Re Brightlife Ltd* [1987] Ch 200, artful drafting by the debenture-holder allowed the debenture-holder to give a notice converting the floating charge in its favour into a fixed charge a week before liquidation commenced. That meant that when liquidation occurred, the floating charge was already converted into a fixed charge and therefore did not have to suffer the preferential debts. This was subsequently struck at by the IA 1986 s 251 which states that any charge created as a floating charge (despite any subsequent conversion) is treated as a floating charge in the context of transactions at an undervalue and preferences in England and Wales – and can therefore be struck down by the liquidator or be treated as a floating charge and suffer the depredations of the preferential debts.

Judgment creditors in England, Wales and Northern Ireland
A judgment creditor is someone who has successfully raised an action against a company for payment of a debt, and has taken steps to enforce the judgment against the debtor company. He can do this by means of a garnishee order, which involves the removal of funds from a company's bank account for payment to the creditor. He could obtain a charging order which is a form of charges against the debtor company's land and buildings and which prevents it selling the land and buildings until the debt is paid. Alternatively bailiffs or sheriffs can remove assets of the debtor company and sell them to defray the debt.

Landlords can also distrain for rent, *i.e.* sell certain of the debtor company's tangible assets to pay for the outstanding rent.

All of these take priority over the receivership provided they have been completed prior to the crystallisation of the floating charge. Unlike a liquidator, a receiver cannot challenge the judgment creditors, and the floating charge-holder may thereby obtain less from the receivership than he expected.

In Northern Ireland judgment debts are enforced by the Enforcement of Judgments Office under the Judgments Enforcement (Northern Ireland) Order 1981. The Office has power to make similar enforcement orders to those listed here except for the power of the landlord to distrain for rent arrears, which has been abolished in Northern Ireland.

Effectually executed diligence in Scotland
This is the Scottish equivalent of the above section. Where a creditor has obtained a decree against a company, that decree can be enforced by various means including arrestment (the seizing of assets in the hands of a third party, such as the company's money in a bank account), poinding (pronounced "pinding", and being the enforced sale by sheriff officers or messengers at arms of the debtor company's assets by means of a public auction or roup), inhibition (an order against the debtor company preventing it selling land and buildings until the debt is paid). Any of these, if properly completed prior to the attachment of a floating charge, take precedence over the receivership, and diminish the sums due to the floating charge-holder. Effectually executed diligence cannot be challenged by a receiver.

Hire-purchased goods
A receiver may be appointed over a company, only to find that some of the company's assets are in fact subject to a hire-purchase agreement. Those assets then belong to the hire-purchase company and not the company in receivership, and the hire-purchase company is entitled to retrieve them.

Undisclosed charges

Charges arising by operation of law, such as a repairer's lien, or the right of the unpaid seller to retain goods, may take precedence over a receiver. In Scotland a landlord's hypothec also takes priority, provided it is in place before the appointment of the receiver (*Grampian Regional Council* v *Drill Stem (Inspection Services) in receivership*, 1994 SCLR 36 (Sh Ct)).

Invalid charges

Lack of registration

Any charge not registered within 21 days of execution will not be a secured charge and will be void against a liquidator, administrator or creditors (CA 1985 ss 395 and 410).

Gifts by the company in England and Wales

In the context of a winding-up or an administration order, if a company within certain time periods grants a charge for more than the value of the asset secured, so that in effect the company is making a gift or partial gift to the recipient of the gift (the "donee"), the gift is said, in England and Wales, to be a transaction at an undervalue (IA 1986 s 238). By making a charge in favour of a donee, the donee will be able to realise his security, thus diminishing the pool of assets available to the company's other creditors. It might be very tempting for a company director, who might wish to prevent the general body of creditors getting their hands on his company's assets, to give his spouse, or someone else close to him, some valuable company asset in order to keep it out of the creditors' grasp. However, any charge which is ascertained to be a transaction at any undervalue may be struck down by the courts on the application of the liquidator or administrator.

While not all such charges are invalid, in England and Wales they may be invalid if:

(a) the company has had an administration order granted over it, or
(b) the company has gone into liquidation (IA 1986 s 238(1)),

and the donee is either:

(c) a connected person (a director or associate), in which case any such charges within the preceding two years (IA 1986 s 240(1)(a)) can be set aside on application to the court (IA 1986 s 238(3)), or
(d) any other person, in which case any such charges within the preceding six months (IA 1986 s 240(1)(b)) can be set aside on application to the court (IA 1986 s 238(3))

or if the charge is granted at any time between the presentation of a petition for the making of an administration order and the granting of an administration order (IA 1986 s 240(1)(c)).

While any such charge is potentially able to be set aside if the donee is a connected person, if the donee is not a connected person the charge will only be invalid if:

(e) the company was unable to pay its debts at the time of the granting of the charge (IA 1986 s 240(2)(a)), or
(f) the transaction for which the charge was granted made the company unable to pay its debts (IA 1986 s 240(2)(b)).

If the donee is a connected person, the company or the donee has to prove that at the timing of the granting of the charge, the company was able to pay its debts or was able to pay its debts despite the granting of the charge (IA 1986 s 240(2)). This is deliberately intended to place the connected donee at a disadvantage. However, if the court is satisfied that the charge relative to the gift was given in good faith by the company, and that the company believed that it would benefit its business, the charge will stand (IA 1986 s 238(5)).

Preferences in England and Wales
In the context of a winding-up or an administration order, a preference is the repayment, within certain time periods, of one creditor, or the granting of some form of security (in this context a charge) in favour of that creditor, so that that creditor is in a better position than he might otherwise have been when the company goes into insolvent liquidation. This is seen as unfair to other creditors of the company. It commonly arises in the context of a loan by a director to the company. If the company looks as though it may not be able to repay his loan, a director might well wish to obtain the benefit of a floating charge to safeguard his loan at the expense of the other creditors. By this means he would be repaid his loan even if other creditors were not. However, any charge granted to a connected person, or any other person as the case may be, which is designed to afford that person a preference (IA 1986 s 239(5)) may be set aside by the courts (IA 1986 s 239(3)) provided it comes within the terms of the rules (a) to (f) applicable to transactions at an undervalue in the preceding section. However, the good faith requirement and the belief that the preference will benefit the company (as specified in IA 1986 s 238(5)) do not apply in the context of preferences. This is because the concept of preference implies a deliberate intention to act without good faith towards the other creditors.

Gratuitous alienations in Scotland
In the context of a liquidation or an administration order, a transaction by a company within certain time periods at an undervalue is known as a gratuitous

alienation in Scotland. The reasons for prohibiting gratuitous alienations are the same as those preventing transfers at an undervalue in England and Wales (to which reference should be made). The law on charges in respect of these is stricter in Scotland than in England and Wales. Charges which are ascertained to be gratuitous alienations can be set aside by the courts if they are within five years of insolvency if they were granted to connected persons or two years to anyone else (IA 1986 s 242(3)). However, if the donee can prove that when the charge was granted in his favour:

(a) the company's assets were greater than its liabilities (IA 1986 s 242(4)(a)), or
(b) the charge was not a gift at all but was properly paid for (IA 1986 s 242(4)(b)), or
(c) the gift was (endearingly) a birthday, Christmas or some other gift suitable for a special occasion (IA 1986 s 242(4)(c)(i)), or
(d) the gift was a charitable one to someone not connected with the company and was a reasonable gift for the company to make (IA 1986 s 242(4)(c)(ii))

the charge will still be a valid charge.

Unfair preferences in Scotland
What is a preference in England and Wales is known as an unfair preference in Scotland. The reasons for the rules prohibiting unfair preferences are the same as the English law rules prohibiting preferences (to which reference should be made). Any charge given in respect of an unfair preference within six months of a company's winding-up or the making of an administration order can be reduced (*i.e.* set aside) by the courts (IA 1986 s 243(5)), unless it was:

(a) a transaction in the ordinary course of business (IA 1986 s 243(2)(a));
(b) a debt due and payable, unless it was collusively done in order to prejudice other creditors (IA 1986 s 243(2)(b));
(c) part of some reciprocal obligations between the company and the preferred creditor (unless it was collusively done to prejudice the other creditors) (IA 1986 s 243(2)(c));
(d) the grant of instructions by the company to a third party to pay out funds that had been arrested (*i.e.* seized following due process of law) in the hands of that third party to the creditor (IA 1986 s 243(2)(d)).

Transactions at an undervalue and preferences in Northern Ireland
Under the Insolvency (Northern Ireland) Order 1989, ("I(NI)O 1989") charges which are transactions at an undervalue may be struck at in the same manner as in England and Wales (I(NI)O 1989 art 202), the same applies to preferences (I(NI)O 1989 art 203).

Avoidance of floating charges in all jurisdictions in the context of a company's insolvency or administration
Under the IA 1986 s 245 a floating charge over the company's undertaking or property will be invalid if:

(a) it is granted within two years of the company's insolvency to someone who is connected (*i.e.* a director or associate) with the company (IA 1986 s 245(3)(a)); or
(b) it is granted at any time between the presentation of a petition for the making of an administration order and the making of that order (IA 1986 s 245(3)(c)).

Where the charge is granted within 12 months of insolvency to a person not connected with the company (IA 1986 s 245(3)(b)), the charge will be invalid if:

(c) at the time of granting the security the company was unable to pay its debts in terms of the IA 1986 s 123 (see Chapter 21) (IA 1986 s 245(4)(a)), or
(d) the company became unable to pay its debts because of the transaction for which the charge was granted (IA 1986 s 245(4)(b)).

Despite the above, any floating charge may still be valid if the charge was granted in respect of:

(e) monies paid, or goods or services supplied at the same time or after the creation of the charge (IA 1986 s 245(2)(a)); or
(f) the value of any reduction or discharge of debt of the company in exchange for which the charge was granted (IA 1986 s 245(2)(b)); or
(g) any interest payable in respect of (e) or (f) above (IA 1986 s 245(2)(c)).

What this section is designed to achieve is to prevent those close to the company (directors and associates) from being able to obtain a floating charge protecting their own transactions with the company at the expense of other creditors. A well known fraud used to involve the company directors taking a floating charge over the company's assets to protect their own loans to the company. If the company went into liquidation, they could appoint a receiver who would be able to sell off the company's assets to repay the company directors' loans. Such a ruse is still possible provided the charge has been in existence for at least two years and provided the company directors are aware of the risks of being caught by the Company Directors Disqualification Act 1986 or such other provisions of the IA 1986 such as the wrongful trading provisions at s 214. To avoid those latter problems company directors sometimes make sure the loan is in the name of a director's spouse – who is not a director.

The second effect of s 245 is that while a charge may be validly granted for a new loan or a new transaction, or the new reduction or discharge of a loan, it is not valid for a creditor to obtain a preferential position for an old loan relative to other creditors. If a creditor wants a security for a loan he should ask for it at the time it is made. To ask for it later places him in a better position than other creditors. Furthermore, if every creditor was able to obtain a retrospective security in this manner it would be difficult to work out which security related to which transaction. So a charge is only valid for the new loan or transaction it relates to.

In Northern Ireland the equivalent legislation is to be found in the I(NI)O 1989 art 207.

Proposals for reform of the law relating to charges

In 1989 the Government, anxious to save money for the Treasury, enacted the Companies Act 1989 which amongst other reforms was meant substantially to reform the rules applying to the registration of securities. In his report ("A Review of Security Interests in Property" 1989 HMSO) Professor Diamond had suggested that the issue of certificates or registration of charges was putting the Government into a difficult position in the event that a charge was registered when it should not have been – or indeed, that one was not registered when it should have been. Massive damages might become payable. The issue of charge certificates as effective guarantees of a charge's certainty was a potential drain on the Exchequer.

Furthermore, Companies House could save much money by taking away the time-consuming and expensive business of having an army of clerks checking the thousands of charges that arrive every day by post. In this connection it is interesting to note that there have been new DTI proposals to charge companies for having their charges registered.

The 1989 legislation, (Part IV of the Companies Act 1989) on the strength of the Diamond report, proposed that the law relating to the registration of charges be substantially changed. However, Part IV of the Companies Act 1989 has not been enacted and apparently is unlikely to be. Among the proposals were:

(i) that the Government no longer provide a guarantee of a charge's validity: all it would provide is a certificate confirming that the charge was lodged within a 21-day period, but the accuracy of its contents would not be guaranteed;

(ii) that late registration of a charge be permitted, providing no liquidator, administrator or creditors had properly exercised his rights over the company's assets secured by the charge;

(iii) that it became easier to amend a charge or correct an inaccurate charge by providing further particulars of the charge.

Some of these proposals have generally been welcomed. It is, for example, unsatisfactory that at present the only way to register a charge late is to petition the court. What proved the most controversial point, however, was the demise of the issue of the effective guarantee by the Registrar of Companies confirming that the registration of the charge is valid. The intention was to put the lawyers on their mettle and make them draft the charges so well that the charges would be faultless, or more cynically, that if there was a problem with the registered charge, the client could then sue the lawyer, not the Registrar of Companies.

The lawyers responded to this by saying such a course of action would result in higher fees because of the increased risk of a claim against them and the consequent high cost of indemnity premiums; that it would lead to litigation and that it was strange of the Government to promote a policy that would increase the workload of the civil courts rather than diminish it; that it was bad for commerce as it led to uncertainty generally; and that it was against the national interest as bankers would clearly prefer to lend in countries where a charge certificate was a valid certificate. Bankers took the view that the new proposals increased their risk.

Companies House employees may well also have been unhappy as the new proposals might possibly have led to job losses.

Finally the lawyers stated that if they were to be seen as the ones who were bearing much of the risk, then as far as registration of land mortgages in England and Wales and standard securities in Scotland were concerned, they would copy onto the then proposed new Forms M395 and M410 (replacing the existing Forms 395 and 410 used for registering charges) all the documentation and wording coming from the Government's own property registers. As Government offices guarantee the title to land ownership in areas covered by the Land Registry in England and the Land Register in Scotland, any liability for errors would find its way back to the Government again. The solicitors' suggestions were not well received by the Land Registry or the Land Register.

At the time of writing, extensive negotiations are taking place, and the relevant sections of the Companies Act 1989 (ss 92 to 107) relating to the registration of charges have not yet been brought into force. It is generally agreed that there is room for improvement and clarification of the whole registration procedure: further reform proposals are therefore expected. The DTI has published consultation papers in respect of registration of charges generally and the creation of new types of charge in Scotland. The uncertain position of negative pledges in England and Wales; the restrictive rules for missing the 21-day registration period; the absence of compulsory memoranda of satisfaction of discharged charges; the ambiguities of (English) charges which are described simultaneously as "fixed and floating": all these and other issues are well known to be unsatisfactory and await further attention by the Government.

Summary

1. If a company wishes to borrow money it may need to provide the lender with a charge over an asset or assets of the company. The assets can then be sold by the lender to repay the loan if the company fails to do so.

2. An acknowledgement of debt by a company is generally known as a debenture. Debentures commonly incorporate a charge (either fixed or floating or both) over assets of the company. Debentures attract a fixed rate of interest and will repay a fixed sum on redemption. Debentures in quoted companies, sometimes known as bonds, can be traded on the stock market in the same manner as other securities. Unlike shares, they can be issued at a discount. The debentures of a private company cannot be traded in this manner.

3. Most charges granted by companies need to be registered with the Registrar of Companies within 21 days of the granting of the charge. Failure to register the charge makes it void against a liquidator, administrator or other creditors. Registration makes it clear to the outside world what of the company's assets are already charged and therefore not available to a liquidator in the event of a company's insolvency. Registration also provides a degree of certainty for the charge-holder that his charge is a valid one.

4. Fixed charges are charges that can only be released with the consent of the charge-holder. The company is thus normally unable to sell assets subject to a fixed charge, though the company is entitled to the reversionary interest on the discharge of the charge. Common fixed charges are legal mortgages over real property in England, Wales and Northern Ireland, and standard securities over heritage in Scotland. Charges over real property and heritage require additional registration in the appropriate registers of land ownership. On default by the company the charge-holder can take over the property subject to the charge and sell it to recover its loss.

5. Floating charges are charges over the assets of a company even though those assets may be changing from time to time in the course of the company's business. Such charges are particularly useful for companies that have no assets for which a fixed charge would be suitable. If the company defaults on the terms of the floating charge, the floating charge-holder will be entitled to appoint an administrative receiver, or in Scotland a receiver, who will gather in the assets caught by the floating charge. He will then sell those assets to pay any debts due to the floating charge-holder from the company. Floating charges are subject to the payment of preferential debts.

6. Normally the order of priority of charges is that the earliest in time take precedence, and fixed charges have precedence over floating charges – unless there is an agreement that says otherwise. Some floating charges prohibit the company from granting any other prior-ranking charges by means of negative pledges.

7. Sometimes charges will be found to be defeated by other creditors or persons with a better right to the assets gathered in by the administrative receiver or receiver. In addition, other floating charges may be invalid if granted within certain time-limits prior to a company's insolvent liquidation or administration. The rules on this vary according to whether the chargeholder is connected with the company or any other person.

8. It is well recognised that the current system or registration of charges is not entirely satisfactory. The 21-day rule can be too severe, and it is not clear why some charges are registrable and others are not.

18. MEETINGS AND SHAREHOLDER DEMOCRACY

Types of meetings – the need for meetings – methods of limiting members' opportunities for unwelcome criticism – who can go to meetings? – the rules relating to annual general meetings – the rules relating to extraordinary general meetings – class meetings – board meetings – procedure at meetings generally – types of resolutions – written resolutions

Any association of people, whether a sports club, a political party or a town council needs to have regular meetings at which the following matters may be discussed:

- the accounts of the association;

- the appointment of managers or office bearers of the association;

- a review of the year's activities and prospects for the future;

- any alterations to the constitution of the association.

A company is no different. The rules relating to the organisation and operation of meetings are set out in the CA 1985 and in the company's articles of association. These rules must in general be followed strictly. If they are not, the decisions approved at company meetings may be invalid.

Types of meeting

In company law there are several different types of meetings. They comprise:

- annual general meetings ("AGMs");

- extraordinary general meetings ("EGMs");

- class meetings;

- board meetings.

A general meeting is any meeting to which all the members of the company are invited. Most companies hold an annual general meetings at which it is common to present the annual accounts and directors' report on the company's activities before the members.

Any meeting to which all the members are invited but which is not described as an annual general meeting is an extraordinary general meeting (Table A art 36).

A class meeting is a meeting of all the members of a given class of shares, and in many respects is organised in the same manner as a general meeting unless the articles state otherwise.

A board meeting is a meeting of the board of directors. Only the directors are present (though the company secretary may attend) and members are not normally permitted to see the board minutes.

It is open to companies to have such other types of meetings as they may choose to have, provided such meetings are permitted under the memorandum or articles of association. Such meetings will, however, not be regulated by statute and the company will have to devise its own procedure for organising them. Such procedure would normally be contained in the articles.

The need for company meetings

Under art 70 of Table A directors are given considerable power to manage their companies, subject to the provisions of the CA 1985, the memorandum and articles, and any directions given by special resolution. Although many companies vary art 70, most companies will have an article that allows the directors similar powers. Those powers are nonetheless circumscribed to prevent the directors taking all the decisions that affect the company. Some decisions, under statute, the memorandum or the articles, can only be taken by the company in general meeting (or, alternatively, in the case of a private company only, by written resolution), which means that the members must be consulted and must approve the decisions. For example, the alteration of the company's articles can only take place following the passing, by a 75% majority of those members voting and entitled to vote in person or in proxy, of a special resolution (CA 1985 s 9). However much directors might wish to be able to alter the articles themselves, such an alteration is not valid without members' approval obtained at a general meeting, or, alternatively, in the case of a private company only, by means of a written resolution. This does not prevent the directors, in their personal capacity as members, from voting to alter the articles. But they do so as members, not as directors.

There are other reasons for holding members' meetings regularly. These include:

(i) Directors, by virtue of their privileged position, may believe that they are best placed to run the company. Their belief may not in fact be justified, and meetings give the members the opportunity to make the directors justify their actions. Sadly in some companies there is sometimes a "them and us" attitude displayed by members and directors towards each other: the members view directors as arrogant and only interested in their own remuneration; the directors view members, particularly those with a small shareholding as less significant members, administratively inconvenient, ignorant of business and fickle.

(ii) Unscrupulous directors are often tempted to use their companies' assets as their own. Directors can be called to account at members' meetings to prevent such practices.

(iii) The members are the ones who contributed to its capital. It is only reasonable that they should have some say in what is done with the money that they invested in the company. Members may not wish to be involved in every commercial decision – that being a job for the directors – but they will wish to be involved if there is anything that affects the constitution of the company, their investment in the company or the senior management of the company.

(iv) Certain personal actions by the directors need disclosure to and the approval of the members. Such actions include the purchase by the company of assets owned by the directors in their personal capacity (CA 1985 s 320). This is to prevent the directors taking advantage of the company – though directors are normally allowed to vote in their own interests if they are also members of the company.

(v) Directors of unprofitable companies may be tempted to mislead investors about their companies' prospects. General meetings provide a forum to force the directors to divulge information on the basis of which the investors can take an informed decision whether or not to continue their investment.

(vi) Directors of large listed companies can sometimes become distanced from the practices and effects of the business that they run. Shareholder criticism, sometimes coupled with employee shareholder criticism, may force the directors to gain a more realistic view of the company's need for improvements.

The above paragraphs give the impression that members and directors are always at loggerheads. Naturally this is not the case, but should it be the case, general meetings offer legally constituted occasions when any differences can be aired. While this may be true of meetings generally, the efficiency and effect of meetings may in practice depend on the size and type of company in question. For example:

• The directors of many small companies are also their sole members, so disputes will be rare. Accordingly general meetings of such companies will be of little significance.

- On a wider scale, if some investors in a major listed company are unhappy about the directors, they are more likely to raise the issue quietly and discreetly in private meetings with selected other members and the directors than battle it out in the full view of the press and the other members. A public slanging match does little for the credibility of the major investors, the company itself or the directors. It may also drive the share price of the company down.

- When general meetings of publicly quoted companies are held, it is often the case that the important procedural matters required under the Companies Acts are not greatly heeded by the minority members, often because the issues are too complicated and boring or because it does not immediately affect the members' dividends.

- Another issue involving minority shareholders is that the major investors (commonly the institutions) are unlikely to pay much attention to them precisely because they are smaller investors. Indeed, there have been many complaints by minority investors about the high level of directors' pay and the extent of directors' pay-offs on dismissal, yet the lesser investors' objections are easily overruled by the far greater voting power of the institutions. This leads to a cynical attitude amongst lesser investors as to major investors' own motives. This issue was addressed to some extent in the Cadbury and Greenbury Reports discussed in Chapter 14.

- Where minority members wish to air a grievance, or believe that some matter should receive more attention than perhaps the directors are willing to give it, they may have to fund their own campaign themselves without the benefit of any legal aid or an indemnity from the company – unless perhaps if they are successful. "Making a fuss" about some action proposed by the directors may be prohibitively expensive – as the directors, backed by the company's funds, often well know.

- Where member are also employees, it may be unwise for those employees to criticise the directors.

- Most general meetings are not particularly interesting anyway. From some companies' point of view, a good meeting is a quiet one. Because of this, and the fact that meetings are often held during working hours when only the most interested or the unemployed can be present, general meetings are not widely attended. However, some company meetings are well attended particularly by lobby groups, using their shares to protest about environmental issues or human rights issues.

- Many members do not care very much about meetings anyway. They just want a good return on their investment.

Method of limiting members' opportunities for unwelcome criticism

Few directors welcome trenchant criticism, and the ability to handle awkward questions gracefully is not always given to chairmen of leading companies. However, skillful drafting of the articles, or the presence of substantial majority shareholders may prevent objecting shareholders from doing much other than lay their objections.

- The articles may provide that apart from certain obligatory matters, such as the tabling of the accounts and the reappointment of the auditors, only "competent business" may be discussed at meetings. In these circumstances, the articles might perhaps provide that "competent" means questions which have been notified to the company secretary three or more weeks in advance, or which have to be supported by a minimum number of members.

  This prevents awkward questions being sprung on the directors, as impromptu questions will be ruled incompetent and out of order by the chairman. What is meant by "competent" may vary from company to company.

- The directors may be the majority shareholders. They are thus in a position to approve their own actions, except where there is clear evidence of fraud or unfairly prejudicial conduct directed towards a minority. If there is, the minority can use the provisions of the CA 1985 ss 459–461 to obtain a suitable remedy, or if necessary, seek to put the company into liquidation under the IA 1986 s 122(1)(g).

- The directors may, in their personal capacity as members, have the benefit of weighted voting. Weighted voting means that, according to the articles, on certain specified occasions a particular member's votes will count, say, for five times their normal voting power. This first case example of this arose in the case of *Bushell* v *Faith* [1970] AC 1099, where a director was entitled to three times his normal votes in the event of a resolution to dismiss that director, or a resolution to alter the articles to remove the weighted voting rights. This made the removal of Mr Faith as a director practically impossible because his multiple voting power was greater than the votes of those who wished to have him removed as a director. The courts held that such voting rights were acceptable.

- Another ingenious trick is to have the presence of a director or a majority member named in the articles as being necessary for a quorum. In other words, if the named director absents himself from a meeting, the meeting is inquorate, and no decisions passed at that meeting will be valid. This could also be achieved by means of a shareholder agreement, whereby a majority of the members agree always to vote in a certain way, thus preventing the minority shareholders succeeding in their objections.

- A less reputable technique is for the directors to arrange for nominated individuals or stooges to ask suitably flattering questions during the meeting, in order to minimise the opportunities for others to ask embarrassing questions.

The above devious methods, although affording temporary protection for the directors and/or majority shareholders at general meetings, may in the long run be counter-productive. Companies with restrictive articles that prevent open discussion of problems will tend to ossify, to be run autocratically and to be unable to adapt to unfamiliar circumstances. Furthermore, new investors would be unwilling to invest in companies where they have little or no say or faith in what takes place. However, it is also true that provided there is a satisfactory return on their investment, many investors will not be concerned by their lack of opportunity to play an active part in the management of the company.

Who can go to meetings?

Those who go to company meetings fall into two categories. Those who go to general or class meetings as members are said to be present. Those who go to a meeting in some other capacity, such as the company secretary, the auditor or an expert called to speak to the meeting, are said to be in attendance. Minutes of a company meeting should state who was present and who was in attendance.

General meetings

Under Table A art 38 the following are entitled to go to a general meeting:

- members with voting rights;
- persons entitled to a share in consequence of the death or bankruptcy of a member;
- the auditor;
- the directors;
- the company secretary.

For major companies the press are often invited as well as that they can report on the proceedings.

Class meetings

Unless the articles provide otherwise, only members of the class of members are entitled to go to class meetings, along with the company secretary and persons representing dead or bankrupt members. As before, the directors and company secretary can vote only if they are members of the class.

Board meetings

Only directors are entitled to go to meetings of the board of directors. The company secretary will attend in his capacity as company secretary, though he can vote as a director if he is also a director – except in the case of a single member company, with a sole director, since a sole director cannot also be the company secretary (CA 1985 s 283(2)). A board meeting of a single member, sole director company need not have the company secretary in attendance (though it is prudent to have him there) but there must nevertheless be a written record of any resolution taken by the director at his board meeting.

Annual general meetings

AGMs are held annually by definition, but unless the articles say otherwise what is dealt with at an AGM could equally well be dealt with at an EGM. As a matter of convention it is common to find the following matters dealt with at an AGM:

- the tabling of the accounts and the directors' report for the last financial year;
- the approval of any dividend recommended by the directors;
- the reappointment of auditors or appointment of new auditors;
- the direction to the directors to fix the auditors' remuneration;
- the re-election or election of directors.

Tabling of the accounts and directors' report

For details of the accounts and the contents of directors' reports, see Chapter 11. Strictly speaking the accounts merely have to be presented to the company in general meeting (CA 1985 s 241(1)). There is no requirement to have the accounts approved. However, it is very common for the members to be asked to approve the accounts.

Declaration of dividend

Under Table A art 102 the members may reduce the amount of the dividend suggested by the directors but may not increase it. If the directors do not recommend a dividend, the members cannot do so.

Appointment of auditors

This is dealt with in Chapter 16.

The remuneration of auditors

By convention, the fee to be paid to the auditors is agreed by the members at a general meeting. However, under the CA 1985 s 390A(1) the members are allowed to delegate that task to the board of directors.

The election or re-election of directors

In a company using arts 73–80 of Table A, at the first AGM of the company all the directors resign and make themselves eligible for re-election. Each year thereafter in turn one-third of the directors retire and may put themselves forward for re-election. Any directors brought in to fill a casual vacancy also need to be formally elected onto the board. Other companies may have different rules under their articles.

The organisation of a AGM

Normally the AGM is held round about the same date each year, but strictly speaking there can be up to 15 months between one AGM and the next (CA 1985 s 366(3)). An AGM must be held each calendar year (CA 1985 s 366(1)) though the gap between incorporation and the first AGM may, in an exception to the rules in s 366(1) and (3), be as great as 18 months (CA 1985 s 366(2)). This can lead to the following situation: ABC Ltd is incorporated on 1 October 19X3. It need not hold an AGM in 19X3. Nor need it hold an AGM in 19X4. But it must hold its first AGM by 31 March 19X5. In order to call an AGM, the directors normally hold a board meeting at which they instruct the company secretary to inform the members of the forthcoming AGM. The calling of a meeting is known as convening a meeting. Normally an AGM is convened by sending the members and others entitled to attend the AGM a notice convening the meeting. The notice must state that the meeting is an AGM (CA 1985 s 366(1)).

Other methods of calling an AGM

If the directors are unable or unwilling to call an AGM (or any general meeting), the Secretary of State, on the application of any member, may call or arrange the calling of an AGM (CA 1985 s 367).

It is also possible under the CA 1985 s 371 for any member or any director to apply to the court to obtain an order that a general meeting be held, on such terms as the court sees fit. The court can also make an order on its own motion.

A court-ordered meeting is only likely to occur where there is no other method of calling a meeting, perhaps because of some complicated provision of the articles which the members cannot overcome, such as the physical impossibility of obtaining a quorum.

Avoidance of AGMs

If a private company has passed an elective resolution under the CA 1985 s 366A(1) it is possible for it to dispense with holding AGMs entirely. Such an elective resolution continues in force until such time as any member decides that he does wish the company to hold an AGM. In that event, within three months of the end of the calendar year he must serve notice of his desire for the company to hold an AGM (CA 1985 s 366A(3)).

Length of notice for calling AGMs

Under the CA 1985 s 369(1) the members must receive at least 21 days' notice in writing of the date of the meeting. This is normally seen as clear days notice, *i.e.* exclusive of the day the notice is sent out and exclusive of the day of the meeting (Table A art 38). Following the case of *Aberdeen Combworks Co Ltd, Petitioners*, (1902) 10 SLT 210, in Scotland alone the clear days do include the day of the meeting itself if the articles are drafted to that effect. Any provisions in articles of a company which provided for less than 21 days' notice would be void (CA 1985 s 369(1)). However, it is possible, if all the members entitled to attend and vote agree, to hold an AGM at lesser notice (CA 1985 s 369(3)(a)). The agreement is usually confirmed by having a specific consent to short notice form signed by all the members. This means that the members do not have to wait for 21 days before holding the AGM.

The reason for the 21-day period was originally to permit members to have plenty of time to consult their professional advisers as to the matters to be discussed at the AGM.

The notice must be sent to all those entitled to receive the notice as indicated above, but the accidental omission to send the notice, or the failure by a member to receive it, does not invalidate the proceedings of the meeting (Table A art 39). The notice must indicate the date, time and place of the meeting (Table A art 38).

Contents of the notice

In addition to the above and the statement that the meeting is an AGM, the notice must specify the general nature of the business to be transacted (Table A art 38). Any special or extraordinary resolutions must be stated as such (CA 1985 s 378(1), (2)).

It is open to members to demand that a resolution be considered at a meeting. This is known as requisitioning a resolution.

Requisitioning of resolutions

The requisition procedure is normally only necessary where the directors are unwilling to include a particular resolution on the agenda for the meeting. One reason for their unwillingness might be that the resolution is critical of the directors, or calls for their dismissal.

In order to requisition a resolution, the requisitionists (those requisitioning the resolution) must:

(a) either hold 5% of the voting rights of all those entitled to vote, or
(b) together amount to 100 shareholders each of whom on average have paid £100 to the company by way of share capital (CA 1985 s 376(2)).

The requisitionists must lodge a copy of the proposed resolution, signed by all the requisitionists, at the registered office of the company at least six weeks prior to the annual general meeting (CA 1985 s 377(1)(a)(i)). The date of the next general meeting will normally be obtainable from the minutes of the previous general meeting.

The six-week period is designed to allow the directors time to include the resolution in the notice of the meeting to be sent out to the members. The resolution itself will be highlighted in the notice as having been requisitioned by members. If it is not practicable to send out the terms of the requisitioned resolution to the members in the notice of the AGM, it must be sent out as soon as convenient thereafter (CA 1985 s 376(5)). Under the CA 1985 s 376(1)(a) the company is obliged to send the members notice of the resolution, along with a statement of up to 1,000 words in length about the resolution, albeit at the expense of the requisitioning members. The statement must not serve as a vehicle for needless defamatory matter. If the court agrees that the matter is defamatory, the company is not obliged to send it to the members (CA 1985 s 377(3)).

Unscrupulous directors might be tempted to get round these rules by bringing forward the date of the AGM so that the requisitionist's six-week notice to the company becomes out of time. This might mean that the requisitionists' resolution could not be heard. Unfortunately for directors, CA 1985 s 377(2) states that where the AGM is brought forward in this manner, the requisitionists' notice is still deemed to be in time. Curiously, the complete failure by the directors to do anything about the requisitioned resolution merely results in a fine (CA 1985 s 367(7)) – if the police ever choose to become involved. This is in contrast to the requisitioning of an EGM discussed later.

Other information on notices of AGMs

Notices of AGMs should indicate the authority of the person sending out the notice of the meeting, commonly the company secretary. He will state that he acts "By order of the Board" or the court or the Secretary of State as the case may be. He will indicate the date of the notice, the registered office of the company, and the right of a member to appoint a proxy, who need not be a member, to attend and vote in the member's place (CA 1985 s 372(3)).

Proxies

A proxy is a substitute for a member who cannot be present. Under the CA 1985 s 372(1) a proxy can attend and vote on behalf of another person, but only in a private company can a proxy speak on behalf of the absent member. This was apparently originally to prevent members hiring barristers or advocates to harangue and bamboozle the other members at general meetings of public companies.

It is possible in some companies (depending on their articles) to have different proxies for different issues, but it is quite common for company articles to follow the forms laid out in Table A arts 60 and 61. Art 60 allows a member to appoint a nominated person (commonly the chairman) as the proxy, with the proxy voting as the proxy sees fit; art 61 contains a definite instruction to make the proxy vote in specific ways for specific resolutions. As the chairman can often end up as a proxy for a large number of members all voting in different ways, it is common for the articles to require proxy forms to be sent in to the company in advance so that the votes the chairman will be casting on behalf of his members can be sorted out and allocated to the various resolutions. It is not permitted for companies to have articles that say the proxy forms must be handed in more than 48 hours before the meeting (CA 1985 s 372(5)). This is to prevent unscrupulous companies having articles that could demand that proxy forms be handed in, say, at least two weeks before the meeting, thus limiting the opportunities for all but the most organised members to vote. Proxies are entitled to call for a poll (CA 1985 s 373(2)).

Corporate representatives

A company is obviously physically unable to attend a meeting of another company, so under the CA 1985 s 375(1) it can send someone on its behalf to speak and vote for the company. That person is known as a corporate representative and normally has to confirm his presence with the company secretary by producing a certificate of his authority from his own company's board of directors.

Extraordinary general meetings

In many respects EGMs operate in the same way as AGMs. Most of the rules applying to AGMs, such as those relating to proxies, votes and quorums, apply to EGMs. EGMs can be called:

- by the directors instructing the company secretary to convene an EGM (as with an AGM);

- by the court under the CA 1985 s 371 (as with an AGM);

- on a requisition by the members under the CA 1985 s 368;

- on a requisition by the auditors under the CA 1985 s 392A.

Convening any general meeting can be an expensive business, particularly for a large company with many shareholders, all of whom have to be written to. It is not therefore lightly undertaken, and companies will generally try to carry over any business until the next AGM if they can. However, if a company needs the approval of its members for a certain course of action, such as issuing new shares or buying back its own shares, it will have no option but to convene an EGM.

If the company is a public limited company and its net assets fall to one-half or less of its called-up share capital the directors, within 28 days of becoming aware of the fact, are obliged to convene an EGM within 56 days of their awareness of the fact (CA 1985 s 142(1)). At the EGM the company is supposed to consider what steps should be taken to deal with the situation.

EGMs can take place at any time, but they only require 14 days' notice unless the company is an unlimited company, in which case seven days' notice is necessary (CA 1985 s 369(2)). However, if a special or an extraordinary resolution is to be discussed at a meeting of any company, the meeting will then require 21 days' notice, irrespective of the type of company (CA 1985 s 366(2)).

As with AGMs, the required length of notice may be shortened. Short notice of an EGM is possible if 95% of the voting members approve (CA 1985 s 369(4)). If a private company has passed an elective resolution to the requisite effect, the figure of 95% may be reduced to 90% (CA 1985 s 369(4)).

Members' requisition of an EGM

Members can demand the holding of an EGM rather in the same manner as they can demand that a particular resolution be considered at an AGM. Under the CA 1985 s 368, members who hold:

(a)   either 10% or more of the paid-up capital of the company, or
(b)   10% or more of the voting rights of the company

can requisition an EGM. Such members are said to be qualified to requisition an EGM.

They must lodge their signed requisition, stating the purpose of the EGM, at the registered office. The directors then have 21 days in which to convene the holding of the EGM (CA 1985 s 368(4)), and the meeting itself must then take place with the normal notice for an EGM depending on the type of resolutions that will be discussed:

(i)   21 days' notice for an EGM including a special or extraordinary resolution,
(ii)   14 (or in the case of an unlimited company, seven) days' notice otherwise (CA 1985 s 368(7)).

If the directors propose to hold the meeting more than 28 days after the date of the notice convening the meeting, they are deemed not to have convened the meeting at all (CA 1985 s 368(8)).

This provision was inserted because some companies got round the rules requiring the directors to convene an EGM on a members' requisition by convening the EGM for a date many months later. This effectively defeated the members' purposes. To prevent the repetition of that abuse, as can be seen by the next paragraph, the CA 1985 s 368(8) has the practical effect of encouraging directors to convene the requisitioned EGM within a month of the notice.

If the directors do not get round to convening an EGM within 21 days of receiving the requisition, or are deemed to have failed to convene one in terms of the CA 1985 s 368(8), the requisitionists themselves can organise the EGM. It must be held within three months from the date of the deposit of the notice of the requisitioned EGM at the registered office (CA 1985 s 368(4)). Any reasonable expenses incurred by the requisitionists in the organising of the EGM can be drawn from the company which in turn can draw them from the remuneration of the directors who failed to convene the requisitioned EGM (CA 1985 s 368(6)).

Requisition by the auditor

If an auditor resigns his office for any reason during the period that he has been appointed auditor, he is required to state under the CA 1985 s 394 if there are any circumstances connected with his ceasing to hold his office which in his view ought to be brought to the attention of the members or the creditors of the company. Such circumstances as might provoke resignation are pressure by the directors, not to qualify the accounts, or discovery of a fraud which the directors are trying to persuade him to ignore.

If this happens, the auditor is entitled to requisition a meeting under the CA 1985 s 392A. The directors have 21 days from the date of receiving the requisition from the auditor to organise an EGM. This must take place within 28 days of the date of the notice to the members convening the EGM (CA 1985 s 392A(5)). The directors must also circulate a copy of the auditor's statement (CA 1985 s 392A (3)) unless the statement is needlessly defamatory. In the statement he can explain to the members the circumstances occasioning the resignation. If the directors ignore his requisition there is no mechanism under statute for compelling the directors to convene the meeting, other than the criminal sanction of a fine. However, if the directors did ignore the requisition, no doubt an auditor would complain to the DTI.

Notice of an EGM

An EGM notice is similar to the notice of an AGM except that it must state that the meeting is an EGM. The requirements as to the organisation of the meeting, the authority of the person convening the meeting and the instructions to proxies remain the same.

The chairman of a general meeting

At any general meeting, annual or extraordinary, the proceedings are conducted by the chairman. It is his job to make sure that a meeting is called to order, that all the items on the agenda are dealt with, that proper discussion is held on each point and that decisions are made. Being an effective chairman is a task that requires skill, tact, firmness and efficiency. In this task he is helped by the company secretary who will generally have prepared the agenda with him, who takes the minutes (the record of the decisions reached) of the meeting and who advises the chairman on any unclear procedural matters. Although a chairman may have the discretion to deal with any points not mentioned in an agenda, and in many cases would be wise to do so to avoid giving an impression of high-handedness, a company is not obliged to discuss anything not mentioned on the agenda.

Under Table A art 42 if the chairman fails to turn up within 15 minutes of the start of the meeting, the directors can nominate someone else to be chairman; and if no director is willing to act as chairman, the members can nominate a member to be chairman (Table A art 43).

The chairman can demand a poll (Table A art 46) and he has a casting vote (Table A art 50) in the event of an equality of votes.

He can also decide that a meeting be adjourned to a more suitable occasion.

Quorums

Before a meeting can begin, the meeting must be quorate. This means that there must be a sufficient and prescribed number of people there to conduct business validly. If the articles state that there must be a quorum of five persons and only four are present, no decisions made by those four are valid or binding upon the company.

Under the CA 1985 s 370(3) and Table A art 40 two members form a quorum at a general meeting, unless the articles provide otherwise. In a single member company, one member present in person or in proxy is a quorum (CA 1985 s 370A). If the meeting is inquorate, the meeting should be adjourned to such other time as may be convenient (Table A art 41).

Some companies have articles that say the meeting must be quorate throughout (Table A art 41). This means that members will have to stay to the very end if there is a danger that the meeting would become inquorate without them. Other companies' articles say that the meeting merely has to start quorate, even if most people leave five minutes later. The purpose of quorums is to prevent the company being run by a small unrepresentative clique who happen to be very good at turning up to meetings and pushing their own business through without proper debate by the members of the company.

Voting on resolutions

Voting on each resolution is normally initially done by means of a show of hands by those in favour of the resolution (Table A art 46). This means that each person present, whether in person or a proxy for another, raises his hand to approve a resolution. However, his raised hand can only be counted once irrespective of the number of people he represents or the size of his shareholding. If the resolution is clearly approved the chairman does not need to count the hands in favour, though he may choose to do so. Unless a poll is demanded, the chairman's declaration that the show or hands was in favour, or the extent to which the resolution was approved or rejected, will be conclusive evidence of the extent of the approval or rejection (Table A art 47).

Polls

If there is any doubt as to whether the resolution has been carried, the chairman can demand a poll (*i.e.* ask that each member's and each proxy's votes be counted by scrutineers) (Table A art 46).

Any two members, or a member who holds 10% of the voting rights or the share capital can also ask for a poll (Table A art 46). It is not permitted to draw up restrictive articles which make it difficult for members to request a poll (CA 1985 s 373(1)). An unscrupulous company might otherwise draw up articles which limited the right of members to call for a poll. This would mean that decisions could be made on the basis of a show of hands. As a show of hands involves publicly revealing your intentions, the failure to be seen supporting a particular proposal might result in intimidation. Forcing matters through on a show of hands is also potentially unfair in that those who have most capital in the company, and therefore most to lose, may be denied the opportunity to use the votes that normally are a right attaching to share ownership.

A poll is likely to be requested where:

- it may not be clear how many members actually approved the resolution;

- there are doubts as to the impartiality of the chairman;

- the show of hands is not actually a true reflection of the way that votes would be cast if members were voting according to the number of votes they hold or represent;

- members wish to keep their voting intentions secret, or if not entirely secret, at least less obvious to their fellow members.

Proxy votes will be counted in a poll.

It is not unusual for a decision reached on a show of hands to be overturned on a poll, because proxy votes will be counted (both for and against) and because members will be voting according to the extent of their shareholdings.

As discussed earlier, following the case of *Bushell* v *Faith* [1970] AC 1099 members can, if the articles permit them, have weighted voted rights.

Class meetings

As stated earlier, a class meeting is in most respects organised like a general meeting (CA 1985 s 125(6)) except that only members or the class are present.

One consequence of having a class of shares is that once a class has been set up, it is difficult for the other non-class shareholders to alter the rights attaching to that class, especially if the articles are well drafted. This may be an advantage to certain investors and may encourage them to invest where they might not otherwise have done so. Once the class of shares has been constituted, the rights attaching to that class of shares can only be altered with the consent of the members of that class.

If the members of a class wish to vary the rights attaching to their shares, then under the CA 1985 s 125(2) the members of that class must:

(i)   at a meeting of that class first pass an extraordinary resolution to approve the variation, or
(ii) the holders of three-quarters of the nominal value of the issued shares of that class must consent in writing instead, and
(iii) subsequently have the company as a whole pass a special resolution to alter the articles to take account of the variation.

If for some reason the company's articles or memorandum prescribe some other procedure, that procedure should be followed instead except in respect of the allotment of shares under the CA 1985 s 80 or reduction of capital under the CA 1985 s 135, in which case the above CA 1985 s 125(2) procedure is followed as well.

It is possible to have a class of shares comprising one member. He is not obliged to have a meeting on his own. A written record of his decision is equivalent to the holding of a meeting.

Board meetings

Table A arts 88–99 prescribe rules applicable to the holding of board meetings. The rules on the conduct of meetings are flexible and a company may choose to draw up its own rules instead. Many of the provisions that apply to general meetings apply to board meetings. The following matters are referred to in Table A:

1. Board meetings can be held whenever and however the directors see fit (art 88), though commonly they are held monthly. Reasonable notice of meetings is required.

2. The chairman has a casting vote (art 88).

3. There is a quorum of two directors (art 91).

4. At a board meeting, even if it is subsequently discovered that one of the directors was in fact disqualified to vote or was technically no longer a director or was not entitled to vote, the decisions of that meeting will still be valid (art 92).

5. If the directors do not actually hold a meeting, but agree in writing to a decision that would have been approved at a meeting had the directors attended one, the decision is deemed to have been validly made as if it had been passed at a board meeting (art 93).

6. Directors should not vote at board meetings on matters where they have a material conflict of interest with the company (art 94). If there is doubt as to whether or not a director could vote, the directors could obtain the approval of the members permitting the director to vote (art 96), or refer the matter to the chairman for his decision (art 98).

At board meetings each director has one vote unless the articles say otherwise. A board of directors can delegate matters to a committee of directors. If this happens, the committee is normally required to report back to the board with its decisions or findings. The terms of the remit to the committee from the board will vary according to circumstances, but generally a committee must not act beyond its terms of instruction except with the consent of the board.

Board meetings are used for the normal commercial and administrative direction of the company and for all matters that do not require the approval of the members either under statute, the memorandum or the articles. At board meetings it is common to approve the signing of contracts, the hiring of staff, the convening of general meetings, the approval of accounts, the level of dividends to be recommended to the members and the general policy of the company. Board minutes are evidence that matters have been discussed and considered. They can only be inspected by the directors and the auditors and the company secretary. Members normally have no right of access to the board minutes. This is because there may be members who are also members of rival companies and who might be tempted to use inside information to benefit the rival company. It is also to preserve necessary commercial confidentiality.

Procedure at meetings generally

In company meetings, class meetings, board meetings, indeed meetings of almost any association, there are commonly accepted practices. In companies the practices are laid down to some extent in statute, in the articles, and in the company's own internal and sometimes informal practices, but most meetings follow the same basic procedure:

1. The chaiman calls the meeting to order and the secretary notes who is present (in person or by proxy), who sends his apologies for absence and who is attending. If the meeting is inquorate the meeting is adjourned.

2. Sometimes the secretary reads out the notice of the meeting, or the agenda of the meeting. In a well-run company the members will already have read the notice and any other papers sent out with the notice. These papers will include the unapproved minutes of the previous meeting and any accounts or documents that will need to be considered at the meeting.

3. The minutes of the previous meeting are tabled and, if considered by any members who were present at that previous meeting to be a true reflection of the previous meeting, are signed by the chairman.

4. Matters arising or outstanding from that previous meeting are discussed and dealt with.

5. Any specific resolutions required under the CA 1985 or the company's articles are dealt with.

6. Any other competent or necessary business is also dealt with.

7. The date of the next meeting is fixed.

Sometimes members object strongly to decisions that are made at meetings, in which case they may wish their dissent to be noted in the minutes. This means that if the company them embarks upon a disastrous project they can say that they had voted against the project and that they are not responsible. Such dissent may also be useful for directors wishing to be seen to be dissociating themselves from practices that could make them liable to compensate the company under the IA 1986 ss 212–216 or liable to disqualification under the CDDA 1986.

Minutes of the meeting

The minutes of a meeting are a record of the proceedings and decisions of a meeting. Commonly they are prepared by the company secretary or minutes secretary and presented to the chairman for his scrutiny prior to the next meeting. Assuming there are no significant errors, the minutes are tabled at the next meeting and the chairman, as stated above, asks if the minutes are a true reflection of what was decided at the meeting. If the minutes are not a true reflection, the minutes have to be rewritten by the company secretary and re-presented at the next meeting – unless the error is trivial or can be corrected there and then. If the minutes are agreed to be a correct record of the meeting, the chairman usually asks someone who was present at the previous meeting to propose that the minutes be signed by the chaiman as being a true record of the previous meeting. In some companies a seconder is required. The chaiman signs the minutes, and from that moment the minutes are deemed to be prima facie evidence of the matters decided upon at the meeting (CA 1985 s 382(2)). This means that if the minutes are in fact incorrect, it is up to the person who objects to the accuracy of the minutes to prove that the minutes are wrong – otherwise the minutes will be deemed to be correct (CA 1985 s 382(2)).

Minutes of general meetings can be inspected by all the members (CA 1985 s 383(1)). Minutes of board meetings are privy to the directors alone. Auditors can inspect any minutes of any meeting. Single member private limited companies can have general meetings since the company may have more than one director and in any event will need a separate company secretary. Single member private limited companies must keep minutes of their decisions, whether done in a meeting or by means of a written resolution (CA 1985 s 382B(1)).

Types of resolutions

There are five main types of resolution which can be passed at a general meeting. They are:

- special resolutions

- extraordinary resolutions

- ordinary resolutions

- elective resolutions

- ordinary resolutions with special notice.

Resolutions in private companies, with certain exceptions, can be passed by means of written assent by all the members. This is discussed later. In addition, under exceptional circumstances, the courts have been prepared to treat certain agreements, not drafted as resolutions or passed at a general meeting, as deemed resolutions, as in *Re Home Treat Ltd* [1991] BCLC 705. The company had for many years run a nursing home without there being power to do so under the company's objects clause. The administrator wished to sell the company as a going concern but was unable himself to pass the necessary resolution to alter the objects clause. Harman J held that as the company's shareholders had clearly agreed to carry on the business of a nursing home without changing the memorandum, the company was deemed to have changed its memorandum – a decision that would have been unthinkable earlier this century when objects clauses were treated with far greater respect.

In terms of the majority required for each of the various resolutions, the majority is a majority of those members who are:

(i)   present at the general meeting in person or in proxy

(ii)   holding shares which entitled the holder to vote, and

(iii) eligible to vote (*i.e.* are not barred under the articles or because of a court order or because a conflict of interest).

Although the requisite number of days' notice is specified for each resolution, companies may hold their general meetings at short notice, in which case the requisite number of days' notice is ignored. Alternatively the undernoted resolutions may, in the case of private companies only, be passed by written resolutions (CA 1985 s 381A(1)), with the exception of resolutions dismissing directors or auditors (CA 1985 Schedule 15A Part 1). Many resolutions require registration with the Registrar of Companies under the CA 1985 s 380. This is to tell future investors of changes to the original constitution and capital of the company as revealed on the company's fiche at Companies House.

1. **Special resolutions** require a majority of 75% and 21 days' notice (CA 1985 s 378(2)). They are used mainly for matters that affect the constitution of the company, its capital or the rights of the members. The high percentage requires that a substantial majority of those with most capital invested in the company approve the proposed resolution and recognise the benefits it offers. The 21-day period is so that members can consult their professional advisers as to how to vote. Certified copies of all special resolutions must be sent to the Registrar of Companies within 15 days (CA 1985 s 380).

2. **Extraordinary resolutions** require a majority of 75% and 14 days' notice (CA 1985 s 378(1)). They are used mainly for varying class rights and for winding up a company voluntarily. Extraordinary resolutions must be registered with the Registrar of Companies within 15 days (CA 1985 s 380).

3. **Ordinary resolutions** require a bare majority and 14 days' notice. They are used in all other circumstances where statute or the memorandum or articles state that the members in general meeting must approve some act. The issues that can be decided upon by an ordinary resolution are deemed to be not as significant and far-reaching in their effects as those decided upon by special resolution. With a few exceptions, such as the increase in authorised share capital and authority to directors to allot shares under the CA 1985 s 80 most ordinary resolutions do not need to be sent to the Registrar of Companies.

4. **Elective resolutions** were introduced in the Companies Act 1989 following consultation with the proprietors of small businesses. It was ascertained that many small companies found the statutory requirements of holding general meetings a pointless formality. Accordingly private companies (but not public companies) can now pass elective resolutions which are designed to lighten the small company's load.

Elective resolutions can be used for five purposes:

(i) to give directors the authority to allot shares for an indefinite period or for a period in excess of five years (CA 1985 s 80A);

(ii) to dispense with the requirement to lay annual accounts at a general meeting (CA 1985 s 252), except where a member or the auditor requires that a meeting be held at which the accounts could be tabled (CA 1985 s 253(2));

(iii) to dispense with the requirement to hold annual general meetings (CA 1985 s 366A(1)) except where a member insists on one being held (CA 1985 s 366A(3));

(iv) to lower the percentage of the majority required to hold an EGM at short notice from 95% to 90% (CA 1985 ss 369(4) and 378(3));

(v) to dispense with the requirement to appoint auditors annually (CA 1985 s 386).

Of these five elective resolutions, (iv) is probably of least benefit because of its marginal nature. (i) is certainly to be welcomed, because the s 80 five-year rule was widely ignored anyway. As for (iii), if a company is not going to lay its accounts at a general meeting, and the auditors can be appointed for an indefinite period, there is not much point in having AGMs, and (iii) reflects this pragmatic approach.

The drawback of elective resolutions (i), (ii), (iii) and (v) is that once the resolutions have been passed, members have less opportunity to call directors' actions into question. The above elective resolutions diminish the accountability of the directors. But this may be a price worth paying in return for the administrative convenience of not having unnecessary meetings. Furthermore in a small family company, all important matters may well be decided on an informal basis anyway.

In order to pass an elective resolution, the following rules apply:

(i) the company must be a private company (CA 1985 s 379A(1));

(ii) shareholders must have received 21 days' notice of the meeting for discussing the elective resolution (CA 1985 s 379A(2)(a));

(iii) all those present at the meeting in person or in proxy and entitled to vote must vote in favour of the resolution (CA 1985 s 379A(2)(b));

(iv) a certified copy of the resolution must be sent to the Registrar of Companies (CA 1985 s 380(4)(bb)).

Elective resolutions can be revoked by ordinary resolutions (CA 1985 s 379A(3)) which in turn must be registered with the Registrar of Companies (CA 1985 s 380(4)(bb)). As can be seen, elective resolutions remove some of the normal methods by which directors are accountable to members – as for example, the holding of AGMs. The law considers that it should be difficult to remove those safeguards but easy to reinstate them. Accordingly to revoke an elective resolution requires the approval of only a majority of the members, while to pass an elective resolution requires the approval of all members voting at the meeting.

5. **Ordinary resolutions with special notice.** In three situations, it is necessary to give special notice to the company of the intention to move certain resolutions. These arise when:

(i)   the members wish to dismiss a director before the expiry of his term of office (CA 1985 s 303);

(ii) in a public company or one of its subsidiaries the members wish to appoint or reappoint a director who has attained the age of 70 (CA 1985 s 293(5));

(iii) the members wish:

    (a) to fill a casual vacancy in the office of auditor (CA 1985 s 388(3)(a));

    (b) to reappoint as auditor a retiring auditor who was appointed by the directors to fill a casual vacancy (CA 1985 s 388(3)(b));

    (c) to remove an auditor before the expiry of the auditor's term of office (CA 1985 s 391A(1)(a));

    (d) to appoint as auditor a person other than a retiring auditor (CA 1985 s 391A(1)(b)).

Companies may, if they wish, require special notice for other resolutions. If so, such provisions must be stated in the articles. The procedure for an ordinary resolution requiring special notice is as follows:

(i)   Those wishing to propose the resolution (directors or members as the case may be) must give the company notice of the intention to move the resolution at the general meeting at which the resolution is to be proposed. That notice must be given 28 days before the meeting takes place (CA 1985 s 379(1)).

(ii) In the notice of the forthcoming general meeting that the company sends out to its members, there must be a statement to the effect that the company has received special notice of the relevant resolution. If this is not practicable, there may need to be newspaper advertisements instead (CA 1985 s 379(2)).

(iii) Directors might be tempted to bring forward the date of the general meeting in order to make the special notice of the relevant resolution time-barred by not being given within 28 days. They might be particularly tempted to do this if the relevant resolution was to dismiss one of the directors. If the directors do this, the CA 1985 s 379(3) states that the requisite notice will be deemed still to have been validly given even if it was less than 28 days.

Where the resolution concerns the dismissal of a director or auditor, the director or auditor is given a right of protest and the right to issue a statement which is to be circulated to the members (CA 1985 ss 303 and 392A).

The purpose of the special notice procedure is to highlight to members that the resolution in question is one to which they should pay particular attention, since the dismissal of a director or auditor does raise serious questions about the management or the accounts of the company. It is arguable, however, how much attention members actually pay to the words "special notice" in any notice of a general meeting; and in any event, if there is a pre-arranged majority in favour of passing the resolution, no amount of special notice is going to make any difference. The dismissed director or auditor may however feel that at least he was given the opportunity to present his case.

Written resolutions

Just as it was established that many small family companies saw no benefit in holding annual general meetings, it was also established that many such companies did not really understand the rules for holding meetings anyway. The requisite number of days' notice, the different types of resolution and all the other paperwork was beyond them. It was decided that it should be possible for companies to pass resolutions without actually convening meetings. Such resolutions are passed by all the members who are entitled to vote at meetings signing a copy of the relevant resolution. This saves all the inconvenience of convening meetings. The rules applying to written resolutions are as follows:

(i)   only private companies may use them;
(ii)   they can be used both for almost all matters that would otherwise be dealt with at general meetings (CA 1985 s 381A(1)(a)) or at class meetings (CA 1985 s 381A(1)(b)); and in each case they are treated as validly approved resolutions (CA 1985 s 381A(4));
(iii) in order to be a valid written resolution all members who are entitled to attend and vote at meetings must sign a copy of the resolution, either on one single document or on separate copies (CA 1985 s 381A(2));
(iv)   the date of the resolution is the date of the last signature (CA 1985 s 381A(3));
(v)   written resolutions cannot be used to dismiss directors under the CA 1985 s 303 or auditors under the CA 1985 s 391: the resolutions for both of these require special notice (as discussed above) and entitle the director or auditor to a right of protest at a general meeting properly convened (CA 1985 s 381A(7));

(vi) a copy of the terms of the proposed written resolution must be sent to the auditors at or before the time the resolution is supplied to a member for signature (CA 1985 s 381B(1)).

Summary

1. The common types of meetings are:

   - annual general meetings
   - extraordinary general meetings
   - class meetings
   - board meetings

   though a company may have other types of meetings if the articles provide for them.

2. General meetings are held so that the members can give their approval to certain decisions which under statute, the company's memorandum or articles can only be taken by the members. General meetings are also a limited form of shareholder democracy, on the grounds that those with the greatest investment in the company should have the most say in what is done with their money.

   Class meetings are for the members of a class of shares only. Board meetings are meetings of the board of directors, and they deal with all the administrative and commercial matters that do not require the approval of the members in general meeting.

3. All members are invited to general meetings, as are the directors and company secretary. Only members of the class of shares are invited to a class meeting. Only directors and the company secretary are invited to board meetings. The auditors can attend any meeting.

4. AGMs normally deal with the following:

   - tabling of accounts and directors' report
   - approval of directors' recommendations for dividend
   - reappointment of auditors and directing the directing to fix their remuneration
   - appointment of directors.

   AGMs are called by means of a notice (CA 1985 s 369(1)), sent out on the instruction of the board of directors, the Secretary of State (CA 1985 s 367), or the court (following a successful application by a director or member (CA 1985 s 371)). The notice must make clear the date, time and place of the meeting, the general nature of the business to be transacted, and indicate how proxies can stand in for members (CA 1985 s 372).

Members can requisition individual resolutions if suitably qualified (CA 1985 s 376).

AGMs require 21 days' notice (CA 1985 s 369).

An AGM may be held at short notice if all members entitled to vote and voting agree to do so (CA 1985 s 369A).

5. EGMs can deal with any matters that require approval at a general meeting. They are usually called by the directors, but can be called by the court (CA 1985 s 371), or requisitioned by the members (CA 1985 s 368) or the auditors (CA 1985 s 392A).

EGMs require 14 days' notice (CA 1985 s 369) unless a special resolution is being considered.

An EGM may be held at short notice if 95% of the members voting and entitled to vote in person or in proxy approve the holding of the meeting at short notice (CA 1985 s 378(3)). The figure of 95% may be reduced to 90% if the members have previously agreed that by elective resolution.

6. Most companies insist on a quorum at any meeting, though the actual quorum for each company will be specified in its articles. Decisions passed at an inquorate meeting will generally be invalid.

7. Voting is normally initially done on a show of hands, but as that is sometimes not representative of the true wishes of the voting members, a poll can be demanded instead. On a poll, members voted according to the number of voting shares they hold. A poll can overturn a decision made on a show of hands.

8. Classes of shareholders have meetings that usually resemble general meetings, but a company may choose to have additional rules relating to class meetings in its articles.

9. Board meetings normally follow an established pattern that is laid down in good practice without any force of law. However, a company could put its rules for board meetings in its articles if it wished. Board meetings must be quorate and each director normally has one vote.

10. All meetings should be minuted, usually by the company secretary. The minutes provide a record of what was decided at the meeting. The minutes are also prima facie evidence of what was decided at the meeting.

11. Although a company could invent other types of resolution if it wished, and refer to them in its articles, the common types of resolution are:

- special (CA 1985 s 378(2));
- extraordinary (CA 1985 s 378(1));
- ordinary;

- elective (CA 1985 s 379A);
- ordinary with special notice (CA 1985 s 379);
- written (CA 1985 s 381A).

12. Special resolutions require 21 days' notice and 75% majority of those entitled to vote and voting in person or in proxy. Special resolutions are generally for the more contentious issues that affect the company's constitution, its capital or members' rights: there must be a substantial majority who agree that it is appropriate to change the company's existing arrangements. All special resolutions need to be registered with the Registrar of Companies.

13. Extraordinary resolutions require 14 days' notice and 75% majority as above. They are used for varying class members' rights and putting companies in voluntary liquidation though they could be used in other circumstances if the articles permitted it. All extraordinary resolutions need to be registered with the Registrar of Companies.

14. Ordinary resolutions require 14 days' notice and a bare majority as above. Ordinary resolutions are used wherever statute, the memorandum or the articles state that the company in general meeting approves a resolution. Ordinary resolutions are generally for the less problematic issues for the company. A few ordinary resolutions require to be registered with the Registrar of Companies.

15. Elective resolutions are available for private companies only for the following five purposes:

- to dispense with the five-year rule for the directors' authority to allot shares under CA1985 s 80A;
- to dispense with the requirement to table the accounts and directors' report at a general meeting under the CA 1985 s 252;
- to dispense with the requirement to hold AGMs under the CA 1985 s 366A;
- to reduce the members' authority required to have short notice of an EGM from 95% to 90% under the CA 1985 s 369(4) and s 378(3);
- to dispense with the requirement to reappoint auditors annually under CA 1985 s 386.

To pass an elective resolution at a general meeting, all members entitled to vote and present in person or in proxy must vote in favour. Twenty-one days' notice is required of an elective resolution to be passed at a general meeting (CA 1985 s 379A), though short notice is permissible, as is the passing of an elective resolution by means of a written resolution.

All elective resolutions must be registered with the Registrar of Companies. An elective resolution can be revoked by means of an ordinary resolution. A revoking resolution must also be lodged with the Registrar of Companies.

16. Ordinary resolutions with special notice are used in conjunction with:

- the dismissal of directors under the CA 1985 s 303;
- the appointment of directors over the age of 70 in public limited companies and their subsidiaries (CA 1985 s 293(5));
- the appointment of a new auditor before the expiry of the former auditor's term of office (CA 1985 s 388) or the removal of auditors before the expiry of their term of office (CA 1985 s 391A).

In the case of directors and auditors, the directors and auditors who are under threat of dismissal are entitled to a right of protest to the members at a general meeting.

The special notice procedure requires those moving the resolution to give notice to the company of the intention to move the resolution at least 28 days prior to the meeting at which the resolution is to be moved (CA 1985 s 379).

Companies may choose to have articles which require special notice of other matters as well.

17. Written resolutions are available to private companies only. They can be used for any resolutions suitable for a general meeting or class meeting with the exception of the dismissal of a director under the CA 1985 s 303 or the dismissal of an auditor under the CA 1985 s 391A. This is because directors and auditors are entitled to the right of protest at a general meeting.

Written resolutions must be signed by all the members entitled to vote. The terms of the resolution must be communicated to the company's auditors.

19. TAKEOVERS AND MERGERS

Purpose and effect of takeovers – Monopolies and Mergers Commission and the Office of Fair Trading – the practice of takeover bids – buying out the minority – reconstructions in the course of voluntary arrangements – schemes of arrangements.

This chapter deals with the expansion of companies through the acquisition of or merger with other companies.

Strictly speaking a takeover of a company occurs when one company buys either all or the greater part of the share capital of the other. The company carrying out the takeover is sometimes called the acquiring company, the bidder, the offeror, or in the case of an unwelcome takeover bid, the "predator". The company whose shares are being bought by the acquiring company is known as the "target" company. In the circumstances of a takeover bid, the acquiring company will wish to buy sufficient of the share capital of the target to be able either to control its board of directors or to pass special resolutions. The acquiring company will give the shareholders of the target company either cash or shares in the acquiring company in exchange for their shares in the target company. Takeovers are usually either agreed or hostile, according the the degree to which the existing management of the target company welcomes the approach of an acquiring company. An agreed takeover usually means that the target company will be given access to more capital and its existing directors will not lose their jobs – or if they do, they will generally be given generous compensation packages. A hostile takeover may not be welcome to the existing directors at all, as they may lose their jobs, the company may be broken up and its various parts sold off at a profit to the predator company.

In a takeover situation, the value of the acquiring company after the takeover is the sum of the existing value of both the acquiring company and the target company less what was paid to acquire the shares in the target company.

Takeovers tend to arise in the context of:

- one private or unquoted company taking over another private or unquoted company;

- a quoted company taking over an unquoted company;

- a quoted company taking over another quoted company.

A takeover can be contrasted with a merger, also sometimes known as an amalgamation. In a merger two companies unite to become one company, which may be a brand new company designed to absorb both businesses. The controllers of both original businesses become controllers of the new combined business and are given shares in the new merged company in exchange for their shares in the two old companies. The value of the new merged company will be the sum of the value of the two old companies. Mergers tend to be less aggressive affairs than takeovers.

Purpose and effect of takeovers

There are various reasons why one company should wish to take over another. These include the following:

1. A strong company may be in the same line of business as a weaker one. A strong company may be able to rationalise the two companies' activities. This should produce a better return on the pooled assets of the two companies than on the two companies separately.

2. A company may wish to ensure access to certain supplies and it may therefore be in its interest to take over the supplier. Equally a company may wish to control the retail of the goods it produces and therefore may wish to buy out the retailer.

3. A company may be cash-rich and wish to diversify into new areas where it feels its commercial acumen could achieve a good return on its investment.

4. A company may be run by directors who wish to retire and sell their shares to an acquiring company willing to take over the business and to pay a premium for it.

5. Existing shareholders of a target company may have lost confidence in the existing management and may wish to dispose of their shares before they lose any more of their investment. Accordingly they may be willing to sell their shares to the acquiring company; the price paid will usually be more favourable than if the shares were sold on the open market.

6. An acquiring company may embark upon a takeover in order to make it more difficult for other companies to take it over. This is because the acquiring company may be funding its takeover bid by means of a large loan. Any other company trying to take over the acquiring company may ultimately find itself liable for the loan.

7. Occasionally an acquiring company may wish to raise its own profile by being seen to be able to acquire other companies, thereby presenting an image of a bigger and more prestigious business.

8. Occasionally some directors obtain a personal "buzz" out of the excitement of acquiring another company and dealing with high-powered city financiers. They may also obtain personal satisfaction in being in control of ever larger and more powerful commercial organisations.

9. Some predator companies intend to asset-strip target companies. This is done by acquiring the shares of a company whose assets are undervalued perhaps because the company's management has been poor or because commercial opportunities have not been seized. The predator, usually using a "war-chest" of cash (or by borrowing) immediately breaks up the target company into smaller units which it sells to other businesses. The predator may choose to keep some parts back for itself. The predator makes a profit on the difference between the price it paid for the target company's shares and the total price it obtains by selling off the constituent parts of the target company. As asset-stripping is considered to be sharp practice, ingenious financiers such as the late Sir James Goldsmith have used the less pejorative term "unbundling".

10. A target company may set itself up for takeover by being large and unwieldy. This is sometimes a fate of conglomerates, companies that have built themselves up by acquisition of other businesses up to the point where their own management cannot cope and there is no coherent strategy unifying all the disparate businesses.

11. An acquiring company may wish to corner the market in a particular product by buying out its competitors. Having taken over its competitors, it can then charge whatever sum it likes for its products. However, in such an event the Monopolies and Merger Commission (referred to later) may well take steps to prevent the takeover taking place.

12. The directors of an acquiring company may believe that it is best to spread the company's commercial risk through a variety of businesses.

13. It may be cheaper and easier to buy an existing business than to set up a new one.

14. A company may wish to integrate all stages of a product, from raw supplies to selling the finished goods, under one management. This is known as "vertical integration".

The cycle of takeovers

A study of the history of many companies reveals that commonly a company starts off as a small concern. Using internally generated funds the company expands and takes over other companies, initially in the same line of business. The holding company can charge each new subsidiary a management fee and receives dividends from it. Economies of scale are achieved by centralising management and stripping out unnecessary layers of middle management. As the company becomes yet more profitable it continues to acquire more companies. Eventually it becomes so large that even its formerly efficient management cannot cope. The original directors who found the company retire, die or lose interest having made their millions. Their children and grandchildren inherit the company but not necessarily their forebears' business skills. The company starts to underperform, and because of the poor management the value of the shares dips below the value of the underlying assets. A predator appears. It takes over the company, breaks it up and sells the assets to young new teams of entrepreneurs or managers – who repeat the whole process.

Effect of takeovers

There are various advantages claimed for takeovers, most of which appeal to the self-interest of either the directors of the acquiring company or the shareholders of the target company.

The advantages for directors in mounting a successful takeover of another company are:

1. with the increase in the size of the new company, the directors can command greater power;

2. as directors' salaries and share options are often related to certain performance targets, some of which are a high share price or the achievement of certain levels of profit, it may well be in directors' personal interest to ensure successful takeovers from time to time;

3. on the principle that attack is the best form of defence, it is clearly better for the retention of directors' own jobs if they take over other companies rather than let their company be a victim of a takeover itself. On the other hand, an overambitious takeover could saddle the acquiring company with more debt or other obligations than it can cope with, so most takeovers are a matter of fine judgment for the takeover company.

The advantages for the target company's shareholders in being taken over include:

1. an opportunity to sell their shares at a high price which may not be repeated and which is unlikely to be equalled by the target company under its present management;

2. an opportunity to acquire shares in the takeover company.

Target companies' directors are often very unhappy at the prospect of their companies being taken over. This is mainly for understandable and emotional reasons:

1. a target company could have been a family-controlled business for many generations: to lose control of it would be losing the family inheritance;

2. the members' rejection of the current management in favour of a takeover bidder is a personal criticism of the way the company has been managed by the existing directors. This may seem to the directors to be both ungrateful and treacherous;

3. existing directors will nearly always lose their jobs. Crafty directors, however, will have well drawn up contracts which entitle them to massive compensation in the event of a takeover. This may prove a deterrent to an acquiring company, but equally may provide a certain secret incentive to a director to ensure that the takeover takes place;

4. takeovers commonly result in job losses throughout the target company as administration, marketing and other functions are centralised and ranks of middle management removed. Conscientious employers/directors of the target company may be genuinely distressed at many of their loyal employees losing their jobs through no fault of their own.

5. resisting a takeover is an extremely stressful business for the directors, as well as being an expensive one for the company as a whole. Much management time may be spent in dealing with the threat of the takeover rather than in dealing with other more manageable operations.

Directors can find themselves in a difficult position with a takeover. On the one hand they stand to lose their jobs, personal standing, careers and perquisites. On the other hand being dismissed may entitle them to enormous pay-offs to soothe their pain. In addition, they are supposed to exercise their fiduciary duty to act in the best interests of the company as a whole. If it is clear that a predator can pay a great deal more for the members' shares than the existing management could produce, or that a predator could generate more income for the shareholders than the existing management could, then the directors would be failing in their duty to their members if they rejected the predator's offer. If they decide that the best course of action is to reject the predator's offer, they will have to mount a defence to the takeover. There is a number of methods used by way of defences:

1. The directors could undertake to sell off a number of underperforming assets to make the company more efficient and give a better return on investors' capital.

2. The directors could dismiss staff – although in the long run this often damages the efficiency of the company as well as lowering morale amongst the employees. It does, however, usually lead to a short-term increase in the share price.

3. The directors could introduce a number of poison pill tactics, so that if the company is taken over the predator will incur liabilities in terms of designated contracts being broken, senior employees having to be paid off, substantial premiums needing to be paid to shareholders, etc.

4. A common unscrupulous technique is to employ researchers to uncover unsavoury information about the predator's directors and their personal behaviour. The dangers of so called "dirty tricks" are that two can play at that game, or that a predator possessed of a high degree of integrity could hold the moral high ground and show the other company to be devious and sharp.

Despite the various defences that are available, it is usually the case that most shareholders, particularly the institutional shareholders, are interested in maximising their returns, and they will back whichever side looks as though it will be most rewarding in both the short and long term. Directors employing defence tactics must therefore remember that loyalty counts for little: what matters is cash.

Political attitudes to takeovers

Although within the UK, Government policies in general tend, broadly speaking, to favour a non-interventionist approach to takeovers, traditionally Labour policies used not to favour takeover activity as takeovers nearly always lead to job losses. Similarly the distaste for takeover activity in Europe is to a great extent because of the awareness there of the effect of takeovers on the unemployment figures. In addition, there are some takeovers which may affect the national interest or may have other political effects. For example, a takeover by a foreign company of an arms-producing business, or of a company involved in radar and defence systems, might not be considered to be in the national interest. A takeover that would lead to high unemployment in a sensitive area, or in a marginal Parliamentary constituency, might be injudicious. A takeover that would result in a monopoly of a supply of a particular commodity such as beer or energy might be unwelcome since the acquiring company could put itself in the position of being able to name its price for its products. Under such circumstances, the Monopolies and Mergers Commission becomes involved, as may the Office of Fair Trading.

On the other hand, suppression of takeover activity may result in sluggish economic activity as without takeover activity there may be no incentive to keep businesses efficient. This may deter outside investors and lead to poor standards of production. It also means that when a change of policy occurs and takeover activity is allowed, the company is even less well equipped to deal with it. The City generally is not keen on suppression of takeovers: this is because any takeover bid results in substantial fees for the merchant banks, the accountants and lawyers involved both in supporting and fighting against the bid.

Speculators would also regret suppression of takeover bids. In the 1980s large sums of money were made by speculators taking positions in undervalued companies which could be subject to takeover bids. At the mere hint of a takeover investors would rush to buy shares in the hope that they would have to be bought out at a very high price a few weeks later.

Takeovers and mergers matter not just to companies themselves, but also to the public generally, because of the dangers of industrial giants "cornering the market" in particular products. Takeovers and mergers also matter to the economy of the UK as a whole, because of the enormous sums of money involved, most of it being dealt with in the City of London. The City of London, with all its financial markets and resources, generates enormous invisible earnings for the UK, but it can only do so while the City is seen to be a place where honest businessmen can practise. Should the conduct of takeovers and mergers in Britain attract a reputation for dishonesty and sharp practice, the City would cease to attract foreign capital, resulting in diminished opportunities for all who work there. It is therefore in the City's interest that takeovers and mergers are properly policed to ensure that shareholders are treated properly and that there is a fair and established set of rules for takeovers and mergers. This set of rules is known as the City Code. The next two parts of this chapter deal with (a) the regulations limiting the opportunities for "cornering the market" and (b) the City Code.

The Monopolies and Mergers Commission and the Office of Fair Trading

It is not necessarily in the public interest to have companies operating cartels or monopolies, and accordingly there is extensive legislation, both at a national and at a European level, to limit the opportunity for cartels or monopolies to arise. Inevitably some cartels and monopolies do arise, either because without them the business in question may disappear or may lower its standards to a level injurious to the common good, or because the Government has given the cartel or monopoly its blessing – as initially happened with the privatised utilities. In such circumstances the cartel or monopoly may be allowed to continue in existence.

If, however, there is a possibility of a cartel or monopoly arising through a takeover or a merger, and where such a cartel or monopoly might adversely affect the public interest, under the Monopolies and Mergers Act 1965 and the Fair Trading Act 1973, the Secretary of State for Trade and Industry can refer a takeover or merger to the Monopolies and Mergers Commission. While the reference takes place, the takeover bid is deemed to lapse in terms of the City Code (see later) and cannot be renewed during the period of the reference.

What triggers a reference will be the size of the prospective monopoly. For these purposes a monopoly arises where at least 25% of the available goods or services are supplied by or to a particular company (Fair Trading Act 1973 s 64). A monopoly also arises where the values of the assets taken over amount to more than £70 million or such figure as is promulgated from time to time (Fair Trading Act 1973 s 64).

The Monopolies and Mergers Commission

The Monopolies and Mergers Commission is made up of senior industrialists, financiers, academics, politicians and civil servants. Their task is to prepare a report, within six months,

(i)   to establish whether or not the reference is within the terms of the Fair Trading Act 1973, and assuming it is,

(ii) to investigate to see if the proposed merger or takeover operates against the public interest, and if so,

(iii) to consider what should be done about it.

Operating against the public interest would, broadly speaking, occur where the competition between suppliers of certain goods is reduced, where consumer interests are likely to be threatened, where potential competitors will be limited in their opportunities for breaking into the market, or where there would be significant and adverse implications for employment. After the report has been made by the Commission stating that in its view the takeover or merger should not proceed, the Secretary of State can either accept the report and forbid the takeover or merger; allow it to proceed subject to conditions; or allow the takeover or merger to proceed anyway.

The role of the Secretary of State

When the Secretary of State makes the reference to the Commission, he may also receive advice from the Director-General of Fair Trading (Fair Trading Act 1973 s 76) although there is no obligation on the Secretary of State to accept the Director General's advice. Equally the Secretary of State is not obliged to accept the Commission's recommendation, but if he does accept it, he has various powers under Fair Trading Act 1973 s 73 to prohibit or limit mergers or takeovers. Another options is that the Director-General of Fair Trading can negotiate voluntary undertakings from the parties concerned, on the basis of which he may let a merger or takeover proceed (Fair Trading Act 1973 s 75G–K). Failure to adhere to the undertaking could entitle a third party to obtain an injunction or interdict to compel the company to perform its undertaking (Fair Trading Act 1973 s 137(5)).

Approval for proposed takeovers and mergers

As the prospect of a takeover or a merger being refused would be highly significant for the companies involved, it is possible to refer the proposed takeover or merger in advance to the Commission. Alternatively the Secretary of State can make a reference in connection with a proposed takeover or merger (Fair Trading Act 1973 s 75). While the reference takes place the companies either agree to defer the takeover or merger, or if necessary, under the Fair Trading Act 1973 s 74, can be forced to defer the takeover or merger while the Commission deliberates. The acquiring company (in the case of a takeover) may not continue to acquire shares beyond the level of 15% of the target company's shares. This is both required under the City Code (see later) and under the Fair Trading Act 1973 s 74. Further acquisitions, however, may be permitted with the consent of the Secretary of State.

There have been various attempts to overturn the decision of the Commission by means of judicial review, such as *R v Monopolies and Mergers Commission, ex parte Elders IXL Ltd* (1986) 2 BCC 99, 179. None so far has been successful.

As the Commission's or the Secretary of State's decision is highly significant, their decisions can influence share prices wildly. A refused merger or takeover may involve the loss of great deal of money by speculators hoping that the bid will be allowed. Inevitably it is also likely to affect the share price of both the target and acquiring company.

The European dimension

Under EC Regulation 4064/89 the Commission of the European Communities has an exclusive power to investigate cross-border mergers in the EC, especially in the context of limiting competition or establishing or strengthening a dominant position within the Common Market. The Regulation does not prevent individual countries from having their own internal takeover and merger rules, as outlined above in the case of the UK, but the Regulation applies in a wider European context and on a cross-border basis. The Regulation was introduced because Article 86 of the Treaty of Rome 1957, although capable of dealing with the abuse of a dominant position within the Common Market, was not designed to deal with the issue of setting aside takeovers and mergers. Readers who wish to find out more about this area should refer to specialist publications on this matter.

The City Code

In addition to the matters outlined above, there is a further set of regulations applicable to takeovers and mergers. This set of regulations is known as the City Code and is administered by the Panel on Takeovers and Mergers. The Panel is controlled by members of the leading accountancy bodies and representatives from banking, insurance, stockbroking, industry and various financial regulatory authorities. It applies to all those involved in takeovers and mergers of major companies, whether as directors or in any other capacity in connection with the company, such as its corporate advisers, lawyers, bankers or accountants. Companies mounting takeovers and mergers, and those connected with such companies are expected to abide by the regulations promulgated by the Panel, but the regulations have no statutory authority. The principle behind the regulations is that the spirit rather than the letter of the regulations should be followed, and furthermore the regulations are deemed to apply even in circumstances not specifically mentioned in the regulations. The regulations are in effect a set of best commercial practices which directors and their advisers in the context of takeovers and mergers are expected to follow. The advantage of having regulations drafted in this way is their commendable flexibility and adaptability, as well as their appeal to the integrity of the participants. Although there are no legal sanctions for non-compliance, the non-legal sanctions are not without effect: delisting and the denial of access to the securities markets would have a serious effect on a company, and those working in the financial services industry would find that they ceased to be authorised by their appropriate self-regulatory authority under the Financial Services Act 1986 to carry on their business.

Notwithstanding the above, there is a cynical view that if someone is determined to bend the rules, there is very little anyone can do about it at the time because the damage, such as it is, will already have been done and cannot be undone. The main sanction against outrageous behaviour by companies and merchant banks involved in sharp practice in the course of a takeover is the tarnishing of a company's or merchant bank's good name. This may lead to a future loss of business. Despite that, occasionally it has been found that the ability to "get away with it" sometimes impresses clients more than the absolute adherence to more virtuous standards. Equally, where there has been a breach of the City Code, whose who administer the Code are sometimes all too aware that they are sitting in judgment upon their professional rivals and are reluctant to discipline them too fiercely, lest one day the accused become the accusers.

The City Code is drawn up on the basis of:

- providing all shareholders with sufficient and accurate information to enable them to decide whether or not to accept the bid;

- providing the same information to all shareholders;

- treating all shareholders fairly, so that none receives a better price for his shares than others and all shareholders are offered an equal chance to sell their shares;

- treating all shareholders within a class of shareholders equally;

- making directors of the target company obtain approval of the members before disposing of any assets that could prejudice the desirability of the takeover bid;

- making directors, when advising the members on the terms of any takeover, disregard their own personal interest in the company, and concentrate on what in their view would be best for the members generally;

- preserving the strictest confidentiality in relation to price-sensitive information (to prevent insider dealing);

- preventing the operation of a false market in shares on the basis on inadequate or inaccurate information;

- ensuring that offers for takeovers should only be made when the acquiring company believes he can indeed implement the takeover: "testing the water" is not acceptable;

- making it difficult for takeover bids to be withdrawn without the consent of the Panel; and

- making all parties conform to strict guidelines and time-limits failing which the bid will lapse unless it has been withdrawn.

After such a lapse or withdrawal the acquiring company cannot try again for at least a year.

Those involved in takeovers and mergers are expected to consult the executive of the Panel on Takeovers and Mergers where they are unsure of their proposed course of conduct. Where there has been a breach of the City Code there is a disciplinary hearing which may be appealed if necessary. Where decisions have not been well received by the protagonists, the Panel's decision has from time to time been challenged in the courts by means of judicial review, though not always to the satisfaction of the challengers (*R v Panel on Takeovers and Mergers, ex parte Guinness* (1988) 4 BCC 714.

The City Code is well regarded because every honest businessman stands to gain by adhering to sensible common standards of integrity and fair play. In addition, the City Code tells foreign investors that the British capital markets are well regulated and reasonably free from market manipulation. The City Code to a certain extent is the basis for the proposed 13th Company Law Directive on Takeovers promulgated by the EC Commission. If the Directive is ever brought into force (which remains to be seen) it would supplant the City Code. In the UK the proposed Directive has so far been vehemently rejected on the grounds that the UK already has satisfactory informal and non-legislative mechanisms via the City Code for dealing with takeovers, and that the Directive from Brussels is bureaucratic, unresponsive and unnecessary. A further argument against it is that a legal structure would be contrary to the flexible approach at present being adopted by the City Code: a legal structure would lead, it is thought, to litigation (of which there has been little concerning the City Code) and delay.

The practice of takeovers and mergers

In quoted companies, in the absence of a reference to the Monopolies and Mergers Commission and assuming adherence to the City Code, the normal practice is for the acquiring company to offer, by means of an offer document, the shareholders of the target company a price for their shares which the acquiring company hopes they will accept. The offer is first communicated to the directors or advisers of the target company who must consider its terms and approve or reject them, bearing in mind, as they do so, not their own personal interests, but the interests of the company as a whole. The directors of the target company may agree with the proposed takeover and the terms of the offer document. In this case they will recommend acceptance. This does not preclude the directors from subsequently changing their minds even if they have previously indicated to the acquiring company that they favour the terms of the agreed takeover (*Coates Viyella v Dawson International* [1989] BCLC 233). Before the directors issue their decision to the shareholders as to whether or not the offer is a fair one, they must take independent advice as to the terms of the offer.

Alternatively the directors of the target company may reject the takeover and the terms of the offer document, in which it is known as a "hostile takeover". This naturally excites a great deal more media attention, particularly as the takeover becomes personalised and is seen as a fight between rivals for shareholders' affections. Military stratagems and metaphors are used, with the use of "defence tactics", threats of libel suits and the use of private detectives to obtain scurrilous stories about the leading protagonists in the fight. Media campaigns are mounted to make the target company directors look incompetent and sluggish, or to make the acquiring company's directors look like unscrupulous asset-strippers.

Usually after a certain amount of posturing, the acquiring company either gives up or increases its offer price, issues a revised offer document and persuades the target company's shareholders that it is worth selling out or that the alternative of shares in the acquiring company is a satisfactory alternative to the cash price offered. Sometimes, however, the offer fails to attract enough acceptances and it lapses. It then usually takes some years for the target company to recover during which time it is at risk from other takeover bidders.

The offer document

The offer price will be contained in an offer document which in essence is an invitation to the target company shareholders to sell their shares to the acquiring company. Amongst other things the offer document will contain:

- the terms of the offer;

- the acquiring company's proposals and intentions for the target company;

- the commercial justification for the offer;

- the acquiring company's intentions with regard to the target company's employees;

- information about the acquiring company, including the extent of the acquiring company's existing shareholding in the target company;

- information about the target company;

- whether or not the offer is conditional on receiving more than a certain percentage (commonly 50%) of acceptances;

- the date by which the shareholders must accept the offer (normally 21 days, though it may be extended following a revised bid);

- the reasons why the acquiring company's directors think their offer so well worth accepting;

- a statement to the effect that if the acquiring company acquires 90% of the target company's shares it is entitled to acquire the remaining 10% compulsorily (this is discussed later).

The response to an offer document

The directors of the target company usually wish to issue a response to the offer, either agreeing with it, rejecting it, or sometimes agreeing with some of it. It too must take independent advice on the offer and comment on the offer as it relates to the acquiring company's intentions and the effect of the takeover on employees. The target company's directors are very likely to query the figures produced by the acquiring company, and just as the acquiring company may try to present an optimistic picture of how it could improve the target company's results, so may the directors of the target company try to convince its members that the acquiring company's plans are inadequate and that theirs are much better. Accordingly, any forecasts about the expected profitability of the target company either under the acquiring company or under the existing management of the target company must be vouched for in each case by auditors.

Substantial Acquisition Rules

It is important for a listed company that it should know if it is likely to be taken over, and to have maximum warning of the threat of a takeover. Equally it is in an acquiring company's interest to take over a company as quickly as possible, as the more publicity there is, the higher and the faster the share price will rise, thus making it more difficult for an acquiring company to acquire a target company for a reasonable price. There is accordingly a strong incentive for acquiring companies to be furtive and to disguise the secret acquisition of a company by the use of nominee companies and offshore companies. Some of the less reputable practices of acquiring companies are detailed later in the section on "Abuses of takeover procedure".

Should an acquiring company, either inadvertently or deliberately, acquire 30% of the voting rights of a listed company, it will be required to make a mandatory bid for the company (discussed shortly). Up to the 30% limit, however, the acquisition of shares by a potential acquiring company is covered by the Substantial Acquisition Rules ("SAR"), issued by the Panel on Takeovers and Mergers. These Rules are published as part of the City Code.

The SAR do not apply to acquiring companies which have announced their intention to make an offer, because in that case the City Code applies to their offer. Nor do the SAR apply to those who have 30% or more of the voting rights in a listed company, because they are covered by the Mandatory Bid Rules.

The SAR state that a purchaser may not within a seven-day period acquire shares representing 10% or more of the voting rights if he already holds shares representing between 15% and 30% of the voting rights.

There are exceptions to this rule, these being:

(i) where a "single shareholder" is involved (this being a shareholder and his immediate family or a company and the group of which the company is a member) whereupon one acquisition within the seven-day period is acceptable;

(ii) where a tender offer is made (*i.e.* a firm offer to buy a specified number of shares for cash at a fixed price or up to a maximum price);

(iii) if the acquisition precedes a formal offer (as discussed above).

The SAR also state that whenever a purchase of shares entitled the member to control 15% or more of the voting rights, and every subsequent percentage point thereafter, this must be disclosed to the Stock Exchange. Contravention of the SAR is contrary to the City Code and attracts the same penalties as other contraventions of the City Code.

Mandatory bids

Where a shareholder has, either on his own account or in conjunction with others, acquired 30% or more of the voting rights of the company, and subsequently acquires more than 1% more of the voting rights within a 12-month period, he is obliged to make a mandatory bid for the company. This must be addressed to all the members, and must be for cash or for a cash alternative (*i.e.* shares in the acquiring company, of if the seller prefers cash, cash). There is certain discretion in the way that the Panel applies this rule: for example, when a company redeems or repurchases its shares, an inadvertent effect of the redemption or repurchase may be that, say, a 28% shareholder finds that his shareholding has increased to 31% because of the repurchase of other shareholders' shares. This can be cured by the "whitewash" procedure, whereby the independent shareholders vote to absolve the 31% shareholder from his duty to make a mandatory bid.

Share for share offers

The acquiring company may offer the shareholders of the target company shares in the acquiring company as consideration for the target company's shares. Alternatively the acquiring company may offer cash or a mixture of cash and shares.

If in the above process it is necessary for the acquiring company to issue more shares as consideration for the shares transferred to the acquiring company by the target company's shareholders, the acquiring company may need to pass an ordinary resolution to give directors authority under the CA 1985 s 80 to allot sufficient shares to enable the takeover to go ahead. Pre-emption rights under the CA 1985 s 89 will not apply as the acquiring company's shares will be offered for non-cash consideration. It will not be necessary to obtain an independent valuation of the shares being acquired because the market will be giving its own indication of the price, and because under the CA 1985 s 103(3)–(5) where all the shares of the target company (or a class thereof) are being acquired in exchange for shares in the acquiring company, no valuation is required. If shares are issued, the issue must be accompanied by a prospectus approved in the normal manner by the Stock Exchange for a listed company or prepared in conjunction with the relevant advisers in the case of companies quoted on the AIM, all as discussed in Chapter 8.

Share for assets offers

Sometimes the acquiring company purchases, not the shares of the target company, but the assets and undertaking of the target company. The consideration for the assets and undertaking is shares in the acquiring company, or as the case may be, cash.

Should:

(a) there be a transfer of assets and undertaking rather than shares,
(b) whereby one or more public companies ("Company A") obtains the assets of another company, public or not ("Company B")
(c) so that there is either a takeover by Company A of Company B's assets and undertaking or a merger of the Company B's assets and undertaking with the business of Company A,

and

(d) should the consideration for Company B's assets and undertaking be shares in Company A,

and

(e) should the mechanism for such a takeover or merger be a scheme of arrangement under the CA 1985 ss 425–427 (schemes of arrangement are discussed later in this chapter) under the CA 1985 s 427A the procedure involved should follow the terms of the CA 1985 Schedule 15A. This Schedule, broadly speaking, requires there to be disclosure of all relevant information to the members of both companies, together with experts' reports and draft documentation for the members' approval prior to the court's approval. In effect, as much information is presented to the members as would be presented in a prospectus – though under the above circumstances a prospectus would not be needed. The above set of rules, enacting the terms of the Sixth Company Law Directive (78/855), is not in practice much used in the UK, partly because of its complexity, but mainly because it is more usual in the UK to effect takeovers and mergers by way of purchases and sales of shares rather than of assets.

The above set of rules also applies when public companies split off and transfer their assets and undertaking to another company by means of a demerger and a scheme of arrangement.

Abuses of the takeover procedure

Financial assistance

If an acquiring company is offering shares in itself as the consideration for buying the shares in the target company, it is in the acquiring company's interest to keep its own share value as high as possible in order to make the offer as attractive as possible. A well-known method of ensuring this is to persuade individuals to buy shares in the acquiring company. The purchase on a large scale of the acquiring company's shares will drive up the share price. However, the individuals who buy shares in order to drive up the share price would be unlikely to buy such shares for nothing. They would expect either a reward from the company, an indemnity against the subsequent fall in price, or some other tangible favours in exchange for their helpfulness. In the case of the Guinness scandal, where such activity took place, indemnities were granted to some individuals, while others received the benefit of lucrative contracts as their reward. Such assistance to favoured individuals to buy shares is a contravention of the City Code, distorts the market and is unfair on other shareholders who are deprived of these opportunities to buy shares at the expense of their own company. Accordingly such practices are forbidden under the CA 1985 s 151, referred to in Chapter 9, under the rules relating to financial assistance. However, it is arguable how well these rules operate. In particular they do not appear to be able to operate outside the UK or at best the European Union, and are difficult to detect.

Concert Parties

A further abuse is the use of concert parties. This is where a group of nominally separate investors buy a large number of shares in a target company. As they are on the face of it unconnected, there is no need to tell the target company of the fact that in reality they are connected and should be disclosing their interests in each new acquisition of shares (CA 1985 s 199(5)). At a later date the members of the concert party sell their shares to the acquiring company. They may be indemnified against any loss in the process. Under the CA 1985 s 212 there are mechanisms for target companies to find out who is involved in concert parties by asking who has the beneficial ownership of the acquired shares. Failure to answer may result in loss of dividends and voting rights. Companies can also ask for a DTI investigation to ascertain the true ownership. But in the heat of a takeover such formalities may be overlooked, and in any event establishing the beneficial ownership may be a time-consuming and fruitless exercise, only completed once the company has been taken over. In addition, if the beneficial ownership is traced to an offshore company, it may prove impossible to establish who the true owner is anyway.

Warehousing is a variant of the above, where a predator pays certain parties (sometimes foreign banks) to buy shares in the target company. As the banks will hold the shares in their own names and disclose their ownership, the target company may be aware that something is going on but will not easily be able to prove who controls the interest held by the banks.

Dawn raids

Dawn raids occur when on start of business there is a substantial purchase of shares in a target company before the market has really woken up. The acquirers commonly buy up to 10% of the target company at great speed first thing in the morning from selected sellers. This is very pleasant for those sellers who have agreed to sell their shares at a high price, but unfortunate for small shareholders whose shareholding is usually too insignificant to be worth buying. They thus do not have the chance to sell their shares at such a good price.

Buying out the minority

Once an acquiring company owns 30% of the target company, under the City Code it is obliged to make an offer in the form or an offer document. Once the acquiring company has obtained acceptances from over 50% of the members it has effective control of the company as it can then control the board of directors. However, although the acquiring company could state that its offer was binding even with a bare majority shareholding, it is common for the acquiring company to state that the offer will only be unconditional and binding once it has acceptances from 90% of the target company's shareholders. From the point of view of the acquiring company, it may wish to have at least 90% or complete control of the company if it is going to invest substantial sums in the company.

Furthermore, the acquiring company may not wish to trouble itself with the problem of possibly dissentient minorities.

If the acquiring company is able to obtain 90% of the target company's shares, there are statutory provisions to enable it to acquire the remaining shares. There are good practical reasons for this:

- In any company, there are likely to be some shareholders who fail to respond to correspondence, perhaps because they have moved without a forwarding address, have died without any executor knowing of their shareholdings, or have forgotten that they ever had shares and failed to keep up with their personal affairs. The acquiring company will understandably wish to be free of these difficulties.

- There may be other shareholders holding out for an even higher price as a form of blackmail against the acquiring company, on the basis of "buy us out or we shall be an annoying minority for ever".

Statute has therefore provided a remedy to help the acquiring company. In order to obtain the benefit of the provisions under statute, the acquiring company must have made a takeover offer under the CA 1985 s 428(1). A takeover offer is one where the acquiring company undertakes to buy all the shares of a target company, or all the shares of a class of shares in the target company, other than those already held by the acquiring company, on terms that apply equally to all the shares to which the offer relates.

Where the offer is accepted by 90% of the shareholders within four months from the beginning of the offer (CA 1985 s 429(3)), the acquiring company can serve a notice on the remaining shareholders stating that it proposes to buy their shares (CA 1985 s 429(1)). A copy must also be sent to the company along with a statutory declaration confirming that the grounds under which the notice can be given have been satisfied (CA 1985 s 429(4)).

The notice will state that the acquiring company can buy the remaining shares at a price the same as that offered to all the other shareholders. If the remaining shareholders are dissatisfied with this for a valid reason they can apply within six weeks of the date of the notice to the courts under the CA 1985 s 430C(1) for an order that the acquiring company may not buy their shares or may only do so on different terms. If the complaint is that the offer is not high enough, it is for the complainers to explain why it was clearly good enough for 90% of the other shareholders to accept it. The complaint may succeed where, as in *Re Bugle Press Limited* [1961] Ch 270,

(i)   those 90% shareholders were the instigators of the offer, and
(ii)   there were very few or no other shareholders available to provide a different view as to the fairness of the price the majority shareholders were offering.

Assuming there is no objection, the purchase of the outstanding shares may take place after the expiry of the six-week period (CA 1985 s 430(2)). The acquiring company sends the target company the consideration for the purchased shares and the target company holds the consideration monies (or shares, as the case may be) in trust for the target company's shareholders (CA 1985 s 430(5)). If after 12 years some untraced shareholders have still not emerged, the funds held to their account are paid into court (CA 1985 s 430(11), and for Scotland only, s 430 (13)).

Just as the acquiring company can buy out a 10% minority, so can the 10% minority ask to be bought out. Under the CA 1985 s 430A, a minority shareholder can write to the acquiring company requiring it to purchase his shares. It then has one month in which to tell the shareholder of his rights under the takeover offer, and it must give the shareholder a period of at least three months after the expiry of the takeover offer in which to take up the offer (CA 1985 s 430A(4)) after which the offer may lapse. If the acquiring company chooses to buy the minority shareholder's shares, he can do so in terms of the offer or under any other terms as may be agreed (CA 1985 s 430B(2)).

It should be pointed out that the above methods of buying out the 10% minority apply in respect both of public and private companies.

Reconstruction in the course of a voluntary arrangement

This is a valid if somewhat cumbersome method by which one company can take over another, or two companies can be merged in a new company. Under the IA 1986 s 110 a company ("A"), having first put itself into voluntary liquidation, can pass a special resolution (IA 1986 s110(3)) to permit the liquidator to sell all or part of A's assets and business to another company B. B will in return give the liquidator of A shares in B to be distributed to the shareholders in A according to their shareholdings in A and according to the shareholders' rights as expressed in A's articles of association. If A is in creditors' voluntary liquidation, either the creditors' approval or the court's approval is required for this course of action (IA 1986 s 110(3)(b)).

This process is known as reconstruction. It can also be done by two companies being put into liquidation and the assets and business of both being transferred to a new company. The liquidators receive shares in the new company and distribute them to the shareholders of the two former companies.

Assuming the relevant resolution or consent is given, the sale of the assets and business is binding on all the members of the company, whether they like it or not (IA 1986 s 110(5)).

If they do not like it, but the resolution is passed or the consent given, the objectors can within seven days write to the liquidator asking him to refrain from carrying out the sale or to buy out the objectors' interests at a price to be agreed or if necessary, settled by arbitration (IA 1986 s 111(2)). The winding-up is not then allowed to continue until the objectors have been paid off (IA 1986 s 111(3)).

The liquidator will need to take account of any creditors, because if there are insufficient funds to pay them the creditors could petition the court for compulsory liquidation by the court. This will have the effect of invalidating the special resolution and indeed invalidating the whole sale unless the court gives leave for the sale to proceed (IA 1986 s 110(6)).

Schemes of arrangement

The problems with the IA 1986 s 110 method are that:

- the company has to be in liquidation,

- shareholders' rights have to be strictly adhered to,

- creditors' rights cannot be altered,

- its only options are sales or amalgamations.

A more flexible method had to be found which could accommodate such matters as the continuation of the company's trade, and variations to shareholders' and creditors' rights. Indeed so inflexible is the s 110 method that it is very rarely used nowadays. A more satisfactory method is to be found in what is known as a s 425 compromise or, more commonly, s 425 scheme of arrangement.

The word "compromise" is apt. The essence of a scheme of arrangement is that all interested parties are fully aware of what is being suggested. The courts give approval to various rearrangements of a company's or companies' debts and shareholdings which reconcile various differing interests and effect a compromise between those interests. There must be an element of give and take for a compromise, and without some give and take between all or most of the interests the courts will not sanction the arrangement. Once the courts have given their approval to the scheme of arrangement it is binding on all the parties, even though there may be some objectors. Unlike a s 110 voluntary arrangement neither the objecting shareholders nor creditors can prevent the scheme of arrangement taking place, once the court has given its approval.

The procedure for a s 425 scheme of arrangement is as follows:

1. If a company is proposing to have a s 425 scheme of arrangement, the company, a member, a creditor, the administrator or the liquidator may apply to the court for an order for meetings of the creditors, classes of creditors,

members, or any classes of members to be called. At each meeting the terms of the arrangement are explained and those present can vote on it. In order for the scheme of arrangement to take place, under the CA 1985 s 425 at each meeting those in favour of the scheme of arrangement must:

(i)   in each meeting be at least a majority in number, and
(ii)   in the case of a creditors' meeting, hold at least 75% of the debt due to all the creditors collectively, or
(iii) in the case of a meeting of a class of creditors, hold 75% of the debt due to the collective debt of that class of creditors, or,
(iv)   in the case of members, hold 75% in value of the issued share capital or,
(v)   for a class of members, have 75% of the capital relating to that class of shares.

Voting will be in person or by proxy in the normal manner (CA 1985 s 425(2)).

2. The notice calling the various meetings must be accompanied by an explanatory note detailing what the scheme of arrangement proposes and in particular how it may affect the material interests of the directors, either in their capacity as directors or in their capacity as members or in any other capacity such as a lender to the company (CA 1985 s 426(2)). In the case of trustees for debenture trust deeds, a similar disclosure must be made (CA 1985 s 426(4)).

3. Assuming the meetings approve the scheme of arrangement, the scheme of arrangement and confirmation of the approval from the relevant meetings are sent to the court. The court can then sanction the arrangement (CA 1985 s 425(2)) and the scheme of arrangement becomes binding on the company, the members and the creditors (CA 1985 s 425(2)). A copy of the scheme of arrangement must be sent to the Registrar of Companies and the court's order is ineffective until this has been done (CA 1985 s 425(3)).

4. The court has wide powers under the CA 1985 s 427 to implement whatever the scheme of arrangement proposes, to transfer property, to allot shares, debentures or other interests, to institute legal proceedings, to dissolve any unwanted companies, to deal with dissentient members or creditors or to carry out whatever else needs to be done.

The main advantage of a scheme or arrangement is that only a majority in number and 75% in value of the members and creditors need approve the scheme. This can be compared with the requirement that 90% of the shares in a takeover or merger be acquired before the remaining 10% can be compulsorily bought out.

The main disadvantage is that the whole procedure is extremely expensive, as there have to be two applications to court, meetings need to be convened, and extensive negotiations between all the interested parties have to take place before the meetings take place. On the other hand, once the court's sanction has been given, the scheme of arrangement can be fully implemented without reference to any other authority.

Summary

1. Takeovers arise where one company acquires most or all of the shares of another company to make a holding company and a subsidiary. A merger is the mingling of two companies into one of the existing companies or sometimes into a new company.

2. Takeovers and mergers may result in a concentration of products or services in the one company. This may not necessarily be in the best interest of the public generally. The Monopolies and Mergers Commission and the Office of Fair Trading may be required to assess the risk of a monopoly or cartel arising, and if there is such a risk, the Secretary of State may forbid the takeover taking place.

3. A listed company taking over another listed company is expected to abide by the City Code, a set of rules for the proper regulation of takeovers. The City Code is non-statutory but failure to adhere to the rules may result in the companies involved being suspended from listing. The City Code ensures a fair and orderly mechanism for the takeover procedure.

4. Takeover offers are normally done by means of an offer document, an offer to the shareholders of the target company encouraging them to sell their shares. The offer document will be closely vetted by the Stock Exchange, the press and other bodies and is treated in much the same way as a prospectus.

5. Once the acquiring company has acquired 50% of the target company it has control of the board of directors but not necessarily of the company since it cannot pass a special resolution. Once the acquiring company has 90% of the shares of the target company, under the CA 1985 s 428 it can compulsorily purchase the shares of the 10% minority. Equally the 10% minority can ask to be bought out under the CA 1985 s 430A.

6. Other methods of ensuring a takeover include reconstruction in the course of a voluntary arrangement under the IA 1986 s 110. This requires the company being put into liquidation, its assets given to another company, and that company's shares given to the liquidator as the consideration for the assets. The liquidator distributes the acquiring company's shares to the

shareholders of the liquidated company. This procedure is still valid but is inflexible and rarely used.

7. An alternative to 6. is a s 425 scheme of arrangement. The court orders meetings of all members and creditors to seek their approval of a scheme of arrangement that effects a compromise between the interests of the company and its creditors. Once approval has been given and the court's sanction obtained, the court order permits such takeovers, rearrangements of debts or such other issues all to be dealt with in terms of the scheme.

20. RECEIVERSHIP

Purpose and effect of receivership – receivership in England and Wales – the administrative receiver's liability as agent for the company – the administrative receiver's relationship with the unsecured creditors of the company – the administrative receiver's relationship with the directors of the company and with the company as a whole – distribution of the assets secured by the floating charge – receivership in Scotland – receivership in Northern Ireland – the defeat of the receiver (in all jurisdictions)

A receiver is a person who is employed to receive or extract goods or monies from a debtor. These goods or monies are used to repay the receiver's client. In the context of insolvency law:

(i)   the receiver is usually an insolvency practitioner, and must be in the case of an administrative receiver,

(ii) his client is usually the holder of a floating charge and/or lender, (though in England and Wales and Northern Ireland a receiver can also be appointed by a fixed charge-holder), and

(iii) the debtor from whom the receiver receives the goods or monies is as far this chapter is concerned the company that granted the charge.

This chapter has only a short section dealing with the position of receivers appointed under fixed charges, as this is a topic more relevant to property law. This chapter mainly deals with receivers appointed under floating charges. The receiver's task is to gather in the assets secured by the floating charge, and to use the sale proceeds of those assets to meet the obligations due by the company to the floating charge-holder.

Purpose and effect of receivership

If the concept of receivership did not exist, lenders might be reluctant to lend against the value of moveable assets. This is because short of obtaining a court order it would be difficult for lenders to get their hands on those moveable assets quickly. Receivership gives both a prior right to those assets and the right to seize those assets quickly. The prior right will defeat most other creditors' rights. Without the right to appoint a receiver lenders would either refuse to lend or charge a very high interest rate to compensate for the risk of not getting their money back.

Accordingly a receiver is given extensive powers to carry out his task. If the powers he is given under the floating charge and by statute are insufficient to obtain satisfaction for the floating charge-holder, the receiver can, if necessary, apply to the courts for further powers. The receiver's reward is his fee from the floating charge-holder who appointed him, albeit that the company provides out of its assets the funds for his fee. The receiver's duty is to the floating charge-holder and subject to any other obligations imposed by law, he need not be concerned about the effect of his actions upon others – even if his actions cause the demise of the company. At the same time, however, he owes a fiduciary duty and a duty of care to the company in receivership, and may not therefore take unauthorised advantage of his position.

A receiver is a creature of English law, but so useful a concept has it proved that it has been adopted into Scots law by statute. However, in all three jurisdictions, the basic operating principle is the same, although the terminology and the grounds for appointment differ between jurisdictions. A receivership operates as follows:

1. The company contravenes some requirement of a debenture, a floating charge and/or statute, entitling the holder of the floating charge to appoint a receiver. Once appointed, the floating charges crystallises.

2. Following appointment the receiver quickly assumes control of the assets secured by the floating charge.

3. Following publicity and various meetings with creditors, he proceeds to deal with the company's assets or business in as advantageous a method as possible from the point of view of the floating charge-holder. It may be better to keep the business trading in order to be able to sell it as a going concern, thus realising a better price than if the company were broken up.

4. If the secured assets or the business (or the charged part thereof) can be sold and the obligation to the charge-holder easily repaid, the charge-holder will be satisfied and the receivership discharged. The company can then continue trading. This is very rare.

5. More commonly, the sale proceeds of the secured assets or of the business barely cover the obligation to the floating charge-holder or any preferential debts. There is then so little left over that the company cannot continue trading. It must then go into liquidation, and the liquidator will divide the remaining assets between the unsecured creditors. Sometimes there is nothing left over after the receivership, in which case there is nothing for a liquidator to divide amongst the creditors.

The difference between receivers and liquidators

The essential difference between a receiver and a liquidator is that the receiver's only concern is to satisfy the charge-holder out of the assets caught by the crystallised floating charge. By contrast, the liquidator is normally not concerned with assets subject to any form of charge, floating or fixed. He is normally concerned only with the unsecured assets, and his task is to realise or divide them up to satisfy (first) the unsecured creditors and (secondly), if there is anything left over, the shareholders. There can occasionally be disputes between receivers and liquidators as to who has rights over certain assets if the extent of the charge-holder's security is unclear.

However, on a consensual basis, or as ordered by the courts, it is also possible for a liquidator to be appointed prior to the appointment of a receiver and for that liquidator to be granted responsibility for dividing up the company's assets between all classes of secured and unsecured creditor. This process would save incurring the expense of a receiver.

The difference between receivers and administrators

Receivership and administration are mutually incompatible. Once a company is in receivership, it cannot (normally) be put into administration (IA 1986 s 9(3)). An administration order can only be granted where an existing receiver agrees, with the consent of the floating charge-holder, to stand down, or where the floating charge-holder, though entitled to put an ailing company into receivership, declines to do so on the grounds that administration might be a better remedy. Once a company is in administration, it cannot be put into receivership and any existing receivership will lapse if the receiver has not already vacated office (as he generally would have done anyway) (IA 1986 s 11). Accordingly floating charge-holders are in a strong position to prevent administration orders being put in place, and will need to be convinced of the superior merits of an administration order before granting their consent to the appointment of an administrator. An administration order places the company temporarily beyond the grasp of all its creditors while the administrator either tries to salvage the company or attempts to sell off or otherwise deal with its constituent parts in a manner that will best satisfy all the various creditors.

We shall now proceed to look at the practice of receivership in greater detail.

Receivership in England and Wales

In England and Wales there is a distinction between a receiver and an administrative receiver.

Receivers

A receiver is a person, usually a chartered surveyor, who is appointed manager of a property on behalf of a fixed charge-holder exercising one of his rights under a fixed charge, this being the right to manage the property and collect the rights therefrom.

A second meaning of the word "receiver" is a manager appointed under a floating charge which only covers a small amount of the company's assets. A receiver in these two contexts need not be an insolvency practitioner.

There are technical differences in insolvency law between receivers and administrative receivers, but in view of the greater quantity and complexity of the law relating to administrative receivership, this chapter will concentrate on administrative receivership. As a matter of practice, in the majority of cases the charges, if securing assets by way of a fixed charge, will also take a floating charge, so as to gain the advantage of appointing an administrative receiver. A dual charge such as this is known as a "composite" charge, sometimes also referred to as a "light-weight floating charge".

Administrative receivers

An administrative receiver is a receiver who is appointed over all or most of a company's assets (IA 1986 s 29(2)). In any event most floating charges are worded so as to be over "the entire assets and undertaking of the company", so that an administrative receiver would be appropriate. Confusingly an administrative receiver is still colloquially known as a "receiver". Most administrative receivers are appointed under the terms of a floating charge contained in a debenture, but it is still technically possible for an administrative receiver to be appointed by the courts. This might be necessary where the debenture was poorly drafted and the normal entitlement to appoint an administrative receiver was not explicit. As this procedure is rare nowadays it will not be considered further.

Who can be an administrative receiver?

An administrative receiver cannot be a body corporate (IA 1986 s 30). A body corporate is a company registered under the Companies Acts or incorporated in any other form such as a friendly society of a chartered company. Equally an administrative receiver, appointed by debenture-holders, must not be a bankrupt, except with the leave of the court (IA 1986 s 31) – though it seems unlikely that debenture-holders would wish to appoint a bankrupt as receiver.

This definition effectively allows only an individual to be an administrative receiver (IA 1986 s 390(1)). In addition, he must also be a qualified insolvency practitioner (IA 1986 s 230(2), s 388(1)(a)). An insolvency practitioner is someone, generally a lawyer or accountant, who has been authorised to act as an insolvency practitioner by virtue of being a member of the recognised professional body of insolvency practitioners (IA 1986 s 391). To become a member requires the passing of a number of highly technical examinations on insolvency law and practice. An insolvency practitioner must have professional indemnity insurance (IA 1986 s 390(3)).

The Official Receiver

The Official Receiver can be appointed by the court as administrative receiver where the company is being wound up and the debenture-holders need an administrative receiver to gather in their secured assets (IA 1986 s 32). An occasion where the Official Receiver might be appointed is where the terms of a debenture unusually did not allow for the appointment of an administrative receiver. The Official Receiver is a specialist in insolvency work (although he does not have to be an insolvency practitioner) and is appointed by and reports back to the courts. He is a court official and is like an administrative receiver of last resort when no one else will do the job. If there are insufficient funds in the company's assets to pay him, the Government pays him (IA 1986 s 399(2)). The advantage of using the Official Receiver is that as he is an officer of the court, to obstruct him in the course of his duty is contempt of court (IA 1986 s 400(2)). It may thus be possible to obtain information and sources of funds more effectively by using the Official Receiver rather than any other receiver.

How is an administrative receiver appointed?

In England and Wales floating charges are normally contained within a debenture. The debenture will specify the occasions which will "trigger" the appointment of a receiver. The trigger occasions are purely contractual, but most lending institutions will specify in their standard debenture documentation some or all of the following triggers:

- default by the company on payment of interest on any loan to the lender;

- default by the company on repayment of the loan after the expiry of a period of notice;

- default by the company in failing to maintain certain financial ratios, such as borrowing relative to assets;

- failure by the company to maintain a predetermined net asset value;

- failure to adhere to certain prudent management requirements such as insuring any property, or not paying directors too much;

- the company being unable to pay its debts as they fall due;

- the company being wound up for any reason;

- the appointment of any other receiver under any other charge over the company's assets;

- the petition for an administration order over the company.

The advantage of these triggers is that there is then no need to go to court to appoint an administrative receiver, though the lender could if it wished obtain a court order appointing an administrative receiver. The courts might be involved when there was doubt as to whether the appointment was justified, either because of the unsatisfactory wording of the debenture or because the financial circumstances of the company were uncertain. As a matter of practice and courtesy normally a company is warned that if it fails to pay its interest in time or repay the full loan within a specified time the debenture-holder will appoint an administrative receiver. However, there is no statutory requirement to give such warning, and if the warning or the debenture says that payment must be made on demand, payment may have to be made very quickly indeed – in the case of *Cripps (Pharmaceuticals) Ltd* v *Wickenden; R. A. Cripps & Son Ltd* v *Wickenden* [1973] 2 All ER 606 failure to pay within two hours was sufficient to allow the receiver to be appointed. In *Bank of Baroda* v *Panessar* [1987] Ch 335 the debtor company found itself in receivership within one hour of the demand being served even though the demand did not state how much needed to be paid.

It would be possible for a debenture-holder to exercise his right to appoint a receiver either oppressively, in bad faith or for a fraudulent purpose. This issue was touched on in the New Zealand case of *Downsview Nominees Ltd* v *First City Corporation Ltd* [1993] AC 295, a Privy Council case. Although this case will be discussed later in the context of the duty of a receiver to act in good faith, the case highlighted the need for the floating charge-holder to act in good faith as well: in this case the floating charge-holder appointed its controlling shareholder to be the receiver of a company in financial difficulty, and while in that position the receiver acted in an improper manner. While this would not be possible, or at least unlikely in the UK because of the requirement that a properly qualified insolvency practitioner be appointed receiver, the case is still appropriate for the general proposition that the floating charge-holder must exercise his rights in good faith and for a proper purpose.

Sometimes if a company appears to be getting into financial difficulties its bankers will ask for an independent report by an investigating accountant. This is designed to establish whether or not it would be wise to put the company into receivership. There have been suggestions that a few independent reporting accountants may not be quite as independent as they seem, since it will generally be in the independent accountant's interest to recommend receivership with the independent accountant as receiver. By this method they can obtain the fee for the independent report and the fee for the receivership. This assertion can be countered by the fact that a receiver who is the same person as the independent accountant does not need to acquaint himself with the company all over again.

Once the debenture-holder has served the demand for repayment, and the company has failed to meet the demand, the debenture-holder generally notifies the company that it is in administrative receivership. The debenture-holder will then formally appoint the administrative receiver to be administrative receiver. The administrative receiver, if appointed under the terms of the debenture and not by the court, must accept the appointment by the end of next succeeding business day after he receives the notice of appointment (IA 1986 s 33(1)). Unless the administrative receiver accepts his appointment in writing using the Form 3.1, he must confirm it in writing within seven days (Insolvency Rules 1986 r 3.1(2)) and on the confirmation state the time and date of receipt of the instrument of appointment and the time and date of acceptance (Insolvency Rules 1986 r 3.1(5)). There may be more than one receiver (Insolvency Rules 1986 r 3.1(1)), joint receiverships being quite common when there are very large sums of money involved and when the workload would be so great that it would need to be shared between two people.

On the appointment of an administrative receiver, either by court order or under the terms of the debenture, the debenture-holder must inform the Registrar of Companies (CA 1985 s 405(1)).

Under the IA 1986 s 46(1) an administrative receiver must also immediately tell the company of his appointment and within 28 days tell all creditors whose addresses he can obtain of his appointment (IA 1986 s 46(2)). He must also arrange for publication of his appointment within a newspaper where it is likely most of the company's creditors will see it, and in the Gazette (Insolvency Rules 1986 r 3.2(3)).

What happens after an administrative receiver has been appointed?

The administrative receiver's primary task is:

(i)   to ascertain what assets are covered by the floating charge,
(ii) to realise them as advantageously as possible,
(iii) to use the proceeds to pay any preferential debts under the IA 1986 s 40(2) (which will be discussed later) and

(iv) to repay the debenture-holder.

To do this he is entitled to exercise extensive powers outlined in the IA 1986 Schedule 1. These powers include the right to dispose of assets, borrow money, give security, raise actions, obtain professional advice, carry on the business of the company, set up subsidiaries and many other powers that might be useful to him. A common task of a receiver is to set up a subsidiary or new company into which will be transferred the marketable assets of the company in receivership. This is sometimes known as a "hive-down". The subsidiary company can be sold, sometimes to existing managers, or to other purchasers, and the funds realised therefrom are used to repay the floating charge-holder's claims. The debts of the receivership company stay with the company in receivership and the newly hived down company starts life with a clean slate. On occasion, the existing directors buy the hived down company from the receiver, thus effectively buying back their own business. If a company asset has a prior-ranking fixed security over it in favour of some other creditor, the administrative receiver can apply to the court to be authorised to sell that asset if to do so would lead to a more advantageous realisation of the asset. The fixed security holder would still be given the proceeds of sale he would expect to receive (IA 1986 s 43).

During the administrative receivership all invoices, orders etc. issued by the company must state that the company is in administrative receivership (IA 1986 s 39(1)).

Normally an administrative receiver will be paid out of the assets or receipts that he ingathers before he passes the balance on to the debenture-holder. If the company is in liquidation, the liquidator can apply to the court to fix the amount due to be paid to the receiver (IA 1986 s 36). This is to prevent the receiver extracting a large fee from the company at the expense of the unsecured creditors whose interest the liquidator will be guarding.

While the company is in administrative receivership neither the members nor the directors have any say over the management of the company except in the limited circumstances outlined below. This does not, however, absolve the directors of their remaining responsibilities to the company such as preparing outstanding accounts and returning documents to the Registrar of Companies. In addition, under the IA 1986 ss 234–7, the administrative receiver has extensive powers to demand the handover of important company assets and paperwork, and to make the directors and officials of the company co-operate with him to supply such assets and information as he needs. If the directors and other officials prove obstructive, the court has the power to demand the presence of the directors or officials and, if necessary, arrest them and seize any necessary assets or paperwork.

The law has imposed certain restraints upon the administrative receiver. These are as follows:

(1) The administrative receiver, while deemed only to be an agent of the company, is nonetheless liable for new contracts he enters into in his capacity as administrative receiver unless the contract says otherwise – though he is not liable for existing contracts.

(2) The more of the company's assets are applied to the debenture-holder, the less there is for the unsecured creditors. The unsecured creditors therefore need reassurance that the administrative receiver does not ignore their collective position.

(3) The administrative receiver has a duty to act competently and to observe his fiduciary relationship to the company and to the floating charge-holder.

The administrative receiver's liability as agent for the company

The administrative receiver is deemed to be the company's agent unless and until the company goes into liquidation (IA 1986 s 44(1)(a)) when the company will be in no position to have any continuing agents or to enter into any contracts.

This means that:

(i)   there is an automatic assumption that the administrative receiver is doing what he does on behalf of the company and that therefore he will not be liable for what the company does at his instigation (except as specified in (iii) below;

(ii)   he is not acting on his own behalf and not on his own account, unless he breaches the authority under which he was appointed and/or the fiduciary duty which any agent should have towards his principal;

(iii) the debenture-holder will not be liable for his acts and omissions in the course of his administrative receivership, though the company will be – except where the administrative receiver enters upon any new contracts, or, to a certain extent, where he adopts contracts of employment (IA 1986 s 44(1)(b)).

Notwithstanding the above, in practice the administrative receiver is working ultimately for the benefit of the floating charge-holder, so that while legally he is the agent of the floating charge-holder, his duty is to the floating charge-holder. Furthermore, advantageously for the floating charge-holder, the company is responsible for the administrative receiver's actions except in the context of (ii) and (iii) above.

The administrative receiver's liability for new contracts

When the administrative receiver enters into any new contract in his capacity as administrative receiver and as agent for the company, he will normally be personally liable for that contract (IA 1986 s 44(1(b)). Naturally he will not wish to be personally liable so he will seek to limit his liability. Statute permits him to limit his liability by being indemnified out of the assets of the company (IA 1986 s 44(1)(c)). This is reasonable, because:

(i)   he will only be likely to embark upon a contract if by doing so it will result in a more advantageous realisation of the assets of the company for the debenture-holder;
(ii)   the administrative receiver in his own personal capacity is not going to gain from the contract;
(iii) it would accordingly be unfair to expect him to bear any losses if the contract is unsuccessful;
(iv)   if he stood to lose his own money, he might refuse to start a new contract which by completion would result in more money for the debenture-holder and by the same token, leave more remaining for the unsecured creditors.

If there is a danger that the company's assets will not meet the administrative receiver's liability, the prudent administrative receiver might also seek an indemnity from the debenture-holder.

Another method of limiting his liability would be to persuade the other party to the contract not to make him personally liable (IA1986 s 44(1)(b)) and to make the company liable instead, since he would be only acting as its agent. If the other contracting party is willing to do that, it is perfectly acceptable for the administrative receiver thereby to avoid any liability. It may not, however, always be in the other party's interest to do this, especially if the company's assets are slender. Nonetheless it is common practice for administrative receivers at least to try to contract out of any personal liability.

The administrative receiver's liability for existing contracts

Normally a company's contracts continue in operation after the appointment of an administrative receiver unless the contract says otherwise, and an administrative receiver can adopt an existing contract if it might be advantageous to do so.

However, the administrative receiver can, if he thinks fit, break existing company contracts. This entitles the other party to sue the company in administrative receivership if it thinks it worthwhile. However, even if the other party won, it would only be able to obtain damages from what was left of the company's assets after satisfaction of the debenture-holder's debt.

Where there is a pre-existing contract and the receiver's actions in repudiating the contract may damage the goodwill of the company or make it more difficult to realise the company's assets, the receiver may be prevented from breaking the contract, as happened in *Re Newdigate Colliery Ltd* [1912] 1 Ch 468. However, in that case the receiver was a court-appointed receiver who was meant to act neutrally in his dealings with the company and the debenture-holder – and this he was failing to do. Where a modern administrative receiver, not appointed by the court and thereby not required to act neutrally, is used there are conflicting cases concerning whether or not damaging the company's goodwill, making it difficult to realise the company's assets, or breaking an undertaking previously contracted for by the company are matters that need concern the administrative receiver.

Airline Airspares Ltd v *Handley Page Ltd* [1970] 1 All ER 29. Airline Airspares Ltd had by contract expected to receive from Handley Page commission on the sales of Jetstream aircraft. An administrative receiver was appointed over Handley Page. He arranged for a subsidiary called Aircraft Ltd to be set up to deal with the sale of Jetstream aircraft. He made it clear to Airline Airspares that he would not be paying it any commission. Airline Airspares then obtained an injunction prohibiting the administrative receiver from selling Aircraft's shares to a third party until a mechanism had been set up for the payment of commission on Jetstream aircraft sales to Airline Airspares. When Airline Airspares applied for the continuation of the injunction the court refused the motion on the ground that an administrative receiver was entitled to break contracts provided it did not adversely affect the goodwill of the company or make it difficult to realise its assets – thus placing the administrative receiver in a stronger position than the company.

Ash & Newman Ltd v *Creative Devices Research Ltd* [1991] BCLC 403. A company, subsequently in administrative receivership, had formerly granted another company a right of pre-emption over certain machinery. The administrative receiver proposed to ignore this right but was barred by an injunction from doing so. When the administrative receiver tried to have the injunction discharged, the courts refused him. This was because the existence of the pre-emption right did not in any case prejudice the administrative receiver's right to realise the company's assets for the best available price. However, the court varied the pre-emption right to the extent that the company having the benefit of the right of pre-emption was not to tell other potential purchasers of its right, and if another purchaser was willing to offer for the machinery, the company having the benefit of the right of pre-emption was to match that offer in terms of price and terms and conditions promptly or lose its right of pre-emption.

Freevale Ltd v *Metrostore Ltd* [1984] 1 All ER 495. Before the completion of the sale by Metrostore to Freevale of some land, Metrostore went into administrative receivership. Freevale successfully applied for specific performance of the transfer of the land. The administrative receiver was thereby obliged to complete the sale.

Of these three cases, the first is about preventing a breach of contract by the administrative receiver, the second is a pragmatic compromise and the third is about making the administrative receiver honour a term of a contract. It is perhaps possible to argue that there is a difference between (i) administrative receivers' breaches of existing contracts and (ii) injunctions and/or actions for specific performance. This might distinguish the three above cases from the normal entitlement of an administrative receiver to breach a contract if he feels it appropriate to do so. Pending a case to reconcile these three cases, or a judicial pronouncement that one of them is wrong, there is no present solution to this inconsistency – and given that the cases are apparently irreconcilable, a wise litigator in any of the above situations would no doubt try to effect a settlement rather than incur enormous costs trying to clarify the point at his client's expense.

The administrative receiver's liability for contracts of employment

Although the receiver is personally liable for any new contract he enters into in his capacity as administrative receiver, there is a further qualification to this rule where the contract is a contract of employment;

(i) The administrative receiver has 14 days from the date of his appointment during which he can make up his mind whether or not to continue any contracts of employment amongst the company's current employees. During that period of 14 days his actions (or inaction) with regard to employees do not constitute either a continuation or cessation of those employees' employment (IA 1986 s 44(2));

(ii) Outside the 14-day period, under the IA 1986 s 44(1)(b) the administrative receiver is liable to the extend of a qualifying liability where:

(a) he adopts an employee's contract of employment, or

(b) introduces a new contract between the employee and the company in administrative receivership.

The administrative receiver is, however, entitled to an indemnity out of the assets of the company for any qualifying liability (IA 1986 s 44(1)(c)).

A qualifying liability is a liability to pay wages, salary or pension contributions, incurred while the administrative receiver is in office, and solely in respect of services rendered wholly or partly after the contract of employment was adopted or introduced (IA 1986 s 44(2A)). The IA 1986 s 44(2B) makes it clear that where there is a qualifying liability which is partly in respect of services after the adoption of the contract, the receiver is only liable for that part of the contract relating to services rendered after the adoption of the contract.

The reason for the IA 1986 s 44(2B) and (2C) is because in 1994 in *Powdrill v Watson* [1995] 2 WLR 312, and *Re Paramount Airways No 3* [1994] BCC 172, the House of Lords, to everyone's surprise, ruled that the receivers could be liable for outstanding salary and other expenses incurred before the adoption of certain contracts of employment by the administrative receivers. It had formerly been understood, but never challenged, that the wording of the IA 1986 s 44, prior to the changes of the Insolvency Act 1994 s 2, allowed the receivers effectively to lay off employees prior to the 14-day adoption period without having to give them redundancy pay. The House of Lords' interpretation of the legislation as it then stood changed that understanding. Not surprisingly, administrative receivers, concerned at the thought of being liable for large sums of money in respect of outstanding redundancy payments and wages, implored the Government to change the law. This the Government did, albeit on a non-retrospective basis, in the Insolvency Act 1994, with effect from 15 March 1994.

The effect of the present legislation is that administrative receivers are now only liable for redundancy and other payments incurred:

(a) in respect of services performed during the receivership and
(b) in respect of which contracts of employment were adopted by the administrative receiver.

The current legislation on these matters benefits preferential creditors, unsecured creditors and administrative receivers. This is because an administrative receiver may not have to use up the company's funds making redundancy payments to employees, except for those employees whose contracts of employment were adopted by the receiver. Equally it disadvantages employees dismissed because their contracts of employment were not adopted by the administrative receiver.

Although the administrative receiver is liable for contracts to which (a) and (b) above apply, he is still entitled to an indemnity out of the company.

The administrative receiver's relationship with the unsecured creditors of the company

Although the primary duty of the receiver is to obtain repayment of the sums due to the debenture-holder, he has to consider the views of other creditors. There are two sets of creditors who may wish to express a view on his activities. These are the preferential creditors and the unsecured creditors.

Preferential creditors

Preferential creditors are those creditors to whom specific debts are owed under the IA 1986 s 386(1) and Schedule 6. They are as follows:

- debts due to the Inland Revenue in respect of PAYE contributions which the company ought to have paid out of employees' wages in the preceding 12 months;

- Value Added Tax due to Customs and Excise within the last six months;

- insurance premium tax within the preceding six months;

- car tax due within the preceding 12 months;

- betting and gaming duties within the preceding 12 months;

- beer duties within the preceding six months;

- lottery duty within the preceding 12 months;

- air passenger duties within the preceding 12 months;

- social security and pension scheme contributions within the preceding year;

- wages and salaries due to employees, including outstanding holiday pay, money borrowed from a bank to pay for such wages, and including payments in respect of Reserve Forces, up to a maximum of £800 arising within the preceding four months;

- levies on coal and steel production.

Although the administrative receiver is not himself a preferential creditor, he will ensure that out of the monies he gathers in for the debenture-holder the terms of the floating charge allow him to pay himself first, and the preferential creditors next, in full if possible. If there is insufficient to pay the preferential creditors, he pays the preferential creditors on a proportional basis. The administrative receiver is obliged to pay the preferential creditors the sums due to them under the IA 1986 s 40(2). The issue of preferential creditors will not, however, arise where the debenture-holder has a fixed charge over one or more of the company's assets, which are then sold by the debenture-holder to cover its claims. Fixed charges do not attract preferential creditors' claims: only floating charges demand that preferential creditors be paid before settlement of the debenture-holder's claim.

At the time of the Cork Report (Cmnd 8558) which carried out a review of insolvency law generally, there were calls for the Inland Revenue and Customs and Excise to relinquish their privileged position as preferential creditors since this deprived unsecured ordinary creditors of funds. The Government however refused to move from its advantageous position, no doubt surmising that banks and other lenders would be more likely to benefit from this relaxation than would unsecured creditors.

Unsecured creditors

Unsecured creditors comprise those creditors who do not have the benefit of a charge to protect their interests. They may include in their ranks preferential creditors, fixed charge-holders and floating charge-holders where those persons' claims will not be met in full by the realisation of assets secured in their favour, thus enabling them to be unsecured creditors in respect of the balance owed to them.

The unsecured creditors, with the exception of the preferential creditors, are in an invidious position in a receivership. They commonly see their contracts rejected by the administrative receiver. Alternatively they are told by him that after payment of the preferential debts and after satisfaction of the debt due to the debenture-holder there will be nothing left over for them. Guarantors for the company may be in a similar position in that on administrative receivership they will have to honour their guarantees.

Some unsecured creditors, excluding suppliers of unstorable supplies such as electricity, may be able to protect their position by means of supplying goods on terms and conditions which include a retention of title clause.

Providing the supplied goods are still identifiable, stored in the purchasing company's premises or somewhere else where they can be easily obtained, not substantially altered and not sold to a third party, the seller should be able to retrieve his goods. He can thus prevent the receiver keeping them and claiming them as part of the company's assets caught by the crystallising floating charge.

To protect their position, or at least to be advised of what is happening when the administrative receiver convenes a meeting of all the creditors under the IA 1986 s 48 to explain to them the financial state of the company and likelihood of payment of creditors' debts, the creditors may form a committee of unsecured creditors to advise the administrative receiver as to his best course of action. He chairs the committee's meetings. Despite this, an administrative receiver is ultimately looking after the debenture-holder and it is his duty to obtain the best return for the debenture-holder. There is therefore a conflict between the administrative receiver and the unsecured creditors. His interests are fundamentally opposed to theirs, and he is not obliged to take account of their interest – though such powers as he exercises must be exercised in good faith and not in such a way as to prejudice unsecured creditors.

However, commercially it would be unwise to alienate the company's unsecured creditors, since the continuation of worthwhile contracts or the possibility of future contracts would make selling the business of the company in receivership a great deal easier. The committee could also complain if the administrative receiver was incompetent or failed to exercise a duty of care towards all those who might be affected by his actions, such as the unsecured creditors, the members or guarantors. In *Standard Chartered Bank Ltd* v *Walker* [1982] 3 All ER 938, the administrative receiver was found to have failed to obtain the best possible price when disposing of assets of the company. The administrative receiver was held to have a duty of care to guarantors who were affected by his inability to obtain a better price for the company's assets.

The administrative receiver's relationship with the directors of the company and with the company as a whole

On administrative receivership the directors' role is much reduced. They still remain as directors, still have control of assets not secured by the floating charge and have continuing duties such as the duty to prepare accounts. Directors may resume their office on the discharge of the administrative receivership. They could convene a meeting to wind up the company, or do certain other acts depending on the exact circumstances: *Newhart Developments Ltd* v *Co-operative Commercial Bank Ltd* [1978] 1 QB 814. After the bank appointed a receiver to Newhart, the directors of Newhart claimed that the bank itself had breached a contract with the company. The receiver refused to raise an action against the bank, so the directors of the company did so instead. The receiver tried to prevent them doing this, asserting that the directors no longer had any status to raise actions. It was held that in these circumstances, since the receiver refused to act, the directors were entitled to do so instead. This was despite the fact that any damages the company received would merely be added to the assets caught by the crystallised floating charge. This in turn could have meant there was more available for unsecured creditors, or less need to call upon guarantors, if the company subsequently went into liquidation.

This decision was extensively doubted in *Tudor Grange Holdings Ltd* v *Citibank NA* [1991] BCLC 1009 which stated that in principle it was unwise for both directors and the administrative receiver to be in a position to raise an action on behalf of the company. On other grounds concerning the inability of the directors to ensure that the company they purported to represent was able to meet its costs, the courts held that the decision in *Newhart* did not apply, and that the directors could not raise an action. It would appear that until satisfactory guidelines are established each case will have to be decided on its particular circumstances.

The administrative receiver is under a duty to prepare proper accounts of his receivership (IA 1986 s 41) and to exercise a fiduciary duty towards the assets of the company in his control, much as in the same manner as a director. He does not owe any duty of care towards the company, but he should exercise his powers properly and for a proper purpose. In *Downsview Nominees Ltd* v *First City Corporation Ltd* [1993] AC 295, referred to earlier, the receiver, in carrying out a favour for the managing director of a company in financial difficulty, exercised his powers as a receiver improperly. Instead of accepting a good offer to redeem the charge under which he was appointed, he continued in office, incurring further expenditure, thus prejudicing the position of a postponed security holder. The receiver and the debenture-holder (a company controlled by the receiver) were both held liable to compensate the postponed security holder.

If the receiver is guilty of misfeasance towards the company or its property under the IA 1986 s 212 he may become personally liable for the company's debts. Under the CDDA 1986 an administrative receiver can be banned from being an administrative receiver in the same manner as a director can be banned from being a director.

Distribution of the assets secured by the floating charge

Once the administrative receiver has gathered in all the assets, he must be aware of any competing claims on the property and must also pay certain bodies in priority to the floating charge-holder.

Competing claims may come from fixed charge-holders, suppliers who supplied goods under retention of title agreements and judgment creditors. Other bodies that have a prior claim to the debenture-holder's funds include the receiver's own creditors, expenses and fees and the preferential creditors.

The order of distribution will be as follows:

1. Normally a fixed charge will defeat a floating charge unless there is some agreement to the contrary. If the administrative receiver obtains leave from the court to sell an asset subject to a prior-ranking fixed charge under the IA 1986 s 43, or the fixed charge-holder agrees to such a sale, the administrative receiver must account to the fixed charge-holder for all sums due to him from the sale of the asset.

2. The administrative receiver's expenses and fees and any creditors whose debts were incurred by the administrative receiver, plus any claims the administrative receiver may have against the company arising out of its indemnity for his actions.

3. Any expenses of any debenture trust deed or debenture-holder in appointing the administrative receiver.

4. The preferential creditors under the IA 1986 s 40.

5. The capital and interest due to the debenture-holder.

After payment of the above, other administrative receivers under postponed floating charges may claim any balance. If there are no other administrative receivers, the balance is returned to the company if still solvent, or to the liquidator if one is appointed.

The administrative receiver may find, however, that goods he thought were subject to the floating charge may not be available to him because they are subject to a valid retention of title agreement or to a hire-purchase or other conditional sale agreement. Goods subject to any of these are not truly owned by the debtor company and therefore cannot be seized by the administrative receiver. Equally other assets may be held by judgment creditors (plaintiffs who have successfully raised an action against the defendant company). Judgment creditors are entitled to use a number of methods for enforcing their judgments, including distraining for rent, garnishee orders and the seizing and sale of a debtor's goods by sheriff's officers or by bailiffs. While in Scotland it is possible to apply to the courts to have such execution set aside provided the creditor obtains his monies ultimately, it is not possible in England to do this. An administrative receiver should also be careful not to sell assets that are not subject to his floating charge, such as equipment lent to a company by a third party.

Cross-border provisions

In order to smooth out potential cross-border problems, an administrative receiver in England can exercise his powers over a company's assets in Scotland, and a Scottish receiver can exercise his powers over a company's assets in England by virtue of the IA 1986 s 72. This is subject to the requirement that the exercise of that power must be consistent with the law of the place where the assets are situated.

This was an issue in *Norfolk House plc (in receivership)* v *Repsol Petroleum Ltd*, 1992 SLT 235. Norfolk had granted a fixed and floating charge, one of the terms of which was that under certain circumstances the floating charge would convert to a fixed charge. This duly took place. Such conversion is not possible for heritage (*i.e.* land and buildings) under Scots law but is under English law. A receiver was appointed and the question arose as to whether the receiver could sell the company's heritage in Scotland on the basis of the conversion of the floating charge to a fixed charge. It was decided that he could not sell on the basis of the conversion to a fixed charge but he could sell heritage following his appointment as receiver, since that was consistent with the law of Scotland.

Receivership in Scotland

Receivership in Scotland is entirely statutory in origin. When floating charges were originally introduced to Scotland by the Companies (Floating Charges) (Scotland) Act 1961 the legislation failed to provide for the appointment of receivers. The only remedy a floating charge-holder had in the event of the company's default was to put the company into liquidation. This was usually more than the occasion required, and eventually the concept of receivers was admitted to Scots law. The rules relating to receivers are to be found in the IA 1986 ss 50–71, the Insolvency (Scotland) Rules 1986 (SI 1986/1915) and the receivers (Scotland) Regulations 1986 (SI 1986/1917).

The appointment of a receiver in Scotland can only be done following the statutory procedure. There is no common law of receivership in Scotland. A receiver in Scotland is the equivalent of an administrative receiver in England and Wales, and Scots law does not entertain the English idea of a receiver who acts as a manager of, say, a large office block. Furthermore there is no Official Receiver in Scots law.

In most respects the Scottish receiver acts in very similar ways to the English receiver, particularly as regards such matters as:

- appointment (IA 1986 ss 53, 54);

- intimation to the Registrar of Companies (IA 1986 s 53(1));

- publicity (IA 1986 ss 64, 65);

- the powers of joint receivers (IA 1986 s 56(2), (3));

- cessation of appointment (IA 1986 s 62);

- the conveying of information about the receivership to the unsecured creditors (IA 1986 ss 66–67);

- the appointment and management of creditors' committees (IA 1986 s 68, Insolvency (Scotland) Rules 1986 Chap. 3));

- the duty to report and make returns to the Registrar of Companies and other interested parties such as the debenture-holder, the creditors' committee and the liquidator (if appointed) (IA 1986 ss 67, 69, Insolvency (Scotland) Rules 1986 Chap. 4);

- liability for new contracts (IA 1986 s 57(2));

- liability for contracts of employment (IA 1986 ss 57(2), (2A–2D));

- applying to the court to sell an asset subject to a prior-ranking security or seized under a court order by a creditor (IA 1986 s 61(1));

- the powers that a receiver can exercise by way of selling the company's assets, maintaining the company as a going concern, borrowing and giving security etc. (IA 1986 Schedule 2);

- preferential debts (IA 1986 ss 59, 386 and Schedule 6).

The basic procedure that applies to administrative receivers in England applies to receivers in Scotland, the main difference being that the procedure is spelt out in the Scottish legislation whereas in the English legislation the common law deals with matters that are omitted under statute. For the matters specified above, the reader should refer to the equivalent passages in the section of this chapter devoted to English procedure and practice.

There is, however, a number of differences generally between English and Scottish receiverships.

- A Scottish receiver can be appointed over the assets comprised within the floating charge, irrespective of the extent of the floating charge. To appoint an administrative receiver in England the floating charge must be over all or substantially all of the company's assets and undertaking. When a receiver is appointed, the floating charge through which he was appointed is said to "attach" to the property of the company as if it were a fixed charge (IA 1986 s 53(7)).

  "Attachment" in this context means the same as crystallisation. Increasingly, under the influence of English law, the term "crystallisation" is used.

- Following the case of *Sharp* v *Thomson*, 1997 SCLR 328 (HL), the House of Lords has thrown the law relating to the attachment of property under a floating charge into some confusion. In this case, purchasers of a new house paid the builders the purchase price of the new house. The purchasers and the builders had concluded missives (the contract for the sale) but the disposition (the legal document transferring the property to the purchasers, which must be registered in the appropriate land registers for Scotland) had not been swiftly registered as it normally would have been on payment of the price. This is because in Scotland a purchaser does not truly have title to his house until the disposition is properly registered. In addition the purchasers' solicitors neglected to obtain a letter of non-crystallisation from the builders' floating charge-holder (as is normally the practice):

  (i) confirming that within a certain period of days the floating charge-holder would not crystallise the charge, and
  (ii) granting consent to the sale.

Before the disposition was registered, the builders went into receivership. The receiver claimed both the purchase price, which the builders already had in their possession, and the house itself – in effect leaving the unfortunate purchasers penniless and homeless. It was no doubt expected that the purchasers would then have sued their solicitors for failure to obtain a letter of non-crystallisation of floating charge from the builders' floating charge-holder, and the solicitors would then have had to compensate the purchasers. However, this did not take place. Instead, the House of Lords adopted what might be called the "consumer-friendly" approach, permitting the purchasers to retain the house and thus preventing the receivers from having both the house and the money. Although to have held otherwise would have provoked a storm of fury from consumer organisations, it is recognised that the decision is not without its legal difficulties. In particular it suggests that, contrary to what was until then the standard view, once the missives were concluded and the purchase price paid, the house was no longer part of the builders' property, notwithstanding the absence of registration of the disposition. Consequently, although it is still the case that heritage, not subject to a prior ranking security and not the subject of concluded missives with a purchaser and for which no purchase price has been paid, can be caught by the receiver following the attachment of a floating charge, heritage for which concluded missives are in existence and a purchase price paid can no longer be touched by the receiver. It remains to be seen what the practical implications of this decision are, or how much of the purchase price needs to be paid to put the property out of the reach of the receiver.

• The term "debenture", although widely understood, is not common in Scotland. In Scotland the function of a debenture is fulfilled by two separate documents known collectively as a "bond and floating charge". Alternatively, all the obligations therein contained are rolled into one document known loosely as a floating charge.

• As in England, neither a body corporate nor a bankrupt can be a receiver, but in addition, a partnership or firm cannot act as a receiver. This is because a partnership in Scotland has legal personality, unlike a partnership in England, and in order to limit the office of receiver to private individuals, it was necessary to forbid partnerships (IA 1986 s 51(3)). A receiver, however, still needs to be a qualified insolvency practitioner (IA 1986 Part XIII).

• It is competent under statute (IA 1986 ss 51(2), 52(2) and 54) (but not common law) for the court to appoint a receiver, but it is extremely rare, and would only be likely to occur where there was a particularly ineptly worded floating charge or there was doubt about the wisdom of appointing a receiver.

• Whereas English law leaves the grounds for appointment of a receiver to be specified in the debenture or floating charge, in Scotland, the grounds for appointment can be such specific grounds as are specified in the floating charge and/or any of the following events:

(i)   the expiry of a period of 21 days after a demand for payment of the whole or part of the principal sum secured by the charge without payment having been made (IA 1986 s 52(1)(a));

(ii) the expiry of period of two months during which interest has been unpaid and in arrears (IA 1986 s 52(1)(b));

(iii) the making of an order or the passing of a resolution to wind up the company (IA 1986 s 52(1)(c));

(iv) the appointment of a receiver by virtue of any floating charge created by the company (IA 1986 s 52(1)(d)).

• English law permits the directors to raise an action to restore funds to a company when the administrative receiver had refused to do so (*Newhart Developments Ltd* v *Co-operative Commercial Bank Ltd* [1978] 1 QB 814). That decision has been queried in *Tudor Grange Holdings Ltd* v *Citibank NA* [1991] BCLC 1009 where the inherent difficulty of having two different bodies, the administrative receiver and the directors, both apparently in a position to raise actions on behalf of the company was recognised. The court in that case was bound by the *Newhart* case and went to some lengths to distinguish that judgment from their own. Scots law states that following the decision in *Imperial Hotel (Aberdeen) Ltd* v *Vaux Breweries Ltd*, 1978 SLT 113 directors were not in a position to deal at all with the assets of a company in receivership. However, in *Shanks* v *Central Regional Council*, 1987 SLT 410, the courts abandoned this particularly restrictive view and brought the law in Scotland closer to the *Newhart* position. By contrast, a recent case on this issue, *Independent Pension Trustee Ltd* v *Law Construction Co Ltd*, 1996 GWD 33–1956, was decided in favour of the receiver, the judge taking the view that the directors' powers supplanted the receiver's only where the receiver had abandoned some claim or entitlement that he should have retained or where there was a conflict of interest between the receiver and the company.

• Scots law specifies the precedence of receivers to the same effect as English law, namely that the receiver of a prior-ranking floating charge ranks ahead of subsequent receivers even if a postponed floating charge-holder appoints his receiver first (IA 1956 s 56(4) unless there is a ranking agreement to some other effect).

• English and Scots law are similar in their approach to the receiver's liability for new contracts and contracts of employment (IA 1986 ss 44 and 57 respectively). However, unlike English law Scots law specifically states that as regards pre-existing contracts in force prior to the appointment of the receiver those contracts continue in force (subject to their terms) notwithstanding receivership but without the receiver incurring any personal liability for them (IA 1986 s 57(4)). This means that if he makes the company break the contract he cannot be sued personally for this. The position as regards the failure to carry out certain acts, or being barred by interdict from carrying out certain acts, remains, as in England, unclear. In one case the court held that the receiver was not obliged to carry out an undertaking the company was supposed to have completed.

Macleod v *Alexander Sutherland Ltd*, 1977 SLT (Notes) 44. The defenders had been required to erect a particular building on a plot of land sold to them by the pursuer. The defenders were completely unable to do so, and when the defenders went into receivership it was apparent that the receiver had no funds or other means of doing so either. When the pursuers tried to obtain a decree *ad factum praestandum* (an order to force the receiver for the defenders to carry out what the defenders had contracted to do) it was rejected as being physically impossible and it was held that the pursuer could only claim for damages for breach of contract.

• Statute makes it clear that the receiver is paid by the floating charge-holder by agreement between them (IA 1986 s 58(1)) but in the event of failure to agree or a dispute about his remuneration the Auditor of the Court of Session may fix his fee (IA 1986 s 58(2));

• When settling the sums due to the floating charge-holder, sums must be retained for payment of the preferential debts under the IA 1986 s 59(1). However, the receiver need only pay those preferential debts which have been intimated to him within the period of six months from the date of advertisement of the receivership (IA 1986 s 59(2)). There is no such time-limit under the English legislation.

• The IA 1986 s 60 states that the funds the receiver has gathered in must be distributed in the following order of priority (unless a ranking agreement says otherwise, though subject to the fact that preferential debts always will rank above floating charges (IA 1986 s 59(1)):

(i)   to the holder of any prior-ranking or *pari passu* fixed security whose secured asset the receiver has sold either following agreement or court order under the IA 1986 s 61;

(ii)   to those creditors who have effectually executed diligence over property otherwise subject to the floating charge but in respect of which the receiver has received permission from the court to sell subject to reimbursing the creditors under the IA 1986 s 61;

(iii) to creditors in respect of debts incurred by the receiver in the performance of his duty;

(iv)   to the receiver in respect of his own fees and expenses and indemnities from the company;

(v) the preferential creditors;

(vi) the floating charge-holder.

If there are any funds left over after satisfaction of these debts, the balance is paid to any postponed receiver or fixed charge-holder, the company (if still solvent) or its liquidator (if the company is insolvent or otherwise wound up), depending on circumstances and on any agreement there may be between them.

- A receiver's claims are as stated above subject to effectually executed diligence (IA 1986 s 53(3)(a)). Effectually executed diligence means methods of enforcing decrees (*i.e.* civil court decisions) in Scotland. The commonest types of these are:

(i)   poinding (seizing and selling of the debtor or defender's assets from his home or business);

(ii) arrestment (the seizing of assets in the hands of a third party, commonly money in a bank account or wages due to an employee);

(iii) inhibition (the prevention of the sale of heritable property [land and buildings] until payment is made to the pursuer [the person who raised the court action]).

As some of these methods of diligence require the completion of several stages, the words "effectually executed" are used to show that the pursuer must have completed all of the stages before the diligence can be said to defeat a receiver (*Lord Advocate* v *Royal Bank of Scotland Ltd*, 1978 SLT 38). It is possible for the receiver to apply to the court to sell an asset which is the subject of effectually executed diligence. Under the IA 1986 s 61(2) the court has discretion to reject or accept the application on such terms as it sees fit under the circumstances. In *Armour & Mycroft, Petitioners*, 1983 SLT 453 the courts permitted a creditor who had inhibited the company from selling any of its heritable assets to be paid before other creditors following receivership.

In addition, as stated above, following *Sharp* v *Thomson*, under certain circumstances, heritage may not be available to a receiver.

- A receiver's rights may also be subject to a prior-ranking security arising by operation of law.

Grampian Regional Council v *Drill Stem (Inspection Services) Ltd (in receivership) and Smith International (North Sea) Ltd as minuters*, 1994 SCLR 36. Grampian Regional Council were the landlords of premises occupied by Drill Stem. Drill Stem was in arrears of rent. Drill Stem went into receivership and the receiver sold the entire business of Drill Stem to Smith International, which took possession of the premises without, surprisingly, obtaining a proper assignation of the lease. Grampian raised proceedings for sequestration for rent and exercised their right of hypothec over the assets in the premises – which belonged to Smith International. Smith International objected on the grounds that a landlord could not sequestrate for rent a company in receivership. It was held that Grampian had a real right of security over the moveable assets in the premises and could therefore sequestrate for rent – even if the assets it seized belonged to the tenant's assignees – since as far as they were concerned Drill Stem was still the tenant and the landlord's hypothec took priority over any other claims to the assets left in the premises. It was up to Smith International to check that their occupancy of the premises was secure.

A more prudent assignee would have obtained a proper assignation before taking entry to the leased premises, and a proper assignation would almost certainly have required the consent of the landlord anyway. The landlord would not have permitted the assignation without payment of arrears.

• There is no Official Receiver in Scotland.

Receivership in Northern Ireland

The law in Northern Ireland is essentially the same as in England and Wales. The relevant legislation provisions may be found in the Insolvency (Northern Ireland) Order 1989 arts 21–39 (as regards administration) and arts 40–59 (as regards receivership).

The defeat of the receiver (in all jurisdictions)

One of the dangers of being appointed an administrative receiver or a Scottish receiver is that subsequently it might turn out that the floating charge-holder was wrong to have put the company into administrative receivership. Reasons for the invalidity of the appointment of a receiver include:

• the alleged grounds for the appointment might not have been specified in the debenture;

• the charge itself might be invalid for some reason, such as lack of registration under the CA 1985 s 395;

• the charge might have been created within six months (or, in the case of England and Wales only, two years where a charge was created in favour of a person connected with the company) prior to insolvent liquidation and is therefore a preference (*i.e.* unduly favouring a particular creditor) in terms of the IA

1986 s 240(b) for England and Wales, IA 1986 s 243(1) for Scotland and Insolvency (Northern Ireland) Order 1989 art 204(1)(b) for Northern Ireland;

- a floating charge might be invalid in terms of the IA 1986 s 245 having been granted when the company is insolvent and within 12 months (or two years in the case of a person connected with the company) of the company's winding-up;

- a floating charge would be invalid if granted to anyone between the presentation of a petition for the granting of an administration order and the actual granting of the administration order (IA 1986 s 245(3)(c));

- the prior appointment of an administrator, since once an administrator has been appointed all floating charge-holders lose their right to appoint an administrative receiver or receiver (IA 1986 s 11(3(b) and (c));

- the floating charge is part of an extortionate credit transaction under the IA 1986 s 244 and can therefore be set aside.

For further details on invalid floating charges, see Chapter 17.

If the appointment of the floating charge is invalid, there may be a right of action by the company against the receiver personally (*Windsor Refrigerator Co Ltd* v *Branch Nominees Ltd* [1961] Ch 375). A prudent administrative receiver will therefore ask for an indemnity from the debenture-holder appointing him; and if the debenture-holder will not indemnify the receiver, the courts can force the debenture-holder to do so (IA 1986 s 34).

One important task of receivers is to report to the Secretary of State on the conduct of directors or shadow directors in the context of the receivership and the events leading up to it (Insolvent Companies (Reports on Conduct of Directors) (No 2) Rules (SI 1986/2134) and Insolvent Companies (Reports of Conduct of Directors) (No 2) (Scotland) Rules (SI 1986/1916)). On the basis of the information supplied the Secretary of State may cause proceedings for the disqualification of directors to take place under the CDDA 1986. However, a receiver cannot ask the courts to find directors liable to compensate the company under the IA 1986 ss 212–216 for such practices as fraudulent trading, wrongful trading, misfeasance or the operation of phoenix companies. Only a liquidator can do this.

Summary

Administrative receivers in England and Wales

1. Due warning having been given to the company, an administrative receiver is appointed following contravention of some term of the debenture which

contains the floating charge. The administrative receiver must quickly accept his appointment (IA 1986 s 33) which must be notified to the Registrar of Companies and publicised in newspapers (IA 1986 s 39).

2. The administrative receiver then prepares a preliminary report on background and the finances of the company in order to assess the likely repayment of the sums due to the floating charge-holder, the company itself and its creditors (IA 1986 s 48). He prepares this report on the basis of information given to him by the officers and employees of the company (IA 1986 s 47).

3. The administrative receiver is given extensive powers to gather in the property subject to the floating charge (IA 1986 s 42). He can do this by carrying on the company's business, selling the company's assets, raising court actions and if necessary, and with prior consent or court approval, disposing of assets subject to a prior-ranking charge or a claim by a judgment creditor. He is not allowed to touch goods which are not the property of the company, and is therefore unable to realise assets which are subject to hire purchase and other conditional sale agreements, or goods supplied subject to a valid retention of title clause. Assets subject to a prior-ranking charge cannot normally be sold by the administrative receiver.

4. The administrative receiver must make regular reports to and prepare accounts for the benefit of the floating charge-holder, the creditors and the registrar of companies (Insolvency Rules 1986 r 3.32). The creditors may set up a committee to advise the administrative receiver (IA 1986 s 49), though the administrative receiver is not obliged to accept their advice.

5. Until liquidation the administrative receiver is the agent of the company (IA 1986 s 44(1)(a)) and he is not personally liable for any claims against him except:

   (i) in respect of any new contracts he makes the company enter into in the carrying out of his administrative receivership (IA 1986 s 44(1)(b)), and
   (ii) contracts of employment he adopts after a 14-day consideration period (IA 1986 s 44(2)), but only to the extent of a qualifying liability (IA 1986 s 44(1)(B)).

   The qualifying liability is in respect of services rendered by new contracts of employment or services rendered after the adoption of the contract of employment (IA 1986 s 44(2A)) – but not in respect of services prior to the appointment of the administrative receiver and the adoption of the contract of employment (IA 1986 s 44(2A)).

6. The administrative receiver can make the company break contracts. This may result in the other party raising an action against the company in

receivership. This will not generally be worthwhile. It is not clear whether an administrative receiver can make a company refuse to obey the terms of an injunction or a successful action for specific implement.

7. The administrative receiver's main duty is to pay out of the company's assets the sums due by way of capital and interest to the floating charge-holder. Assets charged to prior-ranking charge-holders, belonging to someone other than the company, or validly claimed by judgment creditors, are assets that he cannot realise, or where and if he is allowed to realise them he must account to those charge-holders or creditors. Of the funds that he gathers in he must pay in order of priority:

   (i)   the expenses of realising the property subject to the floating charge;
   (ii)   his own expenses, fees and claims against the company by way of any indemnities he may have given;
   (iii) where appropriate, any debenture trust deed trustee's expenses;
   (iv)   preferential debts in terms of the IA 1986 s 386 and Schedule 6;
   (v)   the sums due to the charge-holder.

   Assuming the debt to the charge-holder is thereby discharged, any surplus is handed over to any postponed receivers, the company, if still solvent or its liquidator, if insolvent.

8. If the floating charge under which the receiver is appointed is invalid, the receiver's appointment and actions will also be invalid. Grounds for invalidity include:

   (i)   lack of registration of the floating charge;
   (ii)   the floating charge was granted to an unfairly preferred creditor in terms of the IA 1986 s 243;
   (iii) the floating charge was granted while the company was insolvent and within certain time-limits under the IA 1986 s 245;
   (iv)   the company was already in administration, thus precluding receivership.

9. Under certain circumstances, the administrative receiver's appointment will not in itself be invalid, but the floating charge-holder will be unable to retain all of the goods or assets apparently seized by the receiver because:

   (i)   the assets are subject to a prior-ranking charge which the prior-ranking (fixed) charge-holder will not release and which the courts are not prepared to overrule;
   (ii)   the assets have been seized by a creditor following upon a judgment and therefore not within the ambit of the receiver unless:
          (a) the creditor concerned is willing to release them or

   (b) the courts grant an order releasing them in the hope of obtaining a
       better price overall; and
   (c) the creditor is ultimately paid the sums he is owed;
(iii) the assets are subject to a valid retention of title agreement or hire
      purchase agreement;
(iv) the administrative receiver is due to pay out of the value of the
     gathered-in assets the expenses of any creditors whose bills he has
     incurred, his own expenses and fees and the preferential debts.

Receivers in Scotland

1. Due warning having been given to the company, a receiver is appointed following contravention of some term of the debenture which contains the
   floating charge of the IA 1986 s 52. The receiver must quickly accept his
   appointment (IA 1986 s 53) which must be notified to the Registrar of
   Companies and publicised in newspapers (IA 1986 s 53).

2. The receiver then prepares a preliminary report on background and the
   finances of the company in order to assess the likely repayment of the sums
   due to the floating charge-holder, the company itself and its creditors (IA
   1986 s 66). He prepares this report on the basis of information given to him
   by the officers and employees of the company (IA 1986 s 66).

3. The receiver is given extensive powers under the IA 1986 Schedule 2 to
   gather in the property subject to the floating charge (IA 1986 s 55). He can
   do this by carrying on the company's business, selling the company's assets,
   raising court actions and if necessary, and with prior consent or court
   approval, disposing of assets subject to a prior-ranking charge or a claim by
   a creditor who has exercised effectually executed diligence against the company. He is not allowed to touch goods which are not the property of the
   company, and is therefore unable to realise assets which are subject to hire-
   purchase and other conditional sale agreements, goods supplied subject to a
   valid retention of title clause. Assets subject to a prior-ranking charge cannot normally be sold by the receiver.

4. The receiver must make regular reports to and prepare accounts for the
   benefit of the floating charge-holder, the creditors and the Registrar of
   Companies (Insolvency (Scotland) Rules 1986 r 3.9). The creditors may set
   up a committee to advise the administrative receiver (IA 1986 s 68), though
   the receiver is not obliged to accept its advice.

5. Until liquidation the receiver is the agent of the company (IA 1986 s 57) and
   he is not personally liable for any claims against him except:

    (i)   in respect of any new contracts he makes the company enter into in the carrying out of his administrative receivership (IA 1986 s 57(2)), and

    (ii)   contracts of employment he adopts after a 14-day consideration period (IA 1986 s 57(5)), but only to the extent of a qualifying liability (IA 1986 s 57(2A)).

The qualifying liability is in respect of services rendered by new contracts of employment or services rendered after the adoption of the contract of employment (IA 1986 s 57(2A)) – but not in respect of services prior to the appointment of the receiver and the adoption of the contract of employment (IA 1986 s 57(2B)).

6. The receiver can make the company break contracts. This may result in the other party raising an action against the company in receivership. This will not generally be worthwhile. It is not clear whether an administrative receiver can make a company refuse to obey the terms of an interdict or a successful action for specific implement.

7. The receiver's main duty is to pay out of the company's assets the sums due by way of capital and interest to the floating charge-holder. Assets charged to prior-ranking charge-holders, belonging to someone other than the company, or validly claimed by creditors following decree in their favour are assets that he cannot realise, or where and if he is allowed to realise them he must account to those charge-holders or creditors. Of the funds that he gathers in he must pay in order of priority:

    (i)   the expenses of realising the property subject to the floating charge;

    (ii)   his own expenses and claims against the company by way of indemnities;

    (iii) where appropriate, any debenture trust deed trustee's expenses;

    (iv) preferential debts in terms of the IA 1986 s 386 and Schedule 6;

    (v)   the sums due to the charge-holder.

Assuming the debt to the charge-holder is thereby discharged, any surplus is handed over to any postponed receivers, the company if still solvent or its liquidator if insolvent.

8. If the floating charge under which the receiver is appointed is invalid, the receiver's appointment and actions will also be invalid. Grounds for invalidity include:

    (i)   lack of registration of the floating charge;

    (ii)   the floating charge was granted to an unfairly preferred creditor in terms of the IA 1986 s 243;

    (iii) the floating charge was granted while the company was insolvent and within certain time-limits under the IA 1986 s 245;

(iv) the company was already in administration, thus precluding receiver-ship.

9. Under certain circumstances, the receiver's appointment will not in itself be invalid, but the floating charge-holder will be unable to retain all of the goods or assets apparently seized by the receiver because:

   (i)   the assets are subject to a prior-ranking charge which the prior-ranking (fixed) charge-holder will not release and which the courts are not pre-pared to overrule;
   (ii) the assets have been seized by a creditor following upon a court decree and therefore not within the ambit of the receiver unless:
         (a) the creditor concerned is willing to release them or
         (b) the courts grant an order releasing them in the hope of obtaining a better price overall; and
         (c) the creditor is paid the sums he is owed;
   (iii) the assets are subject to a valid retention of title agreement or hire purchase agreement;
   (iv) the receiver is due to pay out of the value of the gathered-in assets the expenses of any creditors whose bills he has incurred, his own expenses and fees and the preferential debts.

Administrative receivers in Northern Ireland

1. Due warning having been given to the company, an administrative receiver is appointed following contravention of some term of the debenture which contains the floating charge. The administrative receiver must quickly accept his appointment (Insolvency (Northern Ireland) Order 1989 art 43) which must be notified to the Registrar of Companies and publicised in newspapers (Insolvency (Northern Ireland) Order 1989 art 49).

2. The administrative receiver then prepares a preliminary report on back-ground and the finances of the company in order to assess the likely repay-ment of the sums due to the floating charge-holder, the company itself and its creditors (Insolvency (Northern Ireland) Order 1989 art 58). He prepares this report on the basis of information given to him by the officers and employees of the company (Insolvency (Northern Ireland) Order 1989 art 57).

3. The administrative receiver is given extensive powers to gather in the prop-erty subject to the floating charge (Insolvency (Northern Ireland) Order 1989 art 52). He can do this by carrying on the company's business, selling the company's assets, raising court actions and if necessary, and with prior

consent or court approval disposing of assets subject to a prior-ranking charge or a claim by a judgment creditor. He is not allowed to touch goods which are not the property of the company, and is therefore unable to realise assets which are subject to hire-purchase and other conditional sale agreements, or goods supplied subject to a valid retention of title clause. Assets subject to a prior-ranking charge cannot normally be sold by the administrative receiver.

4. The administrative receiver must make regular reports to and prepare accounts for the benefit of the floating charge-holder, the creditors and the Registrar of Companies. The creditors may set up a committee to advise the administrative receiver (Insolvency (Northern Ireland) Order 1989 art 59), though the administrative receiver is not obliged to accept its advice.

5. Until liquidation the administrative receiver is the agent of the company (Insolvency (Northern Ireland) Order 1989 art 54) and he is not personally liable for any claims against him except:

   (i)   in respect of any new contracts he makes the company enter into in the carrying out of his administrative receivership, and
   (ii) contracts of employment he adopts after a 14-day consideration period, but only to the extent of a qualifying liability (Insolvency Act 1994 s 4, Sch 1, para 2).

   The qualifying liability is in respect of services rendered by new contracts of employment or services rendered after the adoption of the contract of employment – but not in respect of services prior to the appointment of the administrative receiver and the adoption of the contract of employment.

6. The administrative receiver can make the company break contracts. This may result in the other party raising an action against the company in receivership. This will not generally be worthwhile. It is not clear whether an administrative receiver can make a company refuse to obey the terms of an injunction or a successful action for specific implement.

7. The administrative receiver's main duty is to pay out of the company's assets the sums due by way of capital and interest to the floating charge-holder. Assets charged to prior-ranking charge-holders, belonging to someone other than the company, or validly claimed by judgment creditors are assets that he cannot realise, or where and if he is allowed to realise them he must account to those charge-holders or creditors. Of the funds that he gathers in he must pay in order of priority:

   (i)   the expenses of realising the property subject to the floating charge;
   (ii) his own expenses and claims against the company by way of an indemnities;

    (iii) where appropriate, any debenture trust deed trustee's expenses;

    (iv) preferential debts in terms of the Insolvency (Northern Ireland) Order 1989 art 346, Sch. 4;

    (v) the sums due to the charge-holder.

Assuming the debt to the charge-holder is thereby discharged, any surplus is handed over to any postponed receivers, the company if still solvent or its liquidator if insolvent.

8. If the floating charge under which the administrative receiver is appointed is invalid, the administrative receiver's appointment and actions will also be invalid. Grounds for invalidity include:

    (i) lack of registration of the floating charge;

    (ii) the floating charge was granted to an unfairly preferred creditor in terms of the Insolvency (Northern Ireland) Order 1989 art 203;

    (iii) the floating charge was granted while the company was insolvent and within certain time-limits under the Insolvency (Northern Ireland) Order 1989 art 207;

    (iv) the company was already in administration, thus precluding administrative receivership.

9. Under certain circumstances, the administrative receiver's appointment will not in itself be invalid, but the floating charge-holder will be unable to retain all of the goods or assets apparently seized by the administrative receiver because:

    (i) the assets are subject to a prior-ranking charge which the prior-ranking (fixed) charge-holder will not release and which the courts are not prepared to overrule;

    (ii) the assets have been seized by a creditor following upon a (court) judgment and therefore not within the ambit of the administrative receiver unless:

        (a) the creditor concerned is willing to release them or

        (b) the courts grant an order releasing them in the hope of obtaining a better price overall – subject to payment to the creditor of the sums he is owed;

    (iii) the assets are subject to a valid retention of title agreement or hire purchase agreement;

    (iv) the administrative receiver is due to pay out of the value of the gathered-in goods the expenses of any creditors whose bills he has incurred, his own expenses and fees and the preferential debts.

21. WINDING UP

Purpose and effect of liquidation – winding-up by the court – voluntary winding-up – getting in the company's assets – distribution of the company's funds – dissolution

Liquidation is the conversion of all assets into the one commercial commodity that can be used in all circumstances: cash. Irrespective of the sentimental, historic or functional value of any asset, the liquidator's job is to turn a business's assets into money to be disbursed by him to whoever is entitled to it. This is normally done by means of a sale of the business's assets to whoever is prepared to pay most for them.

Winding-up in most respects is the same as liquidation. Strictly speaking a liquidation can only be carried out by a liquidator, whereas a business could wind itself up by paying off all its creditors and returning any surplus assets to the owners of the business without employing a liquidator to do so. Liquidation is a more formal and regulated activity. But in common speech the two terms are quite often synonymous.

Once a liquidation is taking place the directors lose the power to manage the company, all headed paper must indicate that the company is in liquidation, no transfers of property can take place except through the liquidator and no shares may be transferred. The liquidator's job is to sell the assets on the best terms he can manage: this may involve keeping some parts of the business going until a willing buyer appears, but it is not his task to keep the business going until such time as all debts are paid (as can be the case with an administrative receiver). If he has to make employees redundant the employees can claim against the company in their capacity as preferential creditors and the balance of their redundancy money will be paid out of the statutory fund set up by the Employment Protection (Consolidation) Act 1978. This is underwritten by the Government, which will then claim against the liquidator of the liquidated company for the redundancy monies it paid out.

A liquidator must be an insolvency practitioner (IA 1986 s 230) and is treated as an officer of the company. He stands in a fiduciary relationship with the company and must not take any personal and undisclosed advantage from his position. He has to report to the Secretary of State on the conduct of his liquidations and draw the attention of the Secretary of State to any matters which he considers significant. This is to protect the public and to help initiate proceedings for the disqualification of company directors where appropriate.

Purpose and effect of liquidation

The purpose of liquidation is to effect an organised and fair method of tidying up a company that either is unable to trade profitably or unwilling to continue trading, whether profitably or not.

If liquidation did not exist, whenever a company fell into financial difficulties, the pushiest creditors with the heaviest henchmen would be the ones who received full payment while less pressing creditors would find that there was nothing left for them. Many countries have adopted winding-up legislation which is designed to prevent this unjust and unfair behaviour.

A second reason for liquidation is to set up a fair method whereby an entrepreneur whose business has failed is given the chance to start again. In this respect liquidation is like bankruptcy. Historically bankrupts could be imprisoned until their debts were paid. Such a method of dealing with bankrupts was scarcely an encouragement to develop new business opportunities that might benefit everyone. Similarly, if the penalties for the collapse of a limited company are too severe, entrepreneurs will not be willing to set up in business.

Liquidation allows the directors to start again with a clean slate. But if the penalties for a limited company becoming insolvent are too lax, rogue entrepreneurs may take unfair advantage of investors and creditors. The law therefore has to tread a path between these two principles of fairness to unfortunate entrepreneurs and protection for creditors and investors. From time to time the law is seen to favour the entrepreneurs at the expense of the creditors, investors and the public; and from time to time the position is reversed. As an example of protection for creditors and investors, s 216 of the Insolvency Act 1986 was brought in because of public disgust at the sharp practice of certain company directors who set up phoenix companies with virtually the same name and business as companies that had just collapsed, thus misleading creditors and customers.

The effect of liquidation is to remove the company from its current members, to take away the powers of management of the company from its directors, and either bring the company to an end or transfer its business to another group of investors. Broadly speaking liquidations operate as follows:

1. The company goes into liquidation either through the courts or voluntarily. A temporary liquidator is appointed and the entire assets and management of the company are transferred to him. Later on the temporary liquidator may be replaced by the liquidator.

2. The liquidator then investigates the company to ascertain its total assets and its total liabilities. In certain situations he is allowed to question the directors to ascertain the reasons for the company's collapse.

3. The liquidator is given extensive powers to gather in or "get in" the company's assets. He is also allowed to recall transactions made by the company within

certain time-limits prior to liquidation. In certain circumstances he can also ask the courts to make directors personally liable for the company's debts. He thereby increases the pool of funds available to the company's creditors.

4. The liquidator may be advised as to his actions by a liquidation committee consisting of certain members and unsecured creditors.

5. Eventually the liquidator will have gathered in all he can and established how much the unsecured creditors are due. He will then pay the creditors either all they are due or a proportion of what they are due, depending on how much is available. If the unsecured creditors are paid in full there may be sufficient to return the investors their capital and any surplus.

6. Once everyone has been paid what he is due, the liquidator applies to the Registrar of Companies to have the company dissolved and struck from the register. It is, however, possible to have the company revived if it is subsequently discovered that the company owns some asset that has been overlooked by the liquidator. The liquidator would then apply to the court to have the company reawakened for the purpose of selling the asset and dividing the proceeds thereof amongst those entitled to those proceeds.

Rights of secured creditors and others against liquidators

The liquidator is normally only able to deal with those assets which are:

- owned by the company;

- unsecured, *i.e.* not subject to a prior-ranking claim, such as a fixed charge or a floating charge;

- not the subject of a valid retention of title clause or a conditional agreement such as a hire-purchase contract;

- able to be reclaimed by the liquidator from judgment creditors, or in Scotland those who have recently exercised diligence against the company's assets.

It is a common term of a debenture that liquidation will entitle a fixed charge-holder to exercise his rights over the asset subject to the charge. In the case of a large building, and depending on the terms of the charge, this would mean that the fixed charge-holder would be able to sell the building or appoint a receiver or manager to gather in rents from its tenants. But the liquidator would not have any rights to the funds generated by the sale of the building or the rents except to the extent of the excess after the satisfaction of the fixed charge-holder's claim. However, by agreement between the fixed charge-holder and the liquidator, or if necessary with the sanction of the courts (provided it can be established that it would indeed be the most sensible and remunerative course of action), the liquidator may be asked to sell or otherwise deal with all the assets of the company, subject to paying the fixed charge-holder the sums due to him. The advantage to the fixed charge-holder of this course of action would be the elimination of the expenses of a receiver or manager.

If the fixed charge-holder sells the building and the sale proceeds do not cover the amount due to the fixed charge-holder, the fixed charge-holder will be able to claim from the liquidator for the balance due, but only as an unsecured creditor along with all the other unsecured creditors. In other words, if the fixed charge-holder lent more money to the company than the building was worth, the fixed charge-holder will be sure of getting back only the current value of the building, but may perhaps only obtain a proportion of the remaining balance due to him.

Equally it is a common and indeed implicit term of a debenture that liquidation will trigger receivership in any company that has a floating charge over its assets and undertaking. The liquidator will not normally be able to touch any assets subject to the receivership, except where there is an excess in the hands of the receiver after satisfaction of the floating charge-holder's claim. As with a fixed charge, where the assets caught by the floating charge are insufficient to repay the floating charge-holder, the floating charge-holder can claim against the liquidator but only for the balance due, and only as an unsecured creditor.

There can sometimes be disputes between receivers and liquidators as to the extent of the validity of ownership of assets. Although these disputes are interesting from a legal point of view, from the point of view of the parties involved they are time-consuming and expensive. Accordingly they are usually settled out of court before the legal fees start mounting. A good receivership or liquidation is a quick one. This allows the company's business to be sold as quickly and as easily as possible in order to allow continuity of trading and prevent the loss of skilled labour and continuing contracts.

There are three types of winding-up. These are:

- winding-up by the court;

- members' voluntary winding-up;

- creditors' voluntary winding-up.

The initial stages for each of these are slightly different and will be explained in turn. However, once the liquidator is in office, his function and activities are in essence similar under all three methods. The essential difference between a court-appointed winding-up and the voluntary winding-up is that the company has no choice in a court-appointed winding-up, whereas with the voluntary methods it is the members' decision to wind the company up. A voluntary winding-up is cheaper, not least because the courts are not generally involved.

Of the two voluntary methods, the members' voluntary winding-up is done for the benefit of the members because whatever surplus there may be after payment of all debts is handed back to the members.

By contrast in a creditors' voluntary winding-up there will probably only be sufficient funds (if any) to pay the creditors and nothing left over for the members. The winding-up is therefore primarily for the benefit of the creditors. Accordingly, creditors are given considerable say in how a creditors' winding-up should be supervised, since it is they who stand to lose most money and therefore need to have their rights safeguarded. Sometimes what initially appears to be a members' voluntary winding-up turns out to be less solvent than had been thought. It then may turn into a creditors' voluntary winding-up.

Winding-up by the court

Winding-up by the court is where a petition is presented to the court asking that a company be wound up. This is different from voluntary winding-up which is where the members at a general meeting choose to put the company into liquidation without using the courts.

Which court do you use?

England and Wales
The High Court has jurisdiction to wind up any company registered in England and Wales (IA 1986 s 117(1)), but companies with a paid-up share capital of up to £120,000 may instead be wound up in the county court appropriate to the district where the company's registered office for the last six months has been situated (IA 1986 s 117(2)). It is generally cheaper to wind up a company in the county court. Difficult issues in relation to the winding-up in a county court may be transmitted to the High Court (IA 1986 s 119).

Scotland
The Court of Session can wind up any company registered in Scotland (IA 1986 s 120(1)) but companies with a paid-up capital of up to £120,000 may instead be wound up in the sheriff court appropriate to the sheriffdom where the company's registered office for the last six months has been situated (IA 1986 s 120(3)).

Northern Ireland
A company may only be wound up in the High Court (Insolvency (Northern Ireland) Order 1989, art 102).

Grounds for winding-up by the court

IA 1986 s 122 specifies as follows:

"A company may be wound up by the court if –
(a) the company has by special resolution resolved that the company be wound up by the court,
(b) being a public company which was registered as such on its original incorporation, the company has not been issued with a certificate under s 117 of the CA 1985 (public company share capital requirements) and more than a year has expired since it was so registered,
(c) it is an old company within the meaning of the Consequential Provisions Act,
(d) the company does not commence business within a year from its incorporation or suspends its business for a whole year,
(e) except in the case of a private company limited by shares or guarantee, the number of members is reduced below two,
(f) the company is unable to pay its debts,
(g) the court is of the opinion that it is just and equitable that the company should be wound up."

Of (a) to (g) above, (f) and (g) are by far the most common methods. For a company to use (a) by applying to the court following a special resolution would nowadays be a cumbersome and expensive method of winding-up. If the members could agree to wind up the company by special resolution, they might as easily agree to have a voluntary winding-up which would not involve the court.

For (b) the option would be open to the company to be wound up if it failed to get the requisite trading certificate, but it is unlikely that anyone would bother. If the company had traded without the certificate being in existence the directors would be potentially liable for the company's debts. However no creditor would be likely to go against the company when he could sue the directors. (c) is virtually obsolete. It would be open for a company to use (d) but it would generally be easier to write to the Registrar of Companies to have the company struck from the register, especially if there has been no trading. There are virtually no recent cases on this issue. (e) was modified following the arrival of the single member company in 1992. (e) still applies to public limited companies.

There is a residual capacity for Scottish companies to apply to the court to be wound up if there is a floating charge and the court is satisfied that the floating charge-holder's security may be threatened (IA 1986 s 122(2)). This is virtually obsolete now that Scottish companies can be put into receivership.

The inability to pay debts (IA s 122(1)(f))

This is explained in the IA 1986 s 123(1) as follows:

"A company is deemed unable to pay its debts –

    (a) if a creditor (by assignment or otherwise) to whom the company is indebted in a sum exceeding £750 then due has served on the company, by leaving it at the company's registered office, a written demand (in the prescribed form) requiring the company to pay the sum so due and the company has for three weeks thereafter neglected to pay the sum or to secure or compound for it to the reasonable satisfaction of the creditor, or

    (b) if, in England and Wales, execution or other process issued on a judgment, decree or order of any court in favour of any creditor of the company is returned unsatisfied in whole or in part, or

    (c) if, in Scotland, the induciae of a charge for payment on an extract decree, or an extract registered bond, or an extract registered protest, have expired without payment being made, or

    (d) if, in Northern Ireland, a certificate of unenforceability has been granted in respect of a judgment against the company, or

    (e) if it is proved to the satisfaction of the court that the company is unable to pay its debts as the fall due."

£750 due and unpaid (IA 1986 s 123(1)(a))

The sum of £750 is not by any means a large sum of money, and three weeks can be a surprisingly short period of time. Provided the claim is validly made and the correct prescribed form (Form 4.1, also known as the statutory demand) is used, there is little the company can do to save itself going into liquidation unless the debt is paid or security (*i.e.* a guarantee, perhaps from a director, or rights over some asset of the company) given in time. The word "compound" in this context means settle, sometimes for less than the full worth but enough to satisfy the creditor. The debt does not need to be due to one creditor alone: if a number of creditors band together and the collective amount due is over £750, a petition for liquidation can still be raised.

    Occasionally there are disputes as to whether or not the sum alleged by the creditor to be due is in fact due. If there is the possibility of a good defence to the claim for debt the petition will be dismissed. The petitioner will then have to try again once he has an unsatisfied judgment or decree against the company.

Execution on a judgment (IA 1986 s 123(1)(b))

Execution on a judgment is the process in England and Wales of enforcement of the decision of a civil court, commonly done by sending in bailiffs or sheriff's officers to carry out a sale of the debtor's assets. If the sums produced by execution fail to satisfy the creditor, the creditor can petition for the company's liquidation. The debt for which execution is being levied can be of any amount.

Expiry of induciae of a charge (IA 1986 s 123(1)(c))

In Scotland the judgement of a civil court is known as a decree. It can be enforced by various methods, of which one is the serving of a charge with a requirement to pay up within 14 days, this period of time being known as the *induciae*. This is a preliminary step before the seizing and selling of the debtor's assets. Failure to pay within the time-limit is grounds for liquidation. The same principle applies in respect of a bond or loan registered in the Books of Council and Session or the Sheriff Court Books for registration and execution, this being a method of enforcing payment without the need to go to court first. An extract registered protest arises in the case of a dishonoured bill of exchange: the person due to receive the money from a dishonoured bill of exchange (a type of cheque) can also demand liquidation after the expiry of the induciae. The debt for which the decree is being enforced can be of any amount.

The grant of a certificate of unenforceability (IA 1986 s 123(1)d))

The grounds on which a company may be wound up in Northern Ireland are essentially the same as in England and Wales (Insolvency (Northern Ireland) Order 1989 art 103). The one exception concerns unsatisfied execution of a judgment. This process no longer exists in Northern Ireland. Instead, judgments are enforced by the Enforcement of Judgments Office under the Judgments Enforcement (Northern Ireland) Order 1981. If the Office is of opinion that a judgment cannot effectively be enforced it grants a certificate of unenforceability. The grant of this certificate constitutes proof that the company is unable to pay its debts.

Proof that the company is unable to pay its debts as they fall due (IA 1986 s 123(1)(e))

A company may have substantial assets but very little cash with which to pay its debts. It may be technically solvent, in that its overall assets are greater than its liabilities, but if those assets are difficult to realise, it may be unable to pay its bills when required to do so. The fact that a creditor's bill is unpaid and that the company is unable or unwilling to sell any assets with which to pay the debt is good evidence that the company is unable to pay its debts as they fall due. The advantage of a petition under this ground is that no statutory notice is required.

There is a further definition of the inability to pay debts in the IA 1986 s 123(2). This is where it is proved to the court's satisfaction that the company's assets are less than its liabilities if to the actual liabilities are added all the "contingent and prospective" liabilities. Contingent and prospective liabilities are those which might arise, such as:

(i) a claim for damages following an injury caused by the company, or
(ii) liabilities that are likely to arise at some stage in the future even if the exact date is not yet known.

To petition the court under this ground would require a detailed knowledge of the company's accounts. It is therefore likely that a petition under this ground would only arise at the instance of well-informed members of the company, directors, professional advisers worried about sums due to them, the company's bankers, or creditors with a good knowledge of the company.

The just and equitable grounds for winding-up (IA 1986 s 122(1)(g))

These grounds are a catch-all for various grounds where the courts have decided that it would be improper for the company to continue in existence. Most of the following categories of grounds are still valid although it is not very likely that all of them would be followed nowadays. The main categories are:

● the disappearance of the substratum of the company;

● the illegality of the company's activities;

● deadlock in the management of the company;

● quasi-partnership cases;

● oppressive conduct by the majority shareholders or directors.

The disappearance of the substratum of the company
The substratum of the company is the principal purpose or trade for which the company was set up. As has been discussed in Chapter 4, adherence to the objects clause was formerly seen as an essential part of a company's duty to its members. After all, the members had invested their capital in the company with the express intention that the money should be used for the purpose stated in the company's memorandum of association and no other. This was noticeably seen in the case *Re German Date Coffee Co* [1882] 20 Ch D 169. A number of shareholders successfully petitioned the court that their company should be wound up because the directors had failed to obtain the correct patent for the production of a certain coffee. The fact that many shareholders did not mind which patent it was, or that the company was solvent made no difference: the

investors' money had not been used for the purpose for which it was invested, and it was therefore just and equitable that the company should be wound up.

This case has never been overruled, so still stands. However, with the decline in importance of the objects clause, the alternative of what probably would be an easier remedy under the CA s1985 s 35(2), the increased importance of third parties' rights in what previously would have been regarded as *ultra vires* contracts and, in particular nowadays, the greater breadth of objects clauses generally, it is not likely that a shareholder would bring such an action now.

The illegality of the company's activities

Not many companies are set up deliberately to perpetrate a fraud, although it is possible that a company might be set up to carry out an activity that was legal at the time that the company was incorporated but was rendered illegal by subsequent legislation. An example might be if a company was set up to trade with a nation that subsequently was the target for sanctions by the UK Government. If the company were to be set up to perpetrate a fraud, the DTI would nowadays be likely to close it down at the request of disgruntled members. However, there have been cases of companies deliberately set up for fraudulent purposes.

Re Thomas Brinsmead & Sons Ltd [1897] 1 Ch 45. An unscrupulous nephew decided to "cash in" on the goodwill attached to his respectable uncle's well-known piano manufacturing business. The nephew and his associates set up a company and invited subscriptions for shares in what investors believed was the uncle's piano business. When enough money had been received by way of subscriptions, the nephew and his associates decamped with the money. At the same time an injunction from the uncle arrived forbidding the nephew and his company from using the uncle's name. The unhappy investors succeeded in having what was left of the company wound up.

Nowadays it is extremely difficult to carry out such a fraud because of the scrutiny undergone by a company inviting the public to acquire shares. However, it remains a possibility that one day a company quoted on the Alternative Investment Market, where the scrutiny is not so intense, might succeed in hoodwinking regulators, advisers and investors, and thus need to be wound up on the above grounds.

Deadlock in the management of the company

If the management of the company has become impossible due to competing and dissenting interests, one option is for the company to be wound up by the court. This arose in the case of *Re Yenidje Tobacco Co Ltd* [1935] Ch 693. Two successful tobacconists decided to join forces to set up a company. However, no sooner had the company been incorporated that the two members/directors who each had an equal share in the company started squabbling about the value of the assets they had transferred to the company. The acrimony between the two members grew so intense that they could only communicate by means of written messages passed to the company secretary who acted as a go-between. In view of the complete inability of the members to agree it was clear that the company would be wound up. Curiously the company remained solvent throughout the dispute.

Were such circumstances to arise nowadays, well drafted articles, learning from the experience of costly and pointless cases such as the above, will have built-in arbitration clauses to deal with such deadlock.

Quasi-partnership cases
This is a loose title for a series of cases which usually concern the behaviour of directors. The best-known case is *Ebrahimi* v *Westbourne Galleries Ltd* [1973] AC 360, where Ebrahimi was deprived of his directorship but was also unable to sell his shares to the directors who had forced him out of office. His treatment was plainly unjust and inequitable, as throughout the company's existence and for many years he had been an equal partner with the then other director, Nazar. Nazar and his son were held to have abused their legitimate power to dismiss Ebrahimi. Nowadays Ebrahimi would have been able to obtain relief under the CA 1985 s 459, but at the time his action was raised, such relief was virtually impossible to obtain due to the courts' then reluctance to grant remedies to minority shareholders. Similar cases of loss of confidence in the goodwill of those who formerly professed it have arisen; in such circumstances a winding up petition has been granted.

Re Zinotty Properties Ltd [1984] 3 All ER 754. The petitioner had been led to believe that he would be appointed a director after he had subscribed for shares; but the majority shareholders changed their minds. He successfully petitioned for winding up on the just and equitable grounds.

Virdi v *Abbey Leisure Ltd* [1990] BCLC 342. Virdi had made his investment on the incorporation of the company in the understanding that the company would carry on its business of operating a disco and nightclub in a certain way and from certain premises. He was held to be entitled to have the company wound up when the majority shareholders subsequently ignored that understanding.

Normally in similar circumstances the would-be investor protects his position by means of a shareholders' agreement before he makes his investment. Although it is not possible to bind a company by a shareholders' agreement it is always possible to bind the members of a company: consequently misunderstanding and changes of mind by the majority shareholders would be less likely to occur.

However, despite the existence of the right to wind up the company, it is probably the case that nowadays a more sure route of success for an aggrieved member is through the CA 1985 s 459 which allows both the aggrieved member and the court wide discretion as to what remedy might be most appropriate under the circumstances.

Oppressive conduct by the majority shareholders or directors
Although this was once an issue that confronted the courts, it is nowadays unlikely to occur because of the greater attention paid to the unfairly prejudicial conduct provisions of the CA 1985 s 459. However, the previous cases in this category have not been overruled and are still valid.

Loch v *John Blackwood Ltd* [1924] AC 783. The minority shareholders successfully petitioned to have their company wound up on the just and equitable grounds that the directors, who were also the majority shareholders, were deliberately refusing to hold general meetings or to make the company's accounts available to the members. This was in order to make the minority members lose interest in the shares and sell them to the majority members for less than their true value.

In the UK now, due to the greater rigour with which the Registrar of Companies pursues companies that are slow to lodge their accounts, such behaviour would be counter-productive, and in any event members would probably use a petition under the CA 1985 s 459 instead. In addition there are statutory procedures available to requisition meetings (CA 1985 s 368) or demand that an AGM be held (CA 1985 s 367).

Who can petition to wind up the company?

Under the IA 1986 s 124 the following can petition to wind up the company:

(a) the company itself;
(b) the directors;
(c) any creditor or creditors, including prospective and contingent creditors;
(d) any contributory or contributories;
(e) the clerk of a magistrates' court in England and Wales following non-payment of a fine by a company;
(f) the Secretary of State, provided:
  (i) the company is a public limited company and has failed to obtain a s 117 trading certificate within a year of having been registered (*i.e.* IA 1986 s 122(1)(b)), or
  (ii) the company is an old public company within the meaning of the Consequential Provisions Act (*i.e.* IA 1986 s 122(1)(c)), or
  (iii) the Secretary of State believes it is in the public interest that the company should be wound up following DTI inspectors' investigation of various regulatory failures or of fraudulent or criminal matters such as insider dealing (IA 1986 s 124A).

Under other legislation the following can also petition to wind up a company:

(a) an administrator appointed under the IA 1986 s 14(1);
(b) an administrative receiver in England and Wales under the IA 1986 s 42(1) by virtue of the general powers given him under the IA 1986 Schedule 1;
(c) a receiver in Scotland under the IA 1986 s 55(2), and a floating charge-holder in Scotland if the security of the floating charge-holder is in danger (IA 1986 s 122(2)); this latter provision survives as a relic from the time when it was not possible in Scotland to appoint receivers;
(d) an administrative receiver in Northern Ireland under the Insolvency (Northern Ireland) Order 1989, by virtue of the general powers given him by art 52(1) and Sch. 1;
(e) the Bank of England to wind up a deposit-taking business (Banking Act 1987 s 92(1));
(f) the DTI to wind up insurance companies (Insurance Companies Act 1982 s 54(1));
(g) the Attorney-General in England and Wales to wind up charitable companies (Charities Act 1993 s 63);
(h) the Lord Advocate in Scotland to wind up charitable companies (Law Reform (Miscellaneous Provisions) (Scotland) Act 1990 s 14.

The company as petitioner

It would be unusual for the company, through the members, to petition for its own liquidation since it would be expensive to do. However, since it requires a special or extraordinary resolution to wind up a company voluntarily, it may be that the company cannot muster the requisite approval. In that event an ordinary resolution to petition the court for liquidation may enable the company to be wound up by the court.

The creditor as petitioner

A creditor is only a creditor if the company owes him a confirmed debt. So, for example, someone who has a pending claim against the company in tort or delict for injuries received from an employee of the company does not have an immediate claim for payment and cannot have the company wound up. However, once the court has granted judgment (or decree in Scotland) in favour of the claimant, and if the methods of execution (or diligence in Scotland) have not resulted in payment, then the company can be wound up. Assuming a creditor is justified in his claim he is normally entitled to have the company wound up, but under the IA 1986 s 195 there is discretion to the court to consider the interests of other creditors and contributories. It might be, for example, that all the other creditors strongly objected to the winding-up of the company but that the one petitioning creditor was motivated by bad faith or spite or some other objectionable reason. However, the courts have no discretion to consider the interests of the employees or the public generally (*Re Craven Insurance Co Ltd* [1968] 1 All ER 1140). Normally there has to be some benefit to the creditor and all the creditors generally for winding up, since there would be little point in winding up a company only to find that there are no assets or the secured creditors would obtain such assets as there are. Nonetheless a petition cannot be refused on the grounds that the company has no assets or only assets secured to other creditors (IA 1986 s 125(1)).

The contributory as petitioner

A contributory is defined in the IA 1986 s 79 as someone who is liable to contribute to the assets of the company on its winding-up, though in fact a more detailed examination of the wording of the legislation reveals that a contributory need not always be required to contribute to the company; the company may occasionally have to contribute to him.

In effect this means:

(a) a present member who is due to pay money to the company either:
   (i) where he is still due to pay the balance on his partly-paid shares or,
   (ii) where the company is a guarantee company, by being obliged to honour his guarantee to the company in terms of the company's memorandum and articles of association, or
   (iii) where he is liable under the IA 1986 s 76. This refers to the liability of a member receiving payment out of capital under the CA 1985 s 173 for shares repurchased or redeemed by the company and where the company has gone into insolvent liquidation within one year of the payment;
(b) a director in connection with the circumstances of (a)(iii) above save that instead of being a member he as a director authorised the repurchase or redemption of the shares within one year of the company's winding-up;
(c) in the same circumstances as (a)(iii) above, a past member all of whose shares have been purchased or redeemed by the company;
(d) a past member:
   (i) except where he disposed of his partly-paid shares at least a year before the winding-up (IA 1986 s 74(2)(a)); and/or
   (ii) except in respect of debts of the company which arose after he ceased to be a member (IA 1986 s 74(2)(b)); and
   (iii) only if the funds of the present members are insufficient, unless the court decides otherwise (IA 1986 s 74(2)(c).

In any event he cannot be made liable for any sums beyond the amount remaining unpaid on the shares he disposed of (IA 1986 s 74(2)(d)). If its seems unfair that a past member should be liable for the debts of a company it is to be remembered that he would have been transferring partly-paid shares. This might suggest that he knew something about the future prospects of the company that the purchaser of those shares did not;

(e) a present member with fully paid-up shares who expects to have a tangible interest in the winding-up because there may be a surplus. This surprising but necessary interpretation arises because of the wording in the IA 1986 s 74(1) which refers to the "adjustment of the rights of the contributories between themselves".

Contributories within the categories of (a)(iii), (b) and (c) above may petition the court for winding-up on the grounds of the company's inability to pay its debts or on the just and equitable grounds (IA 1986 s 124(3)) without having to comply with the requirements of the next paragraph. However, except in the context of those two particular grounds, such contributories must otherwise comply with the requirements of the next paragraph.

Except as stated directly above, if a contributory wishes to petition the court for the winding-up of a company he can only do so if:

(a) the number of members has dropped below two (IA 1986 s 124(2)(a)), or
(b) the shares in respect of which he is a contributory were allotted to him (IA 1986 s 124(2)(b)), or
(c) the contributory has held the shares registered in his name for at least six out of the 18 months preceding the winding-up petition (IA 1986 s 124(2)(b)), or
(d) the contributory inherited the shares (IA 1986 s 124(2)(b)).

The reason these restrictions on contributories' ability to petition the court for liquidation have been imposed is that in respect of (a) a contributory might wish to avoid the prospect of being personally liable for the company's debts under the CA 1985 s 24.

The six months rule in the IA 1986 s 124(2)(b) is designed to prevent someone buying shares in a company with the express purpose of destroying it by presenting a petition for winding-up.

The allotment rule and the inheritance rule are also designed to give a remedy to members who were unaware of what debts the company was running up at the time of allotment or inheritance because they did not have access to the normal information about a company that a member has.

A contributory normally has to have an interest in the winding-up, either by effectively preventing the directors running up more debts for which he as contributory will become responsible, or because he hopes to obtain a surplus after payment of all creditors after the winding-up. As with creditors, the courts may have regard to the interests of other contributories under the IA 1986 s195 if they strongly oppose the liquidation for good reasons. If the petitioner is acting unreasonably in seeking a winding-up order, the courts may dismiss the petition (IA 1986 s 125(2)).

Winding up by the Secretary of State in the public interest under the IA 1986 s 124A

This takes place from time to time when a company has deceived the public, investors or creditors and has subsequently collapsed. In such circumstances, DTI inspectors or, in England and Wales, the Official Receiver can recommend to the Secretary of State that he apply to the court to have the company wound up. In Northern Ireland the Department of Economic Development may present this petition under the Insolvency (Northern Ireland) Order 1989, art 104A.

A recent remarkable winding-up was that of the Ostrich Farming Corporation Plc which promised enormous returns to its investors if they bought ostriches to be reared by the company and then slaughtered the ostriches for their lean and apparently tasty meat. Seduced by tempting advertisements in quality news-papers and despite the absence of any evidence that there was any real demand for ostrich meat, many gullible investors parted with large sums of money to buy their own ostriches. Although some money was genuinely used for the pur-chase and rearing of ostriches, many of the birds were sold several times over. The farms where the ostriches were reared were in Belgium, sufficiently distant to deter investors from actually checking on their own birds. Furthermore, many of the investors' birds soon died anyway. Shortly before the DTI investigation, £7.5 million of company money was paid in questionable circumstances to a Delaware offshore company owned by an acquaintance of the Ostrich Farming Corporation's directors. DTI inspectors were called in to investigate and subse-quently recommended to the Secretary of State that he apply to the court to have the company wound up. The winding-up duly took place, though there was little left for investors by the time of the liquidation.

The procedure for winding up a company by the court

The court procedure for petitioning the court for winding up is different in each UK jurisdiction, but in principle the system is the same. The petitioner must be competent to raise an action and must assert valid grounds for seeking the granting of the petition with supporting evidence such as the certificate indicat-ing the service of the notice demanding payment within 21 days. The petition must be served on the company at its registered office and, depending on the circumstances, can also be served on such others as may have an interest, such as an administrator, and administrative receiver, a receiver in Scotland, a super-visor under a voluntary arrangement and a liquidator if a liquidator has been already put into voluntary liquidation. It will also need to be advertised in the newspapers and the Gazette (Insolvency Rules r 4.11 and Insolvency (Scotland) Rules r 4.2).

The court can dismiss, adjourn or make any such order as it sees fit (IA 1986 s 125(1)). If there is a danger that perishable items owned by the company may deteriorate the court can appoint a provisional liquidator to dispose of them rather than let them go to waste. This can be done prior to the granting of the winding-up order (IA 1986 s 135). Equally a provisional liquidator may be appointed where there is a risk that the company's employees or creditors will simply "remove" the company's assets if they know the company is in financial danger. In England and Wales the provisional liquidator will commonly be the Official Receiver, but in Scotland, there is no Official Receiver and an insolvency practitioner will act as provisional liquidator. A provisional liquidator must lodge a sum of money with the courts as a guarantee that he will not abscond with the liquidation proceeds. In Scotland this practice is known as "finding caution". In any event insolvency practitioners are required to have professional indemnity both for their own negligence and to cover the risk of default.

There is a distinction to be made between the presentation of a winding-up order or petition and the granting of the order or petition. Although as stated above a provisional liquidator can be appointed on the presentation of the order or petition, this does not constitute full winding-up. On presentation of an order or petition, but before approval for the order or petition is given by the court, any creditor or the company or a contributory can apply to the court to stay or restrain any other court proceedings against the company (IA 1986 s126). This is to prevent unnecessary litigation and to ensure that all creditors and contributories are treated equally and fairly.

Equally, during this period any dispositions of property or transfers of shares are void (IA 1986 s 127). In addition, any attachments or seizing by creditors of assets of the company in satisfaction of creditors' debts is void as far as companies in England and Wales are concerned. In Scotland this issue is dealt with under the IA 1985 s 185, which is discussed later in this chapter.

In Northern Ireland the position is similar to that in England (Insolvency (Northern Ireland) Order 1989 arts 107–108).

Once the winding-up order has been granted, or a provisional liquidator appointed, the Registrar of Companies is informed (IA 1986 s 130(1)) and no one can raise an action against the company except with leave of the court (IA 1986 s 130(2)). There must be advertisement in the newspapers and the relevant Gazettes of the liquidation (IA 1986 s 137(4) and for Scotland s 138(6)). The Official Receiver in England and Wales, the interim liquidator in Scotland, and the Official Receiver in Northern Ireland then are given power to investigate the reasons for the failure of the company and to obtain statements about the company's assets and liabilities from the company's promoters, officers and employees (IA 1986 s 131 and Insolvency (Northern Ireland) Order 1989 art 111). Such persons may if necessary be publicly examined (IA 1986 s 133). If they attempt to flee the country, a warrant can be issued for their arrests and any relevant documents or monies connected with the company can be seized (IA 1986 s 134 and Insolvency (Northern Ireland) Order 1989 arts 113–4).

The Official Receiver may within 12 weeks for England, Wales and Northern Ireland convene separate meetings of the company's creditors and contributories to select a permanent liquidator (IA 1986 s 136(5) and Insolvency (Northern Ireland) Order 1989 art 116). If one-quarter of the creditors demand a meeting, he is obliged to hold one (IA 1986 s 136(5)(c)). The permanent liquidator, known in the legislation as the liquidator to distinguish his office from the Official Receiver, may in practice be the same person as the Official Receiver or the provisional liquidator. Sometimes creditors are keen that a certain insolvency practitioner be appointed liquidator because of his particular expertise, and if that insolvency practitioner is chosen, the Official Receiver will demit office.

In Scotland the interim liquidator must within 28 days convene a meeting of creditors and contributories to be held within 42 days and at which to appoint a permanent liquidator (IA 1986 s 138 and Insolvency (Scotland) Rules r 4.12(2A)). However, where the company is being wound up on the grounds of its inability to pay its debts, he may decide to convene only a meeting of the creditors (IA 1986 s 138(4)). The interim liquidator is often appointed as the permanent liquidator.

In any of the jurisdictions if there is disagreement about whose choice of liquidator should prevail (the creditors' choice or the contributories' choice) the creditors' choice will normally prevail (IA 1986 s 139(3)) unless the court decides otherwise (IA 1986 s 139(4) and Insolvency (Northern Ireland) Order 1989 art 118). In England, Wales and Northern Ireland if the ultimate liquidator is not the Official Receiver, the liquidator still has to report to the Official Receiver concerning his activities and must keep the Official Receiver apprised of any matters that the Official Receiver, in his capacity as a general watchdog in the public interest, may need to know about (IA 1986 s 143(2) and Insolvency (Northern Ireland) Order 1989 art 121(2)).

Once the liquidator has been appointed, the property of the company is vested in him (IA 1986 s 145 and Insolvency (Northern Ireland) Order 1989 art 123) and he is entitled to take in the company's property and keep it under his control (IA 1986 s 144(1) and Insolvency (Northern Ireland) Order 1989 art 122). The court has extensive powers to defer court proceedings, obtain money due from contributories, decide the date by which creditors must intimate their claims, convene meetings, seize property and other powers (IA 1986 ss 147–159 and Insolvency (Northern Ireland) Order 1989 arts 125–137) many of which the court will in practice delegate to the liquidator (IA 1986 s 160).

Voluntary winding-up

A company can be wound up voluntarily on three occasions:

- The company's articles of association may have specified that the company is to exist for a certain period only, or for the promotion of a particular project such as a commemorative event. Once the event has taken place, the company can pass an ordinary resolution to wind up the company (IA 1986 s 84(1)(a)).

- The company may by special resolution and for any reason choose to wind itself up (IA 1986 s 84(1)(b)).

- The company may by extraordinary resolution choose to wind itself up on the specific grounds that it cannot by reason of its liabilities continue its business and that it is advisable to wind itself up (IA 1986 s 84(1)(c)). The advantage of the extraordinary resolution is that it does not require the 21 days' notice of a special resolution. This may be significant where debts are mounting fast.

Once the appropriate resolution has been passed, the Registrar of Companies must be informed within 15 days (IA 1986 s 84(3)) and a notice inserted in the Gazette (IA 1986 s 85(1)). The winding-up is deemed to have commenced as at the date of the resolution (IA 1986 s 86) and from that time onwards the company must cease to carry on business except as required by the liquidator to enable the winding up to take place the more effectively (IA 1986 s 87). No transfers of the company's shares may be made from that date except with the permission of the liquidator (IA 1986 s 88). This is to prevent unscrupulous members dumping their shares on less well informed members or others who might be misled into thinking that there might be a surplus payable on the shares.

Members' voluntary winding-up

Before any members' voluntary winding-up takes place, a majority of directors must make a statutory declaration stating that having made a full inquiry into the company's affairs they are of the view that the company can pay all its debts within a period of up to a year from the date of commencement of the winding-up (IA 1986 s 89(1)). Directors who are not so confident are well advised to refuse to make the declaration and to have their objections noted, as a declaration made without good reason and subsequently found to be unjustified may result in the declaring directors' imprisonment (IA 1986 s 89(4)). The statutory declaration must be made within a period of five weeks or less prior to the resolution for the winding-up (IA 1986 s 89(2)(a)) and must be accompanied by an up-to-date statement of the company's assets and liabilities (IA 1986 s 89(2)(b)). The declaration and the statement must be forwarded to the Registrar of Companies within 15 days (IA 1986 s 89(3)).

A statutory declaration made in the above manner is not required for a creditors' voluntary winding-up because the directors know that the company cannot pay its debts. However, if a statutory declaration is made and it subsequently turns out that the company cannot pay all its debts within the period specified in the declaration, the liquidator converts the members' voluntary winding-up into a creditors' voluntary winding-up (IA 1986 s 96) and thereafter follows the procedure suitable for a creditors' voluntary winding-up (IA 1986 s 95).

Assuming the declaration has been properly made and once the appropriate resolution to wind up the company has been passed, the members can appoint one or more liquidators to carry out the task of winding up the company. The liquidator will then exercise his extensive rights under the IA 1986 s 165 to gather in the company's assets and where necessary convert them into cash. Under the IA 1986 Schedule 4 Part 1 the liquidator needs the approval of the members if he proposes to compromise any claims, as, for example, settling a dispute for less than the full claim, in the interest of cost and efficiency. If he wants to raise or defend any legal action in the name of the company he will need the approval of the court (IA 1986 Schedule 4 Part 11). Most other powers are granted to him without any requirement to seek approval (IA 1986 Schedule 4 Part III).

He will pay off any outstanding preferential debts (assuming there is no administrative receiver or Scottish receiver, who would normally deal with them unless there is agreement otherwise) and all other debts due by the company, call in all monies due to the company and disburse the proceeds to the members in accordance with the rights specified in the company's articles (IA 1986 s 107). He is not obliged to give cash to the members. The proceeds could be given *in specie* (in the form of the company's assets equivalent in value to the sums due) or in shares in some other company which has acquired the business or property of the liquidated company (IA 1986 s 110(2)).

Creditors' voluntary winding-up

As with a members' voluntary winding-up, the appropriate resolution is passed in general meeting. This is generally an extraordinary resolution to wind up the company because the company's liabilities make the company unable to continue in business (IA 1986 s 84(1)(c)). No statutory declaration is made beforehand. Instead the company:

- arranges a creditors' meeting to be held within 14 days of the passing of the resolution (IA 1986 s 98(1)(a));

- ensures that the creditors are informed by post of the meeting at least seven days prior to the meeting (IA 1986 s 98(1)(b));

- arranges for suitable advertisement in local newspapers and the appropriate Gazette of the forthcoming creditors' meeting.

The notice of the meeting must either indicate the name and address of the insolvency practitioner who will be able to inform creditors of the company's affairs (IA 1986 s 98(2)) or where a list of the creditors is being held (IA 1986 s 98(2)(b)).

At the meeting the directors must lay a prepared statement (the statutory Form 4.4) before the creditors (IA 1986 s 99(1)). The statement details the entire assets and liabilities of the company (IA 1986 s 99(2)). The directors must vouch for the accuracy of the statement (IA 1986 s 99(2)) on pain of criminal sanctions (IA 1986 s 99(3)). One of the directors chairs the meeting (IA 1986 s 99(1)(c)) and apart from ascertaining the extent to which the creditors are likely to have their debts paid, the main purpose of the meeting is to choose a liquidator. Ideally both the members and the creditors at the respective meetings will agree on who the liquidator will be, but in the event of a disagreement, the creditors' choice will prevail unless they make no choice (IA 1986 s 100(2)) or the courts decide otherwise (IA 1986 s 100(3)).

As a matter of practice the choice of liquidator can be very significant. Historically there used to be a problem with certain liquidators being too close, personally and financially, to the directors of the company of whose assets they were liquidators. Between them, the directors and the liquidator would arrange matters substantially to the directors' benefit. With the rise of the profession of insolvency practitioner, such practices are less likely to arise. However, one weak point in the appointment of the creditors' choice of liquidator is that if a particular creditor is apparently not told of the creditors' meeting, or fails to read the requisite newspaper where the official notice of liquidation is posted, he is not in a position to turn up to the meeting and express any opinion on his choice of liquidator. As the invitation to the creditors is sent out in the post, it is easy for an unscrupulous director to claim that the invitation letter never arrived but that that is no fault of his. If a creditor is not happy with the choice of liquidator it may be difficult for him to prove that the liquidator in question is in any way unsuitable.

Another ruse involving creditors is to arrange for the directors' friends to submit spurious invoices and claim to be genuine creditors. They can then elect the liquidator of the directors' choice without the innocent creditors knowing. The spurious invoices can also be a devious means of extracting money from the company at the expense of the other genuine creditors. The monies that the liquidator pays in settlement of the spurious invoices can then be passed under the table back to the directors.

The creditors can also form a committee to advise the liquidator. The creditors can appoint up to five of their number to serve on the committee (IA 1986 s 101(1)), and the company can also nominate five members to serve on the same committee (IA 1986 s 101(2)). The creditors can, however, object to the members' choices and those chosen members will then be unable to take their seats on the committee unless the court decides otherwise (IA 1986 s 103). This is because the members who will want to be on the committee may well be the ones who caused the company's financial difficulties in the first place, so the creditors would not wish to have them on the committee. Equally, members who were not responsible for the company's difficulties might well be useful committee members.

Once the liquidator has been appointed, the directors cease to have any say in the management of the company except where the liquidation committee directs otherwise (IA 1986 s 103).

Thereafter the liquidator, broadly speaking, has the same function as a liquidator under a members' voluntary winding-up (IA 1986 s 165). If he is unsatisfactory as a liquidator he can be replaced following a majority vote of the members in favour in the case of members' voluntary winding-up or by a majority vote in favour by the creditors in the case of a creditors' voluntary winding-up (IA 1986 s 171). The court can also remove a liquidator if necessary (IA 1986 s 172).

Getting in the company's assets

Although the three different methods of appointing and to a certain extent directing the liquidator are different, in many respects once the liquidator is appointed his task is the same irrespective of the method of appointment. His initial task is to see what assets the company has and subsequently to divide the assets up fairly between those entitled to them. Legislation has given the liquidator the following powers to enable him to maximise the company's assets and diminish its liabilities:

- disclaiming onerous property (England and Wales only) (IA 1986 s 178);

- making calls upon the contributories (IA 1986 Schedule 3);

- setting aside execution and attachment of goods and land (England and Wales only) (IA 1986 s 183);

- equalising diligence within certain time-limits (Scotland only) (IA 1985 s 185);

- setting aside execution and attachment of goods and land (Northern Ireland) only;

- avoiding certain antecedent transactions and charges in England and Wales under the IA 1986 ss 238 and 239;

- avoiding certain antecedent transactions and charges in Scotland under the IA 1986 ss 242 and 243;

- avoiding certain antecedent transactions and charges in Northern Ireland under Insolvency (Northern Ireland) Order 1989 arts 202–208;

- avoiding extortionate credit transactions (IA 1986 s 244);

- avoiding certain floating charges (IA 1985 s 245) (see Chapter 17);

- obtaining summary remedy against delinquent directors for misfeasance etc. (IA 1986 s 212);

- applying to court to require anyone involved in fraudulent trading under the IA 1986 s 213 to contribute to the company's assets;

- applying to court to require officers of the company involved in wrongful trading under the IA 1986 s 214 to contribute to the company's assets;

- under the IA 1986 s 216 requiring anyone involved in the management of a phoenix company to contribute to the assets of the recently defunct company with a similar name.

Power to disclaim onerous property (IA 1986 s 178)
Sometimes a liquidator discovers that the company owns property or is involved in a contract which is more trouble or expense than is justified under the circumstances. It is then possible for the liquidator to issue a notice in a pre-scribed form, indicating that the company will no longer accept any liability or indeed rights and benefits arising from the property or contract. This will release the liquidator from the burden of trying to service an impossible debt or make a claim it cannot pay. Although this procedure benefits the company in liquidation, it is unfortunate for any other party who has thus lost the benefit of the onerous contract or property. All he can do is intimate a claim for loss or damage to the liquidator in the hope that the liquidator will be able ultimately to repay some of it (IA 1986 s 178(6)). The courts can be asked to transfer any disclaimed property to anyone else who has a valid interest (IA 1986 s 181). This procedure is not available in Scotland.

Power to make calls on contributories (IA Schedule 3)
Although nowadays it is not as common as it once was to have partly paid shares, if there are partly paid shares in existence in a company the liquidator

can make the partly-paid shareholders or contributories pay the balance due on the shares to the company. As was explained earlier, former shareholders who transferred partly-paid shares can, in limited circumstances, also be required to pay the balance due on the shares to the company.

Power to set aside execution and attachment of goods and land (England and Wales only) (IA 1986 s 183)

In England and Wales a creditor can issue execution against the goods of a company or attach a debt due to the company. This means that the goods can be seized and sold to defray the debt, or the monies due to the company can be taken by the creditor, provided the relevant procedure is complied with. If the procedure is complete before liquidation takes place, the creditor is protected (IA 1986 s 183(1)). If it is incomplete, the liquidator can demand the asset from the creditor (IA 1986 s 183(1)), unless the court decides otherwise (IA 1986 s 183(2)(c)).

There are some qualifications to this statement. If the creditor knew by notice that a meeting had been called for the winding-up of the company, then to be safe from the liquidator he must have completed the execution or attachment before the date of the notice (IA 1986 s 183(2)(a)).

If execution takes place, and a sheriff (a court-registered official whose task is to sell debtors' assets to release funds to their creditors, and sometimes known as a bailiff) sells the debtor company's assets, a person buying an asset in good faith from the sheriff acquires a good title to the asset, and cannot be required to return the asset to the liquidator (IA 1986 s 183(2)(b)).

Where the company's goods have been taken by the sheriff prior to sale, but before the sale can take place the sheriff learns that the company is in liquidations, the sheriff must hand the goods to the liquidator although the sheriff is entitled to his execution expenses as a first claim of the proceeds of the assets following their sale by the liquidator (IA 1986 s 184(2)).

Power to equalise diligence within certain time-limits (Scotland only) (IA 1986 s 185)

Diligence is the collective Scottish term for execution, attachment and the other methods of enforcing a court decree. The IA 1986 legislation has been carefully adapted to concur with the Scottish law on bankruptcy (Bankruptcy (Scotland) Act 1985) and indeed refers to it. In essence fully completed diligence that takes place within a period of 60 days prior to the commencement of liquidation, or four months after that date, is all treated as taking place as at the date of commencement of liquidation. In this respect the claims are treated as equal irrespective of the date of the claim and its apparent date priority. Although it may seem odd to try to seize assets of the company after the company is in liquidation, not all creditors will necessarily know that the company is in liquidation, and may instruct sheriff officers (the Scottish equivalent to bailiffs/sheriffs) or messengers-at-arms (who are similar to sheriff officers but attached to the Court of Session) to proceed with the necessary steps towards a sale of the debtor company's assets. They may try, and indeed succeed in doing this even after the company is in liquidation. But if they do so within four months after the commencement of liquidation, the liquidator is entitled to go to the creditor and demand the return of the assets (if unsold) or more likely the proceeds thereof, and to insist that the proceeds be handed back to the liquidator. They will then be added to the pool of assets out of which the liquidator will repay all creditors.

Inevitably creditors who have carried out their diligence within the time-limit of 60 days before the commencement of liquidation and four months after are not always happy about this particular rule. However, it is designed to obviate the problem mentioned at the beginning of the chapter, which is that without this rule, the more threatening creditors would be paid first at the expense of the more patient ones. It also means that overall there are more funds to disburse to all the creditors.

Power to set aside execution and attachment of goods and land in Northern Ireland
Similar provisions exist in Northern Ireland under Part VI of the Judgments Enforcement (Northern Ireland) Order 1981. Essentially the Enforcement of Judgments Office must retain the proceeds of any enforcement order for 21 days after receipt of the same. If no resolution for voluntary winding up is passed or no winding up petition is presented within that time the proceeds are handed over to the creditor. If a resolution is passed or a winding up petition is presented and a winding up order is made the enforcement terminates and the proceeds retained by the Office are handed over to the official receiver or liquidator. Costs and expenses of enforcement are a first charge on these proceeds.

Power to avoid certain antecedent transactions and charges in England and Wales under the IA 1986 ss 238 and 239
When a company goes into liquidation, one of the tasks of the liquidator is to look at antecedent transactions, *i.e.* actions carried out by the company shortly before the commencement of liquidation and which may not be entirely innocent. Common actions include the giving away for less than the full price of the company's assets to the managing directors' relatives and friends, and the repaying of certain loans to favoured individuals in preference to more patient creditors.

If a company was becoming insolvent, it would be very tempting for a director either:

(i)   to give a company asset to a friend or relative (known as a transaction at an undervalue if the value of the gift is greater than any consideration that may have been given), or

(ii) repay in advance a friend or useful supplier who had lent him money, or put
     such a person in a better position than other creditors (known as a preference)

before he paid those who were less important to him socially or who were less
likely to be useful to him later.

Either a transaction at an undervalue or more commonly a preference may be
carried out, or backed up by a secured charge granted by the company, with the
intention or effect that the chargee should benefit at the expense of the other
creditors.

If:

(i)   the transaction at an undervalue or the preference was granted in favour of
      a connected person (*i.e.* spouse, children, partners in business, connected
      companies etc.) within a period of two years ending with the onset of
      insolvency (as defined later) it will, subject to (iv) below, be invalid (IA
      1986 s 240(1)(a));
(ii) any preference (irrespective of the person receiving the benefit of the pref-
      erence) which is not a transaction at an undervalue was given within the
      period of six months ending with the onset of insolvency it will, subject to
      (iv) below, be invalid (IA 1986 s 240(1)(b));
(iii) any transaction at an undervalue or any preference secured by a charge is
      granted between the presentation of a petition for the making of an admin-
      istration order and the making of that order will, subject to (iv) below, be
      invalid (IA 1986 s 240(1)(c)). There may be a gap of some weeks before
      the presentation and the making of the order for administration.

However,

(iv) a transaction at an undervalue or a preference will only be invalid if the
      company is unable to pay its debts (*i.e.* is insolvent) or unable to pay its
      debts as a result of the transaction at an undervalue or the preference (IA
      1986 s 240(2)). But if a transaction at an undervalue is in favour of a con-
      nected person it is up to the connected person to show that the company
      was solvent at the time of the transaction and was not made insolvent by
      the transaction.

The effect of the IA 1986 ss 238 and 239 is to increase the value of the funds
available to the liquidator for subsequent disbursement to all creditors by recall-
ing (by order of the court if necessary) any gifts from their recipients (to the
extent that the gifts are less than the true value) and making those creditors who
had been preferred pay to the liquidator what they had received from the company before it was wound up (IA 1986 s 241). Those who received gifts may

be required to pay the full value; charges granted by the company may be discharged by the court; but those who acquired assets in good faith and for value either:

(a) directly from the company, or
(b) indirectly from a recipient of a transaction at an undervalue or a preference creditor,
(c) without notice of any restriction on the right of the recipient or the preference creditor to dispose of the asset

will normally be under no obligation to repay the value of the asset to the liquidator or return the asset unless they were parties to the transaction or the preference (IA 1986 s 241).

Power to avoid certain antecedent transactions and charges in Scotland (IA 1986 ss 242, 243)
In Scotland transactions at an undervalue are known as gratuitous alienations and preferences are known as unfair preferences. Although the basic principle of the law relating to these two issues is broadly the same in each jurisdiction, there are several details which differ. A gratuitous alienation is a disposition of the company's property either for no consideration or less than full consideration, or in other words a gift or partial gift. Once a company is in liquidation, any creditor due money from the company before the liquidation, or the liquidator, can challenge a gratuitous alienation (IA 1986 s 242(1)). In order to be a valid challenge, the alienation must have taken place within five years of the commencement of the winding-up if the recipient is an "associate" (similar to a "connected person" in the rest of the IA 1986 and CA 1985). If the recipient is anyone else, the period is two years. This is considerably longer than the equivalent periods under English law.

The courts will "reduce" (*i.e.* set aside) the alienation and grant an order for the restoration of the company's property (or the proceeds thereof) to the company or discharge any charge granted by the company by way of a gratuitous alienation unless anyone seeking to uphold the alienation can establish that:

(a) the company's assets were greater than its liabilities at the time of the alienation (IA 1986 s 242(4)(a));
(b) the alienation was made for adequate consideration (IA 1986 s 242(4)(b));
(c) the alienation was a birthday, Christmas or other conventional gift or a gift made for a charitable purpose to someone who was not an associate of the company, on any of which occasions it was reasonable for the company to have made the gift.

In any of the events in (a), (b) or (c) above, anyone acquiring rights in an asset of the company derived from a recipient of a gratuitous alienation is protected provided he acquired his rights in good faith and for value (IA 1986 s 242(4)).

An unfair preference is the early repayment of a loan or some other obligation which has the effect of prejudicing the other creditors because the company's money is available to the preferred creditor instead of all creditors equally. An unfair preference is any preference created within six months before the commencement of the winding-up or the making of an administration order. It is possible to have an unfair preference by way of a charge, thus turning the creditor into a secured creditor in the event of the company's winding-up. For the avoidance of doubt is is specified that the following are not unfair preferences:

- transactions in the ordinary course of business (IA 1986 s 243(2)(a));

- payments in cash when a debt was due and payable, unless the underlying transaction was part of a scheme to prejudice the other creditors generally (IA 1986 s 243(2)(b));

- a transaction in which each party owed obligations to each other, irrespective of the time of performance of those obligations) unless the underlying transaction was part of a scheme to prejudice the other creditors generally (IA 1986 s 243(2)(c));

- the granting of a mandate by a company authorising an arrestee to pay over arrested sums to the arrestor following a proper warrant or decree (IA 1986 s 243(2)(d)).

Any creditor, due money from before the winding-up, and the liquidator can both challenge unfair preferences (IA 1986 s 243(4)). If the court is satisfied that the challenge to the preference is justified, it can order that the preference be reduced (set aside) and the company's property, or the proceeds thereof, sent to the liquidator, or any charge discharged. As with gratuitous alienations, the rights of third parties acquiring company assets for value in good faith are protected.

Power to avoid certain antecedent transactions in Northern Ireland
This is similar to the provisions applicable to England and Wales (Insolvency (Northern Ireland) Order 1989, arts 202–208).

Power to set aside extortionate credit transactions (IA 1986 s 244)
If a company has been unwise enough to obtain a loan which requires "grossly exorbitant payments to be made" within the three years ending on the day when the company went into liquidation, the courts can set aside the loan

or any associated obligation, vary its terms, demand repayment by the lender, return any assets held as security by the lender and demand a proper accounting. This section is designed to prevent loan sharks forcing a company into liquidation at the expense of other creditors. It is not invoked very often, loan sharks in general having other extra-legal methods of ensuring payment from directors personally.

Power to avoid certain floating charges (IA 1986 s 245)
This was also discussed in the context of floating charges (Chapter 17). A liquidator may be able to establish that a floating charge is invalid under certain circumstances. This will mean that funds that the receiver thought he would be obtaining for the floating charge-holder will in fact revert to the liquidator and thence to the general body of creditors.

The circumstances are as follows:

(a) if the floating charge is not registered within 21 days of its creation (CA 1985 s 395 and for Scotland s 410); if the floating charge is not registered before the liquidation of the company but is still registered within 21 days of its creation (even although the company may by then be in liquidation), and there are no other factors invalidating the floating charge, it will be valid;

(b) a floating charge created at a relevant time (as defined later) is deemed to be invalid except for any of the following:

   (i) the value of any money paid or goods or services supplied at the same time as or after the creation of the charge. This means that monies lent to the company, or goods and services supplied to the company prior to the creation of the charge are not covered by the charge, as permitting that would retrospectively put the creditor in a better position than other creditors (IA 1986 s 245(2)(a));

   (ii) the value of any reduction or discharge of any debt of the company carried out at the same time or after the creation of the charge (IA 1986 s 245(2)(b));

   (iii) any interest arising from (i) or (ii) above.

The relevant time, as referred to above, depends on who the floating charge-holder is. If the floating charge-holder is a connected person, then any floating charge granted in his favour created within two years of the date of commencement of the winding-up is invalid (IA 1986 s 245(3)(a)) irrespective of the solvency of the company, except to the extent of (i), (ii) or (iii) above.

If the floating charge-holder is not a connected person, then any floating charge granted in his favour created within 12 months of the date of commencement of winding up is invalid (IA 1986 s 245(3)(b)) provided the company was at the time of the creation of the charge unable to pay its debts in terms of the IA 1986 s 123 (see earlier in this chapter) (IA 1986 s 245(4)(a)) or becomes unable to pay its debts because of the transaction for which the floating charge was granted (IA 1986 s 245(4)(b)) – all except to the extent of (i), (ii) or (iii) above.

As can be seen from the above, floating charges in favour of connected persons within the two-year period are likely to be struck down by the courts even if the company were solvent except to the extent that any new money was lent to the company by the connected person and for which the connected person obtained a contemporaneous floating charge. The reason for this is that a connected person would be more likely than any ordinary creditor to know the future prospects of the company and to take steps to ensure that at least his own debt was repaid. An astute connected person taking a floating charge to secure his own loan to the company ensures that the company survives at least two years before liquidation in order that when the receiver is appointed under his floating charge the appointment of his receiver cannot be invalidated.

Power to obtain summary remedy against delinquent directors for misfeasance etc. under the IA 1986 s 212

This is more extensively discussed in Chapter 14. "Misfeasance" is a term which covers a multitude of sins performed by directors (or other officers of the company and including shadow directors) which amount to breach of fiduciary duty or negligence. Where a director has misappropriated the company's assets, failed to account for them satisfactorily, taken advantage of his position or obtained some secret profit from his work for the company, he may be required by the court on the application of the liquidator, or indeed any creditor, contributory or the Official Receiver in England, Wales or Northern Ireland, to return such assets or pay or repay to the company such amount as the court thinks just (IA 1986 s 212(3)). As directors are often in a strong position to remove the company's assets for their own advantage or use, it is a useful weapon in the liquidator's armoury against unsatisfactory directors.

The power to apply to court to require anyone involved in fraudulent trading under the IA 1986 s 213 to contribute to the company's assets

As will be recalled from Chapter 14, this section is rarely used because of the difficulties in proving fraudulent trading. But in the unusual event of fraudulent trading being established, the court, on the application of the liquidator, could order not just directors but anyone knowingly involved in the fraudulent trading to contribute such amount to the company's assets as the court thinks proper (IA 1986 s 213(2)). The amount of the contribution need not just be compensatory: it can be punitive as well (*Re a Company (No 001418 of 1988)* [1991] BCLC 197) if the circumstances so justify it.

The power to apply to court to require officers of the company involved in wrongful trading under the IA 1986 s 214 to contribute to the company's assets
This is also discussed in greater detail in Chapter 14. In essence, where:

(a) a company has gone into insolvent liquidation (IA 1986 s 214(2)(a)), and
(b) a director, past director or shadow director of that company knew or ought to have known that there was no reasonable prospect that the company would avoid going into insolvent liquidation (IA 1986 s 214(2)(b)), and
(c) unless the court is satisfied that in the circumstances in (a) and (b) above the director took every step with a view to minimising the potential loss to the company's creditors as he ought to have taken (IA 1986 s 214(3)),

the court, on the application of the liquidator, will make the director liable to make such contribution to the company's assets as the court thinks proper (IA 1986 s 214(1)).

The power under the IA 1986 s 216 to require anyone involved in the management of a phoenix company to the pay its debts
This section, which is also discussed in greater detail in Chapter 14, was designed to prevent the unscrupulous reuse of a company name. If the director or shadow director of a liquidated company sets up a new company with the same or a similar name to the liquidated company within five years of the date of liquidation, that director can be jointly and severally liable with the new company for the debts of the new company for the duration of his management (IA 1986 s 217). This rule also applies to nominees of the director who are aware of the misuse of the liquidated company's name. The legislation only operates in the context of a liquidation and not in a receivership, a point not wasted on unscrupulous directors.

Although criminal proceedings will not affect the liability of the directors in any of the above circumstances, it is worth noting that the application to the court by the liquidator (or creditor, contributory or Official Receiver as the case may be) may trigger a criminal investigation (IA 1986 s 218). The liquidator will also report to the Secretary of State on any matters in connection with the directors' management of their company which might occasion disqualification as a director in terms of the CDDA 1986.

By all the above means the liquidator should be able to increase the company's assets for the benefit of the creditors. This process is sometimes known as "swelling the company's assets". There are additional powers to extract information from anyone involved in the company (IA 1986 ss 235, 236) and to ask the court to order persons to give up property to the company or pay money to the company (IA 1986 s 237(1), (2)). The creditors in their turn have to intimate their vouched claims to the liquidator, a process known as proving their claims. The liquidator may not necessarily accept all creditors' claims, and there may be disputes over such matters as retention of title agreements, set-off or refusal to produce further supplies to enable some assets of the company to be sold as a going concern without payment in advance. The utility suppliers (gas, electricity etc.) are entitled to ask for a personal guarantee from the liquidator (IA 1986 s 233(2)(a)), but cannot insist on outstanding charges being paid first before reconnection (IA 1986) s 233(2)(b)). This is because it would prejudice all the other creditors were they able to do so.

Distribution of the company's funds

Once the liquidator has gathered in all the assets he can, he will arrange to have his own fees paid first as otherwise he would not carry out the work. His expenses, such as instructing others to carry out work for him, are paid next as without the certainty of prior payment his contractees would not work for him either. From time to time there are suggestions that liquidators' fees can in small liquidations use up a very great deal of the company's funds. Equally it is sometimes suggested that where liquidators take a long time to deal with a liquidation, the sums due to creditors increases dramatically due to the interest running on the outstanding accounts until payment. The delay makes very little difference to the liquidator who probably takes his fees from time to time as he gathers in the assets, but makes a substantial difference to the directors of the debtor company. The directors may be doing their best to meet their company's creditors' bills lest the creditors exercise their rights under any guarantees the directors may have given them. The greater the delay in distribution of the company's assets the greater the amount due under any guarantee that the creditors may call upon.

After payment of the liquidator and his expenses, the sums due to fixed charge-holders are paid. If there is a floating charge, an administrative receiver or Scottish receiver (as the case may be) will have been appointed and will exercise the rights due to him, unless there is some agreement or court order otherwise. If preferential debts are due to be paid, the administrative receiver or Scottish receiver will pay them; but if there is no floating charge, the liquidator will have to pay the preferential debts out of the sums he gathers in.

Where, in England and Wales only, a landlord has distrained upon the goods or effects of a company (*i.e.* seized the company's goods in settlement of outstanding rent) within a period of three months before the commencement of insolvency, the distrained goods or effects suffer the preferential debts first (IA

1986 s 176(2)). The landlord is able to claim against the liquidator for the value of the preferential debts and is treated as a preferential creditor against the rest of the company's assets, but only to the extent of the amount he has had to pay out already (IA 1986 s 176(3)).

Order or priority of payment

In the (admittedly rare) case of a company in liquidation but without any secured charges, a liquidator would pay out the gathered-in funds in the following order:

- the liquidator's own fees and/or the Official Receiver's fees;
- expenses incurred by the liquidator and/or the Official Receiver;
- in a winding-up by the court, the petitioner's expenses;
- the preferential debts;
- (unsecured) creditors;
- deferred debts (outstanding dividends due to members (IA 1986 s 74(2)(f)) and funds set aside for the redemption or repurchase of shares but at the time of liquidation as yet unpaid (CA 1985 s 178(3)–(5));
- repayment of share capital in accordance with the articles;
- distribution of surplus in accordance with the articles.

It should be noted that the liquidator's fees and expenses, together with the preferential debts, may well exhaust the funds otherwise available to the creditors. If there is only a limited amount available for the creditors, the creditors will have their claims abated. Likewise if there is enough to repay the creditors, there may not be enough to repay the members all their capital: their claims may also be abated. The articles may also prescribe that preference shareholders are paid first before ordinary shareholders, and that preference shareholders can share in any surplus. In Scotland there is no Official Receiver and therefore no fees or expenses are due to him or his creditors.

If the company has granted a fixed charge and a floating charge, liquidation will generally trigger enforcement of both these charges. In that event the fixed charge-holder will exercise his rights over the asset secured by the fixed charge. If the sale proceeds of the charged asset are sufficient to repay the fixed charge-holder's debt, the fixed charge-holder will take his monies and hand over any surplus to the receiver under the floating charge. If the fixed charged asset is worth less than expected, the fixed charge-holder will take what he can and rank as an unsecured creditor for the balance.

The same principle applies to the receiver. If after realisation of the assets secured by the floating charge and repayment to those to whom repayment is due there is a surplus, the surplus is handed to the liquidator. If there is a short-fall, the floating charge-holder ranks as an unsecured creditor for the balance due to him.

Fixed and floating charge-holders may, however, have made their own arrangements in respect of priorities by means of a ranking agreement or deed of priorities.

The order of distribution where there are charges will normally be as follows:

- fixed charge-holder and his expenses;

- administrative receiver's fees or Scottish receiver's fees;

- expenses incurred by administrative receiver/Scottish receiver and his own creditors;

- preferential debts (paid by administrative receiver/Scottish receiver);

- floating charge-holder;

- liquidator's and/or Official Receiver's fees and expenses;

- petitioning creditor's expenses in a winding-up by the court;

- unsecured creditors;

- deferred debts;

- repayment of share capital in accordance with the articles;

- payment of surplus in accordance with the articles;

As each recipient of the company's funds is paid, either in full or rateably as the case may be, he provides a receipt which should eventually show that the company has no further proceeds to pay out and, that no creditors or share-holders are due any money. The liquidator will hold a final meeting at which he will present final accounts under the IA 1986 ss 94, 106 or 172. He prepares his final account, vacates his office and sends the Registrar of Companies the final account and informs him that the liquidation is complete. The Official Receiver in England, Wales and Northern Ireland can make a similar report.

Dissolution of the company

Following the liquidation process, the company will then be struck off the Registrar of Companies within three months of the date of the notice by the liquidator (IA 1986 ss 201 or 205) unless there is an application to the Secretary of State, or in Scotland, the court, to defer the dissolution. The Official Receiver can apply to the Registrar of Companies for early dissolution of the company if there are no funds to enable the liquidation to be carried out and if the affairs of the company do not require any further investigation. The company will then be dissolved within three months of the date of the application, unless there is an application to the Secretary of State to defer the dissolution. In Scotland a similar process applies under the IA 1986 s 204, although the courts rather than the Secretary of State can defer the application for dissolution.

It is possible for a liquidator or any other interested person to revive a dissolved company by application to the court (CA 1985 s 651). This sometimes happens where an overlooked asset is discovered. The company can then be resuscitated and the proceeds divided amongst the creditors. However, such revival can only take place within two years of the company's dissolution except where there is a claim against the company for damages in respect of personal injuries (CA 1985 s 651(5)). This is because some injuries, particular long-term sickness, may take many years to come to anyone's notice. In the meantime the company that caused the sickness may have been put into liquidation, but its insurers still may be underwriting the risk to its former employees.

Summary

1. Winding-up is to permit the fair division of company's assets between primarily its creditors and secondly its members.

2. There are three types of winding-up:

   - by the court;
   - members' voluntary winding-up;
   - creditors' voluntary winding-up.

3. The common grounds for winding up the company are:

   (a) its inability to pay its debts (IA 1986 s 122(1)(f)), as shown by:

      - the company's inability to pay a debt of over £750 within a period of 21 days (IA 1986 s 123(1)(a));
      - the failure to make payment after enforcement procedures arising from a court judgment (or decree or other instrument of debt in Scotland) (IA 1986 s 123(1)(b), (c) and (d));
      - the company's inability to pay its debts as they fall due (IA 1986 s 123(1)(e));
      - proof to the satisfaction of the court that the company's assets are worth less than its liabilities, taking into account its contingent and prospective liabilities (IA 1986 s 123(2));

(b) that it would be just and equitable to wind up the company. Grounds that have been accepted are:

- loss of substratum – *Re German Date Coffee Co* (1882) 20 Ch D 169;
- fraud – *Re Thomas Brinsmead & Sons Ltd* [1897] 1 Ch 45;
- deadlock – *Re Yenidje Tobacco Co Ltd* [1935] Ch 693;
- quasi-partnership/oppression – *Ebrahimi* v *Westbourne Galleries Ltd* [1973] AC 360;
- oppression – *Loch* v *John Blackwood Ltd* [1924] AC 783.

4. Under the IA 1986 s 124 those entitled to petition to have the company wound up are:

- the company;
- the directors;
- a creditor or creditors;
- a contributory or contributories;
- the clerk to a magistrates' court (England and Wales only);
- the Secretary of State (on the grounds of public interest);
- the Official Receiver (England, Wales and Northern Ireland only).

5. The procedure for winding up a company by the court is as follows:

- application by petition to court;
- intimation to all interested parties;
- grant of petition or order by court and appointment of liquidator;
- advertisement of liquidation and invitation to creditors to send in claims and attend meetings;
- investigation of company's demise and preparation of statement of affairs;
- establishment of liquidation committee;
- getting in of company's property;
- payment of creditors' claims and return of capital, if any, to members;
- final meeting and dissolution of company.

6. The procedure for winding up the company voluntarily is broadly similar, save that there is no petition to court. The members resolve by ordinary, special or extraordinary resolution (depending on the circumstances) under the IA 1985 s 84 to wind the company up. The liquidator so appointed (or the Official Receiver in England, Wales and Northern Ireland) then carries out all the other tasks referred to above.

7. A members' voluntary liquidation is done in the expectation that there will be funds repayable to the members. A members' voluntary winding up requires a statutory declaration of solvency by the directors, asserting that

in their view the company can pay all its debts in full within a period of up to 12 months from the commencement of the winding-up.

8. Creditors' voluntary liquidations do not require a statutory declaration. Creditors' voluntary liquidations are carried out for the benefit of the creditors. A members' voluntary winding-up can be converted into a creditors' voluntary winding-up if the company turns out to be insolvent.

9. The liquidator is given a large number of powers to enable him to carry out his task (IA 1986 Schedule 3). He has various methods of maximising the company's assets and minimising its liabilities:

- disclaiming onerous contracts and property (not Scotland) (IA 1986 ss 178–182);
- calling on contributories to pay outstanding sums to the company (IA 1986 Schedule 3);
- setting aside incomplete executions and attachments in England, Wales and Northern Ireland;
- setting aside incomplete diligence in Scotland and equalising diligence within two months before and four months after the commencement of the winding-up (IA 1986 s 185);
- avoidance of antecedent transactions in England, Wales and Northern Ireland being transactions at an undervalue (IA 1986 s 238) and preferences (IA 1986 s 239) within certain time-limits depending on whether or not the recipient is a connected person (two years for both transactions at an undervalue and preferences) or anyone else (two years for a transaction at an undervalue and six months for a preference);
- avoidance of antecedent transactions in Scotland, being gratuitous alienations (IA 1986 s 242) and unfair preferences (IA 1986 s 243) within certain time-limits, depending on whether or not the recipient is an associate (five years for gratuitous alienations, six months for an unfair preference) or anyone else (two years for a gratuitous alienations, six months for unfair preferences);
- avoidance of extortionate credit transactions under the IA 1986 s 244;
- avoidance of certain floating charges under the IA 1986 s 245, if granted in favour of connected persons within the last two years, or in favour of unconnected persons within the last 12 months at a time when the company was already unable to pay its debts, except for new funds advanced by that person, whether connected or not;
- contributions from directors as assessed by the court as a result of the directors' misfeasance (IA 1986 s 212), fraudulent trading (IA 1986 s 213), wrongful trading (IA 1986 s 214) or use of a phoenix name for their new company (IA 1986 s 216).

10. Out of the funds ingathered by the liquidator, he must pay the preferential debts (IA 1986 s 175).

11. The order of distribution of the company's funds is generally as follows:

    - fixed charge-holders;
    - receiver's own fees, expenses and creditors (not dealt with by the liquidator);
    - the preferential debts (not normally dealt with by the liquidator);
    - the floating charge-holder (not normally dealt with by the liquidator);
    - liquidator's own fees, expenses and creditors;
    - preferential debts where there is no floating charge or receiver;
    - unsecured creditors;
    - return of capital to members in accordance with the articles;
    - payment of surplus to members in accordance with the articles.

12. When all sums have been paid out and the final accounts are ready, a last meeting is held and the Registrar of Companies is asked to dissolve the company.

22. INSOLVENCY – CORPORATE RESCUE

The Cork Report and administrative orders – administration generally – procedure – administration compared with receivership – company voluntary arrangements

The problem with receivership is that while it may be viewed as a method of keeping a business going, in reality it is more likely to act to the benefit of the floating charge-holders at the expense of the unsecured creditors.

The problem with liquidation is that breaking up the business and turning it into cash to be distributed between the creditors may be more drastic than is necessary.

Accordingly, during the 1970s and early 1980s it became apparent that there was a need for some other new regime for dealing with corporate insolvency, particularly for companies where there was no floating charge-holder who might have an interest in corporate rescue. What was needed was a form of corporate rescue that kept a business going, that preserved employees' jobs and customers' goodwill, but which did not prejudice creditors.

This was one of the issues that was debated by the Cork Committee which produced the Cork Report (*Insolvency Law and Practice: Report of the Review Committee* 1982, Cmns 8998). The Report suggested that UK law had few satisfactory methods of rescuing companies in financial difficulties. It noted that receivership had saved some companies but that where there was no floating charge there was no alternative to liquidation if a creditor petitioned for winding up. The Report recommended that a new method of corporate rescue should be initiated, to be called administration, which would try to rescue the affairs of companies which would otherwise have gone into liquidation.

The second recommendation was that a financially troubled company ought to be able to come to a voluntary arrangement with its creditors which would be legally binding even on those creditors who disagreed with the terms of the arrangement. This became known as a company voluntary arrangement. These two recommendations received the approval of Parliament within the IA 1986.

Administration

Administration is only available by means of an administration order granted by the courts following a petition by a suitable petitioner. There is no informal method of administration: it must be supervised by the courts and it must follow certain procedural requirements. Under the IA 1986 s 8, the court may make an administration order:

(i)   if it is satisfied that a company is or is likely to become unable to pay its debts within the meaning given in the IA 1986 s 123 (see Chapter 21) and
(ii) that it considers that the making of the order would be likely to achieve one or more of the purposes specified in the IA 1986 s 8(3).

Purposes of administration under the IA 1986 s 8(3)

These are stated as follows:

(a)   the survival of the company and the whole or any part of its undertaking as a going concern;
(b)   the approval of a company voluntary arrangement;
(c)   the sanctioning under the CA 1985 s 425 of a scheme of arrangement;
(d)   a more advantageous realisation of the company's assets than would be effected on a winding-up.

Although in practice there have not been as many petitions for administration as might have been expected, so far the courts have proved reasonably willing to grant administration orders, not least because the alternative in many cases would be the collapse of the company, the loss of jobs and the destruction of the business. To refuse to grant an administration order where one is clearly sought would, especially if there were no objections to the order, lead to suggestions that the courts were refusing to implement the wishes of Parliament, negating the recommendations of the Cork Report, and possibly making the UK a less attractive place in which to do business.

Most successful petitions for administration are brought under grounds (a) and (d) above, mainly because it is not vital to a company voluntary arrangement or a scheme of arrangement that an administration order be granted. The virtues of grounds (a) and (d) are that it is generally both in the company's interest and the creditors' interests that the company either survives or realises more money than might be achieved by a liquidation.

The courts cannot grant an administration order:

- if the company is already in liquidation (IA 1986 s 8(4));

- if the company is an insurance company (IA 1985 s 8(4)(a)) or a money-lending institution (IA 1986 s 8(4)(b));

- where a receiver is in place unless:

(a) the floating charge-holder who appointed the receiver consents to the order (IA 1986 s 9(3)(a)), or

(b) unless the security which permitted the appointment of the receiver would be overturned because:

  (i)   it was a transaction at an undervalue or a preference (IA 1986 s 9(3)(b)(i));

  (ii) a gratuitous alienation or an unfair preference (for Scotland only) (IA 1986 s 9(3)(b)(iii)); or

  (iii) a void floating charge in terms of the IA 1986 s 245 (IA 1986 s 9(3)(b)(ii)).

The effect of this is that once a company is in liquidation it cannot be put into administration, but that where a company is in receivership it could be put into administration only if the floating charge is invalid, or, where the floating charge is valid, if the floating charge-holder consents. Those who wish the company to go into administration must therefore convince the floating charge-holder that administration is a more viable alternative to receivership so far as the floating charge-holder is concerned. Convincing him may not always be easy, but for very large companies, with a large number of loans, each backed by floating charges, the individual floating charge-holders may well consider that the cost of having several receivers each supporting his own floating charge-holder may be more costly than one administrator. Other reasons that would favour an administrator are that:

(i)   where there is a consortium of banks lending to a company no one lender may have an enforceable security;

(ii) receivers are not appointed by the courts but by floating charge-holders: some foreign jurisdictions may only recognise court-appointed officials, such as administrators, rather than charge-holder appointed officials;

(iii) a receiver has no power to apply to set aside antecedent transactions, or other fraudulent practices, whereas an administrator can.

Equally where one obstructive floating charge-holder refuses to co-operate with all the floating charge-holders in appointing an administrator, the other floating charge-holders (which will in practice generally be banks) may prove unco-operative on some future occasion when dealing with the obstructive floating charge-holder.

Suitable petitioners

Under the IA 1986 s 9(1) the following can petition for an administration order:

- the company;

- the directors;

- a creditor or creditors;

- the clerk of a magistrates' court under the Magistrates' Courts Act 1980 s 87A (applicable to England and Wales only);

- by all or any of the above together or separately.

Usually the petition is made by the directors, either acting unanimously or as a board following a resolution approving administration. Ironically, having successfully petitioned for administration, the directors could lose their positions if the administrator saw fit to dismiss them (IA 1986 s 14(2)).

Procedure

Under the Insolvency Rules 1986 r 2.6 (and their Scottish equivalent, Insolvency (Scotland) Rules r 2(1), (2)) when a petition is presented to the court, notice must be given to the following:

- anyone who could appoint a receiver (*i.e.* a floating charge-holder);

- a receiver if one is already in existence;

- anyone who is petitioning for the winding-up of the company;

- any provisional liquidator;

- the proposed administrator;

- in the event of a creditors' petition for administration, the company itself;

- (in Scotland only) anyone else upon whom the court orders the petition to be served.

The court will hear the petition and can dismiss, adjourn or grant the petition. It can give any order it sees fit, including an interim administration order (IA 1986 s 9(4)). During the period between the presentation of the petition and the granting of the order or the dismissal of the petition:

- no order can be granted nor resolution passed for the winding-up of the company (IA 1986 s 10(1)(a));

- no one can begin to enforce any security over the company's property without leave of the court (IA 1986 s 10(1)(b));

- no hirer can repossess any goods used by the company that are subject to a hire-purchase agreement without leave of the court (hire purchase in this context includes any conditional sale agreement, chattel leasing agreement or retention of title agreement) (IA 1986 s 10(1)(b);

- no proceedings or enforcement of court judgments or decrees or, in Scotland, diligence, can take place without leave of the court (IA 1986 s 10(1)(c)).

However, during the period between the presentation of the administration petition and the making of the order, it is still permissible to present a petition for the winding-up of a company (even though the petition will have to lie in abeyance until the court decides what to do about the petition for administration) (IA 1986 s 10(2)(a)). During this same period a company can still be put into receivership (IA 1986 s 10(2)(b)) and if the company is already in receivership, the receiver can carry on with his receivership duties (IA 1986 s 10(2)(c)).

Once the administration order is granted, the company cannot be wound up and no administrative receiver can be appointed (IA 1986 s 11(1)). The floating charge-holder's option to protect his own position lapses on the appointment of the administrator. Any receiver he may have appointed demits office, and the company becomes effectively insulated from its creditors. While the administration order is in place:

- no order can be granted nor resolution passed for the winding-up of the company (IA 1986 s 11(3)(a));

- no receiver can be appointed (IA 1986 s 11(3)(b));

- no one can begin to enforce any security over the company's property without leave of the court or the administrator (IA 1986 s 11(3)(c));

- no hirer can repossess any goods used by the company that are subject to a hire-purchase agreement without leave of the court or the administrator (hire purchase in this context includes any conditional sale agreement, chattel leasing agreement or retention or title agreement) (IA 1986 s 11(3)(c));

- no proceedings or enforcement of court judgments or decrees or, in Scotland, diligence, can take place without leave of the court or the administrator (IA 1986 s 11(3)(d)).

There has been a number of applications for leave from the court for creditors to be able to enforce their security or repossess their goods. In general, the courts are slightly reluctant to grant such leave. In *Re Atlantic Computer Systems plc* [1992] 2 WLR 367 some broad guidelines for administrator were laid down. A creditor seeking leave from the court would need to show that refusal would cause undue hardship to the creditor concerned, would not substantially alter the position for the other creditors, and not impede the fulfilment of the purpose of the administration order.

Benefit of administration

The making of the administration order places the administrator at a great advantage, as it allows the administrator the opportunity to turn the company's business around without being pressed continually by creditors. There is effectively a moratorium on the company's debts. The administrator has extensive powers given to him under the IA 1986 Schedule 1 to do everything to achieve the purpose for which he was appointed, and he can apply to the court for directions or approval of matters of which he is uncertain in law. Replacing the directors who caused the collapse of the company is commonly a high priority.

He can also sell assets or goods used by the company which are subject to a security or a hire-purchase agreement (IA 1986 s 15(1)), but if he wishes to do so, he must obtain the consent either of the creditor concerned or of the court first, having convinced the court that this would promote the better realisation of the company's assets. The security holder or hirer is, however, allowed to retain his priority with regards to the proceeds of the sale of the secured assets or hired goods (IA 1986 s 15(4)). Goods subject to retention of title agreements can also be sold by the administrator, although the owner of the goods has a prior right to the proceeds of sale (IA 1986 s 15(4) and in Scotland s 16(2)).

Other significant matters relating to the administrator

- The administrator is deemed to be the company's agent (IA 1986 s 14(5)) and anyone dealing with him in good faith for value need not be concerned whether or not the administrator is acting beyond the powers that he has been given (IA 1986 s 14(6)).

- All documentation issuing from the company must state that it is in administration (IA 1986 s 412).

- Following his appointment, the administrator must take under his control all the company's assets. In companies with assets spread all over the world, or in politically uncertain areas, retrieval of assets may not always be feasible. The administrators of the fruit and packaging company Polly Peck had a great deal of difficulty in getting hold of assets in Northern Cyprus, a state with limited political recognition.

The administrator's remuneration and his liabilities in the course of the administration

- The administrator's fees and expenses are paid out of any property under his control and in priority to any other sums that may be due to any secured creditors (IA 1986 s 19(4)). Likewise any debts and liabilities, including the employment contracts referred to in the next paragraph, incurred by him in carrying out his duties are also paid out of the property under his control (IA 1986 s 19(5)). Without this provision no administrator would take the position and no one would carry out any work for the administrator, unless perhaps the creditors were paying.

- As regards contracts of employment adopted by him in carrying out his duties, the administrator can pay for these out of the property under his control (IA 1986 s 19(6)), but the amount that can be paid in respect of those contracts of employment is limited to pension contributions (IA 1986 s 19(7)(a)) and wages or salary arising out of services rendered wholly or partly after the adoption of the contracts by the administrator (IA 1986 s 19(7)(b)). This means that the administrator is not responsible for paying out of the property under his control wages or salary in respect of services rendered before he adopted the contracts (IA 1986 s 19(8)). The administrator has 14 days from the date of his appointment during which time he may consider which contracts of employment he will adopt. Employees he retains after that period must either be given a new contract or he will be deemed to have adopted their contracts.

The conduct of the administration

- Following the making of an administration order the administrator is required to publish the fact in the press and in the Gazette (IA 1986 s 21(1)) and to inform all creditors of the order (IA 1986 s 21(2)).

- He must convene creditors' meetings if requested to do so by the courts or by one-tenth in value of the company's creditors (IA 1986 s 17(3)).

- The administrator must obtain "statements of affairs" from such of those involved in the management, promotion or employment of the company as he sees fit (IA 1986 s 22) in order to ascertain the company's financial position. Each such person must make a statement of affairs on a Form 2.9 (or Form 2.6 (Scotland)). This is in order to establish whether any of those persons may be liable to the company in respect of their activities, or can furnish any information on the questionable activities of others involved in the company.

- The administrator is required to make proposals for the achievement of the purposes for which the administration order was granted. These must be made within three months of the order (IA 1986 s 23), sent to all creditors and members and presented to a creditors' meeting for revision and/or approval (IA 1986 s 24(1)). The proposals may be rejected whereupon the matter must revert to the courts for discharge of the administration order or such other remedy as the court sees fit (IA 1986 s 24(5)). The creditors can form a committee to advise the administrator (IA 1986 s 26).

- At any time during the existence of the administration order any member or creditor can apply to the court for relief if he can prove that the administrator is prejudicing the interests of the members or creditors (as the case may be) (IA 1986 s 27(1)) and the court has wide discretion to provide suitable remedies (IA 1986 s 27(4)).

The administrator and antecedent transactions

- In the same manner as a liquidator, an administrator can recall:

  - transactions at an undervalue and preferences under the IA 1986 ss 238 and 239 (see Chapter 21);
  - in Scotland, gratuitous alienations and unfair preferences under the IA 1986 ss 242 and 243 (see Chapter 21);
  - extortionate credit transactions under the IA 1986 s 244 (see Chapter 21);
  - invalid floating charges under the IA 1986 s 245 (see Chapters 17 and 21).

- These powers can be used to increase the total assets at the disposal of the company.

The completion of the administration

If the proposals are effective and carried through, the administrator will be in a position to sell on such parts of the business as can be sold on, thus ensuring the likelihood of greater payment to creditors than might otherwise have been possible. Employees may also be better able to retain their jobs. The parts of the business that cannot be dealt with or sold off, such as unprofitable subsidiaries, will have to be written off or wound up. Creditors will have been paid off in such amounts as will have been agreed between the administrator and the creditors. Finally, after presentation of the final accounts, the fulfilment of the purposes of the administration or a satisfactory explanation of the impossibility of the fulfilment of those purposes, the administrator can apply to court for the discharge of his administration (IA 1986 s 18).

Administration compared with receivership

Administration is recognised to be a reasonable idea in principle, but not without its detractions. From time to time there are various ideas floated amongst insolvency practitioners and academics about the best ways to improve the corporate rescue culture of which administration is a part. The real difficulty is that receivership and administration deal with the same problem from different approaches. Receivership is about satisfying the creditor who lends money to the company and wants to recover his loan, and as part of the recovery of his loan, he expects to be allowed his choice of a suitable insolvency practitioner to look after his interests. By contrast, administration is about satisfying all the creditors generally, and the company, rather than the creditors, normally gets its choice of insolvency practitioner.

Lenders take the view that as they lend most they are most at risk and should therefore be placed in a superior position when it comes to retrieval of their funds. If they are not placed in that position, they will merely charge more for lending money, or demand even more by way of personal guarantees from directors.

At the same time lenders, and banks in particular, are aware of the bad publicity that results from receivership. If a bank obtains a reputation for quickly putting companies into receivership, new enterprises may take their business elsewhere. Trade creditors resent banks which protect themselves at the apparent expense of all other creditors. To avoid this difficulty, some banks insert terms in their loan documentation which allow the bank to take over the management of a client's business (even at the risk of being shadow directors) without the formal process of receivership. This saves the unwelcome publicity of receivership while the insertion of professional management hired through the company, but for the benefit of the bank, will ensure that the bank gets its money back.

Three criticisms of administration

1. One of the main criticisms of administration is that it is expensive because of the need to go to court and the need to prepare reports to back up the administrator's proposals for the company. This means that administration is not really an option for small companies. One solution might be to set up a procedure for an informal appointment of an administrator that does not require going to court. It also appears to be the case that only large companies with a solid core of business and substantial reserves can successfully use and indeed afford an administrator to overcome any temporary financial difficulties.

2. A second common criticism concerns the floating charge-holder's power to block the appointment of an administrator. Some critics complain that this gives too much power to a floating charge-holder at the expense of the other creditors. By way of comparison, in Ireland there is a requirement that where the floating charge-holder wishes to block the appointment of an examiner (the Irish equivalent of an administrator) the receiver must have been in place for at least three days before the presentation of a petition to appoint an examiner (Irish Companies (Amendment) Act 1990, s 3(6)). This was designed to minimise the opportunities for a veto by floating charge-holders. It has not been well received by Irish bankers who complain that whenever a receiver is appointed the debtor company rushes to obtain the appointment of an examiner, thus negating the purpose of the receivership.

3. A third criticism of administration is that an individual director who sees the need for administration is unable at present to apply to the courts for an administration order. Even if he is the one honest director amongst a board-room of rogues, he could, unless he has taken suitable steps to distance himself from the actions of his fellow directors, find himself accused of wrongful trading when the company collapses due to the venality of his colleagues.

The UK position can be compared with its equivalent in the USA, known as Chapter 11 bankruptcy. It is designed to protect the debtor company from the predations of creditors. It is almost too effective in protecting debtor companies at the expense of creditors, and some companies will use the threat of going into Chapter 11 bankruptcy either as a means of demanding lower prices for supplies or borrowings or as a means of postponing any large claims against the company. Once in Chapter 11 bankruptcy the company is insulated from its creditors who may have to wait a very long time for their money. Another feature of Chapter 11 bankruptcy is that the directors remain in control, earning their salaries, a concept alien to UK legislation where the underlying assumption is that if a company is forced into receivership or administration it is probably because the management is incompetent anyway. A common argument against letting directors remain in control is that although it may be relatively cheap to retain the directors, there is always the danger that the directors will abscond with the company's funds.

Company voluntary arrangements

Company voluntary arrangements were designed to be a quick, cheap and efficient way of dealing with the difficulties an insolvent company might face without going into liquidation. The principle is that a company agrees terms with most of its creditors as an alternative to the company failing and the money otherwise available to the creditors being swallowed up by court fees and liquidators' expenses. Sometimes creditors will be prepared to hold their hand if the existing management is replaced by a competent insolvency practitioner who will realise the company's assets more sensibly than the existing management, thus resulting in better payment for everyone.

Although company voluntary arrangements have been a well intentioned experiment, they have been little used and are not popular. It is very likely that the procedure and practice of company voluntary arrangements will be reformed in the near future (as discussed later in this chapter).

The structure of a company voluntary arrangement

The directors of a solvent or about to be insolvent company can apply to the courts for preliminary approval of proposals for a voluntary arrangement for compromising and settling creditors' claims (IA 1986 s 2(2)). The arrangement must provide for an insolvency practitioner, known as the nominee, to oversee the arrangement (IA 1986 s 1(1)–(3)). The nominee must give a report on the viability of the proposals for the arrangement (Insolvency Rules 1986 r 1.7 and Insolvency (Scotland) Rules 1986 r 1.7) and whether or not the members of the company and the creditors should consider the arrangement.

If the company is already in liquidation or administration the liquidator or administrator can make his own proposal and be the nominee. Preliminary court approval is not required (Insolvency Rules 1986 r 1.10 and Insolvency (Scotland) Rules 1986 r 1.10).

The nominee summons meetings of the members and of the creditors. There the terms of the arrangements are considered. No proposals concerning the prior rights or security holders or preferential creditors may be approved without the consent of those security holders or preferential creditors (IA 1984 s 4(3), (4)). The arrangement must be approved at both members' and creditors' meetings. At the creditors' meeting, three-quarters in value of the creditors must vote to approve any proposal or modification of a proposal (Insolvency Rules 1986 r 1.19 and Insolvency (Scotland) Rules 1986 r 7.12(2)) but at the members' meeting one-half in shares (according to the voting rights given in the articles) are necessary to approve any proposal or modification (Insolvency Rules 1986 r 1.20 and Insolvency (Scotland) Rules 1986 r 7.12(1)).

Once the proposal is agreed at both meetings, the arrangement is binding on the members, the creditors and the company (IA 1986 s 5), even including those who voted against the proposals. The decisions of the meetings must be reported to the courts which will not sanction them until a period of 28 days has elapsed. This is because it is open to a creditor to challenge the arrangement under the IA 1986 s 6 provided the challenge takes place within 28 days of first report to the courts of the approval of the arrangement at one of the meetings, and provided:

(a) the applicant can prove that he has suffered or could suffer unfair prejudice if the arrangement were implemented, or

(b) the applicant can prove that there has been some material irregularity at either or both of the meetings.

The court has wide discretion to deal with the challenges in whatever way it sees fit (IA 1986 s 6(4)).

If the company is in liquidation or administration at the time of the approval of the arrangement, the court can then terminate the liquidation or the administration (IA 1986 s 5(3)).

Once the arrangement is sanctioned, the nominee (or liquidator or administrator as the case may be) becomes known as the supervisor, and he carries out the arrangement. If the debtor company cannot honour the terms of the arrangement, he or the creditors can return to court to petition for winding up by the court, or a creditors' voluntary liquidation may take place. If the arrangement works, the company resumes business in the normal way and its debts are paid off on the terms specified in the arrangement.

Problems with company voluntary arrangements

- Company voluntary arrangements are not well regarded mainly because the uncertainty arising from a company's failure to adhere to its own arrangement places all the creditors in no better a position than they had been before. It might therefore have been cheaper and quicker to have had the company wound up anyway.

- Security holders and preferential creditors can, if they wish, refuse to be bound by the arrangement (IA 1986 s 4(3) and (4)), thus effectively preventing it succeeding.

- The procedure is quite time-consuming: as it goes through the courts an impatient creditor could put the company into liquidation.

- There is a perception that company voluntary arrangements are too debtor-friendly, and that there is little a disgruntled minority of 25% of the creditors can do if the 75% majority creditors insist on a certain course of action. This is well illustrated by the following fraud which sometimes occurs in company voluntary arrangements, and indeed personal voluntary arrangements. A company gets into financial difficulties and owes, say, £1 million to genuine creditors. The directors then arrange for their friends to submit spurious invoices amounting to £4.5 million, such that at the creditors' meeting the value of their false claims amounts to over 75% of all the sums apparently due from the company to its creditors. The directors' friends in their guise as creditors then approve a settlement of, say, 5p in the pound. The genuine creditors will be unable to prove the fraudulence of the spurious invoices and have to accept the decision of the majority creditors. The genuine creditors then only receive £50,000 of the £1 million they are due, and the company's debts are clear. It can then continue trading, leaving the genuine creditors out of pocket.

Given these criticisms, the Government issued revised proposals for a new company voluntary arrangement procedure in 1995. Amongst its recommendations are:

- an automatic stay of 28 days of all proceedings by creditors, commencing on the date when notice of an intended voluntary arrangement is lodged in court. During this period the existing management stays in place, subject to some supervision and restrictions to prevent the management disposing of the company's assets;

- holders of floating charges would have to give the company five working days' notice of their intention to appoint an administrative receiver (or Scottish receiver).

It remains to be seen whether, and to what extent, the Government will implement these proposals.

Summary

1. The Cork Report established the need for reform of insolvency methods. Their recommendations were enacted in the Insolvency Act 1986 and by the creation of administration orders and compulsory voluntary arrangements.

2. Administration is only possible where floating charge-holders and/or any existing receivers consent to administration, where the company is not in liquidation already, and where it can be shown that either the whole or part of the business of the company could be saved or that administration would provide a better realisation of the assets of the company than winding up (IA 1986 s 8).

3. Once a company is in administration it is insulated from its creditors. It cannot be wound up, nor can it be put into receivership. Hirers of goods used by the company and security holders cannot usually exercise their rights

under the terms of their hire purchase agreements or security. Owners of goods subject to retention of title agreements usually cannot reclaim their goods (IA 1986 s 11).

4. The administrator can apply to court to sell charged assets, hired goods, goods owned by others on retention of title agreements, provided these creditors have first claim on the proceeds (IA 1986 ss 15, 16).

5. The administrator must formulate proposals for approval by the creditors and if approved, he must carry out the terms of the proposal. He must thereafter deal with the company's assets and pay its debts in the manner stated in the proposal (IA 1986 ss 23, 24).

6. The administrator is released from his office once the tasks in the proposal have been completed. Such parts of the business of the company that he has been unable to sell he can write off or put into liquidation.

7. Administration works reasonably well for large companies, with a good core business, which have suffered a large and unexpected loss. The administrator can help trade such companies back to profitability again or can sell on the main parts of the businesses, thus producing funds for creditors.

8. Recognised problems of administration are:

    (i)   cost;
    (ii)   the fact that a floating charge-holder or receiver can veto it; and
    (iii) the fact that it is not open to an individual director to put a company into administration.

9. Company voluntary arrangements are a less formal method of dealing with the potential or actual insolvency of a company. Following meetings of members and creditors of the company, and having obtained approval from the courts, it is possible for a settlement to be imposed on the company and all creditors even if not all of them are satisfied with its terms. The arrangement is overseen and organised by an insolvency practitioner known as in this context as a supervisor.

    Because some creditors' interests can be overruled by the 75% majority, some creditors feel that the arrangement is too debtor-company friendly and are therefore generally unwilling to use company voluntary arrangements.

23. THE EUROPEAN AND INTERNATIONAL DIMENSION

The effect of European directives on UK corporate law – company law in Europe – company law in the USA and the Commonwealth countries – comparison of UK company law with company law in other jurisdictions – company law in former Iron Curtain countries – philosophic issues in common law – whither company law into the 21st century?

This chapter makes no pretensions towards covering in depth what is a vast subject. It merely serves to provide an overview of issues arising in company law at an international level.

The effect of European directives on UK corporate law

One of the aims of the EU was to set up what used to be known as the "Common Market". This was in effect a market-place where all the businesses in Europe could trade on an equal basis using commonly agreed rules and standards, ideally with a common currency. The principle behind this is that if everyone uses the same weights and measures, and applies broadly speaking the same taxes (such as VAT) and common laws, businesses can trade more effectively, thus creating wealth, employment and a host of other social and economic benefits.

This aim has, as is well known, been constantly subverted by individual Member States of the EU. This subversion naturally occurs whenever a Member State feels that its own national interest is being threatened. A balance has therefore to be found between the establishment of a harmonised or non-nationalist set of legal and commercial norms suitable for all members of the EU and the desire of each Member State to preserve its own distinctive commercial and social culture and traditions.

Although harmonisation of the commercial laws of the EU Member States has not generally been an easy task, and in the case of such matters as the purchase and sale of land has not even been attempted, one area where there has been extensive harmonisation of laws is corporate law. Although there are three main strands to corporate law in the EU, these being the UK, the German and the French, there has been substantial agreement on such issues as disclosure, minimum capital requirements, standard formats for accounts, auditing standards, single member companies and other matters mainly relating to public limited companies. There has been less agreement on the right of employees to influence the management of companies.

Directives applying to company law which have been accepted to date are as follows:

1. *The First Directive (68/151)*
   This applies to all companies and details the information that must be shown on public registers. It imposes a common disclosure requirement, limits the applicability of the *ultra vires* rule and establishes common grounds for the nullity of a company. The effect of this Directive can be seen in Chapter 3.

2. *The Second Directive (77/91)*
   This established the minimum capital requirements for public limited companies (see Chapter 3), the need for independent verification of the capital contributed to public limited companies, and the net asset rule for distributions made by public limited companies (see Chapter 10). Amongst other things the Directive also deals with pre-emption rights, the acquisition by a company of its own shares, redeemable shares, the prohibition on financial assistance and reduction of capital (see Chapter 9).

3. *The Third Directive (78/885)*
   This established rules applying to mergers and acquisitions of companies within a single Member State. It also lays down guidelines for the protection of minorities in the context of takeovers and mergers and methods to ensure that minority shareholders are bought out at a fair price (see Chapter 19).

4. *The Fourth Directive (78/660)*
   This establishes standard formats for company reports and accounts and certain provisions for the valuation of assets (see Chapter 11).

5. *The Sixth Directive (82/891)*
   This deals with the division or "scission" of a public limited company into smaller separate units and the transfer of the company's business into those smaller units. The Directive also ensures that creditors are not prejudiced by this division. It was enacted in the UK by the Companies (Mergers and Divisions) Regulations 1987 (SI 1987/1991) (see Chapter 19).

6. *The Seventh Directive (83/349)*
   This deals extensively with group accounts and consolidated accounts (see Chapter 11).

7. *The Eighth Directive (84/253)*
   This establishes common professional requirements for auditors and the need for annual audits (see Chapter 16).

8. *The Eleventh Directive (89/666)*
   This harmonises the rules that allow branches of a company to be set up in different Member States without the need to cope with many differing sets

of disclosure requirements, particularly as regards accounts. This has been enacted in the CA 1985 s 699AA and Schedule 21D (see Chapter 11).

9. *The Twelfth Directive (89/667)*
This permitted the establishment of single member private limited companies (see Chapter 3).

There have been four draft proposals which have yet to be enacted. These are as follows:

1. *The draft Fifth Directive*
This was strongly influenced by the German model of corporate law which allows considerable worker representation and participation in management. The UK has firmly rejected this Directive on the grounds that it would be expensive to operate and that management is a matter for the directors' discretion. While many companies may choose to have worker representation if they wish to, the UK Government's position used to be that companies should not be forced to have worker representation. This Directive was proposed in 1983 at a time when the Conservative Party (then in power in the UK) was in the midst of its long battle to subdue the power of the trades unions. It was therefore not surprising that worker representation was not looked at favourably.

Other issues in this draft Directive are personal liability of directors, minority rights, conflicts of interests involving shareholders voting in their own interest, and restrictions on shareholders' agreements. In view of the recent change in the UK Government, it is possible that there may be a new attitude to this draft Directive.

2. *The draft Ninth Directive*
This has never been formally issued, but is strongly influenced by German law. It relates to the relationship between members of a group of companies and the liability of a holding company for its subsidiaries where the holding company is in a position to manage or to influence the management of its subsidiaries. This has not been well received in the UK because the position at the moment is that in the absence of fraud or some other clear reason, all companies are separate legal personalities. A holding company can, unless there is documentation to the contrary, walk away from its subsidiaries' debts. The draft Ninth Directive, if enacted, would change that, particularly in the context of public limited companies.

There has been no recent action to promote this particular draft Directive.

3. *The draft Tenth Directive*
This is designed to reconcile national differences in takeover and merger legislation. Cross-border takeovers and mergers should therefore become

easier. This proposal rapidly ran into political difficulties because some
countries are more protectionist than others, and nearly all counties are
unwilling to let their prime commercial gems be taken over by a foreign
company, especially if the takeover or merger causes job losses.

4. *The draft Thirteenth Directive*
   This also deals with takeovers and mergers and is an attempt to set a standard EU-wide mechanism for takeovers and mergers. As takeovers and
   mergers are not very common in the rest of Europe it has been strongly influenced by UK practice. The draft Directive has been ill-received in the UK
   because it is believed that the UK has a reasonably satisfactory system in
   place anyway and that enacting the Directive would require legislation. This
   would result in the granting of legal rights which would lead to endless challenges of the Takeover Panel's decisions and require accommodation with
   other countries' rulings on contested takeovers. It is also suggested that
   takeovers would become less flexible, more bureaucratic and subject to
   prolonged litigation.

   The Takeover Panel could also find itself required to pay compensation
   where it failed in its regulatory duty.

   It remains to be seen what the process of consultation will produce (see
   also Chapter 19).

Other matters that have come from the EU and have been adopted with some
success include:

1. *European Economic Interest Groupings*
   These are cross-frontier partnerships, sometimes involving a mixture of public and private finance and are designed to set up infrastructures of mutual
   benefit to the parties concerned. They are sometimes used in the context of
   joint ventures or supplying consultancy or educational services.

2. The Merger Regulation (Regulation 4064/89). This was designed to deal
   with the danger of anti-competitive practices or the establishment of monopolies within the EU. Where a "dominant influence" may result from a large
   merger, the merger must be referred to the European Commission for consideration and approval (see Chapter 19).

Other issues being considered include the EC Convention on Insolvency
Proceedings, initially delayed by the British beef crisis, and the creation of a
proposed European Company. The European Company is meant to be a company whose nationality is European rather than being based in any one Member
State. The idea is that it will straddle frontiers and will use as its constitution
and legal structure a special EU structure, subject to the practical point that

some matters, such as winding up, will have to take place at a national level. Various choices of worker participation will be encouraged. So far there does not appear to be a great call for such a company. One major problem that has yet to be resolved is where the company will be taxed, as no country will wish to miss the opportunity to extract taxable revenues from it if it is successful.

Company law in Europe

Broadly speaking there are three approaches to incorporation worldwide. There is the Anglo-Saxon approach, which encompasses the USA, the UK, Ireland and the Commonwealth or former Commonwealth countries. There is the French approach, and there is the German approach. There is a large amount of overlap between the three approaches, and there are advantages and disadvantages in each. Former Iron Curtain countries, and countries still professedly socialist, such as China, are adopting a "pick and mix" approach to their company legislation, trying to obtain the best ideas and methods worldwide.

Although there is much to be said on the other forms of economic enterprise such as different types of partnership (limited and unlimited), sole traders, economic interest groupings, co-operatives etc. within Europe, this chapter will restrict itself to companies using contributed capital. What follows must also be seen as broad generalisations to which many significant exceptions could easily be made.

United Kingdom

UK companies are divided, generally speaking, into private and public companies. There are greater standards of accountability for public companies, and only public companies can issue securities to the public. In the UK there is no minimum capital requirement except for public companies and no requirement to have different levels of management or supervision depending on the size of the company or the number of its employees.

France

In France, in addition to the difference between private and public companies, to be discussed shortly, there is a difference between civil companies and commercial companies. This is because certain types of economic activity are deemed to be "civil" rather than "commercial". This arises out of the French Code Civile, originally instituted by Napoleon, which set up the two categories of activity.

Civil activities are such activities as farming, mining, property development, creative arts and certain professional activities such as the law, accountancy, architecture, medicine etc. Commercial activities cover such businesses as retail, manufacturing, financial services, or what perhaps earlier in this century would have collectively been known as "trade". There are different types of courts and procedures for the two types of economic activities. Companies under either set of rules require registration, but generally speaking the rules for civil companies are less restrictive than the rules for commercial companies.

Within the category of commercial companies there are the equivalent to private companies, being *Société à responsabilité limitée* ("SARL"). These continue in existence for up to 99 years and shares must be fully paid on incorporation. Transfers of shares to third parties are restricted. There may not be more than 50 members. The minimum capital is 50,000 French francs. There are the equivalents to articles of association (*statuts*) although there is no memorandum of association. The company can carry on almost any commercial activity. The company is run by managers (*gerants*) and shareholders' meetings take place in a similar fashion to UK shareholders' meetings. Depending on the size of the company, there may need to be worker representation on the company's board.

The equivalent of a public company is a *société anonyme* ("SA"). It can carry on almost any commercial activity. In many respects it is similar to a SARL save that there is no maximum number of shareholders, the minimum capital is 250,000 French francs (or more for companies issuing securities to the public), there is a memorandum of association and there is greater accountability both to the shareholders and to the employees. There are almost no restrictions on the transfer of securities. The company is run by a board of directors with a managing director (*president directeur general*) and one or more general directors to support him. It is possible to have a supervisory board (as in Germany – see later). Shareholders' meetings take place on a similar basis to the SARL although there are different rules where the SA has issued securities to the public. Creditors can even convene meetings through the courts. There are different degrees of worker representation according to the number of employees.

The French model influenced, to greater and lesser extents, other European countries that adopted or adapted the Code Napoleon, such as Belgium, Spain and Italy.

Germany

In Germany one of the commonest forms of trading enterprise is the *Gesellschaft mit beschrankter Haftung & Co Kommanditgesellschaft* ("GmbH & Co KG"). This is similar to a limited partnership where the general partner (which would normally have unlimited liability) is a limited company. First the GmbH (*i.e.* a limited company) is founded and it then sets up a limited partnership agreement with the limited partner(s) who are often the same persons as the shareholders in the GmbH. This form of enterprise is popular in Germany because of favourable tax treatment, limited publicity and considerable flexibility.

The equivalent of a private limited company is the *Gesellschaft mit beschrankter Haftung* ("GmbH"). There is a minimum capital requirement of 50,000 Deutschmark but in most other respects it is very similar to a private limited company. It can be compared with the *Aktiengesellschaft* ("AG") which is the equivalent of a public limited company which can offer its shares to the public. The minimum capital for an AG is DM100,000. The principal difference between the UK public limited company and the AG is the obligatory three-tier system of management. At the top is the supervisory board (*Aufsichtsrat*), next is the managing board (*Vorstand*) and finally the shareholders' meeting (*Hauptversammlung*).

The supervisory board is made up of representatives of the shareholders and of the employees, the number of employee representatives increasing according to the extent of the workforce. The representatives are elected by the shareholders and employees respectively. It is their job to supervise the managing board. The managing board has to report regularly to the supervisory board, and certain actions proposed by the managing board will need the approval of the supervisory board.

The managing board is appointed by the supervisory board (but not the members) and the managing board is broadly similar to a board of directors. The managing board deals with the day-to-day decisions of the AG. The members of the managing board are responsible to the AG and its creditors, and it is arguable that stricter professional standards are expected of such managers than are expected of directors of UK companies. Shareholders' meetings have certain duties and rights reserved to them, particularly in connection with the constitution and capital of the company. The shareholders do not normally become involved in questions of management.

As can be seen, the three-tier management system is particularly favourable to employees, and generally speaking in Germany employees are given a large say in the management of the companies they work for. Germany has a relatively low strike record because the employees' interests are more obviously taken account of. It is sometimes said that in the UK ordinary non-institutional shareholders' interests and employees' interests are ignored by the directors: this appears to be less true for Germany. It is also sometimes said that the German model, for all that it seems to lead to good relations with the workforce, adds an extra layer of bureaucracy, makes companies slow to react, involves almost too much consultation and emphasises employees' jobs at the expense of consumers' interests. UK directors are said to feel uncomfortable with the German model since it removes their autonomy: German directors consider the

UK model leads to labour difficulties, to insensitive management and to a failure to appreciate that co-operation is more effective than antagonism.

In Germany, it is common for local banks to invest in their clients' companies, and for bank officials to be directors of those companies. Germany has many more local banks that the UK (or at least England) does, and the German banks' aim is to invest for the long term for the benefit of the bank, the company and the community. There is extensive worker shareholding in companies in Germany as well. The UK criticism of this approach is that sometimes the German banks are too close to the companies to be objective about them.

Another feature of German corporate life is that the institutions are a less dominant power within the investment community, and that the return demanded by German investors is less than is generally expected by the institutions in the UK.

Germany company law has strongly influenced other German-speaking countries such as Switzerland and Austria. It continues to influence the company law of central European states which are developing their own laws. This is partly because of Germany's propinquity, its strong industrial and financial base, and because the element of employee participation is appreciated in former Communist countries where there had been to some extent an element of worker participation.

Within the rest of Europe, the various countries have adopted various elements of the three above approaches. Some are more nationalist than others, Norway, for example, requiring at least one or more members to be Norwegian or domiciled in Norway. Some countries have a more efficient registration system than others. In some countries company registration is done through local chambers of commerce instead of a national register.

Some counties are more efficient than others in policing registered companies, ensuring that documents are properly completed, accounts filed in time etc. Within the EU there are standard formats for accounts and specific requirements for auditing, but outside the EU, and even in some cases within it, there will be considerable doubt as to the validity or accuracy of company accounts, particularly in areas where there is little tradition of compliance with the law or where government officials are very poorly paid.

Company law in the USA and the Commonwealth

Company law in the USA

Each separate state in the USA has its own company law, although many states have broadly similar models. The reason for the similarity is that if a state has a company law that is too far out of line with the commonly accepted standards of US company law, outside investors and/or entrepreneurs will feel uncomfortable with it and go elsewhere. Until fairly recently some states had strict *ultra vires* laws. They had been drawn up at a time when dubious promoters were using investors' funds for unsuitable purposes and a means had to be found to restrict this behaviour. While this made sense at the time, when later on the *ultra vires* rule came to be regarded as more of a nuisance than a protection, such states had to change their laws if they wished to attract entrepreneurs.

One state that has quite deliberately set up a highly sophisticated and advanced corporate law is the state of Delaware. With the help of skilled attorneys it drew up corporate law legislation that is noticeably manager-friendly. This was originally done to protect the interests of the Du Pont chemical firm which was based in that state, but later it was done to attract substantial businesses to locate their registered offices in the state of Delaware. This strategy has been very effective, and those businesses' annual registration and incorporation dues bring substantial funds to that state. As the state is anxious to keep this good source of income, it devotes substantial resources towards maintaining a highly efficient registration system and an up-to-date legislation. As so many companies are based in that state, substantial litigation takes place there, and because of the size and complexity of the cases the local judiciary has become extremely experienced.

Although the Delaware corporate law was originally markedly manager-friendly, more recently the Delaware authorities have had to find a balance between the interests of managers and of investors. Investors might feel that if the legislation unduly favoured the managers the investors' interests would be overlooked. Investors would then be less likely to invest, and this would have the economic effect of marking down the share price – and ultimately driving business away from Delaware.

Company law in the Commonwealth

Of the present or former Commonwealth countries, most of them, having started with the UK model and been subject to the decisions of the UK House of Lords, have developed their own legislation and judicature. In Canada the *ultra vires* rule has been dropped and Australia has been experimenting with alternative forms of insolvency procedure. Australia has also greatly simplified its procedure for protecting minority rights. Australian company law is also keen on the use of "plain English" so that ordinary investors can understand what their companies are doing with their money. New Zealand has been particularly innovatory in the field of company law, reflecting a political desire to reduce the role of the state in personal and business matters. Many companies are not required to file accounts unless they are offering shares to the public. Annual reports need not be filed with Companies House. There are no residence or nationality requirements for directors and no obligation to have a company secretary. While this amount of deregulation may well attract entrepreneurs, it also means that creditors and investors must be on their guard when dealing with companies that provide so little information about themselves.

Comparison of UK companies with companies in other jurisdictions

Although the terms may be different, most developed countries have limited companies and a system of company registration in many respects similar to those in Europe, the Commonwealth and the USA. In some countries there is no distinction between the memorandum and articles, as those documents are amalgamated in one document called "by-laws" or "statutes". Most countries have shares, debentures and the concept of limited liability, though many countries make greater use of limited partnerships. Some countries have no insider dealing rules or despite being highly advanced economies, have only introduced them recently, Japan being a good example.

Registration requirements

There are differences in the level of registration requirements. Throughout Europe the requirements for plcs are gradually being harmonised, with a large amount of information being available at the various nations' Registrars of Companies offices. There are, however, other jurisdictions where very little information need be supplied to their Registrars of Companies. It is possible in some tax-haven countries, such as the Virgin Islands, to set up companies which, although registered, contain only the barest minimum of information, such as a name, a number and a registered office. No accounts need be published and no information needs be disclosed about the directors or shareholders. Even if that information is disclosed, it is perfectly possible to disguise the true owners or directors of a company by stating that the members or directors are themselves companies, registered preferably in yet another jurisdiction. Those companies in turn can be nominees for trusts, the beneficial owners of which are carefully protected by national laws.

The rationale for these companies is that some very rich people wish to keep their assets away from the eyes of the Inland Revenue or other governmental bodies. Certain small countries are known for their willingness to set up companies without asking awkward questions, and the fees for the incorporation and maintenance of those companies can form a major part of the wealth of those countries. It is also not unknown for businessmen involved in illegal activities such as arms-running, drug-smuggling, or insider dealing to use such companies to hide their wealth. Secrecy can also be maintained by strict national banking laws. For many years Switzerland had strict banking secrecy laws until the authorities became aware that the country was attracting a certain amount of opprobrium for its apparent harbouring of money gained by illegal or at best doubtful activities.

Company law in developing countries and in the former Iron Curtain countries

For countries that never had a company law because private enterprise was forbidden by their socialist rulers, it has been necessary to invent a new company law. This is particularly true for some of the former Iron Curtain countries. Such countries have usually taken advice as to what is the most suitable type of company law for their cultural and commercial traditions. As stated above, the German model is admired, particularly in some of the former Eastern Bloc countries, for its employee involvement. Some such countries are being assisted by help from the UN and other international bodies in drafting and developing modern corporate and commercial laws. Such laws will encourage outside investment by not being markedly different from most other countries' commercial and corporate laws. Such countries are sometimes in the difficult position of not wishing to be seen uncritically to adopt wholesale other countries' ideas (since that suggests they are unable to do it themselves) but equally not wishing to embark upon costly corporate experiments which may not work. Yet it is sensible to adopt commercial and corporate legal practices which are seen to work well elsewhere. In addition, many developing countries look to the US models of corporate law because US investment is seen as desirable, particularly if that country has a high record of emigration to the USA. Returning emigrants, or their children, may wish to bring capital back to the land of their forebears but will not do so unless they know their investment will not be expropriated under an obscure legal system. At the same time many countries specifically have commercial and corporate laws that restrict the involvement of foreigners in companies or the movement of capital out of the country. This is to protect their own economies though it may also have the unintended effect of deterring investment.

There is also the considerable risk of fraud. In some countries, such as Russia, many industries have been privatised. The new owners and managers of the industries are often the same as the former managers. They alone understood the industry, how it worked, and were strongly able to influence the price at which the industry's shares could be sold – and indeed to whom the shares could be sold. An inexperienced, not always very numerate electorate and parliament, combined with corrupt officialdom and an underpaid judiciary, is not always alert to conflicts of interest or the possibilities for secret profits. Auditing can be erratic and death threats to judges do not encourage impartiality in commercial disputes. The risks for a naive investing public were well exemplified by the MMM scandal in Russia in 1994, (referred to in Chapter 10).

The race to the bottom

When each country has its own corporate laws, there is the danger that there might be a "race to the bottom" whereby countries vie with each other to have the most flexible or least demanding corporate laws. For example, Lichtenstein and various other small countries such as the Cook Islands and the Bahamas have corporate laws that demand very little other than an annual registration fee and a registered office in the country. Sometimes no details are required either of directors, shareholders or audited accounts. One might therefore think that companies would wish to relocate there to take advantage of the lax rules and the limited disclosure. However, on the whole major corporations have not tended to run their businesses from these places, mainly because the countries are not in themselves seen as suitable places from which to conduct large businesses. This is because there is a certain suspicion of companies that run their business from laxly regulated offshore bases. There is a concern that companies are registered in those places deliberately to prevent snooping eyes, particularly the Inland Revenue's. Reputable companies should not be ashamed to publish their accounts, and companies that try to avoid doing so may have something to hide. This calls their credibility into question. Suggestions that within the trading block of EU there might be a race to the bottom are therefore unrealistic, and if anything, the EU directives are encouraging ever higher standards of accountability and disclosure, at least as far as public companies are concerned, in order to encourage quality business and fair competition.

Irresolvable issues in company law

As was stated at the beginning of this book, company law is designed to encourage trade and deter fraud. It must allow entrepreneurs to take risks to create wealth and sustain employment. It must prevent rogues from deceiving investors and creditors. It must balance the following competing interests:

- shareholders and directors;

- the company and its employees;

- the company and its clients or customers;

- the creation of private wealth and the public interest;

- promoters' and directors' desire for secrecy and the investors' and creditors' desire for disclosure;

- rules that encourage entrepreneurs and rules that reassure investors.

There are also wider issues still, many of which are irresolvable:

1. At present company reports and accounts do not need to take account of difficult and not easily quantifiable concepts such as the effect of the company's activities on the environment. A company could despoil an area of natural beauty, wind itself up and leave the mess for someone else to sort out.

2. Shareholder democracy does not appear to be working, even if shareholders have only themselves to blame. There is widespread dissatisfaction at the extent of directors' salaries and a perception that directors refuse to take private shareholders' grievances seriously.

3. Private shareholders in the UK are generally speaking not investing in listed companies. Although they may receive free shares in building societies or insurance companies, quite often they are happier selling the shares and taking the money now instead of holding for the long term. Many private shareholders do not read the directors' report and accounts, are not numerate enough to understand the accounts or, even if they do understand the accounts, do not control enough votes to make any difference. Many company reports are boring and baffling to all but sophisticated investors and investment analysts. What investors cannot easily understand they will not invest in. Instead they will rely on institutions to invest for them, thus further distancing companies from their owners and increasing suspicion of directors.

4. Unsecured creditors suffer most in the event of a company's liquidation. Even with the advent of the Insolvency Act 1986 and greater personal liability of directors there is still often little left over for unsecured creditors.

5. It is arguable that employees should be given a greater say in the management of their companies, though it is unlikely that compulsion in this respect would necessarily help.

6. Does profit-sharing for employees work? Yes, while the company is doing well, but what about when it is failing and the employees do not have the voting power to replace or improve incompetent management?

7. Do employee share schemes provide an insignificant incentive to motivate employees to uphold the company's best interests? As before, much

depends on the extent of the employees' collective shareholdings and the extent to which they can influence management.

8. Can common accounting standards be achieved?

9. Are there any satisfactory alternatives to receivership and liquidation?

10. To what extent can a company be held responsible for the unauthorised actions of its employees?

11. Should insider dealing solely be a criminal matter?

12. Is there any longer a need for an *ultra vires* rule?

13. To what extent should directors be personally responsible for their own poor management of their companies?

Whither company law into the 21st century?

Earlier this century directors generally were in a very privileged position, only marginally accountable and rarely liable for their own incompetence. While this is still true to some extent, the law in the UK has been gradually reducing their relative impunity. Their continued relative impunity in listed companies now derives from block votes from supportive institutions; and it may be that methods will be found to make directors more responsive to other shareholders' views. This whole area is known as corporate governance and is the subject of much debate.

A current, and some would say, idealistic popular view is that the law should be revised to take account of the interest of other stakeholders (employees, the public interest, environmental concerns, consumers), rather than being a method for facilitating a good return for shareholders' investment. This would, it is suggested, and if properly drafted, lead to greater commitment, longer term rewards, better morale and productivity. It might also lead to slow decision making, while managers play divide and rule between the competing interests.

Insider dealing is never going to disappear, but the law could undoubtedly be improved to minimise the possibilities of both carrying it out and not getting caught. It is also likely that increased electronic monitoring of transactions will gradually make it more and more difficult to carry out successful insider deals.

It is possible that company law will follow the New Zealand model and become progressively less regulated, and equally possible that after a number of years consumer pressure will force company law to revert to a more regulated environment. It is also possible that we may see a global consensus on what form of corporate law (and what form of accounting) is suitable for companies that offer their shares to the public. Private companies will probably continue to have varying degrees of regulation.

It is unlikely that any corporate legal system would satisfactorily resolve all these competing demands upon the corporate structure. As stated above, company law is all about finding the requisite balance. This is the challenge for the next century's legislators.

Summary

1. European directives have substantially aligned the company laws of the EU members, although there has been opposition, mainly in the UK, to any suggestions of greater worker participation in management.

2. Just as, slowly, there is beginning to be agreement on common accounting standards, so it is likely that, at least in the developed economies or countries that wish to be developed economies, company law will adopt standardised norms, particularly for companies that offer their shares to the public.

3. While the "race to the bottom" is a possibility, it is not generally in the long term interests of companies that wish to grow and prosper to hide behind too manager-friendly a legislation.

4. There are major concerns that will need to be addressed by all company law systems, these being the question of worker participation, common accounting standards, shareholder democracy, the powers and duties of directors and the endless battle against fraud.

Index